ments to the Constitution

Article 6.

The right of the people to be secure in their persons, houses, papers, and effects, against unreasonable searches and seizures, shall not be violated, and no Warrants shall issue, but upon probable cause, supported by Oath or affirmation, and particularly describing the place to be searched, and the persons or things to be seized.

Article 7.

No person shall be held to answer for a capital, or otherwise infamous crime, unless on a presentment or indictment of a Grand Jury, except in cases arising in the land or naval forces, or in the Militia, when in actual service in time of War or public danger; nor shall any person be subject for the same offence to be twice put in jeopardy of life or limb, nor shall be compelled in any Criminal case to be a witness against himself, nor be deprived of life, liberty, or property, without due process of law; nor shall private property be taken for public use, without just compensation.

Article 8.

In all criminal prosecutions, the accused shall enjoy the right to a speedy and public trial, by an impartial jury of the State and district wherein the crime shall have been committed, which district shall have been previously ascertained by law, and to be informed of the nature and cause of the accusation; to be confronted with the witnesses against him; to have compulsory process for obtaining witnesses in his favor, and to have the Assistance of Counsel for his defence.

Article 9.

In suits at common law, where the value in controversy shall exceed twenty dollars, the right of trial by jury shall be preserved, and no fact tried by a jury shall be otherwise re-examined in any Court of the United States, than according to the rules of the common law.

Article 10.

Excessive bail shall not be required, nor excessive fines imposed, nor cruel and unusual punishments inflicted.

Article 11.

The enumeration in the Constitution of certain rights shall not be construed to deny or disparage others retained by the people.

Article 12.

The powers not delegated to the United States by the Constitution, nor prohibited by it to the States, are reserved to t' the people.

THE DOCUMENTARY HISTORY OF THE
RATIFICATION OF THE CONSTITUTION
AND THE BILL OF RIGHTS

VOLUME XXXIX

Ratification of the

BILL OF RIGHTS

[3]

Thomas Jefferson's Tally Sheet

After four months of debate, the First Federal Congress in September 1789 agreed to propose twelve amendments to the Constitution that were submitted to the states for their legislative approval. President George Washington sent manuscript broadsides of the twelve amendments to the state executives on 2 October 1789. When a legislature acted on the amendments, it notified President Washington, who, in turn, notified both Congress and the office of the Secretary of State.

As the official "certifying officer," Secretary of State Thomas Jefferson determined which amendments had been officially adopted. To assist him in cataloging the state ratifications, Jefferson drafted a chart with the twelve amendments listed in the left-hand column and with twenty-six empty boxes in the top row—half for "affirmative" actions and half for "negative" actions. As each state responded, Jefferson inserted its action in the appropriate empty box in a vertical column reserved for that particular state arranged left-to-right in a north-to-south arrangement. When Vermont joined the Union and ratified the twelve amendments, Jefferson did not draft another chart, but rather assigned Vermont (with a "V") on the vertical line between the columns reserved for the states of Connecticut and New York. Jefferson left the columns for Massachusetts, Connecticut, and Georgia blank because these states did not send an official "exemplification" of their actions.

THE DOCUMENTARY HISTORY OF THE
RATIFICATION OF THE CONSTITUTION
AND THE BILL OF RIGHTS

Volume XXXIX

BILL OF RIGHTS

[3]

4 June–31 December 1788

Editors

John P. Kaminski
Elizabeth M. Schoenleber
Sarah K. Danforth
Anna M. Biermeier
Oindrila Chattopadhyay

Thomas H. Linley
Timothy D. Moore
Dustin M. Cohan
Christopher S. Berry
Daniel J. Hoefs

MADISON
WISCONSIN HISTORICAL SOCIETY PRESS
2 0 2 3

The Documentary History of the Ratification of the Constitution is sponsored by the National Historical Publications and Records Commission and the University of Wisconsin–Madison. Preparation of this volume was made possible by grants from the National Historical Publications and Records Commission; the Division of Research Programs of the National Endowment for the Humanities, an independent federal agency; the Lynde and Harry Bradley Foundation; the William Nelson Cromwell Foundation; and the Hamilton Roddis Foundation. Any views, findings, conclusions, or recommendations expressed in this publication do not necessarily reflect those of the National Endowment for the Humanities.

Copyright © 2023 by
THE STATE HISTORICAL SOCIETY OF WISCONSIN
All rights reserved

⊚ This paper meets the requirements of ANSI/NISO Z39.48-1992 (Performance of Paper).

LIBRARY OF CONGRESS CATALOGING IN PUBLICATION DATA [REVISED]
Main entry under title:
The Documentary history of the ratification
    of the Constitution.
    Editors for v. 38: John P. Kaminski, Thomas H. Linley, Elizabeth M. Schoenleber, Timothy D. Moore, Dustin M. Cohan, Oindrila Chattopadhyay, Anna M. Biermeier, Christopher S. Berry, Sarah K. Danforth, Daniel J. Hoefs.
    CONTENTS: v. 1. Constitutional documents and records, 1776–1787.—v. 2. Ratification of the Constitution by the States: Pennsylvania.—v. 3. Ratification of the Constitution by the States: Delaware, New Jersey, Georgia, Connecticut.—v. 4–7. Ratification of the Constitution by the States: Massachusetts (1–4).—v. 8–10. Ratification of the Constitution by the States: Virginia (1–3).—v. 11–12. Ratification of the Constitution by the States: Maryland (1–2).—v. 13–18. Commentaries on the Constitution, public and private (1–6).—v. 19–23. Ratification of the Constitution by the States: New York (1–5).—v. 24–26. Ratification of the Constitution by the States: Rhode Island (1–3).—v. 27. Ratification of the Constitution by the States: South Carolina.—v. 28. Ratification of the Constitution by the States: New Hampshire.—v. 29. Ratification of the Constitution by the States: Confederation Congress Implements the Constitution/Vermont.—v. 30–31. Ratification of the Constitution by the States: North Carolina (1–2).—v. 32–34. Ratification of the Constitution by the States: Pennsylvania Supplemental Documents (1–3)—v. 35. Cumulative Name Index.—v. 36. Cumulative Subject Index.—v. 37. Bill of Rights (1).—v. 38. Bill of Rights (2).—v. 39. Bill of Rights (3).
    1. United States—Constitutional history—Sources.
    I. Jensen, Merrill. II. Kaminski, John P. III. Saladino, Gaspare J. IV. Leffler, Richard. V. Schoenleber, Charles H. VI. Reid, Jonathan M. VII. Flamingo, Margaret R. VIII. Lannér-Cusin, Johanna E. IX. Fields, David P. X. Conley, Patrick T. XI. Moore, Timothy, D. XII. Stevens, Michael E. XIII. Muller, H. Nicholas III. XIV. Linley, Thomas H. XV. Cohan, Dustin M. XVI. Chattopadhyay, Oindrila.
KF4502.D63   342'.73'029   75-14149
ISBN 978-1-9766-0001-2   347.30229   AACR2

To

JACK N. RAKOVE

EXPOSITOR OF THE U.S. CONSTITUTION

EDITORIAL ADVISORY COMMITTEE
R. B. Bernstein
Charlene N. Bickford
Kenneth R. Bowling
Joanne B. Freeman
Michael J. Klarman
Richard Leffler
Andrew Jackson O'Shaughnessy
Jack N. Rakove

Contents

Frontispiece	ii
Acknowledgments	xvi
Organization	xvii
Editorial Procedures	xx
General Ratification Chronology, 1786–1939	xxi
Calendar for the Years 1787–1792	xxv
Symbols	xxviii
Introduction	3
An American Citizen, Pennsylvania Gazette, 4 June 1788	7
THE VIRGINIA CONVENTION AND A BILL OF RIGHTS, 7–27 JUNE 1788	8
Patrick Henry: Speech in the Virginia Convention, 7 June 1788	8
Henry Lee: Speech in the Virginia Convention, 9 June 1788	9
Edmund Randolph: Speech in the Virginia Convention, 9 June 1788	11
Edmund Randolph: Speech in the Virginia Convention, 10 June 1788	12
James Monroe: Speech in the Virginia Convention, 10 June 1788	13
George Nicholas: Speech in the Virginia Convention, 10 June 1788	14
Edmund Pendleton: Speech in the Virginia Convention, 12 June 1788	16
Patrick Henry: Speech in the Virginia Convention, 12 June 1788	18
James Madison: Speech in the Virginia Convention, 12 June 1788	22
George Mason: Speech in the Virginia Convention, 16 June 1788	22
Patrick Henry: Speech in the Virginia Convention, 16 June 1788	23
William Grayson: Speech in the Virginia Convention, 16 June 1788	27
George Nicholas and George Mason: Speeches in the Virginia Convention 16 June 1788	27
Patrick Henry: Speech in the Virginia Convention, 17 June 1788	30
Edmund Randolph: Speech in the Virginia Convention, 17 June 1788	32
Patrick Henry: Speech in the Virginia Convention, 19 June 1788	36
John Marshall: Speech in the Virginia Convention, 20 June 1788	37
Patrick Henry: Speech in the Virginia Convention, 23 June 1788	39
George Wythe: Speech in the Virginia Convention, 24 June 1788	41
George Wythe's Resolution for Ratification, 24–25 June 1788	42
Patrick Henry: Speech in the Virginia Convention, 24 June 1788	43
Edmund Randolph: Speech in the Virginia Convention, 24 June 1788	49
George Mason to John Lamb, Richmond, Va., 9 June 1788	51
Joshua Atherton to John Lamb, Amherst, N.H., 11, 14 June 1788	57
Bon Mot—à propôs, Massachusetts Centinel, 11 June 1788	59
Sydney, New York Journal, 13 June 1788	59
Edmund Pendleton to Richard Henry Lee, Richmond, Va., 14 June 1788	61
Cassandra, Philadelphia Independent Gazetteer, 14 June 1788	64
Many, Virginia Independent Chronicle, 18 June 1788	66
Thomas Jefferson to Thomas Lee Shippen, Paris, 19 June 1788	66
Joshua Atherton: Speech in the New Hampshire Convention, 19 June 1788	67
New Hampshire Convention Recommends Amendments to Constitution 21 June 1788	67
Extract of a Letter from Richmond, Va., 25 June 1788	67

Windham, Conn., Celebrates Ratification of the Constitution by New Hampshire 25 June 1788	68
Extract of a Letter from Richmond, Va., 26 June 1788	69
Virginia Convention Recommends Amendments to Constitution, 27 June 1788	69
Richard Henry Lee to John Lamb, Chantilly, Westmoreland County, Va. 27 June 1788	69
Undelivered speech in the New York Convention, c. 2 July 1788	71
A Real Federalist, Albany Register, 5 January 1789 (Supplement)	71
Antifederalists Celebrate the Fourth of July, Carlisle, Pa., 4 July 1788	82
Exeter, N.H., Freeman's Oracle, 4 July 1788	83
Solon, jun., Rhode Island Providence Gazette, 5 July 1788	85
Thomas Jefferson to John Brown Cutting, Paris, 8, 11 July 1788	86
Peleg Arnold to Welcome Arnold, New York, 11 July 1788	86
Ebenezer Hazard to Mathew Carey, New York, 15 July 1788	87
Caleb S. Riggs to John Fitch, New York, 15 July 1788	87
Republican I, Virginia Independent Chronicle, 16 July 1788	87
Francis Hopkinson to Thomas Jefferson, Philadelphia, 17 July 1788	90
Abraham Clark to Thomas Sinnickson, New York, 23 July 1788	91
A Friend to Good Government, Rhode Island Newport Herald, 24 July 1788	92
Petersburg Virginia Gazette, 24 July 1788	92
NORTH CAROLINA HILLSBOROUGH CONVENTION AND A BILL OF RIGHTS 24–30 JULY 1788	94
James Gallaway: Speech in the North Carolina Convention, 24 July 1788	94
Samuel Spencer: Speech in the North Carolina Convention, 28 July 1788	94
Archibald Maclaine: Speech in the North Carolina Convention, 28 July 1788	96
Samuel Johnston: Speech in the North Carolina Convention, 28 July 1788	97
Timothy Bloodworth: Speech in the North Carolina Convention, 28 July 1788	97
Joseph McDowall: Speech in the North Carolina Convention, 28 July 1788	98
Richard Dobbs Spaight: Speech in the North Carolina Convention 28 July 1788	99
James Iredell: Speech in the North Carolina Convention, 28 July 1788	99
Joseph McDowall: Speech in the North Carolina Convention, 28 July 1788	102
Samuel Spencer: Speech in the North Carolina Convention, 29 July 1788	103
William R. Davie: Speech in the North Carolina Convention, 29 July 1788	105
Archibald Maclaine: Speech in the North Carolina Convention, 29 July 1788	106
Samuel Spencer: Speech in the North Carolina Convention, 29 July 1788	107
James Iredell: Speech in the North Carolina Convention, 29 July 1788	108
Timothy Bloodworth: Speech in the North Carolina Convention, 29 July 1788	110
Samuel Spencer: Speech in the North Carolina Convention, 29 July 1788	111
James Iredell: Speech in the North Carolina Convention, 29 July 1788	111
Henry Abbot: Speech in the North Carolina Convention, 30 July 1788	113
James Iredell: Speech in the North Carolina Convention, 30 July 1788	114
David Caldwell: Speech in the North Carolina Convention, 30 July 1788	117
Samuel Spencer: Speech in the North Carolina Convention, 30 July 1788	118
William Lenoir: Speech in the North Carolina Convention, 30 July 1788	118
Richard Dobbs Spaight: Speech in the North Carolina Convention 30 July 1788	121
William Lancaster: Speech in the North Carolina Convention, 30 July 1788	122
Edward Carrington to William Short, New York, 26 July 1788	123
Marquis de Lafayette to Jeremiah Wadsworth, 26 July 1788	123
New York Convention Recommends Amendments to Constitution, 26 July 1788	123

CONTENTS ix

James McHenry to George Washington, Baltimore, Md., 27 July 1788	124
Thomas Jefferson to James Madison, Paris, 31 July 1788	124
George Washington to James McHenry, Mount Vernon, Fairfax County, Va. 31 July 1788	126
Ezra Stiles to John Adams, Yale College, New Haven, Conn., 1 August 1788	127
A Real German, Maryland Journal, 1 August 1788	128
Comte de Moustier to Comte de Montmorin, New York, 2 August 1788	128
First North Carolina Convention Recommends Amendments to Constitution 2 August 1788	129
Pamphlet Compilation of the Amendments Proposed by the State Conventions Richmond, Va., post-2 August 1788	129
Tench Coxe to Robert Smith, Philadelphia, 5 August 1788	130
Westmoreland County, Pa., Desires Amendments, 5 August 1788	131
Proceedings of a Meeting at Greensburg, Pa., 5 August 1788	131
Amendments Proposed by Westmoreland County Committee post-5 August 1788	132
Pennsylvania Gazette, 6 August 1788	135
Abraham B. Bancker to Evert Bancker, Kingston, N.Y., 9 August 1788	135
Thomas Jefferson to James Monroe, Paris, 9 August 1788	135
New Hampshire President John Langdon to Governor George Clinton Portsmouth, N.H., 11 August 1788	136
James Madison to George Washington, New York, 11 August 1788	136
Thomas Jefferson to William Carmichael, Paris, 12 August 1788	137
Edmund Randolph to James Madison, Richmond, Va., 13 August 1788	137
Pennsylvania Gazette, 13 August 1788	138
Martin's North Carolina Gazette, 13 August 1788	139
Thomas B. Wait to George Thatcher, Portland, Maine, 15 August 1788	140
"X," Connecticut Gazette, 15 August 1788	141
George Washington to Charles Pettit, Mount Vernon, Fairfax County, Va. 16 August 1788	142
Philadelphia Independent Gazetteer, 16 August 1788	144
Abigail Adams Smith to John Quincy Adams, Jamaica, N.Y., 20 August 1788	144
Joseph Clay to John Wright Stanly, Savannah, Ga., 20 August 1788	145
A Friend of Society and Liberty, Pennsylvania Carlisle Gazette, 20 August 1788	145
James Madison to Edmund Randolph, New York, 22 August 1788	145
James Madison to Thomas Jefferson, New York, 23 August 1788	146
Solon, Jr., Rhode Island Providence Gazette, 23 August 1788	147
James Madison to George Washington, New York, 24 August 1788	149
James Tilghman to Tench Coxe, Chestertown, Md., 24 August 1788	150
St. John de Crevecoeur to James Bowdoin, New York, 26 August 1788	151
Hortensius, Massachusetts Centinel, 27 August 1788	151
George Washington to Benjamin Lincoln, Mount Vernon, Fairfax County, Va. 28 August 1788	152
A Friend to Amendments, Boston Independent Chronicle, 28 August 1788	153
Solon, Boston Independent Chronicle, 28 August 1788	154
Philadelphia Independent Gazetteer, 28 August 1788	155
A Federalist, Massachusetts Centinel, 30 August 1788	156
James Gordon, Jr., to James Madison, Germanna, Orange County, Va. 31 August 1788	158
George Washington to Thomas Jefferson, Mount Vernon, Fairfax County, Va. 31 August 1788	159
A Republican, Boston Gazette, 1 September 1788	160

Boston Gazette, 1 September 1788	161
George Mason to John Mason, Gunston Hall, Fairfax County, Va.	
2 September 1788	162
Pennsylvania Packet, 2 September 1788	163

HARRISBURG CONVENTION, 3–6 SEPTEMBER 1788 — 163

Cumberland County, Pa., Desires Amendments, 3 July 1788	164
Benjamin Blyth to John Nicholson, Cumberland County, Pa., 3 July 1788	164
Cumberland County Meeting: Proceedings and Resolutions, 3 July 1788	164
Cumberland County Circular Letter, 3 July 1788	165
New York Daily Advertiser, 14 July 1788	167
Germantown, Pa., Antifederalist Meeting, 14 August 1788	167
James Hanna to John Vandegrift, Nathan Vansant, and Jacob Vandegrift	
Newtown, Bucks County, Pa., 15 August 1788	169
Fayette County, Pa.: Certificate of Election of Delegates to Harrisburg	
Convention, 18 August 1788	170
Pennsylvania Gazette, 20 August 1788	170
Robert Galbraith et al. to President Benjamin Franklin, Huntingdon, Pa.	
23 August 1788	171
Bucks County, Pa., Meeting: Proceedings and Resolutions, 25 August 1788	172
Thomas Willing to William Bingham, Philadelphia, 27 August 1788	174
"A.B.," Pennsylvania Gazette, 27 August 1788	174
Thomas McKean to Robert Magaw, Philadelphia, 28 August 1788	175
Extract of a Letter from Carlisle, Pa., 28 August 1788	175
William Shippen, Jr., to Thomas Lee Shippen, Philadelphia	
2 September 1788	175
Pennsylvania Gazette, 3 September 1788	176
Harrisburg Convention: Proceedings, Resolutions, and Petition	
3–6 September 1788	176
Alexander Graydon to Lambert Cadwalader, Louisburg, Pa.	
7 September 1788	182
Benjamin Lincoln to Theodore Sedgwick, Boston, 7 September 1788	182
Thomas Hartley to Tench Coxe, York, Pa., 9 September 1788	183
Pennsylvania Gazette, 10 September 1788	183
A Freeman, Pennsylvania Gazette, 10 September 1788	184
Philadelphia Committee of Correspondence to Timothy Pickering	
11 September 1788	185
James McLene to William Irvine, Philadelphia, 12 September 1788	186
New York Packet, 12 September 1788	186
A Word to the Wise, Pennsylvania Mercury, 13 September 1788	187
Pennsylvania Mercury, 13 September 1788	187
James Madison to Edmund Randolph, New York, 14 September 1788	188
James Madison to George Washington, New York, 14 September 1788	188
Richard Peters to George Washington, Philadelphia, 17 September 1788	188
A Freeman, Pennsylvania Gazette, 17 September 1788	189
Pennsylvania Gazette, 17 September 1788	190
DeWitt Clinton to Charles Clinton, Jr., New York, 19 September 1788	191
Civis, Pennsylvania Packet, 19 September 1788	192
A Despiser of Demagogues, Would-be-ats, and Wheelbarrow-men	
Pennsylvania Mercury, 20 September 1788	193
Pittsburgh Gazette, 20 September 1788	194

CONTENTS   xi

Massachusetts Centinel, 27 September 1788   196
Cassius, Philadelphia Federal Gazette, 9 October 1788   196

Edmund Randolph to James Madison, Richmond, Va., 3 September 1788   198
Steady, Massachusetts Centinel, 3 September 1788   198
Solon, Boston Independent Chronicle, 4 September 1788   199
James Madison to James Madison, Sr., New York, 6 September 1788   201
Massachusetts Centinel, 6 September 1788   201
Tench Coxe to James Madison, Philadelphia, 10 September 1788   203
A Federal Centinel, Pennsylvania Gazette, 10 September 1788   203
Boston Independent Chronicle, 11 September 1788   206
Boston Independent Chronicle, 11 September 1788   208
Edmund Randolph to James Madison, Richmond, Va., 12 September 1788   208
A Marylander, Baltimore Maryland Gazette, 12 September 1788   208
Albert, Baltimore Maryland Gazette, 12 September 1788   211
Henry Lee to George Washington, New York, 13 September 1788   213
William Widgery to George Thatcher, New Glocester, Maine
    14 September 1788   214
Boston Herald of Freedom, 15 September 1788   215
John Brown Cutting to Thomas Jefferson, London, 16 September 1788   215
Charles Nesbit to the Earl of Buchan, Carlisle, Pa., 16 September 1788   216
Massachusetts Centinel, 17 September 1788   217
The Voice of the People, Boston Independent Chronicle, 18 September 1788 218
Boston Herald of Freedom, 18 September 1788   219
Senex, Massachusetts Centinel, 20 September 1788   219
John Jay to George Washington, New York, 21 September 1788   221
James Madison to Thomas Jefferson, New York, 21 September 1788   221
William Samuel Johnson to Samuel Peters, New York, 22 September 1788   222
George Washington to Henry Lee, Mount Vernon, Fairfax County, Va.
    22 September 1788   223
Abraham Yates, Jr., to William Smith, New York, 22 September 1788   224
Samuel Huntington to Samuel Johnston, Norwich, Conn., 23 September 1788   224
Theodore Sedgwick to Benjamin Lincoln, Springfield, Mass.
    23 September 1788   225
An Old German, Baltimore Maryland Gazette, 23 September 1788   226
Benjamin Lincoln to George Washington, Hingham, Mass., 24 September 1788 228
Truth, Philadelphia Independent Gazetteer, 24 September 1788   230
Solon, Boston Independent Chronicle, 25 September 1788   231
Tarantula, Baltimore Maryland Gazette, 26 September 1788   232
Federalism, Maryland Journal, 26 September 1788   233
Federal Commonwealth, Massachusetts Centinel, 27 September 1788   237
Camillus, Baltimore Maryland Gazette, 30 September 1788   238
A Federalist, Baltimore Maryland Gazette, 30 September 1788   239
Massachusetts Centinel, 1 October 1788   242
"A.B.," Maryland Journal, 3 October 1788   243
Philadelphia Federal Gazette, 4 October 1788   245
Thomas Mifflin to Jeremiah Wadsworth, Schuylkill Fall, Pa., 5 October 1788 245
Edmund Pendleton to James Madison, Edmundsbury, Caroline County, Va.
    6 October 1788   245
A Freeman, Philadelphia Federal Gazette, 6 October 1788   246
Anti, Philadelphia Federal Gazette, 7 October 1788   248
Centinel XIX, Philadelphia Independent Gazetteer, 7 October 1788   250

Thomas Tudor Tucker to St. George Tucker, New York, 9 October 1788	252
Thomas Johnson to George Washington, Frederick, Md., 10 October 1788	252
Edward Carrington to James Monroe, Baltimore, Md., 12 October 1788	253
Pennsylvania Mercury, 14 October 1788	254
John Jay to Edward Rutledge, New York, 15 October 1788	254
Richard Henry Lee to Theodorick Bland, Chantilly, Westmoreland County, Va. 15 October 1788	255
Alfred II, Massachusetts Spy, 16 October 1788	255
James Madison to Thomas Jefferson, New York, 17 October 1788	256
Philadelphia Federal Gazette, 18 October 1788	260
Edward Carrington to James Madison, Fredericksburg, Va., 19 October 1788	261
Joseph Jones to James Madison, Richmond, Va., 20 October 1788	262
James Madison to Edmund Pendleton, New York, 20 October 1788	262
George Lee Turberville to James Madison, Richmond, Va., 20 October 1788	263
Francis Corbin to James Madison, Richmond, Va., 21 October 1788	263
Foreign Spectator I, Philadelphia Federal Gazette, 21 October 1788	264
Honestus, Maryland Journal, 21 October 1788	267
Edward Carrington to James Madison, Richmond, Va., 22 October 1788	272
A Federalist, Massachusetts Centinel, 22 October 1788	273
A Friend to Consistency and Stability in Government Philadelphia Federal Gazette, 22 October 1788	274
Edmund Randolph to James Madison, Richmond, Va., 23 October 1788	276
Alfred III, Massachusetts Spy, 23 October 1788	277
Christian Farmer, Connecticut Norwich Packet, 23 October 1788	280
Centinel XX, Philadelphia Independent Gazetteer, 23 October 1788	282
Edward Carrington to James Madison, Richmond, Va., 24 October 1788	284
Benjamin Franklin to Thomas Jefferson, Philadelphia, 24 October 1788	285
Foreign Spectator II, Philadelphia Federal Gazette, 24 October 1788	285
George Washington to Benjamin Lincoln, Mount Vernon, Fairfax County, Va. 26 October 1788	289
John Dawson to James Madison, Richmond, Va., 27 October 1788	290
George Lee Turberville to James Madison, Richmond, Va., 27 October 1788	290
Theodorick Bland to Richard Henry Lee, Richmond, Va., 28 October 1788	291
John Harris to Tench Coxe, Harrisburg, Pa., 28 October 1788	293
Jonathan Trumbull, Jr., to George Washington, Lebanon, Conn. 28 October 1788	293
Foreign Spectator III, Philadelphia Federal Gazette, 28 October 1788	293
Switch, Baltimore Maryland Gazette, 28 October 1788	296
Charles Lee to George Washington, Richmond, Va., 29 October 1788	297
Richard Bland Lee to James Madison, Richmond, Va., 29 October 1788	298
Honestus, Boston Independent Chronicle, 30 October 1788	299
Solon, Boston Independent Chronicle, 30 October 1788	303
Boston Herald of Freedom, 30 October 1788	305
Foreign Spectator IV, Philadelphia Federal Gazette, 31 October 1788	305
Governor John Hancock: Draft of a Speech to the General Court c. 31 October 1788	309
A Friend to the People, Exeter, N.H., Freeman's Oracle, 1 November 1788	310
James Madison to Edmund Randolph, New York, 2 November 1788	311
James Madison to George Lee Turberville, New York, 2 November 1788	312
Theodore Sedgwick to Alexander Hamilton, Boston, 2 November 1788	314
Jeremiah Wadsworth to Henry Knox, Hartford, Conn., 2 November 1788	315

CONTENTS xiii

Thomas Brand-Hollis to John Adams, The Hyde, Essex, England 4 November 1788	315
New York Antifederalist Society: Proceedings of a Meeting on Calling a Second Convention, New York, 4 November 1788	317
Foreign Spectator V, Philadelphia Federal Gazette, 4 November 1788	321
From Collin McGregor, New York, 5 November 1788	323
Massachusetts Centinel, 5 November 1788	324
Lucullus, Pennsylvania Gazette, 5 November 1788	325
Virginia Independent Chronicle, 5 November 1788	325
Coxe and Frazier to Wilson and Boyd, Philadelphia, 6 November 1788	327
Honestus, Boston Independent Gazetteer, 6 November 1788	327
Foreign Spectator VI, Philadelphia Federal Gazette, 7 November 1788	329
A Friend to Liberty and Union, Philadelphia Federal Gazette 7 November 1788	332
Friend to Amendments, Exeter, N.H., Freeman's Oracle, 8 November 1788	337
Theodorick Bland to Richard Henry Lee, Richmond, Va., 9 November 1788	339
Alexander Hamilton to Theodore Sedgwick, New York, 9 November 1788	340
George Lee Turberville to James Madison, Richmond, Va., 10 November 1788	340
Foreign Spectator VII, Philadelphia Federal Gazette, 11 November 1788	341
Francis Corbin to James Madison, Richmond, Va., 12 November 1788	344
Pennsylvania Carlisle Gazette, 12 November 1788	344
Philadelphia Federal Gazette, 12 November 1788	345
Virginia Centinel, 12 November 1788	345
George Lee Turberville to James Madison, Richmond, Va., 13 November 1788	345
Annapolis Maryland Gazette, 13 November 1788	346
Centinel XXII, Philadelphia Independent Gazetteer, 14 November 1788	348
Foreign Spectator VIII, Philadelphia Federal Gazette, 14 November 1788	349
Edward Carrington to James Madison, Richmond, Va., 15 November 1788	352
Patrick Henry to Richard Henry Lee, Richmond, Va., 15 November 1788	354
Massachusetts Centinel, 15 November 1788	355
George Lee Turberville to James Madison, Richmond, Va., 16 November 1788	356
Peter S. Du Ponceau to Edward Jones, Philadelphia, 17 November 1788	357
Richard Bland Lee to James Madison, Richmond, Va., 17 November 1788	358
George Washington to James Madison, Mount Vernon, Fairfax County, Va. 17 November 1788	359
Edward Carrington to James Madison, Richmond, Va., 18 November 1788	360
Thomas Jefferson to James Madison, Paris, 18 November 1788	360
William Shippen, Jr., to Thomas Lee Shippen, Philadelphia, 18 November 1788	361
Foreign Spectator IX, Philadelphia Federal Gazette, 18 November 1788	361
Joseph Willard to Richard Price, Cambridge, Mass., 19 November 1788	364
A Federalist, Pennsylvania Carlisle Gazette, 19 November 1788	364
A Federalist, Pennsylvania Packet, 19 November 1788	367
Joseph Jones to James Madison, Richmond, Va., 21 November 1788	368
Foreign Spectator X, Philadelphia Federal Gazette, 21 November 1788	368
A Federalist who is for Amendments, New York Daily Advertiser 22 November 1788	372
A Real Patriot, Philadelphia Federal Gazette, 22 November 1788	374
Philadelphia Independent Gazetteer, 22 November 1788	375
Philadelphia Independent Gazetteer, 22 November 1788	376
Abraham Baldwin to Joel Barlow, New York, 23 November 1788	376
Alexander Hamilton to James Madison, New York, 23 November 1788	377

William Duer to James Madison, post-23 November 1788	377
DeWitt Clinton to Charles Clinton, Jr., New York, 25 November 1788	378
Edward Carrington to James Madison, Richmond, Va., 26 November 1788	378
Foreign Spectator XI, Philadelphia Federal Gazette, 28 November 1788	379
David Humphreys to Thomas Jefferson, Mount Vernon, Fairfax County, Va. 29 November 1788	381
James Madison to Henry Lee, Philadelphia, 30 November 1788	382
James Madison to George Washington, Philadelphia, 2 December 1788	383
Foreign Spectator XII, Philadelphia Federal Gazette, 2 December 1788	383
Massachusetts Salem Mercury, 2 December 1788	386
Thomas Jefferson to George Washington, Paris, 4 December 1788	386
George Washington to Jonathan Trumbull, Jr., Mount Vernon Fairfax County, Va., 4 December 1788	387
Alexander White to James Madison, Richmond, Va., 4 December 1788	387
A True Federalist, Worcester, Mass., American Herald, 4 December 1788	387
François de la E———., Boston Herald of Freedom, 4 December 1788	388
Sidney, New York Journal, 4 December 1788	389
New York Journal, 4 December 1788	395
St. John de Crevecoeur to William Short, New York, 5 December 1788	395
Foreign Spectator XIII, Philadelphia Federal Gazette, 5 December 1788	396
Massachusetts Centinel, 6 December 1788	400
Thomas Jefferson to William Short, Paris, 8 December 1788	400
Henry Lee to James Madison, Alexandria, Va., 8 December 1788	401
James Madison to Thomas Jefferson, Philadelphia, 8 December 1788	401
Foreign Spectator XIV, Philadelphia Federal Gazette, 9 December 1788	402
James Madison to Philip Mazzei, Philadelphia, 10 December 1788	405
The Conversion, Massachusetts Centinel, 10 December 1788	406
An American Citizen, Philadelphia Federal Gazette, 10 December 1788	407
An American, Boston Independent Chronicle, 11 December 1788	409
A Federal Republican II, New York Journal, 11 December 1788	410
George Clinton to John Dawson, New York, 12 December 1788	413
Richard Bland Lee to James Madison, Richmond, Va., 12 December 1788	413
James Madison to Thomas Jefferson, Philadelphia, 12 December 1788	415
George Lee Turberville to James Madison, Richmond, Va., 12 December 1788	415
New Hampshire Spy, 12 December 1788	416
Foreign Spectator XV, Philadelphia Federal Gazette, 12 December 1788	417
Nobody, Massachusetts Centinel, 13 December 1788	420
George Lee Turberville to James Madison, Richmond, Va., 14 December 1788	420
Consistency, Boston Herald of Freedom, 15 December 1788	421
North End, Boston Herald of Freedom, 15 December 1788	423
An Elector, Boston Herald of Freedom, 15 December 1788	424
Boston Gazette, 15 December 1788	425
Hardin Burnley to James Madison, Richmond, Va., 16 December 1788	425
Foreign Spectator XVI, Philadelphia Federal Gazette, 16 December 1788	426
Massachusetts Centinel, 17 December 1788	429
George Mason to John Mason, Gunston Hall, Fairfax County, Va. 18 December 1788	431
A Bostonian, Boston Herald of Freedom, 18 December 1788	432
A Citizen of New-Haven, Connecticut New Haven Gazette, 18 December 1788	433
Massachusetts Spy, 18 December 1788	436

CONTENTS

John Francis Mercer Declares His Candidacy, Annapolis, Md. 20 December 1788	436
John Wright Stanly to Joseph Clay, New Bern, N.C., 20 December 1788	437
Massachusetts Centinel, 20 December 1788	438
Thomas Jefferson to Francis Hopkinson, Paris, 21 December 1788	438
Meriwether Smith: Campaign Address, c. 21 December 1788	439
Foreign Spectator XVII, Philadelphia Federal Gazette, 23 December 1788	440
An American Citizen, Philadelphia Federal Gazette, 24 December 1788	442
Thomas Jefferson to William Carmichael, Paris, 25 December 1788	445
An Inhabitant, Maryland Journal, 26 December 1788	445
Samuel Sterett: Circular letter and Address on His Candidacy 27 December 1788	447
Antilocalis, Massachusetts Centinel, 27 December 1788	448
Kentucky Gazette, 27 December 1788	448
John Adams to Abigail Adams, Braintree, Mass., 28 December 1788	449
Edward Carrington to Henry Knox, Richmond, Va., 30 December 1788	449
Foreign Spectator XVIII, Philadelphia Federal Gazette, 30 December 1788	449
A Marylander, Baltimore Maryland Gazette, 30 December 1788	453
An American Citizen, Philadelphia Federal Gazette, 31 December 1788	454
Address Supporting the Election of James Monroe to the U.S. House of Representatives, c. 31 December 1788	456
Biographical Gazetteer	458
Appendix I: Amendments Proposed by the Maryland Convention Minority As Remarked Upon by Foreign Spectator	472
Index	477

Acknowledgments

This Bill of Rights volume was supported principally by grants from the National Historical Publications and Records Commission, the National Endowment for the Humanities, and the Lynde and Harry Bradley Foundation. Substantial aid was also provided by the William Nelson Cromwell Foundation, the Hamilton Roddis Foundation, and the Wisconsin Alumni Research Foundation.

We thank Christopher Eck and R. Darrell Meadows of the NHPRC; Adam Wolfson, Peter Scott, and Jason Boffetti of the NEH; Richard W. Graber, Dianne J. Sehler, Daniel P. Schmidt, and Ingrid Gregg of the Bradley Foundation; John D. Gordan III, Charles Dowling, and L. Browning VanMeter, Jr., of the Cromwell Foundation; and Thomas H. Roddis and Philip Hamilton Prange of the Hamilton Roddis Foundation.

A continuing debt of gratitude is owed to the administration and staff of the University of Wisconsin–Madison, especially Assistant Dean Emerita Linda J. Neusen, Kelly Mallon, Tae Kidd, Jana Valeo, and John G. Varda of the College of Letters and Science; Russell Schwalbe of the UW Graduate School; and Dawn-Marie M. Roberts and John Douglas of Research and Sponsored Programs. In the Department of History, we thank, Todd Anderson, Michael R. Burmeister, Davis Fugate, Lauren Rusch, John J. Persike, and Leslie Abadie.

In addition to being our publisher, the Wisconsin Historical Society is our primary research library. The Society's staff continues its invaluable support as does the staff at the University of Wisconsin–Madison Memorial Library, especially Peter C. Gorman and Jill Kambs of the Library's Digital Collections.

This volume is dedicated to Jack N. Rakove, W.R. Coe Professor of History and American Studies emeritus at Stanford University and a recipient of a Pulitzer Prize, who has written extensively on the origins of the Constitution with special emphasis on James Madison.

Organization

The Documentary History of the Ratification of the Constitution is divided into:
  (1) *Constitutional Documents and Records, 1776–1787* (1 volume),
  (2) *Ratification of the Constitution by the States* (27 volumes),
  (3) *Commentaries on the Constitution: Public and Private* (6 volumes),
  (4) *Cumulative Index* (2 volumes).
  (5) *The Bill of Rights* (5 volumes).

Internet Availability

The DHRC volumes will be found on the website of "Rotunda: The American Founding Era," maintained by the University of Virginia Press (http://rotunda.upress.virginia.edu), and at UW Digital Collections on the website of the University of Wisconsin–Madison Libraries (https://digital.library.wisc.edu/1711.dl/Constitution). The latter platform also contains the supplemental documents for the state volumes.

Constitutional Documents and Records, 1776–1787 (Vol. I)

This introductory volume, a companion to all of the other volumes, traces the constitutional development of the United States during its first twelve years. Cross-references to it appear frequently in other volumes when contemporaries refer to events and proposals from 1776 to 1787. The documents include: (1) the Declaration of Independence, (2) the Articles of Confederation, (3) ratification of the Articles, (4) proposed amendments to the Articles, proposed grants of power to Congress, and ordinances for the Western Territory, (5) the calling of the Constitutional Convention, (6) the appointment of Convention delegates, (7) the resolutions and draft constitutions of the Convention, (8) the report of the Convention, and (9) the Confederation Congress and the Constitution.

Ratification of the Constitution by the States (Vols. II–XII, XIX–XXXIV)

The volumes are arranged roughly in the order in which the states considered the Constitution. Although there are variations, the documents for each state are organized into the following groups: (1) commentaries from the adjournment of the Constitutional Convention to the meeting of the state legislature that called the state convention, (2) the proceedings of the legislature in calling the convention, (3) commentaries from the call of the convention until its meeting, (4) the election of convention delegates, (5) the proceedings of the convention, and (6) post-convention documents.

Commentaries on the Constitution: Public and Private (Vols. XIII–XVIII)

This series contains newspaper items, pamphlets, and broadsides that circulated regionally or nationally. It also includes some private letters that give the writers' opinions of the Constitution in general or that report on the prospects for ratification in several states. Except for some grouped items, documents are arranged chronologically and are numbered consecutively throughout the six volumes. There are frequent cross-references between *Commentaries* and the state series.

Cumulative Index (Vols. XXXV–XXXVI)

These two volumes comprise a name index (vol. XXXV) and subject index (vol. XXXVI) for all thirty-four ratification volumes and fourteen state and Congress supplements.

Supplements to Ratification of the Constitution by the States

Supplemental documents were originally placed on microfiche and are available in that form for Pennsylvania (Vol. II), Delaware, New Jersey, Georgia, and Connecticut (all four, Vol. III), and Virginia (Vols. VIII–X). The original microfiche editions of supplemental documents for Pennsylvania, Delaware, New Jersey, Georgia, Connecticut, and Virginia were digitized for online viewing. These digitized supplements can be located at UW Digital Collections on the website of the University of Wisconsin–Madison Libraries (https://digital.library.wisc.edu/1711.dl/Constitution). Supplemental documents for all of the states will be made available in digital form in the coming years. (Because of the importance of the Pennsylvania Supplemental Documents to both the Pennsylvania and the national debate over the Constitution, these documents have been published as RCS volumes XXXII–XXXIV. The supplemental documents for Rhode Island were printed as an unnumbered and privately funded volume by the Center for the Study of the American Constitution.)

Much of the material for each state is repetitious or peripheral but still valuable. Mostly literal transcripts of this material are placed in the supplements. (Any exceptions to this rule have been clearly indicated.) Many facsimiles are also included.

The types of documents in the supplements are:

(1) newspaper items that repeat arguments, examples of which are printed in the state volumes,

(2) pamphlets that circulated primarily within one state and that are not printed in the state volumes or in *Commentaries*,

(3) letters that contain supplementary material about politics and social relationships,

(4) images of petitions with the names of signers,

(5) images of manuscripts such as notes of debates, and
(6) miscellaneous documents such as election certificates, attendance records, pay vouchers and other financial records, etc.

The Bill of Rights (Vols. XXXVII–XLI)

The public and private debate on the Constitution continued in several states after ratification. It was centered on the issue of whether there should be amendments to the Constitution and the manner in which amendments should be proposed—by a second constitutional convention or by the new U.S. Congress. A bill of rights was proposed in the U.S. Congress on 8 June 1789. Twelve amendments were adopted on 25 September and were sent to the states by President George Washington on 2 October. These volumes will contain the documents related to the public and private debate over amendments, to the proposal of amendments by Congress, and to the ratification of the Bill of Rights by the states.

Editorial Procedures

All documents are transcribed literally. Obvious slips of the pen and errors in typesetting contemporary newspapers, broadsides, and pamphlets are silently corrected. When spelling, capitalization, punctuation, paragraphing, and spacing between words are unclear, modern usage is followed. Superscripts and interlineations are lowered to the line, and marginalia are inserted where the author intended. The thorn is spelled out (i.e., "ye" becomes "the"). Crossed-out words are included when significant. Obsolete meanings of words are supplied in footnotes.

Square brackets are used for editorial insertions. Conjectural readings are enclosed in brackets with a question mark. Illegible and missing words are indicated by dashes enclosed in brackets. However, when the author's intent is obvious, illegible or missing text (up to five characters in length) is silently provided.

All headings are supplied by the editors. Salutations, closings of letters, addresses, endorsements, docketings, and postmarks are deleted unless they provide important information, in which case they are retained in the document or placed in editorial notes. Contemporary footnotes and marginal citations are printed after the text of the document and immediately preceding editorial footnotes. Symbols used by contemporaries, such as stars, asterisks, and daggers, have been replaced by superscripted letters (a), (b), (c), etc.

Many documents, particularly letters, are excerpted when they contain material that is not relevant to ratification. Whenever an excerpt is printed in this edition and a longer excerpt or the entire document appears elsewhere in this edition or in other editions, this is noted.

General Ratification Chronology, 1786–1939

1786

21 January	Virginia calls meeting to consider granting Congress power to regulate trade.
11–14 September	Annapolis Convention.
20 September	Congress receives Annapolis Convention report recommending that states elect delegates to a convention at Philadelphia in May 1787.
11 October	Congress appoints committee to consider Annapolis Convention report.
23 November	Virginia authorizes election of delegates to Convention at Philadelphia.
23 November	New Jersey elects delegates.
4 December	Virginia elects delegates.
30 December	Pennsylvania elects delegates.

1787

6 January	North Carolina elects delegates.
17 January	New Hampshire elects delegates.
3 February	Delaware elects delegates.
10 February	Georgia elects delegates.
21 February	Congress calls Constitutional Convention.
22 February	Massachusetts authorizes election of delegates.
28 February	New York authorizes election of delegates.
3 March	Massachusetts elects delegates.
6 March	New York elects delegates.
8 March	South Carolina elects delegates.
14 March	Rhode Island refuses to elect delegates.
23 April–26 May	Maryland elects delegates.
5 May	Rhode Island again refuses to elect delegates.
14 May	Convention meets; quorum not present.
14–17 May	Connecticut elects delegates.
25 May	Convention begins with quorum of seven states.
16 June	Rhode Island again refuses to elect delegates.
27 June	New Hampshire renews election of delegates.
13 July	Congress adopts Northwest Ordinance.
6 August	Committee of Detail submits draft constitution to Convention.
12 September	Committee of Style submits draft constitution to Convention.
17 September	Constitution signed and Convention adjourns *sine die*.
20 September	Congress reads Constitution.
26–28 September	Congress debates Constitution.
28 September	Congress transmits Constitution to the states.
28–29 September	Pennsylvania calls state convention.
17 October	Connecticut calls state convention.
25 October	Massachusetts calls state convention.
26 October	Georgia calls state convention.
31 October	Virginia calls state convention.
1 November	New Jersey calls state convention.

6 November	Pennsylvania elects delegates to state convention.
10 November	Delaware calls state convention.
12 November	Connecticut elects delegates to state convention.
19 November–7 January 1788	Massachusetts elects delegates to state convention.
20 November–15 December	Pennsylvania Convention.
26 November	Delaware elects delegates to state convention.
27 November–1 December	Maryland calls state convention.
27 November–1 December	New Jersey elects delegates to state convention.
3–7 December	Delaware Convention.
4–5 December	Georgia elects delegates to state convention.
6 December	North Carolina calls state convention.
7 December	Delaware Convention ratifies Constitution, 30 to 0.
11–20 December	New Jersey Convention.
12 December	Pennsylvania Convention ratifies Constitution, 46 to 23.
14 December	New Hampshire calls state convention.
18 December	New Jersey Convention ratifies Constitution, 38 to 0.
25 December–5 January 1788	Georgia Convention.
31 December	Georgia Convention ratifies Constitution, 26 to 0.
31 December–12 February 1788	New Hampshire elects delegates to state convention.

1788

3–9 January	Connecticut Convention.
9 January	Connecticut Convention ratifies Constitution, 128 to 40.
9 January–7 February	Massachusetts Convention.
19 January	South Carolina calls state convention.
1 February	New York calls state convention.
6 February	Massachusetts Convention ratifies Constitution, 187 to 168, and proposes amendments.
13–22 February	New Hampshire Convention: first session.
1 March	Rhode Island calls statewide referendum on Constitution.
3–27 March	Virginia elects delegates to state convention.
24 March	Rhode Island referendum: voters reject Constitution, 2,711 to 239.
28–29 March	North Carolina elects delegates to state convention.
7 April	Maryland elects delegates to state convention.
11–12 April	South Carolina elects delegates to state convention.
21–29 April	Maryland Convention.
26 April	Maryland Convention ratifies Constitution, 63 to 11.
29 April–3 May	New York elects delegates to state convention.
12–24 May	South Carolina Convention.
23 May	South Carolina Convention ratifies Constitution, 149 to 73, and proposes amendments.
2–27 June	Virginia Convention.
17 June–26 July	New York Convention.
18–21 June	New Hampshire Convention: second session.

General Ratification Chronology, 1786–1939 xxiii

21 June	New Hampshire Convention ratifies Constitution, 57 to 47, and proposes amendments.
25 June	Virginia Convention ratifies Constitution, 89 to 79.
27 June	Virginia Convention proposes amendments.
2 July	New Hampshire ratification read in Congress; Congress appoints committee to report an act for putting the Constitution into operation.
21 July–4 August	First North Carolina Convention.
26 July	New York Convention Circular Letter calls for second constitutional convention.
26 July	New York Convention ratifies Constitution, 30 to 27, and proposes amendments.
2 August	North Carolina Convention proposes amendments and refuses to ratify until amendments are submitted to Congress and to a second constitutional convention.
13 September	Congress sets dates for election of President and meeting of new government under the Constitution.
20 November	Virginia requests Congress under the Constitution to call a second constitutional convention.
30 November	North Carolina calls second state convention.

1789

4 March	First Federal Congress convenes.
1 April	House of Representatives attains quorum.
6 April	Senate attains quorum.
30 April	George Washington inaugurated first President.
8 June	James Madison proposes Bill of Rights in Congress.
21–22 August	North Carolina elects delegates to second state convention.
24–26 September	Congress adopts twelve amendments to Constitution to be submitted to the states.
16–23 November	Second North Carolina Convention.
20 November	New Jersey ratifies proposed amendments.
21 November	Second North Carolina Convention ratifies Constitution, 194 to 77, and proposes amendments.
19 December	Maryland ratifies proposed amendments.
22 December	North Carolina ratifies proposed amendments.

1790

17 January	Rhode Island calls state convention.
19 January	South Carolina ratifies proposed amendments.
25 January	New Hampshire ratifies proposed amendments.
28 January	Delaware ratifies proposed amendments.
8 February	Rhode Island elects delegates to state convention.
27 February	New York ratifies proposed amendments.
1–6 March	Rhode Island Convention: first session.
10 March	Pennsylvania ratifies proposed amendments.
24–29 May	Rhode Island Convention: second session.
29 May	Rhode Island Convention ratifies Constitution, 34 to 32, and proposes amendments.
11 June	Rhode Island ratifies proposed amendments.

1791

6–10 January	Vermont Convention
10 January	Vermont Convention ratifies Constitution
18 February	Vermont admitted to the Union.
3 November	Vermont ratifies proposed amendments.
15 December	Virginia ratifies proposed amendments.
15 December	Bill of Rights adopted.

1792

1 March	Secretary of State Thomas Jefferson notifies states of the adoption of ten amendments.

1939

2 March	Massachusetts adopts Bill of Rights.
18 March	Georgia adopts Bill of Rights.
13 April	Connecticut adopts Bill of Rights.

Calendar for the Years 1787–1792

1787

JANUARY
S	M	T	W	T	F	S
	1	2	3	4	5	6
7	8	9	10	11	12	13
14	15	16	17	18	19	20
21	22	23	24	25	26	27
28	29	30	31			

FEBRUARY
S	M	T	W	T	F	S
				1	2	3
4	5	6	7	8	9	10
11	12	13	14	15	16	17
18	19	20	21	22	23	24
25	26	27	28			

MARCH
S	M	T	W	T	F	S
				1	2	3
4	5	6	7	8	9	10
11	12	13	14	15	16	17
18	19	20	21	22	23	24
25	26	27	28	29	30	31

APRIL
S	M	T	W	T	F	S
1	2	3	4	5	6	7
8	9	10	11	12	13	14
15	16	17	18	19	20	21
22	23	24	25	26	27	28
29	30					

MAY
S	M	T	W	T	F	S
		1	2	3	4	5
6	7	8	9	10	11	12
13	14	15	16	17	18	19
20	21	22	23	24	25	26
27	28	29	30	31		

JUNE
S	M	T	W	T	F	S
					1	2
3	4	5	6	7	8	9
10	11	12	13	14	15	16
17	18	19	20	21	22	23
24	25	26	27	28	29	30

JULY
S	M	T	W	T	F	S
1	2	3	4	5	6	7
8	9	10	11	12	13	14
15	16	17	18	19	20	21
22	23	24	25	26	27	28
29	30	31				

AUGUST
S	M	T	W	T	F	S
			1	2	3	4
5	6	7	8	9	10	11
12	13	14	15	16	17	18
19	20	21	22	23	24	25
26	27	28	29	30	31	

SEPTEMBER
S	M	T	W	T	F	S
						1
2	3	4	5	6	7	8
9	10	11	12	13	14	15
16	17	18	19	20	21	22
23	24	25	26	27	28	29
30						

OCTOBER
S	M	T	W	T	F	S
	1	2	3	4	5	6
7	8	9	10	11	12	13
14	15	16	17	18	19	20
21	22	23	24	25	26	27
28	29	30	31			

NOVEMBER
S	M	T	W	T	F	S
				1	2	3
4	5	6	7	8	9	10
11	12	13	14	15	16	17
18	19	20	21	22	23	24
25	26	27	28	29	30	

DECEMBER
S	M	T	W	T	F	S
						1
2	3	4	5	6	7	8
9	10	11	12	13	14	15
16	17	18	19	20	21	22
23	24	25	26	27	28	29
30	31					

1788

JANUARY
S	M	T	W	T	F	S
		1	2	3	4	5
6	7	8	9	10	11	12
13	14	15	16	17	18	19
20	21	22	23	24	25	26
27	28	29	30	31		

FEBRUARY
S	M	T	W	T	F	S
					1	2
3	4	5	6	7	8	9
10	11	12	13	14	15	16
17	18	19	20	21	22	23
24	25	26	27	28	29	

MARCH
S	M	T	W	T	F	S
						1
2	3	4	5	6	7	8
9	10	11	12	13	14	15
16	17	18	19	20	21	22
23	24	25	26	27	28	29
30	31					

APRIL
S	M	T	W	T	F	S
		1	2	3	4	5
6	7	8	9	10	11	12
13	14	15	16	17	18	19
20	21	22	23	24	25	26
27	28	29	30			

MAY
S	M	T	W	T	F	S
				1	2	3
4	5	6	7	8	9	10
11	12	13	14	15	16	17
18	19	20	21	22	23	24
25	26	27	28	29	30	31

JUNE
S	M	T	W	T	F	S
1	2	3	4	5	6	7
8	9	10	11	12	13	14
15	16	17	18	19	20	21
22	23	24	25	26	27	28
29	30					

JULY
S	M	T	W	T	F	S
		1	2	3	4	5
6	7	8	9	10	11	12
13	14	15	16	17	18	19
20	21	22	23	24	25	26
27	28	29	30	31		

AUGUST
S	M	T	W	T	F	S
					1	2
3	4	5	6	7	8	9
10	11	12	13	14	15	16
17	18	19	20	21	22	23
24	25	26	27	28	29	30
31						

SEPTEMBER
S	M	T	W	T	F	S
	1	2	3	4	5	6
7	8	9	10	11	12	13
14	15	16	17	18	19	20
21	22	23	24	25	26	27
28	29	30				

OCTOBER
S	M	T	W	T	F	S
			1	2	3	4
5	6	7	8	9	10	11
12	13	14	15	16	17	18
19	20	21	22	23	24	25
26	27	28	29	30	31	

NOVEMBER
S	M	T	W	T	F	S
						1
2	3	4	5	6	7	8
9	10	11	12	13	14	15
16	17	18	19	20	21	22
23	24	25	26	27	28	29
30						

DECEMBER
S	M	T	W	T	F	S
	1	2	3	4	5	6
7	8	9	10	11	12	13
14	15	16	17	18	19	20
21	22	23	24	25	26	27
28	29	30	31			

1789

JANUARY	FEBRUARY	MARCH	APRIL
S M T W T F S	S M T W T F S	S M T W T F S	S M T W T F S
1 2 3	1 2 3 4 5 6 7	1 2 3 4 5 6 7	1 2 3 4
4 5 6 7 8 9 10	8 9 10 11 12 13 14	8 9 10 11 12 13 14	5 6 7 8 9 10 11
11 12 13 14 15 16 17	15 16 17 18 19 20 21	15 16 17 18 19 20 21	12 13 14 15 16 17 18
18 19 20 21 22 23 24	22 23 24 25 26 27 28	22 23 24 25 26 27 28	19 20 21 22 23 24 25
25 26 27 28 29 30 31		29 30 31	26 27 28 29 30

MAY	JUNE	JULY	AUGUST
1 2	1 2 3 4 5 6	1 2 3 4	1
3 4 5 6 7 8 9	7 8 9 10 11 12 13	5 6 7 8 9 10 11	2 3 4 5 6 7 8
10 11 12 13 14 15 16	14 15 16 17 18 19 20	12 13 14 15 16 17 18	9 10 11 12 13 14 15
17 18 19 20 21 22 23	21 22 23 24 25 26 27	19 20 21 22 23 24 25	16 17 18 19 20 21 22
24 25 26 27 28 29 30	28 29 30	26 27 28 29 30 31	23 24 25 26 27 28 29
31			30 31

SEPTEMBER	OCTOBER	NOVEMBER	DECEMBER
1 2 3 4 5	1 2 3	1 2 3 4 5 6 7	1 2 3 4 5
6 7 8 9 10 11 12	4 5 6 7 8 9 10	8 9 10 11 12 13 14	6 7 8 9 10 11 12
13 14 15 16 17 18 19	11 12 13 14 15 16 17	15 16 17 18 19 20 21	13 14 15 16 17 18 19
20 21 22 23 24 25 26	18 19 20 21 22 23 24	22 23 24 25 26 27 28	20 21 22 23 24 25 26
27 28 29 30	25 26 27 28 29 30 31	29 30	27 28 29 30 31

1790

JANUARY	FEBRUARY	MARCH	APRIL
S M T W T F S	S M T W T F S	S M T W T F S	S M T W T F S
1 2	1 2 3 4 5 6	1 2 3 4 5 6	1 2 3
3 4 5 6 7 8 9	7 8 9 10 11 12 13	7 8 9 10 11 12 13	4 5 6 7 8 9 10
10 11 12 13 14 15 16	14 15 16 17 18 19 20	14 15 16 17 18 19 20	11 12 13 14 15 16 17
17 18 19 20 21 22 23	21 22 23 24 25 26 27	21 22 23 24 25 26 27	18 19 20 21 22 23 24
24 25 26 27 28 29 30	28	28 29 30 31	25 26 27 28 29 30
31			

MAY	JUNE	JULY	AUGUST
1	1 2 3 4 5	1 2 3	1 2 3 4 5 6 7
2 3 4 5 6 7 8	6 7 8 9 10 11 12	4 5 6 7 8 9 10	8 9 10 11 12 13 14
9 10 11 12 13 14 15	13 14 15 16 17 18 19	11 12 13 14 15 16 17	15 16 17 18 19 20 21
16 17 18 19 20 21 22	20 21 22 23 24 25 26	18 19 20 21 22 23 24	22 23 24 25 26 27 28
23 24 25 26 27 28 29	27 28 29 30	25 26 27 28 29 30 31	29 30 31
30 31			

SEPTEMBER	OCTOBER	NOVEMBER	DECEMBER
1 2 3 4	1 2	1 2 3 4 5 6	1 2 3 4
5 6 7 8 9 10 11	3 4 5 6 7 8 9	7 8 9 10 11 12 13	5 6 7 8 9 10 11
12 13 14 15 16 17 18	10 11 12 13 14 15 16	14 15 16 17 18 19 20	12 13 14 15 16 17 18
19 20 21 22 23 24 25	17 18 19 20 21 22 23	21 22 23 24 25 26 27	19 20 21 22 23 24 25
26 27 28 29 30	24 25 26 27 28 29 30	28 29 30	26 27 28 29 30 31
	31		

1791

		JANUARY				
S	M	T	W	T	F	S
						1
2	3	4	5	6	7	8
9	10	11	12	13	14	15
16	17	18	19	20	21	22
23	24	25	26	27	28	29
30	31					

		FEBRUARY				
S	M	T	W	T	F	S
		1	2	3	4	5
6	7	8	9	10	11	12
13	14	15	16	17	18	19
20	21	22	23	24	25	26
27	28					

		MARCH				
S	M	T	W	T	F	S
		1	2	3	4	5
6	7	8	9	10	11	12
13	14	15	16	17	18	19
20	21	22	23	24	25	26
27	28	29	30	31		

		APRIL				
S	M	T	W	T	F	S
					1	2
3	4	5	6	7	8	9
10	11	12	13	14	15	16
17	18	19	20	21	22	23
24	25	26	27	28	29	30

		MAY				
1	2	3	4	5	6	7
8	9	10	11	12	13	14
15	16	17	18	19	20	21
22	23	24	25	26	27	28
29	30	31				

		JUNE				
			1	2	3	4
5	6	7	8	9	10	11
12	13	14	15	16	17	18
19	20	21	22	23	24	25
26	27	28	29	30		

		JULY				
					1	2
3	4	5	6	7	8	9
10	11	12	13	14	15	16
17	18	19	20	21	22	23
24	25	26	27	28	29	30
31						

		AUGUST				
	1	2	3	4	5	6
7	8	9	10	11	12	13
14	15	16	17	18	19	20
21	22	23	24	25	26	27
28	29	30	31			

		SEPTEMBER				
				1	2	3
4	5	6	7	8	9	10
11	12	13	14	15	16	17
18	19	20	21	22	23	24
25	26	27	28	29	30	

		OCTOBER				
						1
2	3	4	5	6	7	8
9	10	11	12	13	14	15
16	17	18	19	20	21	22
23	24	25	26	27	28	29
30	31					

		NOVEMBER				
		1	2	3	4	5
6	7	8	9	10	11	12
13	14	15	16	17	18	19
20	21	22	23	24	25	26
27	28	29	30			

		DECEMBER				
				1	2	3
4	5	6	7	8	9	10
11	12	13	14	15	16	17
18	19	20	21	22	23	24
25	26	27	28	29	30	31

1792

		JANUARY				
S	M	T	W	T	F	S
1	2	3	4	5	6	7
8	9	10	11	12	13	14
15	16	17	18	19	20	21
22	23	24	25	26	27	28
29	30	31				

		FEBRUARY				
			1	2	3	4
5	6	7	8	9	10	11
12	13	14	15	16	17	18
19	20	21	22	23	24	25
26	27	28	29			

		MARCH				
				1	2	3
4	5	6	7	8	9	10
11	12	13	14	15	16	17
18	19	20	21	22	23	24
25	26	27	28	29	30	31

		APRIL				
1	2	3	4	5	6	7
8	9	10	11	12	13	14
15	16	17	18	19	20	21
22	23	24	25	26	27	28
29	30					

		MAY				
		1	2	3	4	5
6	7	8	9	10	11	12
13	14	15	16	17	18	19
20	21	22	23	24	25	26
27	28	29	30	31		

		JUNE				
					1	2
3	4	5	6	7	8	9
10	11	12	13	14	15	16
17	18	19	20	21	22	23
24	25	26	27	28	29	30

		JULY				
1	2	3	4	5	6	7
8	9	10	11	12	13	14
15	16	17	18	19	20	21
22	23	24	25	26	27	28
29	30	31				

		AUGUST				
			1	2	3	4
5	6	7	8	9	10	11
12	13	14	15	16	17	18
19	20	21	22	23	24	25
26	27	28	29	30	31	

		SEPTEMBER				
						1
2	3	4	5	6	7	8
9	10	11	12	13	14	15
16	17	18	19	20	21	22
23	24	25	26	27	28	29
30						

		OCTOBER				
	1	2	3	4	5	6
7	8	9	10	11	12	13
14	15	16	17	18	19	20
21	22	23	24	25	26	27
28	29	30	31			

		NOVEMBER				
				1	2	3
4	5	6	7	8	9	10
11	12	13	14	15	16	17
18	19	20	21	22	23	24
25	26	27	28	29	30	

		DECEMBER				
						1
2	3	4	5	6	7	8
9	10	11	12	13	14	15
16	17	18	19	20	21	22
23	24	25	26	27	28	29
30	31					

Symbols

FOR MANUSCRIPTS, MANUSCRIPT DEPOSITORIES, SHORT TITLES, AND CROSS-REFERENCES

Manuscripts

FC	File Copy
MS	Manuscript
RC	Recipient's Copy
Tr	Translation from Foreign Language

Repositories

DLC	Library of Congress
MB	Boston Public Library
MHi	Massachusetts Historical Society
NHi	New-York Historical Society
NN	New York Public Library
PHi	Historical Society of Pennsylvania
ViU	University of Virginia

Short Titles

Abbot, *Washington, Confederation Series*	W. W. Abbot, ed., *The Papers of George Washington: Confederation Series* (6 vols., Charlottesville, Va., 1992–1997).
Abbot, *Washington, Presidential Series*	W. W. Abbot, Dorothy Twohig et al., eds., *The Papers of George Washington: Presidential Series* (Charlottesville, Va., 1987–).
Adams, *Defence of the Constitution*	John Adams, *A Defence of the Constitutions of Government of the United States of America* . . . (3 vols., London, 1787–1788).
Adams Family Correspondence	Margaret A. Hogan, C. James Taylor et al., *Adams Family Correspondence*, vols. VIII–IX (Cambridge, Mass., and London, 2007, 2009).
Blackstone, *Commentaries*	Sir William Blackstone, *Commentaries on the Laws of England. In Four Books* (Reprinted from the British Copy, Page for Page with the Last Edition, 5 vols., Philadelphia, 1771–1772). Originally published in London from 1765 to 1769.

SYMBOLS   xxix

Boyd   Julian P. Boyd et al., eds., *The Papers of Thomas Jefferson* (Princeton, N.J., 1950–).
DHFFE   Merrill Jensen, Robert A. Becker, and Gordon DenBoer, eds., *The Documentary History of the First Federal Elections, 1788–1790* (4 vols., Madison, Wis., 1976–1989).
Evans   Number of documents found in the micro card or online version of Early American Imprints, Series I, 1639–1800.
Hening   William Waller Hening, ed., *The Statutes at Large; Being A Collection of All the Laws of Virginia, from the First Session of the Legislature, in the Year 1619* (13 vols., Richmond and Philadelphia, 1809–1823).
JCC   Worthington C. Ford et al., eds., *Journals of the Continental Congress, 1774–1789*... (34 vols., Washington, D.C., 1904–1937).
Montesquieu,   Charles, Baron de Montesquieu, *The Spirit of Laws*
  Spirit of Laws (translated from the French by Thomas Nugent, 5th ed., 2 vols., London, 1773). Originally published in Geneva in 1748.
OED   *Oxford English Dictionary* (Internet version)
*Papers of John   Sara Georgini, Sara Martin et al., eds., *Papers of
  Adams*   John Adams*, Vols. 19–20 (Cambridge, Mass., and London, 2018, 2020).
*Pennsylvania   Samuel Hazard et al., eds., *Pennsylvania Archives*
  Archives*   (119 vols., Philadelphia 1852–1935).
Rutland, *Madison* Robert A. Rutland et al., eds., *The Papers of James Madison*, Volumes VIII–XVII (Chicago and Charlottesville, Va., 1973–1991).
Rutland, *Mason*   Robert A. Rutland, ed., *The Papers of George Mason, 1725–1792* (3 vols., Chapel Hill, N.C., 1970).
Smith, *Letters*   Paul H. Smith, ed., *Letters of Delegates to Congress* (26 vols., Washington, D.C., 1976–2000).
Syrett   Harold C. Syrett et al., eds., *The Papers of Alexander Hamilton* (27 vols., New York, 1961–1987).
Thorpe   Francis N. Thorpe, ed., *The Federal and State Constitutions*... (7 vols., Washington, D.C., 1909).

Cross-references to Volumes of
The Documentary History of the Ratification of the Constitution

BoR   References to the series of volumes titled Bill of Rights are cited as "BoR" followed by the vol-

	ume and page number. For example: "BoR, I, 200."
CC	References to *Commentaries on the Constitution* are cited as "CC" followed by the number of the document. For example: "CC:25."
CDR	References to the first volume, titled *Constitutional Documents and Records, 1776–1787,* are cited as "CDR" followed by the page number. For example: "CDR, 325."
Mfm or RCS Supplement	References to the supplements to the "RCS" volumes are referred to in two ways. In Volumes II–XXXI the supplements are cited by "Mfm" followed by the state and sometimes the document number. For example "Mfm:N.C. 2." The supplemental documents for The Confederation Congress Implements the Constitution are denoted by "Mfm:Cong. 1." The supplement documents for Pennsylvania have subsequently been published by the Wisconsin Historical Society Press, and those for Rhode Island by the Center for the Study of the American Constitution. Hence starting with Volume XXXII the change has been made to referring to the supplemental documents as "RCS: State Name or Congress, the actual page number(s)." For example "RCS: Pa. Supplement, 241–42." Book quality supplements for all fourteen states and Congress will soon be available at UW Digital Collections on the University of Wisconsin–Madison Libraries web site (https://digital.library.wisc.edu/1711.dl/Constitution). Access to the documents can be either through the Mfm document number or the supplement pages. However, the two Cumulative Index volumes (XXXV–XXXVI) use only the page numbers as well as this and all future Bill of Rights volumes.
RCS	References to the series of volumes titled *Ratification of the Constitution by the States* are cited as "RCS" followed by the abbreviation of the state and the page number. For example: "RCS:N.C., 200."

The Ratification
of the Constitution
and Bill of Rights

BILL OF RIGHTS
[3]

Introduction

This third volume in the Bill of Rights series of the *Documentary History of the Ratification of the Constitution* covers the public debate over amendments to the Constitution from June through December 1788. During this time, three states ratified the Constitution with recommendatory amendments—New Hampshire, Virginia, and New York. The North Carolina Convention, meeting in July and August, voted not to ratify the Constitution without many amendments. This volume contains the portions of those speeches in the Virginia and North Carolina conventions concerning amendments. Speakers include Patrick Henry, James Madison, John Marshall, George Mason, Edmund Randolph, Timothy Bloodworth, William R. Davie, James Iredell, and Richard Dobbs Spraight. Also included is a newspaper report of one speech in the New Hampshire Convention and a newspaper printing of what was purported to be an undelivered speech in the New York Convention. Two letters, one by Mason and the other by Joshua Atherton, respond to New York Antifederalist efforts to get Antifederalist convention delegates in other states to cooperate in securing amendments previous to ratification of the Constitution.

Although New Hampshire's ratification on 21 June satisfied the nine-state requirement in Article VII of the Constitution, it was only when Virginia became the tenth state to ratify four days later on 25 June that it seemed likely that the Constitution would be successfully implemented. Details and logistics pertaining to the Constitution's implementation were to be handled by the Confederation Congress. On 2 July, after it received New Hampshire's form of ratification, Congress appointed a committee to consider the implementation of the Constitution. Delaying its action out of deference to New York, whose Convention was still meeting, Congress finally adopted an ordinance on 13 September calling the first federal elections and specifying that the first federal Congress should meet in New York City on 4 March 1789.

With the adoption by Virginia and New York, the focal point of the public debate shifted from a contest between adopting amendments before or after the implementation of the Constitution to a question of the procedure to be used to propose amendments—either to be proposed by Congress or by a second constitutional convention. Those Federalists who believed that some amendments might be necessary wanted them proposed by Congress rather than by a second convention that might emulate the previous convention in abandoning its mandate and proposing a new form of government. Antifederalists, however, persisted in calling for another convention.

The New York Convention proposed a second convention in its 26 July 1788 circular letter to the other states. Federalists expressed concern over the impact of the circular letter in private letters and newspaper pieces. In Pennsylvania opposition to the Constitution remained strong. A public meeting in Cumberland County on 3 July asserted that "unless prudent Steps be taken to combine the friends of amendments, in some place in which they may confidently draw together and exert their power in unison, posterity, [will] become Slaves to the Officers of Government." The circular letter was sent by Antifederalists to the state's other counties asking them to send delegates to a convention to meet in Harrisburg to propose amendments to the Constitution and to nominate candidates for the U.S. House of Representatives. Thirty-three delegates from thirteen counties and the city of Philadelphia attended the convention from 3 to 6 September. They resolved that Pennsylvanians should acquiesce in the adoption of the Constitution but that amendments were essential to safeguard liberty. The convention approved twelve amendments which were to be sent to the state Assembly in the form of a petition and a slate of candidates was prepared for the ensuing statewide election of federal representatives. The convention's proceedings were printed in newspapers throughout the country, but no record of the Assembly's receipt of the petition has been located. The call of the convention, its proceedings and amendments, and reactions by especially Federalists to it are a large grouping of documents in this volume.

The New York circular letter received its most favorable response from the Virginia legislature. On 21 October 1788, Governor Edmund Randolph submitted it to the state legislature. Eight days later, Patrick Henry, a dominant force in the Virginia House of Delegates, declared that he would "oppose every measure" for putting the Constitution into motion in Virginia unless the legislature called for a second convention. Henry offered several resolutions, one of which provided that the legislature should request Congress to call a second convention. Henry maintained that "the most precious rights of the people if not cancelled are rendered insecure" by the Constitution. Federalists condemned Henry's language as "a direct and indecent censure on all those who have befriended the new constitution holding them forth as the betrayers of the dearest rights of the people" (Charles Lee to George Washington, 29 October). Henry's resolutions did not surprise Federalists who had been concerned that Virginia and New York would lead "an effort for early amendments" (Washington to Benjamin Lincoln,

26 October). But while, "many amendments and explanations might and should take place," some Federalists conceded, the greater worry was that New York's circular letter would, "set every thing afloat again" (Washington to Lincoln, 28 August). After considerable debate, the Virginia legislature on 20 November adopted a resolution requesting Congress to call a second convention. Federalists denounced the resolution. James Madison complained that "The measures pursued at Richmond are as impolitic as they are otherwise exceptionable—if alterations of a reasonable sort are really in view, they are much more attainable from Congress than from attempts to bring about another Convention—It is already decided that the latter mode is a hopeless pursuit" (to Henry Lee, 30 November).

In Virginia Federalists and Antifederalists also fought over who would be elected to serve in the first congress under the Constitution. In numerous letters both sides plotted strategy. In the end, Antifederalists Richard Henry Lee and William Grayson were elected U.S. senators by the legislature, defeating James Madison. Because Madison was still in New York City serving in the Confederation Congress, there are many letters back and forth from Richmond. This volume also includes documents on the beginning of the contest between Madison and Antifederalist James Monroe for a seat in the U.S. House of Representatives.

In Maryland the contest over amendments and the elections for Congress began with the struggle over who would control the state legislature. Federalist and Antifederalist pieces appeared in the state's newspapers. Much of the debate involved Samuel Chase's candidacy from Baltimore. Even though Chase voted to ratify the Constitution in the state Convention, he supported the amendments proposed by the Antifederalist minority in the Convention. (See Appendix I, BoR, III, 472–76.)

The debate in Massachusetts involved both amendments and elections. The sincerity of the conciliatory proposal of amendments in the Massachusetts Convention was discussed in newspaper pieces. Federalists ranged from supporting some amendments, primarily of a bill of rights type, and opposing all amendments. Samuel Adams was caught up in the debate over how much support for amendments made a candidate a safe supporter of the Constitution. Governor John Hancock drafted an address to the legislature supporting amendments but never delivered it because he said he was too ill.

The New York legislature did not meet until 8 December 1788 and its response to the Virginia legislature's 20 November resolutions took place in early 1789. A group of New York City Antifederalists did try to coordinate efforts on behalf of a second convention in early November.

They addressed circular letters to the various counties in the state and the other states. Two major Antifederalist essay appeared in New York papers in December—by "Sidney" (Abraham Yates, Jr.) and "A Republican Federalist" (perhaps Melancton Smith).

This volume also contains the first eighteen of the twenty-eight essays by a "Foreign Spectator." Written by Nicholas Collin, the essays appeared in the Philadelphia *Federal Gazette* beginning on 21 October 1788. They are the only substantial series of essay to discuss comprehensively the amendments proposed by the state conventions and what amendments might be appropriate for Congress to propose to the states for ratification. Another series of four essays on amendments signed "An American Citizen" was written by Tench Coxe. They also appeared in Philadelphia newspapers on 4 June and 10, 24, and 31 December. "A Citizen of New-Haven," written by Roger Sherman, appeared in the Connecticut *New Haven Gazette* on 18 December.

This volume contains over 350 documents—153 newspaper items, broadsides, and pamphlets, 148 letters, 52 speeches, and 7 proceedings of town and county meetings. The letter writers include such prominent individuals as Alexander Hamilton, Thomas Jefferson (from Paris, France), Richard Henry Lee, Benjamin Lincoln, James Madison, Edmund Randolph, and George Washington. A biographical gazetteer at the end of the volume identifies letter writers, speech makers, and newspaper essayists and an appendix contains the amendments proposed by the Antifederalist minority in the Maryland Convention.

An American Citizen
Pennsylvania Gazette, 4 June 1788[1]

On the SOVEREIGNTY, or Supreme Power of the United States of America, as it will stand, according to the true interest and operation of the fœderal and state constitutions, in the event of the adoption of the new act of confederation, proposed to the people by the late general convention in September, 1787.

The actual seat of the sovereign power in every country, or the body in which it is really invested, is that, which can *at all times* alter, amend or add to the constitution of the government. The following article of the proposed fœderal constitution effectually and absolutely reserves that sovereign power to the state legislatures and state conventions, chosen by the people.

"The Congress, when two thirds of both houses shall deem it necessary, shall *propose* amendments to this constitution, or, on the application of the legislatures of two thirds of the several states, *shall* call a convention for proposing amendments, which in either case shall be valid to all intents and purposes, as part of this constitution, when ratified by *the legislatures of three fourths* of the several states, or by *conventions in three fourths* thereof, as the one or the other mode of ratification may be proposed by the Congress."

Congress, we see, may *propose* any amendments that appear necessary, but cannot *adopt* or *ratify* one. As to important business of amendments or alterations of the constitution, they will be a mere council of advice, whose proposed alterations will always be rejected, if four states of the thirteen shall disapprove them. It appears clearly, then, that Congress cannot make or alter the supreme law of the land—that is, the constitution of government,—and of course that *they will not hold the sovereign power.*

Where then will this power, paramount to all others, lie? The above article says that Congress, on the application of two thirds of the state legislatures, *shall* call a convention for proposing amendments. Here is an instance of *high powers* wisely deposited in the hands of *the state legislatures,* for they can *compel* the fœderal legislature, who we have seen are not the sovereign, to institute amendments which Congress absolutely disapprove, and which may diminish and reduce their powers. But should the state legislatures wish dangerously or unwisely to enlarge their own jurisdiction, by depriving Congress of such powers as are *safe and necessary,* there is left in the hands of the fœderal legislature, a right to require that the amendments and alterations proposed shall be considered by a convention in every state, *chosen by the people themselves.*

The powers of THE PEOPLE OF THE UNITED STATES OF AMERICA it appears therefore will be,

1st. That they alone will chuse *all* the legislative, executive, judicial and military officers of their general and state governments, or that they will chuse those who are to appoint them.

2dly. That they *alone* will chuse all the members of the state legislatures and state conventions, to which bodies are specially reserved the right to ratify alterations and amendments of the fœderal constitution, not only *independently of Congress,* but altho' such alterations and amendments should be contrary to *the unanimous opinion* of that body. Truly then may we affirm, that the supreme or sovereign power of the United States of America, in the event of the adoption of the proposed fœderal constitution, will not be vested in Congress, but that it will remain in the people themselves.

1. Reprinted: *New York Packet,* 6 June; New York *Daily Advertiser,* 9 June; Charleston, S.C., *City Gazette,* 5 July. Tench Coxe was probably the author of this essay. He wrote four "An American Citizen" essays between 26 September and 21 October 1787 (CC:100, 109, 112, and BoR, II, 56–58) and informed James Madison on 9 September 1789 that he wrote "near thirty lengthy publications" supporting the Constitution (Rutland, *Madison,* XII, 396). For other "American Citizen" essays in this volume, see the Philadelphia *Federal Gazette,* 10, 24, 31 December (BoR, III, 407–9, 442–45, 456–57).

The Virginia Convention and a Bill of Rights
7–27 June 1788

The speeches in the Virginia Convention have been transcribed from *Debates and Other Proceedings of the Convention of Virginia* . . . (3 vols., 1788–1789) (Evans 21551 and 22225), printed by Miles Hunter and William Prentis of the Petersburgh *Virginia Gazette.* The text was taken in shorthand notes by David Robertson, a prominent Petersburgh lawyer who had emigrated from Scotland to serve as a tutor. In 1805, Robertson published a new edition. Significant changes in this later edition are placed within angle brackets. For full transcriptions of excerpted speeches, see RCS:Va., 1035–47, 1072–87, 1092–1103, 1103–15, 1127–37, 1192–1202, 1219–26, 1347–54, 1393–95, 1474–88.

On 27 June 1788, the Virginia Convention approved a declaration of rights and a list of amendments (each with twenty articles) that were to be submitted to Congress. See BoR, I, 251–56.

Patrick Henry: Speech in the Virginia Convention
7 June 1788 (excerpt)

. . . Trial by jury and liberty of the press, are also on this foundation of implication. If they encroach on these rights, and you give your implication for a plea, you are cast; for they will be justified by the last part of it, which gives them full power, "To make all laws which shall be necessary and proper to carry their powers into execution." Implication is dangerous, because it is unbounded: If it be admitted at all, and no limits be prescribed, it admits of the utmost extension. They say that every thing that is not given is retained. The reverse of the proposition is true by implication. They do not carry their implication so far when they speak of the general welfare. No implication when the sweeping clause comes. Implication is only necessary when the existence of privileges is in dispute. The existence of powers is sufficiently established. If we trust our dearest rights to implication, we shall be in a very unhappy situation.

Implication in England has been a source of dissention. There has been a war of implication between the King and people. For 100 years did the mother country struggle under the uncertainty of implication. The people insisted that their rights were implied: The Monarch denied the doctrine. Their Bill of Rights in some degree terminated the dispute.[1] By a bold implication, they said they had a right to bind us in all cases whatsoever.[2] This constructive power we opposed, and successfully. Thirteen or fourteen years ago, the most important thing that could be thought of, was to exclude the possibility of construction and implication. These, Sir, were then deemed perilous. The first thing that was thought of, was a Bill of Rights. We were not satisfied with your constructive argumentative rights.

Mr. *Henry* then declared, a Bill of Rights indispensably necessary; that a general positive provision should be inserted in the new system, securing to the States and the people, every right which was not conceded to the General Government; and that every implication should be done away. It being now late, he concluded by observing, that he would resume the subject another time.

1. For the English Bill of Rights (1689), see BoR, I, 4–8.
2. A reference to the Declaratory Act of 1766.

Henry Lee: Speech in the Virginia Convention
9 June 1788 (excerpt)

... It was necessary to provide against licentiousness, which is so natural to our climate. I dread more from the licentiousness of the people, than from the bad government of rulers. Our privileges are not however in danger: They are better secured than any bill of rights could have secured them.

I say that this new system shews in stronger terms than words could declare, that the liberties of the people are secure. It goes on the principle that all power is in the people, and that rulers have no powers but what are enumerated in that paper. When a question arises with respect to the legality of any power, exercised or assumed by Congress, it is plain on the side of the governed. *Is it enumerated in the Constitution?* If it be, it is legal and just. It is otherwise arbitrary and unconstitutional. Candour must confess, that it is infinitely more attentive to the liberties of the people than any State Government.

(Mr. *Lee* then said, that under the State Governments the people reserved to themselves certain enumerated rights, and that the rest were vested in their rulers. That consequently the powers reserved to the people, were but an inconsiderable exception from what was given to their rulers. But that in the Federal Government the rulers of the people were vested with certain defined powers, and that what was not delegated to those rulers were retained by the people. The consequence of this, he said, was, that the limited powers were only an exception to those which still rested in the people, that the people therefore knew what they had given up, and could be in no danger. He exemplified the proposition in a familiar manner. He observed, that if a man delegated certain powers to an agent, it would be an insult upon common sense, to suppose, that the agent could legally transact any business for his principal, which was not contained in the commission whereby the powers were delegated. But that if a man empowered his representative or agent to transact all his business, except certain enumerated parts, the clear result was, that the agent could lawfully transact every possible part of his principal's business except the enumerated parts; and added, that these plain propositions were sufficient to demonstrate the inutility and *folly*, were he permitted to use the expression, of Bills of Rights.) He then continued,—I am convinced that that paper secures the liberty of Virginia, and of the United States.—I ask myself, if there be a single power in it, which is not necessary for the support of the Union; and as far as my reasoning goes, I say, that if you deprive it of one single power contained in it, it will be "*Vox et præterea nihil.*"[1] Those who are to go ⟨to⟩[2] Congress will be the servants of the people. They are created and deputed by us, and removeable by us. Is there a greater security than this in our State Government? To fortify this security, is there not a constitutional remedy in the Government, to reform any errors which shall be found inconvenient? Although the Honorable Gentleman [i.e., Patrick Henry] has dwelt so long upon it, he has not made it appear otherwise.—The Confederation can neither render us happy at home, nor respectable abroad; I conceive this system will do both. The two Gentlemen [James Madison and Edmund Randolph] who have been in the Grand Convention have proved incontestibly, that the fears arising from the powers of Congress, are groundless. Having now gone through some of the principal parts of the Gentleman's [Patrick Henry's] harangue, I shall take up but a few moments in replying to its conclusion. . . .

1. Latin: "A voice and nothing more," or empty words.
2. Added in the 1805 edition.

Edmund Randolph: Speech in the Virginia Convention 9 June 1788 (excerpt)

. . . I am going to correct a still greater error which he [i.e., Patrick Henry] has committed, not in order to shew any little knowledge of history I may have (for I am by no means satisfied with its extent) but to endeavor to prevent any impressions from being made by improper and mistaken representations.

He said that Magna Charta destroyed all implication. That was not the object of Magna Charta, but to destroy the power of the King, and secure the liberty of the people. The Bill of Rights was intended to restore the Government to its primitive principles.[1]

We are harrassed by quotations from Holland and Switzerland, which are inapplicable in themselves, and not founded in fact.

I am surprised at his proposition of previous amendments, and his assertion, that subsequent ones will cause disunion.—Shall we not loose[2] our influence and weight in the Government, to bring about amendments, if we propose them previously? Will not the Senators be chosen, and the electors of the President be appointed, and the Government brought instantly into action after the ratification of nine States? Is this disunion, when the effect proposed will be produced? But no man here is willing to believe what the Honorable Gentleman says on this point. I was in hopes we should come to some degree of order. I fear that order is no more. I believed that we should confine ourselves to the particular clause under consideration, and to such other clauses as might be connected with it.

Why have we been told, that maxims can alone save nations—that our maxims are our Bill of Rights—and that the liberty of the press, trial by jury, and religion, are destroyed? Give me leave to say, that the maxims of Virginia are Union and Justice.

The Honorable Gentleman has past by my observations with respect to British debts. He has thought proper to be silent on this subject. My observations must therefore have full force. Justice is, and ought to be our maxim; and must be that of every temperate, moderate and upright man. I should not say so much on this occasion were it not that I perceive that the flowers of ⟨reasoning⟩ ⟨rhetoric⟩[3] are perverted in order to make impressions unfavorable and inimical to an impartial and candid decission. What security can arise from a Bill of Rights? The predilection for it, has arisen from a misconception of its principles. It cannot secure the liberties of this country. A Bill of Rights was used in England to limit the King's prerogative: He could trample on the liberties of the people, in every case which was not within the restraint of the Bill of Rights.

Our situation is radically different from that of the people of England. What have we to do with Bills of Rights? Six or seven States have none.[4] Massachusetts has declared her Bill of Rights as part of her Constitution. Virginia has a Bill of Rights, but it is no part of the Constitution.[5] By not saying whether it is paramount to the Constitution or not, it has left us in confusion. Is the Bill of Rights consistent with the Constitution? Why then is it not inserted in the Constitution? Does it add any thing to the Constitution? Why is it not the Constitution? Does it except any thing from the Constitution; why not put the exceptions in the Constitution? Does it oppose the Constitution? This will produce mischief. The Judges will dispute which is paramount: Some will say, the Bill of Rights is paramount:—Others will say, that the Constitution being subsequent in point of time, must be paramount. A Bill of Rights therefore, accurately speaking, is quite useless, if not dangerous, in a republic. . . .

1. For the Magna Carta, see BoR, I, 3–4. For the English Bill of Rights, see BoR, I, 4–8.
2. "Lose" in 1805 edition.
3. "Rhetoric" replaced "reasoning" in the 1805 edition.
4. See note 2 to "One of the People," *Maryland Journal,* 25 December 1787 (BoR, II, 210).
5. For the Massachusetts and Virginia declarations of rights, see BoR, I, 75–80, 111–13.

Edmund Randolph: Speech in the Virginia Convention
10 June 1788 (excerpt)

. . . The Constitution provides, that "the Senators and Representatives before mentioned, and the members of the several State Legislatures, and all Executive and Judicial officers, both of the United States and of the several States, shall be bound by oath, or affirmation, to support this Constitution; but no religious test shall ever be required as a qualification to any office or public trust under the United States." It has been said, that if the exclusion of the religious test were an exception from the general power of Congress, the power over religion would remain. I inform those who are of this opinion, that no power is given expressly to Congress over religion. The Senators and Representatives, members of the State Legislatures, and Executive and Judicial officers, are bound by oath, or affirmation, to support this Constitution. This only binds them to support it in the exercise of the powers constitutionally given it. The exclusion of religious tests is an exception from this general provision, with respect to oaths, or affirmations. Although officers, &c. are to swear that they will support this Constitution, yet they are not bound to support one mode of worship, or to adhere to one particular sect. It puts all sects on the same footing. A man of abilities and character, of any sect whatever, may be admitted to any office or public trust under the United States. I am a friend to a variety of sects, because they keep one another in order. How many different sects are we composed of throughout the United States? How many different sects will be in Congress? We cannot enumerate the sects that may be in Congress.—And there are so many now in the United States, that they will prevent the establishment of any one sect in prejudice to the rest, and will forever oppose all attempts to infringe religious liberty. If such an attempt be made, will not the alarm be sounded throughout America? If Congress be as wicked as we are foretold they will, they would not run the risk of exciting the resentment of all, or most of the religious sects in America....

James Monroe: Speech in the Virginia Convention 10 June 1788 (excerpt)

... As it will operate on all States and individuals, powers given it generally should be qualified. It may be attributed to the prejudice of my education, but I am a decided and warm friend to a *Bill of Rights*—the polar star, and great support of American liberty; and I am clearly of opinion, that the general powers conceded by that plan, such as the impost, &c. should be guarded and checked by a Bill of Rights.

Permit me to examine the reasoning, that admits, that all powers not given up are reserved. Apply this. If you give to the United States the power of direct taxation—In making all laws necessary to give it operation (which is a power given by the last clause, in the eighth section, of the first article) suppose they should be of opinion, that the right of the trial by jury, was one of the requisites to carry it into effect; there is no check in this Constitution to prevent the formal abolition of it. There is a general power given to them, to make all laws that will enable them to carry their powers into effect. There are no limits pointed out. They are not restrained or controuled from making any law, however oppressive in its operation, which they may think necessary to carry their powers into effect. By this general unqualified power, they may infringe not only the trial by jury, but the liberty of the press, and every right that is not expressly secured, or excepted, from that general power. I conceive that such general powers are very dangerous. Our great unalienable rights ought to be secured from being destroyed by such unlimited powers, either by a Bill of Rights, or by an express provision in the body of the Constitution. It is immaterial in which of these two modes rights are secured. . . .

George Nicholas: Speech in the Virginia Convention 10 June 1788 (excerpts)

. . . The worthy member [i.e., Patrick Henry] has enlarged on our Bill of Rights. Let us see whether his encomiums on the Bill of Rights be consistent with his other arguments. Our Declaration of Rights[1] says, that all men are by nature equally free and independent. How comes the Gentleman to reconcile himself to a Government wherein there are a hereditary Monarch and nobility? He objects to this change although our present federal system is totally without energy—He objects to this system, because he says, it will lay prostrate your Bill of Rights. Does not the Bill of Rights tell you, that a majority of the community have an indubitable right to alter any Government, which shall be found inadequate to the security of the public happiness? Does it not say, "that no free Government, or the blessings of liberty can be preserved to any people, but by a firm adherence to justice, moderation, temperance, frugality, and virtue, and by frequent recurrence to fundamental principles"? Have not the inadequacy of the present system, and repeated flagrant violations of justice, and the other principles recommended by the Bill of Rights, been amply proved? As this plan of Government will promote our happiness and establish justice, will not its adoption be justified by the very principles of your Bill of Rights? . . .

But it is objected to for want of a Bill of Rights. It is a principle universally agreed upon, that all powers not given, are retained. Where by the Constitution, the General Government has general powers, for any purpose, its powers are absolute. Where it has powers with some exceptions, they are absolute, only as to those exceptions. In either case, the people retain what is not conferred on the General Government, as it is by their positive grant that it has any of its powers. In England, in all disputes between the King and people, recurrence is had to the enumerated rights of the people to determine. Are the rights in dispute secured—Are they included in Magna Charta, Bill of Rights, &c.? If not, they are, generally speaking, within the King's prerogative. In disputes between Congress and the people, the reverse of the proposition holds. Is the disputed right enumerated? If not, Congress cannot meddle with it. Which is the most safe? The people of America know what they have relinquished, for certain purposes. They also know that they retain every thing else, and have a right to resume what they have given up, if it be perverted from its intended object. The King's prerogative is general, with certain exceptions. The people are therefore less secure than we are. Magna Charta, Bill of Rights, &c. secure their liberty. Our Constitution itself contains an English Bill of Rights. The English Bill of Rights declares, that Parliaments shall be held frequently. Our Constitution says, that Congress shall sit annually. The English Declaration of Rights provides, that no laws shall be suspended. The Constitution provides, that no law shall be suspended, except one, and that in times of rebellion, or invasion, which is the writ of *habeas corpus*. The Declaration of Rights says, that there should be no army in time of peace *without the consent of Parliament*. Here we cannot have an army even in time of war, *with* the approbation of our Representatives, for more than two years.

The liberty of the press is secured. What secures it in England? Is it secured by Magna Charta, the Declaration of Rights, or by any other express provision? It is not. They have no express security for the liberty of the press. They have a reliance on Parliament for its protection and security. In the time of King William, there passed an act for licensing the press. That was repealed.[2] Since that time it has been looked upon as safe. The people have depended on their Representatives. They will not consent to pass an act to infringe it, because such an act would irritate the nation. It is equally secure with us. As to the trial by jury, consider in what situation it is by the State Constitution. It is not on a better footing. It is by implication under the controul of the Legislature; because it has left particular cases to be decided by the Legislature. Here it is secured in criminal cases, and left to the Legislature in civil cases. One instance will prove the evil tendency of fixing it in the Constitution. It would extend to all cases. Causes in Chancery, which, strictly speaking, never are, nor can be well tried by a jury, would then be tried by that mode, and could not be altered though found to be inconvenient. . . .

1. For the Virginia Declaration of Rights, see BoR, I, 111–13.
2. The Printing Act of 1662 authorized the licensing of the press in England. The act was renewed several times until in 1694 the House of Commons opposed another renewal, thereby ending licensing (Frederick S. Siebert, *Freedom of the Press in England, 1476–1776* [Urbana, Ill., 1952], 237–63).

Edmund Pendleton: Speech in the Virginia Convention
12 June 1788 (excerpt)

... The happiness of the people is the object of this Government, and the people are therefore made the fountain of all power. They cannot act personally and must delegate powers. Here the worthy Gentleman who spoke last [William Grayson], and I, travelling not together indeed, but in sight, are placed at an immeasurable distance—as far as the poles asunder. He recommends a Government more energetic and strong than this—abundantly too strong ever to receive my approbation. A first Magistrate borrowed from Britain, to whom you are to make a surrender of your liberty, and you give him a seperate interest from yours. You intrench that interest by powers and prerogatives undefined—implant in him self-love, from the influence of which he is to do, what—to promote your interest in opposition to his own?—An operation of self-love, which is new! Having done this, you accept from him a charter of the right you have parted with—present him a Bill of Rights—telling him, *thus far shall you oppress us and no farther.*[1] It still depends on him whether he will give you that charter, or allow the operation of the Bill of Rights. He will do it as long as he cannot do otherwise, but no longer. Did ever any free people in the world, not dictated to, by the sword of a conquerer, or by circumstances into which licentiousness may have plunged them, place themselves in so degrading a situation, or make so disgraceful a sacrifice of their liberty? If they did, sure I am that the example will not be followed by this Convention. This is not all; we are to look some where for the chosen few to go into the ten miles square, with extensive powers for life, and thereby destroy every degree of true responsibility. Is there no medium, or shall we recur to extremes? As a republican, Sir, I think that the security of the liberty and happiness of the *people*, from the highest to the lowest, being the object of Government, the people are consequently the fountain of all power. They must, however, delegate it to agents, because from their number, dispersed situation, and many other circumstances, they cannot exercise it in person. They must therefore by frequent, and certain elections, choose Representatives to whom they trust it. Is there any distinction in the exercise of this delegation of power? The man who possesses twenty-five acres of land, has an equal right of voting for a Representative, with the man who has twenty-five thousand acres. This equality of suffrage, secures the people in their property. While we are in pursuit of checks and balances, and proper security in the delegation of power, we ought never to loose sight of the representative character. By this we preserve the great principle, of the primary right of power in the people, and should deviations happen from our interests, the spirit of liberty in future elections will correct it.—A security I esteem far superior to Paper-Bills of Rights.

When the bands of our former society were dissolved, and we were under the necessity of forming a new Government, we established a Constitution, founded on the principle of representation, preserving therein frequency of elections, and guarding against inequality of suffrage. I am one of those who are pleased with that Constitution, because it is built on that foundation. I believe that if the Confederation had the principles and efficacy of that Constitution, we should have found that peace and happiness which we are all in search of. In this State Constitution, to the Executive you commit the sword,—to the Legislative you commit the purse, and every thing else without any limitation. In both cases the representative character is in full effect, and thereby responsibility is secured.—The Judiciary is separate and distinct from both the other branches, has nothing to do with either the purse or sword, and for obvious reasons, the judges hold their office during good behaviour.

There will be deviations even in our State Legislature thus constituted. I say, (and I hope to give no offence when I do) there *have been* some. I believe every Gentleman will see that it is unconstitutional to condemn any man without a fair trial. Such a condemnation is repugnant to the principles of justice. It is contrary to the Constitution, and the spirit of the common law. Look at the Bill of Rights. You find there, that no man should be condemned without being confronted with his accusers and witnesses—that every man has a right to call for evidence in his favor, and above all, to a speedy trial by an impartial jury of the vicinage, without whose unanimous consent he cannot be found guilty.— These principles have not been attended to. An instance has been mentioned already, where they have been in some degree violated.[2] (Here Mr. *Pendleton* spoke so very low that he could not be heard.) My brethren in that department (*the judicial*) felt great uneasiness in their minds, to violate the Constitution by such a law. They have prevented the operation of some unconstitutional acts.[3] Notwithstanding those violations, I rely upon the principles of the Government—that it will produce its own reform, by the responsibility resulting from frequent elections.— We are finally safe while we preserve the representative character. I made these observations as introductory to the consideration of the paper on your table. I conceive that in those respects where our State Constitution has not been disapproved of, objections will not apply against that on your table: When we were forming our State Constitution we were confined to local circumstances. In forming a Government for the Union, we must consider our situation as connected with our neighbouring States. We have seen the advantages and blessings of the Union. Every intelligent and patriotic mind must be convinced that it is essentially necessary to our happiness. God grant we may never see the disadvantages of disunion....

1. An adaptation of Job 38:11, which reads: "And [God] said, Hitherto shalt thou come, but no further: and here shall thy proud waves be stayed?"

2. Pendleton refers to the attainder of Josiah Philips, who was executed in 1778. See the speeches of Edmund Randolph, Patrick Henry, and Benjamin Harrison, Convention Debates, 6, 7, and 10 June (RCS:Va., 972, 1004, note 5, 1038, 1127).

3. For example, in May 1788 Pendleton himself, as President of the Court of Appeals, sent Governor Edmund Randolph the court's remonstrance which asserted that the act for establishing district courts (passed in January 1788) was unconstitutional. (See Charles Lee to George Washington, 14 May, note 2, RCS:Va., 797–98.) For the case of *Commonwealth* v. *Caton* (1782), also concerned with the principle of judicial review, see Bernard Schwartz, ed., *The Roots of the Bill of Rights: An Illustrated Source Book of American Freedom* (5 vols., New York, 1980), II, 404, 410–16.

Patrick Henry: Speech in the Virginia Convention
12 June 1788 (excerpt)

... The Honorable Gentleman has endeavored to explain the opinion of Mr. Jefferson our common friend, into an advice to adopt this new Government.[1] What are his sentiments? He wishes nine States to adopt, and that four States may be found somewhere to reject it? Now, Sir, I say, if we pursue his advice, what are we to do?—To prefer form to substance? For, give me leave to ask what is the substantial part of his counsel? It is, Sir, that four States should *reject.* They tell us, that from the most authentic accounts, New-Hampshire will adopt it. When I denied this, Gentlemen said they were absolutely certain of it. Where then will four States be found to reject, if we adopt it? If we do, the counsel of this enlightened and worthy countryman of ours, will be thrown away,—and for what? He wishes to secure amendments and a Bill of Rights, if I am not mistaken. I speak from the best information, and if wrong, I beg to be put right. His amendments go to that despised thing *a Bill of Rights,* and all the rights which are dear to human nature—Trial by jury, the liberty of religion, and the press, &c—Do not Gentlemen see, that if we adopt under the idea of following Mr. Jefferson's opinion, we amuse ourselves with the shadow, while the substance is given away? If Virginia be for adoption, what States will be left, of sufficient respectability and importance, to secure amendments by their rejection? As to North Carolina it is *a poor despised place.* Its dissent will not have influence to introduce any amendments.—Where is the American spirit of liberty? Where will you find attachment to the rights of mankind, when Massachusetts the great Northern State, Pennsylvania the great middle State, and Virginia the great Southern State, shall have adopted this Government? Where will you find magnanimity enough to reject it? Should the remaining States have this magnanimity, they will not have sufficient weight to have the Government altered. This State has weight and importance. Her example will have powerful influence—Her rejection will procure amendments—Shall we by our adoption hazard the loss of amendments?—Shall we forsake that importance and respectability which our station in America commands, in hopes that relief will come from an obscure part of the Union? I hope my countrymen will spurn at the idea. The necessity of amendments is universally admitted. It is a word which is re-echoed from every part of the Continent. A majority of those who hear me, think amendments are necessary. Policy tells us they are necessary. Reason, self-preservation, and every idea of propriety, powerfully urge us to secure the dearest rights of human nature—Shall we in direct violation of these principles, rest this security upon the uncertainty of its being obtained by a few States more weak, and less respectable than ourselves—and whose virtue and magnanimity may be overborne by the example of so many adopting States?—*Poor* Rhode-Island and North-Carolina, and even New-York, surrounded with Federal walls on every side, may not be magnanimous enough to reject, and if they do reject it, they will have but little influence to obtain amendments. I ask, if amendments be necessary, from whence can they be so properly proposed as from this State? The example of Virginia is a powerful thing, particularly with respect to North-Carolina, whose supplies must come *through* Virginia. Every possible opportunity of procuring amendments is gone—Our power and political salvation is gone, if we ratify unconditionally. The important right of making treaties is upon the most dangerous foundation. The President with a few Senators possess it in the most unlimited manner, without any real responsibility, if from sinister views they should think proper to abuse it. For they may keep all their measures in the most profound secrecy as long as they please. Were we not told that war was the case wherein secrecy was most necessary? But by the paper on your table, their secrecy is not limited to this case only. It is as unlimited and unbounded as their powers. Under the abominable veil of political secrecy and contrivance, your most valuable rights may be sacrificed by a most corrupt faction, without having the satisfaction of knowing who injured you. They are bound by honor and conscience to act with integrity, but they are under no constitutional restraint. The navigation of the Mississippi, which is of so much importance to the happiness of the people of this country, may be lost by the operation of that paper. There are seven States now decidedly opposed to this navigation. If it be of the highest consequence to know who they are who shall have voted its relinquishment, the Federal veil of secrecy will prevent that discovery. We may labor under the magnitude of our miseries without knowing or being able to punish those who produced them. I did not wish that transactions relative to treaties should when unfinished, be exposed; but that it should be known after they were concluded, who had advised them to be made, in order to secure some degree of certainty that the public interest shall be consulted in their formation.

We are told that all powers not given are reserved. I am sorry to bring forth hackneyed observations. But, Sir, important truths lose nothing of their validity or weight, by frequency of repetition. The English history is frequently recurred to by Gentlemen. Let us advert to the conduct of the people of that country. The people of England lived without a declaration of rights, till the war in the time of Charles Ist. That King made usurpations upon the rights of the people. Those rights were in a great measure before that time undefined. Power and privilege then depended on implication and logical discussion. Though the declaration of rights [i.e., the Petition of Right of 1628] was obtained from that King, his usurpations cost him his life. The limits between the liberty of the people, and the prerogative of the King, were still not clearly defined. The rights of the people continued to be violated till the Steward [i.e., Stuart] family was banished in the year 1688. The people of England magnanimously defended their rights, banished the tyrant, and prescribed to William Prince of Orange, *by the Bill of Rights*,[2] on what terms he should reign. And this Bill of Rights put an end to all construction and implication. Before this, Sir, the situation of the public liberty of England was dreadful. For upwards of a century the nation was involved in every kind of calamity, till the Bill of Rights put an end to all, by defining the rights of the people, and limiting the King's prerogative. Give me leave to add (if I can add any thing to so splendid an example) the conduct of the American people. They Sir, thought *a Bill of Rights* necessary. It is alledged that several States, in the formation of their governments, omitted a Bill of Rights. To this I answer, that they had the substance of a Bill of Rights contained in their Constitutions, which is the same thing. I believe that Connecticut has preserved by her Constitution her royal charter, which clearly defines and secures the great rights of mankind—Secure to us the great important rights of humanity, and I care not in what form it is done. Of what advantage is it to the American Congress to take away this great and general security? I ask of what advantage is it to the public or to Congress to drag an unhappy debtor, not for the sake of justice, but to gratify the malice of the plaintiff, with his witnesses to the Federal Court, from a great distance? What was the principle that actuated the Convention in proposing to put such dangerous powers in the hands of any one? Why is the trial by jury taken away? All the learned arguments that have been used on this occasion do not prove that it is secured. Even the advocates for the plan do not all concur in the certainty of its security. Wherefore is religious liberty not secured? One Honorable Gentleman[3] who favors adoption, said that he had had his fears on the subject. If I can well recollect, he informed us that he was perfectly satisfied by the powers of reasoning (with which he is so happily endowed) that those fears were not well grounded. There is many a religious man who knows nothing of argumentative reasoning;—there are many of our most worthy citizens, who cannot go through all the labyrinths of syllogistic argumentative deductions, when they think that the rights of conscience are invaded. This sacred right ought not to depend on constructive logical reasoning. When we see men of such talents and learning, compelled to use their utmost abilities to convince themselves that there is no danger, is it not sufficient to make us tremble? Is it not sufficient to fill the minds of the ignorant part of men with fear? If Gentlemen believe that the apprehensions of men will be quieted, they are mistaken; since our best informed men are in doubt with respect to the security of our rights. Those who are not so well informed will spurn at the Government. When our common citizens, who are not possessed with such extensive knowledge and abilities, are called upon to change their Bill of Rights, (which in plain unequivocal terms, secures their most valuable rights and privileges) for construction and implication, will they implicitly acquiesce? Our Declaration of Rights tells us, "That all men are by nature free and independent, &c." (Here Mr. *Henry* read the Declaration of Rights.)[4] Will they exchange these Rights for logical reasons? If you had a thousand acres of land, dependent on this, would you be satisfied with logical construction? Would you depend upon a title of so disputable a nature? The present opinions of individuals will be buried in entire oblivion when those rights will be thought of. That sacred and lovely thing Religion, ought not to rest on the ingenuity of logical deduction. Holy Religion, Sir, will be prostituted to the lowest purposes of human policy. What has been more productive of mischief among mankind than Religious disputes. Then here, Sir, is a foundation for such disputes, when it requires learning and logical deduction to perceive that religious liberty is secure....

1. Henry refers to Edmund Pendleton's effort earlier in the day (RCS:Va., 1201–2) to explain what Thomas Jefferson wrote in his 7 February 1788 letter to Alexander Donald (BoR, II, 308), upon which Henry himself had commented in the Convention on 9 June (RCS:Va., 1051–52).
2. For the English Bill of Rights, see BoR, I, 4–8.
3. See Edmund Randolph's speech, Convention Debates, 10 June (BoR, III, 13).
4. For the Virginia Declaration of Rights, see BoR, I, 111–13.

James Madison: Speech in the Virginia Convention 12 June 1788 (excerpt)

... The honorable member [i.e., Patrick Henry] has introduced the subject of religion.—Religion is not guarded—There is no Bill of Rights declaring that religion should be secure.—Is a Bill of Rights a security for religion? Would the Bill of Rights in this State exempt the people from paying for the support of one particular sect, if such sect were exclusively established by law? If there were a majority of one sect, a Bill of Rights would be a poor protection for ⟨religion⟩ ⟨liberty⟩.[1] Happily for the States, they enjoy the utmost freedom of religion. This freedom arises from that multiplicity of sects, which pervades America, and which is the best and only security for religious liberty in any society. For where there is such a variety of sects, there cannot be a majority of any one sect to oppress and persecute the rest. Fortunately for this Commonwealth, a majority of the people are decidedly against any exclusive establishment—I believe it to be so in the other States. There is not a shadow of right in the General Government to intermeddle with religion.—Its least interference with it would be a most flagrant usurpation.—I can appeal to my uniform conduct on this subject, that I have warmly supported religious freedom.[2]—It is better that this security should be depended upon from the General Legislature, than from one particular State. A particular State might concur in one religious project.—But the United States abound in such a vast variety of sects, that it is a strong security against religious persecution, and is sufficient to authorise a conclusion, that no one sect will ever be able to out number or depress the rest....

1. "Liberty" replaced "religion" in the 1805 edition.
2. For Madison's role in the debate over religious liberty in Virginia in 1784 to 1786, see BoR, I, 130–38.

George Mason: Speech in the Virginia Convention, 16 June 1788

Mr. *George Mason*, still thought that there ought to be some express declaration in the Constitution, asserting that rights not given to the General Government, were retained by the States. He apprehended that unless this was done, many valuable and important rights would be concluded to be given up by implication. All Governments were drawn from the people, though many were perverted to their oppression. The Government of Virginia, he remarked, was drawn from the people; yet there were certain great and important rights, which the people by their Bill of Rights declared to be paramount to the power of the Legislature.—He asked, why should it not be so in this Constitution?—Was it because we were more substantially represented in it, than in the State Government? If in the State Government, where the people were substantially and fully represented, it was necessary that the great rights of human nature should be secure from the encroachments of the Legislature; he asked, if it was not more necessary in this Government, where they were but inadequately represented? He declared, that artful sophistry and evasions could not satisfy him. He could see no clear distinction between rights relinquished by a positive grant, and lost by implication. Unless there were a Bill of Rights, implication might swallow up all our rights.

Patrick Henry: Speech in the Virginia Convention, 16 June 1788

Mr. Chairman.—The necessity of a Bill of Rights appears to me to be greater in this Government, than ever it was in any Government before. I observed already, that the sense of the European nations, and particularly Great-Britain, is against the construction of rights being retained, which are not *expressly* relinquished. I repeat, that all nations have adopted this construction—That all rights not expressly and unequivocally reserved to the people, are impliedly and incidentally relinquished to rulers; as necessarily inseparable from the delegated powers. It is so in Great-Britain: For every possible right which is not reserved to the people by some express provision or compact, is within the King's prerogative. It is so in that country which is said to be in such full possession of freedom. It is so in Spain, Germany, and other parts of the world. Let us consider the sentiments which have been entertained by the people of America on this subject. At the revolution, it must be admitted, that it was their sense to put down those great rights which ought in all countries to be held inviolable and sacred. Virginia did so we all remember. She made a compact to reserve, expressly, certain rights. When fortified with full, adequate, and abundant representation, was she satisfied with that representation? No.—She most cautiously and guardedly reserved and secured those invaluable, inestimable rights and privileges, which no people, inspired with the least glow of the patriotic love of liberty, ever did, or ever can, abandon. She is called upon now to abandon them, and dissolve that compact which secured them to her. She is called upon to accede to another compact which most infallibly supercedes and annihilates her present one. Will she do it?—This is the question. If you intend to reserve your unalienable rights, you must have the most express stipulation. For if implication be allowed, you are ousted of those rights. If the people do not think it necessary to reserve them, they will be supposed to be given up. How were the Congressional rights defined when the people of America united by a confederacy to defend their liberties and rights against the tyrannical attempts of Great-Britain? The States were not then contented with implied reservation. No, Mr. Chairman. It was expressly declared in our Confederation that every right was retained by the States respectively, which was not given up to the Government of the United States.[1] But there is no such thing here. You therefore by a natural and unavoidable implication, give up your rights to the General Government. Your own example furnishes an argument against it. If you give up these powers, without a Bill of Rights, you will exhibit the most absurd thing to mankind that ever the world saw—A Government that has abandoned all its powers—The powers of a direct taxation, the sword, and the purse. You have disposed of them to Congress, without a Bill of Rights—without check, limitation, or controul. And still you have checks and guards—still you keep barriers—pointed where? Pointed against your weakened, prostrated, enervated State Government! You have a Bill of Rights to defend you against the State Government, which is bereaved of all power; and yet you have none against Congress, though in full and exclusive possession of all power! You arm yourselves against the weak and defenceless, and expose yourselves naked to the armed and powerful. Is not this a conduct of unexampled absurdity? What barriers have you to oppose to this most strong energetic Government? To that Government you have nothing to oppose. All your defence is given up. This is a real actual defect.—It must strike the mind of every Gentleman. When our Government was first instituted in Virginia, we declared the common law of England to be in force.[2]—That system of law which has been admired, and has protected us and our ancestors, is excluded by that system.—Added to this, we adopted a Bill of Rights. By this Constitution, some of the best barriers of human rights are thrown away. Is there not an additional reason to have a Bill of Rights? By the ancient common law, the trial of all facts is decided by a jury of impartial men from the immediate vicinage. This paper speaks of different juries from the common law, in criminal cases; and in civil controversies excludes trial by jury altogether. There is therefore more occasion for the supplementary check of a Bill of

Rights now, than then. Congress from their general powers may fully go into the business of human legislation. They may legislate in criminal cases from treason to the lowest offence, petty larceny. They may define crimes and prescribe punishments. In the definition of crimes, I trust they will be directed by what wise Representatives ought to be governed by. But when we come to punishments, no latitude ought to be left, nor dependence put on the virtue of Representatives. What says our Bill of Rights? "That excessive bail ought not to be required, nor excessive fines imposed, nor cruel and unusual punishments inflicted."[3] Are you not therefore now calling on those Gentlemen who are to compose Congress, to prescribe trials and define punishments without this controul? Will they find sentiments there similar to this Bill of Rights? You let them loose—you do more—you depart from the genius of your country. That paper tells you, that the trial of crimes shall be by jury, and held in the State where the crime shall have been committed.—Under this extensive provision, they may proceed in a manner extremely dangerous to liberty.—Persons accused may be carried from one extremity of the State to another, and be tried not by an impartial jury of the vicinage, acquainted with his character, and the circumstances of the fact; but by a jury unacquainted with both, and who may be biassed against him.—Is not this sufficient to alarm men?— How different is this from the immemorial practice of your British ancestors, and your own? I need not tell you, that by the common law a number of hundredors were required to be on a jury,[4] and that afterwards it was sufficient if the jurors came from the same county. With less than this the people of England have never been satisfied. That paper ought to have declared the common law in force.

In this business of legislation, your Members of Congress will lose the restriction of not imposing excessive fines, demanding excessive bail, and inflicting cruel and unusual punishments.—These are prohibited by your Declaration of Rights. What has distinguished our ancestors?—That they would not admit of tortures, or cruel and barbarous punishments. But Congress may introduce the practice of the civil law, in preference to that of the common law.—They may introduce the practice of France, Spain, and Germany—Of torturing to extort a confession of the crime. They will say that they might as well draw examples from those countries as from Great-Britain; and they will tell you, that there is such a necessity of strengthening the arm of Government, that they must have a criminal equity, and extort confession by torture, in order to punish with still more relentless severity. We are then lost and undone.—And can any man think it troublesome, when we can by a small interference prevent our rights from being lost?—If you will, like the Virginian Government, give them knowledge of the extent of the rights retained by the people, and the powers themselves, they will, if they be honest men, thank you for it.—Will they not wish to go on sure grounds?—But if you leave them otherwise, they will not know how to proceed; and being in a state of uncertainty, they will assume rather than give up powers by implication. A Bill of Rights may be summed up in a few words. What do they tell us?—That our rights are reserved.—Why not say so? Is it because it will consume too much paper? Gentlemen's reasonings against a Bill of Rights, do not satisfy me. Without saying which has the right side, it remains doubtful. A Bill of Rights is a favourite thing with the Virginians, and the people of the other States likewise. It may be their prejudice, but the Government ought to suit their geniuses, otherwise its operation will be unhappy. A Bill of Rights, even if its necessity be doubtful, will exclude the possibility of dispute, and with great submission, I think the best way is to have no dispute. In the present Constitution, they are restrained from issuing general warrants to search suspected places, or seize persons not named, without evidence of the commission of a fact, &c.[5] There was certainly some celestial influence governing those who deliberated on that Constitution:—For they have with the most cautious and enlightened circumspection, guarded those indefeasible rights, which ought ever to be held sacred. The officers of Congress may come upon you, fortified with all the terrors of paramount federal authority.—Excisemen may come in multitudes:—For the limitation of their numbers no man knows.—They may, unless the General Government be restrained by a Bill of Rights, or some similar restriction, go into your cellars and rooms, and search, ransack and measure, every thing you eat, drink and wear. They ought to be restrained within proper bounds. With respect to the freedom of the press, I need say nothing; for it is hoped that the Gentlemen who shall compose Congress, will take care as little as possible, to infringe the rights of human nature.—This will result from their integrity. They should from prudence, abstain from violating the rights of their constituents. They are not however expressly restrained.—But whether they will intermeddle with that palladium of our liberties or not, I leave you to determine.

1. See note 1 to William Grayson's 16 June speech (immediately below).
2. See note 2 to "Brutus," *Virginia Journal*, 6 December 1787 (BoR, II, 189n).
3. See Article 9 of the Virginia Declaration of Rights (BoR, I, 112).
4. In his *Commentaries on the Laws of England*, William Blackstone states: "by the policy of the antient law, the jury was to come *de vicineto*, from the neighbourhood of the vill or place where the cause of action was laid in the declaration; and therefore some of the jury were obliged to be returned from the hundred in which such vill lay; and, if none were returned, the array might be challenged for defect of hundredors" (Book III, chap-

ter 23, p. 359). A hundred was a subdivision of an English county which had its own court, and the hundredor, an inhabitant of a hundred, was liable to serve on a jury.
5. See Article 10 of the Virginia Declaration of Rights (BoR, I, 112–13).

William Grayson: Speech in the Virginia Convention, 16 June 1788

Mr. *Grayson* thought it questionable, whether rights not given up were reserved. A majority of the States, he observed, had expressly reserved certain important rights by Bills of Rights, and that in the Confederation there was a clause, declaring expressly, that every power and right not given up, was retained by the States.[1] It was the general sense of America, that such a clause was necessary; otherwise why did they introduce a clause which was totally unnecessary? It had been insisted, he said, in many parts of America, that a Bill of Rights was only necessary between a Prince and people, and not in such a Government as this, which was a compact between the people themselves. This did not satisfy his mind: For so extensive was the power of legislation, in his estimation, that he doubted, whether when it was once given up, *any thing* was retained. He further remarked, that there were some negative clauses in the Constitution, which refuted the doctrine contended for by the other side: For instance, the second clause, of the ninth section, of the first article, provided, that "The privilege of the writ of *habeas corpus* shall not be suspended, unless when in cases of rebellion or invasion, the public safety may require it."—And by the last clause, of the same section, "No title of nobility shall be granted by the United States."—Now if these restrictions had not been here inserted, he asked, whether Congress would not most clearly have had a right to suspend that great and valuable right, and to grant titles of nobility? When, in addition to these considerations, he saw they had an indefinite power to provide for the general welfare, he thought there were great reasons to apprehend great dangers. He thought therefore, that there ought to be a Bill of Rights.

    1. Article II of the Articles of Confederation states: "Each state retains its sovereignty, freedom and independence, and every Power, Jurisdiction and right, which is not by this confederation expressly delegated to the United States, in Congress assembled."

George Nicholas and George Mason: Speeches in the Virginia Convention, 16 June 1788

Mr. *George Nicholas*, in answer to the two Gentlemen last up [Patrick Henry and William Grayson], observed, that though there was a Declaration of Rights in the Government of Virginia, it was no conclusive reason that there should be one in this Constitution. For, if it was unnecessary in the former, its omission in the latter could be no defect. They ought therefore to prove, that it was essentially necessary to be inserted in the Constitution of Virginia: That there were five or six States in the Union, which had no Bill of Rights, separately and distinctly as such.[1] But they annexed the substance of a Bill of Rights to their respective Constitutions. These States, he further observed, were as free as this State, and their liberties as secure as ours. If so, Gentlemen's arguments from the precedent were not good. In Virginia, all powers were given to the Government without any exception. It was different in the General Government, to which certain special powers were delegated for certain purposes. He asked, which was the more safe?—Was it safer to grant general powers, than certain limited powers? This much as to the theory, continued he. What is the practice of this invaluable Government? Have your citizens been bound by it? They have not, Sir. You have violated that maxim, "That no man shall be condemned without a fair trial."—That man who was killed, not *secundum artem*, was deprived of his life, without the benefit of law, and in express violation of this Declaration of Rights, which they confide in so much.[2] But, Sir, this Bill of Rights was no security.—It is but a paper check.—It has been violated in many other instances. Therefore from theory and practice it may be concluded, that this Government with special powers, without any express exceptions, is better than a Government with general powers, and special exceptions. But the practice of England is against us.—The rights there reserved to the people, are to limit and check the King's prerogative. It is easier to enumerate the exceptions to his prerogative, than to mention all the cases to which it extends.—Besides, these reservations being only formed in acts of the Legislature, may be altered by the Representatives of the people, when they think proper. No comparison can be made of this, with the other Governments he mentioned.—There is no stipulation between the King and people. The former is possessed of absolute unlimited authority.

But, Sir, this Constitution is defective, because the common law is not declared to be in force—What would have been the consequences if it had? It would be immutable. But now it can be changed or modified as the Legislative body may find necessary for the community. But the common law is not excluded. There is nothing in that paper to warrant the assertion. As to the exclusion of a jury from the vicinage, he has mistaken the fact:—The Legislature may direct a jury to come from the vicinage. But the Gentleman says, that by this Constitution, they have power to make laws to define crimes, and prescribe punishments; and that consequently we are not free from torture. Treason against the United States is defined in the Constitution, and the forfeiture limited to the life of the person attainted.—Congress have power to define and punish piracies and felonies committed on the high seas; and offences against the law of nations: But they cannot define or prescribe the punishment of any other crime whatever, without violating the Constitution. If we had no security against torture, but our Declaration of Rights, we might be tortured to morrow: For it has been repeatedly infringed and disregarded. A Bill of Rights is only an acknowledgement of the pre-existing claim to rights in the people. They belong to us as much as if they had been inserted in the Constitution.— But it is said, that if it be doubtful, the possibility of dispute ought to be precluded. Admitting it was proper for the Convention to have inserted a Bill of Rights, it is not proper here to propose it, as the condition of our accession to the Union. Would you reject this Government for its omission, dissolve the Union, and bring miseries on yourselves and posterity? I hope the Gentleman [Patrick Henry] does not oppose it on this ground solely. Is there another reason? He said, that it is not only the general wish of this State, but of all the States to have a Bill of Rights. If it be so, where is the difficulty of having this done by way of subsequent amendments? We shall find the other States willing to accord with their own favourite wish. The Gentleman last up [William Grayson], says, that the power of legislation includes every thing. A *general* power of legislation does. But this is a special power of legislation: Therefore it does not contain that plenitude of power which he imagines. They cannot legislate in any case, but those particularly enumerated. No Gentleman who is a friend to the Government ought to withhold his assent from it for this reason.

Mr. *George Mason* replied, that the worthy Gentleman [George Nicholas] was mistaken in his assertion, that the Bill of Rights did not prohibit torture. For, that one clause expressly provided, that no man can give evidence against himself;[3] and that the worthy Gentleman must know, that in those countries where torture is used, evidence was extorted from the criminal himself. Another clause of the Bill of Rights, provided, that no cruel and unusual punishments shall be inflicted;[4] therefore torture was included in the prohibition.

Mr. *Nicholas* acknowledged the Bill of Rights to contain that prohibition, and that the Gentleman was right with respect to the practice of extorting confession from the criminal in those countries where torture is used; but still he saw no security arising from the Bill of Rights as separate from the Constitution, for that it had been frequently violated with impunity.

1. See note 1 to "One of the People," *Maryland Journal*, 25 December 1787 (BoR, II, 210n).

2. Nicholas refers to the case of Josiah Philips. See note 2 to Edmund Pendleton's 12 June speech (BoR, III, 18n). *"Secundum artem"* means "according to rule."
3. See Article 8 of the Virginia Declaration of Rights (BoR, I, 112).
4. See Article 9 of the Virginia Declaration of Rights (*ibid.*).

Patrick Henry: Speech in the Virginia Convention, 17 June 1788

The 7th clause read.[1]

Mr. Chairman.—We have now come to the ninth section, and I consider myself at liberty to take a short view of the whole. I wish to do it very briefly. Give me leave to remark, that there is a Bill of Rights in that Government. There are express restrictions which are in the shape of a Bill of Rights: But they bear the name of the ninth section. The design of the negative expressions in this section is to prescribe limits, beyond which the powers of Congress shall not go. These are the sole bounds intended by the American Government. Where abouts do we stand with respect to a Bill of Rights? Examine it, and compare it to the idea manifested by the Virginia Bill of Rights, or that of the other States. The restraints in this Congressional Bill of Rights, are so feeble and few, that it would have been infinitely better to have said nothing about it. The fair implication is, that they can do every thing they are not forbidden to do. What will be the result if Congress, in the course of their legislation, should do a thing not restrained by this ninth section? It will fall as an incidental power to Congress, not being prohibited expressly in the Constitution. The first prohibition is, that the privilege of the writ of *habeas corpus* shall not be suspended, but when in cases of rebellion, or invasion, the public safety may require it. It results clearly, that if it had not said so, they could suspend it in all cases whatsoever. It reverses the position of the friends of this Constitution, that every thing is retained which is not given up. For instead of this, every thing is given up, which is not expressly reserved.—It does not speak affirmatively, and say that it shall be suspended in those cases. But that it shall not be suspended but in certain cases; going on a supposition that every thing which is not negatived, shall remain with Congress. If the power remains with the people, how can Congress supply the want of an affirmative grant? They cannot do it but by implication, which destroys their doctrine. The Virginia Bill of Rights interdicts the relinquishment of the sword and purse without controul. That Bill of Rights secures the great and principal rights of mankind. But this Bill of Rights extends to but very few cases, and is destructive of the doctrine advanced by the friends of that paper.

If *ex post facto* laws had not been interdicted, they might also have been extended by implication at pleasure. Let us consider whether this restriction be founded in wisdom or good policy. If no *ex post facto* laws be made, what is to become of the old continental paper dollars? Will not this country be forced to pay it in gold and silver, shilling for shilling? Gentlemen may think that this does not deserve an answer: But it is an all important question. Because the property of this country is not commensurate to the enormous demand. Our own Government triumphs with infinite superiority when put in contrast with that paper.—The want of a Bill of Rights will render all their laws, however oppressive, constitutional.

If the Government of Virginia passes a law in contradiction to our Bill of Rights, it is nugatory. By that paper the national wealth is to be disposed of under the veil of secrecy: For the publication from time to time, will amount to nothing; and they may conceal what they may think requires secrecy. How different is it in your own Government?— Have not the people seen the journals of our Legislature every day during every session? Is not the lobby full of people every day? Yet, Gentlemen say, that the publication from time to time is a security unknown in our State Government! Such a regulation would be nugatory and vain, or at least needless, as the people see the journals of our Legislature, and hear their debates every day. If this be not more secure than what is in that paper, I will give up that I have totally misconceived the principles of the Government. You are told, that your rights are secured in this new Government. They are guarded in no other part but this ninth section. The few restrictions in that section are your only safeguards. They may controul your actions, and your very words, without being repugnant to that paper. The existence of your dearest privileges will depend on the consent of Congress: For these are not within the restrictions of the ninth section.

If Gentlemen think that securing the slave trade is a capital object; that the privilege of the *habeas corpus* is sufficiently secured; that the exclusion of *ex post facto* laws will produce no inconvenience; that the publication from time to time will secure their property; in one word, that this section alone will sufficiently secure their liberties, I have spoken in vain.—Every word of mine, and of my worthy coadjutor [George Mason], is lost. I trust that Gentlemen, on this occasion, will see the great objects of religion, liberty of the press, trial by jury, interdiction of cruel punishments, and every other sacred right secured, before they agree to that paper. These most important human rights are not protected by that section, which is the only safeguard in the Constitution.— My mind will not be quieted till I see something substantial come forth in the shape of a Bill of Rights.

1. Henry's remarks are ostensibly on Article I, section 9, clause 7 of the Constitution. He actually discusses clauses 1, 2, and 3 and section 5, clause 3.

Edmund Randolph: Speech in the Virginia Convention 17 June 1788 (excerpt)

... On the subject of a Bill of Rights, the want of which has been complained of, I will observe that it has been sanctified by such reverend authority, that I feel some difficulty in going against it. I shall not, however, be deterred from giving my opinion on this occasion, let the consequence be what it may. At the beginning of the war we had no certain Bill of Rights: For our charter cannot be considered as a Bill of Rights. It is nothing more than an investiture in the hands of the Virginian citizens, of those rights which belonged to the British subjects. When the British thought proper to infringe our rights, was it not necessary to mention in our Constitution, those rights which ought to be paramount to the power of the Legislature? Why are the Bill of Rights distinct from the Constitution? I consider Bills of Rights in this view, that the Government should use them when there is a departure from its fundamental principles, in order to restore them. This is the true sense of a Bill of Rights. If it be consistent with the Constitution, or contains additional rights, why not put it in the Constitution? If it be repugnant to the Constitution, there will be a perpetual scene of warfare between them. The Honorable Gentleman has praised the Bill of Rights of Virginia, and called it his guardian angel, and vilified this Constitution for not having it. Give me leave to make a distinction between the Representatives of the people of a particular country, who are appointed as the ordinary Legislature, having no limitation to their powers, and another body arising from a compact and certain delineated powers. Were a Bill of Rights necessary in the former, it would not in the latter; for the best security that can be in the latter is the express enumeration of its powers. But let me ask the Gentleman [Patrick Henry] where his favourite rights are violated? They are not violated by the tenth section, which contains restrictions on the States. Are they violated by the enumerated powers? (Here his Excellency read from the eighth to the twelfth article of the Declaration of Rights.)[1]—Is there not provision made in this Constitution for the trial by jury in criminal cases? Does not the third article provide, that the trial of all crimes shall be by jury, and held in the State where the said crimes shall have been committed? Does it not follow, that the cause and nature of the accusation must be produced, because otherwise they cannot proceed on the cause? Every one knows, that the witnesses must be brought before the jury, or else the prisoner will be discharged. Calling for evidence in his favor is co-incident to his trial. There is no suspicion, that less than twelve jurors will be thought sufficient. The only defect is, that there is no speedy trial.—Consider how this could have been amended. We have heard complaints against it, because it is supposed the jury is to come from the State at large. It will be in their power to have juries from the vicinage. And would not the complaints have been louder, if they had appointed a Federal Court to be had in every county in the State?—Criminals are brought in this State from every part of the country to the General Court, and jurors from the vicinage are summoned to the trials. There can be no reason to prevent the General Government from adopting a similar regulation.

As to the exclusion of excessive bail and fines, and cruel and unusual punishments, this would follow of itself without a Bill of Rights. Observations have been made about watchfulness over those in power, which deserve our attention. There must be a combination—We must presume corruption in the House of Representatives, Senate, and President, before we can suppose that excessive fines can be imposed, or cruel punishments inflicted. Their number is the highest security.—Numbers are the highest security in our own Constitution, which has attracted so many eulogiums from the Gentleman. Here we have launched into a sea of suspicions. How shall we check power?—By their numbers. Before these cruel punishments can be inflicted, laws must be passed, and Judges must judge contrary to justice. This would excite universal discontent, and detestation of the Members of the Government. They might involve their friends in the calamities resulting from it, and could be removed from office. I never desire a greater security than this, which I believe to be absolutely sufficient.

That general warrants are grievous and oppressive, and ought not to be granted, I fully admit. I heartily concur in expressing my detestation of them. But we have sufficient security here also. We do not rely on the integrity of any one particular person or body; but on the number and different orders of the Members of the Government: Some of them having necessarily the same feelings with ourselves. Can it be believed, that the Federal Judiciary would not be independent enough to prevent such oppressive practices? If they will not do justice to persons injured, may they not go to our own State Judiciaries and obtain it?

Gentlemen have been misled to a certain degree, by a general declaration, that the trial by jury was gone. We see that in the most valuable cases, it is reserved. Is it abolished in civil cases? Let him put his finger on the part where it is abolished. The Constitution is silent on it.— What expression would you wish the Constitution to use, to establish it? Remember we were not making a Constitution for Virginia alone, or we might have taken Virginia for our directory. But we were forming a Constitution for thirteen States. The trial by jury is different in different States. In some States it is excluded in cases in which it is admitted in others. In Admiralty causes it is not used. Would you have a jury to determine the case of a capture? The Virginian Legislature thought proper to make an exception of that case. These depend on the law of nations, and no twelve men that could be picked up would be equal to the decision of such a matter.

Then, Sir, the freedom of the press is said to be insecure. God forbid that I should give my voice against the freedom of the press. But I ask, (and with confidence that it cannot be answered) where is the page where it is restrained? If there had been any regulation about it, leaving it insecure, then there might have been reason for clamours. But this is not the case. If it be, I again ask for the particular clause which gives liberty to destroy the freedom of the press.

He has added religion to the objects endangered in his conception. Is there any power given over it? Let it be pointed out. Will he not be contented with the answer which has been frequently given to that objection? That variety of sects which abounds in the United States is the best security for the freedom of religion. No part of the Constitution, even if strictly construed, will justify a conclusion, that the General Government can take away, or impair the freedom of religion.

The Gentleman asks with triumph, shall we be deprived of these valuable rights? Had there been an exception, or express infringement of those rights, he might object.—But I conceive every fair reasoner will agree, that there is no just cause to suspect that they will be violated.

But he objects, that the common law is not established by the Constitution. The wisdom of the Convention is displayed by its omission; because the common law ought not to be immutably fixed. Is it established in our own Constitution, or the Bill of Rights which has been resounded through the House? It is established only by an act of the Legislature,[2] and can therefore be changed as circumstances may require it. Let the Honorable Gentleman consider what would be the destructive consequences of its establishment in the Constitution. Even in England, where the firmest opposition has been made to encroachments upon it, it has been frequently changed. What would have been our dilemma if it had been established?—Virginia has declared, that children shall have equal portions of the real estates of their intestate parents,[3] and it is consistent to the principles of a Republican Government.—The immutable establishment of the common law, would have been repugnant to that regulation. It would in many respects be destructive to republican principles, and productive of great inconveniencies. I might indulge myself, by shewing many parts of the common law which would have this effect. I hope I shall not be thought to speak ludicrously, when I say, that the *writ* of *burning heretics*,[4] would have been revived by it. It would tend to throw real property in few hands, and prevent the introduction of many salutary regulations. Thus, were the common law adopted in that system, it would destroy the principles of Republican Government. But it is not excluded. It may be established by an act of the Legislature. Its defective parts may be altered, and it may be changed and modified as the convenience of the public may require it.

I said when I opened my observations, that I thought the friends of the Constitution were mistaken, when they supposed the powers granted by the last clause of the eighth section,[5] to be merely incidental; and that its enemies were equally mistaken when they put such an extravagant construction upon it.

My objection is, that the clause is ambiguous, and that that ambiguity may injure the States. My fear is, that it will by gradual accessions gather to a dangerous length. This is my apprehension, and I disdain to disown it. I will praise it where it deserves it, and censure it where it appears defective. But, Sir, are we to reject it, because it is ambiguous in some particular instances? I cast my eyes to the actual situation of America; I see the dreadful tempest, to which the present calm is a prelude, if disunion takes place. I see the anarchy which must happen if no energetic Government be established. In this situation, I would take the Constitution were it more objectionable than it is.—For if anarchy and confusion follow disunion, an enterprising man may enter into the American throne. I conceive there is no danger. The Representatives are chosen by and from among the people. They will have a fellow-feeling for the farmers and planters. The twenty-six Senators, Representatives of the States, will not be those desperadoes and horrid adventurers which they are represented to be. The State Legislatures, I trust, will not forget the duty they owe to their country so far, as to choose such men to manage their federal interests. I trust, that the Members of Congress themselves, will explain the ambiguous parts: And if not, the States can combine in order to insist on amending the ambiguities. I would depend on the present actual feelings of the people of America, to introduce any amendment which may be necessary. I repeat it again, though I do not reverence the Constitution, that its adoption is necessary to avoid the storm which is hanging over America, and that no greater curse can befal her, than the dissolution of the political connection between the States. Whether we shall propose previous or subsequent amendments, is now the only dispute. It is supererogation to repeat again the arguments in support of each.—But I ask Gentlemen, whether, as eight States have adopted it, it be not safer to adopt it, and rely on the probability of obtaining amendments, than by a rejection to hazard a breach of the Union? I hope to be excused for the breach of order which I have committed.

    1. For the text of these articles, see BoR, I, 112–13.
    2. See note 2 to "Brutus," *Virginia Journal,* 6 December 1787 (BoR, II, 189n).
    3. Randolph refers to an act revising the rule of primogeniture, drafted by Thomas Jefferson between 1776 and 1779 and adopted by the legislature on 30 November 1785, which stipulated the order of inheritance for owners of real property who died intestate (Hening, XII, 138–40; Boyd, I, 563n; II, 301–2, 305–35, 391–93; and Rutland, *Madison,* VIII, 391–99).
    4. Randolph refers to the writ *de hæretico comburendo.* A statute of 1677 abolished the writ (see Blackstone, *Commentaries,* Book IV, chapter 4, pp. 46–49).
    5. The necessary and proper clause.

Patrick Henry: Speech in the Virginia Convention
19 June 1788 (excerpt)

. . . We are told that the State rights are preserved.—Suppose the State right to territory be preserved, I ask and demand how do the rights of persons stand, when they have power to make any treaty, and that treaty is paramount to Constitutions, laws, and every thing?—When a person shall be treated in the most horrid manner, and most cruelly and inhumanly tortured, will the security of territorial rights grant him redress?—Suppose an unusual punishment in consequence of an arrest similar to that of the Russian Ambassador[1]—can it be said to be contrary to the State rights? I might go on in this discrimination, but it is too obvious that the security of territory is no security of individual safety. I ask, how are the State rights, individual rights, and national rights secured?—Not as in England—For the authority quoted from Blackstone, would, if stated right, prove in a thousand instances, that if the King of England attempted to take away the rights of individuals, the law would stand against him.—The acts of Parliament would stand in his way—The Bill, and Declaration of Rights would be against him. The common law is fortified by the Bill of Rights. The rights of the people cannot be destroyed even by the paramount operation of the law of nations, as the case of the Russian Ambassador evinces. If you look for a similar security in the paper on your table, you look in vain.— That paper is defective without such a Declaration of Rights.—It is unbounded without such restrictions. If the Constitution be paramount, how are the Constitutions and laws of the States to stand? Their operation will be totally controuled by it:—For, it is paramount to every thing, unless you can shew some guard against it.—The rights of persons are exposed as it stands now. . . .

> 1. According to William Blackstone, Peter the Great's ambassador to Great Britain was arrested for a debt of fifty pounds in July 1708. Instead of claiming diplomatic privilege, the ambassador posted bail and was released, after which he protested to the British Crown. The attorney general then charged the persons involved in the arrest, and a jury convicted them of the facts, but the criminality of the defendants' actions was never determined. In the meantime, Peter demanded that the officials who made the arrest be executed. Queen Anne replied "that she could inflict no punishment upon any, the meanest, of her subjects, unless warranted by the law of the land." To appease Peter and various foreign ministers, Parliament passed a law making it a punishable crime to arrest diplomats who were entitled to the diplomatic immunity under the law of nations (*Commentaries*, Book I, chapter 7, pp. 254–57).

John Marshall: Speech in the Virginia Convention
20 June 1788 (excerpts)

. . . The exclusion of trial by jury in this case, he [George Mason] urged to prostrate our rights. Does the word Court only mean the Judges? Does not the determination of a jury, necessarily lead to the judgment of the Court? Is there any thing here which gives the Judges exclusive jurisdiction of matters of fact? What is the object of a jury trial? To inform the Court of the facts. When a Court has cognizance of facts, does it not follow, that they can make enquiry by a jury? It is impossible to be otherwise. I hope that in this country, where impartiality is so much admired, the laws will direct facts to be ascertained by a jury. But, says the Honorable Gentleman, the juries in the ten miles square will be mere tools of parties, with which he would not trust his person or property; which, he says, he would rather leave to the Court. Because the Government may have a district ten miles square, will no man stay there but the tools and officers of the Government?— Will no body else be found there?—Is it so in any other part of the world, where a Government has Legislative power?—Are there none but officers and tools of the Government of Virginia in Richmond?— Will there not be independent merchants, and respectable Gentlemen of fortune, within the ten miles square?—Will there not be worthy farmers and mechanics?—Will not a good jury be found there as well as any where else?—Will the officers of the Government become improper to be on a jury?—What is it to the Government, whether this man or that man succeeds?—It is all one thing. Does the Constitution say, that juries shall consist of officers, or that the Supreme Court shall be held in the ten miles square? It was acknowledged by the Honorable Member, that it was secure in England. What makes it secure there?—

Is it their Constitution?—What part of their Constitution is there, that the Parliament cannot change?—As the preservation of this right is in the hands of Parliament, and it has ever been held sacred by them, will the Government of America be less honest than that of Great Britain? Here a restriction is to be found. The jury is not to be brought out of the State. There is no such restriction in that Government; for the laws of Parliament decide every thing respecting it. Yet Gentlemen tell us, that there is safety there, and nothing here but danger. It seems to me, that the laws of the United States will generally secure trials by a jury of the vicinage, or in such manner as will be most safe and convenient for the people.

But it seems that the right of challenging the jurors, is not secured in this Constitution. Is this done by our own Constitution, or by any provision of the English Government? Is it done by their Magna Charta, or Bill of Rights? This privilege is founded on their laws. If so, why should it be objected to the American Constitution, that it is not inserted in it? If we are secure in Virginia, without mentioning it in our Constitution, why should not this security be found in the Federal Court? . . .

We are satisfied with the provision made in this country on the subject of trial by jury. Does our Constitution direct trials to be by jury? It is required in our Bill of Rights,[1] which is not a part of the Constitution. Does any security arise from hence? Have you a jury when a judgment is obtained on a replevy bond, or by default? Have you a jury when a motion is made for the Commonwealth, against an individual; or when a motion is made by one joint obligor against another, to recover sums paid as security? Our Courts decide in all these cases, without the intervention of a jury; yet they are all civil cases. The Bill of Rights is merely recommendatory. Were it otherwise, the consequence would be, that many laws which are found convenient, would be unconstitutional. What does the Government before you say? Does it exclude the Legislature from giving a trial by jury in civil cases? If it does not forbid its exclusion, it is on the same footing on which your State Government stands now. The Legislature of Virginia does not give a trial by jury where it is not necessary. But gives it wherever it is thought expedient. The Federal Legislature will do so too, as it is formed on the same principles.

The Honorable Gentleman says, that unjust claims will be made, and the defendant had better pay them than go to the Supreme Court. Can you suppose such a disposition in one of your citizens, as that to oppress another man, he will incur great expences? What will he gain by an unjust demand? Does a claim establish a right? He must bring his witnesses to prove his claim. If he does not bring his witnesses, the expences must fall upon him. Will he go on a calculation that the defendant will not defend it; or cannot produce a witness? Will he incur a great deal of expence, from a dependance on such a chance? Those who know human nature, black as it is, must know, that mankind are too well attached to their interest to run such a risk. I conceive, that this power is absolutely necessary, and not dangerous; that should it be attended by little inconveniences, they will be altered, and that they can have no interest in not altering them. Is there any real danger?— When I compare it to the exercise of the same power in the Government of Virginia, I am persuaded there is not. The Federal Government has no other motive, and has every reason of doing right, which the Members of our State Legislature have. Will a man on the Eastern Shore, be sent to be tried in Kentuckey; or a man from Kentuckey be brought to the Eastern Shore to have his trial? A Government by doing this, would destroy itself. I am convinced, the trial by jury will be regulated in the manner most advantageous to the community.

1. Article 11 of the Virginia Declaration of Rights provides "That in controversies respecting property, and in suits between man and man, the ancient trial by jury is preferable to any other, and ought to be held sacred" (BoR, I, 113).

Patrick Henry: Speech in the Virginia Convention 23 June 1788 (excerpt)

... Mr. Chairman, I feel myself particularly interested in this part of the Constitution,[1]—I perceive dangers must and will arise, and when the laws of that Government come to be enforced here, I have my fears for the consequences. It is not on that paper before you we have to rely, should it be received; it is on those that may be appointed under it. It will be an empire of men and not of laws—Your rights and liberties rest upon men—Their wisdom and integrity may preserve you— but on the contrary, should they prove ambitious, and designing, may they not flourish and triumph upon the ruins of their country?

He then proceeded to state the appellate jurisdiction of the Judicial power, *both as to law and fact, with such exceptions and under such regulations as Congress shall make.* He observed, that as Congress had a right to organize the Federal Judiciary, they might or might not have recourse to a jury as they pleased. He left it to the candour of the Honorable Gentleman to say, whether those persons who were at the expense of taking witnesses to Philadelphia, or wherever the Federal Judiciary may sit, could be certain whether they were to be heard before a jury or not. An Honorable Gentleman, (Mr. *Marshall*) the other day observed, that he conceived the trial by jury better secured under the plan on the table, than in the British Government, or even in our Bill of Rights. I have the highest veneration and respect for the Honorable Gentleman, and I have experienced his candour on all occasions; but, Mr. Chairman, in this instance, he is so materially mistaken, that I cannot but observe, he is much in an error. I beg the Clerk to read that part of the Constitution which relates to trial by jury.—(The Clerk then read the eighth article of the Bill of Rights.)[2]

Mr. [John] *Marshall* rose to explain what he had before said on this subject: He informed the Committee, that the Honorable Gentleman (Mr. *Henry*) must have misunderstood him. He said, that he conceived the trial by jury was as well secured, and not better secured, in the proposed new Constitution, as in our Bill of Rights.—(The Clerk then read the eleventh article of the Bill of Rights.)[3]

Mr. *Henry*,—Mr. Chairman.—The Gentleman's candour, Sir, as I informed you before, I have the highest opinion of—and am happy to find he has so far explained what he meant—but, Sir, has he mended the matter? Is not the antient trial by jury preserved in the Virginia Bill of Rights,—and is that the case in the new plan? No, Sir,—they can do it if they please. Will Gentlemen tell me the trial by a jury of the vicinage where the party resides, is preserved? True, Sir, there is to be a trial by a jury in the State where the fact was committed—but, Sir, this State, for instance, is so large that your juries may be collected 500 miles from where the party resides—no neighbours who are acquainted with their characters, their good or bad conduct in life, to judge of the unfortunate man who may be thus exposed to the rigour of that Government. Compare this security then, Sir, in our Bill of Rights to that in the new plan of Government, and in the first you have it—and in the other, in my opinion, not at all. But, Sir, in what situation will our citizens be, who have made large contracts under our present Government? They will be called to a Federal Court, and tried under retrospective laws;—for it is evident, to me at least, that the Federal Court must look back, and give new remedies, to compel individuals to fullfil them. The whole history of human nature cannot produce a Government like that before you:—The manner in which the Judiciary and other branches of the Government are formed, seem to me, calculated to lay prostrate the States, and the liberties of the people:— But, Sir, another circumstance ought totally to reject that plan, in my opinion—which is, that it cannot be understood—in many parts even by the supporters of it. A Constitution, Sir, ought to be like a beacon, held up to the public eye so as to be understood by every man. Some Gentlemen have observed, that the word jury, implies a jury of the vicinage.—There are so many inconsistencies in this, that, for my part,

I cannot understand it. By the Bill of Rights of England, a subject has a right to a trial by his peers—what is meant by his peers?—Those who reside near him—his neighbours—and who are well acquainted with his character and situation in life. Is this secured in the proposed plan before you? No, Sir, I think not. But, Sir, as I have observed before, what is to become of the purchases of the Indians?—Those unhappy nations who have given up their lands to private purchasers—who by being made drunk, have given a thousand—nay, I might say 10,000 acres, for the trifling sum of six pence?—It is with true concern, with grief I tell you, that I have waited with pain to come to this part of the plan—because, I observed Gentlemen admitted its being defective—and I had my hopes—would have proposed amendments;—but this part they have defended—and this convinces me of the necessity of obtaining amendments before it is adopted: They have defended it with ingenuity and perseverence,—but by no means satisfactory. If previous amendments are not obtained, the trial by jury is gone: British debtors will be ruined by being dragged to the Federal Court—and the liberty and happiness of our citizens gone—never again to be recovered.

1. Article III, sections 1 and 2.
2. For the eighth article of the Virginia Declaration of Rights, see BoR, I, 112.
3. For the eleventh article of the Virginia Declaration of Rights, see BoR, I, 113.

George Wythe: Speech in the Virginia Convention, 24 June 1788

Mr. *Wythe* arose and addressed the Chairman, but he spoke so very low, that his speech could not be fully comprehended. He took a cursory view of the situation of the United States, previous to the late war, their resistance to the oppressions of Great-Britain, and the glorious conclusion and issue of that arduous conflict. To perpetuate the blessings of freedom, happiness, and independence, he demonstrated the necessity of a firm indissoluble Union of the States. He expatiated on the defects and inadequacy of the Confederation, and the consequent misfortunes suffered by the people. He pointed out the impossibility of securing liberty without society; the impracticability of acting personally, and the inevitable necessity of delegating power to agents. He then recurred to the system under consideration. He admitted its imperfection, and the propriety of some amendments.—But the excellency of many parts of it could not be denied by its warmest opponents. He thought that experience was the best guide, and could alone develope its consequences. Most of the improvements that had been made in the science of Government, and other sciences, were the result of experience. He referred it to the advocates for amendments, whether if they were indulged with any alterations they pleased, there might not still be a necessity of alteration?—He then proceeded to the consideration of the question of previous or subsequent amendments. The critical situation of America,—the extreme danger of dissolving the Union, rendered it necessary to adopt the latter alternative. He saw no danger from this. It appeared to him most clearly, that any amendments which might be thought necessary, would be easily obtained after ratification, in the manner proposed by the Constitution, as amendments were desired by all the States, and had already been proposed by several States. He then proposed, that the Committee should ratify the Constitution, and that whatsoever amendments might be deemed necessary, should be recommended to the consideration of the Congress which should first assemble under the Constitution, to be acted upon according to the mode prescribed therein.

The resolution of ratification proposed by Mr. *Wythe* was then read by the Clerk, which see hereafter in the report of the Committee [of the Whole] to the Convention.

George Wythe's Resolution for Ratification, 24–25 June 1788[1]

Mr. President now resumed the Chair and Mr. *Mathews* reported, that the Committee had according to order, again had the proposed Constitution under their consideration, and had gone through the same and come to several resolutions thereupon, which he read in his place, and afterwards delivered in at the Clerk's table, where the same were again read, and are as followeth:

WHEREAS the powers granted under the proposed Constitution are the gift of the people, and every power not granted thereby, remains with them, and at their will: No right therefore of any denomination, can be cancelled, abridged, restrained or modified by the Congress, by the Senate or House of Representatives, acting in any capacity, by the President, or any department or officer of the United States, except in those instances in which power is given by the Constitution for those purposes: And among other essential rights, liberty of conscience and of the press cannot be cancelled, abridged, restrained or modified by any authority of the United States:

AND WHEREAS any imperfections which may exist in the said Constitution ought rather to be examined in the mode prescribed therein for obtaining amendments, than by a delay with a hope of obtaining previous amendments, to bring the Union into danger:

Resolved, That it is the opinion of this Committee, That the said Constitution be ratified.

But in order to relieve the apprehensions of those, who may be solicitous for amendments, *Resolved, That it is the opinion of this Committee, That whatsoever amendments may be deemed necessary be recommended to the consideration of the Congress, which shall first assemble under the said Constitution, to be acted upon according to the mode prescribed in the fifth article thereof.*

The first resolution being read a second time, a motion was made and the question being put to amend the same by substituting in lieu of the said resolution and its preamble, the following resolution;

"*Resolved,* That previous to the ratification of the new Constitution of Government recommended by the late Federal Convention, a declaration of rights asserting and securing from encroachment the great principles of civil and religious liberty, and the unalienable rights of the people, together with amendments to the most exceptionable parts of the said Constitution of Government, ought to be referred by this Convention to the other States in the American confederacy for their consideration."

It passed in the negative—Ayes 80—Noes 88.[2]

1. Wythe's preamble and resolutions do not exist as a separate document but only as part of the report of the Committee of the Whole presented on 25 June.

2. For the names of the delegates voting aye and no, see RCS:Va., 1558–59. Patrick Henry, seconded by Theodorick Bland, demanded that the names be recorded.

Patrick Henry: Speech in the Virginia Convention
24 June 1788 (excerpt)

Mr. *Henry* after observing, that the proposal of ratification was premature,[1] and that the importance of the subject required the most mature deliberation, proceeded thus:—The Honorable Member must forgive me for declaring my dissent from it, because if I understand it rightly, it admits that the new system is defective, and most capitally: For immediately after the proposed ratification, there comes a declaration, that the paper before you is not intended to violate any of these three great rights—the liberty of religion, liberty of the press, and the trial by jury. What is the inference, when you enumerate the rights which you are to enjoy? That those not enumerated are relinquished. There are only three things to be retained. Religion, freedom of the press, and jury trial. Will not the ratification carry every thing, without excepting these three things? Will not all the world pronounce, that we intended to give up all the rest? Every thing it speaks of by way of right is comprised in these three things. Your subsequent amendments, only go to these three amendments. I feel myself distressed, because the necessity of securing our personal rights, seems not to have pervaded the minds of men: For many other valuable things are omitted. For instance:—General warrants, by which an officer may search suspected places, without evidence of the commission of a fact, or seize any person without evidence of his crime, ought to be prohibited. As these are admitted, any man may be seized; any property may be taken, in the most arbitrary manner, without any evidence or reason. Every thing the most sacred, may be searched and ransacked by the strong hand of power. We have infinitely more reason to dread general warrants here, than they have in England; because there, if a person be confined, liberty may be quickly obtained by the writ of *habeas corpus*. But here a man living many hundred miles from the Judges, may rot in prison before he can get that writ.—Another most fatal omission is, with respect to standing armies. In your Bill of Rights of Virginia, they are said to be dangerous to liberty, and it tells you, that the proper defence of a free State consists in militia;[2] and so I might go on to ten or eleven things of immense consequence secured in your Bill of Rights, concerning which that proposal is silent. Is that the language of the Bill of Rights in England?—Is it the language of the American Bill of Rights, that these three rights, and these only, are valuable? Is it the language of men going into a new Government? Is it not necessary to speak of those things before you go into a compact? How do these three things stand? As one of the parties, we declare we do not mean to give them up. This is very dictatorial. Much more so, than the conduct which proposes alterations as the condition of adoption. In a compact there are two parties,—one accepting, and another proposing. As a party, we propose that we shall secure these three things; and before we have the assent of the other contracting party, we go into the compact, and leave these things at their mercy. What will be the consequence?—Suppose the other States will call this dictatorial? They will say, Virginia has gone into the Government, and carried with her certain propositions, which she says, ought to be concurred in by the other States. They will declare, that she has no right to dictate to other States, the conditions on which they shall come into the Union. According to the Honorable Member's [George Wythe] proposal, the ratification will cease to be obligatory unless they accede to these amendments. We have ratified it. You have committed a violation, they will say. They have not violated it. We say we will go out of it. You are then reduced to a sad dilemma: To give up these three rights, or leave the Government. This is worse than our present Confederation, to which we have hitherto adhered honestly and faithfully. We shall be told we have violated it, because we have left it for the infringement and violation of conditions, which they never agreed to be a part of the ratification. The ratification will be complete. The proposal is made by one party. We, as the other, accede to it, and propose the security of these three great rights; for it is only a proposal. In order to secure them, you are left in that state of fatal hostility, which I shall as much deplore as the Honorable Gentleman. I exhort Gentlemen to think seriously, before they ratify this Constitution, and persuade themselves that they will succeed in making a feeble effort to get amendments after adoption. With respect to that part of the proposal, which says, that every power not granted remains with the people; it must be previous to adoption, or it will involve this country in inevitable destruction—To talk of it, as a thing subsequent, not as one of your unalienable rights, is leaving it to the casual opinion of the Congress who shall take up the consideration of that matter. They will not reason with you about the effect of this Constitution. They will not take the opinion of this Committee concerning its operation. They will construe it as they please. If you place it subsequently, let me ask the consequences? Among ten thousand implied powers which they may assume, they may, if we be engaged in war, liberate every one of your slaves if they please. And this must and will be done by men, a majority of whom have not a common interest with you. They will therefore have no feeling for your interests. It has been repeatedly said here, that the great object of a national Government, was national defence. That power which is said to be intended for security and safety, may be rendered detestable and oppressive. If you give power to the General Government to provide for the general defence, the means must be commensurate to the end. All the means in the possession of the people must be given to the Government which is intrusted with the public defence. In this State there are 236,000 blacks, and there are many in several other States. But there are few or none in the Northern States, and yet if the Northern States shall be of opinion, that our numbers are numberless, they may call forth every national resource. May Congress not say, that every black man must fight?—Did we not see a little of this last war?—We were not so hard pushed, as to make emancipation general. But acts of Assembly passed, that every slave who would go to the army should be free.[3] Another thing will contribute to bring this event about—slavery is detested—we feel its fatal effects—we deplore it with all the pity of humanity. Let all these considerations, at some future period, press with full force on the minds of Congress. Let that urbanity, which I trust will distinguish America, and the necessity of national defence:— Let all these things operate on their minds. They will search that paper, and see if they have power of manumission.—And have they not, Sir?—

Have they not power to provide for the general defence and welfare?—May they not think that these call for the abolition of slavery?—May they not pronounce all slaves free, and will they not be warranted by that power? There is no ambiguous implication, or logical deduction—The paper speaks to the point. They have the power in clear unequivocal terms; and will clearly and certainly exercise it. As much as I deplore slavery, I see that prudence forbids its abolition. I deny that the General Government ought to set them free, because a decided majority of the States have not the ties of sympathy and fellow-feeling for those whose interest would be affected by their emancipation. The majority of Congress is to the North, and the slaves are to the South. In this situation, I see a great deal of the property of the people of Virginia in jeopardy, and their peace and tranquillity gone away. I repeat it again, that it would rejoice my very soul, that every one of my fellow beings was emancipated. As we ought with gratitude to admire that decree of Heaven, which has numbered us among the free, we ought to lament and deplore the necessity of holding our fellow-men in bondage. But is it practicable by any human means, to liberate them, without producing the most dreadful and ruinous consequences? We ought to possess them in the manner we have inherited them from our ancestors, as their manumission is incompatible with the felicity of the country. But we ought to soften, as much as possible, the rigour of their unhappy fate. I know that in a variety of particular instances, the Legislature listening to complaints, have admitted their emancipation.[4] Let me not dwell on this subject. I will only add, that this, as well as every other property of the people of Virginia, is in jeopardy, and put in the hands of those who have no similarity of situation with us. This is a local matter, and I can see no propriety in subjecting it to Congress. With respect to subsequent amendments, proposed by the worthy Member [George Wythe], I am distressed when I hear the expression.—It is a new one altogether, and such a one as stands against every idea of fortitude, and manliness, in the States, or any one else.—Evils admitted, in order to be removed subsequently, and tyranny submitted to, in order to be excluded by a subsequent alteration, are things totally new to me. But I am sure he meant nothing but to amuse the Committee. I know his candour. His proposal is an idea dreadful to me. I ask—does experience warrant such a thing from the beginning of the world, to this day?—Do you enter into a compact of Government first, and afterwards settle the terms of the Government? It is admitted by every one, that this is a compact.—Although the Confederation be lost, it is a compact Constitution, or something of that nature. I confess I never heard of such an idea before. It is most abhorrent to my mind. You endanger the tranquillity of your country—you stab its repose, if you accept this Government unaltered. How are you to allay animosities?— For such there are, great and fatal. He flatters me, and tells me, that I could influence the people, and reconcile them to it. Sir, their sentiments are as firm and steady, as they are patriotic. Were I to ask them to apostatize from their native religion, they would despise me. They are not to be shaken in their opinions, with respect to the propriety of preserving their rights. You never can persuade them, that it is necessary to relinquish them. Were I to attempt to persuade them to abandon their patriotic sentiments, I should look on myself as the most infamous of men. I believe it to be a fact, that the great body of yeomanry are in decided opposition to it. I may say with confidence, that for nineteen counties adjacent to each other, nine-tenths of the people are conscientiously opposed to it. I may be mistaken, but I give you it as my opinion, and my opinion is founded on personal knowledge in some measure, and other good authority.[5] I have not hunted popularity by declaiming to injure this Government. Though public fame might say so, it was not owing to me that this flame of opposition has been kindled and spread. These men never will part with their political opinions.—If they should see their political happiness secured to the latest posterity, then indeed they might agree to it. Subsequent amendments will not do for men of this cast. Do you consult the Union in proposing them? You may amuse them as long as you please, but they will never like it. You have not solid reality, the hearts and hands of the men who are to be governed. Have Gentlemen no respect to the actual dispositions of the people in the adopting States? Look at Pennsylvania and Massachusetts. These two great States have raised as great objections to that Government as we do. There was a majority of only nineteen in Massachusetts. We are told, that only 10,000 were represented in Pennsylvania, although 70,000 had a right to be represented.[6] Is not this a serious thing?—Is it not worth while to turn your eyes for a moment from subsequent amendments, to the situation of your country?—Can you have a lasting Union in these circumstances? It will be in vain to expect it. But if you agree to previous amendments, you shall have Union, firm and solid. I cannot conclude without saying, that I shall have nothing to do with it, if subsequent amendments be determined upon. Oppressions will be carried on as radically by the majority when adjustments and accommodations will be held up. I say, I conceive it my duty, if this Government is adopted before it is amended, to go home.—I shall act as I think my duty requires.—Every other Gentleman will do the same. Previous amendments, in my opinion, are necessary to procure peace and tranquillity. I fear, if they be not agreed to, every movement and operation of Government will cease, and how long that baneful thing *civil discord*, will stay from this country, God only knows. When men are free from restraint, how long will you suspend their fury? The interval between this and bloodshed, is but a moment. The licentious and wicked of the community, will seize with avidity every thing you hold. In this unhappy situation, what is to be done? It surpasses my stock of wisdom. If you will in the language of freemen, stipulate, that there are rights which no man under Heaven can take from you, you shall have me going along with you:—Not otherwise.—(Here Mr. *Henry* informed the Committee, that he had a resolution prepared, to refer a declaration of rights, with certain amendments to the most exceptionable parts of the Constitution, to the other States in the Confederacy, for their consideration, previous to its ratification. The Clerk then read the resolution, the declaration of rights, and amendments, which were nearly the same as those ultimately proposed by the Convention, which see at the conclusion.)[7] He then resumed the subject. I have thus candidly submitted to you Mr. Chairman, and this Committee, what occurred to me as proper amendments to the Constitution, and a declaration of rights containing those fundamental unalienable privileges, which I conceive to be essential to liberty and happiness. I believe, that on a review of these amendments it will still be found, that the arm of power will be sufficiently strong for national purposes, when these restrictions shall be a part of the Government. I believe no Gentleman who opposes me in sentiments, will be able to discover that any one feature of a strong Government is altered; and at the same time your unalienable rights are secured by them. The Government unaltered may be terrible to America; but can never be loved, till it be amended. You find all the resources of the Continent may be drawn to a point. In danger, the President may concentre to a point every effort of the Continent. If the Government be constructed to satisfy the people, and remove their apprehensions, the wealth and strength of the Continent will go where public utility shall direct.—This Government, with these restrictions, will be a strong Government united with the privileges of the people. In my weak judgement, a Government is strong when it applies to the most important end of all Governments,—the rights and privileges of the people.—In the Honorable Member's proposal, jury trial, the press, and religion, and other essential rights, are not to be given up.—*Other essential rights*—What are they?—The world will say, that you intended to give them up....

1. Patrick Henry is responding to a speech by George Wythe on 24 June in the committee of the whole in which Wythe ended with a resolution to adopt the Constitution

unconditionally with the recommendation of a few amendments protecting several sacred rights (immediately above).

2. See Article 13 of the Virginia Declaration of Rights (BoR, I, 113).

3. In 1775 the legislature passed an act stipulating that, with certain exceptions, "all free male persons, hired servants, and apprentices" between the ages of sixteen and fifty were liable to serve in the militia. Some runaway slaves enlisted as soldiers. In 1777 the legislature, seeking to end this practice, required that any black or mulatto wishing to enlist should produce a certificate from a justice of the peace of his home county certifying that he was a freeman. During the course of the Revolution, many slaveowners "caused their slaves to enlist ... as substitutes for free persons" by informing the recruiting officers that these slaves were freemen. After the term of enlistment, some slaveowners tried to force these enlistees back into slavery, "contrary to the principles of justice, and to their own solemn promise." Consequently, in 1783 the legislature freed these enlistees if they had served faithfully (Hening, IX, 27, 280; XI, 308–9).

4. In 1779 and 1780 the legislature, acting upon "applications," passed acts freeing individual slaves (Hening, X, 211, 372). In 1782 the legislature adopted an act which allowed owners to emancipate their slaves under certain restrictions without having to petition the legislature for a special act (*ibid.*, XI, 39–40). Despite this act, some slaves still had to petition the legislature to make certain that wills were properly executed. (For example, see an act passed in 1784, *ibid.*, 362–63.) The 1782 act contributed to an increase in the number of free blacks in Virginia. In 1782 there were fewer than 3,000; while in 1790 there were 12,866 (John H. Russell, *The Free Negro in Virginia, 1619–1865* [1913; reprint ed., New York, 1969], 61).

5. Henry probably meant the counties south of the James River of which his home county of Prince Edward was approximately the geographical center. The delegates from these counties voted overwhelmingly against ratification.

6. The minority of the Pennsylvania Convention claimed (in its "Dissent") "that of upwards of *seventy thousand* freemen who are intitled to vote in Pennsylvania, the whole convention has been elected by about *thirteen thousand* voters ..." (*Pennsylvania Packet*, 18 December, CC:Vol. 3, page 17. For the "Dissent" in Virginia, see RCS:Va., 401–2.).

7. The resolution presented by Patrick Henry was probably the resolution that, on 25 June, was defeated by a vote of 88 to 80 (BoR, III, 43). The George Mason Papers at the Library of Congress include a one-page manuscript in Mason's handwriting that contains versions of a resolution that are similar to the one defeated on 25 June. For a photographic reproduction of this manuscript, see RCS:Va. Supplement, 79. The declaration of rights and structural amendments presented by Henry have not been located. For the declaration of rights and amendments "ultimately proposed by the Convention" on 27 June, see BoR, I, 251–56.

Edmund Randolph: Speech in the Virginia Convention
24 June 1788 (excerpt)

... The Honorable Gentleman [Patrick Henry] says, there is no restraint on the power of issuing general warrants. If I be tedious in asking where is that power, you will ascribe it to him who has put me to the necessity of asking. They have no such power given them:—If they have, where is it?

Again he recurs to standing armies, and asks if Congress cannot raise such. Look at the Bill of Rights provided by the Honorable Gentleman himself, and tell me if there be not great security by admitting it when necessary? It says, that standing armies should be avoided in time of peace: It does not absolutely prohibit them.[1]—Is there any clause in it, or in the Confederation, which prevents Congress from raising an army?—No—it is left to the discretion of Congress. It ought to be in the power of Congress to raise armies, as the existence of the society might at some future period depend upon it. But it should be recommended to them to use the power only when necessary. I humbly conceive, that you will have as great security as you could desire from that clause in the Constitution, which directs that money for supporting armies will be voted for every two years; as by this means, the Representatives who will have appropriated money unnecessarily, or imprudently, to that purpose, may be removed, and a new regulation made. Review the practice of the favourite nation of that Honorable Gentleman. In their Bill of Rights, there is no prohibition of a standing army, but only that it ought not to be maintained without the consent of the Legislature.[2] Can it be done here without the consent of the Democratic branch? Their consent is necessary to every bill, and money bills can originate with them only. Can an army then be raised or supported without their approbation?

(His Excellency then went over all the articles of Mr. *Henry*'s proposed Declaration of Rights, and endeavoured to prove, that the rights intended to be thereby secured, were either provided for in the Constitution itself, or could not be infringed by the General Government, as being unwarranted by any of the powers which were delegated therein; for that it was in vain to provide against the exercise of a power which did not exist.) He then proceeded to examine the nature of some of the amendments proposed by the Honorable Gentleman. As to the reservation of rights not expressly given away, he repeated what he had before observed, of the 2d article of Confederation, that it was interpreted to prohibit Congress from granting passports, although such a power was necessarily incident to that of making war.[3] Did not this, says he, shew the vanity of all Federal authority? Gentlemen have displayed great wisdom in the use they make of the experience of the defects in the old Confederation. When we see the defect of that article, are we to repeat it? Are those Gentlemen zealous friends to the Union, who profess to be so here, and yet insist on a repetition of measures which have been found destructive to it? I believe their professions, but they must pardon me, when I say, their arguments are not true. . . .

1. The declaration of rights and structural amendments presented by Patrick Henry have not been located, but, according to stenographer David Robertson, they "were nearly the same as those ultimately proposed by the Convention." Consequently, Rob-

ertson did not include them in the debates for 24 June. Nor do they appear in the manuscript or printed Convention Journal.

For the amendment on standing armies (number 17) that the Convention adopted as part of its declaration of rights, see BoR, I, 253. The Convention also adopted a structural amendment (number 9) concerning standing armies in time of peace (BoR, I, 254). Both amendments are nearly identical to those adopted by the committee of Antifederalist Convention delegates chaired by George Mason and sent by him to New York Antifederalists on 9 June (BoR, III, 55, 56).

2. The sixth article of the English Bill of Rights (1689) provided "That the raising or keeping a standing army within the kingdom in time of peace unless it be with consent of parliament is against law."

3. For Randolph's earlier references to passports, see Convention Debates, 4 and 6 June (RCS:Va., 936, 985).

George Mason to John Lamb
Richmond, Va., 9 June 1788 (excerpts)[1]

In mid-May 1788 the Federal Republican Committee of New York, a group of Antifederalists in and around New York City, wrote letters to prominent Antifederalists in New Hampshire, Pennsylvania, Maryland, Virginia, and North and South Carolina calling for cooperation in obtaining amendments to the Constitution before it was ratified by nine states. (Pennsylvania and Maryland had ratified in December 1787 and April 1788, respectively, but there was substantial support in each for amendments.) These letters were signed by John Lamb, the committee's chairman.

The New York Federal Republican Committee, targeting Virginia as the most important state, addressed letters to Patrick Henry, George Mason, and William Grayson, among "the most influential Delegates" to the Virginia Convention. The committee also wrote to Richard Henry Lee, possibly because it assumed (incorrectly) that Lee would also be a delegate (CC:750-A). Fearful lest the letters be intercepted if sent through the post office, the letters were carried to Richmond by Eleazer Oswald, the highly partisan Antifederalist printer of the Philadelphia *Independent Gazetteer*. Only in the case of Virginia does it appear that a special carrier was employed. While Oswald was en route, the committee learned that New York Antifederalists had won a landslide victory in the election of convention delegates and that South Carolina had ratified the Constitution. Therefore, on 6 June the committee again wrote to Virginia and New Hampshire Antifederalists, hoping that the news of the New York election would stimulate "a communication" among the conventions of New York, Virginia, and New Hampshire (CC:750-B).

Eleazer Oswald arrived in Richmond on 7 June. Presumably, the delivery of the letters had been scheduled to coincide with the first days of the Virginia Convention. Federalist Convention delegates, such as James Madison and Henry Lee of Westmoreland County, knew about Oswald's arrival, his meetings with Virginia Antifederalists, and the movement to obtain amendments prior to ratification. (See Madison to Alexander Hamilton, 9, 16, and 20 June, and Lee to Hamilton, 16 June, RCS:Va., 1589, 1630, 1631, 1657. See also Robert Smith to Tench Coxe, 31 July, quoted in RCS:Va., 812.)

On 9 June, or shortly thereafter, Eleazer Oswald started back for New York, carrying letters from William Grayson (CC:750–C), Patrick Henry (CC:750–D), and George Mason (printed here) responding to Lamb's May letters. The Virginians, all writing on 9 June, informed Lamb that they had formed a "Comm[itt]ee of Opposition" or a "Republican Society" and had drafted some amendments to the Constitution. Other amendments were being prepared. George Mason, the chairman of the committee, enclosed a copy of the amendments. There is no evidence that Virginia Antifederalists ever responded to the 6 June letter of the New York Federal Republican Committee.

The three Virginians expressed concern that their state Convention was evenly divided between Federalists and Antifederalists. If ratification could be postponed, Mason told Lamb "that an official Communication will immediately take place between the Conventions of this State and yours." He also said that, at the present time, Virginia did not have an Antifederalist organization equivalent to the Federal Republican Committee of New York. If such an organization "should hereafter become necessary," Mason continued, "it is hoped that System and Order will every where appear suitable to the Importance and Dignity of the Cause." According to Patrick Henry, if the Virginia Convention ratified the Constitution, the state's Antifederalists should form their own Republican Society, perhaps composed of multiple associations because of "our dispersed Situation." Before leaving Richmond, Oswald told the Virginians that in the future they could safely write the Federal Republican Committee by addressing their letters to Captain Jacob Reed, Jr., of New York City. In his letter, Mason advised Lamb to address future correspondence by way of George Fleming, a Richmond merchant. (For Richard Henry Lee's 27 June response to Lamb, see BoR, III, 69–70.)

Eleazer Oswald, not wanting "to risque" the Virginia letters "with any other Person," passed through Philadelphia and arrived in New York City on 16 June. He informed John Lamb that Patrick Henry and other Virginians had recommended that the New York Convention take the lead and appoint a delegation to meet with one from the Virginia Convention to discuss amendments. The next day, after copies were made, Lamb sent the Virginia letters to Governor George Clinton at the New York Convention in Poughkeepsie, recommending that, if the New York Convention appointed a delegation to meet with a Virginia group, an express rider carry the news to Virginia immediately (CC:750–H).

On 21 June Clinton, the president of the New York Convention, wrote Lamb that he had turned the Virginia letters over to "a Special Committee of Correspondence" chaired by Convention delegate Robert Yates (CC:750–I). On the same day, Yates wrote to George Mason acknowledging the receipt of the Virginia amendments and enclosing a copy of amendments to which "many" New York Antifederalists had agreed. Yates told Mason that the New Yorkers were willing to correspond with the Virginians, but that it seemed unlikely that the Virginia Antifederalists would win their struggle and that the New York Convention would probably adjourn before the Virginia response could get back to Poughkeepsie (CC:750–J). Given the fact that it would have taken express riders about a week to get from Poughkeepsie to Richmond, Yates's 21 June letter did not reach Richmond on 25 June, the day the Virginia Convention ratified the Constitution, or on 27 June, the day it adopted amendments.

COMMENTARIES, 9 JUNE 1788

For Joshua Atherton's 11, 14 June response to the Federal Republican Committee, see BoR, III, 57–59. For other responses by Samuel Chase of Maryland, Rawlins Lowndes of South Carolina, Timothy Bloodworth of North Carolina, Aedanus Burke of South Carolina, and Thomas Person of North Carolina, see CC:750–G, K, M and P, N, Q, respectively.

I have had the Honor to receive your Letter dated the 18th. of May, in behalf of the fœderal republican Committee of New York, upon the Subject of the Government proposed by the late Convention to the respective States for their Adoption; and have communicated it to several respectable Gentlemen of the Convention now met in this City, who are opposed to the Adoption without previous Amendments:

They receive, with pleasure, the proposition of your Committee for a free Correspondence on the Subject of Amendments, and have requested me to transmit to your committee such as we have agreed on as necessary for previous Adoption.

Although there is a general Concurrence in the Convention of this State that Amendments are necessary, yet, the Members are so equally divided with respect to the Time and Manner of obtaining them, that it cannot now be ascertained whether the Majority will be on our Side or not; if it should be so, I have no doubt but that an official Communication will immediately take place between the Conventions of this State and yours.

As the Amendments proposed by the Convention of Massachusets are the first which have been offered to the public,[2] and contain in them many things that are necessary, it is deemed proper to make them the Basis of such as may finally be agreed on; and it may also be proper to observe. . . .

[Enclosure][3]
Amendments to the New Constitution of Government.

That there be a Declaration or Bill of Rights, asserting and securing from Encroachment, the Essential and unalienable Rights of the People, in some such Manner as the following.—

1. That all Freemen have certain essential inherent Rights, of which they cannot by any Compact, deprive or divest their Posterity; among which are the Enjoyment of Life and Liberty, with the means of acquiring, possessing and protecting Property, and pursuing and obtaining Happiness and Safety.

2. That all Power is naturally vested in, and consequently derived from the People; that Magistrates therefore are their Trustees and Agents, and at all Times amenable to them.

3. That Government ought to be instituted for the Common Benefit, Protection and Security of the People; and that whenever any Government shall be found inadequate or contrary to these purposes, a Ma-

jority of the Community hath an indubitable unalienable and indefeasible Right to reform, alter or abolish it, and to establish another, in such manner as shall be judged most conducive to the public Weal; and that the Doctrine of non-resistance against arbitrary Power and Oppression is absurd, slavish and destructive of the good and Happiness of Mankind.

4. That no man or Set of Men are entitled to exclusive or separate public Emoluments or privileges from the Community, but in Consideration of public Services; which not being descendable neither ought the Offices of Magistrate, Legislator or Judge, or any other public Office, to be hereditary.

5. That the Legislative, Executive and Judicial powers of Government should be separate and distinct; and that the Members of the Two first may be restrained from Oppression, by feeling and participating [in] the public Burthens, they should, at fixed periods, be reduced to a private Station, return into the Mass of the people, and the Vacancies be supplied by certain and regular Elections, in which all, or any part of the Former Members to be eligible or ineligible, as the Rules of the Constitution of Government and the Laws shall direct.

6. That the Right of the People to participate in the Legislature is the best Security of Liberty, and the Foundation of all Free Governments; for this purpose Elections ought to be free and frequent; and all men having sufficient Evidence of permanent common Interest with, and Attachment to the Community, ought to have the Right of Suffrage:[4] And no Aid, Charge, Tax or Fee can be set, rated or levied upon the People without their own Consent, or that of their Representatives so elected; nor can they be bound by any Law to which they have not in like manner assented for the Public Good.

7. That all power of suspending Laws, or the Execution of Laws by any Authority, without Consent of the Representatives of the People in the Legislature, is injurious to their Rights, and ought not to be exercised.

8. That in all Capital or Criminal Prosecutions, a Man hath a Right to demand the Cause & Nature of his Accusation, to be confronted with the Accusers and Witnesses, to call for Evidence and be admitted Counsel in his Favor, and to a fair and speedy Trial by an impartial Jury of his Vicinage, without whose unanimous Consent he cannot be found guilty, (except in the Government of the Land and Naval Forces in Time of actual War, Invasion or Rebellion) nor can he be compelled to give Evidence against himself.

9. That no Freeman ought to be taken, imprisoned, or desseized of his Freehold, Liberties, Privileges or Franchises, or outlawed or exiled,

or in any manner destroyed, or deprived of his Life, Liberty or Property, but by the Law of the Land.

10. That every Freeman restrained of his Liberty is entitled to a Remedy, to enquire into the Lawfulness thereof, and to remove the same if unlawful, and that such Remedy ought not to be denied or delayed.

11. That in Controversies respecting Property, and in Suits between Man and Man, the ancient Trial by Jury of Facts, where they arise, is one of the greatest Securities to the Rights of a Free people, and ought to remain sacred and inviolable.

12. That every Freeman ought to find a certain Remedy, by Recourse to the Laws, for all Injuries or Wrongs he may receive in his person, property or Character: He ought to obtain Right and Justice freely, without sale, compleatly and without Denial, promptly and without Delay; and that all Establishments or Regulations contravening these Rights are oppressive and unjust.

13. That excessive Bail ought not to be required, nor excessive Fines imposed, nor cruel and unusual Punishments inflicted.

14. That every[5] Freeman has a Right to be secure from all unreasonable Searches and Seizures of his Person, his papers, and his property; all Warrants therefore to search suspected places, or to seize any Freeman, his Papers or property, without[6] Information upon Oath (or Affirmation of a person religiously scrupulous of taking an Oath) of legal and sufficient Cause, are grievous and Oppressive; and all General Warrants to search suspected Places, or to apprehend any suspected Person, without specially naming or describing the Place or Person, are dangerous and ought not to be granted.

15. That the People have a Right peaceably to assembly together to consult for their common Good, or to instruct their Representatives, and[7] that every Freeman has a Right to petition or apply to the Legislature for Redress of Greivances.

16. That the People have a Right to Freedom of Speech, and of writing and publishing their Sentiments; that the Freedom of the Press is one of the great Bulwarks of Liberty, and ought not to be violated.

17. That the People have a Right to keep and to bear Arms; that a well regulated Militia, composed of the Body of the People, trained to arms, is the proper, natural, and safe Defence of a free State; that Standing Armies in Time of Peace are dangerous to Liberty, and therefore ought to be avoided as far as the Circumstances and Protection of the Community will admit; and that in all Cases, the Military should be under strict Subordination to, and governed by the Civil Power.

18. That no Soldier in Time of Peace ought to be quartered in any House without the Consent of the Owner; and in Time of War, only by the civil Magistrate in such Manner as the Laws direct.

19. That any Person religiously scrupulou[8] of bearing Arms[9] ought to be exempted upon payment of an Equivalent to employ another to bear Arms in his stead.

20. That Religion or the Duty which we owe to our Creator, and the Manner of discharging it, can be directed only by Reason and Conviction, not by Force or Violence, and therefore all Men have an equal, natural, and unalienable Right to the free Exercise of Religion according to the Dictates of Conscience, and that no particular Religious Sect or Society of Christians ought to be favored or established by Law in preference to others.

That each State in the Union shall retain its Sovereignty, Freedom and Independence, and every Power, Jurisdiction and Right which is not by this Constitution expressly delegated to the Congress of the United States. . . .

No Standing Army or Regular Troops shall be raised or kept up in Time of Peace without the Consent of Two-Thirds of the Members of both Houses.

Neither the president, nor Vice President of the United States, nor any Member of the Council, shall command the Army or Navy of the United States in person, without the Consent of Two-Thirds of the Members of both Houses.

No Soldier shall be enlisted for a longer Term than four Years, except in Time of War, and then for no longer Term than the Continuance of the War.

No Mutiny Act shall be passed for any longer Term than Two Years. . . .

1. RC, Lamb Papers, NHi. This letter is in the handwriting of Meriwether Smith, an Essex County member of the Virginia Convention, but the signature and the inside address are in the handwriting of George Mason. The Lamb Papers also contains a contemporaneous copy of this letter that includes the Virginia committee's proposed amendments to the Constitution (printed as an enclosure immediately below). The recipient's copy of the amendments has not been located. Copies of Mason's letter and the accompanying amendments, both in Smith's handwriting, are in the Virginia Historical Society (Mss2 Sm624 a4 and Mss 13:1788 June 27:1, respectively). The former is docketed "Meriwether Smith." (For the copy of the amendments in Smith's handwriting, see note 3, below.) On 25 June Mason voted against ratification of the Constitution in the Virginia Convention.

2. For the Massachusetts amendments, see BoR, I, 243–45n.

3. MS, Lamb Papers, NHi. The recipient's copy has not been located. The copy printed here, made at the time by the New York Federal Republican Committee, is divided into two parts. A working draft for each part, in George Mason's handwriting, is in the Mason Papers in the Library of Congress. Significant portions lined out in the drafts are indicated in notes 4 to 9 (below). See RCS:Va. Supplement, 79 for photographic reproductions of the drafts, in which some of the amendments appear in a different sequence.

An incomplete copy of the amendments in the handwriting of Meriwether Smith is located in the Virginia Historical Society (Mss 13:1788 June 27:1). There are no significant differences between Smith's copy and the copy made by the New York Federal Republican Committee. (For the copy in the Virginia Historical Society, see RCS:Va. Supplement, 79.) Another copy (not in Smith's hand) is in the Smith Papers at the New-York Historical Society.

The amendments printed here, particularly the first twenty which are largely taken from the Virginia Declaration of Rights (BoR, I, 111–13), formed the basis for the amendments that the Virginia Convention adopted on 27 June (BoR, I, 251–56) and ordered to be sent (along with the Form of Ratification) to Congress and to all of the state executives or legislatures.

4. At this point in Mason's draft the following words are lined out: "the People can not be deprived of their Property for Public Uses."

5. At this point in the draft Mason originally wrote "free Citizen." He then lined out "Citizen" and replaced it with "Man."

6. At this point in Mason's draft the word "previous" is lined out.

7. At this point in Mason's draft the following words are lined out: "apply to the Legislature for Redress of Grievances, by Address, Petition, or Remonstrance."

8. At this point in Mason's draft the following words are lined out: "of the Lawfulness."

9. At this point in Mason's draft the words "shou'd be" are lined out.

Joshua Atherton to John Lamb
Amherst, N.H., 11, 14 June 1788[1]

This letter is a response to the New York Federal Republican Committee's effort to obtain cooperation from Antifederalists in the several states that had not yet ratified the Constitution in obtaining amendments to the Constitution before it was ratified. Atherton received the committee's letter signed by John Lamb, the committee's chairman, on 10 June and responded on 11 and 14 June. (For a similar letter written to Nathaniel Peabody on 18 May, see RCS: N.H., 311–13.) On 20 June, Atherton received another letter from the committee dated 6 June. Atherton responded to this letter on 23 June, two days after the New Hampshire Convention ratified the Constitution (CC:750–L).

For a full discussion of the Federal Republican Committee's effort to foster interstate cooperation among Antifederalists to obtain amendments previous to ratification of the Constitution, see George Mason to John Lamb, 9 June (immediately above).

I have the Honour to recognize the Reception of your very great favour, which came to hand Yesterday.

Long anxiously desirous of the Communication proposed, I shall leave nothing unattempted in my power to effect a unanimity of Sentiment with respect to Amendments: I cannot persuade myself however, that the Method adopted by the Convention of Massachusetts is by any means eligible:[2] To ratify, and then propose Amendments is to surrender our all, and then ask our new Masters if they will be so gracious as to return to us, some, or any part, of our most important Rights and Privileges. Can this be acting the Part of Wisdom or good Policy?

I have the Honour, Gentlemen, perfectly to coincide with you in Sentiment, that the Amendments should be procured *previous* to the

Adoption of the new System, and all local Advantages rejected as unworthy the Attention of those who are contending for the general Liberty.

There has hitherto been a fair Majority in the Convention of New Hampshire, as far as their sentiments could be collected (for the decisive Question has not yet been put) against ratifying the proposed Constitution in its present form: This the candid Consolidarians confess. But I need not inform you how many Arts are made use of to increase their Party. The presses are in a great measure secured to *their* side—inevitable Ruin is held up on non-compliance—while the new System is represented as fraught with every species of Happiness—The opponents are enemies to their Country, and they often make them say what they never thought. In the Exeter Advertiser (New Hampshire) they had the disingenuity to say, that "Mr. Atherton seemed to give up the Idea of all cases between Citizens of different States originating in the federal Courts &c."[3] Nothing could be more the reverse of Truth than this assertion—Their views are obvious—But I will not trouble you with particulars, some future publications, I flatter myself, will brush off the mask of Falsehood.

Permit me to hope you will lead the Way, and delineate the Method of a Correspondence between the States who have not yet resigned their Lives, Liberties, and Properties, into the hands of this new and unlimited Sovereignty: Your central Situation, and great Importance as a State, gives us a Right to expect it of you, while nothing shall be wanting, here, to second such a desireable Event; nor, indeed, shall any part of your public spirited and benevolent proposals want the attention they so highly merit.

No Amendments being yet fixed on here, or even attempted, that subject must be left for future Consideration. Could our Convention receive your Resolution not to adopt, without the necessary Amendments, before they have proceeded too far, together *with your amendments*, I have not the least Doubt but a great Majority would immediately close with your views and wishes.

The Convention of this State sits next Wednesday at Concord, by adjournment,[4] on the conclusion of which Session, I will cause to be transmitted to the Anti-federal Committee of the County of Albany, the Result of our Deliberations, who will be good enough to forward them to you: The Subject of Amendments shall not be forgot.

June 14th

I yesterday received the Supplement to the Albany Journal of the tenth Instant, by which it appears you will have a Majority of two to one at least against the adoption.[5] I congratulate you on so fortunate an Event!

and have the highest Confidence, that the power and opportunity thus put into your hands to save our devoted Country from impending Ruin, will be exercised with Firmness, Integrity and Wisdom.

1. Copy, Lamb Papers, NHi. This letter, in the handwriting of Charles Tillinghast, the secretary of the New York Federal Republican Committee and son-in-law of John Lamb, is docketed "Copy of a Letter from Joshua Atherton Esqr. (New Hampshire) dated June 11th & 14th. 1788." Atherton's letter was sent to New York (via New Haven) by a Mr. Woodworth.

2. On 6 February 1788 the Massachusetts Convention ratified the Constitution unconditionally but recommended that the state's members of the first federal Congress seek the approval of nine amendments to the Constitution through the amending process provided in Article V of the Constitution (BoR, I, 243–45n). Following Massachusetts' example, six of the remaining seven states ratified unconditionally with recommendatory amendments.

3. On 7 March the Exeter, N.H., *Freeman's Oracle* reprinted the version of the 20 February debates of the New Hampshire Convention that the *New Hampshire Spy* had printed in its issue on 23 February. For the *Spy*'s report of Atherton's comments, see RCS:N.H., 212.

4. The New Hampshire Convention met in Exeter on 13 February 1788. Sensing a majority in opposition to ratification, Federalist delegates got the Convention to adjourn on 22 February to reconvene in Concord on 18 June.

5. This issue of the *Albany Journal* has not been located, but on 12 June the *New York Journal* noted in a widely reprinted item that "This state [New York] sends 65 members to the convention, of which, it appears, that 46 are decidedly opposed to the constitution" (RCS:N.Y., 1582, 1583 note 11).

Bon Mot—à propôs
Massachusetts Centinel, 11 June 1788[1]

BON MOT—à propôs.

Two honest natives of the *land of clover*, being in conversation the other day on the subject of the nearly *adopted* Constitution—one of them defended it *in toto*—while the other wished for *amendments.*— "*Where now, my dear, could you amend it*"—asked the federal son of Hibernia. The other readily pointed out the defective part, and proposed the amendment.—"*Faith, and my dear,*" replied the federalist, "*I really think now, that what you propose, would only* AMEND *it for the* WORSE, *by my shoul.*[2]"

1. Reprinted: *New York Morning Post*, 19 June; Hartford, Conn. *American Mercury*, 5 January 1789.
2. A variation of the word "soul" (OED).

Sydney
New York Journal, 13 June 1788 (excerpt)[1]

Abraham Yates, Jr., wrote this two-part essay appearing on 13 and 14 June, under the signature of "Sydney," not "Sidney" as he had done for the articles that he published in the *Albany Gazette* in February and March. On 15 June he wrote to Abraham G. Lansing that on the next day he would send fifty sets of the essay to Poughkeepsie, where the New York Convention was scheduled to convene on 17 June. He also reserved ten sets of which he would send six to Lansing in Albany. The sixty sets, he said, cost him thirty shillings and six pence. He cautioned Lansing that, if the essay was reprinted, "Some Mistakes" would have to be corrected (RCS:N.Y., 1174). On 22 June, Lansing replied from Albany that the essay had been received and "partly distributed among our Friends." If Yates wanted the essay reprinted, declared Lansing, "I shall have it done, but for the present I should think it of more service if they were republished under the Nose of the Convention at Poghkepsie and perhaps a period may arrive at which they will be of more Service in this quarter than just at this present time—your instructions and opinion shall determine me" (RCS:N.Y., 1208).

In the course of his argument, Yates quotes or summarizes parts of the New York state constitution of 1777 with which he was familiar since he was chairman of the thirteen-member committee that drafted that document.

TO THE CITIZENS OF THE STATE OF NEW-YORK,

. . . The omission of a bill of rights in this state,[2] has given occasion to an inference, that the omission was equally warrantable in the constitution for the United States. On this it may be necessary to observe, that while the constitution of this state was in agitation, there appeared doubts upon the propriety of the measure, from the peculiar situation in which the country then was; our connection with Britain dissolved, and her government formally renounced—no substitute devised—all the powers of government avowedly temporary, and solely calculated for defence: it was urged by those who were in favor of a bill of rights, that the power of the rulers ought to be circumscribed, the better to protect the people at large from the oppression and usurpation of their rulers. The English petition of rights, in the reign of Charles the first, and the bill of rights in the reign of king William,[3] were mentioned as examples to support their opinions. Those in opposition admitted, that in established governments, which had an implied constitution, a declaration of rights might be necessary to prevent the usurpation of ambitious men, but that that was not our situation, for upon the declaration of independence it had become necessary that the exercise of every kind of authority "under the former government should be totally suppressed, and all the power of government exerted under the authority of the people of the colonies;"[4] that we could not suppose that we had an existing constitution or form of government, express or implied, and therefore our situation resembled a people in a state of nature, who are preparing "to institute a government, laying its foundation on such principles, and organizing its powers in such form as to them shall seem most likely to effect their safety and happiness," and as such the constitution to be formed would operate as a bill of rights.⁵

These and the like considerations operated to induce the convention of New-York to dismiss the idea of a bill of rights, and the more especially as the legislative state officers being elected by the people at short periods, and thereby rendered from time to time liable to be displaced in case of mal-conduct. But these reasons will not apply to the general government, because it will appear in the sequel, that the state governments are considered in it as mere dependencies, existing solely by its toleration, and possessing powers of which they may be deprived whenever the general government is disposed so to do.

If then the powers of the state governments are to be totally absorbed, in which all agree, and only differ as to the mode, whether it will be effected by a rapid progression, or by as certain, but slower, operations: what is to limit the oppression of the general government? Where are the rights, which are declared to be incapable of violation? And what security have the people against the wanton oppression of unprincipled governors. No constitutional redress is pointed out, and no express declaration is contained in it, to limit the boundaries of their rulers; besides which the mode and period of their being elected tends to take away their responsibility to the people, over whom they may, by the power of the purse and the sword, domineer at discretion; nor is there a power on earth to tell them, What dost thou? or, why dost thou so? . . .

1. For the full essay, which continued in the *New York Journal* on 14 June, see RCS: N.Y., 1153–68n.

2. The committee of thirteen that drafted the state constitution was also instructed to draft a bill or declaration of rights but it failed to do so and no objection was raised in the state convention. Nevertheless, the state constitution does protect a number of rights. (See BoR, I, 88–89.) In January 1787 the legislature enacted a bill of rights entitled "An Act Concerning the Rights of the Citizens of this State" (BoR, I, 89–90).

3. Adopted, respectively, in 1628 and 1689.

4. Quoted from the preamble (15 May 1776) to a resolution adopted by Congress on 10 May 1776 that recommended that the colonies adopt new constitutions to replace their colonial charters (JCC, IV, 342, 357–58). Both the preamble and the resolution are quoted in full in the preamble to the New York constitution of 1777.

5. Quoted from the Declaration of Independence, adopted by Congress on 4 July 1776. The full text of the Declaration is included as part of the preamble to the New York constitution of 1777.

Edmund Pendleton to Richard Henry Lee
Richmond, Va., 14 June 1788 (excerpt)¹

I have to beg yr. Pardon For having so long neglected to acknowledge the Obligations I am under For yr. esteemed Favr. of the 26th. past; to revive a correspondence I always had pleasure in, was not among the smallest of it's benefits, but the Assistance of yr. Sage Counsels in Forming my Judgment on the great Question which has called us together, was the greatest; especially at a time when the wishes of my old constituents & not my own had called me to the decision, in the decline of mental Powers never very strong, grown rusty in Politics From a Supposition that I had long since taken a final leave of that line,[2] and retaining little more than a conscious Integrity, & unshaken Attachment to the Peace & happiness of my Countrey. You have been truly informed of my Sentiments being in favr. of Amendments, but against the insisting on their Incorporation previous to, and as a Sine qua Non of Adoption, or of a Convention being previously called to consider them, before the Government was brought into Action to give it a fair Experiment, & secure the great good it contains. The Amendments I wished, rather tended to eradicate the *seeds* of Future *mischief*, than to remove dangers immediately emminent in Operation—And considering as I do, that certain ruin must attend on a dissolution of the Union—That Union is only to be preserved by a *Fœdral Energetic* Government, and that the Articles of Confederation Possess not an Atom of such a Government,—I confess the evils I wish to remove Vanish, even if they remain in the Plan upon this Comparison on wch. side danger lies; and the rather when I consider that *perfection* would have been a Vain expectation, & that I esteem the great *Barriers* of liberty not *violated* in the Plan, tho' I may not think them sufficiently *Secured*. Prevs. Amendments either as a Sine qua Non, or to be the Subject of Consideration in a Future Convention of the States, impress on my mind a *Fatal* tendency to *rejection*, & it's consequent *evils*, & therefore I feel unconquerable repugnance to that *risque*—But viewing the Prospect of Success in Our *hopes* of Amendment, I think they are strongly Fortified by the mode of making them accompany *Ratification*, rather than to precede it. 8 states have already *Ratified*, some with, & some without Amendments proposed;[3] to *those* at least, & *others* who may so adopt, we shall appear wth. *Hostile* Countenances, unfavorable to a cordial reception—they will cons[ide]r Our Proposals as coming From Men, refusing to make a Common Stock with them of Interests, under the direction of the General Government, And therefore as *dictating* the admission of local *Interests*; Circumstances all unfavorable to *Patient* hearing & *candid* investigation, but say Gentn. Virga. is too *important* in the Union, to risque her *Separation* by refusing her *reasonable* propositions. Alas Sir, with *Irritated* minds, reason has small force, and if those 8 states should make the Supposition of that ground's having produced our Conduct, it will add that of *Insult* to the other causes of *Resentment*, And will any Gentn.

say that Virginia, Respectable as she is, is able to *sustain* the Conflict? does any wish to see the experiment even put in risque? No Sir, that circumstance of Importance it appears to me, will have it's due weight, when those states shall behold Virginia coming Forth as a United friend, with proposed Alterations For Common good, & will secure at least a Candid & Full examination, if not in some degree an influential decision. And thus, Sir, you have the grounds of my Judgmt. upon this All-important question of Previous or Subseqt. Amendments.

As to the Amendments themselves, I feel the Fullest Conviction of the Importance of those great rights, so favourable to Liberty, the trial by *Jury*, the Liberty of the *Press*—the *Fre[e]dom* & *Frequency* of *Elections*, & that *responsibility* of the Representative to his Constituents, by *residing* amongst, & *sharing* with them in all *benefits* & *Injuries*. I am unfortunate enough to differ From you in Opinion as to the best means of Securing them, being that of a *Bill* of *Rights*, my Objection to that is founded not on it's *strength*, but my Fear of it's *weakness* & *Danger*, and the *impropriety* of it's *Principle*. The *Magna Charta* of England wch. our Ancestors so much valued themselves upon, had it's merits; it unfettered them From some of those shackles which the dictated Will of a Conq[uero]r had in the Formation of their Government imposed upon them:[4] It was all they could do, the struggle was *noble* & the *Acquisition* valuable; but supposing it Recur'd to as a model For a *free* people in *Forming* a Governmt. For themselves, it appears in Principle, *humiliating* & *unsafe*, the former in accepting From any *Agent* of their *Power* a Charter of their rights, which they *Possess*, & derive From a *higher* Source. *Unsafe* because it *admits* a Power in the *Donor* to *take* away; a mischief which produced the Subsequent Struggles about the Great Charter, to be found in it's numerous Ratifications.[5] The *Petition* of Rights there, was a further Progress in wch. the humiliating Part of the principle was kept up; the *Bill* of Rights indeed, was a further step in wch. that principle was dropt, and a *Protest* made agt. Violations of Right, still *opposed* to a Ruler in Possessn. of *Dangerous* Powers. Whether that has produced the Apparent Repose of that nation, and the Safety, as some Gentn. Suppose, of their liberty; or whether the first of those effects, if it exists at all, has not been produced by a cause by Far more dangerous to, and annihilating the other, the change of the Instrument For Power From *vain Coertion*, to *effectual Bribery* & *corruption*, is at least *Problematical*: I fear that a review there would Find the Power of the Crown in it's greatest *Altitude*. However if they are happy 'tis well, & I wish not to disturb their *repose*.

But after this view is it not Safer to trust the two first rights to the Broad & Sure ground of this Principle—that the people being Established in the Grant itself as the *Fountain* of Power, *retain* every thing which is not granted? Is not the Principle true & Sound? does the Landlord in a grant For a term, reserve his own right? does the donor in grants For life or intail, reserve his Inheritance? no—when what is granted is at an end, his Original right Occurs—the Case of Escheat is still stronger—when ever an Absolute Fee Simple Estate ceases to Operate, by there being no legal, or Appointed Successor, the Original Source of the Grant comes Forth with it's Indisputable claim. In all these the Principle [retains?] it's Force, & will, I believe be Found to have in every investigation of Grants, or Delegations of Power. Again is there not danger in the Enumeration of Rights? may we not in the progress of things, discover *some* great & important, which we don't now think of? there the principle may be turned upon Us, & what is not reserved, said to be granted: If therefore Gentn. think something should be done, it would seem to me more proper to do as Massachussets proposes—Declare the *Principle*—as more Safe than the *Enumeration*.[6] or after all if Gentn. think a Bill of Rights best, I am satisfied; approving the *End*, I will not divide with them about the *means*, unless I saw more danger than in this. . . .

1. RC, Emmet Collection, NN. The name of the addressee does not appear, but Pendleton answers Richard Henry Lee's 26 May letter (CC:755). For Pendleton's entire letter, see CC:782.
2. Since he became president of the High Court of Chancery in 1778, Pendleton had not held elective office.
3. Of the eight conventions that had ratified the Constitution, only those of Massachusetts and South Carolina had recommended amendments.
4. Pendleton refers to William the Conqueror, the first Norman king of England (1066 to 1087). William introduced the legal theory that all land in the last resort was held of the king. He confiscated the lands of Anglo-Saxon rebels and gave the lands to his followers. He also restored lands to the great Anglo-Saxon landowners, so that they now held the lands from him. Since all public and political rights were intimately related to rights in land, all such rights were also derived from him. William established this feudal structure without the passage of any laws.
5. The Magna Carta (1215), which reaffirmed the feudal rights and privileges of the barons, was reissued with changes in 1216, 1217, and 1225, and it was confirmed more than forty times by 1422, the end of the reign of Henry V.
6. The first proposed Massachusetts amendment provided "That it be explicitly declared, that all Powers not expressly delegated by the aforesaid Constitution, are reserved to the several States to be by them exercised" (BoR, I, 243).

Cassandra
Philadelphia Independent Gazetteer, 14 June 1788

Mr. PRINTER, The cry of adopting the constitution proposed by the late federal convention IN TOTO, seems to have subsided. Even those who of late so very devoutly held it up as the work of divine legation, to which whosoever should add, or from which whosoever should take away, his part should be taken out of the book of life;—even these blind persecuting zealots relent. It seems now to be admitted that amendments are absolutely necessary; and amendments too of the most essential consequence to the liberty of the subject and the security of the individual states. To this principle the states of Massachusetts and South-Carolina have formally borne testimony by the acts of their state conventions;[1] and though the conventions of some of the other states have ratified the plan of government without exception or reserve, yet the sense of the people seems to be sufficiently manifest, that the proposed system of government is calculated more for the benefit of the future rulers than for the good of the people; and that some alterations, either in the form of a bill of rights or otherwise, are indispensably necessary. Few men are found hardy enough to contradict this opinion. In fact, the people of this continent are infinitely better agreed than they are aware of; and yet they are in great danger of being played off one against another and set together by the ears, when, if the votes of the freemen were fairly taken, ninety-nine in a hundred would be found to be still attached to the same principles of liberty which first united us against the tyrannical attempts of Great-Britain. We have still one common interest. Different orders of men are not yet established, except in contemplation; and those who bestride the continent in the fancied views of their own future importance, dare not as yet fully discover themselves. Why is it then, that we may not yet be a happy and united people? Every part of the continent seems agreed that the powers of Congress should be increased; that the regulation of foreign trade should be in their hands, and that they should be clothed with every power that is not destructive of those liberties which are secured by the constitutions of the separate states. Is there any man who wishes to go farther? If there be, he must have interested motives and sinister views; such as he will hardly venture to explain.

The only question that seems to make any difference amongst us appears to be, Whether we shall adopt those amendments, in which we seem all to be agreed, before we raise up a body of governors and rulers with a separate interest, whose wish and inclination it will be, to leave the people as small a share of liberty as possible; or whether we shall trust to our future rulers to do it hereafter? At present it is in our own power; hereafter it will be at the will and pleasure of our rulers to secure the liberties of the people.

The continent most certainly ought to be united; but we ought as certainly to secure our liberties before the new government is set in motion.

WE SHALL NEVER DO IT AFTERWARDS.

1. For the amendments proposed by the Massachusetts and South Carolina conventions, see BoR, I, 243–45n, 247–49.

Many
Virginia Independent Chronicle, 18 June 1788 (excerpt)[1]

MR. DAVIS, The public is under great obligations to you, for the fund of entertainment and instruction, your paper has afforded since the publication of the proposed fœderal constitution: the most illiterate may now discern the usefulness of the press in a free state. It gives all the people an opportunity to learn and be wise, to choose or refuse, in an important affair: indeed it is the noblest exhibition, the new world has yet witnessed. Let us therefore seek after truth, no matter where, or from whom.

We see our way now more clearly than at first outset; several of our objections have been ably answered. But so attached are we to old forms, or from some other cause, we are not yet satisfied, with the want of what is called a BILL of RIGHTS.—What, if the expression was varied, and it should be termed *incontrovertable truths*, or *fundamental laws*—Why might not the new constitution be prefaced by such an instrument of writing? The use we would wish to see made of it, is a resort, or recurrence, a test, to try all the acts of the national legislature by.—It is known that the bulk of the people do not understand abstruse, or lengthy political disquisitions. The fundamental laws of a nation, might be expressed in a few articles, and those in a few words, yet plain, and pithy, to which the people would pay a similar deference, as to the decalogue.

The explanations we have seen respecting the trial by jury, the freedom of the press, election of representatives, rotation in office, and responsibility to constituents are plausible, but not altogether satisfactory....

1. This essay was reprinted in the Philadelphia *Independent Gazetteer* on 2 October 1788. For the entire essay, see RCS:Va., 1638–40. "Many" was Arthur Campbell, who sent a draft of the essay to Augustine Davis, the printer of the *Virginia Independent Chronicle*, with this postscript: "My friend Mr. Davis will be so good as critically to examine and correct the above. Time will not permit to revise and copy it." Either Davis or someone else drastically revised Campbell's draft, although the essence of Campbell's objections to the Constitution was retained. For the draft, see RCS:Va. Supplement, 87–89.

Thomas Jefferson to Thomas Lee Shippen
Paris, 19 June 1788 (excerpt)[1]

... Genl. Washington writes me word he thinks Virginia will accept of the new constitution. it appears to me in fact from all information that it's rejection would drive the states to despair, and bring on events which cannot be foreseen: and that it's adoption is become absolutely necessary. it will be easier to get the assent of 9 states to correct what is wrong in the way pointed out by the constitution itself, than to get 13 to concure in a new convention and another plan of confederation. I therefore sincerely pray that the remaining states may accept it, as Massachusetts has done, with standing instructions to their delegates to press for amendments till they are obtained. They cannot fail of being obtained when the delegates of 8 states shall be under such perpetual instructions. . . .

1. RC, Shippen Family Papers, DLC. For the entire letter, see Boyd, XIII, 276–77. On the same day Jefferson informed Jan Ingenhousz that "we are at present occupied in some amendments of our federal constitution, which I think will take place, and I have the happiness to inform you that our new republicks thrive well" (*ibid.*, 261–62).

Joshua Atherton: Speech in the New Hampshire Convention 19 June 1788[1]

Mr. *Atherton* then rose, and in his usual stile of eloquence, took a general view of the proposed constitution, which he reprobated as a system calculated to forge the chains of tyranny upon the citizens of the United States. He was careful in pointing out its supposed defects—the federal city was noticed—standing armies, the power granted to Congress to alter the times and places of holding the elections for representatives, to collect taxes, duties, imposts, and excises—to raise and support standing armies—vesting Congress with the purse and the sword—the great powers granted to the President—the insecurity of the liberty of the press—want of a religious test—bill of rights, &c. &c. He adverted to the ease with which citizens might be deprived of a trial by jury, when a majority of the Senate should consider it no longer necessary, (he said such an event might happen)—of the great danger which would result from standing armies, &c. &c.—The above are only a part of the honourable gentleman's objections, the whole of them would nearly fill this paper.

1. Printed: *New Hampshire Spy,* 21 June.

New Hampshire Convention Recommends Amendments to Constitution, 21 June 1788

For the amendments recommended by the New Hampshire Convention, see BoR, I, 249–50.

Extract of a Letter from Richmond, Va., 25 June 1788[1]

"Permit me to congratulate you on the happy termination of the elaborate and ingenious deliberations of the convention of this state, who have this day agreed to ratify the proposed constitution, without the insertion of previous amendments, which were long advocated and strenuously urged by the opposition; but determined against them by a majority of ten, say 89 for, 79 against the ratification. The subsequent amendments which are proposed for the consideration of the first Congress, which may be elected under the new plan, it is supposed will take up two or three days discussion. The majority of the minority have declared themselves firmly attached to the Union, and generously offered their influence in support of the new system—indeed many who voted against the Constitution were compelled to it, in violation of their own judgments though in conformity to the positive instructions of their constituents—notwithstanding which there are a few individuals who are evidently influenced by prejudice or interest, that continue obdurate and inflexible, and who have boldly asserted, they are not without hopes of obtaining a better government at some favourable juncture, when the liberties of the people are endangered by that supineness which the operation of the government will naturally introduce among its rulers. The 28th of the month is proposed as a day of rejoicing."

1. Printed: *Pennsylvania Packet*, 2 July. Also printed in the *Pennsylvania Gazette*, 2 July, and reprinted in the *Pennsylvania Mercury*, 3 July; *New York Journal*, 4 July; *Connecticut Journal*, 9 July; Rhode Island *Providence Gazette*, 12 July (excerpt); and *Massachusetts Centinel*, 12 July.

Windham, Conn., Celebrates Ratification of the Constitution by New Hampshire, 25 June 1788 (excerpts)[1]

Windham,[2] 26 June, 1788

Yesterday at eight o'clock A.M. intelligence was received from the State of New-Hampshire, of the adoption of the Federal Constitution, by their convention, which raises the NINTH PILLAR and completes the most magnificent edifice of government and liberty that was ever erected—which agreeable information infused the patriotic spirits of this place with universal joy and hilarity, and every breast glowed with the most sincere and heartfelt satisfaction. Every son of liberty exulted in the prospect of being secured, under the balmy wings of energetical government, from anarchy and tyranny its infallible consequence, and all those concomitant evils, which were so lately menacing us with political ruin and destruction.—At four o'clock in the Afternoon, on this joyful occasion, a numerous and respectable concourse of people assembled on the Federal Green before the courthouse, where were discharged nine cannon, while the bells rung, as a salutation to each of the States

that had ratified the constitution:—After which they repaired to the court chamber, where the greatest unanimity and good order prevailed; and the following toasts were drank.
1. The happy states that have ratified the constitution.
2. Confusion to amendments. . . .
After which nine cheers were given by the whole assembly, and the remainder of the day was spent in merriment and festivity.

1. Printed: *Connecticut Gazette*, 4 July. Reprinted: Rhode Island *Providence Gazette*, 5 July; Hartford, Conn., *American Mercury*, 7 July; Rhode Island *Newport Herald*, 10 July; *Boston Gazette*, 14 July; *Massachusetts Gazette*, 15 July. The *Massachusetts Centinel*, 12 July, printed the following summary and the first three toasts: "Among the toasts drank by the patriotick inhabitants of Windham on the arrival of the news of the completion of the federal edifice by the adoption of the Constitution by nine States, are the following, viz."
2. Most of the reprints inserted "Conn." at this point.

Extract of a Letter from Richmond, Va., 26 June 1788[1]

"The amendments proposed in our convention for the consideration of the first Congress under the new adopted government are, chiefly, that the state shall have power to collect its own taxes and pay Congress by requisitions; and it is expected they will pass the convention without opposition. Many of the Federal party being equally interested with the Anti's in the objects of them—though many fears are entertained of the new Congress not acceeding to these amendments—and such are the apprehensions of the holders of military certificates, finding the certain resource, in their own revenue, for the payment of the annual interest, likely to be superceded by a national establishment, that is uncertain in its operations and remote in its effects, that they are already selling out at a lower price than when the constitution was agitating. The convention, we think will break up tomorrow—and on the next day we shall have a general rejoicing."

1. Printed: *Pennsylvania Packet*, 3 July. Reprinted seven times by 25 July: N.H. (1), Mass. (2), R.I. (1), N.Y. (2), Pa. (1).

Virginia Convention Recommends Amendments to Constitution
27 June 1788

For the amendments recommended by the Virginia Convention, see BoR, I, 251–56.

Richard Henry Lee to John Lamb
Chantilly, Westmoreland County, Va., 27 June 1788[1]

It is but this day I received the letter that you did me the honor to write to me on the 18th. of May last.[2] Repeated experience having shewn me that I could not be at Richmond and be in health prevented me from attempting to be a Member of our State Convention; but I have omitted no occasion of enforcing, to the utmost of my power, the propriety of so stating Amendments as to secure their adoption, as you will see by the letter I wrote to the president of our Convention, copy of which I have the honor to enclose to you.[3] I lament that your letter did not reach me sooner, because I think your plan of correspondence would have produced salutary consequences; as it seems to have been the idea of our Assembly when they sent the proposed plan to a Convention. Every attempt has failed, either to get previous amendments or effectually to secure the obtaining them hereafter. Yet you will see Sir that the ratifying majority feel the propriety of amendments, altho, in my judgement, the mode they have pursued for obtaining them is neither wise or manly. But, if nothing better can be obtained in the States that have not yet ratified, even this Mode of expressing the sense of the approving states, may operate to the obtaining amendments hereafter, as well as to prevent in the exercise of power, such abuses as would, in all probability, take place. It will be considered, I believe, as a most extraordinary Epoch in the history of mankind, that in a few years there should be so essential a change in the minds of men. Tis realy astonishing that the same people who have just emerged from a long & cruel war in defence of liberty, should now agree to fix an elective despotism upon themselves & their posterity! It is true indeed, for the honor of human nature, that this has not been a general acquiescence— In respectable States there have been formidable Minorities—In this, a majority of ten only out of near 200 Members, neither demonstrates that a majority of the people approve the plan, nor does it augur well for the prosperity of the new government—Unless the wisdom & goodness of those who first act under this System shall lead them to take effectual measures for introducing the requisite amendments. And this 1 hope, for the honor and safety of the U. States, will be obtained by the mediation of wise and benevolent Men. Accept my thanks Sir for the enclosures, in your letter, which I shall read with great pleasure.[4]

1. RC, Lamb Papers, NHi.
2. Lamb's letter of 18 May to Lee (CC:750–A) was probably among those letters carried to Richmond by Eleazer Oswald and then forwarded to Lee at his plantation in Westmoreland County.
3. Lee refers to his letter of 26 May to Edmund Pendleton (BoR, II, 475–79n). The copy of the letter that Lee sent to Lamb, misdated 22 May, is in the Lamb Papers in the New-York Historical Society.
4. See note 2 (above).

Undelivered speech in the New York Convention, c. 2 July 1788

After the publication of Francis Childs's *Debates and Proceedings of the Convention of the State of New-York* . . . (Evans 21310) on 16 December 1788, "A Real Federalist" complained that the *Debates* were biased against "the advocates for Amendments." He declared that he was taking "the liberty to publish [i.e., make known], for the information of the people . . . a Speech, which was actually prepared and intended to have been made by an Honorable Member in the Convention." "A Real Federalist" suggested that Childs might publish the speech "as an appendix" to his published *Debates.* Childs probably read the "Speech" in the *Albany Register* since he was in Albany taking notes of the legislative debates for publication in his *Daily Advertiser.* Childs, however, did not print a second edition of the *Debates,* nor did he reprint the "Speech" in any other venue.

"A Real Federalist" did not identify either the New York Convention delegate who intended to deliver the speech nor the day on which it was to be delivered. In fact, the speech could have been a ploy to publish an Antifederal essay. The speech and the preface by "A Real Federalist" were reprinted in installments by the Poughkeepsie, N.Y., *Country Journal,* 20, 27 January 1789, and by the Philadelphia *Independent Gazetteer,* 23, 25 February and 4 March.

In the 1820s and 1830s, Jonathan Elliot, the editor of a multi-volume edition of the debates of the state ratifying conventions, discovered the "Speech" and published it under 2 July 1788, the last day in which Childs published full debates. Elliot attributed the speech to Antifederalist delegate Thomas Tredwell of Suffolk County, a strong proponent of amendments in the Convention who voted against ratification of the Constitution. Elliot offered no explanation for his identification of Tredwell nor did he give any reason for placing the speech under 2 July. Perhaps, Elliot chose 2 July because the next day Antifederalists proposed a large number of amendments, two of them submitted by Tredwell. (The amendments concerned Article I, sections 8 and 9 of the Constitution, both alluded to in the speech.) Tredwell could have submitted the speech for publication in the *Albany Register* because he was in Albany representing the Southern District in the state Senate. Another possible author of the speech could have been John Lansing, Jr., the mayor of Albany, who drafted several plans of amendments in the New York Convention. Furthermore, Lansing had revised his speeches for Childs's *Debates,* and perhaps he had not gotten the speech ready in time for publication in the *Debates.*

A Real Federalist
Albany Register, 5 January 1789 (Supplement)

Messrs. Printers,[1] Having constantly attended the late Convention of this state during its sitting, my curiosity led me to an attentive perusal of the Debates of that Honorable body, published by Mr. Childs for the amusement of the public and the promotion of that cause, which, by a strange abuse of language, has been termed *Federal.*[2] As those debates, as published, furnish several instances in which both sense and diction have been most wantonly perverted—others in which arguments are stated in a much more plausible manner than that in which they were delivered—not a few in which, from prudential motives, the whole sentiment has been suppressed—and some in which there are cogent reasons to suppose that speeches prepared for and intended to have been delivered in the Convention, but which never were, had, perhaps by the inadvertence of the authors been handed to Mr. Childs with those which had been actually made, and, in his great zeal, introduced by him in his compilation—and as the advocates for Amendments have not been on such a footing with Mr. Childs as to have common justice extended to them, I take the liberty to publish, for the information of the people of the United States, a Speech, which was actually prepared and intended to have been made by an Honorable Member in the Convention; which Mr. Childs, if he pleases, may annex as an appendix to his pamphlet.

A REAL FEDERALIST.

Mr. CHAIRMAN, Little accustomed to speak in public, and always inclining, in such an assembly as this, rather to be a hearer than a speaker, on a less important occasion than the present I should have contented myself with a silent vote: But when I consider the nature of this dispute, that it is a contest, not so much between little states and great states (as we have been told), as between little folks and great folks; between patriotism and ambition; between freedom and power; not so much between the navigating states and the non-navigating states, as between navigating and non-navigating individuals (for not one of the amendments we contend for has the least reference to the clashing interests of states): When I consider likewise that a people jealous of their liberties, and strongly attached to freedom, have reposed so entire a confidence in this assembly, that upon our determination depends their future enjoyment of those invaluable rights and privileges, which they have so lately and so gallantly defended at every risque and expence both of life and property, it appears to me so interesting and important, that I cannot be totally silent upon the occasion, lest lisping babes may be taught for ages to come to curse my name, as a betrayer of their freedom and happiness.[3]

The Gentleman, who first opened this debate,[4] did, with an emphasis, which I believe convinced every one present of the propriety of the advice, urge[d] the necessity of proceeding in our deliberations on this important subject coolly and dispassionately. With how much candor this advice was given, appears from the subsequent parts of a long speech, and from several subsequent speeches, almost totally addressed to our fears.

The people of New-Jersey and Connecticut are so exceedingly exasperated against us, that, totally regardless of their own preservation, they will take the two rivers of Connecticut and Delaware by their extremities, and, by dragging them over our country, will, with a sweeping deluge, wash us all into the Hudson, leaving neither house or inhabitant behind them: But if this event should not happen, doubtless the Vermonteers, with the British and Tories, our natural enemies, would, by bringing down upon us the great Lake Ontario, sweep hills and mountains, houses and inhabitants, in one large flota into the Atlantic.[5]

These, Sir, indeed would be terrible calamities; but, terrible as they are, they are not to be compared with the havocs and desolations of tyranny. The arbitrary courts of Philip in the Netherlands, in which life and property were daily confiscated without a jury, occasioned as much misery, and a more rapid depopulation of the provinces, before the people took up arms in their own defence, than all the armies of that haughty Monarch were able to effect afterwards:[6] And it is doubtful in my mind whether governments, by abusing their powers, have not occasioned as much misery and distress, and nearly as great devastations of the human species, as all the wars that have happened since Milton's battle of the Angels to the present day.[7]

The design of government is the safety, peace and welfare of the governed; unwise therefore, and absurd in the highest degree, would be the conduct of that people, who, in forming a government, should give to their rulers power to destroy themselves and their property, and thereby defeat the very purposes of their institution; or, in other words, who should give unlimited power to their rulers, and not retain in their own hands the means of their own preservation.

The first governments in the world were the parental, the powers of which were restricted only by the laws of nature; and doubtless the early succeeding governments were formed upon the same plan, which we may suppose answered tolerably well in the first ages of the world, while the moral sense was strong, and the laws of nature well understood, there being then no lawyers to explain them away. But in after times, when Kings became great and courts became crouded, it was discovered that to govern meant a right to tyrannize, and to rule, a power to oppress; and at the present day, when the jurisperiti[8] are become so skilful in their profession, and quibbling is reduced to a science, it is become extremely difficult to form a constitution which will secure liberty and happiness to the people, or laws under which property is safe; hence, in modern times, the design of a people in forming a constitution of government, is not so much to give powers to their rulers, as to guard against their abuse of them.

Sir, I introduce these observations to combat certain principles, which have been daily and confidently advanced by the favorers of the present Constitution, and which appear to me to be totally indefensible.

The first and grand leading, or rather misleading principle in this debate, and which the advocates for this system of unrestricted powers must chiefly depend upon for its support, is, that in forming a Constitution, whatever powers are not expressly granted or given to the government are reserved to the people; or that rulers cannot exercise any powers, but those expressly given to them by the Constitution.

Let me ask the Gentlemen who advance this principle whether the commission of a Roman dictator, which was in these few words, "To take care that the state receives no harm,"[9] does not come up fully to their ideas of an energetic government? or, whether an invitation from a people to one or more persons, to come and rule over them would not cloath the rulers with sufficient powers? If so, the principle they advance is a false one.

Besides, the absurdity of this principle will obviously appear when we consider the great variety of objects to which the powers of Government must necessarily extend, and that an express enumeration of them all, would probably fill as many volumes, as Poole's Synopsis of the Critics,[10] or Van Sweeten's Commentaries on Boerhaeve:[11] But we may reason with sufficient certainty upon this subject, from the sense of all the public bodies in these United States who have had occasion to form new Constitutions; they have uniformly acted upon a directly contrary principle, not only in forming the State Constitutions and the old Confederation, but also in forming this very Constitution; for do we not find in every state constitution express reservations made in favor of the people?[12] and in the old Confederation a clause, reserving to the several states all the powers, not therein expressly given to Congress?[13] And it is clear, that the late Convention at Philadelphia, whatever might have been the sentiments of some of its members, did not adopt the principle; for they have made certain reservations and restrictions, which upon that principle would have been totally useless and unnecessary: and can it be supposed that that wise body, whose only apology for the great ambiguity of many parts of that performance, and the total omission of some things, which many esteem as essential to the security of liberty, was a great desire of brevity, should so far sacrifice that great and important object, as to insert a number of provisions which they esteemed totally useless? Why is it said that the privilege of the writ of habeas corpus shall not be suspended, unless when in cases of rebellion or invasion the public safety may require it? What clause in the Constitution, except it be this very clause itself, gives the general Government a power to deprive us of that great privilege so sacredly secured to us by our state Constitutions? Why is it provided that no bill of attainder shall be passed, or that no title of nobility shall be granted? Are there any clauses in the Constitution extending the powers of the general Government to these objects? Some Gentlemen say, that these though not necessary, were inserted for the greater caution.—I could have wished, Sir, that as great caution had been used in securing to us the freedom of election, a sufficient and responsible representation, the freedom of the press, and the trial by jury both in civil and criminal cases; these, Sir, are the rocks on which the foundations of this Constitution should have rested, no other foundation can any man lay, which will secure the sacred temple of freedom against the power of the great, the undermining arts of ambition, and the blasts of profane scoffers, for such there will be in every age, who will tell us that all religion is vain, that is, that our political creeds, which have been handed down to us by our forefathers, as sacredly as our bibles, and for which more of them have suffered Martyrdom, than for the creed of the Apostles,[14] are all nonsense; who will tell us that paper constitutions are mere paper; and that parchment is but parchment; that jealousy of our rulers is a sin, &c. I could have wished also that sufficient caution had been used to have secured to us our religious liberties, and to have prevented the general government from tyrannizing over our consciences by a religious establishment, a tyranny of all others the most dreadful; and which will assuredly be exercised, whenever it shall be thought necessary for the promotion & support of their political measures. It is ardently to be wished, Sir, that these and other invaluable rights of freemen, had been as cautiously secured, as the paltry local interests of some of the individual states. But it appears to me that in forming this Constitution, we have run into the same error which the Lawyers and Pharisees were charged with of old; i.e. while we have secured the tythes of mint and anise and cumin, we have neglected the weightier matters of the law, judgment, mercy & faith.[15]

Have we not neglected to secure to ourselves the weighty matter of judgment or justice, by empowering the general Government to establish one supreme, and as many inferior courts as they please, whose proceedings they have a right to fix and regulate as they shall think fit: so that we are ignorant, whether they will be according to the common, the civil, the Jewish or the Turkish law?

What better provision have we made for mercy, when a man for ignorantly passing a counterfeit continental note or bill of credit, is liable to be dragged to a distant county, two or three hundred miles from home, deprived of the support and assistance of friends, to be tried by a strange jury ignorant of his character, ignorant of the character of the witnesses, unable to contradict any false testimony brought against him by their own knowledge of facts, and with whom the prisoner being unacquainted, he must be deprived totally of the benefit of his challenges;[16] and besides all this, he may be exposed to lose his life merely for want of property, to carry his witnesses to such a distance. And after all this solemn farce and mockery of a trial by jury, if they should acquit him, it will require more ingenuity than I am master of to shew, that he does not still hold his life at the will and pleasure of the supreme court, and consequently depend upon the tender mercies, perhaps of the wicked (for judges may be wicked) and what those tender mercies are I need not tell you, you may read them in the history of the Star Chamber Court in England, and in the Courts of Philip,[17] and in your Bibles.

This brings me to the third and last weighty matter mentioned in the text, to wit, faith. The word faith may be with great propriety applied to the articles of our political creed; which it is absolutely necessary should be kept pure and uncorrupted, if we mean to preserve the liberties of our country and the inestimable blessings of a free Government.

And, Sir, I cannot but be seriously alarmed on this head, when I hear, as has frequently been the case during the present discussion, gentlemen of the first rank and abilities, openly opposing some of the essential principles of freedom, and endeavoring by the most ingenious sophistry, and the still more powerful weapons of ridicule, to shake or corrupt our faith therein—have we not been told, "that if Government is but properly organized, and the powers suitably distributed among the several members, it is unnecessary to provide any other security, against the abuse of power? that power thus distributed needs no check, no restrictions?" Is this, Sir, a Whig Principle? does not every Constitution on the Continent contradict this position? Why are we told that all restrictions of powers are found to be inconvenient; that we ought to put unlimited confidence in our rulers; that it is not our duty to be jealous of men in power? Have we not had the idea of an aristocracy in a country, an idea founded on invariable experience, openly ridiculed?

What the design of the preachers on this occasion is, I will not pretend to determine; far be it from me to judge men's hearts, but thus much I can say from the best authority, that they are deceitful above all things and desperately wicked: but whatever be the design of the preachers, the tendency of the doctrines is clear: they tend to corrupt our political faith; to take us off our guard, and to lull to sleep that jealousy, which we are told by all writers, and it is proved by all experience, is essentially necessary for the preservation of freedom.

But notwithstanding the strongest assertions that there are no wolves in our country, yet, if we should see their footsteps in every path, we should be very credulous and unwise to trust our flocks abroad, or to believe that those who advised us to do it were very anxious for their preservation.

In this constitution, sir, we have departed widely from the principles and political faith of 76, when the spirit of liberty ran high, and danger put a curb on ambition. Here we find no security for the rights of individuals; no security for the existence of our state governments: here is no bill of rights, no proper restrictions of power: our lives, our property and our consciences are left wholly at the mercy of the legislature, and the powers of the judicial may be extended to any degree short of almighty.

Sir, in this Constitution we have not only neglected, we have done worse; we have openly violated our faith, that is, our public faith. The seventh article, which is in these words, "The ratification of the Conventions of nine states shall be sufficient for the establishment of this Constitution between the states so ratifying the same," is so flagrant a violation of the public faith of these states, so solemnly pledged to each other in the Confederation,[18] as it makes me tremble to think of; for however lightly some may esteem *paper* and *parchment* Constitutions, they are recorded, Sir, in that high Court of Appeals, the Judge of which will do right; and I am confident, that no such violation of public faith ever did, or ever will go unpunished.

The plan of the Federal Town, Sir, departs from every principle of Freedom, as distant as the two polar stars from each other: for the subjecting the inhabitants of that district to the exclusive legislation of Congress, in whose appointment they have no share, or vote, is laying a foundation on which may be erected as complete a tyranny as can be found in the eastern world, nor do I see how this evil can possibly be prevented without razing its very foundations. How dangerous this city may be, and what its operations on the general Liberties of this country, time alone must discover; but I pray God it may not prove to this western world, what the city of Rome, enjoying a similar Constitution, did to the eastern.

There is another clause, Sir, in this Constitution, which, though there is no prospect of getting it amended,[19] I think ought not to be passed over in silence, lest such silence may be construed into a tacit approbation: I mean the clause which restricts the general Government from putting a stop for a number of years to a commerce, which is a stain to the character of any civilized nation, and has already blackened half the plains of America with a race of wretches, made so by our cruel policy and avarice, and which appears to me to be clearly repugnant to every principle of humanity, morality, religion and good policy.

There are other objections to this Constitution, which are weighty and unanswerable; but they have been so clearly stated, and so fully debated in the course of this discussion, that it would be an unjustifiable intrusion on the patience of the Committee [of the Whole] to repeat them: I shall therefore content myself with a few observations on its general plan and tendency.

We are told that this is a federal government. I think, Sir, there is as much propriety in the name, as in that which its advocates assume, and no more. It is, in my idea, as complete a consolidation as the government of this state, in which legislative powers to a certain extent are exercised by the several towns and corporations. The sole difference between a state government under this Constitution, and a corporation under the state government, is, that a state being more extensive than a town, its powers are likewise proportionably extended; but neither of them enjoy the least share of sovereignty: For let me ask, what is a state government, what sovereignty—what power is left to it, when the control of every source of revenue, and the total command of the militia, are given to the general government? That power that can command both the property and the persons of the community is the sovereign, and the sole sovereign; the idea of two distinct sovereigns in the same country, separately possessed of sovereign or supreme power, at the same time, is as supreme an absurdity as that two distinct separate circles can be bounded by exactly the same circumference. This Sir, is demonstration, and from it I would draw one corollary, which I think clearly follows, altho' it is in favor of the Constitution, to wit, that at least that clause in which Congress guarantees to the several states a republican *form* of government, speaks honestly; that is, that no more is intended by it than is expressed. And I think it is clear, that whilst the mere form is secured, the substance, to wit, the whole power and sovereignty of our state governments, and with them the liberties of the country, are swallowed up by the general government; for it is well worth observing, that while our state governments are held up to us as the great and sufficient security of our rights and privileges, it is carefully provided that they shall be disarmed of all power, and made totally dependent on the bounty of Congress for their support, and consequently for their existence; so that we have scarce a single right secured to us under either. Is this, Sir, a government for freemen? Are we thus to be duped out of our liberties? I hope, Sir, that our affairs have not yet arrived to that long wished-for pitch of confusion, that we are under the necessity of accepting such a system of government as this.

I cannot, Sir, express my feelings on a late occasion, when I considered with what indignation the spirits of a Montgomery, a Herkeimer, a Paris,[20] &c. must have been fired, at the insult offered to their memories on this floor, and that not by a stranger, but by a brother; when their names, which will ever be dear to freemen, were so profanely called upon, as an inducement to us to surrender up those rights and privileges, in the defence of which they so gallantly fought, and so gloriously died.[21] We are called upon at this time, I think it is an early day, to make an unconditional surrender of those rights which ought to be dearer to us than our lives; but I hope, Sir, that the memory of those Patriot Heroes will teach us our duty upon this occasion; if we follow their example, we are sure not to err.

We ought, Sir, to consider, and it is a solemn consideration, that we may now give away by a *vote*, what it may cost the *dying groans* of thousands to recover; that we may now surrender with a little *ink*, what it may take seas of *blood* to regain.

The dagger of ambition is now pointed at the fair bosom of Liberty; and, to deepen and complete the tragedy, we her sons are called upon to give the fatal thrust. Shall we not recoil at such a deed, and all cry out with one voice, Hands off! Hands off! what distraction hath seized us—is she not our mother? And, if the frenzy of any should persist in the parricidical attempt, should we not instantly interpose and receive the fatal point in our own bosoms? A moment's hesitation would prove us to be bastards, and not sons.

The liberties of the country are a deposit in the hands of individuals; they are an entailed estate, which the possessors have no right to dispose of; they belong to our children, and to them we are bound to transmit them; as a representative body, the trust becomes tenfold more sacred in our hands, especially as it was committed to us, with the fullest confidence in our sentiments, integrity and firmness. If we should betray that trust upon this occasion, I fear, I think there is reason to fear, that it will teach a lesson dangerous to liberty, to wit, that no confidence is to be placed in man.

But why, Sir, must we be guilty of this breach of trust? Why surrender up the dear-bought liberties of our country? Because we are told in very positive terms, that nothing short of this will satisfy, or can be accepted of by our future rulers. Is it possible, Sir, that we can be at a loss for an answer to such declarations as these? Can we not—ought we not to speak like freemen on this occasion (this perhaps may be the last time we may ever dare to do it) and declare in as positive terms, that we cannot, we will not give up our liberties—that if we cannot be admitted into the Union as freemen, we will not come in as slaves? This I fully believe to be the language of my constituents, this is the language of my conscience; and though I may not long dare to make it the language of my tongue, yet I trust it will ever be the language of my heart.

If we act with coolness, firmness and decision upon this occasion, I have the fullest confidence that that God, who hath so lately delivered us out of the paw of the lion and out of the paw of the bear,[22] will also deliver us from this Goliah, this uncircumcised Philistine.

We are told, Sir, that government is like a mad horse, which, notwithstanding all the curbs you can put upon him, will sometimes run away with his rider. The idea is undoubtedly a just one: Would he not therefore be justly deemed a madman, and deserve to have his neck broke, who should trust himself on this horse without any bridle at all?

This government, Sir, is founded in sin, and reared up in iniquity; the foundations are laid in a most sinful breach of public trust, and the top-stones in the most iniquitous breach of public faith; and I fear, if it goes into operation, we shall be justly punished with the total extinction of our civil liberties. We are invited in this instance to become partakers of other men's sins;[23] if we do, we must likewise be contented to take our share of the punishment.

We are threatened, Sir, if we do not come into this Union, with the resentment of our neighboring states. I do not apprehend we have much to fear from this quarter:[24] For our neighbors must have the good sense to discover, that not one of our objections is founded on motives of particular state interest; they must see likewise from the debates, that every selfish idea that has been thrown out, has come from those who very improperly call themselves the federal side of the house.

A Union with our sister states I as ardently wish as any man, and that upon the most generous principles; but a Union under such a system as this, I think, is not a desirable thing. The design of a Union is safety; but a Union upon the proposed plan is certain destruction to liberty. In one sense, indeed, it may bring us to a state of safety; for it may reduce us to such a condition, that we may be very sure nothing worse can happen to us, and consequently we shall have nothing to fear. This, Sir, is a dreadful kind of safety; but I confess it is the only safety I can see in this Union.

There are no advantages, that can possibly arise from a Union, which can compensate the loss of freedom; nor can any evils be apprehended from a disunion, which are so much to be dreaded as tyranny.

1. In October 1788, the *Albany Register*, an Antifederalist newspaper, was established by Robert Barber, with the assistance of Antifederalists, as a counter to Albany's Federalist newspapers.

2. On the title page of the *Debates* Childs himself referred to the form of government recommended by the "GENERAL CONVENTION" at Philadelphia on 17 September 1787 as a "FEDERAL GOVERNMENT." For the Antifederalist charge that the supporters of the Constitution misused the words "federal" and "Federalists," see "A Countryman" II (De Witt Clinton), *New York Journal*, 13 December 1787 (RCS:N.Y., 406).

3. Perhaps a variation on a comment made about George Washington by the Comte de Mirabeau in his *Reflections on the Observations on the Importance of the American Revolution . . . By Richard Price* (Philadelphia, 1786) (Evans 19804). On page 3 of this translation of his work, Mirabeau stated: "*Begin with the infant in the cradle: Let the first word he lisps be* WASHINGTON!" This became a popular phrase. (See CC:251.)

4. Robert R. Livingston opened the debates on the Constitution on 19 June with a long speech (RCS:N.Y., 1682–99).

5. A response to Robert R. Livingston's speech of 19 June (RCS:N.Y., 1684–85).

6. The reference is to King Philip II of Spain (1527–1598) and the Council of Troubles or the Council of Blood. Established in 1567 by the Duke of Alba, one of Philip's councilors, this council in The Netherlands condemned more than 12,000 persons for rebellion and heresy without due process. Some of the condemned were executed or banished, while most of them paid heavy fines or forfeited their property. In 1568 the Dutch began a revolt against Spanish rule that continued until 1609.

7. A reference primarily to Book VI of John Milton's *Paradise Lost* (1667) in which God appoints archangels Michael and Gabriel to lead the heavenly angels against the rebellious angels led by Satan. The battle of angels predates the expulsion of Adam and Eve from the Garden of Eden.

8. Latin: learned or skilled in the law.

9. In Latin *at consules darent operam ne quid detrimenti respublic caparet*—the decree the Senate of the Roman Republic used to confer dictatorial power upon a consul in times of crisis.

10. Matthew Poole (1624–1679) published in Latin *Synopsis Criticorum aliorumque Sacræ Scripturæ Interpretum* (London, 1669–1676)—a five volume synopsis of the work of biblical commentators.

11. In 1708 Herman Boerhaave (1668–1738), a Dutch physician and botanist, published his *Institutiones Medicae . . .* (Leyden), a work that would go into several editions and would be translated into other languages. The next year Boerhaave became a professor of medicine and botany at the University of Leyden, and he added to the earlier work *Aphorismi de cognoscendis et curandis morbis* (Leyden). This work would also be translated into other languages and go into several editions. Between 1742 and 1772 Gerard Van Swietan (1700–1772), a student of Boerhaave, published in Latin his *Commentaries* on Boerhaave's *Aphorisms*. An English translation of the *Commentaries* was published in London in eighteen volumes between 1744 and 1773.

12. For example, the New York constitution of 1777 provided in its first article "that no authority shall, on any pretence whatever, be exercised over the people or members of this State but such as shall be derived from and granted by them" (Thorpe, V, 2628). This right was restated in "An Act Concerning the Rights of the Citizens of this State" (26 January 1787) (BoR, II, 89).

13. Article II of the Articles of Confederation states: "Each state retains its sovereignty, freedom and independence, and every Power, Jurisdiction and right, which is not by this confederation expressly delegated to the United States, in Congress assembled."

14. The Apostles' Creed affirms the basic beliefs of Christianity and is often recited aloud by Western Christian congregations and responded to in the affirmative during baptism.

15. Matthew 23:23. "Woe unto you, scribes and Pharisees, hypocrites! for ye pay tithe of mint and anise and cummin, and have omitted the weightier matters of the law, judgment, mercy, and faith: these ought ye to have done, and not to leave the other undone." See also Luke 11:42.

16. Most of the American colonies and states had long allowed challenges to jurors for cause or peremptory challenges which allowed the plaintiff or defendant to dismiss potential jurors without giving cause.

17. The Court of Star Chamber evolved in 15th century England from the judicial sittings of the King's Council at Westminster. It began as a court of equity and prerogative, but extended its jurisdiction, particularly under the Tudors, to criminal matters. Under James I and Charles I, the Star Chamber became tyrannical and arbitrary, and the Long Parliament abolished it in 1641. See note 6 (above) for the courts of Philip II.

18. Under Article XIII of the Articles of Confederation, the Union was to be perpetual, and any alteration in the Articles had to be agreed to by Congress and confirmed by the legislatures of every state (CDR, 93).

19. A reference to Article I, section 9, clause 1, of the Constitution, which prohibits Congress from banning the African slave trade before 1808. Article V outlines the method by which the Constitution can be amended; it provided that no amendment made prior to 1808 could alter the restriction on Congress to prohibit the African slave trade.

20. Generals Richard Montgomery and Nicholas Herkimer, both of whom were New Yorkers, were killed in battle during the Revolution, the former at the siege of Quebec (1775) and the latter from wounds suffered during the Battle of Oriskany (1777) in the Mohawk Valley. "Paris" was probably Colonel Isaac Paris, a Tryon (later Montgomery) County member of the Second, Third, and Fourth Provincial congresses, 1775–77, who was killed after being taken prisoner at the Battle of Oriskany.

21. "A brother" is probably a reference to Robert R. Livingston, a brother-in-law of General Richard Montgomery, who had married Livingston's sister Janet. For the reference, see De Witt Clinton Journal, 17 July (RCS:N.Y., 2219).

22. 1 Samuel 17:27. "The Lord that delivered me [David] out of the paw of the lion, and out of the paw of the bear, he will deliver me out of the hand of this Philistine." In this case, "the paw of the lion" refers to Great Britain and "the paw of the bear" refers to the Iroquois, most of whom were allied with the British during the Revolution.

23. See note 19 (above).

24. For instance, see Robert R. Livingston's speech of 19 June (RCS:N.Y., 1684–85).

Antifederalists Celebrate the Fourth of July
Carlisle, Pa., 4 July 1788 (excerpts)[1]

On Friday the 4th July instant, being the anniversary of the 13th year of American Independence, a number of the respectable inhabitants of the borough of Carlisle, and the adjacent townships, together with the volunteer company of militia, and detachments from other militia companies, convened in the public square of this borough....

[13 Toasts offered] 2. May such amendments be speedily framed, and unanimously adopted, as may render the proposed constitution for the United States truly democratical....

1. Printed: Pennsylvania *Carlisle Gazette*, 9 July 1788. Reprinted: *Pennsylvania Packet*, 18 July; Philadelphia *Independent Gazetteer, Pennsylvania Journal,* and *Pennsylvania Mercury*, 19 July; Baltimore *Maryland Gazette*, 25 July.

Exeter, N.H., Freeman's Oracle, 4 July 1788 (excerpt)[1]

Messi'rs. Printers, Nothing but the last paragraph, in the piece under the signature of Alfredus, in the Freeman's Oracle of Friday 13th inst. should have induced me to pay any further attention to his writing; for he appears to have laid aside all that truth, candor, and fair reasoning a gentleman ought to be possest of. Let us turn our thoughts for a moment to his observations on the jury—he says, "*suppose for instance, in an action of trespass, eleven of the jurors should without hesitation pronounce the defendant guilty, the twelfth says he is not, and obstinately persists in it, against every argument of his brethren; the Law says they must agree to a man, and as he will not agree to a man; as he will not agree with the rest in pronouncing him guilty they must agree with him in acquiting him, for the law requires it*"—In answer, I say the law requires no such thing, for in that case, it would be a jury of *one man*, and not of twelve as the law requires; and if they do agree to acquit him, contrary to law and evidence, they forswear themselves. I wish the Gentleman would attend to the rules and customs of courts: In cases when a jury cannot agree, it is often agreed upon by the parties to take the verdict of eleven, ten, or nine, and judgment recorded accordingly—But in cases where the jury cannot agree, nor the parties, to take a less number than twelve, that jury is set aside, and a new one called, and the cause goes over again, or is continued, till the next term; for it would be an absurdity always to make the jury agree contrary to their own sentiments and solemn oaths.

I will now pass on to his last paragraph, not being contented with throwing out many hard things, because I objected to the new constitution without amendments, this gentleman (if he deserves the name) has taken a large stride, and virulently attacked my character, as a soldier through the late war. I confess, it is the first time I ever heard a hint of the kind, although I served in the army almost nine years—No man then disputed my courage, and no man has attempted to do it since, and if any gentleman disputes it at this late hour, let him call and try it.

But Mr. Alfredus's writings appear to be all of a piece, not founded upon that truth and candor they ought to be—And, as there has been much said by gentlemen, in favor of the New-Constitution, against those who are opposed to it, in a way of reflection calling them antifederalists, shayites, tories, enemies to all order and good government, involved in debt, for paper money, tender acts, Justifery acts &c. &c. and as I have taken an active part against the Constitution, it induces me to take up my political and military character, from the commencement of the war down to the present day—when the power of Great Britain resolved they had a right to tax us in all cases whatsoever,[2] I opposed that power, for I considered representation and taxation to be inseperable companions—War ensued, and on the memorable 19th of April 1775, I girded on my sword, and marched for Lexington Battle, in defence of my country and never laid it aside till the 15th of January 1784,—eight years and nine months, in which time I shared the dangers and fatigues of a soldier, and retired, with as good credentials of my service, as a reasonable man could wish for, (which I shall endeavour to evince presently)—As to being in debt, I owe no man any thing, but what I have got property enough and a disposition to pay him—as to the late proposal for paper money, I opposed it with all my might, for I considered it if made, only to serve as a key to lock up all the silver, and gold, and a door open to cheat the unwary—as to the tender act, I bore that down, with all my might, for I considered it as a stretch of power in the legislature, that they ought not to have taken, it was interfering with private contracts, which ought to be held sacred—as to the justifery act, I opposed that with the same zeal, for I considered it, as an inlet for many little tyrants,[3] and agreeing with the Hon. Justice Blackstone, who justly observes, *"that every new tribunal, erected for the decision of facts, without the intervention of a jury, whether composed of justices of the peace; commissioners of the revenue, judges of a court of conscience; or any other standing magistrates, is a step towards establishing aristocracy, the most oppressive of absolute government"*[4]—As to shayites, I believe every honest man condemned his proceedings, and he has lived to see and acknowledge his own folly—and as to tories, I think it is high time for that epithet to be laid aside—there is of that class of Gentlemen on both sides the question for and against the Constitution for my own part, when I first read it, I had no idea of its being received without amendments, and I verily believe that to be the case, with many of the gentlemen, who were in convention at Philadelphia.—Let us attend to what his Excellency General Washington says: *"I am not blind to its faults, it is the best we could obtain in the Convention; it is now open for the revision of each state"*[5]—What says that aged and venerable politition Dr. Franklin; *"I do not like the Constitution, it has its faults, if they may be considered as such, and will end in monarchial government:"*[6]—What says Gov. Hancock, *"If the proposed amendments take place then the constitution will be complete:"*[7]—In short I have not conversed with any person, not even the most sanguine, but what wish for an alteration; but they say, let us adopt and then propose amendments; but, are we sure amendments will take place in this way? No, by no means; for the views, interests, and designs will be the same in Congress, as they were in the convention, and power once given is hard to recall—In fine, I opposed the constitution upon *fair and honest principles*; for I considered, that the *Liberties* of the people were not sufficiently secured without some amendations. . . .

1. This unsigned article is a response to "Alfredus," Exeter, N.H., *Freeman's Oracle*, 13 June (RCS:N.H., 340–43n). In that article, "Alfredus" identified "The Farmer," a prominent New Hampshire Antifederalist author, as Colonel Thomas Cogswell, a Revolutionary War veteran. From the detailed text, one could argue that the writer of this unsigned article was a soldier, probably Cogswell. And, in fact, "Alfredus" in his response in the *Oracle* on 11 July (RCS:N.H. Supplement, 43–44) identifies the author as Cogswell. (For a discussion of the authorship of "A Farmer" and "Alfredus," see BoR, II, 248n. "Alfredus" was identified as Samuel Tenney.

For the entire essay, see RCS:N.H. Supplement, 39–42.

2. A reference to the Declaratory Act of 1766.
3. For the legislative struggles over these issues, see RCS:N.H., liii–liv.
4. Blackstone, *Commentaries*, Book III, chapter 23, 380.
5. A paraphrase of George Washington's 14 December 1787 letter to Charles Carter that was printed in the *Virginia Herald* on 27 December 1787 and then widely reprinted (CC:386).
6. A reference to Benjamin Franklin's last speech in the Constitutional Convention on 17 September 1787, which was printed in the *Boston Gazette* on 3 December and reprinted throughout America (CC:77).
7. A reference to John Hancock's 27 February 1788 speech to the Massachusetts General Court which was first printed on 28 February in two Boston newspapers—the *American Herald* and the *Independent Chronicle*. It was reprinted in whole or in part more than thirty times throughout America (RCS:Mass., 1667–69).

Solon, jun.
Rhode Island Providence Gazette, 5 July 1788[1]

Before *Nine States* had adopted the New Federal Constitution, the ground of argument on that subject was very different from that on which it *now* stands.

Then, there was hope of procuring amendments thereto, before its operation:—*Now*, all hope of that sort has vanished.

Then, the federal compact among the States, under the old Confederation, was entire and unimpaired:—*Now*, there is in fact a secession of Nine States from the old Union, whereby the others are left to shift for themselves.

Then, those who voted against the New Constitution, only preferred the old one, or a chance for another:—*Now*, those who vote against the New Constitution, vote themselves out of the New Federal Union, which may be considered as inchoative.

Those, therefore, who had rather adopt the New Constitution, with its defects, under a prospect of future corrections, than hazard the consequences of being repudiated from the Grand American Confederacy, will give their voices accordingly *now*, whatever part they may have taken *heretofore*.

1. Reprinted: *Massachusetts Centinel*, 16 July. "Solon, jun." was perhaps David Howell. On 3 June 1790 Howell sent Thomas Jefferson a copy of the Providence, R.I., *United States Chronicle*, 25 February 1790, "containing some of my sentiments under the signature of *Solon, Junior*." Howell also indicated that "Both the papers in this Town contain other peices under the same signature" (Boyd, XVI, 452). Other essays signed "Solon, jun.," "Solon, junior," or "Solon, Jr.," appeared in the Rhode Island *Providence Gazette* in 1788 (12 July and 2, 9, 23 August) and 1790 (27 February) and in the Providence, R.I., *United States Chronicle* in 1790 (25 February and 4 March). All of the essays are printed in RCS:R.I.

Thomas Jefferson to John Brown Cutting
Paris, 8, 11 July 1788 (excerpts)[1]

... The first vessels will probably bring us news of the accession of S. Carolina and Virginia to the new Confederation. The glorious example of Massachusetts, of accepting unconditionally, and pressing for future amendment, will I hope reconcile all parties. The argument is unanswerable that it will be easier to obtain amendments from nine states under the new constitution, than from thirteen after rejecting it. As our information here is much less quick than at London, you will much oblige me by dropping me a line of information as the accession of the other states becomes known to you....

July 11. Since writing this letter I receive from America information that S. Carolina has acceded to the new constitution by a vote of 149 against 72. I hope Virginia will now accede without difficulty.

1. FC, Jefferson Papers, DLC. Printed: Boyd, XIII, 315–16.

Peleg Arnold to Welcome Arnold
New York, 11 July 1788 (excerpt)[1]

... The information from this State[']s Convention has generally Been that they would not addopt the New Constitution; But the Last Reports Say that the Federal Party gain Strength and it is generally believed here that it will be addopted I presume the amendments by the Virginia Convention have had Considerable influence on the minds of the Members of this State Convention which has ocationed this change ...

1. RC, Gratz Collection, PHi. For the entire letter, see RCS:Cong., 14.

Ebenezer Hazard to Mathew Carey
New York, 15 July 1788 (excerpt)[1]

... What N York will do is still uncertain: present appearances lead to an Apprehension that she will stipulate for certain Amendments as the *Condition* of her continuing in the Union:—if she should, she will throw herself out of it. Congress have treated her with Politeness by postponing the Consideration of the Report of their Committee for organizing the new Government; but Regard for the Dignity of the Union will not let them wait very long; & if this State does not soon determine as she ought to do, the *Blank* for the Place at which the new Congress are to meet, will be filled with *Philadelphia*. ...

1. RC, Lea and Febiger Collection, PHi. This excerpt was printed in the Philadelphia *Pennsylvania Mercury* on 19 July and reprinted in the Baltimore *Maryland Gazette* on 25 July.

Caleb S. Riggs to John Fitch
New York, 15 July 1788 (excerpt)[1]

... *Politicks* to be or not to be is now the question,[2] time is pregnant with som[e]thing which must soon appear, but in what shape or colour is left at present at best but to conjecture: by the last accounts from the Convention, it is yet a doubt whether they will follow the example of Virginia by adopting and recommending amendments or have the amendments to preceed which I call rejecting it; the federalists by their writings from Poughkeepsie express great doubts, though some of the opposition have actually come over, and those of popular characters too—The antifederalists in this City very few excepted expect and seeme to hope for its adoption and recommend amendments as the least evil of the two—If it should not be adopted and that without previous amendments, Congress will certainly remove from hence, and Philadelphia probably will be their place of abode: And we shall not only loose them, but I think, have riot, confusion, and blood-shed introduced amongst us—I have only to add that my prayer is Heaven give them wisdom and avert the impending danger.

Pardon me for troubling You this much and You will much oblige Your sincear friend

1. RC, Fitch Papers, DLC.
2. Adapted from Shakespeare, *Hamlet*, Act III, scene 1, line 55.

Republican I
Virginia Independent Chronicle, 16 July 1788

On 9 July this announcement appeared in the *Chronicle:* "The Printer is authorised to inform the public, that a SERIES of LETTERS, addressed to the citizens of Virginia, on the subject of the new Constitution, will be hereafter published in this paper weekly, until the plan upon which they are written shall be fully executed. As the Author abhors, so will he avoid personalities. His sole object is to view with candour the objections, which were urged in the late Convention of this state, and to answer such others, as may from time to time appear. His only wish is to undeceive his fellow-citizens; not by an indiscriminate defence of parts, which he himself censures, but by opposing plain reasoning to any misconstruction, which may take place."

A second letter possibly appeared in the no longer extant issues of the *Virginia Independent Chronicle* on 23 July and 13 August, because on the latter day Governor Edmund Randolph sent the first two numbers to James Madison who had requested them after reading the above announcement. (See Madison to Randolph, 22 July, and Randolph to Madison, 13 August, Rutland, *Madison*, XI, 191–92, and BoR, III, 137–38, respectively. These letters suggest that the "Republican" letters might have been written by Randolph.) On 27 August the "Republican" published this statement in the *Chronicle*: "Since the publication of my last number, a proposition has been received from the convention of New-York, for a new convention of the states. Thus a new scene is presented; and a mode suggested, which will, I trust, be effectual in satisfying scrupulous minds. As therefore my only object in writing was to answer this purpose, I expect the accomplishment of it rather from the expedient proposed, than any reasoning, which I can use. With a hope, that a second convention will produce harmony, and a general support of the constitution, I shall not trouble you further." (The proposition from the New York Convention was the New York circular letter of 26 July. See BoR, I, 153–80, for the circulation letter and the Virginia legislature's response to it.)

LETTER, No. 1.
To the PEOPLE *of* VIRGINIA.

It is a fact, not less honorable to our country, than demonstrative of the respectful attention, with which her propositions are received, that she laid the ground-work of the new government. She invited the other States to the convention at Annapolis, and was the first, which appointed deputies to that of Philadelphia. By them and their associates, all of whom possessed the public confidence, the constitution was recommended for adoption. This recommendation was embraced by eight States, and by some of them unanimously, before Virginia met in convention. It is at least allowable to say of those who composed it, that their situation in life was so interwoven with the fate of their fellow citizens, that a government, bad in its original form, or its subsequent operation, would oppress the whole alike. What passed after they had assembled, corresponded with the hopes which had been previously entertained. A plan of debate was fixed, to the satisfaction of the friends and foes to the constitution; and was conducted with civility, temper, and patience, and with every allowance of time, which any of the speakers desired. Nay the final question was postponed, until the minutest parts had been severely examined, and until the opposition itself had declared, that they were ready to decide.—It was at length adopted.

After these auspicious events, the constitution would now seem to require no farther patronage. But there are among you some, who have conceived honest, though ill founded objections, to it; who may perhaps have been misled by constructions, which were formidable only, while they lurked in secret, and who, not being present at the late convention, know not the answers which were given, nor the little stress, which was placed on many of the most popular terrors.

The design therefore of these letters is to convince and undeceive you—to inlist your hearts and hands into a fair experiment of the constitution. They will differ from former publications, in being confined to the proceedings of our convention. No past arguments will be repeated which are not directly subservient to this particular end; and personalities will be banished, as being injurious to every cause, and disgraceful to their author.

Hence you perceive, that you are addressed by a friend of the constitution. But whosoever he may be, he claims the character of a republican, and pledges himself to labor for the destruction of the government, if at any time it shall cease to yield the blessings of liberty.

I freely confess that Virginia would be unwise, were she to entangle herself, even by a treaty, in the fortunes of the other States, without a clear necessity or the prospect of advantage. But when the advocates of the constitution were shewing the necessity of a general union to Virginia, from the exposure of her territory, the thinness of her population, her inability to raise a fleet or army of defence, the danger from foreign enemies and foreign politics—When they were exhibiting the advantages which such an union would create to her commerce, to her revenue, and to republicanism itself,—They were informed, that this was a wasteful display of truths, which none but an enemy to the honor and happiness of his country would deny.

The point then, next in order for consideration was, whether the confederation had betrayed no radical defect, fatal to the welfare of America. Here too the unanimity was compleat. From every corner of the house was its inefficacy resounded; and from those, who were the least partial to the constitution or most splendid in their encomiums on the confederation, the most ample acknowledgments of this inefficacy were extorted.

By this train of enquiry, the convention were led to seek a remedy for our national distress. From one of the following expedients only could relief be drawn; to form an confederacy with a number of the States, less than the whole, and to treat the rest as aliens; to incorporate more extensive powers into the confederation; to adopt the constitution without amendments; to adopt it on certain specified conditions; or to adopt it, and recommend subsequent amendments. The first expedient was reprobated by all, as infinite in mischief, and almost treasonable in idea; and, if it was even remotely meditated, no man had the hardiness to avow it.

The other expedients will be discussed, by arranging the debates of the convention under these heads. 1. What new powers are necessary for the general government? 2. Whether they could be introduced into the confederation without an alteration of its essence? 3. Whether they be not duly organized by the constitution? 4. And whether it was not better, under the existing circumstances of America, and especially of Virginia, to rely for amendments on some future, more favorable opportunity. According to this order, the subject will be handled; with no other deviation, than that which may be occasioned by the matter flowing from adversary pens.

Francis Hopkinson to Thomas Jefferson
Philadelphia, 17 July 1788 (excerpts)[1]

... You will perceive that our great object for near a Twelve month past has been the Formation & Ratification of a new System of Federal Government—I sent you the Plan proposed by the General Convention, long ago—Since the World began, I believe no Question has ever been more repeatedly & strictly scrutenized or more fairly & freely argued, than this proposed Constitution—It has now been solemnly ratified by 10 States viz. New Hampshire, Massachusetts, Connecticut, New Jersey, Pennsylvania, Delaware, Maryland, Virginia, South Carolina and Georgia—New York now hesitating—North Carolina to determine the last of this month,—Rhode-Island has not even call'd a Convention but seems disposed to do it—Whether *This* is the best possible System of Government, I will not pretend to say—Time must determine; but I am well persuaded that without an efficient federal Government, the States must in a very short Time sink into Contempt & the most dangerous Confusion—Many Amendments have been proposed by the ratifying States, but discordant with each other—A Door is left open in the Constitution itself for Amendments; but so large a Concurrence is made necessary that, it may be supposed none will be admitted but such as shall co-incide with *general* Opinion & *general* Interest.—The new System was long argued & powerfully opposed in Virginia;—however, she made the 10th. assenting State, by a Majority of 11 in Convention—Nothing can equal the Rejoicings in the Cities Towns & Villages thro'out the States on the late fourth of July in Celebration of the Declaration of Independence & the Birth of the new Constitution—The Papers are fill'd with Accounts of Processions, Toasts &c—As a Specimen, I enclose the Exertions of Philadelphia on this Occasion[2]—Altho' the State of New York hath not ratified, & it is very doubtful whether she will or no,—yet the City is making grand Preparations for an Exhibition on the 22d.[3] It is confidently talk'd that if the Convention should reject, the City of New York, with Staten & Long Islands, will seperate themselves from the State & join the Union. . . .

. . . I wish you was here during the Formation of our new Government—we shall be in Want of Men of Ability & Integrity to fill important Departments—much will depend upon our first off-set. . . .

1. RC, Jefferson Papers, DLC. For the entire letter, see Boyd, XIII, 369-71. The letter was carried from Philadelphia to New York City by Rodolphe Tillier, who was planning on leaving for France. Tillier, a former resident of Berne, Switzerland, who had married an American from Philadelphia, did not leave for France until at least 10 August when Edward Carrington also gave him a letter to take to Jefferson. In a letter of 21 December 1788, Jefferson acknowledged the receipt of Hopkinson's letter (Boyd, XIII, 495-96; XIV, 369-71).

2. Hopkinson probably included his account of Philadelphia's "Grand Federal Procession" that had been printed in the *Pennsylvania Gazette* and *Pennsylvania Packet* on 9 July. This account was also printed in a pamphlet entitled *Account of the Grand Federal Procession, Philadelphia, July 4, 1788* . . . that Hopkinson himself probably put together (Evans 21149, 21150; CC:805).

3. For the New York City celebration on 23 July 1788, see RCS:N.Y., 1584-1666.

Abraham Clark to Thomas Sinnickson
New York, 23 July 1788 (excerpt)[1]

. . . As to my sentiments respecting the New System of Government, altho' you do not ask, yet, as I find by your Letter it will be Acceptable, I think it not amiss to give them.—They have at no time been concealed.—I never liked the System in all its parts. I considered it from the first, more a Consolidated government than a federal, a government too expensive, and unnecessarily Oppressive in its Opperation; Creating a Judiciary undefined and unbounded.—with all these imperfections about it, I nevertheless wished it to go to the States from Congress just as it did, without any Censure or Commendation,[2] hoping that in Case of a general Adoption, the Wisdom of the States would soon amend it in the exceptionable parts; Strong fears however remained upon my mind untill I found the Custom of Recommending amendments with the Adoptions began to prevail.[3]—This set my mind at ease. It became clear in my opinion from the Oppositions, and the general concurrence in proposing amendmts. that the present plan must undergo some alterations to make it more agreable to the minds of the great Numbers who dislike it in its present form. The Amendments I wish are not numerous;—many proposed by the different Conventions appear of but little Consequence, yet some are important and must be Acceded to if ever the Government sits easy. From this State of the matter, wishing amendmts. as I do, you will readily conclude I anxiously wish every state may come into the adoption in order to effect a measure with me so desireable; in which case, from the general current of amendments proposed, we shall retain all the important parts in which New Jersey is interested.

1. RC, Conarroe Autograph Collection, PHi. For the entire letter, see CC:812.

2. In late September 1787 Clark took an active part in the debate in Congress over the manner in which the Constitution should be submitted to the states. In the end, Congress adopted his proposal that it be submitted without approbation or censure (CC:95).

3. The Massachusetts Convention was the first to propose recommendatory amendments on 6 February 1788 (BoR, I, 243–45n).

A Friend to Good Government
Rhode Island Newport Herald, 24 July 1788 (excerpt)[1]

... The warmest federalists have always had the candor to acknowledge that the system of government presented to us is imperfect—at the same time they generously allow for the imperfections of human nature—and console themselves under a moral certainty, that once the Constitution [is] ratified, another general Convention will be immediately summoned for the express purpose of taking into consideration the several amendments proposed by the different State Conventions;—thus we may by degrees expect to approach as near perfection as mortals are capable of, allowing for the extent of America, and its various habits, prejudices and clashings of interests; in short, we are now on the verge of realizing all we have been fighting for.

1. Reprinted: *Massachusetts Centinel*, 30 July; *Pennsylvania Mercury*, 12 August. For the entire essay, see RCS:R.I., 363–64.

Petersburg Virginia Gazette, 24 July 1788

On Monday last the Convention of the State of North-Carolina met at Hillsborough. We learn, there is a considerable majority of the members of that convention against the new government—but the supporters of it, have great hopes, since this state has acceded to it. Had Virginia rejected the government, it is generally agreed, that North-Carolina would certainly have followed her; but that state having South-Carolina on one side and Virginia on the other, might it is feared, place herself in a disagreeable situation by rejecting the government altogether—it is therefore expected, that some mode of reconciliation will be concluded on, so as to render it more satisfactory to the opposition.[1]

The general joy which has diffused throughout America, in consequence of the adoption of the new Constitution, is a striking proof of that philantropic disposition, which has hitherto so eminently distinguished the enlightened patriots of America—Willing to relinquish whatever might be found necessary for the preservation of the whole, they have generously given up all local advantages, with a firm and determined resolution of supporting the Union, and establishing that friendship and reciprocity of interest, which cannot but contribute to the general welfare. Fears and apprehensions have arisen in the minds of those, whose characters deserve our highest veneration, from the powers vested in the General Government by this Constitution: but these, if they are found dangerous to our liberties, will doubtless be removed; for America has yet citizens who have wisdom and circumspection enough to discern them. Our first and principal care ought to be, in being watchful of whom we trust—and to chuse none but those who are undeniably friends to the rights of human nature. Those who wish to preserve their liberty, ought to remember, that their dignity, their honor and happiness, rests with those they appoint to represent them—And let the government be what it will, if the representatives are virtuous, the people may live happy. But when the citizens neglect this great and important privilege, and forget that they are freemen, designing men may step into authority—that predominant principle, ambition, will most assuredly follow, the usurpation must be the natural consequence.

(*There is no great danger but men will be honest if they dare not be villains. Lead us not into temptation is a petition that would not only suit for our rulers, but for their creators*).[2]

1. This paragraph was reprinted in whole or in part in the July issue of the Philadelphia *American Museum* and in twenty-seven newspapers by 21 August: N.H. (1), Mass. (5), R.I. (3), Conn. (6), N.Y. (1), Pa. (10), Md. (1). Because the Petersburg *Virginia Gazette* for 24 July is not extant, this item has been transcribed from the Philadelphia *Independent Gazetteer*, one of three newspapers that first reprinted it on 1 August, under a dateline of Petersburg, 24 July.

2. The Petersburg *Virginia Gazette* of 24 July 1788 is not extant. The transcription of these two paragraphs is taken from the Philadelphia *Freeman's Journal*, 6 August under the dateline "PETERSBURG, *July* 24."

North Carolina Hillsborough Convention and a Bill of Rights, 24–30 July 1788

The first North Carolina Convention met in Hillsborough from 21 July through 4 August 1788. Without ratifying or rejecting the Constitution, the Convention recommended that a declaration of rights and amendments be added to the Constitution before North Carolina would ratify (BoR, I, 264–70). The transcriptions of these speeches are taken from *Proceedings and Debates of the Convention of North-Carolina, Convened at Hillsborough on Monday the 21st Day of July, 1788* . . . (Edenton, N.C., 1789) (Evans 22037).

James Gallaway: Speech in the North Carolina Convention 24 July 1788

I trust we shall not take up more time on this point. I shall just make a few remarks on what has been said by the gentleman from Halifax [William R. Davie]. He has gone through our distresses, and those of the other states. As to the weakness of the Confederation, we all know it. A sense of this induced the different states to send Delegates to Philadelphia. They had given them certain powers; we have seen them, they are now upon the table.[1] The result of their deliberations [i.e., the Constitution] is now upon the table also. As they have gone out of the line which the states pointed out to them, we, the people are to take it up and consider it. The gentlemen who framed it, have exceeded their powers, and very far. They will be able perhaps to give reasons for so doing. If they can shew us any reasons, we will no doubt take notice of them. But, on the other hand, if our civil and religious liberties are not secured, and proper checks provided, we have the power in our own hand to do with it as we think proper. I hope gentlemen will permit us to proceed.

1. Perhaps a reference to Congress' resolution of 21 February 1787 (CC:1), calling for a convention to revise the Articles of Confederation. This resolution, along with other state papers, was read in the North Carolina Convention on 23 June 1788 (RCS:N.C., 228).

Samuel Spencer: Speech in the North Carolina Convention 28 July 1788 (excerpt)[1]

. . . Our rights are not guarded. There is no declaration of rights, to secure to every member of the society those unalienable rights which ought not to be given up to any government. Such a bill of rights would be a check upon men in power. Instead of such a bill of rights, this

Constitution has a clause, which may warrant encroachments on the power of the respective state Legislatures.[2] I know it is said that what is not given up to the United States will be retained by the individual states.[3] I know it ought to be so, and should be so understood; but, Sir, it is not *declared* to be so. In the confederation it is expressly declared that all rights and powers, of any kind whatever, of the several states, which are not given up to the United States, are expressly and absolutely retained to be enjoyed by the states.[4] There ought to be a bill of rights, in order that those in power may not step over the boundary between the powers of government and the rights of the people, which they may do, when there is nothing to prevent them. They may do so without a bill of rights; notice will not be readily taken of the encroachments of rulers, and they may go a great length, before the people are alarmed. Oppressions may therefore take place by degrees, but if there were express terms and bounds laid down, when these were passed by, the people would take notice of them, and oppressions would not be carried on to such a length. I look upon it therefore that there ought to be something to confine the power of this government within its proper boundaries. I know that several writers have said that a bill of rights is not necessary in this country;[5] that some states had them not, and that others had. To these I answer, that those states that have them not as bills of right, strictly so called, have them in the frame of their constitution, which is nearly the same.

There has been a comparison made of our situation with Great-Britain. We have no crown or prerogative of a King like the British Constitution. I take it, that the subject has been misunderstood. In Great-Britain, when the King attempts to usurp the rights of the people, the declaration and bill of rights are a guard against him. A bill of rights would be necessary here to guard against our rulers. I wish to have a bill of rights, to secure those unalienable rights, which are called by some respectable writers the *residuum* of human rights,[6] which are never to be given up. At the same time that it would give security to individuals, it would add to the general strength. It might not be so necessary to have a bill of rights in the government of the United States, if such means had not been made use of, as endanger a consolidation of all the states; but at any event it would be proper to have one, because though it might not be of any other service, it would at least satisfy the minds of the people. It would keep the states from being swallowed up by a consolidated government. . . .

1. For the entire speech, see RCS:N.C., 349–52.
2. A reference to the supremacy clause (Article VI, clause 2).

3. See James Wilson's speech of 6 October 1787 (BoR, II, 25–28).
4. Article II of the Articles of Confederation reserved to the states "every Power, Jurisdiction and right" that was not "expressly delegated" to the Confederation government (CDR, 86).
5. See note 3 (above).
6. The words "residuum of human rights," attributed to Sir William Blackstone, were used by Richard Henry Lee in a letter to Edmund Randolph of 16 October 1787 (BoR, II, 9). Blackstone made reference to "that *residuum* of natural liberty, which is not required by the laws of society to be sacrificed to public convenience" (*Commentaries*, Book I, chapter 1, p. 125). In a letter to Samuel Adams of 5 October 1787, Lee accurately quoted Blackstone, though in this instance he did not attribute the words to Blackstone (BoR, II, 18). See also "Cassius" II, *Virginia Independent Chronicle*, 9 April 1788 (BoR, II, 409), and the *New York Journal*, 23 January 1788 (RCS:N.Y., 643, at note 5). The writer in the *Journal* quoted Blackstone further, identifying "that *residuum* of natural liberty" with "three primary articles": "The right of personal security; the right of personal liberty; and the right of private property."

Archibald Maclaine: Speech in the North Carolina Convention 28 July 1788 (excerpt)[1]

... The gentleman [Samuel Spencer] has wandered out of his way, to tell us what has so often been said out of doors; that there is no declaration of rights, that consequently all our rights are taken away. It would be very extraordinary to have a bill of rights, because the powers of Congress are expressly defined, and the very definition of them is as valid and efficacious a check as a bill of rights could be, without the dangerous implication of a bill of rights.[2] The powers of Congress are limited and enumerated. We say we have given them those powers, but we do not say we have given them more. We retain all those rights which we have not given away to the general government. The gentleman is a professional man. If a gentleman had made his last will and testament, and devised or bequeathed to a particular person the sixth part of his property, or any particular specific legacy, could it be said that that person should have the whole estate? If they can assume powers not enumerated, there was no occasion for enumerating any powers. The gentleman is learned: Without recurring to his learning, he may only appeal to common sense, it will inform him, that if we had all power before, and give away but a part, we still retain the rest. It is as plain a thing as possibly can be, that Congress can have no power but what we expressly give them. There is an express clause, which, however disingenuously it has been perverted from its true meaning, clearly demonstrates that they are confined to those powers which are given them.[3] This clause enables them to make all laws which shall be necessary and proper for carrying into execution the foregoing powers, and all other powers vested by this Constitution in the government of the United States, or any department or officers thereof. This clause specifies that they shall make laws to carry into execution, *all the powers vested*[4] by this Constitution, consequently they can make no laws to execute any other power. This clause gives no new power, but declares that those already given are to be executed by proper laws. I hope this will satisfy gentlemen.

1. For the entire speech, see RCS:N.C., 352–54.
2. Maclaine was re-stating the Federalist view, first expressed publicly by James Wilson on 6 October 1787, that the Constitution created a government of delegated powers and that rights not included in a bill of rights were by implication not protected (BoR, II, 25–28).
3. A reference to the necessary and proper clause (Article I, section 8, clause 18).
4. Maclaine misquotes the necessary and proper clause. The text of the Constitution refers to "the foregoing Powers, and all *other* Powers" (italics not in original).

**Samuel Johnston: Speech in the North Carolina Convention
28 July 1788 (excerpt)**[1]

... But the gentleman [Samuel Spencer] says that a bill of rights was necessary. It appears to me, Sir, that it would have been the highest absurdity to undertake to define what rights the people of the United States were entitled to: For that would be as much as to say, they were entitled to nothing else. A bill of rights may be necessary in a monarchical government, whose powers are undefined. Were we in the situation of a monarchical country? No, Sir. Every right could not be enumerated, and the omitted rights would be sacrificed, if security arose from an enumeration.[2] The Congress cannot assume any other powers than those expressly given them, without a palpable violation of the Constitution. Such objections as this, I hope will have no effect on the minds of any Members in this House. ...

1. For the entire speech, see RCS:N.C., 354–55.
2. See James Wilson's speech of 6 October 1787 (BoR, II, 25–28).

**Timothy Bloodworth: Speech in the North Carolina Convention
28 July 1788**

Mr. Chairman, The worthy gentleman up last [Samuel Johnston], has given me information on the subject, which I had never heard before. Hearing so many opinions, I did not know which was right. The honorable gentleman has said that the state courts and the Courts of the United States, would have concurrent jurisdiction.[1] I beg the committee to reflect what would be the consequences of such measures. It has ever been considered that the trial by jury was one of the greatest rights of the people. I ask whether, if such causes go into the Federal Court, the trial by jury is not cut off, and whether there is any security that we shall have justice done us. I ask if there be any security that we shall have juries in civil causes. In criminal cases there are to be juries, but there is no provision made for having civil causes tried by jury. This concurrent jurisdiction is inconsistent with the security of that great right. If it be not, I would wish to hear how it is secured. I have listened with attention to what the learned gentlemen have said, and have endeavoured to see whether their arguments had any weight, but I found none in them. Many words have been spoken, and long time taken up, but with me they have gone in at one ear and out at the other. It would give me much pleasure to hear that the trial by jury was secured.

1. See RCS:N.C., 354 for this statement by Samuel Johnston.

Joseph McDowall: Speech in the North Carolina Convention
28 July 1788

Mr. Chairman, The objections to this part of the Constitution have not been answered to my satisfaction yet. We know that the trial by a jury of the vicinage, is one of the greatest securities for property. If causes are to be decided at such a great distance, the poor will be oppressed; in land affairs particularly, the wealthy suitor will prevail. A poor man, who has a just claim on a piece of land, has not substance to stand it. Can it be supposed that any man, of common circumstances, can stand the expence and trouble of going from Georgia to Philadelphia, there to have a suit tried? And can it be justly determined without the benefit of a trial by jury? These are things which have justly alarmed the people. What made the people revolt from Great-Britain? The trial by jury, that great safeguard of liberty, was taken away,[1] and a stamp duty was laid upon them.[2] This alarmed them, and led them to fear that greater oppressions would take place. We then resisted. It involved us in a war, and caused us to relinquish a government which made us happy in every thing else. The war was very bloody, but we got our independence. We are now giving away our dear bought rights. We ought to consider what we are about to do before we determine.

1. A reference to the Revenue Act of 1764 (the "Sugar Act"), which strengthened the customs service. Under earlier navigation acts, seizures were tried in colonial vice admiralty courts or common law courts where the seizures took place. The Revenue Act of 1764 allowed cases involving seizures to be tried under a vice admiralty court to be established in Halifax, Nova Scotia, far from the reach of colonial juries. There were no jury trials in vice admiralty courts. The Revenue Act also protected customs officials from civil suits in colonial courts. Other vice admiralty courts were established in New York City, Philadelphia, and Charleston.

2. A reference to the Stamp Act of 1765.

Richard Dobbs Spaight: Speech in the North Carolina Convention 28 July 1788

Mr. Chairman, The trial by jury was not forgotten in the [Constitutional] Convention; the subject took up a considerable time to investigate it. It was impossible to make any one uniform regulation for all the states, or that would include all cases where it would be necessary. It was impossible, by one expression, to embrace the whole. There are a number of equity and maritime cases in some of the states, in which jury trials are not used. Had the Convention said, that all causes should be tried by a jury, equity and maritime cases would have been included. It was therefore left to the Legislature to say in what cases it should be used; and as the trial by jury is in full force in the states courts, we have the fullest security.

James Iredell: Speech in the North Carolina Convention, 28 July 1788 (excerpts)[1]

Mr. Chairman, I have waited a considerable time, in hopes that some other gentleman would fully discuss this point. I conceive it to be my duty to speak on every subject, whereon I think I can throw any light, and it appears to me that some things ought to be said which no gentleman has yet mentioned. The gentleman from New-Hanover [Timothy Bloodworth] said, that our arguments went in at one ear and out at the other. This sort of language, on so solemn and important an occasion, gives me pain. (Mr. *Bloodworth* here declared, that he did not mean to convey any disrespectful idea by such an expression—that he did not mean an absolute neglect of their arguments, but that they were not sufficient to convince him—that he should be sorry to give pain to any gentleman—that he had listened, and still would listen with attention to what would be said. Mr. *Iredell* then continued.) I am by no means surprised at the anxiety which is expressed by gentlemen on this subject. Of all the trials that ever were instituted in the world, this, in my opinion, is the best, and that which I hope will continue the longest. If the gentlemen who composed the Convention had designedly omitted it, no man would be more ready to condemn their conduct than myself. But I have been told, that the omission of it arose from the difficulty of establishing one uniform unexceptionable mode; this mode of trial being different in many particulars in the several states. Gentlemen will be pleased to consider, that there is a material difference between an article fixed in the constitution, and a regulation by law. An article in the constitution, however inconvenient it may prove by experience, can only be altered by altering the Constitution itself, which manifestly is a thing that ought not to be done often. When regulated by law, it can easily be occasionally altered, so as best to suit the conveniences of the people. Had there been an article in the Constitution taking away that trial, it would justly have excited the public indignation. It is not taken away by the Constitution. Though that does not provide expressly for a trial by jury in civil cases, it does not say that there shall not be such a trial. The reasons of the omission have been mentioned by a Member of the late General Convention, (Mr. Spaight). There are different practices in regard to this trial in different states. In some cases they have no juries in admiralty and equity cases; in others they have juries in these cases, as well as in suits at common law. I beg leave to say, that if any gentleman of ability, and knowledge of the subject, will only endeavour to fix upon any one rule, that would be pleasing to all the states under the impression of their present different habits, he will be convinced that it is impracticable. If the practice of any particular state had been adopted, others probably, whose practice had been different, would have been discontented. This is a consequence that naturally would have ensued, had the provision been made in the Constitution itself. But when the regulation is to be by law, as that law when found injudicious can be easily repealed, a majority may be expected to agree upon some method, since some method or other must be first tried, and there is a greater chance of the favourite method of one state being in time preferred. It is not to be presumed, that the Congress would dare to deprive the people of this valuable privilege. Their own interest will operate as an additional guard, as none of them could tell how soon they might have occasion for such a trial themselves. The greatest danger from ambition is in criminal cases. But here they have no option. The trial must be by jury in the state wherein the offence is committed, and the writ of *habeas corpus* will in the mean time secure the citizen against arbitrary imprisonment, which has been the principal source of tyranny in all ages. . . .

A gentleman [Joseph McDowall] has said, that the stamp-act, and the taking away of the trial by jury, were the principal causes of resistance to Great-Britain, and seemed to infer, that opposition would therefore be justified to this part of the system. . . . In respect to the trial by jury, its being taken away in certain cases, was to be sure one of the causes assigned in the declaration of independence.[2] But that was done by a foreign Legislature, which might continue it so forever, and therefore jealousy was justly excited. But this Constitution has not taken it away, and it is left to the discretion of our own Legislature, to act in this respect, as their wisdom shall direct. In Great-Britain the people speak of the trial by jury with admiration. No Monarch or Minister, however arbitrary in his principles, would dare to attack that noble palladium of liberty. The enthusiasm of the people in its favour would in such a case produce general resistance. That trial remains unimpaired there, although they have a considerable standing army, and their Parliament has authority to abolish it if they please. But woe be to those who should attempt it! If it be secure in that country, under these circumstances, can we believe that Congress either would or could take it away in this? Were they to attempt it, their authority would be instantly resisted. They would draw down on themselves the resentment and detestation of the people. They and their families, so long as any remained in being, would be held in eternal infamy, and the attempt prove as unsuccessful as it was wicked.

With regard to a bill of rights, this is a notion originating in England, where no written Constitution is to be found, and the authority of their government is derived from the most remote antiquity. Magna Charta itself is no Constitution, but a solemn instrument ascertaining certain rights of individuals, by the Legislature for the time being, and every article of which the Legislature may at any time alter. This, and a bill of rights also, the invention of later times,[3] were occasioned by great usurpations of the crown, contrary, as was conceived, to the principles of their government, about which there was a variety of opinions. But neither that instrument or any other instrument ever attempted to abridge the authority of Parliament, which is supposed to be without any limitation whatever.[4] Had their Constitution been fixed and certain, a bill of rights would have been useless, for the Constitution would have shewn plainly the extent of that authority which they were disputing about. Of what use therefore can a bill of rights be in this Constitution, where the people expressly declare how much power they do give, and consequently retain all they do not? It is a declaration of particular powers by the people to their Representatives for particular purposes. It may be considered as a great power of attorney, under which no power can be exercised but what is expressly given. Did any man ever hear before that at the end of a power of attorney it was said, that the Attorney should not exercise more power than was there given him? Suppose for instance a man had lands in the counties of Anson and Caswell, and he should give another a power of attorney to sell his lands in Anson; would the other have any authority to sell the lands in Caswell? or could he without absurdity say, " 'Tis true you have not expressly authorised me to sell the lands in Caswell, but as you had lands there, and did not say I should not, I thought I might as well sell those lands as the other." A bill of rights, as I conceive, would not only be incongruous, but dangerous. No man, let his ingenuity be what it will, could enumerate all the individual rights not relinquished by this Constitution. Suppose therefore an enumeration of a great many, but an omission of some, and that long after all traces of our present disputes were at an end, any of the omitted rights should be invaded, and the invasion be complained of; what would be the plausible answer of the government to such a complaint? Would they not naturally say, "We live at a great distance from the time when this Constitution was established. We can judge of it much better by the ideas of it entertained at the time, than by any ideas of our own. The bill of rights passed at that time, shewed that the people did not think every power retained which was not given, else this bill of rights was not only useless, but absurd. But we are not at liberty to charge an absurdity upon our ancestors, who have given such strong proofs of their good sense, as well as their attachment to liberty. So long as the rights enumerated in the bill of rights remain unviolated, you have no reason to complain. This is not one of them." Thus a bill of rights might operate as a snare, rather than a protection. If we had formed a General Legislature, with undefined powers, a bill of rights would not only have been proper, but necessary; and it would have then operated as an exception to the legislative authority in such particulars. It has this effect in respect to some of the American Constitutions, where the powers of legislation are general. But where they are powers of a particular nature, and expressly defined, as in the case of the Constitution before us, I think, for the reasons I have given, a bill of rights is not only unnecessary, but would be absurd and dangerous.

1. For the entire speech, see RCS:N.C., 356–61.
2. Among the "repeated injuries and usurpations" leveled against "the present King of Great Britain" in the Declaration of Independence was his deprivation of the "benefits of Trial by Jury" (CDR, 73–74). See note 1 to Joseph McDowall's speech, 28 July (BoR, III, 98n).
3. The English Bill of Rights (1689), BoR, I, 4–8.
4. Blackstone, *Commentaries*, Book I, chapter 2, p. 156. Blackstone, drawing on the jurist Sir Edward Coke, wrote, "The power and jurisdiction of parliament . . . is so transcendent and absolute, that it cannot be confined, either for cause or persons within any bounds. . . . It [i.e., Parliament] hath sovereign, and uncontrolable authority in making, confirming, enlarging, restraining, abrogating, repealing, reviving, and expounding of laws, concerning matters of all possible denominations, ecclesiastical, or temporal, civil, military, maritime, or criminal: this being the place where that absolute despotic power, which must in all governments reside somewhere, is entrusted by the constitution of these kingdoms."

Joseph McDowall: Speech in the North Carolina Convention 28 July 1788

Mr. Chairman, The learned gentleman [James Iredell] made use of several arguments to induce us to believe, that the trial by jury in civil cases was not in danger, and observed, that in criminal cases it is provided, that the trial is to be in the state where the crime was committed. Suppose a crime is committed at the Missisippi—the man may be tried at Edenton. They ought to be tried by the people of the vicinage; for when the trial is at such an immense distance, the principal privilege attending the trial by jury is taken away: Therefore the trial ought to be limited to a district or certain part of the state. It has been said by the gentleman from Edenton [James Iredell], that our Representatives will have virtue and wisdom to regulate all these things. But it would give me much satisfaction, in a matter of this importance, to see it absolutely secured. The depravity of mankind militates against such a degree of confidence. I wish to see every thing fixed.

**Samuel Spencer: Speech in the North Carolina Convention
29 July 1788 (excerpt)**[1]

Mr. Chairman, I hope to be excused for making some observations on what was said yesterday, by gentlemen in favour of these two clauses. The motion which was made that the committee should rise, precluded me from speaking then. The gentlemen have shewed much moderation and candour in conducting this business: But I still think that my observations are well founded, and that some amendments are necessary. The gentlemen [Samuel Johnston and James Iredell] said all matters not given up by this form of government, were retained by the respective states. I know that it ought to be so; it is the general doctrine, but it is necessary that it should be expressly declared in the Constitution, and not left to mere construction and opinion. I am authorised to say it was heretofore thought necessary. The Confederation says expressly, that all that was not given up by the United States, was retained by the respective states.[2] If such a clause had been inserted in this Constitution, it would have superceded the necessity of a bill of rights. But that not being the case, it was necessary that a bill of rights, or something of that kind, should be a part of the Constitution. It was observed, that as the Constitution is to be a delegation of power from the several states to the United States, a bill of rights was unnecessary. But it will be noticed that this is a different case. The states do not act in their political capacities, but the government is proposed for individuals. The very caption of the Constitution shews that this is the case. The expression, "We the people of the United States," shews that this government is intended for individuals; there ought therefore to be a bill of rights. I am ready to acknowledge that the Congress ought to have the power of executing its laws. Heretofore, because all the laws of the

Confederation were binding on the states in their political capacities, courts had nothing to do with them; but now the thing is entirely different. The laws of Congress will be binding on individuals, and those things which concern individuals will be brought properly before the courts. In the next place, all the officers are to take an oath to carry into execution this general government, and are bound to support every act of the government, of whatever nature it may be. This is a fourth reason for securing the rights of individuals. It was also observed, that the Federal Judiciary and the courts of the states under the federal authority, would have concurrent jurisdiction with respect to any subject that might arise under the Constitution. I am ready to say that I most heartily wish that whenever this government takes place, the two jurisdictions and the two governments, that is, the general and the several state governments, may go hand in hand, and that there may be no interference, but that every thing may be rightly conducted. But I will never concede that it is proper to divide the business between the two different courts. I have no doubt but there is wisdom enough in this state to decide the business in a proper manner, without the necessity of federal assistance to do our business. The worthy gentleman from Edenton [James Iredell], dwelt a considerable time on the observations on a bill of rights, contending that they were proper only in monarchies, which were founded on different principles from those of our government; and therefore, though they might be necessary for others, yet they were not necessary for us. I still think that a bill of rights is necessary. This necessity arises from the nature of human societies. When individuals enter into society, they give up some rights to secure the rest. There are certain human rights that ought not to be given up, and which ought in some manner to be secured. With respect to these great essential rights, no latitude ought to be left. They are the most inestimable gifts of the great Creator, and therefore ought not be destroyed, but ought to be secured. They ought to be secured to individuals in consideration of the other rights which they give up to support society.

The trial by jury has been also spoken of. Every person who is acquainted with the nature of liberty, need not be informed of the importance of this trial. Juries are called the bulwarks of our rights and liberty; and no country can ever be enslaved as long as those cases which affect their lives and property, are to be decided in a great measure, by the consent of twelve honest, disinterested men, taken from the respectable body of yeomanry. It is highly improper that any clause which regards the security of the trial by jury should be any way doubtful. In the clause that has been read, it is ascertained that criminal cases are to be tried by jury, in the states wherein they are committed. It has been objected to that clause, that it is not sufficiently explicit. I think that it is not. It was observed, that one may be taken at a great distance. One reason of the resistance to the British government was, because they required that we should be carried to the country of Great-Britain, to be tried by juries of that country.[3] But we insisted on being tried by juries of the vicinage in our own country. I think it therefore proper, that something explicit should be said with respect to the vicinage. . . .

1. For the entire speech, see RCS:N.C., 367–70.
2. Article II of the Articles of Confederation reserved to the states "every Power, Jurisdiction and right" that was not "expressly delegated" to the Confederation government (CDR, 86).
3. A reference to the Administration of Justice Act (20 May 1774), one of the four "Intolerable Acts" passed between 31 March and 2 June 1774. Three of the four acts—the Boston Port Act, the Massachusetts Government Act, and the Administration of Justice Act—were directed at Massachusetts, where revolutionary fervor was greatest in response to British policies. Under the Administration of Justice Act, British customs officials on trial could be removed to another British colony or Great Britain, which would put them beyond the reach of American juries. Witnesses in such proceedings could also be compelled to attend.

William R. Davie: Speech in the North Carolina Convention 29 July 1788 (excerpt)[1]

. . . As to a bill of rights, which has been brought forward in a manner I cannot account for, it is unnecessary to say any thing. The learned gentleman [Samuel Spencer] has said, that by a concurrent jurisdiction the laws of the United States must necessarily clash with the laws of the individual states, in consequence of which the laws of the states will be obstructed, and the state governments absorbed. This cannot be the case. There is not one instance of a power given to the United States, whereby the internal policy or administration of the states is affected. There is no instance that can be pointed out, wherein the internal policy of the state can be affected by the Judiciary of the United States. He mentioned impost laws. It has been given up on all hands, that if there was a necessity of a Federal Court, it was on this account. Money is difficult to be got into the treasury. The power of the Judiciary to enforce the federal laws is necessary to facilitate the collection of the public revenues. It is well known in this state with what reluctance and backwardness Collectors pay up the public monies. We have been making laws after laws to remedy this evil and still find them ineffectual. Is it not therefore necessary to enable the general government to compel the delinquent receivers to be punctual? The honourable gentleman admits that the general government ought to legislate upon individuals instead of states. Its laws will otherwise be ineffectual, but particularly with respect to treaties. We have seen with what little ceremony the states violated the peace with Great-Britain. Congress had no power to enforce its observance.[2] The same cause will produce the same effect. We need not flatter ourselves that similar violations will always meet with equal impunity. I think he must be of opinion upon more reflection, that the jurisdiction of the federal Judiciary could not have been constructed otherwise with safety or propriety. It is necessary that the Constitution should be carried into effect, that the laws should be executed, justice equally done to all the community, and treaties observed. These ends can only be accomplished by a general paramount Judiciary. These are my sentiments, and if the honourable gentleman will prove them erroneous, I shall readily adopt his opinions.

1. For the entire speech, see RCS:N.C., 370–75.
2. See William R. Davie's speech in the North Carolina Convention, 28 July at note 8 and note 8 (RCS:N.C., 336, 364n).

Archibald Maclaine: Speech in the North Carolina Convention 29 July 1788 (excerpt)[1]

Mr. Chairman, I beg leave to make a few observations. One of the gentleman's [Samuel Spencer's] objections to the Constitution now under consideration is, that it is not the act of the states but of the people; but that it ought to be the act of the states, and he instances the delegation of power by the states to the Confederation at the commencement of the war as a proof of this position. I hope, Sir, that all power is in the people and not in the state governments. If he will not deny the authority of the people to delegate power to agents, and to devise such a government as a majority of them thinks will promote their happiness, he will withdraw his objection. The people, Sir, are the only proper authority to form a government. They, Sir, have formed their state governments, and can alter them at pleasure. Their transcendent power is competent to form this or any other government which they think promotive of their happiness. But the gentleman contends that there ought to be a bill of rights, or something of that kind—something declaring expressly, that all power not expressly given to the Constitution, ought to be retained by the states, and he produces the Confederation as an authority for its necessity. When the Confederation was made, we were by no means so well acquainted with the principles of government as we are now. We were then jealous of the power of our rulers, and had an idea of the British government when we entertained that jealousy. There is no people on earth so well acquainted with the nature of government as the people of America generally are. We know now, that it is agreed upon by most writers, and men of judgment and reflection, that all power is in the people and immediately derived from them. The gentleman surely must know, that if there be certain rights which never can nor ought to be given up; these rights cannot be said to be given away, merely because we have omitted to say that we have not given them up. Can any security arise from declaring that we have a right to what belongs to us? Where is the necessity of such a declaration? If we have this inherent, this unalienable, this indefeasible title to those rights, if they are not given up, are they not retained? If Congress should make a law beyond the powers and the spirit of the Constitution, should we not say to Congress, "You have no authority to make this law. There are limits beyond which you cannot go. You cannot exceed the power prescribed by the Constitution. You are amenable to us for your conduct. This act is unconstitutional. We will disregard it, and punish you for the attempt." . . .

1. For the entire speech, see RCS:N.C., 375–77.

Samuel Spencer: Speech in the North Carolina Convention 29 July 1788 (excerpt)[1]

Mr. *Spencer* answered, That the gentleman last up [Archibald Maclaine] had misunderstood him. He did not object to the caption of the Constitution, but he instanced it to shew that the United States were not, merely as states, the objects of the Constitution; but that the laws of Congress were to operate upon individuals and not upon states. He then continued—I do not mean to contend, that the laws of the general government should not operate upon individuals. I before observed that this was necessary, as laws could not be put in execution against states, without the agency of the sword, which instead of answering the ends of government would destroy it.—I endeavoured to shew, that as the government was not to operate against states but against individuals, the rights of individuals ought to be properly secured. In order to constitute this security, it appears to me there ought to be such a clause in the Constitution as there was in the Confederation, expressly declaring, that every power, jurisdiction and right, which are not given up by it, remain in the states.[2] Such a clause would render a bill of rights unnecessary. But as there is no such clause I contend, that there should be a bill of rights, ascertaining and securing the great rights of the states and people. . . .

1. For the entire speech, see RCS:N.C., 377–78.

2. Article II of the Articles of Confederation reserved to the states "every Power, Jurisdiction and right" that was not "expressly delegated" to the Confederation government (CDR, 86).

James Iredell: Speech in the North Carolina Convention, 29 July 1788

Mr. Chairman, I beg leave to make a few observations on some remarks that have been made on this part of the Constitution. The honourable gentleman [Samuel Spencer] said that it was very extraordinary that the Convention should not have taken the trouble to make an addition of five or six lines, to secure the trial by jury in civil cases. Sir, if by the addition, not only of five or six lines, but of five or six hundred lines, this invaluable object could have been secured, I should have thought the Convention criminal in omitting it; and instead of meriting the thanks of their country, as I think they do now, they might justly have met with its resentment and indignation. I am persuaded that the omission arose from the real difficulty of the case. The gentleman says that a mode might have been provided, whereby the trial by jury might have been secured satisfactorily to all the states. I call on him to shew that mode—I know of none—nor do I think it possible for any man to devise one to which some states would not have objected. It is said indeed, that it might have been provided that it should be as it had been heretofore. Had this been the case, surely it would have been highly incongruous.—The trial by jury is different in different states. It is regulated in one way in the state of North-Carolina, and in another way in the state of Virginia. It is established in a different way from either in several other states. Had it then been inserted in the Constitution, that the trial by jury should be as it had been heretofore, there would have been an example, for the first time in the world, of a Judiciary belonging to the same government being different in different parts of the same country. What would you think of an act of Assembly which should require the trial by jury to be had in one mode in the county of Orange, in another mode in Granville, and in a manner different from both in Chatham? Such an act of Assembly, so manifestly injudicious, impolitic and unjust, would be repealed next year. But what would you say of our Constitution, if it authorised such an absurdity? The mischief then could not be removed without altering the Constitution itself. It must be evident therefore, that the addition contended for would not have answered the purpose. If the method of any particular state had been established, it would have been objected to by others, because whatever inconveniences it might have been attended with, nothing but a change in the Constitution itself could have removed them; whereas, as it is now, if any mode established by Congress is found inconvenient, it can easily be altered by a single act of legislation. Let any gentleman consider the difficulties in which the Convention was placed. And union was absolutely necessary. Every thing could be agreed upon except the regulation of the trial by jury in civil cases. They were all anxious to establish it on the best footing, but found they could fix upon no permanent rule that was not liable to great objections and difficulties. If they could not agree among themselves, they had still less reason to believe that all the states would have unanimously agreed to any one plan that could be proposed. They therefore thought it better to leave all such regulations to the Legislature itself, conceiving there could be no real danger in this case from a body composed of our own Representatives, who could have no temptation to undermine this excellent mode of trial in civil cases, and who would have indeed a personal interest in common with others, in making the administration of justice between man and man secure and easy. In criminal cases, however, no latitude ought to be allowed. In these the greatest danger from any government subsists, and accordingly it is provided, that there shall be a trial by jury in all such cases in the state wherein the offence is committed. I thought the objection against the want of a bill of rights had been obviated unanswerably. It appears to me most extraordinary. Shall we give up any thing but what is positively granted by that instrument? It would be the greatest absurdity for any man to pretend, that when a Legislature is formed for a particular purpose, it can have any authority but what is so expressly given to it, any more than a man acting under a power of attorney could depart from the authority it conveyed to him, according to an instance which I stated when speaking on the subject before.[1] As for example— If I had three tracts of land, one in Orange, another in Caswell, and another in Chatham, and I gave a power of attorney to a man to sell the two tracts in Orange and Caswell, and he should attempt to sell my land in Chatham, would any man of common sense suppose he had authority to do so? In like manner, I say, the future Congress can have no right to exercise any power but what is contained in that paper. Negative words, in my opinion, could make the matter no plainer than it was before. The gentleman [Samuel Spencer] says that unalienable rights ought not to be given up. Those rights which are unalienable are not alienated. They still remain with the great body of the people. If any right be given up that ought not to be, let it be shewn. Say it is a thing which affects your country, and that it ought not to be surrendered—this would be reasonable. But when it is evident that the exercise of any power not given up would be an usurpation, it would be not only useless but dangerous to enumerate a number of rights which are not intended to be given up; because it would be implying in the strongest manner, that every right not included in the exception might be impaired by the government without usurpation, and it would be impossible to enumerate every one. Let any one make what collection or enumeration of rights he pleases, I will immediately mention twenty or thirty more rights not contained in it.

1. See Iredell's speech on 28 July (BoR, III, 101).

Timothy Bloodworth: Speech in the North Carolina Convention
29 July 1788

Mr. Chairman, I have listened with attention to the gentleman's [James Iredell's] arguments, but, whether it be for want of sufficient attention, or from the grossness of my ideas, I cannot be satisfied with his defence of the omission with respect to the trial by jury. He says that it would be impossible to fall on any satisfactory mode of regulating the trial by jury, because there are various customs relative to it in the different states. Is this a satisfactory cause for the omission? Why did it not provide that the trial by jury should be preserved in civil cases? It has said that the trial should be by jury in criminal cases, and yet this trial is different in its manner in criminal cases in the different states. If it has been possible to secure it in criminal cases, notwithstanding the diversity concerning it, why has it not been possible to secure it in civil cases? I wish this to be cleared up. By its not being provided for, it is expressly provided against. I still see the necessity of a bill of rights. Gentlemen use contradictory arguments on this subject, if I recollect right. Without the most express restrictions, Congress may trample on your rights. Every possible precaution should be taken when we grant powers. Rulers are always disposed to abuse them. I beg leave to call gentlemen's recollection to what happened under our Confederation. By it nine states are required to make a treaty, yet seven states said that they could, with propriety, repeal part of the instructions given our secretary for foreign affairs, which prohibited him from making a treaty to give up the Missisippi to Spain, by which repeal the rest of his instructions enabled him to make such treaty:[1] Seven states actually did repeal the prohibitory part of these instructions, and they insisted it was legal and proper. This was in fact a violation of the Confederation. If gentlemen thus put what construction they please upon words, how shall we be redressed if Congress shall say that all that is not expressed is given up, and they assume a power which is expressly inconsistent with the rights of mankind. Where is the power to pretend to deny its legality? This has occurred to me, and I wish it to be explained.

1. Since 1779 John Jay engaged in negotiations with the Spanish government in Spain and France. When Jay returned to the United States he was appointed secretary for foreign affairs. Negotiations continued with the arrival of Spanish envoy Don Diego de Gardoqui in New York in 1786. In 1784, the Spanish government prohibited Americans from navigating the Mississippi River. Without American acceptance of this prohibition, Spain would not agree to a commercial treaty with the United States. Jay asked Congress to alter his instructions, allowing him to give up the American right to navigate the Mississippi River for twenty-five years in exchange for commercial privileges for American merchants in Spanish ports. Jay had the support of the Northern States in Congress, but the five Southern States could defeat any proposed treaty because the Articles of Confederation required that at least nine states had to approve treaties as well as all other important actions of Congress.

Samuel Spencer: Speech in the North Carolina Convention 29 July 1788

Mr. Chairman, The gentleman [James Iredell] expresses admiration as to what we object with respect to a bill of rights, and insists that what is not given up in the Constitution, is retained. He must recollect I said yesterday, that we could not guard with too much care, those essential rights and liberties which ought never to be given up. There is no express negative—no fence against their being trampled upon. They might exceed the proper boundary without being taken notice of. When there is no rule but a vague doctrine, they might make great strides and get into possession of so much power, that a general insurrection of the people would be necessary to bring an alteration about. But if a boundary were set up, when the boundary is passed, the people would take notice of it immediately. These are the observations which I made, and I have no doubt that when he coolly reflects, he will acknowledge the necessity of it. I acknowledge, however, that the doctrine is right. But if that Constitution is not satisfactory to the people, I would have a bill of rights, or something of that kind, to satisfy them.

James Iredell: Speech in the North Carolina Convention, 29 July 1788

Mr. Chairman, I hope that some other gentleman will answer what has been said by the gentlemen who have spoken last.[1] I only rise to answer the question of the Member from New-Hanover [Timothy Bloodworth], which was, If there was such a difficulty in establishing the trial by jury in civil cases, that the Convention could not concur in any mode, why the difficulty did not extend to criminal cases? I beg leave to say, that the difficulty in this case does not depend so much on the mode of proceeding, as on the difference of the subjects of controversy, and the laws relative to them. In some states there are no juries in admiralty and equity cases. In other states there are juries in such cases.

In some states there are no distinct courts of equity, though in most states there are. I believe, that if an uniform rule had been fixed by the Constitution, it would have displeased some states so far that they would have rejected the Constitution altogether. Had it been declared generally, as the gentleman mentioned, it would have included equity and maritime cases, and created a necessity of deciding them in a manner different from that in which they have been decided heretofore in many of the states; which would very probably have met with the disapprobation of those states. We have been told, and I believe this was the real reason why they could not concur in any general rule. I have great respect for the characters of those gentlemen who formed the Convention, and I believe they were not capable of overlooking the importance of the trial by jury, much less of designedly plotting against it. But I fully believe that the real difficulty of the thing was the cause of the omission. I trust sufficient reasons have been offered, to shew that it is in no danger. As to criminal cases, I must observe, that the great instrument of arbitrary power is criminal prosecutions. By the privilege of the *habeas corpus* no man can be confined without enquiry, and if it should appear he has been committed contrary to law, he must be discharged. That diversity which is to be found in civil controversies, does not subsist in criminal cases. That diversity which contributes to the security of property in civil cases, would have pernicious effects in criminal ones. There is no other safe mode to try these but by a jury. If any man had the means of trying another his own way; or were it left to the controul of arbitrary Judges, no man would have that security for life and liberty which every freeman ought to have. I presume that in no state on the continent is a man tried on a criminal accusation but by a jury. It was necessary therefore that it should be fixed in the Constitution, that the trial should be by jury in criminal cases, and such difficulties did not occur in this as in the other case. The worthy gentleman [Timothy Bloodworth] says, that by not being provided for in civil cases it is expressly provided against, and that what is not expressed is given up. Were it so, no man would be more against this Constitution than myself. I should detest and oppose it as much as any man. But, Sir, this cannot be the case. I beg leave to say that that construction appears to me absurd and unnatural. As it could not be fixed either on the principles of uniformity or diversity, it must be left to Congress to modify it. If they establish it in any manner by law, and find it inconvenient, they can alter it. But I am convinced that a majority of the Representatives of the people, will never attempt to establish a mode oppressive to their constituents, as it will be their own interest to take care of this right. But it is observed that there ought to be a fence provided against future encroachments of power. If there be not such a fence it is a cause of objection. I readily agree there ought to be such a *fence*. The instrument ought to contain such a definition of authority as would leave no doubt, and if there be any ambiguity it ought not to be admitted. He says this construction is not agreeable to the people, though he acknowledges it is a right one. In my opinion there is no man of any reason at all, but must be satisfied with so clear and plain a definition. If the Congress should claim any power not given them, it would be as bare an usurpation as making a King in America. If this Constitution be adopted, it must be presumed the instrument will be in the hands of every man in America, to see whether authority be usurped; and any person by inspecting it may see if the power claimed be enumerated. If it be not, he will know it to be an usurpation.

1. Matthew Locke. For Locke's speech, see RCS:N.C., 381–83.

Henry Abbot: Speech in the North Carolina Convention, 30 July 1788

Mr. *Abbot*, after a short exordium which was not distinctly heard, proceeded thus—Some are afraid, Mr. Chairman, that should the Constitution be received, they would be deprived of the privilege of worshipping God according to their consciences; which would be taking from them a benefit they enjoy under the present Constitution. They wish to know if their religious and civil liberties be secured under this system, or whether the general government may not make laws infringing their religious liberties. The worthy member from Edenton [James Iredell] mentioned sundry political reasons why treaties should be the supreme law of the land. It is feared by some people, that by the power of making treaties, they might make a treaty engaging with foreign powers to adopt the Roman catholic religion in the United States, which would prevent the people from worshipping God according to their own consciences. The worthy member from Halifax [William R. Davie] has in some measure satisfied my mind on this subject. But others may be dissatisfied. Many wish to know what religion shall be established. I believe a majority of the community are Presbyterians. I am for my part against any exclusive establishment, but if there were any, I would prefer the Episcopal. The exclusion of religious tests is by many thought dangerous and impolitic. They suppose that if there be no religious test required, Pagans, Deists and Mahometans might obtain offices among us, and that the Senate and Representatives might all be Pagans. Every person employed by the general and state governments is to take an oath to support the former. Some are desirous to know how, and by whom they are to swear, since no religious tests are required—

whether they are to swear by Jupiter, Juno, Minerva, Proserpine or Pluto. We ought to be suspicious of our liberties. We have felt the effects of oppressive measures, and know the happy consequences of being jealous of our rights. I would be glad some gentleman would endeavour to obviate these objections, in order to satisfy the religious part of the society. Could I be convinced that the objections were well founded, I would then declare my opinion against the Constitution. (Mr. *Abbot* added several other observations, but spoke too low to be heard.)

James Iredell: Speech in the North Carolina Convention, 30 July 1788

Mr. Chairman, Nothing is more desireable than to remove the scruples of any gentleman on this interesting subject: Those concerning religion are entitled to particular respect. I did not expect any objection to this particular regulation, which in my opinion, is calculated to prevent evils of the most pernicious consequences to society. Every person in the least conversant in the history of mankind, knows what dreadful mischiefs have been committed by religious persecutions. Under the colour of religious tests the utmost cruelties have been exercised. Those in power have generally considered all wisdom centered in themselves, that they alone had a right to dictate to the rest of mankind, and that all opposition to their tenets was profane and impious. The consequence of this intolerant spirit has been, that each church has in turn set itself up against every other, and persecutions and wars of the most implacable and bloody nature have taken place in every part of the world. America has set an example to mankind to think more modestly and reasonably; that a man may be of different religious sentiments from our own, without being a bad member of society. The principles of toleration, to the honour of this age, are doing away those errors and prejudices which have so long prevailed even in the most intolerant countries. In the Roman catholic countries, principles of moderation are adopted, which would have been spurned at a century or two ago. I should be sorry to find, when examples of toleration are set even by arbitrary governments, that this country, so impressed with the highest sense of liberty, should adopt principles on this subject, that were narrow and illiberal. I consider the clause under consideration as one of the strongest proofs that could be adduced, that it was the intention of those who formed this system, to establish a general religious liberty in America. Were we to judge from the examples of religious tests in other countries, we should be persuaded that they do not answer the purpose for which they are intended. What is the consequence of such in England? In that country no man can be a Member in the House of Commons, or hold any office under the Crown, without taking the sacrament according to the rites of the church. This in the first instance must degrade and profane a rite, which never ought to be taken but from a sincere principle of devotion. To a man of base principles, it is made a mere instrument of civil policy. The intention was to exclude all persons from offices, but the members of the church of England. Yet it is notorious, that Dissenters qualify themselves for offices in this manner, though they never conform to the church on any other occasion; and men of no religion at all, have no scruple to make use of this qualification. It never was known that a man who had no principles of religion, hesitated to perform any rite when it was convenient for his private interest. No test can bind such a one. I am therefore clearly of opinion, that such a discrimination would neither be effectual for its own purposes, nor if it could, ought it by any means to be made. Upon the principles I have stated, I confess the restriction on the power of Congress in this particular has my hearty approbation. They certainly have no authority to interfere in the establishment of any religion whatsoever, and I am astonished that any gentleman should conceive they have. Is there any power given to Congress in matters of religion? Can they pass a single act to impair our religious liberties? If they could, it would be a just cause of alarm. If they could, Sir, no man would have more horror against it than myself. Happily no sect here is superior to another. As long as this is the case, we shall be free from those persecutions and distractions with which other countries have been torn. If any future Congress should pass an act concerning the religion of the country, it would be an act which they are not authorised to pass by the Constitution, and which the people would not obey. Every one would ask, "Who authorised the government to pass such an act? It is not warranted by the Constitution, and is a barefaced usurpation." The power to make treaties can never be supposed to include a right to establish a foreign religion among ourselves, though it might authorise a toleration of others.

But it is objected, that the people of America may perhaps chuse Representatives who have no religion at all, and that Pagans and Mahometans may be admitted into offices. But how is it possible to exclude any set of men, without taking away that principle of religious freedom which we ourselves so warmly contend for? This is the foundation on which persecution has been raised in every part of the world. The people in power were always in the right, and every body else wrong. If you admit the least difference, the door to persecution is opened. Nor would it answer the purpose, for the worst part of the excluded sects would comply with the test, and the best men only be kept out of our counsels. But it is never to be supposed that the people of America will trust their dearest rights to persons who have no religion at all, or a religion materially different from their own. It would be happy for mankind if religion was permitted to take its own course, and maintain itself by the excellence of its own doctrines. The divine author of our religion never wished for its support by worldly authority. Has he not said, *that the gates of hell shall not prevail against it?*[1] It made much greater progress for itself, than when supported by the greatest authority upon earth.

It has been asked by that respectable gentleman (Mr. Abbot) what is the meaning of that part, where it is said, that the United States shall *guarantee* to every state in the union a republican form of government, and why a *guarantee* of *religious freedom* was not included. The meaning of the guarantee provided was this—There being thirteen governments confederated, upon a republican principle, it was essential to the existence and harmony of the confederacy that each should be a republican government, and that no state should have a right to establish an aristocracy or monarchy. That clause was therefore inserted to prevent any state from establishing any government but a republican one. Every one must be convinced of the mischief that would ensue, if any state had a right to change its government to a monarchy. If a monarchy was established in any one state, it would endeavour to subvert the freedom of the others, and would probably by degrees succeed in it. This must strike the mind of every person here who recollects the history of Greece when she had confederated governments. The King of Macedon by his arts and intrigues got himself admitted a member of the Amphyctionic council, which was the superintending government of the Grecian republics, and in a short time he became master of them all.[2] It is then necessary that the members of a confederacy should have similar governments. But consistently with this restriction the states may make what change in their own governments they think proper. Had Congress undertaken to guarantee *religious freedom,* or any particular species of it, they would then have had a pretence to interfere in a subject they have nothing to do with. Each state, so far as the clause in question does not interfere, must be left to the operation of its own principles.

There is a degree of jealousy which it is impossible to satisfy. Jealousy in a free government ought to be respected: But it may be carried to too great an extent. It is impracticable to guard against all *possible* danger of people's chusing their officers indiscreetly. If they have a right to chuse, they may make a bad choice. I met by accident with a pamphlet this morning, in which the author states as a very serious danger, that the Pope of Rome might be elected President. I confess this never struck me before, and if the author had read all the qualifications of a President, perhaps his fears might have been quieted. No man but a native, and who has resided fourteen years in America, can be chosen President. I know not all the qualifications for a Pope, but I believe he must be taken from the college of Cardinals, and probably there are many previous steps necessary before he arrives at this dignity. A native of America must have very singular good fortune, who after residing fourteen years in his own country, should go to Europe, enter into Romish orders, obtain the promotion of Cardinal, afterwards that of Pope, and at length be so much in the confidence of his own country, as to be elected President. It would be still more extraordinary if he should give up his Popedom for our Presidency. Sir, it is impossible to treat such idle fears with any degree of gravity. Why is it not objected, that there is no provision in the Constitution against electing one of the Kings of Europe President? It would be a clause equally rational and judicious.

I hope that I have in some degree satisfied the doubts of the gentleman [Henry Abbott]. This article is calculated to secure universal religious liberty, by putting all sects on a level, the only way to prevent persecution. I thought nobody would have objected to this clause, which deserves in my opinion the highest approbation. This country has already had the honour of setting an example of civil freedom, and I trust it will likewise have the honour of teaching the rest of the world the way to religious freedom also. God grant both may be perpetuated to the end of time.

1. Matthew 16:18: "And I say also unto thee, That thou art Peter, and upon this rock I will build my church; and the gates of hell shall not prevail against it."
2. Philip II, father of Alexander the Great.

David Caldwell: Speech in the North Carolina Convention 30 July 1788

Mr. *Caldwell* thought that some danger might arise. He imagined it might be objected to in a political as well as in a religious view. In the first place, he said there was an invitation for Jews, and Pagans of every kind, to come among us. At some future period, said he, this might endanger the character of the United States. Moreover, even those who do not regard religion, acknowledge that the Christian religion is best calculated of all religions to make good members of society, on account of its morality. I think then, added he, that in a political view, those gentlemen who formed this Constitution, should not have given this invitation to Jews and Heathens. All those who have any religion are against the emigration of those people from the eastern hemisphere.

Samuel Spencer: Speech in the North Carolina Convention
30 July 1788

Mr. *Spencer* was an advocate for securing every unalienable right, and that of worshipping God according to the dictates of conscience in particular. He therefore thought that no one particular religion should be established. Religious tests, said he, have been the foundation of persecutions in all countries. Persons who are conscientious will not take the oath required by religious tests, and will therefore be excluded from offices, though equally capable of discharging them as any member of the society. It is feared, continued he, that persons of bad principles, Deists, Atheists, &c. may come into this country, and there is nothing to restrain them from being eligible to offices. He asked if it was reasonable to suppose that the people would chuse men without regarding their characters. Mr. *Spencer* then continued thus—Gentlemen urge that the want of a test admits the most vicious characters to offices. I desire to know what test could bind them. If they were of such principles, it would not keep them from enjoying those offices. On the other hand, it would exclude from offices conscientious and truly religious people, though equally capable as others. Conscientious persons would not take such an oath, and would be therefore excluded. This would be a great cause of objection to a religious test. But in this case as there is not a religious test required, it leaves religion on the solid foundation of its own inherent validity, without any connexion with temporal authority, and no kind of oppression can take place. I confess it strikes me so. I am sorry to differ from the worthy gentleman [David Caldwell]. I cannot object to this part of the Constitution. I wish every other part was as good and proper.

William Lenoir: Speech in the North Carolina Convention
30 July 1788 (excerpts)[1]

Mr. *Lenoir*—Mr. Chairman, I conceive that I shall not be out of order to make some observations on this last part of the system, and take some retrospective view of some other parts of it. I think it not proper for our adoption, as I consider that it endangers our liberties. When we consider this system collectively, we must be surprised to think, that any set of men who were delegated to amend the Confederation, should propose to annihilate it. For that and this system are utterly different, and cannot exist together. It has been said that the fullest confidence should be put in those characters who formed this Constitution. We will admit them in private and public transactions to be good characters. But, Sir, it appears to me and every other Member of this committee, that they exceeded their powers. Those gentlemen had no sort of power to form a new Constitution altogether, neither had the citizens of this country such an idea in their view. I cannot undertake to say what principles actuated them. I must conceive they were mistaken in their politics, and that this system does not secure the unalienable rights of freemen. It has some aristocratical and some monarchical features, and perhaps some of them intended the establishment of one of these governments.[2] Whatever might be their intent, according to my views, it will lead to the most dangerous aristocracy that ever was thought of. An aristocracy established on a constitutional bottom!—I conceive (and I believe most of this committee will likewise) that this is so dangerous, that I should like as well to have no Constitution at all. Their powers are almost unlimited.

A Constitution ought to be understood by every one. The most humble and trifling characters in the country have a right to know what foundation they stand upon. I confess I do not see the end of the powers here proposed, nor the reasons for granting them. The principal end of a Constitution is to set forth what must be given up for the common benefit of the community at large, and to secure those rights which ought never to be infringed. The proposed plan secures no right, or if it does, it is in so vague and undeterminate a manner, that we do not understand it. My constituents instructed me to oppose the adoption of this Constitution. The principal reasons are as follow. The right of representation is not fairly and explicitly preserved to the people; it being easy to evade that privilege as provided in this system, and the terms of election being too long. If our General Assembly be corrupt, at the end of the year we can make new men of them by sending others in their stead.[3] It is not so here. If there be any reason to think that human nature is corrupt, and that there is a disposition in men to aspire to power, they may embrace an opportunity during their long continuance in office, by means of their powers, to take away the rights of the people. The Senators are chosen for six years, and two-thirds of them with the President have most extensive powers. They may enter into a dangerous combination. And they may be continually re-elected. The President may be as good a man as any in existence, but he is but a man. He may be corrupt. He has an opportunity of forming plans dangerous to the community at large. I shall not enter into the minutiæ of this system, but I conceive that whatever may have been the intention of its framers, that it leads to a most dangerous aristocracy. It appears to me that instead of securing the sovereignty of the states, it is calculated to melt them down into one solid empire. If the citizens of this state like a consolidated government, I hope they will have virtue enough to secure their rights. I am sorry to make use of the expression, but it appears to me to be a scheme to reduce this government to an aristocracy. It guarantees a republican form of government to the states; when all these powers are in Congress it will only be a form. It will be past recovery when Congress has the power of the purse and the sword. The power of the sword is in explicit terms given to it. The power of direct taxation gives the purse. They may prohibit the trial by jury, which is a most sacred and valuable right. There is nothing contained in this Constitution to bar them from it. The Federal Courts have also appellate cognizance of law and fact: the sole cause of which is to deprive the people of that trial, which it is optional in them to grant or not. We find no provision against infringement on the rights of conscience. Ecclesiastical courts may be established, which will be destructive to our citizens. They may make any establishment they think proper. They have also an exclusive legislation in their ten miles square, to which may be added their power over the militia, who may be carried thither and kept there for life. Should any one grumble at their acts, he would be deemed a traitor, and perhaps taken up and carried to the exclusive legislation, and there tried without a jury. We are told there is no cause to fear. When we consider the great powers of Congress, there is great cause of alarm. They can disarm the militia. If they were armed, they would be a resource against great oppressions. The laws of a great empire are difficult to be executed. If the laws of the union were oppressive they could not carry them into effect, if the people were possessed of proper means of defence. . . .

. . . There is no assurance of the liberty of the press. They may make it treason to write against the most arbitrary proceedings. . . .

I wish not to be so understood as to be so averse to this system, as that I should object to all parts of it, or attempt to reflect on the reputation of those gentlemen who formed it; though it appears to me that I would not have agreed to any proposal but the amendment of the Confederation. If there were any security for the liberty of the people, I would for my own part agree to it. But in this case, as millions yet unborn are concerned, and deeply interested in our decision, I would have the most positive and pointed security. I shall therefore hope that before this House will proceed to adopt this Constitution, they will propose such amendments to it, as will make it complete; and when amendments are adopted, perhaps I will be as ready to accede to it as any man—One thing will make it aristocratical. Its powers are very indefinite. There was a very necessary clause in the Confederation, which is omitted in this system. That was a clause declaring that every power, &c. not given to Congress, was reserved to the states.[4] The omission of this clause makes the power so much greater. Men will naturally put the fullest construction on the power given them. Therefore lay all restraint on them, and form a plan to be understood by every gentleman of this committee, and every individual of the community.

1. For the entire speech, see RCS:N.C., 411–15.
2. Possibly a reference to Alexander Hamilton's plan of government proposed in the Constitutional Convention on 18 June 1787 (CDR, 253–55).
3. Under the North Carolina constitution of 1776, members of the state Senate and House of Commons were to be chosen annually (RCS:N.C., 826).
4. Article II of the Articles of Confederation reserved to the states "every Power, Jurisdiction and right" that was not "expressly delegated" to the Confederation government (CDR, 86).

Richard Dobbs Spaight: Speech in the North Carolina Convention 30 July 1788 (excerpts)[1]

... The gentleman [William Lenoir] has insinuated, that this Constitution, instead of securing our liberties, is a scheme to enslave us. He has produced no proof, but rests it on his bare assertion—an assertion which I am astonished to hear, after the ability with which every objection has been fully and clearly refuted in the course of our debates. I am for my part conscious of having had nothing in view but the liberty and happiness of my country, and I believe every member of that Convention was actuated by motives equally sincere and patriotic....

... The gentleman has again brought on the trial by jury. The Federal Convention, Sir, had no wish to destroy the trial by jury. It was three or four days before them. There were a variety of objections to any one mode. It was thought impossible to fall upon any one mode, but what would produce some inconveniences. I cannot now recollect all the reasons given. Most of them have been amply detailed by other gentlemen here. I should suppose, that if the Representatives of twelve states, with many able lawyers among them, could not form any unexceptionable mode, this Convention could hardly be able to do it. As to the subject of religion, I thought what has been said would fully satisfy that gentleman and every other. No power is given to the general government to interfere with it at all. Any act of Congress on this subject would be an usurpation. No sect is preferred to another. Every man has a right to worship the Supreme Being in the manner he thinks proper. No test is required. All men of equal capacity and integrity, are equally eligible to offices. Temporal violence might make mankind wicked, but never religious. A test would enable the prevailing sect to persecute the rest. I do not suppose an Infidel, or any such person, will ever be chosen to any office unless the people themselves be of the same opinion. He says that Congress may establish ecclesiastical courts. I do not know what part of the Constitution warrants that assertion. It is impossible. No such power is given them. The gentleman [William Lenoir] advises such amendments as would satisfy him, and proposes a mode of amending before ratifying. If we do not adopt first, we are no more a part of the union than any foreign power. It will be also throwing away the influence of our state to propose amendments as the condition of our ratification. If we adopt first, our Representatives will have a proportionable weight in bringing about amendments, which will not be the case if we do not adopt. It is adopted by ten states already. The question then is, not whether the Constitution be good, but whether we will or will not confederate with the other states. . . . The gentleman [William Lenoir] supposes that the liberty of the press is not secured. The Constitution does not take it away. It says nothing of it, and can do nothing to injure it. But it is secured by the Constitution of every state in the union in the most ample manner.[2] . . .

1. For the entire speech, see RCS:N.C., 416–19.
2. This is not an accurate statement. At least four states—Rhode Island, Connecticut, New York, and New Jersey—did not have a constitutional provision protecting the liberty of the press. Rhode Island and Connecticut were still operating under their royal charters.

William Lancaster: Speech in the North Carolina Convention 30 July 1788 (excerpt)[1]

. . . How do we know that if we propose amendments they shall be obtained after actual ratification? May not these amendments be proposed with equal propriety, and more safety, as the condition of our adoption? If they violate the thirteenth article of the Confederation in this manner, may they not with equal propriety refuse to adopt amendments, although agreed to and wished for by two-thirds of the states?[2] This violation of the old system is a precedent for such proceedings as these. That would be a violation destructive to our felicity. We are now determining a question deeply affecting the happiness of millions yet unborn. It is the policy of freemen to guard their privileges. Let us then as far as we can exclude the possibility of tyranny. . . .

1. For the entire speech, see RCS:N.C., 420–23.
2. Article XIII of the Articles of Confederation provided that Congress could propose amendments which, to be adopted, needed to be ratified by all of the state legislatures.

Article V of the Constitution provided that two-thirds of the state legislatures could request that Congress call a convention for proposing amendments to the Constitution. Congress would then be required to call a convention. Three-fourths of state legislatures—or three-fourths of conventions in the states—would be necessary to ratify any proposed amendments.

Edward Carrington to William Short
New York, 26 July 1788 (excerpt)[1]

... We may now contemplate this Fabrick as erected, and permit me my dear Friend to congratulate you upon the event, so thorough a revolution was never before effected by Voluntary Convention, and it will stand as a lasting monument of a wisdom and congeniality peculiar to America. The system yet requires much to make it perfect, and I hope experience will be our guide in taking from or adding to it: there is however some reason to fear that alterations will be precipitated, so as to prevent some of the benefits which might result from trial. the oponents have acquiesced so far as to attempt nothing unconstitutionally, but, I apprehend it will now be their drift, to get into the Congress men who will promote the measure of a General convention at too early a period. I am persuaded that could the Government operate uninterrupted, for a few years, many of the visionary dangers which have been apprehended, would vanish, and in that time the real defects would be discovered & the remedies suggested....

1. RC, Short Papers, DLC. For the entire letter, see CC:817.

Marquis de Lafayette to Jeremiah Wadsworth
26 July 1788 (excerpt)[1]

... I am Happy thrice Happy to find that Eleven states Have already Adopted the Constitution—May they Be unanimous! I am a foederalist with all my Heart, and (altho I can't Help wishing a few Amendments to Be adopted, However superior Be the Constitution to Every thing that ever existed) I think that America is taking the only way to insure Her own Consequence and prosperity—it seems to me a trader, Circumstanced as you were, that a work so Excellence and so Convenience to all the states may Have Been formed—should some Additions or Alterations take place, I fancy it will Be in the first Congress....

1. RC, Governor Jonathan Trumbull Collection, Connecticut State Library.

New York Convention Recommends Amendments to Constitution
26 July 1788

For the amendments recommended by the New York Convention, see BoR, I, 256–64.

James McHenry to George Washington
Baltimore, Md., 27 July 1788[1]

My dear General,

It is whispered here that some leading characters among you have by no means dropped their resentment to the new constitution, but have determined on some secret plan to suspend the proper organization of the government or to defeat it altogether. This is so serious and alarming a circumstance that it is necessary to be apprised of its truth and extent that we may be on our guard against attempts of the antifederals to get into our assembly, as in all probability the next legislature will meet before the time for commencing proceedings by the new Congress. Here every means is made use of to do away all distincting between federal and antifederal and I suspect with no very friendly design to the federal cause. If such a plan has been hatched I think you must have heard of it. I shall therefore be much obliged to you to give me a hint of it as soon as possible.

With great respect and sincere attachment I am Dr. General Yours

1. RC, Washington Papers, DLC. Washington replied to this letter on 31 July (BoR, III, 126-27).

Thomas Jefferson to James Madison
Paris, 31 July 1788 (excerpt)[1]

... I sincerely rejoice at the acceptance of our new constitution by nine states. it is a good canvas, on which some strokes only want retouching. what these are I think are sufficiently manifested by the general voice from North to South, which calls for a bill of rights. it seems pretty generally understood that this should go to Juries, Habeas corpus, Standing armies, Printing, Religion & Monopolies.

I conceive there may be difficulty in finding general modification of these suited to the habits of all the states. but if such cannot be found then it is better to establish trials by Jury, the right of Habeas corpus, freedom of the press, & freedom of religion in all cases, and to abolish standing armies in time of peace, and Monopolies, in all cases, than not to do it in any. the few cases wherein these things may do evil, cannot be weighed against the multitude wherein the want of them will do evil. in disputes between a foreigner & a native, a trial by jury may be improper, but if this exception cannot be agreed to the remedy will be to model the jury by giving the medietas Anquae[2] in civil as well as criminal cases. why suspend the Hab. corp. in insurrections & rebellions? the parties who may be arrested may be charged instantly with a well defined crime. of course the judge will remand them. if the publick safety requires that the government should have a man imprisoned on less probable testimony in those than in other emergencies; let him be taken & tried, retaken & retried, while the necessity continues, only giving him redress against the government for damages. examine the history of England. see how few of the cases of the suspension of the Habeas corpus law have been worthy of that suspension. they have been either real treasons wherein the parties might as well have been charged at once, or sham-plots where it was shameful they should ever have been suspected. yet for the few cases wherein the suspension of the hab. corp. has done real good, the operation is now become habitual, & the minds of the nation almost prepared to live under it's constant suspension. a declaration that the federal government will never restrain the presses from printing any thing they please, will not take away the liability of the printers for false facts printed. the declaration that religious faith shall be unpunished, does not give impunity to criminal acts dictated by religious error. the saying there shall be no monopolies lessens the incitements to ingenuity, which is spurred on by the hope of a monopoly for a limited time, as of 14 years; but the benefit even of limited monopolies is too doubtful to be opposed to that of their general suppression. if no check can be found to keep the number of standing troops within safe bounds, while they are tolerated as far as necessary, abandon them altogether. discipline well the militia, & guard the magazines with them. more than magazine-guards will be useless if few, & dangerous if many. no European nation can ever send against us such a regular army as we need fear, & it is hard if our militia are not equal to those of Canada or Florida. my idea then is, that tho' proper exceptions to these general rules are desireable & probably practicable, yet if the exceptions cannot be agreed on, the establishment of the rules in all cases will do ill in very few. I hope therefore a bill of rights will be formed to guard the people against their state governments in most instances. the abandoning the principle of necessary rotation in the Senate, has I see been disregarded by many; in the case of the President, by none. I readily therefore suppose my opinion wrong, when opposed by the majority as in the former instance, & the totality as in the latter. in this however I should have done it with more complete satisfaction, had we all judged from the same position....

1. RC, Madison Papers, DLC. For the entire letter, see Rutland, *Madison*, XI, 210–14.
2. Latin legal term: notwithstanding the verdict.

George Washington to James McHenry
Mount Vernon, Fairfax County, Va., 31 July 1788[1]

In reply to your recent favour,[2] which has been duly received, I can only observe; that, as I never go from home except when I am obliged by necessary avocations, and as I meddle as little as possible with politics that my interference may not give occasion for impertinent imputations, so I am less likely than almost any person to have been informed of the circumstance to which you allude. That some of the leading characters among the Opponents [of] the proposed government have not laid aside their ideas of obtaining great and essential changes, through a constitutional opposition, (as they term it) may be collected from their public speeches. That others will use more secret and, perhaps, insidious means to prevent its organization may be presumed from their previous conduct on the subject. In addition to this probability, the casual information received from Visitants at my house, would lead me to expect that a considerable effort will be made to procure the election of Antifederalists to the first Congress; in order to bring the subject immediately before the State legislators, to open an extensive correspondence between the minorities for obtaining alterations, and in short to undo all that has been done. It is reported that a respectable Neighbour of mine has said, the Constitution cannot be carried in execution, without great amendments.[3] But I will freely do the opposition with us the Justice to declare, that I have heard of no cabals or canvassings respecting the elections. It is said to be otherwise on your side of the river. By letters from the eastern States I am induced to believe the Minorities have acquiesced not only with a good grace, but also with a serious design to give the government a fair chance to discover its operation by being carryed into effect. I hope and trust that the same liberal disposition prevails with a large proportion of the same description of men in this State. Still, I think there will be great reason, for those who are well-affected to the government, to use their utmost exertions that the worthiest Citizens may be appointed to the two houses of the first Congress and where State Elections take place previous to this choice that the same principle govern in these also. For much will doubtless depend on their prudence in conducting business at the beginning; and reconciling discordant dispositions to a reasonable acquiescence with candid and honest measures. At the same time it will be a point of no common delicacy to make provision for effecting such explanations and amendments as might be really proper and generally satisfactory; without producing or at least fostering such a spirit of innovation as will overturn the whole system.

I earnestly pray that the Omnipotent Being who hath not deserted the cause of America in the hour of its extremest hazard; will never yeild so fair a heritage of freedom a prey to *Anarchy* or *Despotism*.

1. FC, Washington Papers, DLC.
2. See McHenry's letter of 27 July (BoR, III, 124).
3. A reference to George Mason whose residence, Gunston Hall, was about six miles south of Mount Vernon on the Potomac River in Fairfax County, Virginia.

Ezra Stiles to John Adams
Yale College, New Haven, Conn., 1 August 1788 (excerpt)[1]

... I have received great Instruction from your learned Labors,[2] which will do more, I believe, towards leading & directg the Inquiries of american & European Politicians to a thoro Examination of the antient & modern Politics in Europe, & thence to learn what Government human Nature can & cannot bear, than any publication hitherto made. We have needed and at this Time specially need the very Lights you have furnished. I thank you for your learned Labors.

As sincerely as any Man in America did I rejoyce in your safe Return & Arrival to our native Country;[3] where may the Gd of Heaven make you an extensive & lastg Blessing & Ornament. I rejoyce in the Accession of Eleven States to the federal Government—and I do not wish it to be revised these dozen or 20 years; nor until we shall by cool Experience know & find out what Revisions are either neccessy or expedient. That Amendments in the Polity are necessy I believe; but I wish for Time & Coolness of Reflexion & sage Wisdom to discover & make them.

I believe we shall be a happy & glorious People—& that greater Wisdom of Policy & jurisprudential Sagacity will be displayed in the political Arrangmts Regulations & Institutions of the United States than has ever been displayed among the despotic Sovereignties of Europe or Asia, which have been dictated by & f[or]med in military Conquests or the insidious Intrigues of Policy over Nations unenlightened by the Sciences, Literature, & large Acquaintance with the Histories of all Ages & Nations. It is my Wish that Gen Wash may be President, & Dr Adams Vice-President under the new fœderal Government. But whether it shd be so or not, p[er]mit me to express my Wishes that every Blessg of Heaven may rest upon you. With the most respectful Esteem & would you Accept from me a share in the Tribute of Gratitude from my Country.

1. RC, Adams Papers, MHi. For the entire letter, see the *Papers of John Adams*, XIX, 329–30.

2. A reference to Adams's three-volume *A Defence of the Constitutions of Government of the United States of America* . . . (London, 1787-1788). See CC:16.

3. John and Abigail Adams arrived in Boston from England on 17 June 1788.

A Real German
Maryland Journal, 1 August 1788 (excerpts)[1]

Mr. GODDARD, *You will be pleased to give the enclosed Dialogue a place in your useful and entertaining Paper.*

Yours, &c.

July 31, 1788. A REAL GERMAN.

A DIALOGUE. . . .

ANTI. I hope, however, neighbour, you will admit, that the federal constitution wants amendments.

FEDERAL. And I hope, neighbour, you will admit, that one of the men you want me to vote for, has said a hundred times over, it was so bad it could not be mended. I'll tell you, however, I am for *federal amendments*; but I am against *antifederal amendments*. I am for getting your true federalists to mend it, who will endeavour to make it better; but if we were to employ antifederalists, I am sure they would try hard to make it worse. Set the antifederalists to work upon it, and it will fare with us as it did with the owner of an excellent watch, who sent it to a roguish artist to be regulated. The fellow had no sooner got it into his hands, than, under pretext of cleaning it, he took out all the *new wheels*, and put in old ones in their room; so that altho' the watch looked to be the same, it never went right a single day after, or gave the least satisfaction to the owner. It's an ill procession where the Devil holds the candle; and a foolish sheep that makes the *wolf* his *confessor*.

1. This dialogue, without the prefatory statement, was also printed in the Baltimore *Maryland Gazette* on 1 August.

Comte de Moustier to Comte de Montmorin
New York, 2 August 1788 (excerpts)[1]

The State of Newyork on the 25th of last month finally acceded to the new Constitution, which is now adopted by eleven States. The recommended amendments[2] are so numerous and so important that if the new Congress takes them into account, this Constitution will barely resemble its first form. However, a great blow has been dealt to the individual Sovereignty of the States taken separately. The phantom of Democracy that has seduced the people is about to disappear. The credulous majority, intoxicated by the noblest hopes that it allowed itself to be fed, has itself forged the bonds by which sooner or later the Leaders of the people will be able to subjugate and control them after having appeared to want to obey them. The Constitution is taken on approval until a better one is found. This tendency always to perfect is infinitely favorable to the designs of the ambitious, who, by means of alterations, will manage to weary the American people and make them receive with indifference the yoke that is prepared for them and that they will probably endure much more patiently than expected. The proposed amendments offer a multitude of pretexts at the outset even for a reorganization of Government. This means is open to various parties. It is not doubted that each will profit from it according to its views. . . .

As soon as the decision of North Carolina is known, I will have the honor to send You in the same packet, My Lord, the Constitution as it has been proposed by the general Convention, with the comparison of the different amendments proposed by the individual Conventions. I will separate this statement from the observations that I propose to have the honor of submitting to You on the influence of the Constitution on the foreign policy of the United States and on the probabilities of the system that can prevail in this respect. . . .

1. RC (Tr), Correspondance Politique, États-Unis, Vol. 33, ff. 238–41, Archives du Ministère des Affaires Étrangères, Paris. This is dispatch number 18 and was received on 26 September. For the entire letter, see CC:820.
2. For New York's proposed amendments, see BoR, I, 256–64.

First North Carolina Convention Recommends Amendments to Constitution, 2 August 1788

For the amendments recommended by the North Carolina Hillsborough Convention, see BoR, I, 264–70.

Pamphlet Compilation of the Amendments Proposed by the State Conventions, Richmond, Va., post-2 August 1788

Probably at the suggestion of Edmund Randolph, Augustine Davis, the printer of the *Virginia Independent Chronicle* and the postmaster of Richmond, compiled the proposed amendments in a thirty-two-page pamphlet entitled *The Ratification of the New Fœderal Constitution, Together with the Amendments, Proposed by the Several States* that was published in Richmond some time after the adjournment of the North Carolina Convention (Evans 21529). For the amendments, see BoR, I, 231–77.

Tench Coxe to Robert Smith
Philadelphia, 5 August 1788 (excerpt)[1]

... I am of opinion you are very judiciously employed in Maryland in securing sincere, firm and intelligent federalists for state Representatives. Very much will depend upon the legislatures chosen this year, on the score of Amendments. I also saw Mr. M. [i.e., James Madison] several times on his way thro this city, and found him strongly impressed with the Opinions you mention, and I have since heard from him. I find appearances & information at N. Yk have heightened his belief, and strengthened his Opinion of the necessity of Exertions on our part. His words are somewhat particular—"The combination against direct taxes is *more extensive & more formidable* than some gentlemen suspect. It is clearly seen by the Enemies to the Constitution, that an abolition of that power will re-establish the Supremacy of the state legislatures, *the real object* of all their Zeal in opposing the System."[2]

I have observed, from the adoption of Virga. till this time a strong *profession* of acquiescence in some very cool and artful men, who till then were in the opposition: and it [is] striking that they never enumerate their points of Amendment, without taking in direct taxes, which they say will be impracticable sometimes, & sometimes improper. The persons I allude to are of weight in our federal general politics, and in our Western Counties, but here are lost. They however are formidable for their talents, information, and especially for their political Industry.

A Combination was taken up in the back parts & centre of Pennsa. for the purpose of obtaining amendments in concert with the Opposition in New York, who were then supposed to have an absolute Command in that State. They proposed to meet at Harrisburg, and meant to term themselves a Convention. The unexpected Adoption by the Convention of N Yk. has staggerd them a good deal, but I do not think they will drop their Measures, tho they may be less extravagant and assuming for that check—

A fact of a very curious Nature occurd to me about the time Virginia was determining. Some little question arose in Conversation between a strong & sensible Opponent and myself on the probable nature of the Virginia amendments, as they would be proposed to Congress. We thought differently on them, when he made this remark. "It is not worth making a question about the Amendments for I have *a copy of them in my pocket*." It is but a single fact, but it comes in confirmation of the many Symptoms of *concert* in this plan, which are daily presenting themselves.

On the whole, Sir, I am clearly of Opinion, that the fixed aversion of some to the Government, & the pliancy of temper and want of sufficient apprehension and perception of danger in many, who are disposed to favor it render it necessary to keep up a vigilant attention, a strong and constant Exertion, and to observe a firm and decided, tho a mild deportment towards the Opposition. I would do every thing that could be done, & trust Nothing to the chapter of Accidents. Above all things I would not think too favorably of the Views of the Opposition, nor too lightly of their Exertions or their Strength.—Put in only such men as will not swerve, under any temptations, from maint[a]ining the Energy of the Government—

The enclosed paper addressed to our Western Inhabitants is calculated to remove some very gross errors and prejudices. From Hartford [County] back it may have some Effect in Maryland,[3] and I find the last argument about the representation thought well of in many places. Tis a simple stile, calculated to be understood, where education blesses but few and in a small degree.—I wish you may think it worth republishing. Our principal inducement to it was to shew the opposition, that tho we were successful, we were not disposed to cease from exertion, while a prejudice remained to be done away.

1. FC, Coxe Papers, Series II, Correspondence and General Papers, PHi.
2. A reference to Madison's 30 July letter to Coxe (Rutland, *Madison*, XI, 210).
3. A reference to "A Friend to Society and Liberty," *Pennsylvania Gazette*, 23 July, which was reprinted in the *Maryland Journal* on 12 August (CC:813).

Westmoreland County, Pa., Desires Amendments, 5 August 1788

Proceedings of a Meeting at Greensburg, Pa., 5 August 1788[1]

At a Meeting of a number of Freemen, Inhabitants of the different Townships in the County of Westmoreland, held at Greensburg the 5th day of August, 1788.

JOHN MOORE, Esquire
Was unanimously chosen to the Chair.

Upon motion being made, it was resolved unanimously, That it is the duty of this meeting, to endeavour to procure several amendments to the plan proposed for the general government of the United States, by the late federal convention, and now adopted by the conventions of ten states.

Resolved unanimously, That a committee, consisting of seven persons, be chosen by this meeting to correspond with the different counties of this state, respecting the most proper method of procuring those amendments, in connection with other states, and according to the method laid down in the said plan of general government.

Resolved, That captain Thomas Morton, Christopher Truby, esq; William Jack, esq; Christopher Lovinguire, col. John Shields, Charles Campbell, esq; and James Brison, be a standing committee of correspondence for the aforesaid purpose.

Resolved, That the aforesaid committee, with the chairman, be requested to receive and take charge of the minutes of this meeting.

JOHN MOORE, Chairman.

Amendments Proposed by Westmoreland County Committee post-5 August 1788[2]

A Committee having been chosen at a meeting held in Greensburgh, for the county of Westmoreland, on the 5th day of August, and authorized to correspond with other counties of this state, respecting the propriety of joining with other states in endeavouring to procure amendments to the constitution for the general government of the United States; and the respective citizens present at the said meeting, having unanimously voted that amendments were necessary, and the committee having received letters on the subject, think it their duty to express their own sentiments, and what they believe to be the prevailing sentiments of the people of the county of Westmoreland on this important subject.

They profess to possess sentiments compleatly federal, and do believe that no other than a federal republican form of government can secure political liberty in an empire so extensive as the United States. They are also fully convinced of the necessity of vesting more extensive powers in Congress, than it could exercise under the confederation, consequently they heartily approve of vesting the general government with every power and resource which is of a general nature, and which is generally relating to all the states; such as imposts or duties arising from importation, regulation of commerce, treaties of all sorts, armies, navies, coin, post-office, &c. &c. but they regret that the general government goes much farther than these federal principles will admit, and vests Congress with such extensive local powers, in addition to the necessary general powers, as must eventually destroy the state governments, and absorb the whole sovereignty; consequently prove to be one entire consolidated government, which in our extensive situation must be a despotic one. They therefore wish that it may be expressly stipulated, that Congress shall not assume or exercise any further or other powers than what is expressly defined and clearly vested therein by the express words of the constitution. Secondly, they consider the representation to be disproportioned to the powers wherewith the government is vested, not only because the representatives are too few in number to have that knowledge of and common interest with the people at large, which is essential to political safety, but also because the smallness of the number, together with the greatness of the powers and privileges which the new Congress will possess, will subject the members to the greatest temptation to corruption and undue influence: they therefore [propose] the representatives to be encreased to one to thirty thousand at least, and regularly proportioned to certain districts to be described by the state legislatures; and also that Congress may not be vested with the unnecessary and dangerous powers of lessening their own numbers, and consequently exercising the supreme power, by as few hands as ambition or corruption may see fit. Thirdly, They further consider the power of regulating elections as vested by the new general government, to be unsafely lodged; they apprehend these powers, especially to the place and manner, to be only competent for the state governments, where the most equal and most responsible representation, in the very nature of things will always be found, and where there can be no interest in abusing the powers to dangerous purposes. They conceive this power is not necessary to the general government for any good purpose, but seems rather calculated to secure and promote a corrupt and dangerous influence in the hands of Congress over the election of its own members, highly dangerous to the essential rights of a free people; therefore, they earnestly wish a revision of this part of the general government. Fourthly, They also observe, that the extensive and unlimited powers of internal taxation, added to the resources of the general government, must be in their operation entirely subversive of the state governments, and that this vested without any constitutional check or controul, are sufficient means of absolute power in the most extensive sense, if those who occupy the government think proper to make use of them for that purpose, and we ought not to trust more than is necessary to future men and future measures; but more particularly they wish that Congress may not be vested with the power of levying internal direct taxes upon the citizens of any state, unless when such states proves obstinately delinquent; nor even then to have the power of levying poll taxes as they are in their nature unequal and always oppressive, as they go to tax not only the poor individuals, but the poor and remote counties equal with the more wealthy and more valuable situations. They wish to have the powers of levying excise defined, so that it may be known what the particulars are the citizens eat, drink or wear, which shall be subject to excise.—Fifthly, They apprehend that the unlimited power of having standing armies in time of peace, especially as combined with the power over every source of revenue is inconsistent with the principles of a federal republican government, & the freedom of the citizens; they therefore earnestly recommend, that if keeping standing armies in time of peace should be thought necessary, the power should be put under such checks, as to secure the liberty of the community at large, and the personal safety of individuals; and this they conceive may be accomplished by rendering a majority of three-fourths of the senate and house of representatives agreeing to the necessity and propriety of raising a standing army in time of peace necessary, and by keeping the military in due subordination to the civil law. Sixthly, They conceive that by so imperfect a bill or declaration of rights as the new plan of general government contains, whereby the trial by jury in criminal cases, the habeus corpus act, &c. only is secured; trial by jury in civil cases, and every other essential right of freemen is impliedly given up to the arbitrary will of future men. They therefore wish that such a declaration of rights may be added to the general frame of government as may secure to posterity those privileges which are essential to the proper limiting the extent of sovereign power, and securing those rights which are essential to freemen; and that Congress may not have power to pass any laws which in their effects may infringe on or tend to subvert the constitution of any particular state, except in such cases as are mentioned in the first clause to be of a general nature, and properly belonging to Congress. Seventhly, They further observe, that the undue mixture of legislative and executive powers in the senate is highly corrupting in its nature, and dangerous to liberty in its influence; and that the power of putting the militia under the terrors of martial law in time of peace, or of marching them, perhaps, to destroy the freedom of an oppressed sister state, without any check or controul from the state governments, stand also in absolute need of revision and amendments.

The foregoing particulars the committee have tho't proper to point out as amongst the most obvious exceptionable powers vested by the new system of general government in the future Congress: at the same time they believe that the people of the county of Westmoreland are willing to concur with such further, or other amendments, as shall render the proposed plan a government of freedom, confidence and energy.

WILLIAM JACK, Chairman.

1. Printed: *Pittsburgh Gazette*, 9 August. Reprinted: Pennsylvania *Carlisle Gazette*, 20 August; *Pennsylvania Mercury*, 23 August; Baltimore *Maryland Gazette*, 2 September; and *Virginia Herald*, 4 September.

2. Printed: *Pittsburgh Gazette*, 20 September. Reprinted: Philadelphia *Freeman's Journal*, 24 September; Philadelphia *Independent Gazetteer*, 25 September; and *New York Morning Post*, 1 October.

Pennsylvania Gazette, 6 August 1788[1]

The *alterations* (not amendments) of the fœderal constitution proposed by the Convention of New-York, says a correspondent, are so numerous, that if it were possible to admit them, they would annihilate the constitution, and throw the United States not only back again into anarchy, but introduce poverty, misery, bloodshed and slavery into every state in the union. The authors of these alterations would do well to put on match coats and associate with the lawless Indians who inhabit the borders of the western lakes. They have not sense enough to frame, or understand a system of government fit for a civilized nation.

1. Reprints by 4 October (15): Mass. (3), R.I. (1), Conn. (2), N.Y. (1), N.J. (1), Pa. (2), Md. (1), Va. (2), Ga. (2). See BoR, III, 144 for a criticism of this piece that appeared in the Philadelphia *Independent Gazetteer*, 16 August.

Abraham B. Bancker to Evert Bancker
Kingston, N.Y., 9 August 1788 (excerpts)[1]

Hond. sir

... I ... Expect soon to be called upon again in the Capacity of Clk. of Senate as the Adoption of the New Constitution will render a fall Meeting necessary in Order to forward the Movements of the new Government, and dont doubt but the new Congress will find it necessary in Order to preserve peace and good Order in several of the States, in their first out set to Submit the several Amendments to the Consideration of another General Convention—Our Convention have called upon the Sister States for the purpose and I hope their request will meet with the wished for Success, that Order may take place of our present Confusion and Strength be added to our present Weakness....
Your Ever Affectionate Son ...

1. RC, Bancker Family Papers, NHi. Evert Bancker indicated that this letter was received on 14 August and answered the next day. The address page indicated that the letter was "favd. by Capt. Garret D Witt."

Thomas Jefferson to James Monroe
Paris, 9 August 1788 (excerpt)[1]

... I heartily rejoice that 9 states have accepted the new constitution. as yet we do not hear what Virginia, N. Carolina & N. York have done, & we take for granted R. isld. is against it. this constitution forms a basis which is good, but not perfect. I hope the states will annex to it a bill of rights securing those which are essential against the federal government; particularly trial by jury, habeas corpus, freedom of religion, freedom of the press, freedom against monopolies, & no standing armies. I see so general a demand of this that I trust it will be done. there is another article of which I have no hopes of amendment because I do not find it objected to in the states. this is the abandonment of the principle of necessary rotation in the Senate & Presidency. with respect to the last particularly it is as universally condemned in Europe, as it is universally unanimadverted on in America. I have never heard a single person here speak of it without condemnation, because on the supposition that a man being once chosen will be always chosen, he is a king for life, & his importance will produce the same brigues[2] & cabals foreign & domestic which the election of a king of Poland and other elective monarchies have ever produced, so that we must take refuge in the end in hereditary monarchy, the very evil which grinds to atoms the people of Europe. . . .

1. RC, Monroe Papers, NN. For the entire letter, see Boyd, XIII, 488–90.
2. The noun brigues meant plot, intrigue, or faction. As a verb it means "to engage in plots or intrigues; to solicit or canvass, esp. for election, in an underhand way" (OED).

New Hampshire President John Langdon to Governor George Clinton
Portsmouth, N.H., 11 August 1788[1]

I had the honour a few days since of receiving a letter of 26th Ult. from the Convention of your State[2] in which was Inclosed the ratification of the proposed Constitution for the United States, by the important State of New-York; both which shall be laid before the legislature of this State at their next Session, and I have no doubt the Amendments proposed by the Convention of your State will be taken into their Consideration and every proper Step taken that may be tho't necessary to promote that national Harmony, and good Government which is so earnestly sought after by ev[e]ry honest man. I shall not be wanting in my feeble endeavors to promote this desireable Object.

1. RC, Conarroe Papers, PHi.
2. The copy of the New York circular letter sent to the president of New Hampshire is in the Peter Force Miscellany at the Library of Congress. For the circular letter, see BoR, I, 153–58.

James Madison to George Washington
New York, 11 August 1788 (excerpt)[1]

. . . You will have seen the circular letter from the Convention of this State.[2] It has a most pestilent tendency. If an Early General Convention cannot be parried, it is seriously to be feared that the system which has resisted so many direct attacks may be at last successfully undermined by its enemies. It is now perhaps to be wished that Rho. Island may not accede till this new crisis of danger be over. Some think it would have been better if even N. York had held out till the operation of the Government could have dissipated the fears which artifice had created and the attempts resulting from those fears & artifices. We hear nothing yet from N. Carolina more than comes by the way of Petersburg.

1. RC, Washington Papers, DLC. Printed: CC:824. Madison's copy (Madison Papers, DLC) is misdated 15 August. On 11 August, Madison wrote a similar letter to Virginia Governor Edmund Randolph (Rutland, *Madison*, XI, 227–29).

2. For the New York Convention's circular letter dated 26 July 1788, see BoR, I, 153–58.

Thomas Jefferson to William Carmichael
Paris, 12 August 1788 (excerpt)[1]

Since my last to you, I have been honoured with your's of the 18th. and 29th. of May and 5th. of June. My latest American intelligence is of the 24th. of June when 9. certainly and probably 10. states had accepted the new constitution, and there was no doubt of the 11th. (North Carolina) because there was no opposition there. In New-York ⅔ of the state was against it, and certainly if they had been called to the decision in any other stage of the business, they would have rejected it. But before they put it to the vote, they would certainly have heard that 11. states had joined in it, and they would find it safer to go with those 11. than put themselves into opposition with Rhode island only. Tho' I am much pleased with this succesful issue of the new constitution, yet I am more so to find that one of it's principal defects (the want of a Declaration of rights) will pretty certainly be remedied. I suppose this, because I see that both people and Conventions in almost every state have concurred in demanding it. Another defect, the perpetual re-eligibility of the same president, will probably not be cured during the life of General Washington. His merit has blinded our countrymen to the dangers of making so important an officer re-eligible. I presume there will not be a vote against him in the U.S. . . .

1. FC, Jefferson Papers, DLC. For the entire letter, see Boyd, XIII, 502–3.

Edmund Randolph to James Madison
Richmond, Va., 13 August 1788[1]

Inclosed are the first two numbers of the Republican, according to your request.[2]

Govr. Clinton's letter[3] to me for the calling of a convention is this day published by my order. It will give contentment to many, who are now dissatisfied. The problem of a new convention has many difficulties in its solution. But upon the whole, I believe the assembly of Virginia *perhaps* ought, and probably will concur in urging it. It is not too early;

because it will only incorporate the theory of the people with the theory of the convention; & each of these theories is entitled to equal respect. I do indeed fear, that the constitution may be enervated; if some states should prevail in all their amendments; but if such be the will of America, who can withstand it? For my own part, I fear that direct taxation may be too much weakened. But I can only endeavour to avert that particular evil, and cannot persuade myself to thwart a second convention merely from the apprehension of that evil—This letter will probably carry me sooner into the assembly, than I intended.[4] I will prepare a draught upon this subject, and forward a copy to you, as soon as I can. My object will be (if possible) to prevent instructions from being conclusive, if any should be offered, and to leave the conventioners perfectly free—

The Marquis of Condor[c]et has sent me some strictures on the constitution. But they do not appear to me to have a better title to notice, than the liberties of the Abbe Mably concerning America[5]—

No. Carolina has rejected by a large majority. The fact may be relied on; tho' nothing official has come to hand.

1. RC, Madison Papers, DLC. For Madison's reply of 22 August, see BoR, III, 145–46.
2. See BoR, III, 87–90, for "Republican" I, *Virginia Independent Chronicle*, 16 July 1788. On 22 July Madison asked Randolph to send him the essays (Rutland, *Madison*, XI, 191–92).
3. For the New York Convention's circular letter dated 26 July, see BoR, I, 153–58.
4. Randolph resigned as governor in November to enter the Virginia House of Delegates.
5. Abbé de Mably, *Observations sur le Gouvernement et les lois des États-Unis* . . . (Amsterdam, 1784).

Pennsylvania Gazette, 13 August 1788[1]

The *impertinent* letter sent by the late Convention of New-York to all the states,[2] urging what they *impudently* call amendments in the new constitution, merits the severest treatment from all the friends of good government. It holds out the total annihilation of every useful and wise part of the constitution. The only design of these supposed amendments is to continue a few New-York speculators and land-jobbers in office, who have imposed upon an ignorant but well meaning majority in the convention. Nothing proves this more than the enmity these official certificate and land-brokers shewed to the government *before* it was published.[3] Let the government have a fair tryal. If it should be found faulty, the *faults* will soon shew themselves, and they may be amended. Fortunately for the United States, *six* states have adopted the constitution without a wish for a single alteration. If they continue firm, no alteration can be made until an experiment has been tried with the government. This experiment will certainly be favourable to it, for the demands for alterations in a great majority of the disaffected have arisen from *ignorance* only, which the operations of government will remove in a few years.

1. Reprinted thirteen times by 28 August: N.H. (1), Mass. (4), R.I. (1), Conn. (3), Pa. (1), Md. (1), Va. (2). For a criticism of this piece, see the Philadelphia *Independent Gazetteer*, 16 August (BoR, III, 144).

2. For the New York Convention's Circular Letter, see BoR, I, 153-58.

3. While the Constitutional Convention was still in session, some Federalists attacked state officeholders, especially in Pennsylvania and New York, who they believed would oppose the new Constitution that the Convention was expected to adopt. One such state officeholder was Governor George Clinton of New York, who was accused by Convention delegate Alexander Hamilton, in an anonymous article in the New York *Daily Advertiser*, 21 July 1787, of trying to prejudice the people of New York against any proposals made by the Convention. "A Republican" denied the charge in an article in the *New York Journal*, 6 September. (See RCS:N.Y., 11-14, 16-20, for both essays.)

Martin's North Carolina Gazette, 13 August 1788[1]

It is to be expected that the first business that will come before Congress will be the amendments to the Constitution, that have been recommended by the conventions of several of the states that have adopted it. Very little doubt can be entertained of the success of the advocates of the amendments, when we reflect that a majority of the members who will compose the new Congress, will be strictly and absolutely bound, not only to vote in favor of, but to exert their abilities and use all legal means to support, those amendments.

The states which have proposed amendments, and the number of their representatives are as follow:

New-Hampshire	3
Massachusetts	8
New-York	6
Virginia	10
South-Carolina	5
In all	32

The states that have adopted it without proposing amendments, and the number of their representatives, are as follow:

Connecticut	5
New-Jersey	4
Pennsylvania	8
Delaware	1
Maryland	6
Georgia	3
In all	27

Majority for the amendments 5.

It is further to be believed that the greater number of the representatives of the last mentioned states, the people of which had scarcely the time to read the federal constitution, before they were called upon to vote for delegates, will see the necessity of securing the rights and liberties of their constituents from the encroachments to which a door is opened, by the ambiguous and indefinite expressions in which so large a share of power is granted away.

1. *Martin's North Carolina Gazette*, 13 August is not extant. The transcription was taken from the reprinting in the *Georgia State Gazette*, 11 October, under the dateline "NEWBERN, *August* 13."

Thomas B. Wait to George Thatcher
Portland, Maine, 15 August 1788 (excerpt)[1]

... New York hath at length adopted the Constitution—at which I am greatly rejoiced—But what a spirit of Liberty, of republican jealousy has the Convention discovered—I am charmed with the Form of Ratification—You laugh at a Bill of Rights; but should one ever be annexed to the Constitution, I will fall down, and may worship it.—

No people under Heaven are so well acquainted with the natural rights of mankind, with the rights that ever ought to be reserved in all civil compacts, as are the people of America—Nor perhaps will Americans, themselves be so well acquainted at a future day with those rights as they now are.—During the last fifteen or twenty years, it has been the business of the ablest Politicians (Politicians too, who were contending for the liberties of the people) to discover "and draw a line between those rights which may be reserved"—If not the whole truth, yet, many great truths have been discovered, are now fresh in our minds, and I think
OUGHT TO BE RECORDED.—

The people are now masters of the subject, and should be as explicit with respect to those rights they mean to reserve, as were the Convention with regard to those rights that are to be given up—The same instrument that conveys the weapon, should reserve the shield—should continue, not only the powers of the rulers, but also the defence of the people.—

Politick—ex. . . .

1. RC, Thatcher Papers, MB.

"X"

Connecticut Gazette, 15 August 1788[1]

To their Excellencies the Governors of the several United States of America.

May it please your Excellencies,

I Observe that the late Convention of the State of New-York, have requested a new Continental Convention to be called, in order to take into consideration the proposed amendments, and make a revision of the new Constitution. I have been told by the rules of war, upon the approach of any enemy, it is justifiable in the meanest subject to give the alarm. I can have no conception that those gentlemen who composed that Convention, expected to have any notice taken of their circular letter[2] by your Excellencies, further than a polite answer in the negative; otherwise, though an obscure individual in private life, I should, for myself, view that requisition with that contempt which I think it deserves. I would ever wish to consider New-York in that important scale in which they ought to stand; that is, as a very considerable & valuable member: but they must not have the impudence or expectation to dictate to the union. I observe they conclude that they are the only expositors of the articles in the new Constitution, and that no different construction must hereafter ever be put any of them, by the united wisdom of the continent. May it please your Excellencies, be ye not deceived, if they mean or expect any thing, they certainly mean and expect, from the contrariety of interests, manners, and customs in the different States, (which we all know create prejudices that are difficult to be removed) to procure a delay, increase dissentions, and in the end effect a total destruction of the grand system, and thence reap profit to themselves. And should a new Convention be called, depend upon it that their delegates will go armed with every art and finesse, to increase the natural difficulties, and if possible render them incurable; and at any rate they will gain something by procrastination: one year's delay will give them a further opportunity to fill their pockets out of their neighbours by the impost;[3] in which time many incidents may arise, that will assist them in obstructing or overthrowing our glorious fabric. The present Constitution has made ample provision for alterations and emendations; and whenever conviction or experience shall point out the necessity, I am fully convinced they will be made, in the mode expressly reserved and provided by the Constitution, without the inconceivable damage of a total stagnation to all the power of government, for at least twelve months, and an expense of at least two hundred thousand pounds, in calling town-meetings, general assemblies, &c. all which, if it does no hurt, will certainly, not be productive of one good consequence, unless we send to Europe, or some other quarter of the globe for our men, to make the emendations; as I am fully persuaded we cannot procure better upon this continent, than composed the last Continental Convention; and we may be assured, that no other body of men, we can assemble for the purpose, will be more disposed to make concessions than the last. But when we become firmly united, by an indissoluble union, we shall begin to consider ourselves more and more as one nation and family; our prejudices will gradually remove, wear out and disappear; and the necessary alterations and emendations take place, without all this circumlocution which is meant to overthrow it. I give this hint to the public, in hopes and full expectation, that persons of more leisure, information and abilities, will take up the subject, and do it justice, as I have not yet seen the famous or rather circular letter.

1. Reprinted: Hartford, Conn., *American Mercury*, 18 August; *Massachusetts Centinel*, 23 August; Rhode Island *Newport Herald*, 28 August.
2. For the circular letter, see BoR, I, 153–58.
3. For New York's dominance over the commerce of Connecticut and New Jersey, see RCS:N.Y., Vol. 1, xxxvii.

George Washington to Charles Pettit
Mount Vernon, Fairfax County, Va., 16 August 1788[1]

I have to acknowledge with much sensibility the receipt of your letter, dated the 5th instant,[2] in which you offer your congratulations on the prospect of an established government, whose principles seem calculated to secure the benefits of society to the Citizens of the United States; and in which you also give a more accurate state of fœderal Politics in Pennsylvania than I had before received.

It affords me unfeigned satisfaction to find that the acrimony of parties is much abated. Doubtless there are defects in the proposed system which may be remedied in a constitutional mode. I am truly pleased to learn that those who have been considered as its most violent opposers will not only acquiese peacably, but co-operate in its organization and content themselves with asking amendments in the manner prescribed by the Constitution. The great danger, in my view, was that every thing might have been thrown into the last stage of Confusion before any government whatsoever could have been established; and that we should have suffered a political shipwreck, without the aid of one friendly star to guide us into Port. Every real patriot must have lamented that private feuds and local politics should have unhappily insinuated themselves into, and in some measure obstructed the discussion of a great national question. A just opinion, that the People when rightly informed will decide in a proper manner, ought certainly to have prevented all intemperate or precipitate proceedings on a subject of so much magnitude, Nor should a regard to common decency have suffered the Zealots in the minority to have stigmatized the authors of the Constitution as Conspirators and Traitors. However unfavorably individuals, blinded by passion and prejudice, might have thought of the characters which composed the Convention; the election of those characters by the Legislatures of the several States and the refferrence of their Proceedings to the free determination of their Constituents, did not carry the appearance of *a private combination to destroy the liberties of their Country.*—Nor did the outrageous disposition which some indulged in traducing and vilifying the members seem much calculated to produce concord or accomodation.

For myself, I expected not to be exempted from obloquy any more than others. It is the lot of humanity.

But if the shafts of malice had been aimed at me in ever so pointed a manner, on this occasion, involved as I was in a consciousness of having acted in conformity to what I believed my duty, they would have fallen blunted from their mark. It is known to some of my countrymen and can be demonstrated to the conviction of all, that I was in a manner constrained to attend the general Convention in compliance with the earnest and pressing desires of many of the most respectable characters in different parts of the Continent.

At my age, and in my circumstances, what sinister object, or personal emolument had I to seek after, in this life? The growing infirmities of age and the encreasing love of retirement, daily confirm my decided predilection for domestic life: and the great searcher of human hearts is my witness, that I have no wish which aspires beyond the humble and happy lot of living and dying a private citizen on my own farm.

Your candour and patriotism in endeavoring to moderate the jealousies and remove the prejudices which a particular class of Citizens had conceived against the new government, are certainly very commendable; and must be viewed as such by all true friends to their Country.

In this discription, I shall fondly hope I have a right to comprehend myself; and shall conclude by professing the grateful sense of your favorable opinion for me,

1. FC, Washington Papers, DLC.
2. For this letter, see Abbot, *Washington, Confederation Series,* VI, 423–28.

Philadelphia Independent Gazetteer, 16 August 1788

The paragraphs, which have appeared in the last two numbers of the Pennsylvania Gazettee,[1] exhibit in the clearest point of view the dilemma into which our RED-HOT FEDERALISTS are now driven.

If *trial by jury*, the *liberty of the press*, no *capitation tax*, &c. are to be established as fundamental privileges of freemen; then according to the doctrine of RED-HOT FEDERALISM, "these *alterations*, not *amendments*, would annihilate the constitution, and throw the United States not only back into anarchy, but introduce *poverty, misery, bloodshed*, and *slavery* into every state in the union."

In one paper all the members of the honorable convention of New-York are told that they should associate with Indians in match-coats preparing them for being burned to death, &c. In another (severity subsiding a little) they are branded with the *gentle* epithets of *impudent, impertinent*, &c. in this we are also informed, that the convention of North-Carolina had rejected the constitution by a majority of 100, against 76; instead of saying 176 against 76; and thus, by a pitiful quible, 76 members are hid from the eye of the reader.

But, Mr. Oswald, without making any farther comments, please to let the paragraphs alluded to, have a place in your paper for the use of your readers, and oblige a subscriber.[2]

1. This is a reply to paragraphs that appeared in the *Pennsylvania Gazette* on 6 August (BoR, III, 135; CC:Vol. 6, pp. 401) and 13 August (BoR, III, 138–39).

2. Here Oswald reprints the two paragraphs cited in note one (above) and a third paragraph (CC:Vol. 6, p. 401).

Abigail Adams Smith to John Quincy Adams
Jamaica, N.Y., 20 August 1788 (excerpt)[1]

. . . I Shall not dispute the subject of Federal or antefederal with you, I think that the Constitution is now too generally adopted by the States to be receded from by any one with good intentions, but of the affect I Confess myself doubtfull—there is a great deal to be done to Sattisfy the Sanguine—and perhaps there may be found more perplexity in doing than is yet suspected by any one—it is a most important and critical era in the fate of our Country—may She be so Conducted as to insure peace tranquility and happiness to her Subjects is my wish, and in this I dare say you will not dissent from your affectionate Sister

1. RC, Adams Papers, MHi. Printed: *Adams Family Correspondence*, VIII, 290–93.

Joseph Clay to John Wright Stanly
Savannah, Ga., 20 August 1788 (excerpt)[1]

... tis reported here that your State [i.e., North Carolina] has rejected the New Constitution if its true I am sorry for it—I do not like it altogether as it stands but I presume amendments are attainable—and a rejection is very dangerous at home & discredits us abroad. ...

1. FC, Clay Letterbook, Georgia Historical Society.

A Friend of Society and Liberty
Pennsylvania Carlisle Gazette, 20 August 1788 (excerpts)[1]

To the INHABITANTS of the Western Counties of Pennsylvania
(Concluded from our last.)
Friends and Countrymen. ...

It has been asserted, that the new constitution, when ratified, would be fixed and permanent, and that no alterations or amendments, should those proposed appear on consideration ever so salutary, could afterwards be obtained. A candid consideration of the constitution will shew this to be a groundless remark. It is provided, in the clearest words, that Congress shall be obliged to call a convention on the application of two thirds of the legislatures; and all amendments proposed by such convention, are to be valid when approved by the conventions or legislatures of three fourths of the states.—It must therefore be evident to every candid man, that two thirds of the states can always procure a general convention for the purpose of amending the constitution, and that three fourths of them can introduce those amendments into the constitution, although the President, Senate and Foederal House of Representatives, should be unanimously opposed to each and all of them. Congress therefore cannot hold any power, which three fourths of the states shall not approve, on experience. ...

1. Reprinted: *Pennsylvania Mercury*, 23 August 1788.

James Madison to Edmund Randolph
New York, 22 August 1788 (excerpt)[1]

My dear friend
I have your favor of the 13th.[2] The effect of Clintons Circular letter in Virga. does not surprise me. It is a signal of concord & hope to the enemies of the Constitution every where, and will I fear prove extremely dangerous. Notwithstanding your remarks on the subject I cannot but

think that an *early* convention will be an unadvised measure. It will evidently be the offspring of party & passion, and will probably for that reason alone be the parent of error and public injury. It is pretty clear that a majority of the people of the Union are in favor of the Constitution as it stands, or at least are not dissatisfied with it in that form; or if this be not the case it is at least clear that a greater proportion unite in that system than are likely to unite in any other theory. Should radical alterations take place therefore they will not result from the deliberate sense of the people, but will be obtained by management, or extorted by menaces, and will be a real sacrifice of the public will as well as of the public good, to the view of individuals & perhaps the ambition of the state legislatures. . . .

1. RC, Madison Papers, DLC. For the entire letter, see Rutland, *Madison*, XI, 237–38. The letter lacks an addressee, but from the content, the recipient was Edmund Randolph.
2. For this letter, see BoR, III, 137–38.

James Madison to Thomas Jefferson
New York, 23 August 1788 (excerpt)[1]

My last went via England in the hands of a Swiss gentleman who had married an American lady, and was returning with her to his own country. He proposed to take Paris in his way. By that opportunity I inclosed copies of the proceedings of this State on the subject of the Constitution.[2] North Carolina was then in Convention, and it was generally expected would in some form or other have fallen into the general stream. The event has disappointed us. It appears that a large majority has decided against the Constitution as it stands, and according to the information here received has made the alterations proposed by Virginia the conditions on which alone that State will unite with the others.[3] Whether this be the precise State of the case I cannot say. It seems at least certain that she has either rejected the Constitution, or annexed conditions precedent to her ratification. It cannot be doubted that this bold step is to be ascribed in part to the influence of the minority in Virginia which lies mostly in the Southern part of the State, and to the management of its leader.[4] It is in part ascribed also by some to assurances transmitted from leading individuals here, that New York would set the example of rejection.[5] The event, whatever may have been its cause, with the tendency of the circular letter from the Convention of N. York,[6] has somewhat changed the aspect of things and has given fresh hopes and exertions to those who opposed the Constitution. The object with them now will be to effect an early Convention composed of men who will essentially mutilate the system, particularly in the article of taxation, without which in my opinion the System cannot answer the purposes for which it was intended. An early Convention is in every view to be dreaded in the present temper of America. A very short period of delay would produce the double advantage of diminishing the heat and increasing the light of all parties. A trial for one year will probably suggest more real amendments than all the antecedent speculations of our most sagacious politicians. . . .

1. RC, Madison Papers, DLC. Printed: Boyd, XIII, 539–41.
2. For Madison's letter to Jefferson, 10 August, see RCS:N.Y., 2451–52; Rutland, *Madison*, XI, 225–27.
3. For the Virginia amendments, see BoR, I, 251–56.
4. Patrick Henry.
5. Perhaps a reference to the letters sent by the New York Federal Republican Committee to leading Antifederalists in states that had not yet ratified the Constitution. See the headnote to George Mason to John Lamb, Richmond, Va., 9 June 1788, BoR, III, 51n–53n.
6. For the New York Convention's circular letter of 26 July calling for a second general convention of the states, see BoR, I, 153–58.

Solon, Jr.
Rhode Island Providence Gazette, 23 August 1788[1]

The force of habit is very great.—I have heard of an old highlander, who for many years after he had been denied the pleasure of chopping his enemies with his broad-sword, used, at certain times of the day, regularly to brandish it, as though in action.—It is not strange, therefore, that a writer should divert himself in the same manner with his goose-quill, even when there are no hopes left of doing execution.

Time has at length discovered to us, that a great many of the people, and some respectable States in the Union, are of opinion, that the New Constitution needs amendments.—The ratification of it by the State of New-York bears a singular complexion; and North-Carolina has refused to ratify it.

The most eligible mode of obtaining these amendments is therefore now on the tapis.[2]—Two only strike me at present.—It must be done by the States under the old confederation—or as an operation of the New Constitution.

Eleven States having ratified the Constitution unconditionally, it is not likely that they will so far recede from that measure, as to humour the remaining two States in holding a Convention under the old confederation—this indeed would be an indecent request from the two non-complying States, were they more respectable than they are. It therefore follows, that the necessary amendments are to be sought for by the operation of the New Constitution.—Let us therefore attend to the fifth article thereof, which points out the process.

In case two-thirds of the New Congress are of opinion that amendments are necessary—they have authority to draught such as they please, and transmit them to the States they represent for ratification.—It is at the option of the New Congress to direct that these amendments shall be submitted to the Legislatures of the States, or to Conventions in the several States, for ratification; and in case such amendments shall be ratified by three-fourths either of the Legislatures or Conventions of such States, they become valid and binding. In this method amendments are obtainable under the New Constitution, without another General Convention.

But, secondly, although two-thirds of the New Congress should not be in favour of any amendments, yet if two-thirds of the Legislatures of the States they represent are for amendments, on the application of such two-thirds, the New Congress will call a General Convention for the purpose of considering and proposing amendments, to be ratified in the same manner as in case they had been proposed by the Congress themselves.

From this brief application of the process in obtaining amendments under the operation of the New Constitution, it is clear that the non-complying States can have no agency whatever in the business. They will not be represented on the floor of the New Congress, and so cannot act in amendments originating with that body; nor can they have a seat in any future Convention directed by that body, in which amendments may originate, and so can have neither part nor lot in the matter.

It is scarcely to be expected, that eight of the eleven States, assembled under the powers of the New Constitution, will agree in any amendments at all; and the voices of seven States, being less than two-thirds of that body, cannot originate any amendments—they will be unavailing—the voices of the Legislatures of seven of those States for a General Convention will also be unavailing for the same reason: But let us suppose that the two outstanding States should come in, after the manner of New-York, their two voices, added to the seven in the New Congress, or the voices of their two Legislatures added to the other seven, would make more than two-thirds of the whole—for a moderate skill in arithmetic will discover, that although *seven* is less than two-thirds of *eleven*, *nine* is more than two-thirds of *thirteen*.

The line of policy appears therefore clearly chalked out to the non-complying States, if they wish to facilitate and secure amendments, and more especially if they wish to have a voice in making those amendments. Under this impression, no doubt, the Convention of New-York ratified the Constitution—and what wiser views influenced the North-Carolinians we are yet to learn.

Individuals may talk at random, and many times suffer their passions to over-rule their interest; but we are to hope better things of *States*, assembled in Council by their best and wisest men.

Although it may be only an humiliating reflection, that the State of Rhode-Island, on former occasions holding a dignified rank in the General Councils of this country, should have been able to send no persons qualified to assist in forming the New Constitution[3]—will it not be also chargeable with cruelty to our sister States, who desire our co-operation, to continue to hold ourselves aloof—and refuse to take a situation either to serve ourselves, or them with effect?

1. Reprinted: *New York Packet,* 5 September; *Pennsylvania Journal,* 10 September; Baltimore *Maryland Gazette,* 12 September; Richmond *Virginia Gazette and Weekly Advertiser,* 25 September. David Howell was possibly the author of this essay. See "Solon, jun.," Rhode Island *Providence Gazette,* 5 July, note 1 (BoR, III, 86n).
2. The phrase "on the tapis" means "under discussion or consideration."
3. On 14 March, 5 May, and 16 June 1787, the Rhode Island legislature rejected attempts to appoint delegates to the Constitutional Convention. See RCS:R.I., 8–9.

James Madison to George Washington
New York, 24 August 1788[1]

... The Circular letter from this State is certainly a matter of as much regret, as the *unanimity* with which it passed is matter of surprize.[2] I find it is every where, and particularly in Virginia, laid hold of as the signal for united exertions in pursuit of *early* amendments. In Pennsylva. the antifederal leaders are I understand, soon to have a meeting at Harrisburg, in order to concert proper arrangements on the part of that State. I begin now to accede to the opinion, which has been avowed for some time by many, that the circumstances involved in the ratification of New York will prove more injurious than a rejection would have done. The latter wd. have rather alarmed the well meaning antifederalists elsewhere, would have had no ill effect on the other party, would have excited the indignation of the neighbouring States, and would have been necessarily followed by a speedy reconsideration of the subject. I am not able to account for the concurrence of the federal part of the Convention in the circular address, on any other principle than the determination to purchase an immediate ratification in any form and at any price, rather than disappoint this City of a chance for the new Congress. This solution is sufficiently justified by the eagerness displayed on this point, and the evident disposition to risk and sacrifice every thing to it. Unfortunately the disagreeable question continues to be undecided, and is now in a state more perplexing than ever. By the last vote taken, the whole arrangement was thrown out, and the departure of Rho Island & the refusal of N. Carolina to participate further in the business, has left eleven States only to take it up anew. In this number there are not seven States for any place, and the disposition to relax, as usually happens, decreases with the progress of the contest. What and when the issue is to be is really more than I can foresee. It is truly mortifying that the outset of the new Government should be immediately preceded by such a display of locality, as portends the continuance of an evil which has dishonored the old, and gives countenance to some of the most popular arguments which have been inculcated by the Southern antifederalists....

1. RC, Washington Papers, DLC. For the entire letter, see CC:836. The previous day Madison had written in a similar vein to Thomas Jefferson (BoR, III, 146–47).
2. For the New York Convention's circular letter, which was approved by a unanimous vote, see BoR, I, 153–58.

James Tilghman to Tench Coxe
Chestertown, Md., 24 August 1788 (excerpt)[1]

... You ask me who are like to be our federal Senators You might almost as well proposed your Question to any man in Phila. I have heard one or two Gentlemen of wealth and Ability mentioned as those who will not accept but none who will and the difficulty of getting proper persons to serve that important office, strikes Every body, I have heard speak on the Subject. And it is to be feared it must fall to the share either of Youngsters or Adventurers, two very improper sorts of People. Who is it that will give up his family and affairs for a Seat in the continental Senate? The Sacrifice is too great for the Patriotism of this Age. Every body's Invention is strained to acquire wealth not to apply to the publick good but to the support of Luxury. This is the complexion of the Bulk of America and is totally unfit for republican Government. There is a great deal to do before the present form of Government can get into operation It must first be revised and amended whether by the Congress themselves or by a New Convention is somewhat incertain I am apprehensive the New York circular letter will take with many People I thought I saw many defects and Errors in the Constitution which I imagined the New Congress wd. rectify and supply otherwise I would not have promoted it I still think they will do it if they have any degree of Sense and Prudence. This makes a good choice of delegates and Senators a matter of vast importance We shall see how the mode of chusing delegates will succeed I never did like it The choice of Senators is upon a better plan—I have said much more upon the Subject than I intended

1. RC, Coxe Papers, Series II, Correspondence and General Papers, PHi.

St. John de Crevecoeur to James Bowdoin
New York, 26 August 1788 (excerpt)[1]

I am much obliged to you for the book you have sent me, the history of the late Insurrection of part of your State[2] in the quelling of which you have had so iminent a share by your prudence, firmness & activity, it is elegantly wrote, this work is a manifest proof of the improved & advanced state of Society in America; the account of that effervency, that abuse of freedom degenerated into outrageous licentiousness, may become very useful in a Country like this, where most men read & think for themselves; I hope it will serve to convince your people, how difficult it is to organize by dint of reason alone, & to establish & maintain without force a form of government which may be acceptable to the inhabitants of so large & extensive a territory, the interests of which are so unavoidably various & opposite.

I anxiously long for the first Session of Congress in order to see whether the amending States will have sufficient influence to alter the new Constitution 'ere its effects have been felt; 'tis high time this long Inter-regna shou'd be at an end & be succeeded by coercitive & uniform laws. . . .

1. RC, Bowdoin-Temple Papers, MHi.
2. A reference to George Richards Minot, *The History of the Insurrections, in Massachusetts* . . . (Worcester, Mass., 1788) (Evans 21259).

Hortensius
Massachusetts Centinel, 27 August 1788

Mr. RUSSELL, The general joy which has diffused throughout America, in consequence of the adoption of the new Constitution, is a striking proof of that philanthropick disposition, which has hitherto so eminently distinguished the enlightened patriots of America—Willing to relinquish whatever might be found necessary for the preservation of the whole, they have generously given up all local advantages, with a firm and determined resolution of supporting the Union, and establishing that friendship and reciprocity of interest, which cannot but contribute to the general welfare. Fears and apprehensions have arisen in the minds of some, from the powers vested in the general government by this Constitution: But these, if on trial they are found dangerous to our liberties, will doubtless be removed; for America has yet citizens who have wisdom and circumspection to discern them. But let us be cautious, lest those, who under the mask of obtaining *amendments*, only wish for such alterations, erasements, or additions, as shall utterly destroy the fair fabrick which has caused us so much labour and expense, should get into power, by our own election, to work our ruin. Our first and principal care ought to be, in being watchful of whom we trust—and to choose none but those who are undeniably friends to the rights of human nature.—Friends to justice, publick faith and honour,—who have adequate ideas of the *present state* of the continent, and stability enough to adopt, and to pursue such measures, as the exigencies of the times may require. Those who wish to preserve their liberty, ought to remember, that their dignity, their honour and happiness, rests with those they appoint to represent them—And let the government be what it will, if the representatives are virtuous, the people may live happy. But when the citizens neglect this great and important privilege, and forget that they are freemen, designing men may step into authority—that predominant principle, interest, will most assuredly follow, and anarchy must be the natural consequence.

George Washington to Benjamin Lincoln
Mount Vernon, Fairfax County, Va., 28 August 1788 (excerpt)[1]

... So far as I am able to learn, fœderal principles are gaining ground considerably.—The declaration of some of the most respectable characters in this State (I mean of those who were opposed to the government) is now explicit that they will give the Constitution (as it has been fairly discussed) a fair chance, by affording it all the support in their power.—Even in Pennsylvania the Minority, who were more violent than in any other place, say they will only seek for amendments in the mode pointed out by the Constitution itself.

I will, however, just mention by way of *caveat*, there are suggestions that attempts will be made to procure the election of a number of antifœderal characters to the first Congress, in order to embarrass the Wheels of government and produce premature alterations in the Constitution.—How far these hints, which have come through different channels, may be well or ill founded, I know not; but, it will be advisable, I should think, for the fœderalists to be on their guard so far as not to suffer any secret machinations to prevail, without taking measures to frustrate them.—That many amendments and explanations might and should take place, I have no difficulty in conceding; but, I will confess, that my apprehension is, that the New York circular Letter is intended to bring on a general Convention at too early a period, and in short, by referring the subject to the Legislatures, to set every thing afloat again.—I wish I may be mistaken in imagining, that there are persons, who upon finding they could not carry their point by an open attack against the Constitution, have some sinister designs to be silently effected if possible.—But I trust in that Providence which has saved us in six troubles, yea in seven, to rescue us again from any imminent, though unseen, dangers.—Nothing, however, on our part ought to be left undone.—I conceive it to be of unspeakable importance, that whatever there be of wisdom, & prudence, & patriotism on the Continent, should be concentred in the public Councils, at the first outset.—

Our habits of intimacy will render an apology unnecessary.—Heaven is my witness, that an inextinguishable desire [for] the felicity of my Country may be promoted, is my only motive in making these observations

1. RC, George Washington to Benjamin Lincoln Letters, The Houghton Library, Harvard University. For the entire letter, see Abbot, *Washington, Confederation Series,* VI, 482–83.

A Friend to Amendments
Boston Independent Chronicle, 28 August 1788[1]

Mess'rs. ADAMS & NOURSE, A Writer in the Centinel, under the signature of Laco,[2] has given several specimens of his impertinence. His introducing the names of Hutchinson and Ruggles,[3] is supposed a reflection on Mess'rs Adams and Gerry,[4] recommended in Edes's paper for Senators of this State. The known patriotism of the former of these gentlemen, can never be injured by any reflections thrown on him by certain *time serving busy-bodies,* who are now anxious to introduce themselves and *party* into our new government; & who are eager to share the loaves and fishes among a few of their adherents.

It is not doubted the sentiments of the people will be united in such men as are *known to be* the friends to our country, independent of sinister motives, and who are advocates for amendments in our Federal Constitution; as a large and respectable majority of the States have earnestly recommended them.

A friend to amendments has *now* become the criterion of a federalist, and none but a set of head-strong aristocratics, who will ever disregard the voice of the people, will endeavour to introduce those men into our new government, who are not strenuous advocates for amendments.

As the federal government guarantees a *Republican* form of government to the several States, it is presumed the people will be so prudent as not to chuse any of that party, who already are attempting to destroy this form by recent publications.

1. Reprinted: *New York Journal*, 11 September.
2. For "Laco," *Massachusetts Centinel*, 27 August, see DHFFE, I, 451.
3. Thomas Hutchinson and Timothy Dwight Ruggles, both prominent Massachusetts Loyalists.
4. Samuel Adams and Elbridge Gerry had been nominated as candidates for U.S. senators in the *Boston Globe*, 25 August (DHFFE, I, 450).

Solon
Boston Independent Chronicle, 28 August 1788[1]

Mess'rs ADAMS & NOURSE,

Please to give the following a place in your very useful paper.

To the respectable FREEMEN of the United States of *America.*

Fellow Countrymen and Citizens, Animated by those noble principles of *virtuous freedom,* which are the dignity of human nature, you spurned the idea of dependence and vassalage, asserted your rights, and, under the smiles of Heaven, to the wonder of an admiring world, established your *independence* and sovereignty.

Actuated by sentiments of wisdom, and fore-sight, you have generally adopted a Federal Constitution, which is ere long to be put in practice—and to an eye of reason, promises, if well administered, to *confirm* your independence and sovereignty—to render you prosperous and happy at home, and respected abroad. But it has been, and still is the opinion of many, that *certain amendments* are absolutely necessary to render the Constitution still more perfect, and to secure to you, and your posterity, under every administration, the blessings of that liberty, you have so dearly purchased, and which it is the duty of enlightened freemen ever to provide. These considerations have induced me to address you at this time, and with all deference to interest, that you do not loose sight of the important object so highly interesting to yourselves and posterity. The amendments which have been proposed by the different State Conventions,[2] are not local, they equally concern all the States; but whether all that have been mentioned are absolutely necessary, is not for me to determine: But in some of them, there is such a general concurrence, that but little, if any doubt can remain of their eligibility. It is not improbable that there will be found some who do not wish for *any* amendments; or that any further *checks* should be provided, than are at present in the Constitution; but I assure myself, that a large majority of you think otherwise, and that you will not be diverted from proper and necessary endeavours to obtain the object, by any animadversion, cant, or ridicule, that may be thrown out on the subject; it is to be observed, that this is already beginning to discover itself.—The circular letter from the Convention of New-York,[3] has had the epithets of *impertinent* and *impudent*, bestowed upon it, and probably more will be advanced, as the time draws near. If amendments are necessary, they *claim* an *early consideration*, and measures for the purpose merit your *first* attention. Will it be improper to hint, that in the choice of *Senators* and *Representatives*, this object among others naturally presents itself to your consideration, and that such *instructions* as may be necessary, be *seasonably prepared*; you have hitherto been the peculiar care of a kind Providence, may you, and your posterity after you, be a name and a praise among the nations of the earth, is the ardent wish of   SOLON.

1. Reprinted: Philadelphia *Independent Gazetteer*, 6 September; *New York Journal*, 18 September; Springfield, Mass., *Hampshire Chronicle*, 1 October. "A Federalist," *Massachusetts Centinel*, 30 August, suggested that William Heath, a candidate for the U.S. House of Representatives, was the author of "Solon" (BoR, III, 156–58). Another possible author could be Caleb Strong (note 1 to "Alfred" II, *Massachusetts Spy*, 16 October, BoR, III, 256n). For other essays by "Solon" of 4, 25 September, 30 October, see BoR, III, 199–201n, 231–32, 303–5.
2. For the amendments proposed by the state conventions, see BoR, I, 231–77.
3. For the Circular Letter of the New York Convention, see BoR, I, 153–58.

Philadelphia Independent Gazetteer, 28 August 1788[1]

A correspondent says, that situated as this country is at present, and in intimate alliance with an intriguing, ambitious nation who have taken delight in destroying the liberties of mankind,[2] it would be the part of wisdom in us to guard against *a national* government, and to continue, with proper amendments *a federal* government. It is obvious to a man of reflection, that if our government is national, an attempt to enslave the country can be easily put in execution by the capability that it will have of making the people act unitedly at an unguarded hour for the destruction of their liberties. In a federal government, where there are thirteen or more independent states, an attempt to enslave us will succeed with difficulty. When it is made upon one state, the others will be alarmed before their hour of trial comes on. The government of the United States of America was fabricated upon the model of the government of the Thirteen Cantons of Switzerland, which for about 500 years have flourished in unparalelled prosperity and happy freedom without dangerous commotions. I will transcribe a passage in proof of this from the learned and ingenious Mr. Coxe's letters on Switzerland, who may be considered as impartial, as he is an able judge of the matter which he treats upon. "There is no part of Europe which contains within the same extent of region, so many independent commonwealths, and such a variety of different governments, as are collected together in this remarkable and delightful country; and yet, with such wisdom was the helvetic union composed, and so little have the Swiss of late years been actuated with the spirit of conquest, that since the firm and compleat establishment of their general confederacy, they have scarcely ever had occasion to employ their arms against a foreign enemy, and have had no hostile commotions among themselves that were not very soon terminated. And thus while the several neighbouring kingdoms have suffered, by turns, all the horrors of internal war, this favored nation hath enjoyed the felicity described by Lucretius, and looked down with security upon the various tempests that have shaken the world around them." Coxe's Letters on Switzerland, page 460. And afterwards he says, "but the felicity of Switzerland does not consist merely in being peculiarly exempted from the burdens and miseries of war; there is no country in which happiness and content more universally prevail among the people." Page 462.[3]

1. Reprinted: *New York Journal*, 25 September.
2. Probably a reference to France, a United States ally since 1778.
3. William Coxe, *Sketches of the Natural, Civil, and Political State of Swisserland: In a Series of Letters to William Melmoth* (London, 1779), Letter XLIII.

A Federalist
Massachusetts Centinel, 30 August 1788[1]

Mr. RUSSELL, It is a well known fact, that the *"proposed amendments,"* as they are called, to the Federal Constitution, took their rise from a variety of causes, very few of which, if impartially considered, will be found *honest* or *praise worthy*—so far as they were acceded to, by the *real patriots* of our country, the *prompt* and *steady* advocates for an *unconditional* adoption of the Constitution, a laudable motive may be assigned—that of peace and conciliation.

Let us advert to the conduct of those who are now clamourers for introducing into the Federal Legislature the sticklers for *alterations* while they were members of the Convention—particular reference is now had, to the writer whose signature is *Solon*, in last Thursday's Chronicle[2]—The conduct of this man has been uniformly such, both in the *field* and *legislature*, that he may with propriety be called the *doubting*

General,[3] and the *doubting* Politician.—When the proceedings of the Grand Convention, in their excellent system, were first promulgated, the *vague, doubting* and *inconclusive* lucubrations of this *doubting* statesman, upon the subject, saluted the publick eye: Through some *fatality*, he obtained a seat in the State Convention—and there he added fresh laurels to his *doubting* character—(see his very extraordinary declamation upon the subject without object, spirit or decision—an *enemy* to, and an *advocate* for, the *same thing* in the *same speech*)[4]—What good fruit can ever be expected from such a non-descriptive soil? While the die spun *doubtful*, this *doubting* orator fluttered upon the wings of uncertainty; but when he found a *clear vote* would be obtained for the adoption of this system, the friends of the Constitution were enabled, and *not before*, to count him in the affirmative. Can it be possible that such a character is ever actuated by *independent* principles? However capable of forming adequate ideas upon any subject, no credit is due to, nor can any reliance be placed upon, so equivocal a character.— And yet astonishing as it may appear, THIS MAN is a candidate for a seat in the federal Legislature. And what are the methods by which he is now trying to effect his purpose; are they manly, decisive and patriotick? By no means. Under the appearance of contending for amendments, his design is to draw the publick attention to *himself*, and some *other* characters, who, when in Convention, would have effected a total rejection of the Constitution, had not their *secret* machinations been counteracted by those *inflexible* and *able* patriots, who realized and demonstrated that our ALL was suspended on a decisive system of conduct.

Should the plan of this *camelion* politician succeed; should we be so highly unfortunate as to have persons of *his kidney* introduced into the federal Legislature, the blessed effects to be derived from the operation of the new government, which the people so justly and fondly anticipate, will in all probability be procrastinated to a period that shall exhaust the patience of the States; and may be finally productive of that *despair, anarchy* and *confusion*, from which we have but *just* escaped.

But, Mr. Russell, our FEDERAL REPRESENTATIVES are to be *instructed*—and such instructions are to be "seasonably prepared"!— Blessed proposition! To say nothing of its absurdity, which neither the General himself, nor any of a *similar cut*, could reduce to a *consistent* idea: It has been thought that such a flagellation as *some folks* received from the pen of a very ingenious satirist, for his code of ready "*cut and dried*" instructions, respecting the "annihilation of the Order," would have operated a *little* to prevent a like fruitless essay in future. It is devoutly to be wished that this *stepping stone* may fail, as it did on the above occasion.—"And as we have hitherto been the care of a kind

Providence," we have reason from that circumstance to hope, that our federal councils will be preserved from the direction of *shufflers, shifters, doubters,* and *time-serving politicians.*

1. Reprinted: *New York Journal,* 11 September. For a response, see *Boston Gazette,* 1 September 1788 (BoR, III, 161–62).
2. See "Solon," *Independent Chronicle,* 28 August (BoR, III, 154–55).
3. "A Federalist" evidently thought that William Heath was "Solon." In January 1777, Heath, a major general in the Continental Army, had been ordered to secure the surrender or evacuation of the British garrison at Kingsbridge on the mainland across from the northern tip of Manhattan Island. He failed, and Washington reprimanded him in a public letter and virtually called him a coward in a private letter (to Heath, 3, 4 February 1777, Smith, *Letters,* VIII, 231–32, 240–41). From then until the end of the war Heath did not command troops in the field.
4. The comment about the "extraordinary declamation" is presumably a reference to William Heath's speech in the Massachusetts Convention on 31 January, in which he proposed that the first members of Congress from Massachusetts be instructed to secure amendments to the Constitution (RCS:Mass., 1377–79).

James Gordon, Jr., to James Madison
Germanna, Orange County, Va., 31 August 1788[1]

Your several letters of the 25 & 27 of July I have received and should have answered them ere this but they did not come to hand untill a few days since at Orange C. House.

I am pleased to find the ratification of the constitution by new York was unconditional but I fear from the Circular letter therefrom[2] much disquietude may succeed, in those States where the Majoritys are not large—I expect that letter will be eagerly caught by Mr. P. Henry who in our next assembly will be greatly an over match for any federalist that I know in the same—I trust there are a majority of Federalist[s] in the House who I hope will firmly withs[t]and the artfull Intrigues of designing men; but there are instances of the most heroic conduct being defeated for want of a competant commander; such an one I fear we have not in our House of Delegates.—

I have carefully perused the numbers of the Federalist and am happy to say the arguments therein contained are sufficiently satisfactory to my mind And must carry conviction to every candid reader. we are all in quiet at present; there appears to be little or no opposition from the Anties & have been informed they are generally pretty well satisfied but I rather think their conduct is intended to lull the friends to the new government into a state of security and then in the fall to make a violent attack—I am sorry to find N. York are as the Virginia convention against the power of direct taxation without which I fear nay I am certain the most apparent evils will insue[.] to form a government without such a necessary power would be nearly as ridiculous as for Such a government to send persons to transact business of importance far distant without the sufficient sum of money to enable such persons to make good their journey and therby to obtain requisitions from those who were not compelled to assist: Should such an amendment take place the long and glorious endeavours of our Patriots will be (of little or) far less beneficial consequences than their unwearied attention for the interest of America merited—The conduct of N. Carolina you have seen[.][3] should they be fortunate enough to be seconded by Rhode Island from their local situation, their knowledge in Political Science and numbers the eleven confederated States have every thing to fear; good God what can they promise themselves! being the consumers of two Importing states, and so unable to stand upon their own ground I should have thought they would have greedily caught the union; it is reported Mr. Henry has influenced their councils considerably since the rising of our convention, the truth of which I have not sufficient knowledge—

I had the pleasure of seeing yr. Father & most of yr. Friends who are all well the last week—It will be a matter of satisfaction to yr. Friends in this state to know whether you wish to be in the Senate or in the House of representatives in Congress[.] so soon as the districts are laid out I hope there will be care taken not to send to Congress those who are inimical to the constitution—I shall ever esteem it a singular favor to receive any intelligence from you and your advice upon any subject will be an additional obligation on Dr Sir Your sincere Friend and affectionate Huml Sert.

1. RC, Madison Papers, DLC.
2. For the New York Convention's circular letter, see BoR, I, 153–58.
3. On 2 August the North Carolina Convention had proposed amendments to the Constitution and refused to ratify until amendments had been submitted to Congress and to a second constitutional convention. See BoR, I, 264–70.

George Washington to Thomas Jefferson
Mount Vernon, Fairfax County, Va., 31 August 1788 (excerpt)[1]

... The merits and defects of the proposed Constitution have been largely & ably discussed.—For myself, I was ready to have embraced any tolerable compromise that was competent to save us from impending ruin; and I can say, there are scarcely any of the amendments which have been suggested to which I have *much* objection, except that which goes to the prevention of direct taxation—and that, I presume, will be more strenuously advocated and insisted upon hereafter than any other.—I had indulged the expectation, that the New Government would enable those entrusted with its Administration to do justice to the public creditors and retrieve the National character.—But if no means are to be employed but requisitions, that expectation was vain and we may as well recur to the old Confœderation.—If the system can be put in operation without touching much the Pockets of the People, perhaps, it may be done; but, in my judgment, infinite circumspection & prudence are yet necessary in the experiment.—It is nearly impossible for any body who has not been on the spot to conceive (from any description) what the delicacy and danger of our situation have been. Though the peril is not passed entirely; thank God! the prospect is somewhat brightening.—You will probably have heard before the receipt of this letter, that the general government has been adopted by eleven States; and that the actual Congress have been prevented from issuing their Ordinance for carrying it into execution, in consequence of a dispute about the place at which the future Congress shall meet. It is probable that Philadelphia or New York will soon be agreed upon....

1. RC, Jefferson Papers, DLC. For the entire letter, see Boyd XIII, 554–57.

A Republican
Boston Gazette, 1 September 1788

Messrs. EDES, The political scene is opened, the canvass is begun, in order to prepare the minds of an enlightened people for the choice of their Federal Legislators. Much depends upon the wisdom of the first choice: While the citizens of Massachusetts carefully guard against giving their suffrages for such as wish for an inefficient and feeble government, it is to be hoped; that equal caution will be observed towards those persons who are so ardently desirous of erecting a government of an arbitrary, oppressive and tyrannical complexion; we have many of this last description of men among us; they are violently opposed to any alterations of the new Constitution in favour of the freedom of the people, while they secretly wish for alterations on the side of arbitrary power; but as three fourths of the people are desirous of amendments not favourable to their views, they dare not hazard their principles in public, and content themselves at present in endeavouring to prevent the amendments already recommended, from being adopted: To effect this, they insist upon our trying the Constitution first, in order, they say, by that means to discover its defects, well knowing, if once put in motion under their administration, no amendments favourable to liberty will ever be obtained thereafter. These Aristocratical tyrants are ever insulting and abusing the old patriots and true friends of our country, because they are not as despotically inclined as themselves, and also with the view of raising themselves up on their ruin. They compare the Honorable Mr. [Samuel] Adams with [Royal] Governor [Thomas] Hutchinson and other traitors to our country; a republican is called a Shayite and a destroyer of all government, if he only wishes the adoption of one alteration recommended; although if it had not been for the expectation of amendments, the constitution would have been rejected in this state, by a majority of more than two to one of our Convention.[1] Thus notwithstanding, it is the wish of the people that the alterations recommended should take place, these arbitrary Aristocraticks are perpetually scribbling in the little papers, to induce the people to neglect the true patriots of our country, that themselves may be chosen into the Federal Legislature. How absurd and inconsistent will it appear, Messieurs Printers, after having recommended amendments, to elect such men to administer the Federal Government, as have publicly declared themselves opposed to all amendments which have been recommended? "But as we have hitherto been the care of Divine Providence, we have reason to hope, that our Federal Councils will be preserved from the direction" of *Recanting Tories, British Agents,* and *Aristocratical,* and *Monarchical Tyrants.*

1. For the importance of adopting subsequent amendments in obtaining ratification of the Constitution in Massachusetts and the amendments' impact on ratification in other states, see the headnote to CC:508.

Boston Gazette, 1 September 1788[1]

A correspondent who observed a Piece in the Centinel of Saturday signed 'A Federalist'[2] could not but remark on the Candor of the Writer, who says very few of the propos'd amendments to the Constitution are honest or praiseworthy, when several of the most powerful and wise States of the Union have agreed in and recommended certain Amendments, not merely local, but which have a Reference to the Union at large, and which the People of the Commonwealth think essential and necessary.

The Writer has not more distinguished himself for his candor and moderation in his attack on the suppos'd Writer of the Piece sign'd *Solon* in last Thursday's Chronicle.[3] The Hon. General there alluded to distinguished himself as the firm and decided Friend of his Country, previous to the Revolution, when such Characters as the Federalist and his associates dare not risk their Lives or Fortunes on the issue of the Dispute. He has since been invariably the assertor of the Rights of the people in opposition to the Designs of an *aristocratical junto.*

With respect to "the excellent system of the grand Convention," your correspondent can vouch from its first promulgation, that the General was decidedly in favour of it, although he saw some alterations necessary for the security of the people,—& was while in the Convention, of the same sentiments uniformly and without equivocation. He is still of the same sentiments, and where is the reason for stiling him, A doubtful and equivocal character? But the people are cautioned to beware of a Junto, who are endeavouring to stigmatize with the most opprobrious epithets, those Patriots, who have carried us through the Revolution with the highest honor; who, labouring for the welfare of the people have spent the vigor of their years, and who, this set, are now endeavouring to deprive of the rewards of their faithful and active services.

The Legislature, and the freemen of the county of Suffolk in particular, will mark well their real friends, and decide upon the merits of the several candidates for legislative officers, without the interference of the pretended Federalist.

The flagellation, ("as some folks suppose,") to have been receiv'd upon the Annihilation of the order "from an ingenious Satyrist" will never (this correspondent observes) deter any man from giving his opinion on public men or measures who is zealous in the cause of his fellow citizens.

1. Reprinted: *New York Journal*, 11 September.
2. See "A Federalist," *Massachusetts Centinel*, 30 August 1788 (BoR, III, 156–57).
3. See "Solon," Boston *Independent Chronicle*, 28 August 1788 (BoR, III, 154–55).

George Mason to John Mason
Gunston Hall, Fairfax County, Va., 2 September 1788 (excerpt)[1]

... I sent you, by the Brig, the Proceedings of the Virginia Convention; I have not yet seen a publication of the Debates.—Notwithstanding there was, in the New York Convention, a Majority of two to one against the new Constitution of Government, without previous Amendments; yet after the adoption by Virginia, they thought themselves under the necessity of adopting also; for fear of being left out of the Union, & of Civil Commotions: They have however drawn up Amendments, nearly similar to those of Virginia, & recommended them unanimously, in the strongest manner, they have also written a circular Letter to all the other States, solliciting their Co-operation, in obtaining the Amendments, by Application to the new Congress, at their first meeting; which it is expected will be in March next, at New York; so that there is still Hopes of proper & safe Amendments.[2] The North Carolina

Convention has rejected the new Constitution, unless previous Amendments are made, by a very great Majority; I have not yet seen their Amendments, but am inform'd they are much the same with those recommended by Virginia. Your Brothers have sent You a Number of late Newspapers; which will give You pretty full Information of the present state of American politicks. . . .

1. RC, George Mason Papers, DLC. For the entire letter, see Rutland, *Mason*, III, 1128–30.
2. The New York Convention's circular letter was approved unanimously, but the Convention voted 30 to 27 to ratify the Constitution with recommendatory amendments.

Pennsylvania Packet, 2 September 1788[1]

It is remarked, that there is an amendment which now appears necessary in the new Constitution, which has never been in the contemplation of a single state, and of which recent experience in Congress dictates the necessity—it is *permission for the Senate to vote by proxy*, otherwise the southern states, being at such a distance, and consequently more exposed to have their members frequently absent, may be oppressed by the operation of laws, which could never have passed, if they had had a full representation.

1. Reprinted: *Pennsylvania Journal*, 3 September; New Jersey *Brunswick Gazette*, 9 September; New Bern *State Gazette of North Carolina*, 15 September.

Harrisburg Convention, 3–6 September 1788

Antifederalist opposition to the Constitution in Pennsylvania persisted even after its ratification by the state Convention on 12 December 1787. In January 1788, Philadelphia Antifederalist leaders drafted and circulated petitions requesting (1) that the state Assembly censure the Pennsylvania delegates to the Constitutional Convention for exceeding their authority, (2) that ratification of the Constitution by the state Convention "not be confirmed," and (3) that the Pennsylvania delegates in the Confederation Congress be instructed that the Constitution not be "adopted in the said United States." The petitions were printed in the Pennsylvania *Carlisle Gazette* and the Philadelphia *Independent Gazetteer* and possibly as a broadside. The Assembly received and tabled petitions from six counties signed by 6,005 people. Seven other petitions from Northumberland County arrived after the Assembly adjourned.

Opposition to the Constitution persisted. When news of the ninth and tenth state ratifications reached Carlisle in Cumberland County, Antifederalists from several townships met and agreed to send a circular letter to the other counties asking that they send delegates to a convention to meet at Harrisburg on 3 September to propose amendments to the Constitution and to nominate candidates for the U.S. House of Representatives. Thirty-seven delegates from thirteen counties and the city of Philadelphia attended the Convention. They resolved that Pennsylvanians should acquiesce in the adoption of the Constitution but that amendments were essential to safeguard liberty. The Convention approved twelve amendments to the Constitution to be sent to the Assembly in the form of a petition. The Convention ordered that its proceedings be published; they were printed in the Philadelphia *Independent Gazetteer* and *Pennsylvania Packet* on 15 September and widely reprinted throughout the country. There is no record that the Assembly received the petition or amendments.

This grouping contains documents from 3 July through 9 October 1788 that deal with the efforts to call a convention, the Convention proceedings, and reaction to the Convention's actions.

Cumberland County, Pa., Desires Amendments, 3 July 1788

Benjamin Blyth to John Nicholson
Cumberland County, Pa., 3 July 1788[1]

You are Earnestly requested to Call a meeting of Some of the best informed men of Your County from Each Township with Design to Consider of the Necessity of Sending Delegates from the Countys to represent You in a General Conference of the State in Order to conclude upon Such Amendments and Such mode of Obtaining them as the Conference in their Wisdom may Judge Proper the time and place of Meeting is as you will see by Our resolutions the Necessity of the Measure need not be Urged Confiding in your Friendship & Integrity we hope you will Exert yourself for the good of Mankind—

Benjn. Blyth, C. M

At[test] Mr. James Bells—

Cumberland County Meeting: Proceedings and Resolutions, 3 July 1788[2]

⟨In a meeting of Delegates from the Several Townships of the Before said County³ Benjn Blyth—in the Chair, Called for the purpose of Advising the most Eligible mode of Obtaining Such Amendments in the Constitution proposed by the general Convention for the government of these United States, as May remove the Causes of Jealousy and fears of a Tyranical Aristocracy. The foundation of which Appears to be in many parts of the Said Constitution and Secure and hand Down to Posterity the Blessings of Dear bought Freedom; and thereby most Cordialy Engage Each State and Every Citizen, not Only for wrath but Conscience Sake to Aid and Support the Officers of the Government in the due Execution thereof; After Seriously Considering the Importance of the Subject and the Duty of Citizens; Have come to the following Resolutions Viz—Resolved that it is the Opinion of this meeting that the Constitution proposed by the General Convention of the United States is in Several parts Distructive of that Liberty for which so much blood and Treasure has been Spent—and Subversive of the Several State Governments by which the Rights & Liberties of the People have been Guarded and Secured That it is the Indespensible Duty of Every Citizen to Use all lawfull means to Obtain Such Amendments in the Said Constitution or Take Such measures as shall be Necesary for the Security of religion and Liberty—Resolved that it is the Opinion of the members of this meeting that it will be Expedient to Collect as Soon and as Accurately as Possible the Sentiments of the Citizens of this State Touching Such Amendments and Such mode of Obtain[ing] them as Shall be to said Citizens most Agreeable—Resolved that in order to Effectuate the foregoing resolutions that a Circular Letter be written Signed by the Chairman a[nd] Addressed to such Societys in Each County as have Already be[en] formed for Political purposes and to such as Shall be form[ed] in Any County where none is Yet formed or to Such perso[ns] as shall be Judged fit requesting that measures be Tak[en] to Call a metting of Delegates from Each Township withi[n] the respective Counties to meet as soon as Conveniently may be and take into Consideration the necessity & prop[ri]ety of Amending the Constitution of the United States & for that purpose to Appoint Delegates to meet in a General Conference of the State at Harisburgh on the Third Day of September 1788—then and there to Consider and Devise a plan the most Likely to Suceed in Obtaining the Desired Amendments—Resolved by the meeting tha[t] five members[4] be Chosen by the County Cumberland or thr[ee] Out of the five to represent Said County in the Conference to be held at Harisburgh the 3d Day of Septr. 1788—the place and time Aforesaid—⟩

B. Blyth, C. M

Cumberland County Circular Letter, 3 July 1788[5]

East Pennsborough, Cumberland Co. 3d: July 1788

Sir[,] That ten States have already, unexpectedly, without amending ratifyed the Constitution proposed for the government of these united States, cannot have escaped the notice of the friends of Liberty.—That the way is prepared for the full organization of the government, with all its foreseen and consequent dangers, is too evident, and unless prudent Steps be taken to combine the friends to amendments, in some place in which they may confidently draw together and exert their power in unison, the liberty of the american Citizens must lie at the Discretion of Congress, and most probably, posterity, become Slaves to the Officers of Government.—

The means adopted and proposed by a Meeting of Delegates from the Townships of this County for preventing the alledged Evils and also the calamities of a civil War, are, as may be observed in perusing the proceedings of the said meeting herewith transmitted to request such persons as shall be judged fit within the Counties respectively, to use their influence to obtain a meeting of delegates from each Township to take into consideration, the necessity of amending the Constitution of these united States, and for that purpose to nominate and appoint a number of Delegates to represent the County, in a general conference of the Counties of this commonwealth, to be held at Harrisburg on the third day of September next, then and there, to devise such amendments, and such mode of obtaining them, as in the wisdom of the Delegates shall be judged most satisfactory and expedient.—

A Law will no doubt be soon enacted by the General Assembly for electing eight Members to represent this State in the New Congress. It will therefore be expedient to have proper persons put in nomination by the Delegates in conference, being the most likely method of directing the views of the Electors to the same Object and of obtaining the desired End.—

The Society of which you are chairman is requested to call a meeting agreeably to the foregoing design, and lay before the Delegates the proceeding of this County, to the intent that the State may unite in casting off the Yoke of Slavery and once more establish Union and Liberty—

by order of the meeting

I am, with real Esteem Sir
Your most obedt. Servt—
Benjamin Blyth Chairman

1. RC, Pennsylvania Papers, Harrisburg Convention, NN. The letter was addressed to Nicholson as "Controller General." It is endorsed in Nicholson's handwriting as received on 20 August and answered on 26 August. A note on it, not in Nicholson's handwriting, reads: "Sir, You will be punctual in laying these Resolutions before yr Committe; if there are any Such in the City, and use your Endeavours that they Comply with the Same.— John Nicholson Esqr. C. Genl." As comptroller general of the state, Nicholson often used his office to disseminate Antifederalist communications.

2. MS, Pennsylvania Papers, Harrisburg Convention, NN. Another version of the text within angle brackets is in the Robert Whitehill Papers, Hamilton Library, Cumberland County Historical Society. It differs significantly in wording and paragraphing from the version printed here, but the sentiments expressed are the same. For two key differences, see notes 3 and 4 below.

3. The Whitehill Papers version adds "at Mr James Bell's" here.

4. The Whitehill Papers version contains the five names: Benjamin Blyth, John Jourdan, James Powers, William Sterret, and Robert Whitehill.

5. RC, Peter Force, Pennsylvania Misc., Box 11, 1781–1788, DLC. Another copy of the circular letter is in the Robert Whitehill Papers, Hamilton Library, Cumberland County Historical Society. The *Pennsylvania Gazette*, 10 September; *Pennsylvania Journal*, 13 September; and *New York Morning Post*, 18 September, printed the circular letter.

New York Daily Advertiser, 14 July 1788[1]

Extract of a letter from Philadelphia, dated 11 July 1788.

"I am informed from good authority, that in consequence of the 9th state having adopted the New Constitution, the Anti-Federalists of Cumberland county in this state, held a meeting near Carlisle; the result was, that they were determined to support it, and give it a fair trial, and solicit amendments in a Constitutional way. Only three at the meeting were opposed to it."

1. Reprinted: *Boston Gazette*, 21 July; Poughkeepsie, N.Y., *Country Journal*, 22 July; Massachusetts *Salem Mercury*, 22 July; *Massachusetts Centinel*, 23 July; Providence, R.I., *United States Chronicle*, 24 July; *New Hampshire Spy*, 26 July.

Germantown, Pa., Antifederalist Meeting, 14 August 1788[1]

This unsigned letter dated 17 August describes the events that occurred at a meeting held in a tavern in Germantown on the evening of 14 August in response to the Cumberland County circular letter of 3 July that called for the election of delegates to the Harrisburg Convention (BoR, III, 165–66). Presumably the account was sent to Benjamin Franklin, who was ending his three-year term as president of the Pennsylvania Supreme Executive Council.

An alarm!

Dear Sir,

I have a sincere love for my country & therefore cannot be silent & torpid when I see danger approaching—there is an old adage, i.e., a spoonfull of water will put out a fire at the beginning which if suffer'd to increase into a flame an ocean may prove inadequate to Extinguish its raging violence. but I will come to the point without further procrastination—Last friday morn [15 August] I stoped with a friend at the public school near Germantown when Colonel Dunning the master informd us that Mr. Ashurst had prevailed on him the Evening before to go to a public meeting at Nices's Tavern & that they happened to be the first in the room—soon after which Dr. Finely, Colonel Ingle, & two others Entered the apartment when one of them took a writing out of his pocket & handed it to Mr. Ashurst to read which he attempted but the writing being bad & much interlined he found it too difficult & therefore handed it to Colonel Dunning who read it aloud to the Company; but ere he had perused it a second time with hope of fully developing its real intentions (which the Company appear'd ignorant of) Mr. Blare McClanegan[2] seated himself opposite & instantly declared his disapprobation of any persons being in that private meeting (as he called it) Except those of their own Society. this caused Dunning to lay down the paper which was instantly pocketed by Mc-

Clanegan & an Altercation succeeded. Dunning contended that no meetings of a public nature ought to be under the rose[3] & that he Evidently saw from the tenour of what he had read there was Evil at the root. This Circular Letter was wrote from Cumberland County[4] where Patriotic meetings (as they term em) are Established in all the towns & to meet in Harrisburg the 3 day of September as well for *wrath* as Conscience sake to consider of amendments to the proposed Government previous to its organization. Similar letters it seems are forwarded to all States to ascertain the numbers & strength of the antifederalists & if found sufficient to make Effectual opposition then to stand forth boldly in the cause[.] there are, I'm inform'd very alarming Expressions in the waiting blood & slaughter seem unavoidable unless speedily Counteracted by sufficient authority—we have in Pennsylvania a wise Council & President & their wisdom will direct them to pursue the proper measures perhaps they may see the necessity of issuing a Proclamation suitable to the occasion without loss of time stating the iniquity of these proceedings, the danger of perservering & the humiliating fate of the [majority.?] Shay in his vain opposition to the government of Massachusetts[5] & the necessity of sending a sufficient body of Militia instantly to remove the sinews of war from Carlisle & Philadelphia as likewise to take Effectual measures to secure the insurgents & their papers at their meeting on thursday Evening at the same Tavern[6]—

At the instance of Mr. Ashurst a letter was wrote to Genl: Mifflin[7] on the above [- - -] subject signed by him who declares himself ready to give every particular when [called?] upon by proper authority but the General being in New York the hope of [- - -] secretary was lost thro his means, however it may yet be revived thro [your?] means as the happiness of America is near your heart—should the matter be conducted with due secrecy & prudence in those appointed to go to the Tavern, great discoveries may be made—Mr. Ashurst was the next day informed by [some?] in the secret that Doctor Finelay was selected to go over Schuylkill to sound [out] people—Mr. McClanegan to the Northern Libertys of the City & others to [various?] parts of the Country for the like purpose[.] there appears to be a firm plan to defeat the government if they possibly can & without speedy spirited [measures?], perhaps a Civil war will be unavoidable the horrors of which none [can?] imagine but those who have unhappily Experienced its dreadfull Consequences which may God in his infinite goodness preserve us from—

1. RC, Benjamin Franklin Papers, American Philosophical Society.
2. Blair M'Clenachan was elected to the Harrisburg Convention from Philadelphia County. He was elected chairman of the convention.
3. In secret, i.e., sub rosa.

4. See the Cumberland County circular letter 3 July (BoR, III, 165–66).
5. For Shays's Rebellion, see RCS:Mass., Vol. 1, xxxix–xli.
6. No proclamation was issued, and no militia force was sent against the "insurgents" at Germantown.
7. Because of Benjamin Franklin's infirmities, Thomas Mifflin was serving as acting president of the Pennsylvania Supreme Executive Council. Mifflin was elected president of the Council in November 1788.

James Hanna to John Vandegrift, Nathan Vansant, and Jacob Vandegrift, Newtown, Bucks County, Pa., 15 August 1788[1]

GENTLEMEN, The important crisis now approaching (confident I am you will think with me) demands the most serious attention of every friend of American liberty. The constitution of the United States is now adopted by eleven states in the union, and no doubt the other two will follow their example; for, however just the sentiments of the opposition may be, I do conceive it would be the height of madness and folly, and in fact a crime of very detrimental consequence to our country, to refuse to acquiesce in a measure received in form by so great a majority of our country; not only to ourselves individually, but to the community at large—for the worst that we can expect from a bad form of government is anarchy and confusion, with all its common train of grievances—and by an opposition in the present situation of affairs, we are sure of it. On the other hand, by a sullen and inactive conduct, it will give the promoters and warm advocates of the plan an opportunity (if any such design they have) to shackle us with those manacles, that we fear may be formed under colour of law, and we be led to know it is constitutional, when it is too late to extricate ourselves and posterity from a lasting bondage.

To you it is not worth while to animadvert on the plain and pointed tendency the constitution has to this effect, and how easily it may be accomplished in power under its influence. That virtue is not the standard which has principally animated the adoption of the constitution in this state I believe is too true. Let us, therefore, as we wish to serve our country, and shew the world that those only who wished amendments were truly fœderal, adopt the conduct of our fellow-citizens in the back counties. Let us, as freemen, call a meeting of those citizens who wish for amendments, in a committee of the county, delegated from each township, for the purpose expressed in a copy of the (circular) inclosed.[2] In promoting a scheme of this kind, I hope we shall not only have the satisfaction of seeing the minds and exertions of all who wish for amendments center in this object, which will swallow others more injurious, but that we will enjoy the supreme felicity of having assisted in snatching from slavery a once happy and worthy people.

I therefore hope you will undertake to call together your township, have delegates chosen to represent them in a committee to be held at the house of George Piper, on Monday, the 21st inst. at nine o'clock in the forenoon, for the purpose of appointing delegates to represent them in the state conference, and for giving them instructions, &c.

If you should apprehend the people will not call a town-meeting for the purpose, that you will, as we intend here, write or call on a few of the most respectable people of your township, to attend at the general meeting, as they intend to do at Philadelphia, if they cannot accomplish their purpose in the other way.

Your usual public spirit on occasions of this kind, I am sure, needs no spur. We shall, therefore, rest assured that we will meet a representation of the township *committed to your charge* on the day appointed. *I am, with every sentiment of esteem, Yours, &c.*

1. Printed: *Pennsylvania Gazette*, 10 September. Reprinted: *Pennsylvania Journal*, 13 September; *New York Morning Post*, 18 September. Newtown was the county seat of Bucks County. The letter was addressed to the three men at Bensalem, a township in the extreme southern corner of Bucks County. None of the three men attended the county meeting. See Bucks County Meeting, 25 August (BoR, III, 172–74).

2. See the Cumberland County circular letter of 3 July calling the Harrisburg Convention (BoR, III, 165–66).

Fayette County, Pa.: Certificate of Election of Delegates to Harrisburg Convention, 18 August 1788[1]

We whose names are hereunto subscribed, at a conference held at Union Town for the County of Fayette, being appointed a committee, do certify that the Honorable John Smilie and Mr. Albert Galattin were chosen by the people then convened, to represent them in a general conference of the state to be held at Harrisburg the third day of September, in order to conclude upon such amendments and such mode of obtaining them as the conference in their wisdom may judge proper: Given under our hands at Union Town August the eighteenth Anno Domini 1788.

[Signed:] Nathanial Breading, James Finley, Daniel Cannon, Zadok Springer, Joseph Torrence

1. MS, Gallatin Papers, NHi.

Pennsylvania Gazette, 20 August 1788[1]

Circular letters, it is confidently asserted, have been sent to most of the counties and many townships from Cumberland, to request persons to meet at Harrisburg in September, for the purpose of procuring certain alterations in the fœderal government. Though we cannot think any citizen in the smallest degree censurable for pursuing measures, which he may think necessary or proper, yet the secrecy of this measure, and the omission of such circular letters to the townships in our vicinity and to this city, has a very improper appearance. There is *a fear of open discussion*, and *a depth of manœvering*, which we hope will have *a serious effect* upon the minds of the good people of Pennsylvania. It is evidently calculated to affect the ensuing election. Let the friends of just government and of the peace and happiness of Pennsylvania *not sleep upon the watch*.

1. Reprinted nine times by 22 September: Vt. (1), R.I. (1), Conn. (1), N.Y. (3), N.J. (1), Pa. (2).

Robert Galbraith et al. to President Benjamin Franklin Huntingdon, Pa., 23 August 1788[1]

With the utmost regret we find ourselves once more under the disagreeable necessity of informing Your Excellency that our part of the state is still torn and distracted by the machinations of wicked and evil disposed persons. A few days after our last letter to your honorable board from Messrs. Smith and Henderson,[2] a party armed with bludgeons, about twenty in number, headed by Abraham Smith, William M'Cune and Samuel Clinton, the latter of them a most notorious rioter, came into the town and violently beat Mr. Alexander Irwin, one of our citizens. Some of the same riotous party, whose names and persons we have not been able properly to ascertain, have frequently, at night, assaulted our houses with showers of stones. Threats have been sent from all parts of the county that death—or what is to a man of feeling worse—cropping, tarring, etc., should be inflicted on us or any other officer of the county who should attempt to put the laws in force. On Wednesday last [20 August] about one hundred and eighty men collected from different parts of the county—some few of the townsmen among them—paraded the streets, not with muskets, as before, altho we have reason to believe they had a number secreted. They were headed by William M'Elroy, Abraham Smith, John Smith and John Little, Esq., one of the county justices. What their intentions were we know not, but hearing from many different quarters that they were determined to destroy some of us, we collected a few friends of government and some arms and met at the house of Benjamin Elliot, Esq., our sheriff, resolved, if any attack was made, to repel force with force, and to the utmost defend our own lives. This salutary precaution, of which we are satisfied, their spies had given them information, was without doubt, the reason of their not committing any violence that day. After marching with colors flying and fifes playing thro the town, they held, what they called an election, at the house of William Kerr, for members to meet in convention at Louisburg [i.e., Harrisburg], as we have been informed. At this election they excluded from voting everyone who did not march with them, and admitted promiscuously everyone who did. A number of insults were thrown out against the government, but no personal injury done.

To your honorable board, as the supreme executive power of the state, we apply for such assistance in support of government, as to your wisdoms shall deem proper.

1. Printed: *Pennsylvania Archives*, 1 ser., XI, 379–80. The letter was signed by Robert Galbraith, Thomas Duncan Smith, Andrew Henderson, and Benjamin Elliot. Franklin was president of the Pennsylvania Supreme Executive Council.

2. Thomas Duncan Smith and Andrew Henderson to President Franklin, 5 June, *ibid.*, 305–7.

Bucks County, Pa., Meeting: Proceedings and Resolutions
25 August 1788[1]

The ratification of the Federal Constitution and its expected operation forming a new æra in the American world, and giving cause of hope to some and fear to others, it has been thought proper that the freemen of the state, or delegates chosen by them, should meet together and deliberate on the subject. Accordingly it has been proposed, that a meeting of deputies from the different counties be held at Harrisburg the third day of September next. A circular letter, bearing the above proposition was sent to this county,[2] and in pursuance thereof there met this day at Piper's Tavern, in Bedminster township, the following gentlemen from the townships annexed to their names respectively:—

Newtown,	James Hanna, Esquire.
Warwick,	John Crawford, Hugh Ramsey, Capt. William Walker, Benjamin Snodgrass, Samuel Flack.
Newbritain,	James Snodgrass, Thomas Stewart, David Thomas.
Bedminster,	Jacob Utt, Alexander Hughes, George Piper, Daniel Soliday.
Haycock,	Capt. Manus Yost, John Keller.
Rockhill,	Samuel Smith, Esquire.
Millford,	Henry Blitaz, Henry Hoover.
Springfield,	Col. John Smith, Charles Fleming.
Durham,	Richard Backhouse, Esquire.

HARRISBURG CONVENTION, 3–6 SEPTEMBER 1788

Tinicum,	John Thompson, Jacob Weaver, George Bennet.
Nockamixon,	Samuel Wilson, George Vogle.
Richland,	Benjamin Seagle.
Plumstead,	Thomas Wright, Thomas Gibson, James Ruckman, Major John Shaw, James Farres, Thomas Henry, Moses Kelly, Henry Geddis.
Warrington,	Rev. Nathaniel Erwin, Capt. William Walker.
Buckingham,	Capt. Samuel Smith.
Solesbury,	Henry Seabring.
Hilltown.	Joseph Grier.

Samuel Smith, esquire, chosen chairman, and James Hanna, esquire, secretary. After some time spent in discussing the business of the meeting, Resolved, that the Rev. Nathaniel Erwin, Richard Backhouse, Samuel Smith, John Crawford, and James Hanna, esquires, be a committee to draw up resolves expressive of the sense of this meeting on the subject before them.

In a short time thereafter the following were presented by the gentlemen appointed, and unanimously approved.

Resolved 1. That it is the opinion of this meeting that the plan of government for the United States, formed by the general convention, having been adopted by eleven of the states, ought, in conformity to the resolves of said convention, to come into operation, and have force until altered in a constitutional way.

2. That as we mean to act the part of peaceable citizens ourselves, so we will support the said plan of government and those who act under it against all illegal violence.

3. That the said plan of government will admit of very considerable amendments, which ought to be made in the mode pointed out in the constitution itself.

4. That as few governments once established have ever been altered in favour of liberty without confusion and bloodshed, the requisite amendments in said constitution ought to be attempted as soon as possible.

5. That we will use our utmost endeavours in a pacific way to procure such alterations in the fœderal constitution as may be necessary to secure the rights and liberties of ourselves and posterity.

6. That we approve of a state meeting being held at Harrisburg the third day of September next, on the subject of the above resolves.

7. That four persons ought to be delegated from this county to attend said meeting, and join with the deputies from other counties who may meet with them (in recommendation to the citizens of this state) of a suitable set of men to represent them in the new Congress, and generally to acquiesce and assist in the promotion of such plan or plans

as may be designed by the said state conferres for the purpose of obtaining the necessary amendments of said constitution, as far as is consistent with our views, expressed in the foregoing resolves.

Agreeable to the resolve last past, the Rev. Nathaniel Erwin, Richard Backhouse, John Crawford, and James Hanna, esquires, or any two of them, were appointed to represent us in said conference to be held at Harrisburg.

Resolved, That James Hanna, esquire be requested to hand the foregoing proceedings to the Press for publication.

SAMUEL SMITH Chairman.

1. Printed: *Pennsylvania Packet*, 2 September. Reprinted in whole or in part in twelve newspapers by 2 October: Mass. (2), R.I. (1), Conn. (1), N.Y. (2), Pa. (5), S.C. (1).

2. Possibly the Cumberland County circular letter, 3 July (BoR, III, 165–66).

Thomas Willing to William Bingham
Philadelphia, 27 August 1788 (excerpt)[1]

... [P.S.] Some such boy's as I have mentioned above, are to meet at Harrisburgh—B Mc.—en, was named by a meetg. of 4 or 5 at Germantown to go for the County; and G. B—n C. P—t. Doctr. Ja—n[2] appointed by themselves I believe, for there has been no public meetg. or even one call'd, to give any body such appointment, are going from this City, to co'opperate with other Antis, to take advantage of your tedious delay—

1. RC, Gratz Collection, PHi. For a longer excerpt of this letter, see RCS:Cong., 62–64n.

2. References to Antifederalists Blair M'Clenachan, George Bryan, Charles Pettit, and Dr. James Hutchinson. See Germantown Antifederalist Meeting, 14 August (BoR, III, 167–68).

"A.B."
Pennsylvania Gazette, 27 August 1788[1]

Serious Advice to the GOVERNMENT-MENDERS,
who are to assemble at Harrisburgh, on the 3d of September.

A gentleman once gave his son (a lad about 14 years of age) a handsome new watch. The youth, upon opening it, perceived something in the watch which he took to be a hair which had fallen into it, and instantly pulled it away. It proved to be the pendulum spring, the loss of which rendered his watch good for nothing. Beware, gentlemen Government-Menders, how you touch any part of the new constitution. You may by mistake destroy its pendulum spring.

1. Reprinted: Boston *Independent Chronicle*, 4 September; Massachusetts *Salem Mercury*, 9 September.

Thomas McKean to Robert Magaw
Philadelphia, 28 August 1788 (excerpt)[1]

... It is reported here, that there is to be a convention at Louisburg [i.e., Harrisburg] on the 3d. of next month relating to the new Constitution. The motives for this I have not learnt. I have some apprehensions, that such meetings may prove injurious to good order, and therefore wish that they may not be drawn into practice, nor ever had but upon great and necessary occasions. Persons thus assembled are too apt to work themselves up to an opinion that they are a public legal body, instead of so many individuals collected together; and sometimes assume and exercise actual authority, which must always have a tendency to weaken if not disturb the regular government. May their zeal be tempered with prudence....

1. RC, James Hamilton Collection, PHi.

Extract of a Letter from Carlisle, Pa., 28 August 1788[1]

Our *Friends* the *Antifederals* are not yet quiet; a large Body of them from the East and West Side of the Susquehanna are to assemble next Tuesday at Harrisburg, by private Appointment, secretly communicated.—Mr. Finley, of Washington County, has just passed through this Town, on his way thither, to confer, it is supposed, with Mr. Whitehill, who lives near that Place.—The Object of this Meeting, it is universally believed, is to devise and adopt, in concert with the *Anties* throughout the Continent, some Plan for subverting the Federal Government. May their clandestine Designs be disappointed!

1. Printed: *Maryland Journal*, 2 September. Reprinted: *Virginia Independent Chronicle*, 10 September.

William Shippen, Jr., to Thomas Lee Shippen
Philadelphia, 2 September 1788 (excerpt)[1]

... There is a great convention now sitting at Harrisburgh on the Susquehannah, compos'd of antifœderalists from every county—Blair McClenahan is gone from philad. county & George Bryan & Charles Pettit from the city—their business is to agree upon & recommend such alterations as they may think necessary & there is so respectable a minority in every state that I think one of the first acts of the new Government will be to propose a general convention of the people to make these necessary alterations—till when the minds of a great part of the U States will not be easy.—To effect this measure I am apt to think at our next election the Constitutionalists will prevail.—General

[Thomas] Miflin is to be our next president.—Our Assembly met this morning & [Thomas] Lloyd takes down their debates in short hand—I will preserve them for you. . . .

1. RC, Thomas Lee Shippen Family Papers, DLC. Shippen's letters to his son, who was traveling in Europe, were usually written over a period of time. The above letter is from a letter written between 21 August and 21 September. The excerpt is dated 2 September because Shippen wrote that the Assembly met that morning. The Pennsylvania Assembly met for its fall session on 2 September.

Pennsylvania Gazette, 3 September 1788[1]

A Correspondent has furnished us with the following curious paragraph, extracted from a letter which was forwarded to three gentlemen in a respectable township, by a very active promoter of *The Antifederal Conclave* intended to meet this day (3d September) at Harrisburg—

"If you should *apprehend* the people *will not* call a town meeting for the purpose, that you will, *as we intend here*, write or call on *a few* of the most *respectable* people of your township to attend at *this general* meeting, as they *intend* to do at Philadelphia, *if they cannot accomplish their purpose* the other way."[2]—

Thus we see that these kind gentlemen, knowing *the people at large* are opposed to their scheme, intend that "*a few* respectable" well-born people shall carry it on for them.—Our Correspondent observes further, that it appears this "*general* meeting" is to be made up of "*a few*" particular persons. The circular letter, which was enclosed in the above-mentioned, plainly talks of "*a civil war*," and proposes that the eight federal representatives for Pennsylvania shall be put in nomination by *the Conclave* of "*the respectable few*" at Harrisburg.[3]—These obliging Volunteers, we presume, mean to save all the trouble of *free elections* in future;—for it seems, if the people do not come into their scheme, they intend to accomplish their purpose in another way.

1. Reprinted: New York *Daily Advertiser* and *New York Morning Post*, 6 September; Charleston, S.C., *City Gazette*, 17 September; Annapolis *Maryland Gazette*, 18 September.
2. Quoted from a 15 August letter of James Hanna (BoR, III, 170).
3. See the Cumberland County circular letter (BoR, III, 165–66).

Harrisburg Convention: Proceedings, Resolutions, and Petition 3–6 September 1788[1]

Harrisburgh, Dauphin County, State of Pennsylvania, September 3d, 1788.

Agreeably to a circular letter which originated in the county of Cumberland,[2] inviting to a conference such of the citizens of this state, who conceive that a revision of the federal system, lately proposed for the government of these United States, is necessary; a number of gentlemen from the city of Philadelphia and counties of Philadelphia, Bucks, Chester, Lancaster, Cumberland, Berks, Northumberland, Bedford, Fayette, Washington, Franklin, Dauphin, and Huntingdon,[3] assembled at this place for the said purpose, viz.

Hon. George Bryan, Esq.	William Petricken,
Charles Pettit,	Jonathan Hoge,
Blair M'Clenachan,	John Bishop,
Richard Backhouse,	Daniel Montgomery,
James Hanna,	John Lytle,
Joseph Gardner,	John Dickey,
James Mercer,	Honorable John Smiley,
Benjamin Blyth,	Albert Gallatin,
Robert Whitehill,	James Marshall,
John Jordan,	Benjamin Elliott,
William Sterrett,	Richard Baird,
William Rodgers,	James Crooks,
Adam Orth,	John A. Hanna,
John Rodgers,	Daniel Bradley,
Thomas Murray,	Robert Smith,
Robert M'Kee,	James Anderson.
John Kean,	

Blair M'Clenachan, Esq. was unanimously elected Chairman, and John A. Hanna, Esq. Secretary.

After free discussion and mature deliberation had upon the subject before them, the following resolutions and propositions were adopted.

The ratification of the federal constitution having formed a new æra in the American world, highly interesting to all the citizens of the United States, it is not less the duty than the privilege of every citizen, to examine with attention the principles and probable effects of a system, on which the happiness or misery of the present, as well as future generations, so much depend. In the course of such examination, many of the good citizens of the state of Pennsylvania have found their apprehensions excited that the constitution in its present form, contains in it some principles which may be perverted to purposes injurious to the rights of free citizens, and some ambiguities which may probably lead to contentions incompatible with order and good government: in order to remedy these inconveniencies, and to avert the apprehended dangers, it has been thought expedient that delegates, chosen by those who wish for early amendments in the said constitution, should meet together for the purpose of deliberating on the subject, and uniting in some constitutional plan for obtaining the amendments which they may deem necessary.

We the conferees assembled, for the purpose aforesaid, agree in opinion:

That a federal government only can preserve the liberties and secure the happiness of the inhabitants of a country so extensive as these United States; and experience having taught us, that the ties of our union, under the articles of confederation, were so weak as to deprive us of some of the greatest advantages we had a right to expect from it. We are fully convinced that a more efficient government is indispensably necessary; but although the constitution proposed for the United States is likely to obviate most of the inconveniencies we labored under; yet several parts of it appear so exceptionable to us, that we are clearly of opinion considerable amendments are essentially necessary: In full confidence however of obtaining a revision of such exceptionable parts by a General-Convention, and from a desire to harmonize with our fellow-citizens, we are induced to acquiesce in the organization of the said constitution.

We are sensible that a large number of the citizens both in this and the other states, who gave their assent to its being carried into execution, previous to any amendments, were actuated more by the fear of the dangers that might arise from delays, than by a conviction of its being perfect; we therefore hope they will concur with us in pursuing every peaceable method of obtaining a speedy revision of the constitution in the mode therein provided; and when we reflect on the present circumstances of the union, we can entertain no doubt that motives of conciliation, and the dictates of policy and prudence, will conspire to induce every man of true federal principles, to give his support to a measure which is not only calculated to recommend the new constitution to the approbation and support of every class of citizens, but even necessary to prevent the total defection of some members of the union.

Strongly impressed with these sentiments we have agreed to the following resolutions:

1. *Resolved*, That it be recommended to the people of this state to acquiesce in the organization of the said government; but although we thus accord in its organization, we by no means lose sight of the grand object of obtaining very considerable amendments and alterations, which we consider essential to preserve the peace and harmony of the union, and those invaluable privileges for which so much blood and treasure have been recently expended.

2. *Resolved*, That it is necessary to obtain a speedy revision of said constitution by a general convention.

3. *Resolved*, That in order to effect this desirable end, a petition be presented to the Legislature of this state, requesting that honorable body to take the earliest opportunity to make application for that purpose to the new Congress.[4]

The petition proposed is as follows:
To the Honorable the Representatives of the Freemen of the Commonwealth of Pennsylvania, in General Assembly met.

The Petition and Representation of the Subscribers,
HUMBLY SHEW,

That your petitioners possess sentiments completely federal: being convinced that a confederacy of republican states, and no other, can secure political liberty, happiness, and safety throughout a territory so extended as the United States of *America*. They are well apprized of the necessity of devolving extensive powers to Congress, and of vesting the Supreme Legislature with every power and resource of a general nature; and consequently they acquiesce in the general system of government framed by the late *federal convention*; in full confidence, however, that the same will be revised without delay: For however worthy of approbation the general principles and outlines of the said system may be, your petitioners conceive that amendments in some parts of the plan are essential, not only to the preservation of such rights and privileges as ought to be reserved in the respective states, and in the citizens thereof, but to the fair and unembarassed operation of the GOVERNMENT in its various departments. And as provision is made in the *constitution* itself for the making of such amendments as may be deemed necessary; and your petitioners are desirous of obtaining the amendments which occur to them as more immediately desirable and necessary, in the mode admitted by such provision.

They pray that your honorable House, as the Representatives of the people in this Commonwealth, will, in the course of your present session, take such measures as you in your wisdom shall deem most effectual and proper to obtain a revision and amendment of the constitution of the United States, in such parts and in such manner as have been or shall be pointed out by the conventions or assemblies of the respective states; and that such revision be by a general convention of representatives from the several states in the Union.

Your petitioners consider the amendments pointed out in the propositions hereto subjoined as essentially necessary, and as such they suggest them to your notice, submitting to your wisdom the order in which they shall be presented to the consideration of the United States.

The Amendments proposed are as follow,—viz.

I. That Congress shall not exercise any powers whatsoever, but such as are expressly given to that body by the constitution of the United

States; nor shall any authority, power or jurisdiction, be assumed or exercised by the executive or judiciary departments of the union under colour or pretence of construction or fiction: But all the rights of sovereignty, which are not by the said constitution expressly and plainly vested in the Congress shall be deemed to remain with, and shall be exercised by the several states in union according to their respective constitutions: And that every reserve of the rights of individuals, made by the several constitutions of the states in union to the citizens and inhabitants of each state respectively, shall remain inviolate, except so far as they are expressly and manifestly yielded or narrowed by the national constitution.

Article 1. Section 2. Paragraph 3.

II. That the number of representatives be for the present, one for every twenty thousand inhabitants according to the present estimated numbers in the several states, and continue in that proportion till the whole number of representatives shall amount to two hundred; and then to be so proportioned and modified as not to exceed that number till the proportion of one representative for every thirty thousand inhabitants, shall amount to the said number of two hundred.

Section 3.

III. That senators, though chosen for six years, shall be liable to be recalled, or superseded by other appointments, by the respective Legislatures of the states at any time.

Section 4.

IV. That Congress shall not have power to make or alter regulations concerning the time, place and manner of electing senators and representatives, except in case of neglect or refusal by the state to make regulations for the purpose: and then only for such time as such neglect or refusal shall continue.

Section 8.

V. That when Congress shall require supplies, which are to be raised by direct taxes, they shall demand from the several states their respective quotas thereof, giving a reasonable time to each state to procure and pay the same; and if any state shall refuse, neglect or omit to raise and pay the same within such limited time, then Congress shall have power to assess, levy and collect the quota of such state, together with interest for the same from the time of such delinquency, upon the inhabitants and estates therein, in such manner as they shall by law direct, provided that no poll-tax be imposed.

Section 8.

VI. That no standing army of regular troops shall be raised or kept up in time of peace, without the consent of two-thirds of both Houses in Congress.

Section 8.

VII. That the clause respecting the exclusive legislation over a district not exceeding ten miles square, be qualified by a proviso that such right of legislation extend only to such regulations as respect the police and good order thereof.

Article 1. Section 8.

VIII. That each state respectively shall have power to provide for organizing, arming and disciplining the militia thereof, whensoever Congress shall omit or neglect to provide for the same. That the militia shall not be subject to martial law, but when in actual service in time of war, invasion or rebellion: and when not in the actual service of the United States, shall be subject to such fines, penalties, and punishments only, as shall be directed or inflicted by the laws of its own state: nor shall the militia of any state be continued in actual service longer than two months under any call of Congress, without the consent of the Legislature of such state, or, in their recess, the Executive Authority thereof.

Section 9.

IX. That the clause respecting vessels bound to or from any one of the states, be explained.

Article 3. Section 1.

X. That Congress establish no court other than the supreme court, except such as shall be necessary for determining causes of admiralty jurisdiction.

Section 2. Paragraph 2.

XI. That a proviso be added at the end of the second clause of the second section of the third article, to the following effect, viz. Provided, That such appellate jurisdiction, in all cases of common law cognizance, be by Writ of Error, and confined to Matters of Law only; and that no such writ of error shall be admitted except in revenue cases, unless the matter in controversy exceed the value of three thousand dollars.

Article 6. Paragraph 2.

XII. That to article 6, clause 2, be added the following proviso, viz. Provided always, That no treaty which shall hereafter be made, shall be deemed or construed to alter or affect any law of the United States, or of any particular state, until such treaty shall have been laid before and assented to by the House of Representatives in Congress.

Resolved, That the foregoing proceedings be committed to the Chairman for publication.

BLAIR M'CLENACHAN, Chairman.

Attest.
JOHN A. HANNA, Secretary.

1. Printed: Philadelphia *Independent Gazetteer*, 15 September. This report also appears in the *Pennsylvania Packet* on 15 September. Reprinted twelve times by 14 October: R.I. (1), Conn. (1), Pa. (6), Va. (2), N.C. (1), S.C. (1). The manuscript version of these proceedings are in the Albert Gallatin Papers at the New-York Historical Society. For draft resolutions significantly different from these by Albert Gallatin, see DHFFE, I, 259–60.

2. For the Cumberland County circular letter, see BoR, III, 165–66.

3. Northampton, Montgomery, York, Westmoreland, and Luzerne counties were not represented.

4. No evidence has been found to indicate that these resolutions were delivered to the Pennsylvania Assembly.

Alexander Graydon to Lambert Cadwalader
Louisburg, Pa., 7 September 1788 (excerpt)[1]

... We have had a meeting of the antifederal party in this Town consisting of Deputies from most of the Counties in the State. They have fixed upon several Amendments which they proposed offering to Congress thro' the Medium of the Assembly These Amendments are extremely moderate indeed and by no means such as wou'd justify the violent Opposition given by these Gentlemen to the Constitution But tho' the ostensible Motive for meeting, was to propose Amendments, the real one seems to be to let themselves down as easy as possible and to come in for a Share of the good things the new Government may have to bestow—You will probably see their proceedings published.

1. RC, Cadwalader Papers, PHi. When Dauphin County was established in 1785, Harris's Ferry on the Susquehanna River was made the county seat. The commissions issued to county officers named the place "Louisburg," although most contemporaries called it Harrisburg, which became the official name in 1791.

Benjamin Lincoln to Theodore Sedgwick
Boston, 7 September 1788 (excerpts)[1]

... We are anxious here that any reasonable crises which makes it indefensible to defer an organization of the new government to so late a period—we must however submit for there are so many circumstances constantly turning up and so many different interests to be reconciled that much time must be expended in adjusting them we should therefore be quiet though it is difficult to keep all so.—

I am sorry that North Carolina has rejected the constitution—I cannot feel on the occasion as you do—I am very apprehensive, soldiers may have apprehensions but no fears, that the Anties in Virginia will find aid and support by their brethren in North Carolina besides I think it will have its influence in calling the general convention proposed by New York—may Heaven avert the design—Rhode Island that little trollop of a sister, will take support be flattered in her wickedness and encouraged in her obstinacy....

Truly we cannot think seriously of calling a convention it is a measure of all others to be dreaded—When you say we are pledged not to oppose who do you mean by *We* not surely the *State* that must and I think will oppose and contend earnestly in support of the opposite side of the question—If this measure should take place I shall in that moment bid adieu to those pleasing prospects which I have embraced with so much real satisfaction for months past. Do not let us procrastinate let us begin as soon as possible to secure ourselves as far as we have proceded—Would you not think it a very laughable circumstance should a number of Gardners in possession of the most valuable plants, plants necessary to be cultivated for the very existance of the proprietor quarrel so long respecting that part of the Garden in which they should be cultivated and so finally as to omit the care of them and in the mean while, the goats should enter and devour them.

1. RC, Sedgwick Papers, MHi.

Thomas Hartley to Tench Coxe
York, Pa., 9 September 1788[1]

By a Trusty Friend whom we had at Harrisburg—I have a Transcript of their Proceedings there—The Obvious Intention of those Men is to distract this Country and embarrass the new Counstitution.—

Their Sentiments are known to you and all of us—

They like no part of the System because it operates against their Power—but for the Moment they wish to appear under the plauseable Pretentions of Amendments—

Their Proceedings will probably be published early in the City—but I thought it prudent to send you a Copy as early as possible to be communicated to our Friends—

Besides this I dare say they have fixed upon Tickets &c

I can add no more than that I am in great Haste Your Friend & humble Servt.

1. RC, Coxe Papers, Series II, Correspondence and General Papers, PHi. Coxe became a member of a committee of correspondence for Philadelphia that encouraged Federalists throughout the state to work diligently to elect Federalists to both the state Assembly and the U.S. House of Representatives. See Philadelphia Committee of Correspondence to Timothy Pickering, 11 September 1788 (BoR, III, 185–86).

Pennsylvania Gazette, 10 September 1788[1]

By a gentleman, who passed through Harrisburg a few days ago, we learn that the anti-fœderal conference had met, and appointed Blair

M'Clenachan chairman of their meeting, and George Bryan and Charles Pettit, with some others, a committee to bring in a *string* of amendments to the new constitution—that they were much disappointed in meeting no deputies from several of the most respectable counties in the state[2]—and that of the deputies who were there, many of them were so hampered with moderate instructions, that they could do nothing with them—that the whole squad of Malecontents was dull and dissatisfied, as there appeared to be no chance of kindling a civil war in the United States—and that the opinion of all the considerate men in the neighbourhood of Harrisburg was, that the persons met would be much better employed in mending *themselves*, than in trying to mend a government which was framed by the wisest and best men in America.

1. Reprinted: *Pennsylvania Journal*, 13 September; *Maryland Journal*, 16 September; *New York Morning Post*, 18 September.
2. Northampton, Montgomery, York, Westmoreland, and Luzerne counties were not represented.

A Freeman
Pennsylvania Gazette, 10 September 1788[1]

In a free country, private or *secret* associations for the purpose of taking care of the government are always dangerous, and should be narrowly watched and opposed. The following letters will shew that such a secret association has existed for some time in Pennsylvania. The government over the members of this association is a kind of aristocracy. The heads of it are some of the officers of the state government—one of whom has lately got an appointment in Bucks county, viz. Mr. Hanna. It is to be hoped the independent citizens of Pennsylvania will guard their power and offices, hereafter, from men, who make politics a private business, and who have no other means of maintaining their families.

Germantown, September 4.

P. S. Would it not be proper to obtain the names of the persons to whom the *charge*, or government, of every township in the state is *committed*, so that we might know our new masters, and obey them accordingly?

[Here followed the Cumberland County circular letter of 3 July and James Hanna's letter of 15 August, BoR, III, 165–66, 169–70.]

1. Reprinted: *Pennsylvania Journal*, 13 September; *New York Morning Post*, 18 September.

Philadelphia Committee of Correspondence to Timothy Pickering
11 September 1788[1]

The present important crisis in the affairs of Pennsylvania having induced a considerable number of respectable Inhabitants of this City & neighborhood to meet & consider of such measures as would be most likely to secure to the State a Representation of men in the next Assembly, equally known for their firm attachment to the federal Government, & real interests of this State as well as for their candour, integrity & good sense, a committee, to communicate their sentiments to, & correspond with their friends in the different Counties, was thought essentially necessary.—

We therefore as the Committee of correspondence,[2] take the liberty to address you on this important subject, being not only well assured of your zeal and regard for the new Government, but that you will, on all occasions use your influence with your friends to promote its true interests.

To have persons of the best qualifications elected to represent us in the general Assembly, is at all times an object of very great consequence, but at the present moment, when the new federal Constitution is to be carried into effect, it is a matter of the utmost importance. The ensuing legislature will not only have the ordinary objects of our State affairs before them, but they will have in charge to complete the arrangements of the general Government, so far as the present House shall leave them unfinished. It is probable also that the great subject of amendments may form a part of their deliberations: All those points will require representatives of undoubted integrity and sound judgment. But to revise the new Constitution if that should be brought before them, they should be men of great candour free from prejudices against it, & well disposed to the continuance of an energetic power in our federal head.

The late meeting of the opponents of the new Constitution in the town of Harrisburg must have given serious alarm to its friends, & the Election purposes, both with regard to the federal & State Representatives, which we conceive it was calculated to promote, should excite our most active exertions, & vigilance, & awaken all our caution: You will see at once that as this measure was confessedly intended, so it may seriously affect the Election of the eight federal Representatives, as well as of the State Legislature. Their circular letter plainly recommends the nomination of eight persons for that purpose:[3] You will permit us therefore to put you on your guard concerning that Election also, and to recommend it equally to your attention in due time, according as the same may be ordered by the present or future Assembly.

As we shall on all occasions be happy to communicate to you every necessary information which we may obtain in this business, so we are desirous to receive the same from you.

1. RC, Pickering Papers, MHi. The letter was signed by Samuel Miles, Walter Stewart, Francis Gurney, Tench Coxe, Henry Kammerer, John Nixon, Benjamin Rush, and Hilary Baker. A draft of this letter is in the Coxe Papers, Series II, Correspondence and General Papers, PHi.

2. There is no evidence of a meeting to create such a "committee of correspondence." However, at a meeting on 1 October to plan for forthcoming federal elections, these and other men were appointed to a committee to plan for a meeting at Lancaster to nominate Federalist candidates (See DHFFE, I, 296–98.).

3. This refers to the Cumberland County circular letter, 3 July (printed for the first time in the *Pennsylvania Gazette* on 10 September, BoR, III, 165–66) rather than to the proceedings of the Harrisburg Convention, which were not printed in Philadelphia until 15 September. It is possible, however, that Tench Coxe had received a copy of the proceedings of the Convention by this time (see Thomas Hartley to Coxe, 9 September, BoR, III, 183).

James McLene to William Irvine
Philadelphia, 12 September 1788 (excerpt)[1]

The meeting at harris-burgh has for Some time past been A Subject of much conversation & great enquirey amongst A certain class of people in this city. Mr. [John] Smiley (who attended the meeting) came to town yesterday; by him we Learn that the business was carried on with great harmony & moderation. The proceedings are printing at Lancaster & will be forwarded to you as Soon as possible, The bearer Dr. [Samuel?] Jackson, having Seen Mr. Smiley, can tell you all that we know about it....

1. RC, Irvine Papers, PHi.

New York Packet, 12 September 1788[1]

The intended meeting at Harrisburgh in Pennsylvania having become the topic of much political disquisition—it may not be unacceptable to our readers to see the following resolutions of the Bucks-county meeting[2] in the said State.

The moderation of these resolutions it is to be hoped will be imitated by all the friends to peace and good government.

Let the ill-judged epithet of *Anti*-federal be for ever emerged in the foul channel of folly and impertinence from whence it generated. We are now all Federal-men—and those who shall attempt to divide us into party hereafter, are wretches worthy to know no other happiness than that they now enjoy, pale misery and guilty hearts.

1. Reprinted: Lansingburgh, N.Y., *Federal Herald*, 22 September; Hartford, Conn., *American Mercury*, 22 September.
2. For the Bucks County meeting and resolutions, 25 August, see BoR, III, 172–74.

A Word to the Wise
Pennsylvania Mercury, 13 September 1788[1]

To the Electors *of* Pennsylvania.

The enemies of the new constitution having failed in their attempts to prevent its establishment, are now busily employed in endeavoring to *overset* it in a constitutional way.—For this purpose they have held an electionering conference at Harrisburgh, the design of which is to fill all the elective posts of the state and federal government with antifederal characters. It becomes the friends of the constitution to *keep a good look-out*, and thereby prevent any such persons from seizing the helm of our fœderal barque, in order to run her ashore within sight of the port of liberty and safety.—The times are difficult and critical. Let the wisest and best men, therefore, be fixed upon to compose our representatives in Congress, and in the assembly. It is not enough that they should be men of integrity and fair characters. They should be men of abilities, and perfectly acquainted with the principles of government. They should understand, in a particular manner, the *place* and *use* of every peg in the Fœderal Constitution. Such men will never be imposed upon or surprised by *side motions* or resolves in favor of amendments, which, in the present state of this country, cannot fail of involving us in ruin.

1. Reprinted: Philadelphia *Freeman's Journal*, 17 September.

Pennsylvania Mercury, 13 September 1788

Extract of a letter from Harrisburgh,
(the seat of the self-created Pennsylvania Congress.)

"Our real design in meeting here, is to make the last arrangement in our power for the next General Election, so as, if possible, to keep ourselves and get our friends into the Legislature; and what some of us wish much more, is to get into the general Government; but we cover our real design, by making the people believe that our intentions are to propose amendments to the new Constitution, and you will see petitions handed about, so soon as any of the worthy gentlemen of your city go down. These petitions were printed, and sent over to us from our good friends in London, as you may see by looking at the stamp on the paper, where our favorite GR and crown, plainly appear.— We have been disappointed by not having any representatives from the German counties, viz. Lancaster, York, Berks and Northampton."[1]

1. Only York and Northampton of these four counties were not represented at the Harrisburg Convention.

James Madison to Edmund Randolph
New York, 14 September 1788 (excerpt)[1]

... The result of the Meeting at Harrisburg is I am told in the press & will of course be soon before the public. I am not acquainted with the particulars, or indeed with the general complexion of it. It has been said here that the meeting was so thin as to disappoint much the patrons of the scheme. . . .

1. RC, Madison Papers, DLC. The letter was marked "*private*" on the address page, indicating that it was not an official letter from a member of Congress to Virginia's governor. For the entire letter, see Rutland, *Madison,* XI, 252–54.

James Madison to George Washington
New York, 14 September 1788 (excerpt)[1]

... The meeting at Harrisburg is represented by its friends as having been conducted with much harmony & moderation. Its proceedings are said to be in the press, and will of course soon be before the public. I find that all the mischeif apprehended from Clinton's circular letter in Virginia will be verified. The Antifederalsts lay hold of it with eagerness as the harbinger of a second Convention; and as the Governor[2] espouses the project it will certainly have the co-operation of our Assembly. . . .

1. RC, Washington Papers, DLC. For the entire letter, see Abbot, *Washington, Confederation Series,* VI, 513–14.
2. Virginia Governor Edmund Randolph. See BoR, I, 158–80 for the Virginia General Assembly's actions on the New York Convention's circular letter and Virginia's resolution requesting Congress to call a general convention to amend the Constitution.

Richard Peters to George Washington
Philadelphia, 17 September 1788 (excerpt)[1]

... Our Antifederalists have changed their Battery. They are now very federal. They want Amendments & they must get into the Seats of Government to bring them about—or what is better—to share the Loaves & fishes.—Their Harrisburg Convention have agreed to submit to &

support the Government, & some of them, like the moderate Men & converted Tories formerly, now make up in Sound what they want in Patriotism. In short their Convention was a mere Election Jobb & no Harm is to be expected from it except they get into the Government which in the whole cannot be prevented. When they have got warm in their Seats they will, as it always happens in such Cases, find it their Interest to support a Government in which they are Sharers tho' they may make a little Bustle ad captandum.[2] . . .

1. RC, Washington Papers, DLC. For the entire letter, see Abbot, *Washington, Confederation Series*, VI, 520–22.
2. Latin: capturing popular favor. Often used to describe an argument directed chiefly at the emotions.

A Freeman
Pennsylvania Gazette, 17 September 1788[1]

To the PEOPLE *of the United States.*

So much formality was observed by the opposition to the new fœderal constitution in this state, in forwarding (tho' secretly) a circular letter to every township,[2] and so much pains has been taken to make known every where (but in Pennsylvania) this extraordinary meeting, that to many of you it must have had the appearance of a regular convention.[3] You have been informed, and truly too, that the people were tempted to the measure, by having an exemption from taxes for several years deceitfully promised to them. The authority of Congress was also shamefully asserted to have been obtained. It is not pretended that this was the case universally, for it is believed that in some places no deceptions were observed. At those meetings, however, the numbers were very small, several of them not exceeding one citizen for one hundred who had a right to be there. It appears that several entire counties had so little inclination for the business, that no one inhabitant of them chose to be at the expence or trouble of attending, particularly Lancaster, York, Northampton and Berks,[4] in which four are the great body of the Germans. But to persons at a distance it must have been a matter of curiosity, to know what was the design of this assembly. It is evident that amendments could not be the real object; for the minority of the convention of Pennsylvania, in their address and reasons of dissent, have given their objections, and the principles of the amendments desired by them, with a deal of reasoning and observations. *To muster* their force for THE ENSUING ELECTIONS of state and fœderal representatives was the object. As the opposition in Pennsylvania has been thus industrious and active to obtain their views in our continental elections, they have no doubt *passed on the word*, eastward and southward; and tho' the virtue manifested by the minorities of several of the states has been such as to remove all apprehensions of similar conduct on their part, yet the friends of peace and harmony on both sides of the question ought to know the concealed and unwarrantable measures, which some people have pursued in Pennsylvania. It was the circular letter that called this meeting, that held out to the freemen of this commonwealth, and of the rest of the United States, the menacing alternative of adopting the amendments they should prescribe, or the miseries of a civil war.[5] There cannot be a sincere desire for alterations, favorable to public liberty or happiness, in the minds of men thus dictatorial and outrageous. The pure spirits among the oppositions of the other states, the men among them who devoutly love their country and mankind, must be disgusted with such proceedings. They must be fearful of entering on the discussion of even proper amendments with men capable of such practices, and wrought up to such an unhappy frame of mind. In their intemperate debates WISDOM could have no share. TRUTH would be hard to find, and PEACE, LIBERTY AND SAFETY might be lost for ever.

1. Reprinted: *New York Morning Post*, 19 September; New York *Daily Advertiser*, 29 September. For an earlier essay in the *Pennsylvania Gazette*, 10 September, signed "A Freeman," see BoR, III, 184.
2. See the Cumberland County circular letter calling the Harrisburg Convention, 3 July 1788 (*ibid.*, 165–66).
3. A reference to the Harrisburg Convention, 3–6 September (*ibid.*, 176–82n).
4. Only York and Northampton of these four counties were not represented at the Harrisburg Convention.
5. For an earlier statement that the Cumberland County circular letter encouraged "a civil war," see the *Pennsylvania Gazette*, 3 September (*ibid.*, 176).

Pennsylvania Gazette, 17 September 1788 (excerpt)[1]

A correspondent remarks, with satisfaction, that notwithstanding Judge B——'s assertion last spring that the serious Quakers were against the new government,[2] not one of them could be persuaded to favor the Harrisburg meeting with their presence—nor did one German go thither from any of the respectable counties in which they live. A single man only of that worthy and valuable body of citizens appeared, the place of meeting being near, and subjecting him to *earnest invitation*.

A friend of liberty and government remarks, that however full and fair may be the future consideration of amendments on the part of Pennsylvania, it must give great satisfaction to see the disappointment of the late attempt to procure a *pretended representation* of the counties at Harrisburg. Pennsylvania never manifested more good sense, nor a greater attachment to good government, than by her evident disapprobation of means so deceitful, secret and inflammatory, as were used to effect this meeting.

Pennsylvania, says a correspondent, sends sixty-nine members, by the votes 69000 electors, to her state legislature, but it seems they cannot do our public business, but an *Upper House* must be assembled at Harrisburg. Our state constitution requires that men noted for *wisdom and virtue* should be chosen, but we do not find that any thing of that kind is required for this Upper House. He further remarks, that in proportion to *the electors who met* to chuse this unconstitutional body, the city of Philadelphia, instead of five whole members, only sent a little finger and a thumb, the counties of Montgomery, York, Northampton, &c. not the pairing of a nail, the county of Dauphin a head, &c.[3] so that altogether they may be truly said not to make A BODY....

1. Reprinted six times by 27 September: Mass. (2), N.Y. (2), Pa. (1), Va. (1).
2. In a fake letter purported to be from George Bryan to John Ralston printed in the Federalist *Pennsylvania Gazette*, 26 March, the claim was made that "The solid Quakers greatly dislike" the Constitution (CC:647, p. 489).
3. For the delegates to the Harrisburg Convention, see BoR, III, 177.

De Witt Clinton to Charles Clinton, Jr.
New York, 19 September 1788 (excerpt)[1]

... I always supposed that subsequent amendments. were never the serious design of the great friends of the new govt. and that the idea was only a political maneuvre to lead the people to its adoption. In some of the Philadelphia & Boston Newspapers, emendations to the govt. are evidently reprobated—the circular letter & proposed amendts. of our Convention styled impertinent & destructive, & an attempt to procure alterations, until the govt. is tried, called high treason against the majesty of the people.[2] Messieurs Saml. Adams and [Elbridge] Gerry are nominated in the Massachusetts Newspapers as Senators for that state—the first is earnest for amendments and the second was a member of the Genl. Convention & refused to subscribe to the Constitution. By a cooperation of influence, it is supposed they may get in.
I am sir with the greatest Respect Yours Affectionately

1. RC, De Witt Clinton Papers, Washington's Headquarters Museum, Newburgh, N.Y. De Witt Clinton was a nephew and personal secretary of Governor George Clinton of New York. Dr. Charles Clinton, Jr., was De Witt Clinton's great-uncle.
2. See *Pennsylvania Gazette*, 6, 13 August; "X," *Connecticut Gazette*, 15 August; Philadelphia *Independent Gazetteer*, 16 August; "Republican," *Virginia Independent Chronicle*, 27 Au-

gust; and "Solon," Boston *Independent Chronicle*, 28 August (BoR, III, 135, 138–39, 141–42, 144, 88n, 154–55, respectively).

Civis
Pennsylvania Packet, 19 September 1788

The publication of the proceedings of a late meeting at Harrisburg has afforded to me, and probably to many others, an agreeable disappointment. From what we had heard of the disposition of the people who promoted the meeting, there was reason to expect a result widely different from that which their proceedings exhibit. The moderation they have shewn on this occasion does honor to those who were assembled, and entitles the measures they have recommended to attention and respect. However widely some of them may have heretofore strayed from the line of sound policy, and good citizenship in their conduct concerning the Federal Constitution, they had, or imagined they had, sufficient cause for the opposition they gave. If in the manner of doing it passion should be supposed to have unduly interposed its influence, candid reflection on the occurrences shortly after the promulgation of the plan of government, may extenuate, though it may not excuse the fault. But however this may be, they have now made a conciliatory advance, which ought to be met and cherished by those from whom they have differed in opinion, as well for the sake of promoting harmony in the state, as to give fair operation to the plan of confederation. For although in a free government, the *will* of the majority may, and ought to predominate, a wise and prudent majority will nevertheless calculate and conduct their measures in as conciliating a manner as is consistent with the dignity and energy of government, and cautiously avoid giving unnecessary cause of irritation or disgust to the minority. Success naturally produces moderation, complacency and dignity in cultivated minds. These effects are therefore expected to be found in the conduct of a majority; and when it is otherwise they generally diminish their own strength, by adding to that of the minority, and not unfrequently change places with them. I wish, therefore, as one of the majority, to see our public measures so conducted as to leave no ground for prejudice itself to generate alarms upon, and in such manner as may be most likely to improve the *acquiescence* of the minority into *approbation*.

A large proportion, probably a majority of those who have assented to the ratification of the new Constitution in its present form, are desirous that it should be amended in some parts as early as such amendments can be made without impeding its operation, or hazarding its being destroyed, by being wholly submitted to the arbitration of another general convention. The amendments proposed are but few, and pointed to particular parts, which may be subjected to revision by a general convention, without danger to the general principles or vital parts of the Constitution, and without impeding its organization and operation in the mean time. Several of the most considerable of the states have accompanied their adoption with an instruction to procure amendments as early as possible. As the convention of Pennsylvania omitted this accompanyment to their ratification on a supposition, it is imagined, that their power was limited to the mere adoption or rejection of the instrument laid before them, the Assembly, who are expressly authorised by the Constitution itself to propose amendments, are now requested to do it. Whether they will comply with this request or not, is with them to determine.

May wisdom govern their choice!

A Despiser of Demagogues, Would-be-ats, and Wheelbarrow-men
Pennsylvania Mercury, 20 September 1788 (excerpt)

Mr. Humphreys, Some of your correspondents, in your last Thursday's paper,[1] observes that our Constitution calls for the men of most wisdom and virtue to be put in government—but seems to think this was not attended to in forming the upper house at Harrisburg. The gentleman should remember that only means when the characters are questionable. We sent two gentlemen, or they rather sent themselves, who knew they were the very men the Constitution points out; and further, that they are well qualified for the new government, being able to say, as David said of Golia[t]h's sword, there are none like themselves[2]—and to come forward, without the assistance of a priest, save a friendly shove from the one near College Green. They are good natured gentlemen; for if you will assure them they shall be dog, they care not who shall be miller.—To obtain this object it matters not much whether we cry out for a bill of rights or a bill of wrongs.

Your correspondent further remarks, that the city of Philadelphia only sent to Harrisburg a little finger—but let him take care that it be not nearly related to the little finger of Rehoboam, for it intends by hook or crook, to grow as big as a lion. Be this as it may, there was no need to make this affair too public, when the case was so clear—You know, Sir, that secrecy is the life of trade in some cases; and these gentlemen understand this, for there are few that know them, who will deny, that both nature and necessity have formed them to govern. . . .

1. See the *Pennsylvania Gazette*, 17 September, which was reprinted in the *Mercury* on 18 September (BoR, III, 190–91).
2. 1 Samuel 21:8–10.

Pittsburgh Gazette, 20 September 1788[1]

OBSERVATIONS by a Member of the Convention at Harrisburgh.

Countrymen, This convention had not a Franklin, or a Washington at the head of it, but it had a [Charles] Pettit and [George] Bryan. It may be observed, that in the amendments proposed we have said nothing about *a bill of rights, the liberty of the press, or the trial by jury.* It was found upon examination there was nothing in the constitution which interfered with any of these. The people might try their causes, advertise their stray colts, and wear their breeches just as they used to do. It may be thought wrong to have made such a noise about these things, when there was no ground for it; more especially to have *run away from a house of assembly,*[2] to have *signed protests,* setting forth the want of these particulars, to have *voted against the constitution,* and published a *dissent in writing;*[3] by these means setting the whole country in a flame, & representing those as traitors who did not raise the same clamour. But the people do not consider that they might not have been all villains and rascals who did this, but some of them actually well meaning ignorant men, who believed, at least a great deal of what they said.

It is true the amendments now proposed, are a great part of them unnecessary, contain[in]g little more than what is in the constitution already, but it was expedient to do something to satisfy the people; just as a physician who has led a man to believe that he is sick, and to make him think that he is well again, gives him a little warm water, with the powder of a dried leaf in it perhaps; that if it does no good, it can do him no harm.

There is one thing a little different, viz. the power of "recaling the senators." This is right; and is like a man tying a string to his monkey, or his racoon, that he is afraid will run away; so that when it climbs up the tree a certain distance, he can at his pleasure bring it back again. It will be perfectly expedient in this state, where there are two parties, for the senators will be changed, as these alternately prevail; so that like buckets in a well the one goes down, while the other comes up; and the senate from being the most stable and dangerous body, will become the most fluctuating and absurd. In this case there will be nothing to dread from them and the immediate representatives of the people may do just what they please. Perhaps after all it might have been as well to have proposed lessening the period, for which they are chosen, but make the appointment irrevocable for the time.

It is said the Congress shall not have the power of "altering the places, times and manner of chusing senators." They have not the power as the case now is. The clause in the constitution respects only the choice of representatives in the second house; but this was put into the amendments, either seeming to imply that it was otherwise before, or was a mere blunder and oversight in some of us that drew up the writing.

Take notice that there is to be no *poll tax*, so that the new-comers, the shop-keepers, jobbers, wayfaring-men, and bachelors, that *have no land*, are to go free; and the *farmers*, because they are able, pay the whole.

There is to be no standing army, because it is better that people should go out and be shot themselves, than pay others for doing it. The militia are to serve only two months at a time, because there can be no war that can last longer. And if the time should expire just a day before the battle ought to be, it is only to put it off until the recruit comes, and leave the *baggage and artillery standing there as a scare crow to the enemy*.

There are to be no subordinate courts established, as for instance at Pittsburgh, or in Kentucky, or elsewhere, but must all go to one *supreme court*, at the federal town I suppose, which will help to encrease the domilitium of the empire.

As to the proceeding of the convention, you will hear of them in due time. I will mention only some particulars, viz. It was insisted much amongst us, to put in a clause, that all doctors should tell diseases by the water; but it was thought this would be construed into a slur upon the Germans and the Scotch Irish, and so left out. It was [Robert] Whitehill that proposed this. [William] Findly did not come to the convention; he had thrown out such r[h]apsodies before in speaking and writing, that he was ashamed to appear and support them at this place.

We made a ticket at this meeting for the new Congress. Blair M'Clenachan is one. He may be no conjurer, as the saying is, but he is a good man. Doctor [Joseph] Gardner is also in the ticket; he is a relation by marriage, to the Simpsons in Chester county, and I think will do very well. There is one Simon Drusback pitched upon. I imagine being of the same name with one *Simon a tanner*, who made good leather in the scriptures, a great while ago. It was right that Findly should be put in nomination, because he can "Address the chair," and say, "Myster Spacker." and avoid being "parsenal," and will do great credit to the western country, amongst the orators in the new Congress. I think it would not be amiss to have him sent ambassador to the Barbary states, or some part of the world, where his dialect would be understood as an original language.

I am just thinking with myself, what these [men?] when they first go to the Congress, will propose. I should be glad to get a law passed,

"Myster Spacker," to have all Fridays turned into Saturdays, and all Saturdays into Sundays, for I have observed for several years, that all Saturdays are days of rain; when we might as well be going to sermon as any where else, but can get no work done.

But we must let these things rest, and in the mean time rejoice, that this convention have, with such unanimity, agreed upon what was of no consequence nor ever will be. However, that is as it takes, and so wishing you all health and happiness, and meaning no ill to any man, I am the public's humble servant.

1. Reprinted: Philadelphia *Freeman's Journal*, 24 September; Philadelphia *Independent Gazetteer*, 25 September; and *New York Morning Post*, 1 October. It is evident that this piece was not written by a member of the Harrisburg Convention.

2. On 28–29 September 1787 enough opponents of calling a convention to ratify the Constitution stayed away from the Pennsylvania Assembly to prevent a quorum. Two of these assemblymen were taken forcibly from their lodgings to the Assembly, which then completed the resolutions calling the state Convention. See RCS:Pa., 65–120.

3. For the Dissent of the Minority of the Pennsylvania Convention, see BoR, II, 197–203n.

Massachusetts Centinel, 27 September 1788[1]

About thirty persons from different parts of this State, lately met at Harrisburg, and appointed Blair M'Clenachan, Esq. President, and agreed to present a petition to our Legislature, praying that the Legislature would take measures, that a General Convention of the States be called for the purpose of considering certain amendments proposed *by them* to the federal Constitution. These amendments are similar to some proposed by other States—but, notwithstanding, it is expected that the Legislature will not take any notice of so unconstitutional and insignificant a body.

1. Appearing under a dateline of "Philadelphia, September 17," this item is probably a summary of one of the three Philadelphia reprints of the report of the Harrisburg Convention that appeared that day (See BoR, III, 176–82n). The *Centinel's* summary was reprinted in the *New Hampshire Spy*, 30 September.

Cassius
Philadelphia Federal Gazette, 9 October 1788

The insidious efforts of the anti-federalists, to prevent the adoption of the new constitution, having failed of success, they have now altered their plan, and are applying their strength to secretly undermine what they could not openly and fairly destroy. All their endeavours are now concentrated in the election of federal representatives, in hopes, that by introducing into that eminent body, men who may impede its operations and disgrace its character, by their utter incapacity in some instances, or by their concealed treacheries and artful combinations in others; the government may become inefficient, or at least unpopular in its out-set; and the people consent to relapse into their former systems of weakness, poverty and domestic tyranny—systems in which the leaders of the few remaining anti-federalists naturally delight, as affording means of supporting that ascendancy which the possession of the best offices and emoluments of the state affords.

There is something in this plan so base and contemptible, that the indignation of every honest elector must rise against it. It is like applying to poison when the generous weapons have failed. It is worse than the *Machiavelian* policy with which the scribes of the party have affected to designate the conduct of the friends to American prosperity. It is the true dark and deadly system of the two *Borgias*, who were accustomed to make a feeble attack, in order that by a feigned reconciliation, their adversaries, disarmed of suspicion, might be secretly and safely destroyed.

The meeting at Harrisburg, the affected protestations of submission to the government, are their feigned reconciliation; the proposed amendments, the terms of the fictitious treaty. It is as clear as any thing in human events can be, that their aim is not to amend but to destroy. Their object is not a good federal government; it is to have no solid union whatever. Seduced in some instances by visionary notions of existence as unconnected states, terrified from a sense of the tenure by which they hold their own importance, at the possibility of losing any thing of the state prerogative in the federal compound, the chief object of their wishes is to render the new government as difficult, expensive, and unsatisfactory as possible.

If the misfortunes of this state should still hang over her so far as to determine the election in their favor, and they should attempt on the one hand to introduce the amendments proposed at Harrisburg, we shall at much expence lose a great deal of that valuable time which ought to be immediately applied to the regulation of our finances, commerce, and internal resources, without a chance that the people will consent to diminish any part of that beautiful combination of strength and liberty which forms the character of the structure. But if on the other hand, in pursuance of that secret plan which it is generally believed was laid at Harrisburg, no farther mention is made of amendments, then will all the well known ingenuity and industry of this sect of people be applied to the introduction of discord and dissension, to the general detriment and final dishonor of America.

This is therefore an occasion which ought to excite our alarm and urge our exertion. Whoever holds his liberty dear, whoever detests anarchy and loves government, peace, and independence, should now

press into service all the abilities he possesses. To himself and to his country he now owes all his assiduity and all his labour, till the issue of the election shall have evinced that the good sense of Pennsylvania is incapable of being deceived by the specious assurances and treacherous machinations of her real enemies.
October 7, 1788.

Edmund Randolph to James Madison
Richmond, Va., 3 September 1788 (excerpt)[1]

My dear friend

I am much obliged to you for your favor of the 25th. ulto. Being in Wmsburg, when I received it, I imparted it to our friend, the president[2] who espouses with warmth an early convention. I sincerely wish, that the valuable parts of the constitution may suffer no ill from the temper, with which such a body will probably assemble. But is there no danger, that, if the respect, which the large minorities at present command should be effaced by delay, the spirit of amendment will hereafter be treated as heretical? I confess to you without reserve, that I feel great distrust of some of those who will certainly be influential agents in the government, and whom I suspect to be capable of making a wicked use of its defects. Do not charge me with undue suspicion; but indeed the management in some stages of the convention created a disgustful apprehension of the views of some particular characters. I reverence Hamilton, because he was honest and open in his views.

Perhaps the states may not concur in any particular correction of the new theory. But if dissensions in opinion should prevent an amendment, the constitution remains as it is. If on the other hand they should be in unison as to even one amendment, it will satisfy, and bear down all malcontents....

1. RC, Madison Papers, DLC. For the entire letter, see Rutland, *Madison*, XI, 246–47.
2. The Reverend James Madison (1749–1812), president of the College of William and Mary, was a cousin of James Madison (1751–1836).

Steady
Massachusetts Centinel, 3 September 1788

MISCELLANY.

Mr. RUSSELL, Among the candidates for appointments in the *federal Legislature*, we may expect many who will make a *stalking horse* of the deceiving term "*amendments*"—I shall notice at this time, four different classes of these *seekers*, viz. One description of them will by this device attempt to ingratiate themselves in the favour of many of the good people, whose fears of lurking mischiefs in the Constitution have been excited by the artful misrepresentation of these demagogues—these are totally inadequate in point of abilities to originating or sustaining any amendments, and therefore have no thoughts of exerting themselves to obtain them—their object is to effect their OWN ELECTION.

Another class may be denominated self-opinionated *system-mongers*—who can see no beauty or perfection in any thing, but in their own fabrications.

A third class are those whose volatility of disposition leads them to fly from one thing, to another, doubting, condemning and approving by turns as occasion prompts.

But a fourth, and the most *dangerous* class, are those who are *inveterate enemies* to the system itself; it would not do for them *openly* to avow their sentiments—it being the general idea, that the Constitution is now fixed beyond the power of malice or false patriotism to affect its stability—but under the idea of being friendly to what are termed amendments, they mean to get into power, and when *once elected*, they will leave nothing unattempted that may tend to subvert the Constitution.

It is clearly evident that none of the foregoing characters, can *consistently* receive the suffrages of the *real, decided* friends to the Constitution, or of their country.

If the Constitution is a *bad one*, let it be proved so by experience—if it is a *good one*, let us not choose men to deface and injure it, by *pretended amendments*.

If an ingenious artist had constructed a machine, upon the best principles, after *severe* investigation and labour—should we not consider him as a MAD MAN for making *alterations*, before he had made a trial to ascertain the goodness of his invention? We certainly should.

Solon
Boston Independent Chronicle, 4 September 1788[1]

Mess'rs. ADAMS & NOURSE, It is not at all surprizing to observe how *alarmed* some *particular characters pretend* to be, that any thing should be said respecting measures being taken to *effect any amendments* in the *Federal Constitution*; and that such measures will but *delay* the *operation* and *salutary* effects so ardently wished for, and expected from the new government, as this is a mere *bagatelle*. The Conventions of a number of the States which have adopted the Federal Constitution, and among these are to found *some* [of] the *most populous* and *opulent* in the *Union*, have deemed amendments absolutely necessary, and have proposed sundry accordingly:[2] At the same time, they have discovered their *wisdom* and their *true federalism*, in first adopting and ratifying the Constitution, that no public injury may accrue by a delay of the operation of the system, while the amendments are attended to.

A wise and free people in forming a Constitution of government for *themselves*, should ever provide against their own political annihilation, by reserving to themselves, the *power of amending or altering* the Constitution, whenever they judge it *necessary* and *expedient*, without offering *violence* to the *Legislative or Executive powers*, or even *interrupting* them in the regular discharge of their respective functions, until the alterations or amendments are made, and the administration directed into them. This is an excellence in the Federal Constitution, which is scarcely elsewhere to be found in the world; for in article fifth, it is expressed, that "The Congress whenever two thirds of both Houses shall deem it necessary, shall propose amendments to this Constitution, or on the application of the Legislatures of two thirds of the several States, shall call a Convention for proposing amendments, which in either case, shall be valid to all intents and purposes as part of this Constitution, when ratified by the Legislatures of three fourths of the several States, or by Conventions in three fourths thereof," &c.—Hence proposals for amendments are perfectly constitutional; and since so many States have thought them *necessary*, they become an object of the first attention. More than a sufficient number of the States, constitutionally necessary to put the new government in motion, have already adopted it, (and it is ardently wished that all may soon accede to it)—every moment of delay, unless unavoidable, will be regreted by every friend to his country, while common-sense and reason dictate, that such amendments as have been deemed necessary, be early brought forward, and these will not in the least retard the operations of the government, or prevent its acting. The amendments which have generally been proposed, are a *more explicit definition of*, and *limiting of power*, not a restraint to action. If therefore, the amendments proposed, are necessary to the *security* of the *liberties* of the *people*, they *ought* to be attended to *immediately*; and even if they were not in some particulars so essential as some have imagined, yet if a *great* number of the people, have conceived them to be so, the principles of *national policy*, as well as *natural right*, clearly mark that *those* for whom the *government is formed, should be satisfied*. Will not every man therefore, who is a *real federalist, chearfully* and *zealously* endeavour to *give* that *cement* to the *Union*, which shall *appear most likely to render it indissoluable*; without this, will not *pretensions* to *federalism*, be but a *cloak* to the *ensign* of *faction* and *disunion*.

1. For William Heath as the possible author of this essay, see note 1 to "Solon," *Massachusetts Centinel*, 28 August (BoR, III, 155n). Other essays by "Solon" appeared on 25 September and 30 October (*ibid.*, 231-32, 303-5).

2. For the amendments proposed by the state conventions, see BoR, I, 231-77.

James Madison to James Madison, Sr.
New York, 6 September 1788 (excerpts)[1]

Hond Sir

I forward this by the mail expecting it will be at Fredg. in time for Mr. A. Shepherd who left this a day or two ago. Nothing of much consequence has occurred since my last. The current intelligence you will find in the inclosed gazette. The Antifederalists are every where exerting themselves for an early Convention. The circular letter from this State and the rejection of N. Carolina give them great spirits. Virginia, I suppose from the temper of the present Legislature will cooperate in the plan.

Congress have not yet settled the place for the meeting of the new Govt. It is most probable that the advocates for N. York who form at present the greater number, will prevail. In that case, altho' I think it a very unreasonable thing for the South[er]n & Western parts of the Union, the best face must be put on it. . . .

. . . Remember me affecty to my mother & the family and believe me yr dutiful son

1. RC, Madison Papers, DLC. For the entire letter, see Rutland, *Madison*, XI, 247-48.

Massachusetts Centinel, 6 September 1788[1]

FROM CORRESPONDENTS.

A federal correspondent of the Centinel informs the *serious* correspondent of the Chronicle, that the assertion in the latter paper, previous to the election of Governours, &c. "that a number of the citizens of this town, as well friends to Gen. [Benjamin] *Lincoln* as to Mr. [Samuel] *Adams* had met, and agreed to give up all exertions for the former, and to unite their interests in favour of the latter, as being the candidate most likely to obtain the greatest number of votes elsewhere"— whatever may *be said of it* SINCE, was THEN *acknowledged* to be a *falshood*— a *trick*.

The legislature (thank God *they* chuse the senators) and the freemen of the county of Suffolk, in particular, will undoubtedly fix their eyes upon men of *real* federalism, *consistent, independent* characters, who have judgment to *discern*, and spirit to *pursue* the best interests of their country. You will not find such men pledging themselves to *alter* the Constitution.—The proposition is treason against the majesty of the people. It is their *own Constitution*, by a fairer and better title than any nation under Heaven can boast; having been conceded to in its *present form*, by a greater proportion of the free citizens, than we can naturally suppose, any alterations ever will—and therefore we may safely repeat, that unconditional promises to support and bring about alterations, previous to a *full trial* and experience of its competency to the great purposes of the union, is TREASON AGAINST THE MAJESTY OF THE PEOPLE.[2]

If one half of the *alterations* and *additions impertinently* suggested by the Conventions of some of the States to the new Constitution, are made, this system of government will, *in every respect*, be inferiour to the old Confederation—which has so long been justly complained of. Knowing this, the people ought to be on their guard against your *alteration makers*, before the Constitution has had a *fair* trial. It is the opinion of the most exalted and good characters of the United States, that in obtaining the new government, the people have made the happiest acquisition the children of men were ever blessed with—Let us beware then how we mar it. The people may be assured, that under the cloak of *previous amendments* is hid a *dagger*, aimed at the existence of our *union* and *peace*: But under such a government as this system provides, it is the general sentiment that our union will be cemented, and our peace perpetuated—that dignity and justice will be our characteristicks as a nation—and that the spunge of time will wipe out the many, many stains which *individual* States have made.

If we *divide* we are lost—But if, planted in the soil of *freedom*, and watered with the dews of union, these States will adhere to the great principles of the Constitution, they will multiply and increase like the Indian figtree—so beautifully described by MILTON—

> "Branching so broad and long, that in the ground
> The bending twigs take root—and daughters grow
> About the mother tree—a pillar'd shade—
> High over-arch'd."[3]—Bestowing succour—and
> Affording safety.

1. Reprinted: Worcester, Mass., *American Herald*, 11 September; New York *Daily Advertiser*, 15–16 September; New York *Independent Journal*, 17 September; Rhode Island *Newport Herald*, 2 October. The last two newspapers omitted the first paragraph.

2. For criticisms of these comments, see the Boston *Independent Chronicle*, 11 September (BoR, III, 206–8).

3. John Milton, *Paradise Lost. A Poem in Twelve Books* (2nd edition, revised and augmented, London, 1674), Book 9, p. 246.

Tench Coxe to James Madison
Philadelphia, 10 September 1788 (excerpt)[1]

... We have been made uneasy here by an effort of our opposition, promoted by some of their friends in the adjacent states, to influence the elections for state & federal representatives, not only in Pennsa. but in those states also who elect about this Season of the Year. The paper enclosed will shew you how the matter has been conducted. It is probable it may be of use to republish it, as the facts are carefully stated, and it is addressed to the Union at large. From the temper of a part of the new York opposition it may have some effect there, and indeed there has been such a run upon Amendments, that a little from the friends of the Constitution may not be malapropos. I mean the paper signed a fedl. Centinel.[2] ...

1. RC, Madison Papers, DLC. For the entire letter, see Rutland, *Madison*, XI, 248–50.
2. See "A Federal Centinel," *Pennsylvania Gazette*, 10 September (immediately below). Despite Coxe's suggestion, the essay was not reprinted.

A Federal Centinel
Pennsylvania Gazette, 10 September 1788

To the PEOPLE *of the* United States,
And particularly to the
INDEPENDENT ELECTORS *of* PENNSYLVANIA.

The appearance of an important movement in this state, the present meeting at the town of Harrisburg,[1] renders a little information on the subject absolutely necessary, to prevent your being deceived and misled. The account of the proceedings of a few persons in the county of Bucks, published in our late Gazettes,[2] in which a studied moderation is observed, and an appearance of acting on the public sentiments and feelings is industriously displayed, require some explanation, which will lead to further remarks on the nature and objects of the Harrisburg meeting.

The opposition to the general government in this state, finding that the minorities of the other conventions, after full and fair discussion, had determined to acquiesce in and even to support a fœderal constitution, which appeared to them necessary to preserve our union, and which was sanctioned by *the supreme authority of the majority of a free people*, determined to assume also, at least to the other states, the appearance of moderation and acquiescence. They knew that the conduct, which the dispositions of some of their leaders prompted them to pursue, could not be acceptable to the great body of the opposition, either north or south. Their declarations therefore have been that they would support the government, till altered according to the forms provided, and such is the language of the Bucks county publication referred to above. But at the moment of these declarations, AMENDMENTS and CIVIL WAR were held forth as the alternatives, by which the friends of peace were to be alarmed, and *a large majority* of the independent freemen of Pennsylvania were to be overawed. This is no loose unfounded suggestion, no phantom of the heated brain of a jealous partyman, but is an existing fact, contained in the letters which invited the townships of Bucks county to the meeting at Harrisburg. Submission to the minority, then, or the sword, is their meaning.

It is necessary that you should be informed of the manner in which this meeting has been collected, and let every friend to peace, and every lover of free government, mark the extraordinary proceedings.—In Philadelphia, Lancaster and York, are printed weekly twenty-three news-papers, at ten presses. In not one of these was ever published a single notification to the freemen of the state, that such a measure was in contemplation, nor any call to the freemen of the neighbourhood to meet for the purpose of electing persons to assemble at Harrisburg. In York and Lancaster, and many other places, the matter was discovered or suspected by the enemies to the measure, but nothing was said to *the public* by its *friends*. Some secret whispers, symptoms of the nature of the proceedings, were passed about among those in whom they thought they could confide. In the city of Philadelphia it was not known who meant to assume to represent them, till after their departure. In the county of Philadelphia, where a meeting was discovered, the tenth man of those assembled was not in favor of sending a deputation. In some of the townships of Bucks, the measure was rejected unanimously, but of this not a word is said in the proceedings; in others not more than three or four attended, and yet they undertook to appoint out of their number. So secret have the movements been in some places, that even in Dauphin county, of which Harrisburg is the seat of justice, the matter was carefully concealed, and gentlemen of the first intelligence, now holding the highest public offices *by the voice of the people*, were unacquainted with the intended meeting. But improper as these measures must appear to every genuine commonwealths man, they have been shockingly exceeded in some parts of the state. The most respectable proofs are now in this city, of the people in several places having been informed, that the Harrisburg meeting was to be held *by order of Congress*—that they must therefore elect their deputies as to a lawful and constitutional body, and that it was expected they would be able to procure *a deduction of taxes for three years!* Such has been the abuse of the honest unsuspecting people of the remote counties.

Reflect, my country-men, on such proceedings. Are these open *republican* measures, *seeking the face of day*, or oligarchic stratagems and wicked deceptions, calculated to cheat the electors of this state. Are these the men, who called the convention of the United States *a Conclave*, and the conventions of the people, their constitutional legislators, our Franklin and our Washington, dark conspirators. Ye virtuous patriots of *the Connecticut minority*, who first set the example of acquiescence,[3] who, tho' dissentient yourselves, first pledged your endeavours to support the measures of the majority of that body of freemen to which ye belong, ye genuine republicans among the minorities of the other states, who, waving prejudice, magnanimously followed that noble example, can ye approve of measures such as these, or can ye hope the happiness of your country will result from such proceedings. Measures of this nature are seriously alarming. We cannot but apprehend the worst consequences to *liberty and happiness* from this violence, precipitancy, secrecy and deception in the business of amendments. The objects before the people of America are the most important and the most arduous that ever engaged the attention of mankind. *To perfect a republican system* for each state in the union, and *to balance on general laws the affairs of an extensive confederacy of many members*, is a work of so great difficulty, that no human genius, however profound and comprehensive, can be able by mere force of reason and reflection to effect it at once. Let us then, in such a work, beware of passion. 'Tis a serious task for the coolest minds, and the judgments of many must unite in the work. None must be thus excluded, or shamefully deceived. Experience and observation must guide our labours. We have already acquired great political light in the progress of the American revolution, of which every philosopher and politician must deem this measure a principal part. Time will advance us further, and can alone bring us to perfection. The experience of inconveniencies must correct the mistakes we may have fallen into. In the course of our deliberations, let the wise and good of each opinion remember the duty and indispensible necessity of keeping their minds cool, and fit for discussions so important to liberty, and their hearts full of deference towards each other, as brothers embarked in the same cause.—Let the government be got into motion. The clauses provided for considering amendments will remain. They will always be of force, and can always be recurred to. We want not irregular meetings produced by self-creation and deception, and fostered in secrecy, to procure a reconsideration of the new government. Our state legislatures, who remain and always will continue our immediate guardians, can apply for and procure them, if they shall be found proper on due consideration.

It is a matter of serious consequence to the freemen of this commonwealth, and not unimportant to the people of the union, that all the objects of this meeting should be understood. Our state elections are fast approaching—October is the month fixed by the constitution. To affect those elections is a very principal object. Let the independent electors of Pennsylvania be upon their guard. Take care you do not chuse the friends of paper tenders, or of oppressive test-laws,[4] which are now no longer necessary in their former extent. Let men of sense, information and good moral characters, at least of competent property and industrious habits, be your choice. With such men you will be always safe. If the new constitution proves injurious to your liberty, peace and property, it will be equally so to theirs, and they will apply for and ratify the alterations, or call Conventions for the purpose. Be not inattentive to the importance of the present moment, for on the ensuing Assembly more will depend, than on any that has been elected since you were an independent people.

Another object, which the secret letters soliciting the Harrisburg meeting plainly express, is the election of the eight fœderal representatives. They recommend a plan of concert and union. Let us not then be supine and inactive, when they are thus forward in their operations and united in their plans. A great majority of Pennsylvania is favorable to good government, and sensible that amendments to the new constitution can always be procured. Let them therefore exert themselves to get into all offices, men whom their judgments and consciences approve. Let them beware of the plan of amendments formed and promoted by the deceitful, dangerous and insulting means abovementioned. Means which disgrace those who have stooped to them, would degrade the electors of Pennsylvania from their rank as freemen, and must disgust the honest part of the opposition in all the other states.

1. For the Harrisburg Convention, 3–6 September 1788, see BoR, III, 176–82n.
2. For the Bucks County meeting on 25 August, which appeared in the *Pennsylvania Gazette,* 2 September, see BoR, III, 172–74.
3. For the acquiescence of the minority in Connecticut, see the *Pennsylvania Gazette,* 20 February and 26 March 1788 (CC:Vol. 4, pp. 522, 539).
4. For the conflict from 1777 to 1789 over the laws requiring men over eighteen to renounce their allegiance to King George III and swear allegiance to Pennsylvania, see Robert L. Brunhouse, *The Counter-Revolution in Pennsylvania, 1776–1790* (Harrisburg, Pa., 1942), 16–17, 40–41, 154–55, 167–69, 180–81, 197–98.

Boston Independent Chronicle, 11 September 1788[1]

Mess'rs. ADAMS & NOURSE, A *federal* correspondent observes, that howsoever a *correspondent* of the Centinel of Saturday last,[2] may amuse himself with air, "*thin air*," the *enlightened* freemen of the United States of America, are not so destitute of *common sense*, as not to *see* and *laugh* at any suggestions, direct or implied, that *convey* an *idea*, that it is treason against themselves, to *propose*, and *endeavour* to obtain, in the *constitutional* way, *necessary amendments*, to their *own* Constitution; "*treason against the Majesty of the people*," lies on the *other* hand. The *people* of this *Commonwealth*, in *particular*, by their *very respectable Convention*, in February last, at the ratification of the Federal Constitution, after stating sundry amendments, then enumerated, did, "In the name and in the behalf of the people of this Commonwealth, enjoin it upon their Representatives in Congress, at all times, until the alterations and provisions aforesaid, have been considered, agreeably to the fifth article of the said Constitution, to exert all their influence, and use all reasonable and legal methods to obtain a ratification of the said alterations and provisions, in such manner, as is provided in the said article."[3]

Is it then, this correspondent asks, the *holding* up the *propriety* and *importance*, of *obtaining*, if *possible*, this *enjoined* object of the people; or *sentiments*, advanced in *opposition* to *it*, that *exhibits most*, the complexion of TREASON AGAINST THE MAJESTY OF THE PEOPLE—of this the enlightened people are fully competent to determine for themselves. But not only the Convention of this Commonwealth, but those of several other States, (the whole included, being intitled, as fixed by the Constitution, to a majority of Representatives, of those States which have adopted the system,) have likewise proposed amendments. And it is highly probable, that if the mode of first adopting the Constitution, and then proposing amendments, had been at first thought of, all the ratifying States, would have pursued nearly the same line of conduct. The *freemen* of *those States*, have a *fore-sight* to discern, that their liberties *may* be in *danger*, although *not* attacked, if an *avenue* is left open, *through* which they may at *some future time*, *be* attacked; they will therefore, naturely be anxious, that any *aperture* in the *barrier* between *powers delegated* and *retained*, be *closed, explicitly defined*, and well understood. To leave matters to a *full trial* of experience, as *some* are *urging*, may perhaps, be compared to the loaning a man's money, *untold* and without *proper security* for the payment thereof, in order to *ascertain* his *honor* and *honesty*; or to neglect to *repair* a *breach* in the walls of a city liable to be besieged, in order to discover whether the assailants *would* avail *themselves* of the advantage *offered* them: The *loss* of property however, in the one case, and a *lodgment gained behind the breach*, in the other, would render *after* precaution *unavailable*.

1. Reprinted: *New York Journal*, 25 September.
2. See the *Massachusetts Centinel*, 6 September 1788 (BoR, III 201–2).

3. Quoted from the Massachusetts Form of Ratification, 6–7 February 1788 (RCS: Mass., 1468–71).

Boston Independent Chronicle, 11 September 1788

Mess'rs. ADAMS & NOURSE, A *True federal* correspondent would enquire of the false federal correspondent of the Centinel,[1] whether the Hon. Mr. Adams would not have obtained "*the greatest number of votes elsewhere,*" had it not been for the "*falshood*" and "*trick,*" which was played off by his enemies. The Legislature chuses the federal Senators, and the Freemen of the Commonwealth, chuse the federal Representatives. In their choice "they will undoubtedly fix their eyes upon men of *real* federalism, of consistent and independent principles, who have judgment to *discern,* and spirit to *pursue* the best interests of their country." "You will not find such men pledging themselves," to *oppose* every alteration of the Constitution, which has been *demanded* by the Freemen of America; to *oppose* their adoption is "treason against the majesty of the people." They have demanded their adoption, and conceded to the Constitution in its present form, only with a view of unanimity in the pursuit of necessary alterations. "Therefore we may safely repeat," that all those who declare their opposition to amendments are "GUILTY OF TREASON AGAINST THE MAJESTY OF THE PEOPLE."

1. See the *Massachusetts Centinel,* 6 September 1788 (BoR, III, 201–2).

Edmund Randolph to James Madison
Richmond, Va., 12 September 1788 (excerpts)[1]

... Mr. Bev[erley] Randolph has lately returned from P[rince] Edward [County], where he saw Mr. H [i.e., Patrick Henry], who grows in violence against the constitution, and is much pleased at the idea of a new convention....

I desired Davis to make a collection, of which the inclosed is a copy.[2] ...

1. RC, Madison Papers, DLC. For the entire letter, see Rutland, *Madison,* XI, 251–52.
2. A reference to a pamphlet compilation of the amendments proposed by the state ratifying conventions printed by Augustine Davis after 2 August 1788 (Evans 21529) (BoR, III, 129).

A Marylander
Baltimore Maryland Gazette, 12 September 1788[1]

To the *Inhabitants* of *Baltimore-Town.*

It is industriously held out, that the federal constitution is now so firmly fixed, as to render it immaterial, what are the political sentiments of our representatives in the ensuing assembly—For my part I think a federalist ought to vote against his own brother, who will not unequivocally pledge himself to put the government in motion, vote for no man as a senator, but what has been uniformly an advocate for the adoption of the government, previous to the proposal of amendments, so as to secure the union from dissolution, and support no alterations, which shall subvert or enervate the constitution—No man, who is for depriving the general government of the exclusive direction of foreign affairs, and confirmation or rejection of treaties; of the command of the militia (thereby laying a foundation for civil wars among the different States;) of the direction and appropriation of all excises and duties upon imports and exports to the uses of the union, and the power of laying direct taxes, in cases of emergency, can with propriety be termed a federalist, those being the cardinal points of the new constitution—It is customary here to call out for amendments, amendments, and upbraiding the two Doctors for being opposed to any whatever—Almost every person agrees, that explanatory amendments, more accurately defining the great rights of the people, are necessary, but we should take care, that no *alterations*, sapping the most energetic parts of the government, should be carried, under the popular cry of *amendments*—The two Doctors ought to explain at the Town Meeting, HOW FAR THEY WILL GO, and the two Lawyers, WHERE THEY WILL STOP.[2]

There is a majority of anti-federalists in the present assemblies of New-Hampshire, New-York and Virginia (which are to set the new government in motion) so that we may expect anti-federal senators from those States—There is but a majority of *seven* federals in the present legislature of Pennsylvania, consisting of a single branch, a State continually convulsed by the struggles of two great contending parties,[3] each of which have alternately predominated for these twelve years, so that no dependance can be placed in that State—The present antifederal meeting at Harrisburg, ostensibly for the purpose of proposing amendments (which can only consistently be done either by a representation or the collective body of the *whole* State) but more probably to digest a plan for securing an anti-federal assembly, at the October election, in order to SUBVERT the government in a regular way, must alarm every friend to it—Should their turbulent machinations unfortunately be successful, and that State send anti-federal senators, it may induce Rhode-Island and North-Carolina to join the union on the same principles, which actuated the nonjuring peers of England and Scotland to take the oaths to King William, more effectually to promote the success of a plot for the restoration of King James—In such case it will depend on Maryland, whether there shall be a majority of two federals or anties in the first instance to set the government in motion, therefore the federal town of Baltimore of course will chuse no man, who hesitates unequivocally to pledge himself, at the town-meeting, to vote for no man, as a senator, who has not uniformly been an advocate for the ratification of the constitution—This is not the effusion of party, unless an ardent zeal to preserve the union and prevent the different States from cutting each others throats, can be termed such—I have suggested these hints, that we may be prepared on this subject at the Town meeting.

Some anti-federals, in other counties, have expressed a wish and expectation of Mr. *Paca*'s being a senator, and observed the federals could not reasonably object to him, as he voted for the adoption of the government, but he certainly proposed amendments,[4] subversive of it, and tried to have them accompany the ratification, a measure disagreeable to his constituents, who wished a rejection—I esteem Mr. *Paca*, and wish to see *him one of our six delegates*, but that we should have no *senator, whose federalism has ever been equivocal*—The candidates of the town should therefore pledge themselves not to vote for him as a senator.

I am sorry to see such heats and annimosities prevail, and old transactions ripped up, which are done away and ought to be forgot—We should rather look forward, than back, and the choice of senators is an object of immense magnitude, which we should never lose sight of— I have not enlisted myself under the standard of either party, all my desire being to secure two federal senators, and care not by what instruments that is done—I endeavoured, but in vain, in a former address to check the animosities of party[5]—The contest must be decided by a majority of you, and that your choice may be a good one, is the sincere wish of *A* MARYLANDER.

Baltimore, September 10, 1788.

1. Reprinted: *Pennsylvania Packet,* 10 September 1789. Otho Holland Williams was probably "A Marylander." Earlier essays by "A Marylander" appeared in the Baltimore *Maryland Gazette* on 4 December 1787 and 4 January, 12 February 1788 (RCS:Md., 105–8, 152–55n, 297–301n) supporting ratification of the Constitution.

2. Doctors James McHenry and John Coulter were the Federalist candidates for the House of Delegates from Baltimore; lawyers Samuel Chase and David McMechen were the Antifederalist candidates.

3. The two parties were the Constitutionalists, or radicals, who supported the democratic state constitution of 1776 that created a one-house legislature, and the Republicans, or conservatives, who wanted a new constitution that provided for a bicameral legislature. The Constitutionalists had their greatest strength among the country people, while the Republicans were strongest in Philadelphia and its environs.

4. For William Paca's amendments, see BoR, I, 245–47; BoR, III, 472–76.

5. Four articles by "A Marylander" were printed in the Baltimore *Maryland Gazette,* 20 and 23 May, 3 June, and 29 July. He had urged the voters to elect Federalists to the state

House of Delegates to ensure that proper measures, notably the election of Federalist Senators, would be taken to implement the Federal Constitution. He saw no harm, however, in electing two Antifederalists (including Chase) to the House of Representatives—they would provide a constitutional check on the Federalists and reflect minority opinion in Maryland. He defended McMechen against the charge of Antifederalism and suggested that Federalists could demonstrate moderation by electing him—with McHenry—to the House of Delegates. Once the federal government was operating, "Marylander" favored obliterating all party distinctions and choosing only the ablest men to serve in the state and federal governments.

Albert
Baltimore Maryland Gazette, 12 September 1788 (excerpt)

To the GERMAN VOTERS of *Baltimore-Town.*
... The only plausible objection urged to induce you to believe, that Mr. Chase is an *improper* character to be your delegate, *at this time,* is this, that he opposed the ratification of the new government by this state, unless amendments were *previously* adopted, and made part of the ratification. To decide the weight of this objection it appears to me to be indispensably necessary clearly to understand what *our legislature,* have to do with *amendments* to the constitution of the United States, because if *our legislature* has no power to *propose* any amendments, or to express any opinion respecting the propriety or necessity of any amendments to the said constitution, there can not be an atom of reason in this objection. The fifth article of the constitution provides two modes only by which the national constitution may be amended. First, *Two thirds* of *both* houses of congress, when they shall deem it necessary, shall *propose* amendments, which shall be *part* of the constitution, when RATIFIED by the *legislatures* of *three fourths* of the states, or when *ratified* by *conventions* in *three fourths* thereof; as one or the other mode of *ratification* shall be proposed by congress. Second, On the application of the *legislatures* of *two thirds* of the several states, congress shall call a *convention* for *proposing amendments,* which shall be *part* of the constitution when *ratified,* in the manner before mentioned. Our *legislature* therefore can not do any other whatever, respecting amendments to the constitution, than only apply to congress to call a *convention* to *propose amendments*; and consequently no member of the house of delegates, let him be friendly, or ever so inimical to the new government, can do it any injury by way of amendment.

If I am mistaken, and our *legislature* can, agreeably to the constitution of the United States, *propose amendments,* yet certainly the house of delegates *alone* can have no such power; and the senate will be ample security against any amendments being proposed as will injure, much less *destroy* the new government. But Mr. Chase is so determined an enemy to the constitution that he will carry such amendments as will injure it. This assertion implies an influence which Mr. Chase, and no other gentleman will possess in the house of delegates, or the senate, and not possibly in both.—Mr. Chase has publicly declared "that he was for obtaining, *in the mode prescribed by the constitution and in no other way*, such amendments as, in his opinion, are necessary *to secure the great and essential rights of the people* —" it is now *universaly* agreed that the constitution is defective, and no man can object to amendments to secure essential rights to the people. But the opponents of Mr. Chase express their fears that, under *pretense* of amendments for *these* purposes, he will *artfully* weaken or destroy the government. A powerful proof, (if true) of his understanding, and a high reflection on the members of our legislature. To remove all suspicion, if possible, on this head, let Mr. Chase, *and the two Doctors*,[1] be called on to state what amendments they wish to be made to the new government, if they were to determine on the subject.

But Mr. Chase, *as our delegate,* will *obstruct,* or *clog,* such measures as are necessary to put the new government into motion, and to carry it effectually into execution. In the consideration of this matter it may be proper to understand what measures are to be adopted by our legislature to carry the new government into effect. After congress have fixed the day on which *electors* shall be appointed to choose the president and vice-president, and also the day on which the electors are to assemble and ballot for these officers, our legislature are 1st, to direct the *manner* of choosing the *electors* of the president and vice-president; and of consequence to determine what persons shall be entitled to vote for the electors.[(a)] 2nd, To direct the time, place and manner of holding elections for senators and representatives. 3rd, To choose two senators.—If these are all the measures to be adopted by our legislature to carry the new government into effect, *if inclined,* can any man sincerely believe that Mr. Chase will be able to *clog* or *obstruct* these measures? Mr. Chase has declared, "that he considered it the *duty of every good citizen* to submit to the new government, and to carry it into execution, and that, in his opinion, it ought *immediately* to be carried into *full and vigorous execution,* and that he would use his endeavours for *all* measures and regulation for that purpose"; and he assigned this reason for his declaration that, if the government ratified by ten states was not established, America would be without any national government, and in a state of confusion and anarchy. Those who give faith and credit to this declaration of Mr. Chase will trust him; those who disbelieve him will not trust him.

But Mr. Chase, if elected, will vote for *antifederal* characters to the senate of the United States. He will be bound to give his voice for the persons most capable of representing the State; whether in favour of the new government *without* or *with* previous amendments; and I think he ought to oppose the choice of any person who is averse from all amendments.

But there is a scheme, in *all* the States, to elect *antifederals* into the State legislatures, that they may choose *similar* characters into the senate of the United States. This suggestion is made to *alarm* the advocates of the new government, and if it prevails, no man who was for previous amendments will be elected; for if the objection is reasonable in this town, it will be as just in every other part of America. If the people of this town are of opinion that amendments are necessary, ought they to elect persons opposed to, or in favour of amendments?

The *opponents* of Mr. Chase have endeavoured to make the term ANTIFEDERAL a word of *contempt* and *reproach*, and synonimous to an *enemy of the country*, or a TORY; and the term *federal* as honorable, and friendly to good government, and the rights of men; and they *indiscriminately* apply this appellation to ALL who support his election. This conduct is disgraceful, and indecent. They should remember that a great many of this town were of the *same* opinion with Mr. Chase, that the government ought not to have been adopted without *previous* amendments; and they may observe that many of his advocates were for taking the government as it stood, but who always were for procuring amendments to it, as soon as circumstances would permit.

The *right* of choosing representatives is the distinguishing characteristic of freemen, and one of the greatest *privileges* they possess; and they ought to exercise it with sobriety, peace, order, and decency, without riot or tumult. I make no doubt you will, as heretofore, behave with propriety, and at the same time, with resolution and firmness.

September 11, 1788.

(a) Dr. M'Henry *delivered his opinion, that the legislature might appoint the electors of the President and Vice-President, or give the appointment to others.*

1. The *"two Doctors"* were James McHenry and John Coulter, the Federalist candidates running against Samuel Chase and David McMechen for state representative from Baltimore.

Henry Lee to George Washington
New York, 13 September 1788 (excerpt)[1]

... The new govt tho about to commence its proceedings & r[e]ceived by a large majority of the people with unprecedented unanimity & attachment, must encounter from the nature of human affairs many difficultys—these obstacles to its harmonious progress will receive additional weight & influence from the active & enterprizing characters who continue to inflame the passions & to systemize the measures of opposition—the circular letr from this state,[2] seems to be the standard, to which the various minoritys will repair, & if they should succeed in bringing quickly into action the objects of that letr, new & serious difficu[l]tys must arise, which will cross & may destroy the govt in its infancy—Much will depend on the part which the assembly of Virginia may adopt in this business, & from the complexion of that body, little is to be hoped. They appeared to be generally opposed, & Mr Henry with many other conventional coadjutors, are members of the legislature—Madison will not be there, nor is there a friend to govt in the assembly of comparative ability—It would be fortunate if this gentleman could be introduced into that body, & I think it is practicable—Mr [James] Gordon one of the orange members would readily vacate, to let him in & the county would certainly elect him. In my letr of this date to Doctor [David] Stuart, I have mentioned this suggestion.

It would certainly be unpleasant to you & obnoxious to all who feel for your just fame, to see you at the head of a tumbling system—It is a sacrifice on your part, unjustifiable in any point of view—But on the other hand no alternative seems to be presented.

without you the govt. can have but little chance of success, & the people of that happiness which its prosperity must yield—In this dilemma, it seems wise that such previous measures be in time adopted, which most promise to allay the fury of opposition, to defer amendments, till experience has shewn defects—& to ensure the appointments of able & honest men in the first Congress.

One of the best means to accomplish this seems to me to bring into the assembly of Virga the aid before mentioned.

Indeed I know of nothing so effective, for on the conduct of Virga every thing will depend—Her example will be followed, & if she supports with promptitude the system recommended by this state [i.e., New York], confusion & anarchy may be the substitutes of order & good govt. . . .

1. RC, Washington Papers, DLC. For the entire letter, see Abbot, *Washington, Confederation Series*, VI, 510–13n.
2. For the New York Convention's circular letter of 26 July, see BoR, I, 153–58.

William Widgery to George Thatcher
New Glocester, Maine, 14 September 1788 (excerpt)[1]

Honoured Sir

I received yours of August 24th. Observed the Contents I am very sorry to hear of the Conduct of North Carolina rejecting the constitution,[2] not but that I think it ought to be Amended, but as it is already Adopted by eleven States I think there can be no danger but that the amendments would take place as Sune as the New Congress is organized. I am sorry to hear that the Minority of Carolina are not possessed with that Noble Republican Principal of Adhearing to the voice of a majority in Political Matters. for two Reasons the Minority are [w]rong in Showing any resentment, first because if the Majority are the most Sensible part of the State as well as the most numerous, in vain will the Minority Strive to force, but if they are the more ignorant part it is much better to draw than drive, for you can better Draw ten ignorant men than drive one. I am therefore in hopes they will rather Strive to Draw than Drive, as I think that will be the most likely way to unite the whole. Some men think it degrading to them to Stupe to a man who does not Know so much as they do, but let me tel you it is Victory that crowns the day, this much for Constitution....

1. RC, Thatcher Papers, Chamberlain Collection, MB. Printed: William F. Goodwin, ed., "The Thatcher Papers," *Historical Magazine*, 2nd ser., VI (1869), 352–53.
2. On 2 August 1788, the North Carolina Hillsborough Convention refused to ratify the Constitution before its declaration of rights and amendments were considered by Congress and a second general convention. See BoR, I, 264–70.

Boston Herald of Freedom, 15 September 1788

From a Correspondent.

The absurdity of chusing our federal Rulers, from those characters who are sticklers for amendments to the Federal Constitution in the first instance, or before it's competency to the exigencies of the Union is tried, must appear obvious, when it is considered that upon this plan we must exclude every advocate for the system, or, which is the same thing, every open, decided Federalist who was in favour of adopting it without amendments—there are enough of the *first sort*, to form the whole Continental Legislature & if our suffrages should run in that direction, we should exclude all those worthies to whose exertions we are indebted for that Constitution which must save our Country, if in a salvable State.

John Brown Cutting to Thomas Jefferson
London, 16 September 1788 (excerpt)[1]

Your respective favours of Sepr. 4th and 9th are before me. For both but especially for the last accept my sincere thanks. Truth and certainty are always most grateful to the human mind. Your mode of conveying them and the important objects concerning which you enlighten me, render what is naturally pleasant particularly interesting and grateful. As my passage to South Carolina must be regulated by the intelligence I obtain concerning the probability of a speedy, or more retarded commencement of the operations of the general government, as well of the assembling of the legislature, of the particular state to which I am about to resort, I think you may depend upon the fidelity of my correspondence for some weeks yet to come. Especially if the *new Congress* do not meet until March; and more especially if the circular letter from the Convention of New York[2] shou'd prevail upon two thirds of the states, and among these Carolina, to suspend the functions of *that body* until another general convention can be convoked to consider and decide upon amendments. Or even if the following alteration of the general constitution shou'd by any mean[s] take place as insisted upon by New York, namely "That the judicial power of the United States, in cases in which a state may be a party, does not extend to authorise *any suit by any* person against *a state*";[3] I fear my proposed negotiation with the state of South Carolina wou'd be baffled, or rather so evidently promise to be abortive as not to be worth attempting.

The August Packet tho' momently expected is not yet arriv'd here from New York. By the next post I hope to announce to you the accession of North Carolina which I look to receive by the packet, since it seems she was to sail three days later than the date of any of the papers I inclose. Among these papers you will observe a transcript of the conventional letter from New York, and certain other articles, which I have with some industry collected and committed to writing for your entertainment. The sources whence I derived most of those extracts were not to be purchased nor even purloyn'd. . . .

1. RC, Jefferson Papers, DLC. For the entire letter and the enclosure not printed here, see Boyd, XIII, 608–13n.
2. For the New York Convention's circular letter, see BoR, I, 153–58.
3. The concept of sovereign immunity of the states was embodied in the Eleventh Amendment proposed by Congress on 4 March 1794 and adopted by the states on 7 February 1795.

Charles Nesbit to the Earl of Buchan
Carlisle, Pa., 16 September 1788 (excerpt)[1]

From a Country of so little Curiosity, & so barren of Events as this is, little Information can be expected, but as it is now in a singular & interesting Situation, & the Accounts in the public Papers may be defective or partial, I imagined that a brief Account of its present State might not be unacceptable to your Lordship, as a Citizen of the World, & a lover of Mankind. Last Year a Convention of the Representatives of the thirteen States drew up a Constitution or Plan of Government for this Country, which was submitted to the Conventions of the several States, & agreed to be carried into Execution, if adopted by Nine States. This Constitution, tho' imperfect, defective, & in some Respects impious, was judged however to be the best Form of Government that could be adopted by a People in our Situation, & is Still thought to be so, by all that love Order, Justice & the Happiness of Society. Eleven States have now adopted this Constitution, tho' those of Virginia & New York appear to be least sincere in this Business. Rhode Island has not called a Convention to consider it, & North Carolina appears to be disposed only to accept it conditionally. Your Lordship may easily imagine how few good things can be expected to be agreed to by three Millions of ignorant Peasants, under factious Leaders, & loaded with Debts at home & abroad, habituated likewise, as they have been since the Peace, to the uniform Practice of Injustice to their Creditors & to one another. Wicked Men in this Situation, must be Enemies to an efficient Government, which would oblige them to pay their Debts and Taxes, & put it out of their Power to make Laws against the Practice of Justice, which is all that the State Governments have done hitherto. Accordingly, the Opposers of the New Constitution consist almost wholly of Men of this Description, & considering how much they abound here, it is surprising that the Opposition has not been greater. I hope that no Violence will be attempted, but the Malcontents in every State are setting up Committees of Correspondence in Hopes of ruining the Constitution by Amendments, which they could not hinder by force or Numbers. What they principally point at is to deprive Congress of the Power of imposing general Taxes, & to prevent their keeping a standing Army in time of Peace. Many likewise contend for a Bill of Rights, & that the Congress should not have Power to appoint the Time & Place of the Election of their own Members, but that it should be left to the Direction of the State Assemblies. If they should prevail on the Legislatures of Nine States to agree to these pretended Amendments, or even any of the two first, they would effectually defeat the Intention of the New Constitution, & prolong our present Anarchy. . . .

1. RC, Founders Collection, Dickinson College, Carlisle, Pa. David Steuart Erskine, the 11th Earl of Buchan, had founded the Society of Antiquaries of Scotland in 1780.

Massachusetts Centinel, 17 September 1788[1]

It is very strange to hear people talking about a "clamour" for amendments to the federal Constitution—no such clamour exists—It is true the *antifederalists* have made a pother about certain *alterations*, but in these they are greatly divided, and it would puzzle the most subtle of them, to ascertain the precise meaning of any *two minorities* of any of the State Conventions, respecting one particular alteration—Some talk about a *bill of rights*, others have given up that idea, honestly confessing that it would be a dangerous appendage to the system, in as much that volumes upon volumes, would be insufficient to enumerate those rights, and upon this plan whatever was not designated as a right, would be considered as relinquished—the truth is, the excellency of the federal Constitution consists in its *brevity* and *perspicuity*—it is *now* a complete system, but the proposed *alterations* would mar its beauty and render it a shapeless monster,

"THE MAJESTY OF THE PEOPLE"[2]—yes, "the majesty of the people" is *insulted* by the proposition to introduce into the federal Legislature, certain *sticklers* for *pretended* amendments. The Constitution in its *present form*, is the Constitution of the people, but *mutilated* or *distorted* by the variations of these *sticklers*, it will no longer be the legitimate offspring of the people, but the creature of an antifederal junto.

1. Reprinted: Worcester, Mass., *American Herald*, 25 September; *Pennsylvania Mercury*, 30 September; *Pennsylvania Journal*, 1 October; Trenton, N.J., *Federal Post*, 7 October; *Virginia Independent Chronicle*, 15 October (extraordinary). For a criticism, see "The Voice of the People," Boston *Independent Chronicle*, 18 September (immediately below).
2. See the *Massachusetts Centinel*, 6 September 1788 (BoR, III, 201–2).

The Voice of the People
Boston Independent Chronicle, 18 September 1788[1]

One scarcely knows whether the unparelled affrontery of the contemptible paragraphist of yesterday's Centinel, on the subject of "*amendments*," ought rather to excite our ridicule or resentment.[2] The honour of the Convention who adopted the Constitution, of the good people represented by this highly honourable body, and of every delegate from the State, whether senatorial or popular, are all equally pledged to support the amendments submitted by his Excellency, and highly approved by the *federal* part of the Convention.[3]

No matter what their private sentiments may be,—whether there are pernicious alterations or solid improvements; it is just the same. *The faith of the community is plighted.* THE MAJESTY OF THE PEOPLE will be injured by an attempt to prevent their adoption. Will his Excellency be silent? will the other gentlemen who advocated the proposition for 'amendments' be quiet? Because, forsooth, the paltry scriblers of the Centinel disapprove. When every State, since the ratification of Massachusetts, have adopted the same plan, shall this State be the first to rescind its own resolution? Such a measure would indeed be an insult on *The Majesty of the People*, and will accordingly meet the contempt, rediculc and detestation of the honest and impartial, and of all, indeed, but the few incendiaries who supply their trash to the Centinel, and call it THE VOICE OF THE PEOPLE.

    1. Reprinted: Worcester, Mass., *American Herald*, 25 September; Philadelphia *Independent Gazetteer*, 26 September.
    2. See the *Massachusetts Centinel*, 17 September (immediately above).
    3. See at footnote 3 and footnote 3, Boston *Independent Chronicle*, 11 September (BoR, III, 207, 208n).

Boston Herald of Freedom, 18 September 1788[1]

The *Federal Constitution* (says a Correspondent) in its *present form*, so completely met the *wishes* and *ideas* of the citizens of this metropolis, that they received it as a messenger of good tidings, and the harbinger of future peace and prosperity—and so universally did *federal* sentiments prevail on the happy occasion, that among the whole body of the *natives* of the town, scarcely a breeze of antifederalism was heard.— Have they changed their opinions? Are they less sensible at the *present moment* of the excellency of the Constitution, than they were at the above period? By no means.—Their anticipations of future prosperity, are founded on the Constitution *as it is*—not on what it will be, when the spirit of it is taken away or destroyed by the pretended amendments of the Antifederalists.

We have happily (continues our Correspondent) got rid of the old Confederation, which was emphatically "a rope of sand."—Shall we be so infatuated as to revert to a state of national imbecility and contempt, by electing for our Federal Rulers, men who will by alterations of the new system extract the essence and spirit of it, till nothing but the *shadow* of a Constitution remains? Heaven prevent us from such delusion.

    1. Reprinted: *New Hampshire Gazette*, 25 September. Only the second paragraph was reprinted in the New York *Daily Advertiser*, 26 and 27 September, and in the Poughkeepsie, N.Y., *Country Journal*, 30 September.

Senex
Massachusetts Centinel, 20 September 1788

Mr. RUSSELL, The celebrated writer of Common Sense compared the marches and countermarches of Gen. Howe, in America, to "*a dog running after his tail.*"[1]—The similitude was striking; but it is better applied to the *knot* of scribblers who have been for a long time harping on the subject of "*amendments,*" in our papers. But to what can one compare the folly of these witlings in taking it upon them to call the writings of those who are opposed to them, "*trash,*" &c. when even they *themselves* must confess that they are not competent to judge of composition—and by their writings shew themselves to be not only destitute of every species of political knowledge and pretensions to candour; but of the first rudiments of grammar?—A similitude is to be found only in their ignorance. If the federal paragraphs which have been occasionally inserted, to caution the people against the arts of these designing seekers—were such "*trash*" as they would insinuate, why need they take such unwearied pains to make the publick believe them such? The publick could determine on them—and a consolation is, that the enlightened publick WILL judge of the merits or demerits of the paragraphs on both sides—and I believe there is no occasion for any thing to be said, to convince them which are "*trash.*"

Opposed to these moonshine politicians, are the writings of Publius, and Mr. Adams[2]—of Gen. Washington, Dr. Price, and many other dignified and enlightened characters, both in America and Europe. If one were to ask on whose opinion it was safe for the people to rely—the characters above mentioned, or these wiseacres[3]—who would not smile?

The proposed amendments, Mr. RUSSELL, have effected the purpose for which they were intended—i.e. *conciliation.*[4] Did not a number of gentlemen in our Convention, among whom was our Commander in Chief, declare—and have not a majority in all the other Conventions which have since met—*declared,* that they were willing to receive the Constitution without ANY ALTERATIONS? But, for the sake of conciliation, and a regard for the *weakness* of those who from the want of time to consider the subject maturely—prejudice, and the arts of demagogues, had supposed the Constitution to be dangerous—they consented to the recommendation of amendments. This is the truth, and the object being happily attained, alterations ought not to be further thought of—until found by *experience,* wanting.

While one cannot but smile at the *shrewd guesses* of these wisacres, respecting the authors of the paragraphs they find fault with—and the motives in which they originate—I can assure the publick, that their conjectures on both heads are wholly ill-founded. That their project is contrary to the expressed sentiments of the People of America, need not be told at this time of day.

1. On page 15 of *The American Crisis. Number V. Addressed to General Sir William Howe.* . . . (Lancaster, Pa., 1778) (Evans 15953) Thomas Paine wrote: "The history & figure of your movements be truly ridiculous could they be delineated. They resemble the labors of a puppy pursuing his tail; the end is still at the same distance, and all the turnings round must be done over again."

COMMENTARIES, 21 SEPTEMBER 1788 221

2. A reference to *A Defence of the Constitutions* by John Adams (CC:16).
3. "Wiseacres" was used by Federalists to stigmatize Rhode Island Antifederalists and debt-relief and paper money advocates. See RCS:R.I., 255, 451, 460, 506, 566.
4. The *Massachusetts Centinel*, 2 February 1788, printed the amendments introduced by Governor John Hancock on 31 January under the headline "CONCILIATION." See RCS:Mass., 1387–88.

John Jay to George Washington
New York, 21 September 1788 (excerpt)[1]

... I am not sure that the new Government will be found to rest on Principles sufficiently stable to produce a uniform adherence to what Justice, Dignity and liberal Policy may require: for however proper such Conduct may be, none but great minds will always deem it expedient. Men in general are guided more by conveniences than by Principles. This Idea accompanies all my Reflections on the new Constitution, and induced me to remark to our late Convention at Poughkeepsie, that some of the most unpopular and strong Parts of it appeared to me to be the most unexceptionable. Government without Liberty is a curse but on the other Hand Liberty without Government is far from being a Blessing.

The opponents in this State to the Constitution decrease and grow temperate. many of them seem to look forward to another Convention rather as a Measure that will justify their opposition, than produce *all* the Effects they pretended to expect from it. I wish that Measure may be adopted with a good Grace, and without Delay or Hesitation. So many good Reasons can be assigned for postponing the *Session* of such a Convention for three or four Years, that I really believe the great Majority of its advocates would be satisfied with that Delay. After which I think we should not have much Danger to apprehend from it; especially if the new Governmt should in the mean Time recommend itself to the People by the wisdom of its Proceedings, which I flatter myself will be the Case. The Division of the Powers of Govt into three Departments is a great and valuable point gained; and will give the People the best opportunity of bringing the Question whether they can govern themselves, to a Decision in their Favor.

1. RC, Washington Papers, DLC. For the entire letter, see Abbot, *Washington, Confederation Series*, VI, 527–28.

James Madison to Thomas Jefferson
New York, 21 September 1788 (excerpt)[1]

... The Circular letter from the New York Convention has rekindled an ardor among the opponents of the federal Constitution for an *im-*

mediate revision of it by another General Convention. You will find in one of the papers inclosed the result of the consultations in Pennsylvania on that subject.[2] Mr. Henry and his friends in Virginia enter with great zeal into the scheme. Governour Randolph also espouses it; but with a wish to prevent if possible danger to the article which extends the power of the Government to internal as well as external taxation. It is observable that the views of the Pennsylva. meeting do not rhyme very well with those of the Southern advocates for a Convention; the objects most eagerly pursued by the latter being unnoticed in the Harrisburg proceedings. The effect of the Circular letter on other States is less known.[3] I conclude that it will be the same every where, among those who opposed the Constitution, or contended for a conditional ratification of it. Whether an early Convention will be the result of this united effort, is more than can at this moment be foretold. The measure will certainly be industriously opposed in some parts of the Union, not only by those who wish for no alterations, but by others who would prefer the other mode provided in the Constitution;[4] as most expedient at present for introducing those supplemental safeguards to liberty agst. which no objections can be raised; and who would moreover approve of a Convention for amending the frame of the Government itself, as soon as time shall have somewhat corrected the feverish state of the public mind, and trial have pointed its attention to the true defects of the System....

1. RC, Madison Papers, DLC. For the entire letter, see Rutland, *Madison*, XI, 257–59.
2. A reference to the proceedings and resolutions of the Harrisburg Convention as printed in the *Pennsylvania Gazette*, 10 September 1788 (BoR, III, 176–82n).
3. For the actions of other states on the proposal in the New York circular letter, see BoR, I, 156.
4. Article V of the Constitution provides that two-thirds of both houses of Congress could propose amendments and that Congress, on application of two-thirds of the state legislatures, should call a convention to propose amendments.

William Samuel Johnson to Samuel Peters
New York, 22 September 1788 (excerpt)[1]

... Eleven States, having adopted the proposed Constitution, our Congress have now published their Ordinance directing the necessary steps towards the Organization of the new Government, & that it commence its Operations in this City on the first Wednesday of March next[2]—Very many are extremely sanguine in their Expectations that we shall derive great Blessings from it, while many, on the other hand, are aiming at, & expecting soon to obtain great alterations & emendations of the plan—Both sides will as usual, probably be in some measure, disappointed, & how it will finally operate is known only to the allwise disposer of all Events. . . .

1. RC, Archives and Historical Collections, Historical Society of the Episcopal Church, Austin, Texas. The letter was addressed to the "Revd. Mr. Samuel Peters/Pimlico/Westminster." It was endorsed by Peters as "recd. Nov. 16" and "Ansd. Nov. 17." For the entire letter, see Joseph Hooper, ed., *Diocese of Connecticut, Formative Period 1784–1791* (n.p., 1913), 15–16; reprinted Kenneth Walter Cameron, ed., *Connecticut Churchmanship Records and Historical Papers Concerning the Anglican Church in Connecticut in the Eighteenth and Early Nineteenth Centuries* (Hartford, Conn., 1969), 15–16.

2. For the election ordinance, see CC:845.

George Washington to Henry Lee
Mount Vernon, Fairfax County, Va., 22 September 1788 (excerpt)[1]

. . . Your observations on the solemnity of the crisis & its application to myself, bring before me subjects of the most momentous & interesting nature. In our endeavours to establish a new general government, the contest, nationally considered, seems not to have been so much for glory, as existence. It was for a long time doubtful whether we were to survive as an independent Republic, or decline from our fœderal dignity into insignificant & wretched fragments of Empire. The adoption of the Constitution so extensively, & with so liberal an acquiescence on the part of the Minorities in general, promised the former: until, lately, the Circular letter of New York carried, in my apprehension, an unfavorable, if not an insidious tendency to a contrary policy. I will hope for the best, but before you mentioned it, I could not help fearing it would serve as a Standard to which the disaffected might resort. It is now evidently the part of all honest men, who are friends to the New Constitution, to endeavor to give it a chance to disclose its merits and defects, by carrying it fairly into effect, in the first instance. For it is to be apprehended, that by an attempt, to obtain amendments before the experiment has been candidly made "more is meant than meets the ear"—that an intention is concealed to accomplish slily, what could not have been done openly—to undo all that has been done. If the fact so exists, that a kind of combination is forming to stifle the government in embrio; it is a happy circumstance that the design has become suspected. Preparation should be the sure attendant upon forewarning. Probably, prudence, wisdom, & patriotism were never more essentially necessary than at the present moment: and so far as it can be done in an irreproachable direct manner, no effort ought to be left unessayed to procure the election of the best possible characters to the new Congress. On their harmony, deliberation & decision every thing will depend. I heartily wish Mr Madison was in our Assembly: as I think, with you, it is of unspeakable importance Virginia should set out in her fœderal measures under right auspices. . . .

1. RC, Library of Virginia, Richmond. Washington indicated that the letter was "Private." For the entire letter, see Abbot, *Washington, Confederation Series*, VI, 528–31. Washington is answering Lee's letter of 13 September (BoR, III, 213–14).

Abraham Yates, Jr., to William Smith
New York, 22 September 1788[1]

I have your favour of the 17th before me[2]—In Respect to the New government We exactly Agree in Opinion—The Case now is Simple All agree that Amendments are Indispensably necessary—And Where We had it in our Own power before, the Convention have transferred it to the union at Large And We now Cant get the Amendments unless ⅔ of the States first Agree to a Convention And as Many to Agree to the Amendments—And then ¾ of the Several Legislatures to Confirm them: That this Will be an uphill Affair—You may See When you Call to Mind that Congress lately had ten Weeks before they Could Agree Where the New government Was to meet[3]—But so it is And We must make the best of it—our only safety now is in geting the Amendments Confirmed—I mean to try for it and I believe the first thing Necessary will be to pass a Law to Inhibit the State officers (the Legislative Executive And Judicial) from takeing the Oath to support the New government untill our amendments have been Confirmed in due form—My Next Will Contain More upon this Subject I have no time (your son goes of[f] to Manor) than to Add that I Remain Your sincere frend And Humble Servt

1. RC, Manor of St. George Museum, Center Moriches, N.Y.
2. Not found.
3. See RCS:Congress, passim.

Samuel Huntington to Samuel Johnston
Norwich, Conn., 23 September 1788[1]

I have been honoured with your several letters of the 12th. & 24th. ulto., the former covering an Extract from the Journals of the late Convention of your State & the latter accompanied with two Resolves passed in your Convention.[2]

These papers will be communicated to the General Assembly of this State at their approaching Session.

The Convention in this State, at the time they ratified the new federal Constitution, would have preferred some Alterations & Amendments rather than the present form, if I may judge from the sentiments that were thrown out in discussing the subject; but deemed it too dangerous to hazard Delays under a tottering Constitution, until every difficulty should be removed, so as to obtain a Constitution which would meet the entire approbation of all the States in the Union, which it is not probable would ever be the Case.

Perhaps from the nature of the case, it must be left to the wisdom & virtue of the States to make Amendments in future, in the mode provided by the Constitution, as experience shall dictate: No Constitution of Government can make a people happy without Virtue and Wisdom.

A Bill of Rights in former times hath been judged necessary, but in this enlightened age, when it seems a self evident truth, acknowledged almost as indisputably as any Axiom, that all right & authority in Government is derived from the People, & may be resumed whenever the safety or happiness of the People renders it necessary; is it necessary, or expedient, for them to form a Bill of Rights which seems at least to call in question a truth of such importance & which ought ever to be held indisputable?

1. RC, Misc. Collection, HM22570, Henry E. Huntington Library, San Marino, California. Huntington was governor of Connecticut; Johnston was governor of North Carolina.

2. Governor Johnston's circular letter to the states, 12 August, enclosed an extract from the journal of the first North Carolina Convention, which met 21 July–4 August 1788 and which did not ratify the Constitution. The extract, dated 1 August, included a "Declaration of Rights" containing twenty articles and twenty-six "Amendments to the Constitution." The two resolutions enclosed in Johnston's circular letter of 24 August recommended that the North Carolina General Assembly take steps to redeem the state's paper currency and enact a state impost to match any federal impost enacted by Congress under the new Federal Constitution (RCS:N.C., 484–86n).

Theodore Sedgwick to Benjamin Lincoln
Springfield, Mass., 23 September 1788 (excerpts)[1]

... I wish to be understood in regard to what I said with respect to the obligation we are under not to oppose the meeting of a convention. You remember that attendant in the form of our ratification, was an instruction to our delegates hereafter to be appointed to use their influence to procure the amendments we proposed. My meaning was that we, the federal members of the convention, would do nothing in contradiction of that act. At the same time I am fully in opinion that a convention called at any period not far distant, would probably defeat every beneficial effect to be expected from the un[ob]structed operation of the system. It is therefore my opinion that the business should rest on the natural effort & the vote of our convention & the character of our members so far as respects the agency of Massachusetts. . . .

I hope that every prudent precaution will be taken to secure a good federal representation. The amendment mongers, I trust in Heaven, will be universally excluded. The danger is not that the first operations of the new Govermt. will be too rigorous, but too cautious and timid.— Nothing however I hope will in any part of the state be ultimately decided on untill the Legislature meets when characters will be duly ballanced. . . .

1. RC, Lincoln Papers, MHi. This is a response to Lincoln's letter of 7 September (BoR, III, 182–83).

An Old German
Baltimore Maryland Gazette, 23 September 1788[1]

To the MANUFACTURERS and MECHANICS of Baltimore-Town. *Friends and Fellow-Citizens!*

In my last, I noticed to you that our *old delegates* were friends to civil and religious liberty; as such they claim our respect and attention; for after all the noisy meetings to examine their characters, I have not heard any real objection, sufficient to shake your confidence in them. If we change our servants, we ought to have reason for so doing; and should we act from meer prejudice, and not reason, it may be feared our change and our choice may be for the worse. We know the men we now have, are *experienced* in public business, and that they are willing and ready to abide by our instructions, and will rejoice to do us any service in their power:—We do not know that others can do better for us. It is easy to ridicule and find fault with public men, and bold confident assertions are more easily made than proven. In electioneering seasons, slander will take liberties, parties will be warm, and falsehoods widely circulate.—In the common affairs of life, we may perhaps give credit to half that is told us; but in the contention for election victory, we cannot safely believe one-sixth part of what we are told about any man; and on that account, we should remember to believe no more than what has come within the compass of our own knowledge. Take heed therefore, how you hear, and how you believe.—

But you will say the federalism of these men is doubtful, because they are for amendments.—If that is all that is brought against them, it is trifling indeed. Let us look into the matter fairly and we shall find them not to blame for this opinion, provided they candidly pledge themselves to abide by the instructions that may be given them.

The number of inhabitants in America, according to a publication in the American Museum, is as follows, viz.

For amendments:		Against amendments:	
New-Hampshire	150,000	Connecticut	192,000
Massachusetts	400,000	New-Jersey	150,000
Rhode-Island	59,670	Pennsylvania	300,000
New-York	250,000	Delaware	50,000
Virginia	650,000	Maryland	320,000
North-Carolina	300,000	Georgia	56,000
South-Carolina	225,000		
	2034,670		1068,000
	1068,000		
Majority for amendments,	966,670		

By this calculation, we see there are near two to one for amendments throughout the states; but if we consider there are thousands in Pennsylvania for amendments, who are now taking measures to obtain them; that in Maryland likewise there are great numbers of this way of thinking; and we have reason to assert, there are other states who ratified without proposing amendments, which are now convinced of the necessity of them, surely it can be no objection against any gentleman to serve us in the house of delegates, because he is for amendments, seeing it is the opinion of an amazing majority in America. If because a person is for amendments, he is to be called an antifederalist, the great majority of the United States are antifederalists. Nothing can be more absurd than such a position. What are the views and intentions of those who are for amendments?—*To secure on firm and constitutional foundations, the liberties of their country.* Can such men then be our enemies? It is impossible. I will venture to assert that seven-eighths of the inhabitants of America, except place hunters, except those who are gaping, like young vultures, for profitable offices, are for amendments. This objection then against your old candidates ought to be despised.

The proposing amendments can reflect no dishonor on the members who composed the late convention at Philadelphia; for no man, or body of men is infallible in politics. We acknowledge, we revere their wisdom; but in a matter of such consequence, too much caution cannot be used. It was thought the convention spent a great deal of time in framing the new constitution, because they sat *four months.* I never thought so; for every single clause in that all-important writing, ought to be considered and weighed a thousand times over.—Four years spent in such a work would not be too much. A certain great painter said, *I paint for eternity,* and the members of the convention might truly say, "we are acting for eternity; we are draughting the Magna Charta of

America, which ought to be so carefully worded as to last for ever. Let us not then be in a hurry—let us hear what the people will say of our workmanship, and then let us go at it again, and endeavour to make it agreeable to them, and as perfect as possible.—It is an object worth all our labour, as it concerns the happiness of ourselves, and our children, even to all generations.—"

Married in haste, you may repent at leisure, is an old proverb;[2] and in this case, it may justly be said, adopt a new government in haste, you may repent at leisure—look, before you leap; we are now free, let us then be careful in all our future movements, that we preserve our freedom, and stand fast in that liberty, in which heaven has kindly made us free!

I shall now, my friends, conclude for the present, wishing you may do right and follow good counsels.—Be advised to chuse men of sense, who are generous, open, and manly in their sentiments,—no novices, but tried experienced men, and who have shewed themselves, in the worst of times, lovers of the public good.

Sept. 18, 1788.

1. On 19 September, the *Gazette* announced that this essay would appear in the next issue.

2. This phrase first appeared in print in *The Old Bachelor* . . . by William Congreve (London, 1693).

Benjamin Lincoln to George Washington
Hingham, Mass., 24 September 1788 (excerpts)[1]

I was my dear general a few days since in Boston where I had the pleasure of receiving your favor of the 23d Ulto.[2]

The information which your Excellency has received, respecting the machinations of the antifederal characters, appears from what circulates in this part of the country, but too well founded. I have no doubt, but every exertion will be made to introduce into the new government, in the first instance characters unfriendly to those parts of it, which in my opinion are its highest orniments and its most precious jewels. To this they will be induced from two considerations at the least—The first with a view totally to change the nature of the government immediately—But should they fail of that, they will then have it in their power to introduce into all the important offices in government men of their own sentiments, so that in a short time by their influence they may bring about that change which cannot at first or in any other way be effected by them.

Should these events take place, the situation of the federalists will be humiliating indeed. They will soon have the mortification of seeing that all their exertion for establishing a government, for promoting the honour, & for securing the freedom and felicity of the people have proved ineffectual not only so but they will find themselves buried in such obscurity as to be totally unable to rise with that influence necessary to have any controul over public men or public measures. Their only hope then can be, a forlorn in truth, that when the government established shall be found insufficient to answer the great and interesting purposes which it should embrace and when the distresses of the people in consequence thereof, are evinced by clamours and out rage against it, and things fall back into a state of confusion they may possibly stand on a floor with others. A melancholy consideration however, though the punishment suffered hereby would be but just should this train of evils take place in consequence of our own indolence and in attention.

There never was an instance when it could have been more necessary to call into exercise the wisdom the prudence and patriotism of the United States than it will be in the important transactions of appointing the executive and the legislative branches of the new government. For the first impressions made therein will probably give a tone to all future measures.

We are happy here in finding it to be the unanimous voice of this rising empire, that your Excellency who has so just a claim to the merit of its establishment, should now take it under your protection. The share your Excellency holds in the affections of the people, and the unlimited confidence they place in your integrety and judgment, gives you an elevated stand among them which no other man can or probably ever will command. These things must insure to your Excellency all which a susceptible mind can wish, a power of promoting in the highest degree the happiness of a virtuous and an enlightened country.

But will not these very important considerations alarm those antifederal characters before mentioned? They must know that the influence your Excellency will have in the organization of the new government and in enforcing the precepts of it, will embarrass their Scheams if not totally baffle them. Surely they must know that these consequences will follow your acceptance of the important trust. We must therefore expect and we should be guarded in every point to prevent the influence of the intreagues and combinations of those who wish to set every thing again afloat. They will endeavour, as one of the most probable means by which they can effect their purposes, to prevent your Excellencys acceptance of the Presidency, your election they cannot hinder....

I have my dear General thus freely written from the fullest conviction of duty and in perfect confidence in your Excellency I feel my self exceedingly interested to see such a government as we want and need established without loss of time—I have many motives to wish it besides my regard, for the general good—I hope yet to live and enjoy the blessings of it—I have a large rising family who may share the fate of those about them, if things go well they may be happy if other wise they must partake in the common misery. I wish to see a government in existance and properly administred that I may not suffer the sad mortification which would take place if after all the toils dangers and sufferings of a long and distressing war prosecuted for the purpose of warding off an impending blow and of establishing our country in those rights to which they were justly entitled the people should from any conduct of theirs lose those blessings which to secure was the sole end of the important struggle.

1. RC, Washington Papers, DLC. For the entire letter, see Abbot, *Washington, Presidential Series*, I, 5–9n.
2. The letter was actually dated 28 August (BoR, III, 152–53).

Truth
Philadelphia Independent Gazetteer, 24 September 1788[1]

The "Truth" "handbill" first appeared in Boston on 14 November 1787 as a one-page broadside. This Antifederalist piece signaled the opening of the campaign to elect delegates to the state convention that would decide the fate of the Constitution. (See RCS:Mass., 232–35.) The Philadelphia reprinting was intended to influence voters in the upcoming elections for members of the Assembly who it was believed would decide the fate of amendments to the ratified Constitution.

A gentleman just arrived from Boston has favored us with the following handbill which is in circulation there:

DISADVANTAGES *of* FEDERALISM *upon the* NEW PLAN.

1. The Trade of Boston transferred to Philadelphia; and the Boston Tradesmen starving.
2. The Discouragement of Agriculture by the Loss of Trade.
3. People indolent, dissolute and vicious, by the loss of Liberty.
4. An infinite Multiplication of Offices to provide for ruined Fortunes.
5. A standing Army, and a Navy at all Times kept up, to give genteel Employment to the idle and extravagant.
6. Importance of Boston annihilated.
7. The wealthy retiring to Philadelphia to spend their Revenues, while we are oppressed to pay Rents and Taxes to Absentees.
8. Liberty of the Press restrained.
9. Trial by Jury abolished.
10. Habeas Corpus done away.

11. Representatives chosen in such a manner, as to make it a business for life.
12. The Bill of Rights repealed.
And, 13th. Religion abolished.

All these reasons, and many more, require the plan to be amended, and made conformable to the circumstances of the people. The same objections are made in every state. Rouse then, and regulate the business so as to be friendly to industry, trade and arts. Your ships *now* go to every part of the world, and carry your produce. *Then*, they may go to *Philadelphia.*

1. Reprinted: *New York Journal,* 9 October.

Solon
Boston Independent Chronicle, 25 September 1788[1]

Mess'rs. ADAMS & NOURSE, When the *very respectable Convention* of this *Commonwealth,* adopted the *federal* Constitution, their *wisdom* and *foresight* were truly *conspicuous,* and highly *praise-worthy,* in declaring that it was "The opinion of this Convention, that certain amendments and alterations in the said Constitution, would remove the fears, and quiet the apprehensions of many of the good people of this Commonwealth, and more effectually guard against an undue administration of the federal government, the Convention do therefore recommend, that the following alterations and provisions, be introduced into the said Constitution." *Nine propositions* then follow. And an *injunction* on the *Representatives* of the people to endeavour to obtain a ratification of them.[2] The *wisdom* and *sound* policy of this measure, *produced* a happy conciliatory disposition in the minds of the members of the Convention, and among the *people* at *large,* who could not but *anticipate* every reasonable advantage, to result from a *wise* and *energetic* government, which by the proposed amendments, would in *no part* or *degree,* be *marred* in its *beauty* or *excellence,* and at the same time, be *properly restricted,* from *encroaching* on the *rights* and *liberties* of the *people,* which *have been* rendered *more dear* and *invaluable,* in their *estimation* than *ever, by* the *late* almost *unparalleled exertions,* to *rescue* and *secure* them. It is therefore, NOW, for the *good people* of this Commonwealth, as far as their *weight* in the great political scale *extends,* to *determine* for *themselves,* and *eventually* for *posterity, whether* the *salutary* intentions, of their late *respectable* Convention, and those of several other States, *shall* be carried into *effect,* by *adopting,* and *pursuing* those measures which *tend to insure* it; or *permit* them to be *frustrated,* by *listening* to *men* who are *decidedly* opposed to *any* amendments in the *federal* Constitution, and who view with abhorrence, any instructions or injunctions of the people for obtaining the important object. Would not the latter, *again* awaken those *fears* and *apprehensions*, which the Convention endeavoured to *soothe*, and leave open that door, to the *undue* administration of the federal government, at some *future* time, which they supposed possible; and against which *they* conceived, as the *delegates* of the *people*, it *was their duty to* GUARD.

While therefore, the *people rationally*, and with *good* grounds, *anticipate*, under the new government, the *increase* of their *agriculture, manufactures*, and *commerce*, it is *indispensable*, that they *guard well* the *portals* of their *rights* and *liberties*; *for* what *assurance* can they *have* of the *uninterrupted* enjoyment of *them*, if they do not, in the ONLY proper time, take the *necessary* precautions, for their *security* and *permanence*.

1. Reprinted: Portland, Maine, *Cumberland Gazette*, 9 October. For other essays by "Solon" and William Heath as the possible author, see the Boston *Independent Chronicle*, 28 August, 4 September, and 30 October (BoR, III, 147–49, 154–55, 199–201n).
2. For the Massachusetts Form of Ratification, amendments, and "injunction," see RCS:Mass., 1468–71.

Tarantula
Baltimore Maryland Gazette, 26 September 1788

Mr. HAYES, There is a piece in your last paper signed *Camillus*, which I am induced to notice, not I assure you on account of its being handsomely written, or for its abounding with vulgarities, and illiberal abuse, but because it is said to be the production of Mr. C—— [Samuel Chase], and contains the following opinions respecting the new constitution.

Mr. C. . . . is anxious to be known for a profound Statesman, and one well versed in the constitution of the United States. Take an example of both from his Camillus. "If," says he, (in that elaborate performance) "our Assembly can only apply to Congress to call a convention, and such convention only can propose amendments to the legislatures of the States, of what consequence are the sentiments of Mr. Chase or Dr. M'Henry about amendments? You raised a clamour (speaking to a man who had not addressed him) about amendments, when, if you understood the constitution, you would know that in a representative capacity *no delegate for this town, can have any thing to say to the subject.*"

Let us see whether this writer understands the constitution any better now than he did at the public meeting at Morris's. He would have the people believe (if, this paragraph means any thing) that a convention *only* can propose amendments to the legislatures of the States.[a] This is not true: Congress can *also* propose amendments to the legislatures of the States. Here there are *two* modes in place of one *only*.

Mr. C. . . . asserts in the same paragraph, that "in a representative capacity, no delegate, for this town, can have any thing to say to the subject of amendments." Here again he is wrong even admitting his position, that a convention *only* can propose amendments. Agreeably to the constitution, Congress may refer any amendments proposed by a convention to the legislatures of the States for ratification, consequently they may come before a delegate for this town in his representative capacity. Besides, as the *first Congress* may save the expence, risk, and trouble of a convention, by proposing at their *first session* every necessary amendment to the legislature of the several States, these, of course, must come before the delegates for this town in their representative capacity. Thus, whichever way the subject is viewed, Mr. C. . . . is miserably mistaken.

One cannot help being a little surprised to find a man who has been *five and twenty years* a legislator, and concerned besides in a variety of intricate transactions, so very ignorant of the constitution, especially too after having so recently sat upon it as a judge and condemned it for want of merit. I would advise this writer and Statesman, when he next attempts to explain the constitution, to get Mr. *M*   to correct his opinions before he sends them to the press.

September 23, 1788.

(a) *The* cry *among the antifederalists is a convention to propose amendments.*

Federalism
Maryland Journal, 26 September 1788 (excerpt)[1]

MR. GODDARD,[2] . . .

"Sir, the affairs of our country are at present in the most dangerous, the most alarming situation—and the future happiness and independence of *America* are suspended by a straw.—The glorious fabrick of *American* greatness, the true republican wisdom, secured by our federal government, the pride and the pleasure of every wise friend of this country, and the envy of all its enemies, now totters on its basis, and trembles at approaching fate.

It is said, with great confidence, by all the enemies of the federal constitution, that the government is constitutionally confirmed, and that nothing can prevent its being put in motion as the constitution of *America.* Sir, this is but half the truth—this is an idea which they have carefully circulated, through every part of this continent. It is manifestly intended to make the people at rest—to lull their minds asleep to a further prosecution of the business—and at our present situation, when in reality the constitution is but half established—when recovered from an imperfect, an enfeebled state of infancy, and just obtained a healthful tone, at this imperfect crisis, we hear and see plans forming in several states to give the constitution a secret stab through the medium of *particular amendments,* which will destroy every federal feature, and crush all its efficient powers.—This may be considered a harsh accusation—This kind of conduct in men, may be considered as beneath the utmost depravity of mankind—But I am sorry to see this truth upon record—I am sorry to think and know we have men so base amongst us.

The *inclination* and *power* in men to do *certain acts,* is sufficient ground for the rational mind to conclude that these *acts* will be executed, if not prevented by circumstances opposite, or men of contrary sentiments.—That it is the *will* or *inclination* of certain men, in the different states, to throw our public affairs into confusion and prevent the federal government taking effect, I appeal to facts—I appeal to the proceedings of the minority of the state of *Pennsylvania:*—What was the conduct of these men while in their state convention? When they met in that body, by the voice of their country, and by the consent of themselves, when they found a majority in the house for adopting the constitution, did they not, with violence, attempt to break up the house, and in the fury of their malice bursted the doors; and those who absconded from the house, were they not dragged to their duty, to the business of their country, by force?—And what was their conduct afterwards?—Did they not publish an address to the people in the most inflammatory language that could be penned, and in this address advised the people "to oppose the constitution then offered to them," and adopted by their state, "*in the same manner, and with the same spirit, that they resisted the tyranny of* Great-Britain *in the late revolution.*"[3] Sir, this was the language of these men, it is upon record, and in the hands of almost every person—and this is their language still. The leaders of these very men, and some of the men themselves, were in the late convention that sat at *Harrisburgh*[4]—The names of these men are annexed to and accompany the *amendments,* that are now published by that convention and offered for our acceptance.—Are these men to be trusted?—Can credulity itself place confidence in men who, but a few months since, advised their constituents to take *up arms against each other*—to introduce all the *horrors of civil war* in this country, and *draw the sword* against that *constitution which they now say they mean to put in motion.*

Now permit me to call your attention to the enemies of the constitution, collected in the minority in the late convention of this state:

Although, in fact, their conduct was not as openly expressive of their malicious designs against the constitution; but in proportion to their numbers, compared with those in *Pennsylvania,* they were equally as much so; yet, I say, the final issue of their deliberations were the same, and the amendments of each may be considered this issue.[5]—Every person who can read, may compare the amendments of each minority, and acknowledge their similitude.—In those points that are not materially necessary either way—and those also that are expressed by the one and not mentioned by the other, still of little or no consequence, they differ; but in the great leading points, that are necessary to the execution of their plan, the distruction of the federal constitution, *they exactly agree.*—Does not this shew a premeditated plan?—Does not this discover an inclination to destroy, *by particular amendments,* our federal governments?—This inclination being thus proved, as far as actions are declarative of intentions or wishes, it only remains to shew that these men have it in their power, if their numbers in state-legislatures are sufficient, to defeat the government in a *constitutional manner.*—This will appear evident from the following considerations.

The means by which amendments, agreeably to the constitution, are to be made to the federal government, are two—First, by Congress—Secondly, by the legislatures of the several states—Congress will be composed of a President, of a Senate, and of a House of Representatives—Congress is a body *yet to be formed*—The people appoint immediately the House of Representatives as one part; but the Senate and President, the other parts, are created by other powers.—The President will be appointed by electors, and these electors are to be chosen, out of the body of the people, in such manner as the legislatures of the several states shall order.—Here is great discretionary power.—So that in truth the President of Congress will be the mediate creature of the state-legislatures.—This constitutional truth being duly considered and established, let us suppose, for a moment, that which is much to be feared we will be obliged to admit, an antifederal representation present in the state-legislatures; under these circumstances, I beg leave to ask every friend and foe to the constitution, if it is not probable, if it is not reasonable, if it is not consistent with human nature to expect, that states so represented will choose antifederal electors, and those electors will make choice of an antifederal President.

The Senate is the next object. The same reasons urged above, with respect to the President, apply in the present case, and in a much more forcible manner; because the Senate is appointed by the state-legislatures immediately, and their voice will determine the complexion of the Senate for six years, when it will be in vain to counteract what they have done.

But, Sir, this is not all—These great chances are not the only ones that the enemies to the constitution have to defeat the government—they have another power, if you will permit their numbers to be sufficient, in the state-legislatures, to do what they please—and to have such amendments as they *choose*, without the intervention of Congress or any other power to control them.—All these powers appear evident to every candid and reasonable person, and all clearly expressed on the face of the constitution, as will appear from the following statement of part of the fifth article thereof, *viz.* "The Congress, whenever two-thirds of both houses shall deem it necessary, shall propose amendments to this constitution; *or on the application of the legislatures of two-thirds of the several states, shall call a convention for proposing amendments, which will in either case be valid to all intents and purposes as a part of this constitution, when ratified by the legislatures of three-fourths of the several states,* or by conventions in three-fourths thereof, as the one or the other mode of ratification may be proposed by Congress," &c.

The second means by which amendments are to be made to the constitution, that is by the legislature, I conceive will be the way by which the enemies to the constitution mean to make their first attack upon the government; this will be the unfortunate avenue through which these political serpents mean to insinuate their baneful poison into our public measures—and our next assemblies, I fear, will bear testimony to the sad catastrophe—It will, perhaps, be then in their power to bring forward those amendments which have been already offered to us, and rejected by the real friends to our country; and if their present plan succeeds; that of obtaining a sufficient number of antifederals in the state-assemblies, they will do the business at once.—They will not wait the issue of another election; and before the people will have another voice in the business, our beloved and once befriended federal government will be done away, or rendered useless by the *addition of particular amendments*—and amendments too proposed and incorporated in the government in the above constitutional manner.—This is the reason why we hear the constant cry of antefederalism in every corner—"*We want amendments, and we will pledge ourselves to the people that we will make them in a constitutional manner.*"

Sir, I flatter myself it is now plain to the most domestic capacity, the danger we are yet in, and the great probability of our federal government being defeated.—After all our trouble—after the united exertions of the collected wisdom and virtue of the tried friends of *America,* assembled in General Convention—after the Constitution has passed triumphant thro' the strictest constitutional investigation that freemen can give it, and at length has been adopted by our country by a great majority of states, more than was sufficient, as prescribed by the constitution, to give efficacy to it—I say, after all this labour, there is a great probability that this constitution will yet be defeated.

Sir, what would be the consequence of such a loss? At what point of distress would the affairs of this country pause? Let the complicated miseries of men, without government, act as a lesson in the one case; and the blood of thousands of our countrymen can only give an adequate idea of the other! . . .

Baltimore, September 24, 1788.

(*To be continued.*)

1. Reprinted: Baltimore *Maryland Gazette*, 10, 14 October.
2. In the material omitted here, "Federalism" defended specific charges he had made against Samuel Chase in his earlier 12 August essay in the *Maryland Journal* (DHFFE, II, 110–14n) and responded to other specific statements that Antifederalist writers had made.
3. Possibly based on this passage in "The Dissent of the Minority of the Pennsylvania Convention": "It remains with you whether you will think those inestimable privileges, which you have so ably contended for, should be sacrificed at the shrine of despotism, or whether you mean to contend for them with the same spirit that has so often baffled the attempts of an aristocratic faction, to rivet the shackles of slavery on you and your unborn posterity" (CC:353, p. 20).
4. For the Harrisburg Convention, see BoR, III, 176–82n.
5. For the amendments of the Pennsylvania Convention minority, see BoR, I, 241–43. For those of the Maryland Convention minority, see Appendix I (BoR, III, 472–76).

Federal Commonwealth
Massachusetts Centinel, 27 September 1788

Mr. RUSSELL, The necessity and importance of being on our guard against the secret and open attempts of the antifederalists and other time serving politicians, are daily more and more evidenced—the interval between the present time, and the organization of the new government, affords these restless sons of disunion, an opportunity to bring forward their *last* expedients to defeat the hopes of every decided friend to the UNION and a COMPETENT FEDERAL GOVERNMENT—The old knot of Pennsylvania—the rioters of anti memory—are again at their detestable machinations; and with a string of alterations, subversive of every trace of energy in the Constitution, are seeking to *divide, perplex* and *harrass* the people. Shall we never be at peace among ourselves? Shall the restless sons of anarchy forever disturb us?—Yes—forever, and forever, if the people suffer themselves to be deluded by such demagogues—Let their pretensions be what they will, the object of these "sticklers for alterations," is the subversion of the federal Constitution. Is there a man living whose mind is not involved in prejudice, that does not anticipate the destruction of the *essence* and *spirit* of the adopted Constitution, should a new Continental Convention be suddenly called under the auspices of these alteration-mongers?—But how do they mean to effect this fatal manœuvre? The answer is plain—by first persuading the people that their liberties are in danger—*secondly*, that they are the only true patriots; and *thirdly*, by getting themselves elected into the federal Legislature. It therefore behoves the good people of these States to hold fast their federal integrity. The new Constitution is their *dernier resort*; this is their only retreat from *disunion, anarchy* and *destruction.*

Happy is it for the citizens of this Commonwealth, their *federalism* is daily more and more apparent; and there can be no doubt of their being united at the ensuing FEDERAL ELECTIONS, in truly federal characters. If any alterations in the Constitution should be found necessary on experience, *antifederal* or *equivocal* characters must be the most unsuitable agents to employ in so important a business—None such can therefore expect the suffrages of the people of this
FEDERAL COMMONWEALTH.

Camillus
Baltimore Maryland Gazette, 30 September 1788 (excerpts)[1]

For the MARYLAND GAZETTE, &c.

A *New* writer, under the address of *Federalism,* has appeared in Mr. Goddard's Journal of Friday last.[2] The pedantic sophistry, and the vindictive malice and implacable resentment, that breathes against Mr. Chase in every sentence, discovers the cloven foot, as well as if the author had appeared in all his *fables.* . . .

. . . I shall offer a few remarks on the assertion of *new Fed.* that the national constitution is in danger from the antifederalists, who may destroy it under pretence of amending it. He says, amendments may be made to the federal government in *two* ways. First by congress. Second by the legislatures of the states. Neither of these positions is true. It is provided in the constitution that two-thirds of congress may *propose* amendments to the constitution to the legislatures of the states, or to a convention of the states, and such amendments, as shall be *ratified* by *three-fourths* of the *legislatures,* or *three-fourths* of such *convention,* are to become part of the constitution. This is *one* mode. It is also provided in the constitution that *two thirds* of the legislatures may *apply* to congress to call a convention to *propose* amendments to the legislatures, or a convention of the states; to be ratified in the same manner. This is the *second* mode. The *first* mode is more expeditious than the second, and does not require the interposition of the legislatures to obtain a convention to *propose* amendments, and this is the only difference between the two modes prescribed by the constitution. It is a *self-evident* truth, that the *legislatures* have nothing to say to amendments, they cannot propose any, or give any opinion on the subject. If they think the constitution defective, they can *only apply* to congress to call a convention to *propose* amendments to the legislatures, or a convention. In fact our legislature can never consider *any* amendments but *such only* as *congress*; or a *convention called by congress*, may propose to *them*. The fears of *new Fed.* "that *perhaps* (a salvo by which a writer can go as near telling a lie as possible without doing it) it will be in the power of the assemblies to bring forward amendments rejected," are without any foundation. He either writes to alarm the people with fears he does not feel, or he is very ignorant of the subject.—As *new Fed.* says he will continue his remarks,[3] I call on him to say, whether the assemblies, *agreeably to the constitution*, can have any thing to say to amendments. I pledge myself to maintain, *that they have nothing further to do with the subject than only to apply to congress to call a convention to propose amendments.*—I will give my name to the public, and risk a condemnation of my understanding, if I do not support the position I have advanced. Will *old* or *new Fed.* or any man who respects his character, give his name, and take the same risk? If I am right, it follows as a certain consequence, that no member of our legislature, however averse from, or inimical to the new constitution, can do it any *possible* injury by *way of amendment.* The CRY that the *anties* intend to destroy the government by amendments, is only set up to alarm and frighten weak minds. If in their inclination, it is not in their power. Only artful designing knaves assert that it is in their power, and only ignorant, shallow daws believe it.

Sept. 29, 1788.

1. "Tarantula," Baltimore *Maryland Gazette*, 26 September (BoR, III, 232), suggested that "Camillus" was Samuel Chase.
2. A reference to "Federalism," *Maryland Journal*, 26 September (BoR, III, 233–37).
3. The continuation appeared in the *Maryland Journal*, 4 October.

A Federalist
Baltimore Maryland Gazette, 30 September 1788

Mr. HAYES, The antifederalists in their conversations and writings, labour to have it believed, that since the adoption of the new constitution, the ground of distinction between *federalist* and *antifederalist* is done away; in other words, that those who were for *previous amendments*, and those who were for *subsequent amendments* are now of the *same opinion*. Taking this for granted, they confidently exclaim, that the cry of "anti, anti, anti," is a mere *electioneering trick*; and that (to use the words of Mr. C—— [Samuel Chase]) "*the intention of this low art and dirty cunning, is to inflame the passions of the populace and to catch them by words and sounds.*" A few instances will shew that the distinction still exists in its full force, and who it is would catch the populace by words and sounds.

1st. The *antifederals* are for the different assemblies *applying* to congress to call a convention to propose amendments.

The *federals* are opposed to this mode of obtaining amendments as improper, unnecessary and hazardous. *Improper*, because neither the state assemblies nor congress can confine the deliberations of the convention to certain enumerated amendments. A convention, whenever called, will have a general power to alter every part of the system, and, if they please, to propose the old articles of confederation. *Unnecessary*, because amendments can be obtained in an *easier* and *less expensive mode*. *Hazardous*, from our not knowing what amendments or changes in the constitution may be proposed; from its keeping the minds of the people in a state of agitation, and from its tendency to suspend such regulations as the new constitution authorizes.

2dly. The *antifederals* are against leaving it to congress to propose amendments.

The *federals* prefer this mode, because they expect that congress will propose those only which are necessary.

3dly. The *antifederals* wish to amend the constitution so as to prevent the establishment of *inferior federal courts* in each state.

The *federals* are anxious to preserve that part of the constitution, inasmuch as from *inferior federal courts,* they can only hope for a revival of credit, an extension of *inland trade,* and punctuality in all dealings between the citizens of the different states.

4thly. The *antifederals* are for depriving congress of the power to raise money by direct taxes, without *previous requisitions.*

The *federals* think this power cannot be so abridged without destroying the constitution. Requisitions would be laying a certain foundation for perpetual quarrels between the assemblies, and congress. *Requisitions* would put it in the power of the enemies to the constitution in the state assemblies, to frustrate the most salutary systems of congress, to destroy at any time the national credit, and to disappoint congress in the most perilous emergencies. *Requisitions* would greatly encrease the public expence. In place of one supply-bill framed by congress, we must then have thirteen supply-bills framed by thirteen different assemblies. *Requisitions* in case of partial compliances would fall particularly heavy upon the punctual citizen. Congress could make no distinction between the delinquents and those who had paid under the state law, in consequence of which the *innocent* or honest would be the constant sufferers.

5thly. The *antifederals* propose that congress shall raise no troops in time of peace, unless with the consent of two-thirds of the members present of each branch of congress.

The *federals* are against this amendment. It is in peace that nations provide for invasion or defence. This restriction therefore, gives our enemies an evident and decided advantage over us. A *majority* of the British parliament, for example, may in time of peace, raise an army to *invade us*; but a *majority* of congress may not raise an army to *defend us*. Are we afraid that this power may be turned against our liberties? I am sure we are better secured against its abuse than the people of England. One branch of their legislature is in for seven years, and the other for life and hereditary. One branch of our congress in only for two years, another for six and the president for four; besides one-third of the senate must be chosen every second year. It is a part of the British constitution that no troops can be raised or kept up in time of peace without the consent of parliament. It is a part of our constitution that no troops can be raised or kept up, whether in peace or war, *without the consent of congress*. It is a part of our constitution that no supplies can be granted for a longer period than two years, within which time it is contrived, by the constitution, that the people may change the *whole* of their representatives and *one-third* of the senate. The house of representatives may also impeach the president should he ever prolong a war to the injury of the people. Can reasonable men expect more effectual securities against the abuse of this power?

6thly. The *antifederals* are for amending the constitution so as to prevent the president from commanding the army, in person, without the consent of congress.

The *federals* are for leaving the president at liberty to command the army, in person, whenever in his opinion it may be proper. Congress in all probability will set but a few months in every year, so that before the president could convene them and obtain their consent to take the field, the country might lose some important advantage, or be overrun by an army.

7thly. The *antifederals* are for each state having passed to its credit the revenue collected on its imports.

The *federals* are against this amendment on two accounts: first, because the people who consume the duties goods finally pay the tax;

therefore the *non-importing states*, who consume these goods equally with the *importing states*, have a just right to participate of the revenue; secondly, the non-importing states would not come into the union should this be refused them.

8thly. The *antifederals* are for altering the constitution so as to make the performance of treaties dependant on the several assemblies.

The *federals* are for leaving this power as it is; it being in hands more competent to exercise it to the good of the whole.

These are a few of the amendments the antifederals will endeavour to obtain, either by getting their creatures into congress, or by a general convention, is this like federals and antifederals being *of the same opinion*? Are these amendments the antifederals still advocate a proof that the cry of anti, is a mere *electioneering trick*? Let the antifederals deny their amendments. Let them relinquish the idea of the assembly's applying for a convention to propose amendments. Let them trust to a federal congress to propose those to which no one objects. Let them not mount upon the *one* to obtain the *other*. Let them besides give their votes to federal candidates; and then, and not till then, shall we have some ground to believe that they also are federal. If they do not afford these proofs, we must consider them as ad[d]ing to the crime of antifederalism, the sin of deception.

Baltimore, Sept. 28, 1788.

Massachusetts Centinel, 1 October 1788

Mr. RUSSELL, It appears by the southern papers that the antifederal junto of Pennsylvania are at their old game gain—Notwithstanding they *profess* to be *federal* in their late publications, yet by carefully attending to names, we shall find they are the *same set* that opposed the adoption of the Constitution—"and can the Ethiopean change his skin, &c."[1]

There is a select number of similar geniuses in this Commonwealth, who never knew what would suit them. When we were destitute of a federal government, and all our continental concerns were at "*loose ends*," these persons would talk of the necessity of giving powers to Congress—but when the impost was proposed and voted by a majority of the States, oh then we were going to sacrifice our liberties forsooth—and by the utmost *wit* and *cunning* the measure was finally defeated. When the federal Constitution came upon the carpet, they exerted themselves to nip it in the bud—but THE PEOPLE said they *would* have it adopted—and adopted it was, for they would confide in lying prophets no longer. At present these *antifederal anarchiads*, are trying a new manœuvre and under the specious, delusive idea of *amendments* or *alterations*, to the federal system, they intend to embarrass the operation of the continental government. *Charity* itself, cannot think more favourably of a set of men, let them pretend what they will—who have done nothing but throw impediments in the way, and hang as dead weights upon the business of forwarding the   CONSTITUTION.

1. Jeremiah 13:23.

"A.B."
Maryland Journal, 3 October 1788 (excerpts)[1]

Mr. GODDARD, I take the liberty of your press to submit a few facts to my fellow-citizens, more particularly to those who wish to be thought federal, and yet intend to vote for Mr. C—— [Samuel Chase]. . . .

. . . The party in Pennsylvania which opposed the ratification of the constitution, still continue their exertions against it. They have agreed, through a convention of their creatures at Harrisburg, that the assembly ought to apply to Congress for a convention to propose amendments, and have also no doubt, at the same meeting, (it being essential to the attainment of their object) concerted measures to elect an assembly suited to their purposes. Mr. C—— still in sentiment with these implacable enemies to the constitution, delivered it as his opinion, at the court-house, that our assembly ought to apply for a convention to propose amendments; and by way of impressing this idea upon the minds of the people, he signified, in his first Camillus, that this was the *only* mode in which amendments could be obtained.[a]

These facts reduce it to a certainty that Mr. C—— retains all his original opinions, and that he only waits with Mr. Patrick Henry, of Virginia, for "a favourable opportunity to free him from the misfortune of a ratification."[b] . . .

The constitution prescribes two modes in which it may be altered. By the first, Congress whenever they think proper may propose amendments to the several states. By the second, a convention may be called to propose amendments. In either case the amendments must be referred to the legislatures or conventions, the one or the other as Congress may determine. The first mode is the gentlest and most rational for correcting any ambiguities in the constitution, or for adding such amendments as may free it from any popular objection that has been excited against it. The second mode, from its very nature, can only be intended to be used when the constitution shall be found, by experience, to be so defective as to require a thorough and radical reform. It seems moreover to be particularly meant to guard the *rights* of the state-assemblies, by vesting them with a power to defend themselves from the encroachments of Congress, by means of a convention, which they cannot be denied. The first mode therefore seems established to remedy partial evils, the last to remedy general defects.

Should a general convention be called, neither the legislatures, nor Congress, can limit their powers or define the amendments for their deliberation. But, besides the risk of creating a body of men who may new-model the constitution, years would be consumed in the experiment. A certain number of assemblies must first apply to Congress to call a convention. When this is done, Congress must appoint the time and place for the holding of this convention. The convention then agree upon amendments or a new form of government, which is to be taken up and rejected or ratified by the several state-legislatures or state conventions to be called for that purpose. This is the mode for obtaining amendments preferred by the Harrisburg convention, the antifederal convention of New-York, and Mr. C———. Does this look as if Mr. C——— was in a hurry to obtain amendments? What would be the unavoidable consequences of such an experiment? It would keep the minds of the people, during the time employed in making it, in a constant state of agitation and distraction, very contrary to the establishment of order and good government. It would deter Congress from carrying into effect many of the essential authorities of the constitution. It would keep foreigners of property from settling among us, for who that loves his property would entrust it to an unsettled government? It would afford occasion to men of turbulent characters to avail themselves of the advantages to be obtained in times of public confusion. Shall we dare to risque encountering these evils, when they may be all avoided by a preference of the first mode? . . .

Baltimore, October 1, 1788.

(a) *Mr. C——— corrected this mistake in his second Camillus, but not before he was bit by Tarantula.*[2]

(b) *Mr. Patrick Henry, in a speech in the Virginia convention, said, that "although he should hold himself bound as a peaceable citizen to acquiesce in an adoption, he should hold himself equally bound to seize the first favourable moment for being relieved from the misfortune—but in a constitutional way."*[3]

1. Reprinted: Philadelphia *Federal Gazette*, 11 October 1788.
2. For the essays by "Tarantula" (26 September) and "Camillus" (30 September), see BoR, III, 232–33, 238–39.
3. The printed volumes of the Virginia Convention debates had not yet appeared. This version of a portion of Patrick Henry's speech on 25 June is the same in substance, but quite different in wording, from the printed version of the speech (RCS:Va., 1537).

Philadelphia Federal Gazette, 4 October 1788[1]

A correspondent wishes to awake the friends of federal measures, to a sense of the duty which they owe alike to their country, to posterity, and themselves, in the choice of men to represent them in the federal body—let no lukewarm patriot, no disguised enemy to their glorious cause, be suffered to have a seat in that honorable house; but let them nobly copy the worthy example of our legislature, who have chosen for senators, two gentlemen of inviolable attachment to the great cause of liberty and the union. Should such men be chosen in the different states, the constitution will have a fair trial, our drooping commerce will revive, and our distressed mechanics be enabled to procure bread. Such men will not mutilate, maim, distort, nor deform that plan of government which has been the result of long experience, mature deliberation, tried integrity, and universally acknowledged abilities—by foisting into it, the absurd doctrines of [Luther] Martin, [George] Mason, and our other antifederal ringleaders. In fine, such men will never attempt to make *alterations* in the system, until they appear to be *amendments*.

1. Reprinted: *New York Packet,* 10 October; New York *Hudson Weekly Gazette,* 21 October.

Thomas Mifflin to Jeremiah Wadsworth
Schuylkill Fall, Pa., 5 October 1788 (excerpt)[1]

... The Minority who are termed *Anti* are exerting themselves to obtain a Representation for the New York Amendments.

On Saturday A Motion was introduced to recommend the Letter from Governor Clinton with the Amendments of the New York Convention to the succeeding General Assembly—but it was negatived by a great Majority[2]—Our late House was strongly fœderal & There is great Probability that the next will be equally so....

1. RC, Jeremiah Wadsworth Papers, Connecticut Historical Society.
2. In early October the Federalist-dominated Assembly, by a vote of 38 to 24, defeated an Antifederalist motion to recommend the New York Convention's circular letter (BoR, I, 153-58) to the next Assembly.

Edmund Pendleton to James Madison
Edmundsbury, Caroline County, Va., 6 October 1788 (excerpt)[1]

... I have not been without my fears that Opposition would use the Subject of Amendments, & a New General Convention for the purpose of keeping the New Government from Operation, tho' I have heard little on the Subject—some warm friends to it in this County, suspecting that Procrastinating measures might be pushed in Our Assembly, a Majority of whom are Supposed to be unfriendly, are preparing Instructions to their Delegates, To us[e] no *delay* or *impropriety* in appointing the time & mode of Electing the Delegates—In their votes for Senators or Electors of the President to chuse such only as are known friends to the Governmt.—and not to hasten a Meeting of a Convention to consider of the Amendments, but leave the Government to have previous Operation, that experience may either Sanctify or repel the Alterations proposed, and perhaps discover others not hitherto brought forth....

1. RC, GLC 00099.134, The Gilder-Lehrman Collection, The Gilder-Lehrman Institute of American History, at the New-York Historical Society. For the entire letter, see Rutland, *Madison*, XVII, 529–30.

A Freeman
Philadelphia Federal Gazette, 6 October 1788

To the CITIZENS of PENNSYLVANIA.

Friends and Fellow-Freemen, The time is fast approaching, when you will have an opportunity of exercising that most invaluable privilege of free-citizens—the right of election. A prudent but manly exertion of this important trust, was never more necessary than now.—That independence for which many of you have sustained the rigours of the summer-sun and the nipping frosts of winter, exposed to nakedness and famine, through eight successive years—and for which the frozen regions of the North, and the burning sands of the South, have been deluged with the best blood of our citizens, and strewed with their mangled bodies—that independence, my countrymen, is yet incomplete: one generous effort remains to crown all your past success with glory. The wisdom of America has formed and adopted a constitution which seems well calculated to secure the freedom and establish the national importance of the United States. But in vain have you struggled for liberty, in vain have you formed a constitution, to preserve that liberty, and adopted it in *name*, unless you also adopt it in *practice.*

To effect this, however, is no arduous task, it is only necessary that you should be vigilant and active in your choice of eight federal representatives, whose known abilities, integrity and firm attachment to the constitution should be their chief recommendation; and without which no man should be entitled to your suffrages. Unhappy, indeed, were our case if men of a different stamp should be suffered to creep into the general government, to clog its wheels and retard its motions, by endeavouring to foist in a train of *amendments*, as they are pleased to call their absurd, ill-digested, and contradictory *alterations*, which could not fail to overthrow this hitherto unequalled fabric, and render all your labours abortive.

The liberties of your country can never be endangered but by two things. The first is, an injudicious exercise of this your darling privilege; the second, your total negligence concerning it.

With respect to the first, an injudicious choice changes this blessing into the worst of curses; and, instead of liberty, order, and good government, do not fail to introduce slavery, anarchy and intestine commotions. Be watchful therefore, be stedfast, and let no consideration under Heaven warp your integrity, when the safety and happiness of your country, when your life, liberty, and property, when every thing that is dear to freemen, is at stake. It has been objected by Luther Martin, that the people at large should not be the electors of federal representatives, but that they ought to be chosen by the state legislatures: the worthy framers of our new constitution thought otherwise, and were not afraid to commit this important trust to your charge, relying on your wisdom and firmness for a faithful discharge of it. Consider then, that by every abuse of this privilege you shew yourselves unworthy of the trust reposed in you by your constitution; that by placing unworthy men at the head of affairs, you violate the social compact between you and your fellow-citizens, and exercise this right not only to your own but to their destruction.

Our government flowing, from the people must necessarily be pure while its source remains uncontaminated. But it must also be muddy and impure whenever the fountain becomes corrupted. Let me therefore once more call upon you to guard well your integrity, and act like men of an independent spirit, who will spurn from you with indignation, the wretch who shall dare to insult your understanding, direct your judgment, or bias your choice. Let no electioneering jobber be suffered, with impunity, to lie in wait for the unwary on the day of election with a ticket which he shall have the daring insolence to offer them, without having previously consulted them on the subject. Such treatment is beneath the dignity of freemen; it is only fit to be exercised over stalls of asses. You should therefore consider well whether you are to give up your freedom of election to a wretch, who is not a freeman, but the miserable tool, the drudge of a party. If you wish to preserve this sacred right, you will treat with becoming contempt every endeavour to rob you of it; and will faithfully exercise it to your own, your fellow-citizens, and your country's advantage, by electing men of wisdom, and patriotic firmness, to represent you in the general government; bearing in mind, that even a constitution framed by the creator of the universe himself, would be inadequate to the preservation of your freedom, if it were not well administered: now if you be improperly governed, the fault must be your own, in choosing improper representatives. May you consider this point with the importance it deserves, and be active in choosing men of worth and integrity.

(*To be continued.*)[1]

1. For the 8 October continuation, see DHFFE, I, 309-11.

Anti
Philadelphia Federal Gazette, 7 October 1788

Mr. BROWN, It is really surprising, that the citizens of the United States should be so blind to their real interests, as to discountenance the amendments some have proposed to the new constitution, especially when we consider that our all is now at stake. I profess to be one of those who are convinced, that perfection is not a human attribute, and consequently that it is impossible for any set of men to produce a system free from error; but as I have never yet seen the true reasons why we anti-federalists object to the unconditional (or indeed any) adoption of the code of legislation so blindly consented to by the greater part of this continent, and as you profess impartiality in the conduct of your paper, I trust you will not refuse the following a place in it.

It is a well known fact, that our party is composed principally of men, who at the commencement of the revolution were advocates for monarchy, in defence of which many of us suffered for our improper sentiments, in so severe a manner, that we soon became sincere proselytes to republicanism, altho' we never appeared in the field or cabinet till after the danger was over, when (from a conviction that by appointments to the latter we might make a fortune) we became active, and had soon our utmost wishes gratified, and were raised to an affluence unknown to us before. Now, sir, can you blame us for dissenting to a legislation in which the president possesses so much of the regal power? Or can any suppose us wrong in adhering to principles you first taught us? Tis true indeed you may again have the merit of converting us to your opinions, if you will only assure us that we shall enjoy the most lucrative offices under the new government, for none can doubt the truth of the old adage, that charity begins at home; and as some of us now are fattening in the most profitable posts in this state, would it not be madness in us to afford our influence to measures which we are convinced would render our abilities less necessary, and perhaps sink us into our original obscurity? We assert, that "a federal government will annihilate that of each state." Tho' we do not believe this will really be the case, yet as we are convinced that such an assertion may have some weight among the weaker part of the citizens, and as we heretofore have stuck at nothing to gain our ends, we boldly declare it a fact, knowing that an energetic continental legislation, will afford us fewer opportunities of intriguing for the advancement of our own interests, or make such intrigues more readily detected. "The liberty of the press is not provided for, nor is their any bill of rights." This is a popular topic, and on this we have therefore liberally discanted. The liberty of the press, Mr. Printer, all parties allow, should be preserved inviolate; but they do not agree as to what is really the liberty of the press. Our opinion is (and our constant practice must, ere this, have convinced you, that it is well founded) that it consists in the unrestrained licence of abusing *men* who think differently from us; especially if the popular tide is in their favor, and measures which thwart our darling scheme of exclusively possessing every post to which either honor or profit is annexed. Those of drudgery we have never been anxious about, nor while the least spark of wisdom remains among us, shall we ever solicit.

The bill of rights we care little about; but as one is appended to each of our state constitutions, and custom has made the people at large look upon it as a necessary security of their privileges, we have adduced it, only as a collateral proof of the imperfection and tyranny of the new constitution. "A standing army," is another of our objections, and we think the strongest; for as it is well known, that numbers of us have never paid taxes in this state (though we have been enriching ourselves with those paid by others) we are apprehensive that our delinquency will not in future be overlooked, but that we shall be compelled to contribute to the support of that government we are protected by, and under which we have throve. That these are the true motives which actuate us in our opposition, experience fully evinces; 'tis this which formerly directed us to use every possible argument to prevent the repeal of the test laws of this state,[1] and these you and every thinking man must allow to be arguments irrefutable upon every principle whatever, unless that of the common good, which you know we never attend to, except when our interest happens to be joined with that of the people; then indeed we make a great stir, and magnify our conduct as the height of patriotism.

If these objections are admitted in your paper, I may perhaps hereafter pursue the subject, to, I hope, the conviction of every federalist in the union.

1. See note 4, "A Federal Centinel," *Pennsylvania Gazette*, 10 September, for the test laws (BoR, III, 206n).

Centinel XIX
Philadelphia Independent Gazetteer, 7 October 1788[1]

To the People of Pennsylvania.

Friends, Countrymen and Fellow Citizens!

When I last addressed you on the subject of the new constitution, I had not a doubt of its rejection: the baneful nature and tendency of this system of ambition had been so fully exposed, that its most zealous advocates were constrained to acknowledge many imperfections and dangers, and *seemingly* to acquiesce in the necessity of amendments.— However by the time this general conviction had taken place in the minds of the people, so many states had adopted the constitution, and the public anxiety was so great to have an efficient government, that the votaries of power and ambition, were enabled, by adapting their language and conduct to the temper of the times, to prevail upon a competent number of the states to establish the constitution, without previous alteration, upon the implied condition of subsequent amendments, which they assured would certainly be made, as every body were agreed in their propriety.

My knowledge of the principles and conduct of these men, for many years past, left me no room to doubt of their insincerity[2] on this occasion—I was persuaded that all their professions of moderation, and assurances of future amendments, were founded in deception, that they were but the blind of the moment, the covered way to dominion and empire—Like a barrel thrown to the whale,[3] the people were to be amused with fancied amendments, until the harpoon of power, should secure its prey and render resistance ineffectual. Already the masque of ambition begins to be removed, and its latent features to appear in their genuine hue, disdaining any further veil from policy; the *well-born*, inebriated with success, and dispising the people for their easy credulity, think it unnecessary to dissemble any longer—almost every newspaper ridicules the idea of amendments, and triumphs over the deluded people. Ye patriots of America, arouse from the dangerous infatuation in which ye are lulled, and, while it is yet time, strain every nerve to rescue your country from the servile yoke of bondage and to preserve that liberty which has been so recently vindicated, at the expence of so much blood and treasure. Upon the improvement of the present moment, depends the fate of your country; you have now a constitutional opportunity afforded you, to obtain a safe and a good government, by making choice of such persons to represent you in the new Congress; as have congenial sentiments with yourselves. Suffer not, ye freemen of America, the *well-born*, or their *servile minions*, to usurp the sacred trust, to impose themselves upon you as your guardians; for whatever professions they may make, or assurances they may give you, depend upon it they will deceive you, like the wolf in sheeps clothing they will make you their prey. Treat with contempt the slanderous arts of the well-born to prejudice you against your true friends, and convince them on this great occasion, by your good sense, union and vigour, that you are not to be duped out of your liberties by all the refinements of *machiavelian* policy. The future government of these United States will take its tone from the complexion of the first Congress;—upon this will greatly depend, whether despotic sway, or the salutary influence of a well regulated government, shall hereafter rule this once happy land. As the Legislature of this state have appointed the last Wednesday in November next for the election of the 8 representatives from this state in the new Congress—you ought to be prepared for that *all-important* day; and as success is only to be ensured by unanimity among the friends of equal liberty, local and personal predilections and dislikes should give place to the general sentiment; whatever ticket may be agreed to by the majority of the opposition to the new constitution in its present shape, ought to be supported by all those who are sincere in wishing for amendments.—I trust that all prejudices and antipathies arising from the late war, or from difference of religion, will be sacrificed to the great object of the public welfare, and that all good and well meaning men of whatever description will harmonize on this occasion. For among the various practices & stratagems of the well born, the principal one, and upon which they will the most rely for success, will be the endeavor to divide you, and thus by scattering your suffrages between various candidates to frustrate your object.

From the mode of appointment, the Senate of the general government will be chiefly composed of the *well born*, or their minions, and when we consider the great and various powers which they will possess, and their permanency, it ought to opperate as an additional stimulus with you to obtain faithful representatives in the other branch of legislature, to shield your privileges and property from the machinations of ambition, and the rapacity of power. The Senate, besides their proper share in the Legislature, have great executive and judicial powers—their concurrence is made necessary to all the principal appointments in government—What a fruitful source of corruption does not this present! in the capacity of Legislators they will have the irresistible temptation to institute lucrative and needless offices, as they will in fact, have the appointment of the *officers.*

When I consider the nature of power and ambition; when I view the numerous swarm of hungry office-hunters, and their splendid expectations, anticipation exhibits such a scene of rapacity and oppression, such burthensome establishments to pamper the pride and luxury of a useless herd of officers, such dissipation and profusion of the public treasure, such consequent impoverishment and misery of the people, that I tremble for my country.

Such evils are only to be averted by a vigorous exertion of the freemen of America, to procure a virtuous, disinterested, & patriotic House of Representatives. That you may all view the importance of this election in its true light, and improve the only means which the constitution affords you for your preservation, is the fervent wish of

CENTINEL

Philadelphia, October 3d, 1788.

1. Reprinted: Philadelphia *Freeman's Journal*, 8 October; *New York Journal*, 16 October; New York *Hudson Weekly Gazette*, 21 October. See "Centinel" I, Philadelphia *Independent Gazetteer*, 5 October 1787 (BoR, II, 21n–23n) for the authorship, circulation and response to the "Centinel" essays.

2. "Centinel" obviously meant the word to be "sincerity." The *Hudson Weekly Gazette* reprinting made the correction.

3. "A barrel thrown to a whale" is meant metaphorically to be a diversion. See Jonathan Swift, *A Tale of a Tub* (London, 1704).

Thomas Tudor Tucker to St. George Tucker
New York, 9 October 1788 (excerpt)[1]

... [P.S.] How go on your Elections for the new Constitution? Have you any Expectation of Amendments? And after all, will it be an eligible Mode of Government. I confess that I dislike the Form, even with every Limitation of Power that can be contrived. I see more & more that the Election of Representatives will be attended with a great deal of Intrigue, that it will be a Representation of an Aristocratical Party, will lay a Foundation for consolidating the Governments, & will hold out the Name & Shadow of Freedom in place of the reality....

1. RC, Tucker-Coleman Collection, College of William and Mary.

Thomas Johnson to George Washington
Frederick, Md., 10 October 1788 (excerpt)[1]

On 20 April 1788 George Washington wrote former Maryland Governor Thomas Johnson informing him that if the Maryland Convention deferred to the Virginia Convention and adjourned without ratifying the Constitution it would "be tantamount to the rejection of the Constitution" (RCS:Md., 523). Washington received information that Johnson was so upset with Washington's interference in Maryland politics that Johnson was induced "to take an active part in bringing about the amendments proposed by a Committee of the Convention of Maryland." Washington apologized in a letter to Johnson on 31 August (RCS:Md., 764–65). Johnson replied on 10 October telling Washington that the letter "obliged" him and did not stimulate him to seek amendments to the Constitution in the Maryland Convention. Johnson, however, told Washington that he was dissatisfied with the manner in which the Maryland Convention refused to recommend amendments, suggesting that he favored some of the amendments considered by the Convention's committee. (For the amendments proposed by the committee of the Maryland Convention, see Appendix I, BoR, III, 472–76.)

I lately received your Letter of the 31st of August; scarce any Thing could have surprised me more than the Occasion of it for instead of being displeased I thought myself much obliged by the Letter you wrote me in the Time of our Convention—To strengthen the Friends of the new Constitution and expedite it's Adoption I shewed that and other Letters containing much the same Information and Sentiments to some Gent. and mentioned them to others a strange Conduct had I been under the Impressions suggested! nor do I recollect any Conduct of mine which can be called active to bring about any Amendments—I was not well pleased at the manner of our breaking up I thought it to our discredit and should be better pleased with the Constitution with some Alterations but I am very far from wishing all that were proposed to take place. . . .

1. RC, Washington Papers, DLC. For the entire letter, see RCS:Md., 765.

Edward Carrington to James Monroe
Baltimore, Md., 12 October 1788 (excerpts)[1]

Being this far on my way to Richmond and intending to make several calls on the way, I take the advantage of a leisure moment to acknowledge the Rec't of yours of the 24th Ulto. . . .

We are to meet in the Legislature, where the new constitution is to furnish much business, of which, efforts towards alterations will form no small part: The circular letter of N. York I am told is received with avidity amongst you. I am, however, inclined to think, that a concurrence with it, will not lead to any thing effectual, as to the views of those who are for an early revision, for I suspect there will not be a sufficient number of Concurring States to bring about a Convention:—will it not be better to decline it then, altogether, and strongly recommend the desired alterations to the notice of the first Congress? My sentiments as to an early revision you already know, but at the same time I will not obstinately set myself against a respectable majority. I shall be with you in the course of the week, or perhaps not until the 20th the day for the meeting of the Assembly. . . .

1. RC, Monroe Papers, DLC. For the entire letter, see Daniel Preston, ed., *The Papers of James Monroe* (7 vols. to date, Westport, Conn., and Santa Barbara, Calif., 2003–), II, 455–56.

Pennsylvania Mercury, 14 October 1788 (excerpt)[1]

We are informed that on Friday, at a very large and respectable meeting of the free electors of the county of Philadelphia, held at Germantown, that *George Gray* and *Enoch Edwards*, Esqrs. were unanimously appointed to attend the Federal Conference to be held at Lancaster for the purpose of recommending suitable persons to represent this state in Congress, and also electors to chuse the President of the United States.

It must give pleasure to all honest federal minds to observe, that this business was done openly, at a very public meeting of the county, publicly advertised, and that men of respectable, established, unequivocal federal characters, were appointed to so important a trust. This appointment wears a very different complexion to what the smuggling business which took place in the sending members to Harrisburg did, with the ostensible pretensions of procuring amendments, but in fact to form a ticket for representatives in Congress.[2] A very curious story indeed, that eight antifederal men should represent one of the greatest federal states in the Union! . . .

1. Reprinted: Philadelphia *Federal Gazette*, 15 October; *Pennsylvania Gazette*, 15 October; Baltimore *Maryland Gazette*, 21 October; Pennsylvania *Carlisle Gazette*, 22 October; *Neue Unpartheyische Lancaster Zeitung*, 22 October; *Pittsburgh Gazette*, 25 October.

2. A reference to an Antifederalist meeting in Germantown on 14 August (see BoR, III, 167–69n).

John Jay to Edward Rutledge
New York, 15 October 1788 (excerpts)[1]

I thank you for your friendly letter. . . .

You have seen from the public papers that the new Constitution was with difficulty adopted in this State. The opposition which was violent has daily become more moderate, and the minds of the people will gradually be reconciled to it in proportion as they see the government administered in the manner you mention.[2] The measure of a new convention to consider and decide on the proposed amendments will, I think, be expedient to terminate all questions on the subject. If immediately carried, its friends will be satisfied, and if convened three years hence, little danger, perhaps some good, will attend it. . . . Your sincere and affectionate friend,

COMMENTARIES, 16 OCTOBER 1788

1. Printed: Henry P. Johnston, ed. *The Correspondence and Public Papers of John Jay* . . . (4 vols., New York and London, 1890–1893), III, 362.
2. In his "friendly letter" of 20 June, Rutledge, who had informed Jay that South Carolina had ratified the Constitution, stated that "People become more and more satisfied with the adoption, and if well administered, and administered with moderation they will cherish and bless those who have offered them a Constitution which will secure to them all the Advantages that flow from good government" (*ibid.*, III, 339).

Richard Henry Lee to Theodorick Bland
Chantilly, Westmoreland County, Va., 15 October 1788[1]

Long acquaintance and friendship, with very similar political opinions, will apologize for my troubling you with my wishes that amendments may be procured to the new constitution, by means of the new Congress; and that I am willing to exert my faculties for the obtaining such amendments in the senate of the new legislature, if it shall please the Assembly to send me there; and this information to my friends is the more necessary, because I know it is a common art, in these times, to prevent elections by asserting that persons proposed will not serve, if elected. That amendments are necessary to this system, cannot, I think, be doubted by any sensible and dispassionate man. The thing itself, the judgment of many respectable states, and great numbers of individuals, all proclaim it. Nor will amendments, probably, fail to be made, unless the legislatures should choose men so zealously and blindly devoted as to prevent them from seeing defects that all other men do see. As the subject has been very fully considered, and a majority have received it, professedly under the idea of expected amendments, I should think that, as good citizens, it now becomes us to exert our faculties so to conduct the business as that a wise, energetic, and free government, may result from properly amending the present form. Should this fortunately be your opinion, the community will have the aid of your knowledge and experience in the new legislature.

1. Richard H. Lee, *Memoir of the Life of Richard Henry Lee and His Correspondence* . . . (2 vols., Philadelphia, 1825), II, 95. "Chantilly" was Lee's plantation. On 15 October, Lee also wrote to John Jones (Lee, *Memoir*, II, 94) and William Cabell (Andrew de Coppet Collection, Princeton University Library), repeating essentially what he told Bland. Bland (Prince George) and Cabell (Amherst) were in the House of Delegates; Jones (Brunswick) was in the state Senate. All three had voted against ratification of the Constitution in the state Convention.

Alfred II
Massachusetts Spy, 16 October 1788 (excerpt)[1]

. . . Finding ourselves thus one nation, united by one government, having only one sovereignty, the question will be, whether the constitution needs amendments in order to secure the rights, and liberties of the people?

It is frequently said, that the people cannot be enslaved, or deprived of their liberties—and that therefore it is not material what constitution they have, but the same reasoning would prove, that none at all is necessary, if it proves any thing. He is now called by some, an enemy to his country, who would attempt amendments, and we are told that the propositions for that purpose in the convention, were only conciliatory, and the constitution being adopted, there can be no need of them. And did a [Governor John] Hancock introduce the propositions, did [Samuel] Adams support them, did the leaders in convention advocate, and agree to them, in order to obtain a vote—in order to beguile the majority into what they would not have done, unless they had been thus deceived?

America has not yet made such strides in political vice and deception, as to be contented with such chicanery and cunning, and the people can have no reason to conclude, from the base insinuations of a few individuals, that after his Excellency our Governour, and many other patriots, have sacredly pledged themselves to attempt amendments, that they will now basely desert the people, and avow an unexampled piece of chicanery, that would disgrace the character of a Nero, or a Caligula. Indeed the man who has consented to the adoption of the constitution, upon the propositions introduced in the several conventions, and will now oppose a revision of those propositions in Congress, or vote for a member who would oppose an investigator into the necessity of them, ought to be branded with the odious epithet of a betrayer of his country's freedom—and never can be trusted by the people.

I shall trouble the publick with one paper more, in which I shall consider the necessity of particular amendments.[2]

1. Reprinted: Boston *Herald of Freedom*, 20 October (partial); *Massachusetts Gazette*, 21 October; Boston *Independent Chronicle*, 23 October; Northampton, Mass., *Hampshire Gazette*, 30 October; Providence, R.I., *United States Chronicle*, 30 October and 20 November; Philadelphia *Independent Gazetteer*, 19 November; Portland, Maine, *Cumberland Gazette*, 20 November. The reprinting in the Providence, R.I., *United States Chronicle*, 30 November indicated that "Alfred" was written by Caleb Strong, a candidate for the Massachusetts Senate. For a response to "Alfred," see "A Federalist," *Massachusetts Centinel*, 22 October (BoR, III, 273–74).

2. See *Massachusetts Spy*, 23 October (BoR, III, 277–80).

James Madison to Thomas Jefferson
New York, 17 October 1788 (excerpt)[1]

... The little pamphlet herewith inclosed will give you a collective view of the alterations which have been proposed for the new Constitution.² Various and numerous as they appear they certainly omit many of the *true* grounds of opposition. The articles relating to Treaties—to paper money, and to contracts, created more enemies than all the errors in the System positive & negative put together. It is true nevertheless that not a few particularly in Virginia have contended for the proposed alterations from the most honorable & patriotic motives: and that among the advocates for the Constitution, there are some who wish for further guards to public liberty & individual rights. As far as these may consist of a constitutional declaration of the most essential rights, it is probable they will be added; though there are many who think such additional unnecessary, and not a few who think it misplaced in such a Constitution. There is scarce any point on which the party in opposition is so much divided as to its importance and its propriety. My own opinion has always been in favor of a bill of rights; provided it be so framed as not to imply powers not meant to be included in the enumeration. At the same time I have never thought the omission a material defect, nor been anxious to supply it even by *subsequent* amendment, for any other reason than that it is anxiously desired by others. I have favored it because I supposed it might be of use, and if properly executed could not be of disservice. I have not viewed it in an important light 1. because I conceive that in a certain degree, though not in the extent argued by Mr. Wilson, the rights in question are reserved by the manner in which the federal powers are granted.³ 2. because there is great reason to fear that a positive declaration of some of the most essential rights could not be obtained in the requisite latitude. I am sure that the rights of Conscience in particular, if submitted to public definition would be narrowed much more than they are likely ever to be by an assumed power. One of the objections in New England was that the Constitution by prohibiting religious tests opened a door for Jews Turks & infidels.⁴ 3. because the limited powers of the federal Government and the jealousy of the subordinate Governments, afford a security which has not existed in the case of the State Governments, and exists in no other. 4. because experience proves the inefficiency of a bill of rights on those occasions when its controul is most needed. Repeated violations of these parchment barriers have been committed by overbearing majorities in every State. In Virginia I have seen the bill of rights violated in every instance where it has been opposed to a popular current. Notwithstanding the explicit provision contained in that instrument for the rights of Conscience⁵ it is well known that a religious establishment wd. have taken place in that State, if the legislative majority had found as they expected, a majority of the people in favor of the measure; and I am persuaded that if a majority of the people were now of one sect, the measure would still take place and on narrower ground than was then proposed, notwithstanding the additional obstacle which the law has since created.[6] Wherever the real power in a Government lies, there is the danger of oppression. In our Governments the real power lies in the majority of the Community, and the invasion of private rights is *cheifly* to be apprehended, not from acts of Government contrary to the sense of its constituents, but from acts in which the Government is the mere instrument of the major number of the constituents. This is a truth of great importance, but not yet sufficiently attended to: and is probably more strongly impressed on my mind by facts, and reflections suggested by them, than on yours which has contemplated abuses of power issuing from a very different quarter. Wherever there is an interest and power to do wrong, wrong will generally be done, and not less readily by a powerful & interested party than by a powerful and interested prince. The difference so far as it relates to the superiority of republics over monarchies, lies in the less degree of probability that interest may prompt abuses of power in the former than in the latter; and in the security in the former agst. oppression of more than the smaller part of the society, whereas in the former[7] it may be extended in a manner to the whole. The difference so far as it relates to the point in question—the efficacy of a bill of rights in controuling abuses of power—lies in this, that in a monarchy the latent force of the nation is superior to that of the sovereign, and a solemn charter of popular rights must have a great effect, as a standard for trying the validity of public acts, and a signal for rousing & uniting the superior force of the community; whereas in a popular Government, the political and physical power may be considered as vested in the same hands, that is in a majority of the people, and consequently the tyrannical will of the sovereign is not [to] be controuled by the dread of an appeal to any other force within the community. What use then it may be asked can a bill of rights serve in popular Governments? I answer the two following which thought less essential than in other Governments, sufficiently recommend the precaution. 1. The political truths declared in that solemn manner acquire by degrees the character of fundamental maxims of free Government, and as they become incorporated with the national sentiment, counteract the impulses of interest and passion. 2. Altho' it be generally true as above stated that the danger of oppression lies in the interested majorities of the people rather than in usurped acts of the Government, yet there may be occasions on which the evil may spring from the latter sources; and on such, a bill of rights will be a good ground for an appeal to the sense of the community. Perhaps too there may be a certain degree of danger, that a succession of artful and ambitious rulers, may by gradual & well-timed advances, finally erect an independent Government on the subversion of liberty. Should this danger exist at all, it is prudent to guard agst it, especially when the precaution can do no injury. At the same time I must own that I see no tendency in our governments to danger on that side. It has been remarked that there is a tendency in *all* Governments to an augmentation of power at the expence of liberty. But the remark as usually understood does not appear to me well founded. Power when it has attained a certain degree of energy and independence goes on generally to further degrees. But when below that degree, the direct tendency is to further degrees of relaxation, until the abuses of liberty beget a sudden transition to an undue degree of power. With this explanation the remark may be true; and in the latter sense only is it in my opinion applicable to the existing Governments in America. It is a melancholy reflection that liberty should be equally exposed to danger whether the Government have too much or too little power, and that the line which divides their extremes should be so inaccurately defined by experience.

Supposing a bill of rights to be proper the articles which ought to compose it, admit of much discussion. I am inclined to think that *absolute* restrictions in cases that are doubtful, or where emergencies may overrule them, ought to be avoided. The restrictions however strongly marked on paper will never be regarded when opposed to the decided sense of the public; and after repeated violations in extraordinary cases, they will lose even their ordinary efficacy. Should a Rebellion or insurrection alarm the people as well as the Government, and a suspension of the Hab. Corp. be dictated by the alarm, no written prohibitions on earth would prevent the measure. Should an army in time of peace be gradually established in our neighbourhood by Britn: or Spain, declarations on paper would have as little effect in preventing a standing force for the public safety. The best security agst. these evils is to remove the pretext for them. With regard to monopolies they are justly classed among the greatest nusances in Government. But is it clear that as encouragements to literary works and ingenious discoveries, they are not too valuable to be wholly renounced? Would it not suffice to reserve in all cases a right to the Public to abolish the privilege at a price to be specified in the grant of it? Is there not also infinitely less danger of this abuse in our Governments than in most others? Monopolies are sacrifices of the many to the few. Where the power is in the few it is natural for them to sacrifice the many to their own partialities and corruptions. Where the power, as with us, is in the many not in the few, the danger can not be very great that the few will be thus favored.

It is much more to be dreaded that the few will be unnecessarily sacrificed to the many. . . .

1. RC, Madison Papers, DLC. For the entire letter, see Rutland, *Madison*, XI, 295–300.
2. For the pamphlet collection printed by Augustine Davis sometime after 2 August, see BoR, III, 129.
3. For Wilson's assertion that reserved power remained with the states, see his 6 October 1787 speech in the Pennsylvania state house yard (BoR, II, 25–28).
4. See Amos Singletary's 19 January speech in the Massachusetts Convention (RCS: Mass., 1254–55).
5. A reference to Article 3 of the Virginia Declaration of Rights (BoR, I, 106–7).
6. A reference to Virginia's 1786 Act for Religious Freedom (BoR, I, 136–38).
7. Madison should have written "latter."

Philadelphia Federal Gazette, 18 October 1788[1]

A correspondent has favoured us with the following remarks, upon the subject of the election of the eight federal representatives for this state:—We are to take care, says he, of errors in the outset, and therefore, *avoiding all local ideas*, we are to consider the present business to be an election of representatives for the state, and not for a county, a city, or a borough. Whether the man lives in this county, that borough, or the city, should be no consideration. 'Tis our duty only to consider *the man*, his qualifications and connexions, and not *the place* in which he lives. The first point we are to see to is, that he is a sincere federalist, that he has never opposed the adoption of the constitution upon the plea that amendments should first be made; for such a man has predetermined the question concerning amendments by declaring them indispensible, whereas the propriety or necessity of making amendments is yet to be coolly, fairly and fully considered. Secondly, he should have an evident stake in the hedge; that is, the property he possesses should be in *Pennsylvania*. Riches are by no means necessary; but should any man's name be offered, who has very little property in this state, and a great deal in any other country or state, it will be proper to remember he wants *a common interest* with his fellow citizens. Thirdly, he should really understand the new constitution; for otherwise we may be tricked into insidious and ruinous alterations, or unnecessary and injurious abridgments of the wholesome powers of the federal government, and *this*, says our correspondent, is a matter of the utmost importance; for if we lose the energy of this constitution, we shall be a ruined people. Besides these general requisites, the more he is interested in landed property, the more he is acquainted with the general affairs and interest of Pennsylvania, with foreign commerce, manufactures, and the general principles of civil polity, the better will he be able to perform the various duties which will fall upon a federal representative. Wherever we can find the men who will best answer this description, *there* should our choice be fixed, if we really wish a confirmation and establishment to the constitution. The present moment is *full* as serious as any we have experienced; for in vain have we adopted the government, if we do not bring forward those eight men who are most truly competent to carry it into execution, and to guard and defend it against those *constitutional* attacks, those attacks *under its own forms*, with which it has been openly menaced.

1. Reprinted: Boston *Herald of Freedom,* 30 October.

**Edward Carrington to James Madison
Fredericksburg, Va., 19 October 1788**[1]

Having travelled leisurely I arrived here last evning and shall proceed tomorrow morning for Richmond.

I left Mount Vernon on friday: during my stay there I had much conversation with the General upon the probable policies of the assembly with respect to the Constitution—He is fully persuaded that antifederalism will be the actuating principle, and that great circumspection is necessary to prevent very mischievous effects from a co-operation in the insidious proposition of N. York.[2] He is particularly alarmed for the prospect of an election for the Senate entirely antifederal. it is said in this part of the State, that Mr. Henry & Mr. R. H. Lee are to be pushed. I beleive it is founded only in conjecture but the Genl. is apprehensive it may prove true; that to exclude the former will be impossible; and that the latter, being supported by his influence, will also get in, unless a Federalist very well established in the confidence of the people can be opposed. He is decided in his wishes that you may be brought forward upon this occasion. I told him "that your views were to offer your services to the public in the Legislature in that branch which would be most agreable to the public, but that I had reason to beleive you had a preference for the House of representatives." Upon this he observed that in addition to the considerations first suggested, your services in the Senate will be of more importance than in the other House, as there will be much depending on that branch unconnected with the other. some other observations were made to this purpose, and the issue was his decided opinion that you ought [to] be proposed for the Senate. Upon conversing with some other gentlemen I found you were brought into contemplation pretty generally as to this object; I shall let the idea take its fairest course so as to be placed at last as you may ultimately direct. in the mean time I beg you to be full and confidential in your communications to me. I will write you immediately upon my arrival, and shall constantly keep you informed of the dispositions of the House in all points.

1. RC, Madison Papers, DLC. Carrington was returning to Virginia from serving in Congress in New York City. Madison was still in Congress.
2. For the New York Convention's circular letter of 26 July 1788, see BoR, I, 153–58.

Joseph Jones to James Madison
Richmond, Va., 20 October 1788 (excerpt)[1]

... the new capital will in a few days be in condition to receive the members of assembly, to which building they will probably adjourn when the houses are formed—As yet their politicks are but conjecture a short time will open their designs—The Go——r[2] has it In contemplation to bring forward the adoption of the measure proposed by N. Y. for another genl Convention[3] it is said the Citizens of Wmbg are not fond of the measure and he says unless they will send him unfettered in that respect he shall decline serving this session.[4] ...

1. RC, Madison Papers, DLC. For the entire letter, see Rutland, *Madison*, XI, 308–9n.
2. Edmund Randolph.
3. For the Virginia General Assembly's consideration of the New York Convention's circular letter, see BoR, I, 158–80.
4. Edmund Randolph, whose term as governor was ending, represented Williamsburg in the House of Delegates later at this session.

James Madison to Edmund Pendleton
New York, 20 October 1788 (excerpt)[1]

... I am glad to find you concurring in the requisite expedients for preventing antifederal elections, and a premature Convention. The circular letter from this State[2] has united and animated the efforts of the adverse side with respect to both these points. An early convention threatens discord and mischief. It will be composed of the most heterogenious characters—will be actuated by the party spirit reigning among their constituents—will comprehend men having insidious designs agst. the Union—and can scarcely therefore terminate in harmony or the public good. Let the enemies to the System wait untill some experience shall have taken place, and the business will be conducted with more light as well as with less heat. In the mean time the other mode of amendments may be employed to quiet the fears of many by suppling those further guards for private rights which can do no harm to the system in the judgments even of its most partial friends, and will even be approved by others who have steadily supported it. ...

1. RC, Madison Papers, DLC. For the entire letter, see Rutland, *Madison*, XI, 306–7. Madison is responding to Pendleton's letter of 6 October (BoR, III, 245–46).
2. For the New York Convention's circular letter of 26 July 1788, see BoR, I, 153–58.

George Lee Turberville to James Madison
Richmond, Va., 20 October 1788[1]

Tis only ½ hour to the making up of the mail Excuse therefore a detail of Occurrences I will write you fully by next post—
A proposition is talked of even by the staunchest friends to the new Constitution, to close with N York & propose another convention to amend[2]—your opinion on this subject wou'd assist me Much; especially if you think it improper—I therefore write for this information which I shou'd be gratefully obliged for[3]—
With ever sincere Wish for your health & happiness I remain my dear sir Yrs. most sincerely & Affectionly

1. RC, Madison Papers, NN.
2. For the Virginia Legislature's actions on the New York circular letter, see BoR, I, 158–80.
3. See Madison to Turberville, 2 November (BoR, III, 312–14), for Madison's sentiments.

Francis Corbin to James Madison
Richmond, Va., 21 October 1788 (excerpt)[1]

... A proposition will be brought forward in the assembly for a Second Convention of the States—and I fear it will be carried—altho' I have not yet been able to ascertain the Complexion of the House—this being but the 2d. Day of our meeting[2]—This proposition it is said will be introduced not by Henry but (mirabile dictu!)[3] by our friend Randolph—He will injure his political Reputation by his doubtings and turnings—He is *too Machiavelian* and not *Machiavelian Enough*—
I wish, I sincerely wish that he could be advised and would take advice—but this, I fear, is out of the question—We Virginians are too much accustomed to Solitude and Slavery—too much puff'd up with our own foolish Pride and Vanity even to Entertain any other Idea than that we alone are wise and all the rest of the World Fools. Should any thing occur worth your notice during the Session of Assembly you shall have the Earliest intelligence of it.

1. RC, Madison Papers, DLC. Corbin did not date the letter. Madison docketed it "Ocr. 21. 1788." For the entire letter, see Rutland, *Madison*, XI, 310–11.
2. For Virginia's resolution requesting Congress to call a general convention to amend the Constitution, see BoR, I, 158–80.
3. Latin: strange to say; wonderful to relate.

Foreign Spectator I
Philadelphia Federal Gazette, 21 October 1788

This is the first of twenty-eight numbered essays signed "Foreign Spectator" that appeared in the Philadelphia *Federal Gazette* between 21 October 1788 and 16 February 1789 arguing that the Constitution did not need amendments. An earlier series of twenty-nine unnumbered essays by "Foreign Spectator" appeared in the Philadelphia *Independent Gazetteer* between 6 August and 2 October 1787. In a letter to Matthias Hultgren on 29 March 1788 Nicholas Collin admitted that he was the author of the first series of "Foreign Spectator" essays (CC:651). The 2 October 1787 essay (the last in the first series) is printed as CC:124. The other twenty-eight first series essays are printed in the first volume of RCS:Pa. Supplement.

The *Federal Gazette*, 10 March 1789, identified Collin as the author of the second series of "ingenious" essays by "Foreign Spectator" which showed "the folly and danger of alterations (for no one real amendment has yet been suggested) in the constitution of the United States" (BoR, IV).

The *New York Daily Gazette* reprinted this essay on 3 June 1789 with the following preface:

> Mr. M'LEAN, As Congress will shortly consider of amending the Federal Constitution, you are requested to publish the remarks made by a foreign spectator, on the amendments proposed by the conventions of five of the adopting states, the minority of two others, and the late one of North Carolina. They were published in Philadelphia about six months ago.
>
> The importance of the subject, and the judicious manner in which it is treated, will render it very interesting to your readers.

The *Daily Gazette* continued its reprinting of "Foreign Spectator" numbers two through twenty-eight daily Monday through Saturday until 7 July with two exceptions: On 30 June the *Daily Gazette* announced that No. XXIV would appear the next day, 1 July, and No. XXVIII was reprinted in two issues, 6–7 July. The reprinting was timely as Congress was then considering amendments to the Constitution. Maryland U.S. Representative Benjamin Contee probably sent one of the *Daily Gazette's* printed numbers of "Foreign Spectator" to that state's governor, John Eager Howard, on 7 June (BoR, IV).

The only other newspaper reprinting that has been located was in the North Carolina *Fayetteville Gazette*. Only two issues of this newspaper are extant for this period. The *Fayetteville Gazette* reprinted "Foreign Spectator" II on 14 September and No. VI on 12 October, indicating that it was continuing its reprinting from the last issue and would continue the reprinting in the next. From this, it is almost certain that Nos. I, III–V, and VII were reprinted in the issues of 7, 21, 28 September and 5, 19 October, respectively. How many additional numbers of the "Foreign Spectator" the *Fayetteville Gazette* reprinted in the run-up to the meeting of the second North Carolina Convention in Fayetteville on 16 November is unknown.

The nationally circulated monthly Philadelphia *American Museum* reprinted Nos. I–X in its issues of January–April, June, September, and October 1789.

The *Museum* indentified the author as "the rev. Nicholas Collin, D. D. & M. A. P. S.," i.e., a member of the American Philosophical Society.

"Gehennapolis" in the Philadelphia *Federal Gazette*, 18 February 1789, lamented the end of the "Foreign Spectator" series and hoped for more from the author. He described the author "as a real patriot and wel-wisher to the United States of America," whose essays "ought to be read by every intelligent individual." "His remarks on amendments proposed by the state conventions," asserted "Gehennapolis" "are judicious and solid, and rank him in the first class of honest politicians" (BoR, IV). On the conclusion of the New York reprinting of the "Foreign Spectator" series, "A Federalist" asked the editor of the *Daily Gazette* to reprint a German fable as a final illustration of the arguments made in the "Foreign Spectator" series. The fable appeared on 8 July (BoR, IV).

For the amendments referred to by "Foreign Spectator," see BoR, I, 241–43 (Pennsylvania Minority), 243–45n (Massachusetts), 247–49 (South Carolina), 249–50 (New Hampshire), 251–56 (Virginia), 256–64 (New York), 264–70 (North Carolina); and Appendix I, BoR, III, 472–76 (Maryland Minority).

REMARKS[a] *on the Amendments to the Federal Constitution, proposed by the Conventions of Massachusetts, New-Hampshire, New-York, Virginia, South and North-Carolina, with the minorities of Pennsylvania and Maryland, by a* FOREIGN SPECTATOR.

NUMBER I.

In the history of the United States, the present æra is probably more important than any that has been or ever shall be. The declaration of independence, in 1776, was a bold measure; and its confirmation by the peace, in 1783, a glorious event. But if this independence is not secured by a solid union, fully adequate to the political and civil happiness of the states, it is at the best very doubtful, whether a longer dependance on Great-Britain would have been more calamitous than this premature political existence, fraught in its very stamina with disease and destruction. I shall not repeat the melancholy chime of *anarchy, civil war,* and *foreign conquest*, rung through the whole continent by the feeling and sagacious apprehensions of so many Americans, justly celebrated for political wisdom and patriotic virtue; but only beg leave to present one reflection—Neither the United States, nor any other part of the globe, are yet civilized enough to settle national disputes in the amicable way of reason and equity. Alas! the tinsels of ambition and avarice create frequent and furious contents, which are decided by the sword, that *ultima ratio* of kings and republics. In some future stage of civilization, a close union of the states will be less necessary; but till that happy period arrives, it is undoubtedly a sacred object with every man of sense and virtue.

The federal constitution has, for near a twelve month, undergone the most critical investigation, in the public prints and the conventions of the states. Politicians have been entertained with a grand and interesting spectacle—Thirteen sister-republics debating with all the force of argument, all the powers of oratory, on the form of a common government: this form embraced by great numbers as the guardian angel of America, sent from Heaven to save her from impending ruin: detested by others as a fiend come from the regions of darkness to enslave a vast continent: the constitution rejected by two; and adopted in some of the others, even great states, by small majorities, and with a pressing request of many capital amendments.

That an object of such awful magnitude should be agitated with anxious hopes and fears; that, held up in every point of view, it should, to so many eyes, present an appearance somewhat different, is a natural and pleasing symptom of that keen and solicitous love of liberty, which is the vital principle of republics.—But such difference of opinions on *first principles*, is really very extraordinary: and the *retaking by the left hand what was given by the right*, is a mark of jealousy inconsistent with the most necessary energy of government. The federal constitution will, no doubt, like all other political institutions, require alterations in the process of time. The trial of such a complex machine in operations partly novel, may also very probably point out some very important amendments. But if no essential fault can as yet be discovered, it must be very unwise to undo what has been done with so much difficulty—to frustrate the sanguine hopes and anxious desires of the people—to irritate the numbers that have suffered so long under the cruel tyranny of anarchy—to throw so many who pant for speedy relief, into utter despair—to lock up or banish the little circulating specie and credit, that barely keeps alive our expiring trade—to confirm foreign nations in their contempt of our imbecility, and want of faith; to prevent all beneficial intercourse with any of them; and to urge those who are creditors to violent demands of public and private debts—to do all this, would be absolute folly and madness.

Though a majority in congress may be wise enough not to advise a reform of the new government before it really becomes expedient, yet a persuasion that the present form is pernicious, unjust, and dangerous, must render great numbers of people dissatisfied—make many worthy men bad federal citizens—weaken the union, and impair its benefits—perhaps enable some daring spirits to raise insurrections.

While prejudiced electors fetter their representatives with injunctions to procure visionary amendments, it is to be feared, that many excellent persons will decline a trust so incompatible with their feelings—and that the mercenary and timid will sacrifice honor and conscience to popularity.

In a candid examination of the proposed amendments, we shall find that some are repugnant to an effectual confederacy, others of dubious utility, and the most specious improper, until the union is firmly established, and experience has decided between opposite theories.

(a) *The editor, with the permission of the author, informs the public that one number of these remarks will appear regularly in the Federal Gazette, every Tuesday and every Friday evening, until the subject be finished.*

Honestus
Maryland Journal, 21 October 1788[1]

To the CITIZENS of MARYLAND.

Although the conduct of your Delegates in Convention was not such as to merit your indignant reproaches, it was precisely what an intelligent antifederalist might have wished. A majority of the members determined, out of doors, not to waste time by arguments in favour of a system which, by every sacred obligation, they were bound to adopt; and yet they agreed, in the House, to hear patiently all that might be urged against it, on the general question. Here was the first error.— Had they done, on the first day, that which took place on the fourth; had a member of each delegation declared the powers under which they acted, and the duties to which they considered themselves confined, the business would have been compleated in less than a third of the time, and sophistry would have had no opportunity of making its baneful impressions on capricious wavering minds.

The appointment of the committee was a second error, resulting almost inevitably from the former. But, had the majority of the committee answered fully that inflammatory address of the dissenting twelve,[2] every pernicious consequence from either of these mistakes might have been prevented. This salutary measure, I understand, was declined partly from an idea, that it would tend to keep alive an opposition, which was driven to its last expiring effort, and partly from the difficulty of convening and keeping together gentlemen who, at that time, were too closely occupied by business more interesting to their feelings.

It is certain, that the committee was appointed on a principle of conciliation; and that the Convention never deemed amendments necessary for perfecting the constitution. Perceiving, in the end, that the scheme of proposing amendments[3] to the consideration of the people might produce much mischief, without effecting any real good, they dismissed it, on a conviction, that, in every point of view, it was improper.

⟨It is, perhaps, a matter of little moment to ascertain, from what source is derived the general vague idea respecting the necessity of an early revision of the new constitution.⟩ I believe it, in this state, to have originated from the conduct of the Convention, and the silence of the committee. From the beginning, indeed, I was apprehensive that these things would give countenance to a position that, although the Convention proposed no amendments, a very great majority of its members were convinced, that it was essential to obtain an alteration as early as possible.

⟨There is nothing more hazardous to the interests of America, than the propagation of such a sentiment. It is repugnant to all we have yet done; and I much fear, unless it be diligently guarded against, that the constitution, embraced by eleven states, as the means of their political salvation, will ultimately be defeated.

As the contrivance and institution of men, it is unreasonable to suppose the system absolutely perfect. But, for other men, without a trial of its effects, to point out, with certainty, where the error lies, supposes infallibility in those, whom we know to be actuated by narrow views, interested motives, and inveterate prejudices.—Is it conceivable, that men like these will not only be *able*, but *willing*, to correct the mistakes of the most select assembly, which America ever contained?—of an assembly, composed, in a great measure, of its heroes, sages, and patriots, and possessed of almost all the means of thorough information?

From Americans, far be the base grovelling principles of implicit faith! Were the defects of the constitution plain to common sense; were they such as evidently to endanger your welfare, there is no respect to persons would induce me to defend them. But when, after the most deliberate attention, I think it more than probable, that those things, which sometimes appear wrong, are, in truth, the most excellent; when I perceive there is not a majority of rational men, who can agree on any one amendment; when I am satisfied, that nothing will prevent us from obtaining those alterations, which experience shall dictate; when, above all, I see men still obstinately bent on the ruin of the system, I am clear and decided, that every good citizen should, for the present, lay aside the idea of amendment, and consider only the means of securing and giving motion to the government, such as it is.—Were it loaded with faults, more than the vilest of all demagogues is loaded with offences against candour, truth and justice, an early premature revision, projected by either its enemies, or its friends, would render it far more erroneous and defective.

This baneful plan of revision is suggested by its most bitter and dangerous enemies. The adoption of eleven states has impelled them to change their ground; and, under the specious pretext of amendment, they securely meditate its defeat.—Be assured, my fellow-citizens, that, from one end of the continent to the other, they will practise every art, use every engine, strain every nerve, to crown this their last grand attempt with success.—The indolence and supineness of Americans must be without parallel, should they permit this invidious plan to succeed. As full of resources, as they are, the antifederal tribe can have no hope without obtaining your confidence; and, to gain this, has been universally their aim. Is it possible you can be weak and tame enough to trust them? Can you be persuaded, by mere empty professions, that men who have acted as they have done, and whose last dependence is in the destruction of a system, will have in view no alterations, except those which will improve it. Be assured, there is no possible change will content them, short of taking all energy from the general government, and permitting them to avail themselves still of the distraction, weakness and mutability of the state-councils.

I wish not, after all, to be understood, that I view every enemy to the new constitution as destitute of the spirit of patriotism, and guided only by interest or ambition. There are a few well-meaning men who believe they cannot render their country more signal service, than by averting the ruin impending on its liberties.⟩ I pity their delusion, and lament, that, at this critical moment, their exertions are so shockingly misapplied.—Between those *influenced* by the love of public good, and those *impelled* by dishonourable motives, it is by no means difficult to distinguish. An attention to their *circumstances*, *connexions*, and *pursuits*, will enable you to determine with ease.

⟨But I call upon them all, to demonstrate those evils, in the new constitution, which threaten destruction to our freedom. It is certain, that of one hundred men, who clamour for amendments, there are not ten, who can say with precision, what it is they desire. Perhaps I might go further, and assert, that, of these hundred men, not three have studied coolly the constitution; not twenty have perused it twice; and not fifty have read it at all. I call upon the ablest of them all to appear in the public prints, and demonstrate, that liberty of conscience is in danger; that the establishment of a national church is either within the power of the legislature, or likely to take place if it were practicable at all; that there is danger of oppression from the modes of taxation to be adopted; and that America ought to exhibit to the rest of the world this solecism in politics, a free government precluded for ever, let the exigence be what it may, from some of the best and most obvious resources of government. In short, I call upon its enemies to establish, by fair argument, the charges they have *thundered* in electioneering harrangues. Instead of dealing out their positions to small circles of ignorant and credulous men, let them instruct you all by means of the press. Let them convince you, if they can, that it is not proper to give this constitution a trial; that America can be safe, and the union preserved, without an efficient general government; that it is the perfection of political science to entrust government with no powers, which, by any possibility may be misused; that liberty cannot exist, where government controls the *"free-born will;"* and that it is possible and consistent with society, for every *free-born will* to be gratified.⟩

I have intimated, that the constitution has not been sufficiently perused and understood. I request every man to reflect, which class of its readers, before-mentioned, he belongs to; if he feels any compunction for his negligence, let him make the proper atonement, by considering carefully its provisions, and investigating its principles. Let him not decline the task of instructing others, at least, whenever a fair occasion shall present itself unsought. ⟨One would imagine, in a country like America, it would be impossible to disseminate falsehoods of a constitution, comprised in a single sheet of paper, and published over and over again, for the perusal of all. But he that has never been accustomed to hear confident assertions in public, can have no adequate notion of their effect. On their foundation alone, is erected the fame and power of "*many a*" mighty demagogue. It is notorious, that a number of barefaced falsehoods have lately been propagated with success, to influence the elections in more than one county. A gentleman, some time ago, presented me a list of such as he had collected. It was his intention to stigmatize the inventors, by publishing affidavits, which should fix each calumny on its proper founder. Why he has not done it I cannot say. Here is the list, with the title.

"A list of the political lies, circulated by the myrmidons and yelpers of the antifederal party in ——— county; by means whereof they carried the election.

"No. 1. That the Roman Catholic religion, if the new government be adopted, is to be established in America, with every power which it possesses in any part of the world.—This lie was told to the Methodists.

"No. 2. That the Presbyterians would be mounted on the high horse of ecclesiastic rule. This lie was appropriated for the Quakers, who were reminded, that once in Massachusetts—the Presbyterians made *"no bones"* of hanging them on the first convenient tree, if found in the state, after the time limited for their stay.

"No. 3. That, after the adoption, every man who leaves the state, will be obliged to pay Ten Dollars for each of his family; and that this was a scheme of the rich men, to prevent the poor from quitting the state, in order, that their lands might not want tenants, at the rents they please to demand.

"No. 4. That no person must dare to use a pound of soap, a dozen of candles, or a ceg of cider, although of his own make, without sending for the exciseman, or making him a return, under the most grievous penalties; that this rascal of an exciseman might enter the house of any man, at the dead hour of midnight, and search any place with impunity, yea! even the pockets and petticoats of his wife, or daughters.

"No. 5. That the government was to remit ten thousand of the militia to the Grand Monarque, to pay off part of the debt due to him, at so much a head.

"No. 6. That every poor man's son; at the age of fourteen, is to be enrolled as a soldier, and for the most trifling fault will be drawn up to the halberd; and have nearly his guts lashed out by perhaps a Negro drummer.

"No. 7. That the most sensible of the federalists were obliged to confess the trial by jury, in civil cases, was abolished.

"No. 8. That the federal government was adopted for the purpose of paving the way for Prince William-Henry, the third son of George, the English King, to be made King of all America.

"These are (says my informer) but a part of the lies told in our part of the county. Every one of these I can fix on the party," &c.⟩

To excite apprehension and terror in a weak mind, and by that method to procure a vote, which on a just representation and understanding of the subject, would have been very differently conferred, is in my conception, a crime of no trifling magnitude. It is perhaps the vilest of all cheats. It is much to be regreted, that some proper legal punishment has never been devised. The common usage in canvassing for votes is a plea unworthy of a man; and affords but little extenuation of the crime. The nature of right and wrong being immutable; however the universality of a practice may lessen the disgrace, it cannot, in the slightest degree, diminish the depravity. There arises indeed a too fair presumption, that the man, who shelters himself under example, feels little or nothing of the restraints arising from moral sentiment.

The remarks, I have just made, are intended, my fellow-citizens, for no particular character. Here is no designation of person, and if any man has reason for applying them to himself, the sensations they will excite are but a small part of the punishment he deserves. They are not intended for a single candidate at the recent elections. I have no just cause for insinuating, that any of them has been guilty of such base nefarious conduct. God forbid, that our public councils should be disgraced by the fellowship of such a character!

⟨That partizans have propagated the lies contained in the list, I have not the most distant doubt. My object is to incite an inquiry in the country; and, if possible, to deter men from such flagitious practices. The man, who will detect and hold up to public view, the railer who has either invented, or propagated, any of those calumnies on the constitution, will render, I am certain, an acceptable service to the community. It will be a poor apology for him, who can read, to say, that he relied on the information of another, with respect to the positive provisions in the constitution; although, with regard to the direct consequences, expected to result from its adoption, it may be easy for an artful eloquent man, to impose on the understandings of many, who have actually perused it with attention, and the offence of him, who has relied on the opinion of another, may, in some measure, be excused.⟩

It is some consolation to the lover of his country to reflect, that however guilt may escape the vengeance of the law, the exercise of a free Press permits every man to inflict a punishment by no means slight to the man whose heart, although depraved, is not yet totally callous.

Elk-Ridge, October 15, 1788.

1. The Massachusetts *Salem Mercury*, 23 December 1788, reprinted the text in angle brackets with slight variations after the following introduction:
    ⟨*As the necessity of speedy amendments to the Federal Constitution has become a favourite idea with some, perhaps the following extracts from a piece on that subject, lately published in a Baltimore paper, will not be thought ill timed—by those, at least, who are willing to prove both its excellencies and defects by a fair experiment of it entire.*⟩
2. A reference to the address signed by twelve Antifederalists, the minority in the Maryland Convention, that appeared in the Annapolis *Maryland Gazette* on 1 May (RCS: Md., 659–69).
3. For the amendments, see Appendix I (BoR, III, 472–76).

Edward Carrington to James Madison
Richmond, Va., 22 October 1788 (excerpts)[1]

Yesterday we had a full House. I am apprehensive from the complection of the Body that my predictions in my former letter,[2] as to the dispositions of a Majority of the Members, will be verified—nothing of

any kind has however yet been proposed, and therefore I am enabled to speak only from conjecture as drawn from a view of Characters. . . .
Mr. Henry keeps himself close—Mr. [Benjamin] Harrison & Mr. [William] Grayson discover considerable Malignancy against the Govr. [Edmund Randolph]. The Governor will come into the assembly, and is decidedly for a convention.

1. RC, Madison Papers, DLC. For the entire letter, see Rutland, *Madison*, XI, 311–12.
2. Carrington to Madison, 19 October (BoR, III, 261–62).

A Federalist
Massachusetts Centinel, 22 October 1788

Mr. RUSSELL, A writer, with the signature of ALFRED, in a late Worcester paper vauntingly asks, when speaking of the amendments proposed to the Constitution[1]—"Did a HANCOCK introduce the propositions— Did ADAMS support them—Did the leaders in the Convention advocate, and agree to them, in order to obtain a vote?" I answer—YES— it was to ease the minds of gentlemen who did not rightly understand some articles of the Constitution—and thereby obtain a vote in its favour, that this proposition was introduced. To prove it let us hear what a reverend and worthy member of the Convention says on the subject[2]—"Your Excellency" says he, "depressed with bodily infirmity, and exercised with severe pain, has stepped forth at the critical moment, and from the benevolence of your heart, presented us with a number of proposed amendments, in order, if possible, to quiet the minds of the gentlemen, in the opposition, and bring us together in amity and peace. Amendments which you, Sir, declare YOU DO NOT THINK NECESSARY, except for the SOLE PURPOSE of uniting us in a common, and most important cause."

In the same speech this gentleman said—
"Viewing the Constitution in this light, I stand ready to give my vote for it WITHOUT ANY AMENDMENTS AT ALL. Yet if the amendments proposed by your Excellency will tend to CONCILIATION, I readily admit them, not as a *condition* of acceptance, but as a matter of *recommendation* only; knowing that, *Blessed are the peace-makers.*—I am ready, to submit my life, my liberty, my family, my property, and as far as my vote will go, the interest of my constituents, to THIS general government."

But it is in vain to contend with such characters as ALFRED.—With them, AMENDMENTS—*alias*—*alterations*—are only a stalking-horse of deception—the annihilation of the Constitution is their object:—They wish not to give it a *fair trial*—as they are convinced, that *trial* will demonstrate its superiour efficacy in eradicating the growing evils which now overshadow our country.

1. See "Alfred" II, *Massachusetts Spy*, 16 October (BoR, III, 255–56).
2. The quotations are taken from a speech delivered by Samuel Stillman, a Boston Baptist minister, on 6 February 1788 (RCS:Mass., 1456, 1460).

A Friend to Consistency and Stability in Government
Philadelphia Federal Gazette, 22 October 1788

Mr. BROWN, No person entertains a higher sense of the excellence of that article in the federal constitution which provides for its future amendments, than I do; but I can by no means agree with those who contend that there is a necessity for exercising this privilege now.

The convention well knew, that in forming a plan of government, for our young and growing empire, it would not be sufficient to consider the present situation of the United States; for, by such a limited view of things, they would have been led to patch up a temporary fabric, as an expedient for the present moment; a fabric which, from the very nature of its construction, must have been for ever a patching, and always in need of repair. They also knew the science of government to be yet in its infancy, and like all other progressive sciences, capable of much improvement: that, therefore, to dictate to, or presume to bind posterity by a constitution, accommodated to the present state of the union, and of political knowledge amongst us, would have been the height of injustice, arrogance and absurdity.

They also had wisdom and candor enough to perceive and acknowledge their own fallibility—that, notwithstanding their utmost exertions, some things might escape their notice, and others be capable of further improvement, at no distance period.

Impressed with these ideas, they have raised a stately edifice, in which are combined all the beauteous orders of political mechanism and architecture, and have finished the building agreeably to the most modern taste. But this they have done in such a manner as to admit of any alterations, that may, from time to time, be found necessary, to render it more elegant, or convenient, without altering, or in any manner impairing, the principal parts of the building; they being composed of materials which, from their nature, are incapable of decay.

In short, to speak without allegory, they have formed a constitution which excites the admiration of every enlightened politician in America, or in Europe; a constitution which is not only adapted to our present situation, but is also left open to improvement, as a more enlightened posterity, or a change of our national circumstances may require.

This provision the convention foresaw would be necessary, to effect partial changes in the system, without endangering the ground-work of the plan, without bringing about another revolution in politics, without destroying the stability of our government and laws, and thereby rendering us unworthy the confidence of foreigners, and of each other.

Well aware of the inconveniences and evils attendant on a frequently changing, and constantly fluctuating government, the convention proceeded with cool deliberation: caution and circumspection marked their proceedings; that, if possible, sudden alterations might not be necessary. How amazingly successful they have been in the attempt, is no small cause for wonder, when we remember the various interests they had to unite, the jarring and discordant ones they had to reconcile to each other, and the many other embarrassments, which, in a business so important and arduous, beset them on all hands.

Notwithstanding the many difficulties which they had to encounter in every stage of their proceedings, they at length completed a constitution, which, in the words of the deliverer of his country, is "*the best that can be obtained at this time,*"[1] and, in the opinion of men eminent for their political wisdom, is *the best plan of government that ever was offered to the world.*

Yet strange to tell! the objectors to it hesitate not to give the lie to those respectable opinions—each of them intimating that his alterations would amend it considerably. To such I would only beg leave to remark, that the constitution, as it stands, is much more agreeable to a large majority of their fellow-citizens, than it would be, were the objections of any one man, or set of men, to be regarded so far as to alter the plan accordingly. And to make the constitution, without alterations, still more eligible, no one part of it is disapproved of by a majority of the people; while no two, of all those who are opposed to it, can agree with each other in their proposed amendments, much less can they expect to make them pleasing to the people: as well might we attempt to incorporate and unite fire and water, as endeavour to reconcile to each other, the different objections that have been made.

Here then let the people of America pause, and seriously reflect on that happy disposition of mind which prevailed in the convention, and induced the members to give up their selfish opinions, their local views, and partial interests, for the general good. Let them consider that nothing can please every body—but that whatever is agreeable to a majority, ought to be preferred to the jarring and inconsistent proposals of a much-divided minority. Let each opposer of the constitution enquire what probability there is, that *three-fourths* of the people of the United States (the number necessary to adopt amendments) will come into his opinion, in preference to those of others who propose amendments widely different—or that they will pay more respect to him and his political creed, than to the constitution, and the worthy men who had so much toil in forming it.

When a man vainly imagines that he has more wisdom than the convention, or than the rest of his fellow-citizens, he must hope in vain, if he expects to have this inimitable constitution destroyed, in its best parts, by foisting in those *alterations*, which his disordered imagination or his depraved heart would arrogantly suggest as amendments.—No man of common sense will presume that in such circumstances his single opinion is infallible.

But, sir, it is mistakenly imagined by some, that amendments are generally wished for; at least that a similarity of opinion, with respect to the nature and extent of amendments, is at all prevalent. I will readily agree that many, yea, almost all of us have discovered something in the constitution, that seems objectionable, and in need of being amended: but how, sir, would it be possible to new-model the system agreeably to such objections, when perhaps no two object to the same thing; or, if they do, yet they cannot agree as to the best mode of amending it? Such is the diversity of sentiment that prevails among us, that with men of candour, it will be one more great argument in favour of the excellence of the system; for, were any particular part of it strikingly wrong, we should, methinks, unite in having it amended; to suppose otherwise, would be an insult to our understanding, or to call our patriotism in question. But as no such unanimity of opinion respecting amendments prevails, and as we cannot all be called ideots, nor be charged with a lukewarm attachment to the cause of liberty and our country, it must necessarily follow, that no essential, no radical alteration is generally wished for.

Under these considerations, I trust that no man will be elected to represent any of the states in Congress, who is an advocate for *amending* (would it not be more just to say *destroying?*) the constitution in the first instance—but that men will be chosen who will immediately put it in motion—since no danger can arise from the trial; but much is to be apprehended from previous alterations.

1. Quoted from the *Maryland Journal*, 1 January 1788, which printed an extract from George Washington's letter of 14 December 1787 to Charles Carter (CC:386-A). The extract was widely reprinted.

Edmund Randolph to James Madison
Richmond, Va., 23 October 1788 (excerpt)[1]

Until the meeting of the assembly, which took place the day before yesterday, I have had nothing, with which to repay you for your many friendly attentions.

The hundred and seven members are assembled; among whom is the leader of the opposition [Patrick Henry]. I have not seen him, but I am told, that he appears to be involved in gloomy mystery. Something is surely meditated against the new constitution, more animated, forcible and violent than a simple application for calling a convention. Whether the thing projected will issue forth in language only, or the substance of an act, I cannot divine. But I believe I may safely say, that the elections will be provided for and that no obstruction will arise to the government, or rather will be attempted, so far as a preparation for organizing it goes. . . .

1. RC, Madison Papers, DLC. For the entire letter, see Rutland, *Madison*, XI, 313–14.

Alfred III
Massachusetts Spy, 23 October 1788[1]

On the NEW CONSTITUTION.

Mr. THOMAS, There is not one amendment proposed by the Convention of Massachusetts, but what is quite compatible with the idea of a consolidated government.

As government is composed of three states, which the nature of man seems to point out, as checks for each other, in it, to wit, the Legislative, the Executive and the Judicial; so in the latter, it is necessary, that there should be a democratical balance to the prerogative, which is so strongly represented in the judicial power.

As we know of no other nation besides that of Greatbritain, where those balances in government, are preserved, or indeed thought of; or any, where the people have a hand in the government, or any considerable share of political freedom, we may be allowed to produce some ideas from that kingdom. The whole freedom of that country depends ultimately upon a trial by jury. The House of Commons are not more valuable for any other purpose, than for their tendency when uncorrupted, to preserve this right to the people; yet nevertheless, had it been a mere statute, and not a constitutional right, the House of Commons in their rage, corruption and folly, would have sacrificed it long ago.

"The impartial administration of justice, says Judge Blackstone, which secures, both our persons and property, is the great end of civil society"—and, says a noble Lord in parliament, "for what are seventy regiments, and eighty ships of the line supported, for what does the parliament meet, or royalty fill a throne, but for the administration of civil justice?" And yet says Judge Blackstone, "if that were entirely entrusted to the magistracy, a select body of men, and those generally selected by the prince, *or* such as enjoy the highest offices in the state, their decisions, *in spite of their own integrity*, would have frequently an involuntary bias towards those of their own rank; it is not to be expected from human nature, that the few should be always attentive to the interest of the many. Here therefore, a competent number of sensible and upright jurymen, chosen by lot from among those of the middle rank, will be found the best interpreters of truth AND THE SUREST GUARDIANS OF THE PUBLICK JUSTICE."[2]

A transcript of all the eulogiums bestowed on this part of the British constitution, would fill a large volume. An attempt to overturn it, has brought majesty itself to the block; while the guardians of this privilege have sacrificed their lives and fortunes to its preservation; without it, in this country, each attempt to give the people information of their danger, would be punished in civil actions, as a libel against some one officer of the government, when and where the judges would give their own construction by fanciful innuendoes, to the publication, and crush the first bloomings of patriotism, by examplary and destructive damage.

Tyranny, in a government where this mode of trial is not adopted, can have no check, but from the rising of the people, who are generally patient, because they dread the horrid consequences of a civil war. Thus the people in England suffered the enormities of Charles the first, until by advice of all the judges but two, he taxed the people in ship money without the consent of parliament; then Hampden, immortalized in the annals of freedom, dared to oppose the tyranny. The consequences are well known.

Should we have no trial by jury secured to us in civil actions under the new government, who will dare arraign the rulers before the great tribunal of the publick? Or where shall the press, that only vehicle of publick intelligence find security? In England, when a measure is doubtful as to its legality, and yet to be adopted, the judges are always closseted, and a combination formed with the supreme executive, or with all the other branches of the government, to support each other against the people, or what they call the faction, opposition, &c.

If in our new world, the judges should combine with the senate, and President, to violate the peoples' rights, who should punish them? If they are impeached, that very senate, who are advisory in the executive department, is to try them.

And here I beg leave to propose, as a very important amendment, that there should be devised a tribunal to be taken from the several states, to try all impeachments against president, vicepresident, and judges of the supreme court.

The privilege of trial by jury, in civil cases, is so solemnly thought of in the declaration of independence,[3] in all the previous addresses to the throne, and recognized so carefully in all the constitutions of the states, that one might have expected to have found it, in the new frame of government—But it is not there.

Had nothing at all been said about a trial by jury, we should have supposed, that it was passed over as a principle so interwoven with the nature of the government, and so well fixed and settled, as not to need a preservative provision. But when no notice is taken of a grand jury, and thereby the door left open to *informations*, those grand engines of ministerial despotism; and provision made for trial by jury in criminal cases only, we are led to believe, that it is more owing to design, than "*the want of an apt mode of expression*" that it is neglected. I do not contend for it in questions of seizures for breach of revenue laws, or the laws of trade, but many expressions might be hit upon to secure it in other instances.

The supreme judicial power is lodged in a court. I will not affront the understanding of the people by exposing the weakness of an observation made in the convention by a law character, "that the word Court does not by popular, or technical construction exclude the trial of fact by a jury;"[4] it is enough for the present purpose, that it does not certainly, and necessarily, include it, because it is a point too important to be left constitutionally doubtful. To say it may be provided for by laws as well as by the constitution, is to arraign the wisdom of the people of the whole union; for they have all solemnly adopted it as a fundamental and principal right in their forms of government.

Should Congress make laws for the purpose of fulfilling the expectations of the people at present, they can repeal those laws, in whole, or in part, by subsequent militating ordinances, and do this so imperceptibly, that the privilege may be nearly annihilated before the people shall take the alarm.

I am not such a novice, as to believe that justice between a man and his neighbour, cannot be done without a jury, where the court interest is out of the question: A Jeffrey and a Mansfield were upright judges where the crown had no particular interest.

The power of raising taxes, implies, if Congress shall choose to do it, the power of individual assessment, which will multiply officers, and serve only to vex the people. Should Congress possess those powers over each state in this point, which the governments possess over towns and corporations, it will be sufficient.

The privilege of trial by jury in criminal cases, upon information, and without indictment by grand jury, will subject every friend of the people to be brought to the bar on the information of an Attorney-general, and though he may be acquitted, yet the punishment of imprisonment, trial, and jeopardy, will discourage many, and rob the people of the aid of faithful leaders.

By having power to grant exclusive right to companies in matters of commerce, the Congress may obtain great riches to themselves, and favourites, and destroy the fair and honest merchant by rendering of him tributary.

The amendment proposed by Massachusetts, with regard to trial by jury, is inaccurate, and insufficient; it provides for such trial on cases of common law, which in technical expression, does not extend to trials on acts of Congress.[5]

I shall enlarge no farther on amendments. The convention of Massachusetts in their mode of adopting the constitution, "in the name and behalf of the people, enjoined it upon their representatives in Congress, at all times to use their influence to obtain amendments"—and yet some of the very men who held up their hands to give the solemn charge, openly laugh at the idea, and declare every man who proposed amendments not fit to be trusted. But surely if such unmanly chicane and double dealing, can abuse the candour of the people, so far as not to prevent *their* having a place, it will not prevent the people from voting for such men as are open and manly in their politicks and true to their own sentiments.

1. Reprinted: *Massachusetts Gazette*, 28 October; Boston *Independent Chronicle*, 30 October; Portland, Maine, *Cumberland Gazette*, 28 November; Philadelphia *Independent Gazetteer*, 6 December. See "Alfred" II, *Massachusetts Spy*, 16 October, for the authorship of this series of essays (BoR, III, 256 note 1).
2. Blackstone, *Commentaries*, Book III, Chapter XXIII, 379.
3. The phrase used in the Declaration of Independence is "For depriving us in many cases of the benefits of the Trial by Jury" (CDR, 74).
4. Quoted from the 30 January 1788 Massachusetts Convention speech of Boston lawyer Thomas Dawes, Jr. (RCS:Mass., 1369).
5. The sixth amendment (BoR, I, 244).

Christian Farmer
Connecticut Norwich Packet, 23 October 1788

Mr. TRUMBULL, *Please to insert the following in your impartial Paper, and you will oblige a number of your Readers.*
CHRISTIAN FARMER.

It is of the utmost importance to found our principles on the solid basis of truth; and before we declare ourselves on this or the other side of any question we ought thoroughly to understand the matter in debate, & seriously consider the consequence of adopting this or the other opinion: when we have done this, we are fitted for a manly and uniform prosecution of what we take in hand. Reason points out to us the method; and a consciousness of our being right, supplieth us with resolution and fortitude to pursue it.

It is of the greatest moment to every society, that a just estimate be formed of the powers of government, and the liberties of the people; for on this depends every thing which is held dear; whether of a civil or religious nature; and what makes it still more interesting is, that every one in this case is like Adam the representative of a future race, who are to be rewarded for the virtues or suffer for the guilt of their progenitors.

Never was there a people whom it more immediately concerned to search into the nature and extent of their rights and privileges, than it doth the people of America at this day; what is once dedicated to legislative authority is seldom if ever recovered without bloodshed, although it is improved to the oppression of the people who meant it to be exercised for their benefit.

My Christian Brethren and Fellow Citizens, we cannot easily be too critical in examining a Constitution which has been compiled and thus far approved by the aristocratic or court part of this infant nation, pray dont let us be discouraged and think the trial is over and desided. Remember it is the right of Americans to have a fair trial by Jury. I think their virdict on the trial has been forgotten or not taken in by the court. Except only in the State of Rhode-Island, and their we are informed the democratic or jury part were about four fifths against the Constitution,[1] in North-Carolina a large majority of their Convention were against it, and have wisely and judiciously drawn up a bill of rights, and proposed material amendments, which ought to take place previous to the new government;[2] of those Conventions that have adopted the Constitution, it has, in most of them, been by a small majority, and several of them have proposed amendments. New-York Convention have in a judicious, pertinent and respectful circular letter to the supreme executives of the respective States; proposed, that a national Convention be appointed to make the amendments.[3] Whom else can make the alterations that are proposed? Surely Congress cannot. For the design and subject of a Constitution and Bill of Rights is to be a law to Congress, to teach them what they are impowered to do for the general good of the people; and what they shall not do that might hurt or oppress the community, methinks it could not be rationally expected that the first Convention should do any more than lay a foundation, and prepare the way to bring up the sense and feelings of the nation on so weighty a subject. Especially when we reflect they originated only from a creature or creatures of the people, made by the people at large for another purpose, viz. to legislate under their respective State Constitutions, which gave them no power to make such a great political creature bigger then themselves and their Constituants united. Seeing it did not originate from God by the voice of the people, it seems to be in fear and keeps as far off of them both as possible. Witness the manner of its formation,[a] the matter it contains, its mode of seeking the breath of life at second hand. Let it alone it will die of convulsions; rather than seek life and health of God, by the voice of the people at large: in which way only it can obtain life and a healthful constitution.

How little hath it of purity, which is the first property of that wisdom which is from above, surely neglect of God, breach of solemn covenants, do not indicate purity of heart or life. It may be further examined by the other properties of heavenly wisdom.

In our next Essay,[4] especially whether it hath been hitherto conducted, without partiality and without hypocrisy.

> (a) *It is reported our late national Convention did not attend social public prayers at the opening of, nor through the whole of their sessions, although the subject before them was so important.*

1. A reference to the Rhode Island referendum on 24 March 1788 where the freemen voted 2,714 to 238 against the Constitution (RCS:R.I., 151–217).
2. For the North Carolina Hillsborough Convention amendments, see BoR, I, 264–70.
3. For the New York Convention's circular letter, see BoR, I, 153–58.
4. No "next Essay" has been located. A previous essay by "Christian Farmer" appeared in the *Connecticut Gazette* on 29 August 1788 (DHFFE, II, 11–12).

Centinel XX
Philadelphia Independent Gazetteer, 23 October 1788 (excerpt)[1]

... It has been moreover the policy of the junto, from the beginning, to ruin, by every device of calumny and exertion of influence, the character and circumstances of every leading patriot; well knowing that the people are only important and powerful when united under confidential leaders; and as this policy was supported by a numerous and weighty party, and pursued with unremitted perseverance, the ablest and most influential patrons of the people fell victims to it, character after character were successively attacked and hunted down by the dogs of party, with the most unfeeling rancour, even the death of the victim did not assuage their gall—In this barbarous game of policy, the infamous *Galen*[2] bore away the palm, and shone conspicuous beyond all the imps of the *well-born*; he boasted that the superior malignity of his pen had deprived the illustrious and patriotic *Reed*[3] of his existence, and in his fate had made a signal example to deter others from emulating his virtues, and standing forth the advocates of the privileges of the people, which is so highly criminal in the eyes of the *well-born*. By such means have the well-born attained to their present power and importance, to a situation which has enabled them to dictate and procure the establishment of a form of government for the United States, which, if not amended, will put the finishing stroke to popular liberty, and confirm the sway of the *well-born*. Whilst the fate of the new constitution was doubtful, great was the assumed moderation, specious were the promises of its advocates. The despotic principles and tendency of this system of government were so powerfully demonstrated as to strike conviction in almost every breast, but this was artfully obviated by urging the pressing necessity of having an energetic government and assurances of subsequent amendments. The people were moreover told, "you will have the means in your own power to prevent the oppression of government, viz. the choice of your representatives in the federal legislature, who will be the guardians of your rights and property, your shield against the machinations of the *well-born*.["] But how changed the language, how different the conduct of these men, since its establishment?—the[y] are taking effectual measures as far as in their power to realize the worst predictions of the opponents to the new constitution—Having secured the avenue to offices under the new Congress by the appointment of the senators, they are now exerting all their influence to carry the election of the representatives in the federal legislature, and thereby get the absolute command of the *purse strings* to confirm their domination; every artifice is practising to delude the people on this great occasion, which in all probability will be the last opportunity they will have to preserve their liberties, as the new Congress will have it in their power to establish despotism without violating the principles of the constitution. The proposed meeting at *Lancaster*[4] is a high game of deception; under the appearance of giving the people an opportunity to nominate their representatives, the minions of ambition are to be palmed upon them. Ostensible deputies are to be sent from every county for this purpose, who, if we may judge from those already appointed, will take especial care to prevent the nomination of men who have congenial feelings with the people, as such would prove troublesome obstacles in the way of ambition; the intention is to monopolize both branches of the legislature, and make the government harmonize with the aggrandizement of the *well-born* and their minions. The deputies appointed to go from this city[5] characterise the juggle and designate the intention more strikingly than is in the power of language to express, or the ingenuity of artifice to conceal: the man who confessedly has had a principal share in the framing of a constitution that is universally allowed to be dangerously despotic;[6] and therefore to require great amendments; the man who in every stage of its adoption has been its greatest advocate; whose views of aggrandizement are founded upon the unqualified execution of this government, whose aristocratic principles, aspiring ambition, and contempt of the common people, have long distinguished him; I say this man is now selected as one of that body who are to dictate the choice of the people—to point out *faithful* representatives who are to check ambition and defend their rights and privileges. If the people suffer themselves to be thus fooled upon so momentous an occasion, they will deserve their fate. But I am persuaded they will discern the fraud and act becoming freemen, that they will give their suffrages to real patriots and genuine representatives.

Philadelphia, October 22d, 1788.

1. Reprinted: Philadelphia *Freeman's Journal,* 29 October; *New York Journal,* 30 October. The *Freeman's Journal* printed an errata on 5 November stating "In the note of Centinel Numb. XX, read *Jonathan Morris,* instead of *Jonathan Roberts.*" For the authorship, circulation, and responses to the "Centinel" essays, see the headnote to "Centinel" I, *Independent Gazetteer,* 5 October 1787 (BoR, II, 21n–23n).
2. Benjamin Rush.
3. Joseph Reed.
4. The Lancaster conference composed of delegates from most of the Pennsylvania counties and Philadelphia met on 3 November 1788 to select a slate of candidates for the U.S. House of Representatives and for presidential electors. See DHFFE, I, 313–20n, 321–22, 323–29.
5. James Wilson and George Latimer.
6. James Wilson.

Edward Carrington to James Madison
Richmond, Va., 24 October 1788 (excerpt)[1]

... Since mine of the 22d.[2] I have endeavoured to get into the views of the leaders of the opposition.—they are wicked with regard to the Constitution—every attempt will be made to enthral it, & render it odious to the people—what think you of an Act restricting Judiciary & other Officers of the State, from exercising duties of the same Nature, under the Federal Govt.?—this is in contemplation, & thus, it is intended, that the multiplication of Officers amongst the people, which has been predicted shall be introduced.—Mr. [John] Beckly says that the Majority of Anti's in the House is about 15 whether this is accurate I cannot say as yet; but I am inclined to think there is certainly *a* Majority. No one Measure has yet been brought forward—next monday is assigned for the House to go into Committee upon the State of the

Commonwealth, when I suppose propositions of an antifederal nature will be brought on. . . .

1. RC, Madison Papers, DLC. For the entire letter, see Rutland, *Madison*, XI, 314–16.
2. See BoR, III, 272–73.

Benjamin Franklin to Thomas Jefferson
Philadelphia, 24 October 1788 (excerpt)[1]

. . . Our Disputes here about the new Constitution are subsided, and we are gotten into Order. As the first Meeting of the new Congress, I suppose there will be some Contestation for Amendments, and probably some will be made: And future Congresses may make more as Experience shall make them appear necessary. There is no doubt but that Gen. Washington will be chosen President.

1. RC, Jefferson Papers, DLC. For the entire letter, see Boyd, XIV, 36.

Foreign Spectator II
Philadelphia Federal Gazette, 24 October 1788[1]

REMARKS *on the Amendments to the Federal Constitution, proposed by the Conventions of Massachusetts, New-Hampshire, New-York, Virginia, South and North-Carolina, with the minorities of Pennsylvania and Maryland, by a* FOREIGN SPECTATOR.

NUMBER II.

In treating a momentous and difficult subject, my reasoning may sometimes jar with the principles of many enlightened persons; but my pen shall be guided by a sincere zeal for the liberty and happiness of the union, and by a sacred regard to what I believe to be the truth, without even the least tincture of well-meant dissimulation. This is odious to a candid mind, and justifiable only by extreme necessity. Happily the federal cause does not want such a paltry resource: the better we understand our true situation, the more unanimous, pleasing, and effectual will be the pursuit of our common interest. With a peculiar satisfaction I can also execute my design, without the necessity of reflecting on men or parties: I discuss with modest freedom the actions of public bodies, without any criticism of their motives, or distinction of the individuals that composed them: only observing that the minority of Maryland was but eleven; that the amendments were more or less approved of in the several states; and that those proposed by Massachusetts and South-Carolina are but few; from which we may conclude, that there is much more apparent than real dissention about the constitution.[2]

Our attention is naturally first attracted by this extensive amendment—*That it be explicitly declared, that all powers not expressly delegated by the constitution are reserved to the several states, to be by them exercised.*— Ratification by Massachusetts, 1 am. Ditto 1 by New-Hampshire, North-Carolina, Virginia; 2d by South-Carolina; 1st in the address of the minority of Maryland, and 11th in that of the minority of Pennsylvania— all in words nearly the same. The convention of New-York probably supposed that so many other pointed amendments made this needless. The minority of Pennsylvania inforce it by this addition, *that the sovereignty and independency of the several states shall be retained.* Virginia and North-Carolina strengthen it by this further amendment (17 and 18 respectively) *That those clauses which declare that Congress shall not exercise certain powers, be not interpreted in any manner whatsoever to extend the power of Congress; but that they be construed either as making exceptions to the specified powers, where this shall be the case, or otherwise as inserted merely for greater caution.* The minority of Maryland declare the above amendment to be *absolutely necessary for restraining the general powers given to Congress by the first and last paragraph of the 8th sect. of art. 1st, and the 2d part of the 6th article; those dangerous expressions, by which the bills of rights and constitutions of the several states may be repealed by the laws of Congress, in some degree moderated, and the exercise of constructive power wholly prevented.*

A careless observer must perceive a fearful distrust in these strong barriers. Waving for a moment any superiority, and putting the federal head on a level with the several state governments, would it not be a fair bargain to make this counter declaration, *that every power, whose operation is not evidently confined within the affairs of a particular state, shall explicitly be deemed federal?* The real truth is, that a very nice line cannot be drawn between the federal government and the states, especially in this early stage of the union. The constitution has therefore, in explicitly granting some powers, and expressly refusing others, traced this limit with all the accuracy that is practicable. It leaves, as it were, a small vacant place between the two parties, and says, *the federal government may, in the necessary exertions for the general good, sometimes go out of its usual career; but it shall never trespass on the proper grounds of the states: In the same manner any state may occasionally step over its proper line into this common walk; but shall not touch the federal rights of the union.* This is right and generous; nor will it produce any contention, while both parties have a tolerable share of reason and equity.

I scruple not to assert, that without *some constructive power* the Federal government will not be adequate to every emergency, and I will prove it by examples. Suppose the plague, or a similar epidemic destemper should visit this country: it is a national affair; because it is the interest

COMMENTARIES, 24 OCTOBER 1788   287

of every state, that not only its neighbours, but the remotest states may
stop the rapid contagion:—The Federal government must then concert
general measures; rouse the indolent, and check the selfish, who might
reap some benefit from the calamities of a sister state. How much have
we already suffered, from the Hessian fly,[3] and what may we not suffer
from its rapid progress. Should not the Federal government offer premiums for an effectual remedy, or make other salutary regulations? The
same reasoning might be extended to some other considerable national
objects.

Congress ought then undoubtedly to have the power of *providing for
the general welfare of the United States*, 1st part, 8th sect. 1st art. Again, so
far as the states grant certain specified powers, and others which their
exigencies may require, they necessarily grant all the requisite means
for the execution of them; and the *mode, quality, and degree* of these
means cannot possibly be strictly defined I cannot therefore see any
impropriety in the 18th part of the above sect. and art. *to make all laws,
which shall be necessary and proper, for carrying into execution all the powers
vested by this constitution in the government of the United States, or in any
department or officer thereof.* At the same time this constructive power
cannot be very great. It is limited *first* by the plain sense of the words,
general welfare, laws necessary and proper, which express an object of great
common utility, and the pursuit of it by means the best that can be
had, the easiest, cheapest, most effectual. 2*dly, By all the explicit stipulations of what Congress shall not do*, sect. 9. art. 1. These are clearly and
bona fide meant as checks on the Federal power; and to suspect them
as lurking traps for the people, is indeed very unreasonable.

I verily believe that if the Federal Constitution was charged with a
minute regulation of what may be expedient, and how it should be
done, in every possible situation, and with a scrupulous enumeration
of all the rights of the states and individuals, it would make a larger
volume than the Bible, and yet give rise to more political schisms, than
there have been religious ones in all Christendom, for near 1800 years.
A Federal Government clogged with so many weights, confined in every
motion, and lamed in every limb, would be an unwieldy useless machine; a gigantic monstrous pageant of the union—all the trouble and
expence of it would be fooled away merely to gratify the fickle fancy
of political dreamers, or the spleen of gloomy choleric knight-errants.

After all, this childish jealousy would render liberty less secure, because a bold and artful Congress could safely invade the people through
the holes they had forgot to stop, without any legal charge of treason;
as all that was not reserved in such exact detail, must be supposed fairly
granted.

Every man of business knows, that he cannot employ an agent without giving some discretionary powers. In domestic affairs we cannot pin a servant down to stiff minute rules: a blockhead or knave who wants them, is not worth keeping.

That the Federal Constitution should be *the supreme law of the land, is much complained of by the minorities* of Pennsylvania and Maryland. It is however self-evident that two sovereign powers in the same country are a flat contradiction; and that the United States, in reciprocally giving and receiving certain obligations, cannot keep their original sovereignty and independence separately, though they render the independency of the whole more respectable and happy. It is indispensible, that *all the laws of the United States, made in pursuance of the constitution,* should in case of collision prevail over *the constitution and laws of any state:* even laws made by constructive power for the general welfare, 6th art. 2d. part: But the spirit of the constitution requires an impartial regard to the common good of the union, and by no means warrants a sacrifice of the essential interests of any one state to some general but small advantage of the United States.

That either the explicit or constructive powers of Congress, may gradually abolish the state governments, is a chimera now almost out of date. Those who want more information on this head, may consult the well-written *address to the minority of Pennsylvania,* signed a Freeman. (See Carey's Museum for February, March and April last.)[4] There is, however, yet, a pretty general and strong reluctance among the states, to make the necessary concessions; and it seems requisite to fix a general, simple, and precise idea of the federal government. It is formed by the people, and for the good of the people; its first object is therefore to secure the grand interests of the individuals who compose the states: the second, to preserve the political powers of these states, is but of an inferior quality, and subordinate to the first. It is of the greatest moment to every citizen of America, to be protected in his life, property, liberty, family, and all the dear interests of human nature; but whether the state in which he resides, has such a particular constitution, is less material. If the confederacies did not exist, the several states would in process of time, undergo many capital changes in their legislative, judicial, and executive forms: probably the large ones would even be divided;—why then should we stickle for the exact limits of the state governments, if they encroach upon a necessary federal government, which alone is capable of protecting us against foreign enemies, and a dangerous anarchy? The dispute whether the new government is national or merely federal, is therefore in a great measure equivocal, and has a bad tendency. To a certain degree it is national, because it acts directly on the people, without the intervention of the state governments, in all those cases which are necessary for the general safety and welfare. Indeed, the want of this direct operation, was the principal defect of the old confederacy, as will be seen in the examination of the following amendments.

Note: The readers will find the federal constitution, its ratification by Massachusetts, South-Carolina, New-Hampshire, Virginia, and New-York, the address of the minority of Pennsylvania, ditto of Maryland, and the proceedings of the convention of North-Carolina, in Mr. Carey's Museum for Sept. 1787; Feb. and Aug. 1788; Dec. 1787; May and Sept. 1788, respectively.

1. Reprinted: *New York Daily Gazette,* 4 June 1789; North Carolina *Fayetteville Gazette,* 14 September; and in the February issue of the Philadelphia *American Museum.* For the authorship of the "Foreign Spectator" series, see the headnote to Essay No. I (21 October, BoR, III, 264n).
2. For the proposed amendments, see BoR, I, 241–77.
3. The Hessian fly was a fly that wreaked havoc on cereal crops such as wheat, rye, and barley. A 1786 infestation particularly affected the middle states.
4. "A Freeman," I, II, and III, written by Tench Coxe, were originally printed in the *Pennsylvania Gazette* on 23 and 30 January and 6 February (CC:472, 488, 505). The three essays were reprinted in the Philadelphia *American Museum.*

George Washington to Benjamin Lincoln
Mount Vernon, Fairfax County, Va., 26 October 1788 (excerpt)[1]

I have been lately favored with the receipt of your letters of the 24th. and 30th. of September,[2] with their enclosure, & thank you sincerely for your free & friendly communications.

As the period is now rapidly approaching which must decide the fate of the new Constitution as to the manner of its being carried into execution & probably as to its usefulness, it is not wonderful that we should all feel an unusual degree of anxiety on the occasion.—I must acknowledge my fears have been greatly,[3] but still I am not without hopes.—From the good beginning that has been made in Pensylvania a State from which much was to be feared, I cannot help foreboding well of the others.—That is to say, I flatter myself a majority of them will appoint fœderal Members to the several branches of the New Government.—I hardly should think that Massachusetts, Connecticut, New Jersey, Delaware, Maryland, South Carolina & Georgia, would be for attempting premature amendments.—Some of the rest may, also, in all probability be apprehensive of throwing our affairs into confusion, by such ill-timed expedients.—There will, however, be no room for the advocates of the Constitution to relax in their exertions; for if they should be lulled into security, appointments of Antifœderal men may probably take place; and the consequences, which you so justly dread, be realised.—Our Assembly is now in session; it is represented to be rather antifœderal, but we have heard nothing of its doings.—Mr Patrick Henry, R. H. Lee & Madison are talked of for the Senate.—Perhaps as much opposition, or, in other words, as great an effort for early amendments, is to be apprehended from this State, as from any but New York.—The constant report is, that North Carolina will soon accede to the New Union.—A New Assembly is just elected in Maryland, in which it is asserted the number of Fœderalists greatly predominates; and that being the case, we may look for favorable appointments, in spite of the rancour & activity of a few discontented, and I may say *apparently* unprincipled men....

1. RC, The Original Letters of George Washington to Benjamin Lincoln, Houghton Library, Harvard University. For the entire letter, see Abbot, *Washington, Presidential Series*, I, 70–73.
2. For the 24 September letter, see BoR, III, 228–30 for the 30 September letter, see Abbot, *Washington, Presidential Series*, I, 22.
3. The letterbook copy reads "greatly alarmed" (Washington Papers, DLC).

John Dawson to James Madison
Richmond, Va., 27 October 1788 (excerpt)[1]

... Nothing has yet been said respecting the organization of the New Government—I expect it will be brought forwd to day, and that the Act for that purpose will be accompanid with instructions for another general Convention agreably to the plan propos'd by the President of the N. York convention....

1. RC, Madison Papers, DLC. For the entire letter, see Rutland, *Madison*, XI, 318–19.

George Lee Turberville to James Madison
Richmond, Va., 27 October 1788[1]

Sentiments begin to circulate—the Cloven hoof begins to appear—I want no arguments to convince me—A convention I am opposed to—intrigue antifœderalism and artifice go hand in hand—R. H. L. [i.e., Richard Henry Lee] & Colo. [William] Grayson are the objects of antifœderal choice for the Senate—but I trust they will be deceived & by aiming at too much they will loose every thing—Mr. [Francis] Corbin has precipitated resolutions into the Committee of the whole to day for organizing the Government which with his speech I fear will be productive of ill—however I hope for the best—Governor Clinton's Letter tomorrow[2]—I tremble for the event & must soon put a conclusion to this Letter in order to prepare myself for that subject—do not

conceive me a flatterer when I tell you that I in common with your
Native Countrymen feel most sensibly the want of your ample aid upon
this trying occasion—I only can gratify myself with the Certainty of my
consciencious purity of my intentions. & in being certain that my conduct will be regulated by my Judgement—not my passions—& then
the great Poet of Nature tells me in the language of inspiration almost—that I am safe—

> Thrice is he armed who has his quarrel just
> & he but naked tho locked up in steel
> Whose *conscience* makes a coward of his soul[3]—

We are in the new capitol
God bless you My best respects to the President & to Mr. Brown.[4]

1. RC, Madison Collection, NN.
2. For the New York Convention's circular letter of 26 July 1788, see BoR, I, 153–58.
3. William Shakespeare, *Henry VI*, Part II, Act III, scene 4, lines 241–43.
4. President of Congress Cyrus Griffin and fellow Virginia delegate John Brown.

Theodorick Bland to Richard Henry Lee
Richmond, Va., 28 October 1788[1]

Not lightly unadvisedly or wantonly did I take up my opinion with
regard to the new Constitution, and however matured I considered
those opinions in my own mind—I confess they have received great
additional strength from their concurrence with those of so many of
my Friends, who have long been numbered among the first and most
active Patriots—when I mention this Class of our fellow Citizens I presume Sr. that I need not particularize one who has borne the highest
honors as well as the most heavy Burthens, incident to and consequent
on our virtuous and well *meant* Struggle. A uniform consentaniety of
political opinions grounded on and growing out of a Basis which is the
surest foundation of Political happiness (viz a government in which the
Essential rights of a free People are well secured,) has knit us together
and calls loudly on us to strengthen those Bonds which may enable us
together to stem the Torrent, which bids fair to bear down every thing
before it. The Virtuous Principles which have dictated our political
opinions, I trust do still remain in full vigor in the breasts of some of
us, and will I hope lead us to exertions which will in the end render
that government secure and harmless, which in its outset threatens
Tyranny and oppression. This Sr. in my humble apprehension can only
be done by men wedded to freedom and the rights of *men*, and by
measures carried on in concert and steadily opposed to whatever shall

tend to trample on those rights; Convinced as I am sr. that you hold these principles you may be well assured that my exertions will not be wanting to place you in those councils, where your Experience, abilities, and Inclination will I hope cooperate to introduce such *amendments* as can alone render the new Government *tolerable*, and which I beleive the far greater part of the People of the United States wish to see adopted—Nothing of Consequence has yet been done this Session—I have not yet thought much on the Business now before the house, but the first Blush of that part of it which relates to the Congressional requisitions of men, Money &.c. of the *old Congress* I confess strikes me disagreeably—how can men, money, &.c. be demanded by a Body which died in June last without leaving a last Will and Testament: on what principle can one Government exist, when another is declared to be Established in Lieu of it: but it may be said that Such Ideas, are the cavills of Malcontents—Is not this a resumption of power which they have parted with—Suppose they shd. take it into their heads to reconsider and repeal their act for putting the new government in motion? would they not have as good, nay a better right to do this than they have after an abdication of their right to assess quotas, again to resume that right and by the bye it is somewhat Singular that not one state in the Union as far as I can learn has ratified that resolution of the Convention, which vests a right in the old Congress to put the new Government in motion—thus will doubts and difficulties arise at the threshold of this Business—and while an actual Interregnum prevails—a kind of sham government is carrying on the most Important functions of a real one—The state of the Business of the present Session appears to me to resemble a large Indolent tumor, that is not yet ripened to a head—it contains much matter which wants an issue but the Political Surgeons seem fearfull to cut into it least they shd. wound some great vital organ—we have however taken possession of the Capitol—the Chief Magistrate has (tho not Publickly) anounced his resolution to retire from the helm, and take a birth among the Crew—where he talkes of Joining the mutineers either to trim the Ballast of the new Government or put the Ship about[2]—this is all the intelligence of Importance I am at present able to communicate to you I therefore hope you will be satisfied with that as well as that you will be assured that I am with perfect Esteem Dr. Sr. Yr. obedt. sr.

1. RC, Lee Family Papers, ViU.
2. For Edmund Randolph's plans to resign the governorship, see Joseph Jones to James Madison, 20 October, note 4 (BoR, III, 262n).

COMMENTARIES, 28 OCTOBER 1788   293

John Harris to Tench Coxe
Harrisburg, Pa., 28 October 1788 (excerpts)[1]

... the Meeting at Lancaster will be by one side of the Question, I hope they'l name good men, there will be a party Election, If good men are Elected as our Representatives it will Answer the public Utility, a few Amendments will please every honest man to the Constitution, & none calld for, but whats reasonable (& Neccessary) & not a String of them that wou'd destroy the whole Constitution, wch might be Attended with bad Consequences. I hope for the best, & means to be a good Subject, (as I ever has been[)]. ...
P.S. I write from home with a Very bad pen in haste.

1. RC, Coxe Papers, Series II, Correspondence and General Papers, PHi. For the entire letter, see DHFFE, I, 321. Harris did not include a place of writing, but he had founded the town of Harrisburg.

Jonathan Trumbull, Jr., to George Washington
Lebanon, Conn., 28 October 1788 (excerpt)[1]

... The circular Letter from the Convention of the State of N. York, being among the Letters which the Govr. laid before the Assembly—had of course a reading among the other public communications.—this was all that passed respecting it—for—altho we had in our Assembly the Champion of our Antis:,[2] with some of his principal Aides, yet no one had hardiness enough to call up the consideration of that Letter, or to mention one word of its subject—thus passed, in silent review, that formidable communication.—

Excepting a few—very few—discordant Souls, whose unharmonious principles will never suffer them to act in general concert—we continue very unanimous in sentiment & salutary measures in this State:—and are progressing with much cheerfulness, & great good humour to the commencement of the new Constitution. ...

1. RC, Washington Papers, DLC. For the entire letter, see Abbot, *Washington, Presidential Series*, I, 79–82n.
2. James Wadsworth (BoR, I, 156).

Foreign Spectator III
Philadelphia Federal Gazette, 28 October 1788[1]

REMARKS *on the Amendments to the Federal Constitution, proposed by the Conventions of Massachusetts, New-Hampshire, New-York, Virginia, South and*

North-Carolina, with the minorities of Pennsylvania and Maryland, by a FOREIGN SPECTATOR.

NUMBER III.

The federal power of raising a revenue, is an object of general but various criticism. The minority of Pennsylvania propose, that *no taxes, except imposts, and duties upon goods imported and exported, and postage on letters, shall be levied by the authority of Congress,* addr. 9. Whether they mean to grant duties on exportation, prohibited in the constitution, is not clear. Whatever may be the extent and merit of this amendment, I shall pass by it, as differing from all the rest.

The convention of New-York insists, *that no capitation tax shall ever be laid by the Congress,* am. 15. The minority of Maryland means the same by the word poll-tax, am. 9; and that of Pennsylvania tacitly condemns it among so many others. Capitation taxes are not indeed very eligible: when the degrees of opulence among a people are numerous and very unequal; they cannot be proportional and productive without a troublesome, and in some measure arbitrary, assessment. They may however be occasionally used in America, because the great body of the people is in easy circumstances, and few comparatively rich or poor; consequently a general small capitation tax, of a dollar per annum, would not incommode even day labourers, yet amount to a considerable sum. It must also be remarked, that as the people at large have the important right of directly choosing the federal house of representatives, in which all money-bills must originate, it would be ungenerous to complain of a little disproportion in a general personal tax: if a person in that case pays the same as his rich neighbour, he has also an equal vote with him; and this very tax forms a part of that federal revenue, by which not only property but liberty is protected.

The minority of Maryland request, *that all imposts and duties laid by Congress, shall be placed to the credit of the state in which the same be collected, and shall be deducted out of such state's quota of the common or general expences of government,* am. 13. The meaning, though not clearly expressed, is, that all the expences of the federal government should be apportioned among the states according to the census and number of representatives; and that all imposts and duties, by virtue of a general and uniform law of Congress collected in any state, shall be deducted out of such state's quota.

Virginia and North-Carolina demand, that *excises,* like direct taxes, may be apportioned among the states *according to the census, nor collected by Congress in such state as will pay its quota,* am. 3.

The amendment of the above minority, differs considerably from the two just mentioned; and all three are unsupported by any of the other conventions. I shall therefore leave them without a direct reply, as their impropriety will appear when we come to examine the system of federal revenue, adopted by the constitution. For the same reason I barely take notice of the second amendment, proposed by the convention of New-York, *That the Congress do not impose any excise on any article, except ardent spirits, of the growth, production, or manufacture of the United States, or any of them.*

The general request of amendments, when cleared of contradictory parts, is, that congress may not have recourse to direct taxes, but when the other sources of revenue are insufficient; nor then lay and levy any such, if the several states will in a reasonable time pay their quotas of the general requisition made according to the determined census. Their sense of the matter is thus respectively expressed: *That Congress do not lay direct taxes, but when the monies arising from the impost and excise are insufficient for the public exigencies; nor then until Congress shall have first made a requisition upon the states, to assess, levy, and pay their respective proportions of such requisition, agreeably to the census fixed in the said constitution, in such manner, as the legislatures of the states shall think best; and in such case, if any state shall neglect or refuse to pay its proportion, pursuant to such requisition, then Congress may assess and levy such state's proportion, together with interest thereon, at the rate of six per cent per annum, from the time of payment prescribed by such requisition,* Massachusetts 4th am. New-York 3d, New-Hampshire 4th, with the variation—*impost, excise, and their other resources;* South-Carolina 3d, in words nearly the same, with *duties, imposts, and excise. When Congress shall lay direct taxes or excises, they shall immediately inform the executive power of each state, of the quota of such state, according to the census herein directed, which is proposed to be thereby raised; and if the legislature of any state shall pass a law, which shall be effectual for raising such quota, at the time required by Congress, the taxes and excises laid by Congress shall not be collected in such state—*Virginia and North-Carolina 3d. *That in every law of Congress imposing direct taxes, the collection thereof shall be suspended for a certain reasonable time, therein limited; and on payment of the sum by any state, by the time appointed, such taxes shall not be collected—*min[ority] of Maryland, 3d am.

It is then agreed, that Congress may in some cases levy direct taxes, but not until a state neglects or refuses to pay its quota of the requisition. But why will any state neglect and refuse? Is it because the legislature disapproves of it? or because it cannot make the people comply with it? While the government of a state is popular, its rejecting a federal requisition, or neglecting to collect a tax laid in consequence of it, is a tacit but significant hint to the people not to pay; nay, I may almost say it is an express request, considering how well the opinions of a legislature are generally known by the public prints, and the free mingled conversation of all ranks in a republic. Can we suppose that after this, the assessors and collectors of Congress will dare to shew their faces without being supported by a strong military force! If the legislature approves of a requisition from Congress, it cannot well be odious to a majority of the people, considering what harmony of sentiment there must generally be between the represented and the representatives. Therefore a tax necessary and reasonable may certainly be enforced by the authority of the state government; if it is not done, such neglect must proceed from a wish of throwing the odium of the discontented on the Congress. Let every friend to the union reflect, if the events in either case are favourable to federal sentiments!

The non-compliance with requisitions was an essential defect of the old constitution; and to mutilate the new government by them, is certainly very imprudent. They should therefore be left to the discretion of the United States in Congress assembled, to be made use of or not, according to times and circumstances. As the stability and ease of government depends much on custom and habit, I think that the people should in all federal concerns be directly governed by federal laws; an unusual, though moderate exercise of legal authority, has often produced civil tumults.

The promises of interest of six per cent. on quotas of requisition not paid, and this from the time of payment prescribed by Congress, held out by the conventions of Massachusetts, New-Hampshire, New-York and South-Carolina, are indeed very generous; but I sincerely wish that the defence of the union may never depend on them: generally a bad debtor pays neither an accumulated interest nor the principal.

1. Reprinted: *New York Daily Gazette*, 5 June 1789; North Carolina *Fayetteville Gazette*, 21 September; and in the March issue of the Philadelphia *American Museum*. For the authorship of the "Foreign Spectator" series, see the headnote to Essay No. I (21 October, BoR, III, 264n).

Switch
Baltimore Maryland Gazette, 28 October 1788 (excerpt)[1]

... The new federal system, though admired by some, is yet thought by others (and they not inconsiderable in number and reputation) to stand in need of amendments, for the better security of our most invaluable liberties. The subject is of great importance and worthy the serious attention of every citizen. Here is a field for each party to display their abilities, and when it is done with temper and moderation, with a view to a fair investigation and the public good, it is highly commendable.

Mr. C[has]e has given early and most decided proofs of his attachment to American freedom; and the very same attachment induces him to declare for amendments—But because he happens to differ from *some* men in a great political question, can it justify such a *paltry stripling* as you are, in your attempts to divest him of every virtue, to traduce and misrepresent almost every action of his life? . . .

1. "Switch" requested that the printer publish the essay from which this excerpt comes because of the *Gazette's* "unseasonable re-publication" on 10, 14 October of "Federalism" from the *Maryland Journal,* 26 September (BoR, III, 233–37).

Charles Lee to George Washington
Richmond, Va., 29 October 1788[1]

For a few days past the Assembly has been engaged upon the subject of the federal constitution: The house of delegates in committee has come to several resolutions with respect to putting it into operation. One of them distributes the commonwealth into ten districts each of which is to choose a representative in Congress, and another appoints that there shall be twelve districts each of which is to choose an Elector of the President, and every free man is at this election to have a vote. These matters were introduced by Mr. [Francis] Corbin who seems to me not to have the confidence even of those who are friends to the fair trial of the new government and as they have made but small progress, I cannot tell what will become of them. For Mr. [Patrick] Henry to day took occasion to declare that he should oppose every measure tending to the organization of the government unless accompanied with measures for the amendment of the Constitution for which purpose he proposes that another General Convention of deputies from the different states shall be held as soon as practicable. He offered to the Committee of the whole house several resolutions to be agreed to upon this point, one of them that the Legislature of Virginia should apply to the new Congress expressive of the desire of this state that another General Convention be immediately held to amend the constitution—The language of this resolution contains a direct and indecent censure on all those who have befriended the new constitution holding them forth as the betrayers of the dearest rights of the people—Applying to the constitution these words are used "whereby the most precious rights of the people if not cancelled are rendered insecure." With some difficulty and after much entreaty Mr. Henry *conceded* (I use his expression) to suffer the resolution to lie on the table for consideration till tomorrow.[2] Mr. Corbin who spoke several times but never against the resolution concluded with saying that the resolution as proposed was unobjectionable and Zach. Johnson was the only member who declared his disapprobation in positive terms. If Mr. Henry pleases he will carry the resolution in its present terms, than which none in my opinion can be more exceptionable or inflamatory though as he is sometimes kind and condescending, he may perhaps be induced to alter it. The other resolution proposed that a committee should be appointed, to answer the circular letter of New York and in conformity with the object of that letter, to address the assemblies of the other states.

I am told Mr. Henry has publickly said that no person who wishes the constitution to be amended should vote for Mr. Madison to be in the senate, and there is much reason to fear he will not be elected. Col R. H. Lee is considered as certain—and Col Grayson is expected to be the choice for the Senate.

Mr. Mayo has completed his bridge, & the greater part is strong and substantial; and this is now the common passage for waggons chariots &c across the river[3]—you will please to pardon the abrupt manner of my communication as I have been much fatigued with the business of the court, and have been much chagrined with the conduct of the federalists in the assembly who seem in general to stand in fear of their opponents.

1. RC, Washington Papers, DLC.
2. The resolutions introduced by Henry on 29 October were most likely the same as those the Committee of the Whole reported to the House of Delegates on 30 October. See BoR, I, 162–64.
3. A reference to John Mayo's toll bridge over the James River between Richmond and Manchester.

Richard Bland Lee to James Madison
Richmond, Va., 29 October 1788[1]

Mr: [George Lee] Turberville informs me he has inclosed to you Mr. Henry's resolution concerning the calling of another general Convention to propose amendments to the New Government—I fear we shall not be able to defeat the measure altogether—I hope however, we shall be able to modify it, so as to divest it of it's inflammatory dress[2]—or to postpone its operation to such a distant period as to give the people of America a fair experiment of the government. This however is but a hope as he is old in parliamentory science and is supported by the prejudice and apprehensions of many members of the assembly—We shall however be able I think to carry what we have very much at heart your election for the Senate, notwithstanding, any opposition to the government—the friends and foes to it appearing sufficiently sensible of the propriety of preferring gentlemen of the first merit and integrity to offices of such importance, without regard to their theoretic opinions on government.—Our assembly is *weak*. Mr. [Patrick] Henry is the only orator we have amon[gs]t us—and the friends to the new government, being all young & inexperienced—form but a feeble band against him. We shall do however what We Can and, will endeavor at all events to give our Country a fair view of the subject.—I am in haste, with all the affection I can feel for the highest virtue & patriotism

1. RC, Richard Bland Lee Papers, DLC.
2. On 30 October an attempt was made to replace Patrick Henry's resolutions with a substitute preamble and resolutions. The attempt failed, 39 for the substitute and 85 against (BoR, I, 164–65).

Honestus
Boston Independent Chronicle, 30 October 1788[1]

Mess'rs. ADAMS & NOURSE, I have observed in some late publications a disposition to inculcate among the people, an idea, *that those persons who are in favour of the proposed amendments, are not to be trusted in our federal government;* and some have gone even so far as to brand all such persons with the approbrious epithet of *antifederalists*. This being the case, I conceive it has now become a serious question to be determined—*Whether the amendments were proposed with an intention of having them adopted, or whether they were artfully introduced to deceive the Members of the Convention?* We cannot in candour suppose, that any Members of that respectable Body, (particularly the gentleman [John Hancock] who introduced them) meant to betray their constituents, by pretending to adopt a Constitution under the mask of amendments, and then desert them after its ratification: We cannot in justice to those respectable characters, who composed that august Assembly, conceive that so much cunning and subtilty should prevail among any individuals; neither ought we to presume, that men possessing so much political wisdom, would have been so *impolitic*, as to introduce the new government, by deceiving the people in its first establishment. Such a mode of conduct, they must be sensible, would have a tendency to raise a jealousy in the minds of the public, which would ever operate as a clog on all the future operations of government. No policy can be more destructive, than to raise a distrust of the *integrity* of those with whom we have intrusted our political concerns. What must be the sentiments of the people with respect to the Convention, if we are now told, *that the amendments are not to be regarded*—and that they were only introduced as a measure to pass the Constitution; and that our Members for the federal government, should be of that class of men, who are *openly opposed* to any amendments whatever.—Provided this is the case, (but which I conceive was far from the intention of the Convention) would not a distrust naturally prevail among the body of the people? What must be their conjectures? Will they think more favourably of that government, which needs such deception for its adoption? What decisions can they trust to in future, if this solemn form of ratification, signed by a man in whom they have ever confided, is to be treated as words of no signification? If the determinations of a body of men, consisting of characters as respectable for their wisdom and patriotism as any in the Commonwealth, are to be considered only as the mere trick of State policy, how will the people be ever able to ascertain the reality of any doings hereafter, however solemnly and deliberately resolved? Surely then if we mean to act consistent with the principles of *common prudence,* or wish to effect a lasting and beneficial government, founded on the CONFIDENCE OF THE PEOPLE, we ought at least to avoid those persons whom we have reason to believe are opposed to the proposed amendments. As the Convention have pledged to the people, that exertions shall be made to effect the adoption of the propositions, we should be careful to have such Members as are disposed to comply with these resolutions; that if the amendments are of any importance they may be adopted; if not, that they may be set aside, after that decent investigation which is due to the propositions of this Commonwealth.

If we attend to the words of the recommen[da]tion, we cannot but consider them of some importance,—"*And the Convention do in the name, and in behalf of the people of this Commonwealth, enjoin it upon their Representatives in Congress, at all times, until the alterations and provisions aforesaid, have been considered, agreeably to the 5th article of the said Constitution; to exert all their influence, and use every reasonable and legal method to obtain a ratification of the said alterations and provisions, in such manner as is provided in the said article.*"

After reading the form of the ratification, it is the highest reflection on their probity, to doubt of the sentiments of the Convention, with respect to the *importance* of the amendments. How abusive and uncandid then to stigmatize those who are for adhering to them, as antifederalists? Certainly those who are opposed to them, may with greater propriety be stiled such, as they are opposed to the decided voice of the Convention. If we are to *enjoin* upon our Representatives the alterations and provisions mentioned—and they are *bound to exert* all their influence for these purposes—how absurd to think of chusing men, whom we have reason to suppose will rather use their influence to backward[2] any attempts for their adoption? Real federal men are those who are for the propositions submitted; for REAL FEDERALISM *consists in promoting the harmony and union of all the States*: These happy consequences are most likely to be effected by complying with the decisions of the several States, as far as their proposals can be adopted. But to disregard the several propositions, and pretend to chuse men professedly with a view to backward any attempt to gratify the people, must have a direct tendency to destroy that UNION, which must ever be our national support.

Besides, what dependence can we place in men, who arrogantly presume to disregard the almost unanimous voice of the Conventions of the several States!

To ascertain the real sentiments of some respectable gentlemen of the convention, let us attend to a few extracts from the debates.

Judge [Increase] Sumner said "He sincerely hoped that the propositions would meet with the approbation of the convention, as it appeared to him to remedy all the difficulties, which gentlemen in the course of the debates had mentioned; and concluded by observing, that the probability was very great, that if the amendments proposed were recommended *that they would be adopted by the general government.*" Judge [Francis] Dana and several other gentlemen spoke in favour of the amendments, and the probability of their being adopted—Doctor [Charles] Jarvis said "That the propositions are general, and not local; and that they were not calculated for the peculiar situation of this State; but with indiscriminate justice comprehended the circumstances of every individual on the banks of the Savannah, as well as the hardy and industrious husbandman on the margin of the Kennebeck, and if they were not ingrafted on the Constitution, *it would be our own faults.*"[3]

From the above quotations, we can judge of the sentiments of some of the gentlemen in the convention; How greatly arrogant then, it is for writers to abuse those who are in favour of the amendments, after such explicit declarations from gentlemen whose sincerity cannot be doubted.

I am sensible it is rather unfashionable among some circles, to adhere to our old republican principles.—A republican and an antifederalist with them are synonimous.—The term antifederalist has of late been used by such persons to weaken the influence of some of our old tried republicans. But however lightly they may esteem our staunch patriots, or however contemptible our republican principles may appear to *them*, yet the body of this people I doubt not are convinced that those are the *men* who will work out our deliverance, and those are the *principles* which must eventually secure the rights and liberties of those States.—This country was founded on those principles; actuated by them our fore-fathers, secured to themselves and posterity the previleges of freemen against the arbitrary attempts of their enemies.—Animated by the same sentiments, we opposed Britain; defeated their armies; and finally established our Independence.—Surely then at this period, when we are just about to reap the fruits of our perseverance, we will not relinquish those principles which have been our support, from the first settlement of this country to the present day? neither will we stigmatize our firm, and *aged patriots*, who have helped us in every time of danger.

Let us then while we are anxious to secure a permanent federal government, continue stedfast in our *first principles.*—Let us preserve the spirit of moderation, and carefully avoid the dangerous extremes of *licentiousness* and *inattention.*—On our own prudence and wisdom under God depend the Salvation of our country.—The proceedings of the first Congress will give the leading traits of our future national character; therefore as we regard the happiness of America, let us give our suffrages for those tried patriots, who early stood forth in the cause of their country. We may then be assured that while we act thus, we act safely.

The objects of our federal government, are not to gratify the vanity of the ambitious, or to provide maintenance for seekers, but to restore our national vigour, and to promote our agriculture manufactures and commerce; the *latter* therefore depending so materially on the union of the southern and northern States, and the propositions of Virginia and Carolina being so similar with this, we ought particularly to inculcate that harmony which may produce those mutual advantages, so earnestly wish'd for by every sincere friend to the prosperity, and lasting happiness of America.

To accomplish the important purposes of our government, we need those faithful servants of the public, whose zealous patriotism and *stern integrity*, early rendered them objects of British vengeance; likewise those whose knowledge in European politicks, has rendered them competent to defeat the most subtile measures of our enemies. Thus doubly secured by the goodness of our Constitution, and the virtues of our Legislators, America, under the smiles of Providence, "shall enjoy without further interruption, that WEIGHT and CONSIDERATION, due to its EXTENT, its POPULATION, and the CHARACTER of its INHABITANTS."

1. "Honestus" was a pseudonym used by Benjamin Austin, Jr., in a series of essays that appeared in the *Independent Chronicle* in the spring of 1786 (published in pamphlet form as *Observations on the Pernicious Practice of the Law* [Boston, 1786] [Evans 19481]). The style of those essays is similar to the one printed here, and it is probable that Austin was the author. A political ally of Samuel Adams in Boston during the Revolution, he continued

to be active in popular politics after the war, and could be found at the head of crowds and demonstrations into the 1790s.

2. Obsolete: "To put or keep back, delay, retard" (OED).

3. The quotations are from the 1 February speech of Increase Sumner and the 4 February speech of Charles Jarvis (RCS:Mass., 1400, 1425). The reference is probably to the 1 February speech of Francis Dana (*ibid.*, 1403).

Solon
Boston Independent Chronicle, 30 October 1788[1]

Mess'rs. ADAMS and NOURSE, Some *writers* on the *subject* of the Federal Constitution, *write* with a *candour peculiar* to *themselves*; every man or number of men, who advance sentiments of the propriety, necessity or utility of any amendments in the Constitution, are held up as "*antifederalists*" or "time serving politicians" "sticklers for alterations," "alteration mongers," "shameless seekers of posts and pensions," and the like, who want to "*divide*"—"perplex," and "harrass the people," and are "anticipating the destruction of the essence and spirit of the adopted Constitution":—But such a *mode* of *reasoning* with candid and impartial men, is seldom convincing. A *free* and *enlightened* people are capable of distinguishing between *right* and *wrong*. If the federal Constitution is a system of government, *balanced*, and *sufficiently checked*, by those principles which reason and common sense dictate, and approve, and *experience* hath *taught* and *confirmed*, any attempt needlessly to *alarm, perplex* or *harrass* the people will undoubtedly be treated by them with that inattention and contempt which they deserve;—But if on the other hand, it *appears*, that with all the *excellencies* of the new Constitution, it is *essential* to the *security* and *permanence* of the *rights* and *liberties* of the people, that in some *particulars*, a more *explicit* definition and *express* limitation of power be made,—the men who advance, and hold up to the people, the propriety and necessity of such measures, will *justly merit*, not the character of *antifederalists*, or time serving politicians, but that of *true federalists* and *true patriots*.

The respectable Convention of this State, have stated *nine* propositions[2]—these speak for themselves; will any man say, there were no grounds for, or weight in them, or that it is a matter of indifference, whether there are any such *checks* or *declarations* adopted into the federal Constitution or not? Several other States have likewise proposed amendments, not of a *local* but *general* nature: Is no respect or attention due to these? Hath not every man, and every body of men, in a free country, a right to express their sentiments, with decency and candour, touching public measures; and those objects in which both they and their posterity are deeply interested, to be *heard*, and attended to, as far as the merits of their observations have weight, and not to be *stigmatized?* It is *measures*, and not men, that are to be *scaned, (truth is truth from whomsoever it comes)* and these will ever *stand* or *fall*, as they have their *basis* on *truth* and *reason*, or not—unless *supported* by *arbitrary power.*—*This people*, are not only remarkable for their good sense and discernment, but they live in a peculiar age—and without recurence to ancient story, within the compass of a score of years, have *seen* and *heard* sufficiently, to caution them, carefully to *define* those powers, which *they delegate* to others.

Great-Britain, who stiled herself the mother country, of these now sovereign States, not long since her colonies, *claimed* the *exercise* of those powers over them in *all* cases whatsoever,[3] to which this enlightned people would not submit; and an everlasting seperation has taken place.

A *Prince* and a *virtuous people*, a *Republic* too, we have seen, not long since, disputing of *prerogative*, and of *rights*—a horrid civil war commenced—a *foreign force* commanded *silence*. If *powers delegated*, and *rights retained*, had been *definite*, probably *this dispute* had not happened.

In a *nation* with whom these States have not only a near connection, but for whom they also possess a *warm* affection, and between a *Prince* the most *amiable* and *paternal*, and *a people* the most *filial* and *obedient*, are matters at this moment in a most disagreeable situation[4]—the one *claiming*, what the other suppose ought not to be *conceded*; what the event will be, time must discover,—*Heaven* grant that the *law* of the *Prince* for his people, to whom he has remarkably shewn himself in time past, the *father*; and the *love* of the *people* for their *Prince*, who has been their pride and their boast, may cement, and forever *unite* their affections, in those measures which tend to the *prosperity* and *happiness* of the nation.

But these things *shew*, as was my intention in the mention of them, that *powers delegated*, ought never to be *indefinite*, or *ambiguous*, but *clearly defined*, and well *understood*; as it will not only *prevent* unhappy disputes, but as it heretofore *might*, so it hereafter *may*, prevent *bloodshed, and the loss of liberty*. A celebrated writer has told us, that "in every society there is an effort constantly tending to confer on one part the height of power, and to reduce the other to the extreme of weakness and misery."[5] And *another* has observed, "*Is it not strange, though true, to say that virtue itself has need of limits.*"[6]—Ought then, a *wise* and *free* people carefully to *guard that* which of all human enjoyments, is the *most invaluable*—or, in any essential point, grant it *unlimited* and at *discretion?* Let common sense and reason, in the breasts of those who *determine, and who have virtue to be free*, decide.

1. Reprinted: Philadelphia *Independent Gazetteer*, 4 December. For the authorship and three other essays by "Solon" of 28 August, 4, 25 September, see BoR, III, 154–55, 199–201n, 231–32.
2. For the nine amendments recommended by the Massachusetts Convention on 6 February 1788, see BoR, I, 243–45n.
3. A reference to the Declaratory Act (1766).
4. A reference to France and Louis XVI.
5. Quoted from the first sentence of the introduction to Cesare Bonesana, Marchese di Beccaria's *An Essay on Crimes and Punishments*, which first appeared in Italian in Liverno (Leghorn) in 1764.
6. Montesquieu, *Spirit of Laws*, Book XI, chapter IV, 220.

Boston Herald of Freedom, 30 October 1788[1]

Extract of a letter from a gentleman in New-York, to his friend in this town, dated October 23.

"Anti-federalism, which once held such absolute dominion over the minds of some of our citizens, loses ground daily; in short, very few real Americans pretend to advocate its cause: it is true, there are some who foolishly assert that the new Constitution will not be established yet without blood-shed, but all such meet with the smile of contempt from every honest man.

"I am well assured, that in almost every state where the new system of government met with opposition at first, that that opposition has dwindled almost to a mere cypher, and Federal light illumines the mind of almost every free born son of America.

"Happy, thrice happy will these United States yet be in the enjoyment of every civil and religious blessing, under the administration of a government calculated to establish and secure the dearest rights of man.

"I anticipate with transport the good effects which MUST follow the progression of Federal laws and regulations, and look forward with that pleasure which words cannot express, to the period when the glory of our country will vie with the most celebrated nations of ancient or modern date; true glory may she soon possess, and may it "travel with the sun, and expire with the skies."

1. Reprinted: Northampton, Mass., *Hampshire Gazette*, 5 November; Rhode Island *Newport Herald*, 6 November; *Pennsylvania Mercury*, 11 November; *Pennsylvania Packet*, 11 November; *Pennsylvania Gazette*, 12 November; *Maryland Journal*, 18 November; Portland, Maine, *Cumberland Gazette*, 20 November; *State Gazette of South Carolina*, 11 December.

Foreign Spectator IV
Philadelphia Federal Gazette, 31 October 1788[1]

REMARKS *on the Amendments to the Federal Constitution, proposed by the Conventions of Massachusetts, New-Hampshire, New-York, Virginia, South and*

North-Carolina, with the minorities of Pennsylvania and Maryland, by a FOR-
EIGN SPECTATOR.

NUMBER IV.

Let us now consider the restriction, that Congress may not lay any direct taxes, until the other means of raising money are insufficient. *The impost* is generally regarded as a plentiful source of revenue; it must not, however, be estimated from the late inundation of European superfluities, but from the natural correspondence of imports to exports; it will also, in a great measure, decrease with the desirable increase of home-manufactures. This resource must, like all others, be used with some discretion. First. The opportunity of smuggling is very great in America, from the vast extent of her coast, the length of so many bays and rivers, and the number of creeks and inlets which every where wind, for many miles, into the country; to guard all these avenues, against a host of bold and artful smugglers, would require the expence of a small navy. Very high imposts, will certainly be powerful temptations to fraud, when local situation promises impunity; and nothing but the severest penalties, could check the flattering hopes of making a fortune in such a speedy and easy manner. Numbers would be ruined every year; and smuggling, like many other dangerous trades, would still be very general. In Great-Britain, bloody rencountres happen every week, between the officers of government and parties of smugglers; and cruel punishments are frequent: those scenes, so painful to humanity, would be seen in America, though every navigable water swarmed with armed vessels.

Secondly. An immoderate impost on several articles, which are in themselves good, and have become general luxuries, would not be agreeable to the nation—as tea, sugar, coffee, chocolate. It is only playing with words, to say that such duties cannot be too high, because they may be evaded; it is very hard either to lose a favorite enjoyment, or to purchase it by the money I want for other very useful things. Should Congress raise a pound of common tea to forty shillings, they would injure many of their fair country women; and I doubt not but many of them would prefer a tax on the *female tongue* to such a duty on a darling luxury.

Thirdly. Too high an impost on articles which are necessary ingredients in American manufactures, would prejudice these, i. e. paints, steel springs, furniture of cabinet works, various tools of mechanics and artists. In some cases a valuable native commodity is highly ornamented by foreign articles of moderate price; excessive duties on these would then be prejudicial, i. e. the lining, glass &c. of carri[a]ges.

Fourthly. Imported goods of real value, which cannot at all, or with no advantage be produced in America, nor draw the necessary money from the channels of domestic industry, are not objects of a high duty, i. e. books in foreign languages, and several kinds of the finer manufactures.

The *excise* is another branch of the federal revenue: let us enquire how far this may be used. Excise, properly speaking, is a duty laid on commodities of home-produce and general home-consumption, which are not absolutely necessaries of life. It is very convenient to the consumer, as he pays in piece-meal, and when he can best afford the expence; it may also be lessened by reducing the total consumption, If the excise on whiskey, i. e. is high, a person may buy a quart at a time, and save so many gallons in the year. But with all these advantages, the excise will probably not be so generally and in the same degree practicable in America, as it is in European countries. First. It must be laid with a gentle hand on the materials of the most important domestic manufactures, or on commodities which by affecting them and workmen in other respects, may considerably raise their price. Secondly. Some eatables and drinkables, which, at least as to quantity, may be called luxuries, are yet generally regarded as necessaries, and consequently as less proper objects of a productive excise, as beer, cyder, and butchers meat. Thirdly. As the great body of the people live in the country, there is but little buying and selling of provisions, in comparison with manufacturing and mercantile countries full of cities, towns and villages; therefore the excise cannot profit by the vast home-produce, and home-consumption of private families. Fourthly. It is doubtful how far the independent spirit of the Americans will, even in necessary cases, brook the troublesome and sometimes vexatious visits of excise-officers: at least, will this circumstance prevent any considerable excise within private families? Besides, such modes of taxation, would make the requisite number of collectors very expensive.

The excise upon the materials and manufacture of home-made fermented and spirituous liquors, amounted in England for the year which ended on the 5th of July, 1775, to the amazing sum of 3,341,837l. 9s. 9d. sterling: though it does not extend to beer brewed and liquors distilled in private families.[a] Of this the tax on cyder produced only 3083l. 6s. 8d.[b] In the United States, a sum proportional to the number of people could by no means be raised by this kind of excise. Beer is not yet of very general use, and wants encouragement: when it becomes a national drink, a great deal will probably be brewed in private country-families, as in the northern countries in Europe. The making of cyder will be altogether domestic, and by far the greater part consumed by the country people. The excise on ardent spirits will indeed be very beneficial, but not so productive as the convention of New-York seems to think, by their wish to grant the Congress this alone; because an high duty will hopefully render the use of this pernicious luxury very moderate; and because the number and conveniency of private stills will in a great measure elude the vigilance of most active excise-men.

I observe again, how little the conventions agree about the extent of a federal excise. Virginia and North-Carolina dislike it as much as direct taxes, am. 3. The minority of Maryland deem it worse, and call it *an odious tax* in the conclusion of their address.

As for other *duties*, which do not come under the description of impost or excise, Congress must also lay them with a discreet regard to a variety of circumstances. A duty on newspapers may hinder the general circulation of useful knowledge, and necessary political information. Duties on domestic articles of convenience and elegance, which at present are but in little demand, cannot be considerable without lessening still more the custom and profit on the respective mechanics, i. e. cabinet-makers, upholsterers, painters, silversmiths, &c. The various taxes on trinkets, ornaments, and amusements, which in most parts of Europe yield a great deal, will not in America do so, because of different manners, and less inequality of wealth.

It must then be pretty evident, that the federal revenue from impost, excise, and other duties, may in many cases be very limited by necessary circumstances and prudential considerations; and consequently, it is very improper to force the Congress into an immoderate pernicious use of these means, when direct taxes are more eligible: the Convention of New-Hampshire expressly forbids these, *until all other resources are* insufficient: that of Massachusetts and New-York only mention the impost and excise; but then the last would only allow the excise on distilled liquors.

I shall not enter into a detail of direct taxes, to discuss when or how they may be used; but only endeavour to remove an ill-founded aversion against them by these observations—There being collected with certainty, ease and less expence, is a great advantage: In cases when they cannot be exactly proportioned to the revenue of individuals, this inequality will be less felt in America: They will be apportioned among the states in fixed quotas according to the census mentioned in the constitution.

The general property of these taxes, that *they cannot be evaded*, is perhaps what most displeases individuals. But if we must pay taxes in one shape or another, and all upon the whole pay nearly their proportional part of the public expence, this reason is in a great measure visionary.

It must also be remarked that some kinds of direct taxes are inevitable only in certain civil transactions, consequently only temporary, and then in many cases proportionable to the value of the deeds.

(a) *Smith on the wealth of nations,*[2] 3 vol. p. 261.
(b) 38, 365.

1. Reprinted: *New York Daily Gazette,* 6 June 1789; North Carolina *Fayetteville Gazette,* 28 September; and in the March issue of the Philadelphia *American Museum.* For the authorship of the "Foreign Spectator" series, see the headnote to Essay No. I (21 October, BoR, III, 264n).

2. *An Inquiry into the Nature and Causes of the Wealth of Nations* by Adam Smith was first published in London in 1776.

Governor John Hancock: Draft of a Speech to the General Court c. 31 October 1788[1]

I have directed the Secretary to Lay before You the Letters of a public nature which I have received in the recess of the General Court. amongst them you will find one from the Secretary of Congress containing a notification that Congress have appointed a time and place for the meeting of a Congress under the Constitution of the United States and that they have also fixed upon a day for the appointment of the electors of a President and vice president.

The mode of this appointment as described in the Constitution has already received a different interpretation by two of the states;[2] it would have been well that the mode had been expressed in such technical and unequivocal Language as would have given a uniformity of practice in the whole nation but when the grant of power is doubtfully expressed, or a privilege referred it is in my opinion always safer to give the expression a Construction favourable to the rights of the people.

The deliberations upon these points are of the highest importance and will necessarily call forth the Exercise of all your candor & wisdom.

A decision agreeable to the True Spirit of the Constitution will give Strength to the Union; & increase the harmony of the States, cultivate those good affections amongst the Citizen which is at all times so necessary to their happiness and prosperity, and so much conducive to the good administration of the general Government.

The people have their Expectations Justly raised to the greatest political benefits which can result from a form of government and I am convinced that if the amendments proposed by the people of this state and attended to by those of the others should take place, we may feel ourselves assured of freedom & peace at home and respectability abroad.

I had the satisfaction to propose those amendments in the late Convention of this state. This was a pleasing part of my duty as a member and I feel myself obliged so far as my publick station will admit to use my endeavours that they should meet a candid and thorough investigation in Congress. it would be very fortunate if such measures should be adopted as would give the General Government all the Energy necessary to our National Interest, leave each State in the assured possession of proper & necessary powers and at the same Time secure to each individual his full share of Liberty as a subject.

Whatever I may find necessary in the Course of the session I shall communicate to you, and shall readily approve any measures by you adopted for the benefit of the Commonwealth.

1. Two copies of this address exist. The one printed here is in the Philip H. and A. S. W. Rosenbach Foundation in Philadelphia. The other is in the Hancock Papers, Division of Political History, Smithsonian Institution. Governor Hancock never delivered the speech. On 31 October, Secretary John Avery, Jr., informed the House of Representatives that Hancock "intended respectfully to have addressed the legislature, but was prevented by severe sickness, and that he had directed such papers as he had received during the recess to be laid before them . . . and that His Excellency would address the legislature in person as soon as his health would admit." The Senate received a similar message, along with the papers, which included Congress' Election Ordinance of 13 September, the amendments proposed by the Virginia, New York, and North Carolina conventions, and the New York Convention's circular letter). The Senate passed the papers on to the House (DHFFE, I, 477).

2. The states referred to are Pennsylvania and Connecticut. The Pennsylvania election law of 4 October provided for the popular election of Electors. The Connecticut legislature decided on 14 October "that the General Assembly of this State . . . [shall] choose Electors. . . ." See DHFFE, I, 300, II, 20.

A Friend to the People
Exeter, N.H., Freeman's Oracle, 1 November 1788 (excerpts)[1]

Messrs. Printers, . . . The amendments to the New Constitution is the most important object we are looking for, at the setling of the New Congress. *Vox Populi, est Vox Dei*—the voice of the people cry aloud for it. Every gentleman has a right to give his own sentiments—and his honor the Chief Justice [Samuel Livermore] delivered his in the Convention with a great degree of firmness, '*that the Constitution was now complete without any amendments,*'—if so, why should we send him to Congress to be an instrument to withhold from us the amendments so ardently wished for, and at the same time deprive us of a gentleman on the superior bench that time will scarce ever replace? Were I to recommend any person for the office of Senator, I should be careful to avoid any character who had a hand in framing the Constitution, as it is, in some measure, a child of their own making—consequently, they would wish to support it at any rate—witness the expression of a respectable character in the late Convention,² viz. *"that the Constitution was now complete—the amendments would not take place in five hundred years."*—On the other hand—I should avoid those who wish to destroy the whole. But take the middle path and choose some gentleman who wishes well to the whole community, and whose acquaintance and extensive knowledge will be serviceable in bringing about the amendments.

1. For the entire essay, see DHFFE, I, 776-77. For a response to this item, see "Friend to Amendments," Exeter, N.H., *Freeman's Oracle*, 8 November 1788 (BoR, III, 337-39).
2. Probably John Langdon.

James Madison to Edmund Randolph
New York, 2 November 1788 (excerpt)[1]

I recd. yesterday your favor of the 23d Ult.[2] The first countenance of the Assembly corresponds with the picture which my imagination had formed of it. The views of the greater part of the opposition to the fœderal Government, and particularly of its principal leader, have ever since the Convention, been regarded by me as permanently hostile, and likely to produce every effort that might endanger or embarrass it. The defects which drew forth objections from many quarters, were evidently of little consequence in the eye of Mr. H—ry. His own arguments proved it. His enmity was levelled, as he did not scruple to insinuate agst the *whole System*; and the destruction of the whole System, I take to be still the secret wish of his heart, and the real object of his pursuit. If temperate and rational alterations only were his plan, is it conceivable that his coalition and patronage would be extended to men whose particular ideas on the subject must differ more from his own than those of others who share most liberally in his hatred?

My last letter[3] with Col. Carrington's communications to which it referred, will have sufficiently explained my sentiments with regard to the Legislative Service under the new Constitution. My first wish is to see the Government put into quiet and successful operation; and to afford any Service, that may be acceptable from me, for that purpose. My second wish if that were to be consulted would prefer, for reasons formerly hinted, an opportunity of contributing that service in the House of Reps. rather than in the Senate; provided the opportunity be attainable from the spontaneous suffrage of the Constituents: Should the real friends to the Constitution think this preference inconsistent with my primary object, as Col. Carrington tells me is the case with some who are entitled to peculiar respect; and view my renouncing it as of any material consequence, I shall not hesitate to comply.[4]—You will not infer from the freedom with which these observations are made, that I am in the least unaware of the probability that whatever my inclinations or those of my freinds may be, they are likely to be of little avail in the present case. I take it for certain that a clear majority of the Assembly are enemies to the Govt. and I have no reason to suppose that I can be less obnoxious than others on the opposite side. An election into the Senate therefore can hardly come into question. I know also that a good deal will depend on the arrangements for the election of the other branch; and that much may depend moreover on steps to be taken by the Candidates which will not be taken by me. Here again therefore there must be great uncertainty, if not improbability of my election. With these circumstances in view, it is impossible that I can be the dupe of false calculations, even if I were in other cases disposed to indulge them. I trust it is equally impossible for the result whatever it may be, to rob me of any reflections which enter into the internal fund of comfort & happiness. Popular favor or disfavor, is no criterion of the character maintained with those whose esteem an honorable ambition must court. Much less can it be a criterion of that maintained with ones self. And when the Spirit of party directs the public voice, it must be a little mind indeed that can suffer in its own estimation, or apprehend danger of suffering in that of others. . . .

1. RC, Madison Papers, DLC. For the entire letter, see Rutland, *Madison*, XI, 328–30.
2. For this letter, see DHFFE, II, 264.
3. For Madison's 17 October letter to Randolph, see *ibid.*, 260.
4. See Edward Carrington to Madison, 19 October (BoR, III, 261–62).

James Madison to George Lee Turberville
New York, 2 November 1788 (excerpt)[1]

. . . You wish to know my sentiments on the project of another general Convention as suggested by New York. I shall give them to you with great frankness, though I am aware they may not coincide with those in fashion at Richmond or even with your own. I am not of the number if there be any such, who think the Constitution, lately adopted, a faultless work. On the contrary there are amendments wch. I wished it to have received before it issued from the place in which it was formed. These amendments I still think ought to be made according to the apparent sense of America; and some of them at least I presume will be made. There are others, concerning which doubts are entertained by many, and which have both advocates and opponents on each side of the main question. These I think ought to receive the light of actual experiment, before it would be prudent to admit them into the Constitution. With respect to the first class, the only question is which of the two modes provided be most eligible for the discussion and adoption of them. The objections agst. a Convention which give a preference to the other mode in my judgment are the following 1. It will add to the difference among the States on the merits, another and an unnecessary difference concerning the mode. There are amendments which in themselves will probably be agreed to by all the States, and pretty certainly by the requisite proportion of them. If they be contended for in the mode of a Convention, there are unquestionably a number of States who will be so averse and apprehensive as to the mode, that they will reject the merits rather than agree to the mode. A convention therefore does not appear to be the most convenient or probable channel for getting to the object. 2. A convention cannot be called without the unanimous consent of the parties who are to be bound by it, if first principles are to be recurred to; or without the previous application of ⅔ of the State legislatures, if the forms of the Constitution are to be pursued. The difficulties in either of these cases must evidently be much greater than will attend the origination of amendments in Congress, which may be done at the instance of a single State Legislature, or even without a single instruction on the subject. 3. If a General Convention were to take place for the avowed and sole purpose of revising the Constitution, it would naturally consider itself as having a greater latitude than the Congress appointed to administer and support as well as to amend the system; it would consequently give greater agitation to the public mind; an election into it would be courted by the most violent partisans on both sides; it wd. probably consist of the most heterogeneous characters; would be the very focus of that flame which has already too much heated men of all parties; would no doubt contain individuals of insidious views, who under the mask of seeking alterations popular in some parts but inadmissible in other parts of the Union might have a dangerous opportunity of sapping the very foundations of the fabric. Under all these circumstances it seems scarcely to be presumable that the deliberations of the body could be conducted in harmony, or terminate in the general good. Having witnessed the difficulties and dangers experienced by the first Convention which assembled under every propitious circumstance, I should tremble for the result of a second, meeting in the present temper of America, and under all the disadvantages I have mentioned. 4. It is not unworthy of consideration that the prospect of a second Convention would be viewed by all Europe as a dark and threatening Cloud hanging over the Constitution just established, and perhaps over the Union itself; and wd. therefore suspend at least the advantages this great event has promised us on that side. It is a well known fact that this event has filled that quarter of the globe with equal wonder and veneration, that its influence is already secretly but powerfully working in favor of liberty in France, and it is fairly to be inferred that the final event there may be materially affected by the prospect of things here. We are not sufficiently sensible of the importance of the example which this Country may give to the world: nor sufficiently attentive to the advantages we may reap from the late reform, if we avoid bringg. it into danger. The last loan in Holland and that alone, saved the U.S. from Bankruptcy in Europe; and that loan was obtained from a belief that the Constitution then depending wd. be certainly speedily, quietly, and finally established, & by that means put America into a permanent capacity to discharge with honor & punctuality all her engagements.

1. FC, Madison Papers, DLC. At the top of the letter, Madison noted: "Copy in substance of a letter to G. L. Turberville Esqr." For the entire letter, see Rutland, *Madison*, XI, 330–32. Madison is responding to Turberville's letter of 24 October (DHFFE, II, 266). Turberville wrote: "much talk of closing with New York in her proposal for a new convention prima facia—I see no impropriety in it."

Theodore Sedgwick to Alexander Hamilton
Boston, 2 November 1788[1]

In my last hasty letter,[2] I engaged to write you soon after my arrival in this town.—Various questions will be agitated in the legislature (of considerable magnitude) which respect the organization of the government. There is a party of federalists, who are of opinion that the electors should be chosen by the people, and the representatives not in districts but at large. These will be joined by all the antis probably. I yet hope they will not succeed. We yesterday committed to a committee of both houses the circular letter from your convention. The event is uncertain as a considerable number of federalists have been brought over to the amendment system, the prospect is not withstanding that the real friends of the constitution will prevail. every thing depends upon it; and the exertion will be proportionate to the magnitude of the object.—

Should the electors be chosen by the legislature, Mr. [John] Adams will probably combine all the votes of Massachusetts. I am very certain that the suggestion that he is unfriendly to General Washington is entirely unfounded. Mr. [John] Hancock has been very explicit in patronising the doctrine of Amendments. The other gentleman is for postponing the conduct of that business untill it shall be understood from experience.—

1. RC, Hamilton Papers, DLC.
2. For this letter of 16 October, see DHFFE, IV, 78.

Jeremiah Wadsworth to Henry Knox
Hartford, Conn., 2 November 1788 (excerpt)[1]

... [P.S.] My Cousin James & the rest of the Anties have lost all their influence in our Assembly & the Circular letter from N. York Convention had no other Notice taken of it Than to be read before both houses as all public letters are. no body dared to call it up to Notice— The Anties are making one more effort in the Election of Assembly Men for the new Congress—but will fail—

1. RC, Knox Papers, GL02437.04021, The Gilder Lehrman Collection, The Gilder Lehrman Institute of American History, at the New-York Historical Society. The letter is docketed as "Recd and answered the 5th Nov 1788."

Thomas Brand-Hollis to John Adams
The Hyde, Essex, England, 4 November 1788 (excerpt)[1]

Tho revelling in what you justly call luxury, planting and adorning the place round me, yet you have presented me with the highest luxury in producing a people emancipated and enjoying their natural rights under just & equal laws procured by your exertions.

Did envy enter into my composition you would have no small share of it. but my walk is humble and limited. I endeavour that the good is done but unconcerned who does it.

The more I consider the new constitution of America the more I rejoice and congratulate my self & you. it is the wisdom of ages reduced to practice.

Your writings[2] have pointed out the necessity of a balance in the legislature. by three independent equal branches & by just & equal representations of the people a total seperation of the executive from the legislative power & the judicial from both a free commonwealth will be established which mankind have never yet enjoyed.

a more perfect frame of government may be imagin'd but it is to be consider'd what the people of these times will bear & therefore this is highly to be esteemed and most desirable to be put in execution.

some minuter parts may be reconsidered and lead to more perfection.

By appointing a President Senate & assembly the convention has wisely secured this Balance By giving the President very considerable power, tho not absolute but guarded by deliberation & advisers most wisely & cautiously. perhaps in this we may not agree you may think more power necessary but recollect the constant abuse & tremble.

He has a senate to advise with, if not too numerous of which I have some fear at least may be the case sometime hence, is security to him and safety to the people. The president's power will not be improperly lessened, by his nominations to places & offices being approved by the Senate, for if he behaives well he will have friends, the danger is of too many.

The manner of electing the president tho very cautious & guarded is not clear & distinct & there appears some confusion in the language. Part of the representative being renewed every two years is most wise, Harringtonian & miltonic. The votes of the members being publickly register'd is too democratical even for me, for it may affect the freedom of votes. subjecting the members to party rage. would not instructing their representatives answer the purpose better?

if I remember right in the treaty between America & Prussia. no letters of marque were allowed.[3] it is to be lamented they are permitted by the new constitution. being contrary to the law of Christianity good Policy & a disgrace to human nature. The state alone should be enabled to conduct her own wars and not citizens make a trade of fighting against one another.

"Sunt et Belli, sicut pacis, jura justeque ea, non minus quam fortiter didicimus gerere." Liv.[4]

The suspension of the Habeas corpus cannot be too much guarded against. Liberty suffered in England during the late convulsion & had it not been for a rider tacked to the bill, the best citizens would have been liable to the greatest oppression.

Books should be free & exempted from any tax. to promote the erecting Libraries & as the means of knowledge & for the same reason printing types of all sorts & paper for printing & Ink till America can supply her self.

The Liberty of the press is not mentioned in the new constitution & tho all or most of the states insist on it yet in the new constitution it should appear as an additional star & not shining only in England. it is the Bulwark of Liberty which therefore Despots dread and permit not.

no tax on the postage of letters but what is necessary to bear the expence, which would be trifling, more prevents correspondence & communication of sentiments.

members of each house to have the priviledge of franking under some general line to prevent abuse....

1. RC, Adams Papers, MHi. For the entire letter, see the *Papers of John Adams*, XIX, 209-12. The Hyde was Hollis' estate in Essex, England.
2. A reference to Adams's *A Defence of the Constitutions.* See the headnote to CC:16 for more on *A Defence*.
3. Article 20 of the Prussian-American Treaty of 1785 prohibited letters of marque.
4. Quoted from Livy, *The History of Rome*, Book V, chapter 27, lines 6-7: "There are rights of war as well as of peace, and we have learnt to use them justly no less bravely" (B. O. Foster, *Livy With an English Translation in Fourteen Volumes* [Cambridge, Mass., and London, 1960], III, 94-95).

New York Antifederalist Society: Proceedings of a Meeting on Calling a Second Convention, New York, 4 November 1788[1]

(To the Counties within the State)
New York November 4th. 1788

Gentlemen,

The Circumstances and Situation of Things both before, and some time after, our Convention had met, warranted an universal Opinion among all Federal Republicans, that it was proper to adopt the new Constitution, only on Condition that those important Alterations, which were considered Necessary to the Protection of political and civil Liberty, should be made; and this was founded not only on the defects of the Constitution, but on the Anticipation that there would have been a Majority in several of the State Conventions of the same Sentiment with our own, from whom we should have derived Support; but in pursuing our Opposition in this Form, the Sentiments and Opinions of many in our Convention were changed, not, as we have reason to believe, as to the Principles of Opposition, but as to the expediency of adopting it under an Alteration of Circumstances, so that this State should continue in the Union; at the same time giving such Constructions to some of its Articles, and relying on the Sentiments of a Majority in the United States with Respect to an Opinion of its Defects, that the Government would be restrained in the exercise of its most offensive and dangerous Powers until a new Convention should have an Opportunity of reconsidering and revising it before it should have its full operation—This Alteration of Sentiment with respect to a conditional Adoption, and the Mode of adopting it in its present Manner, it is to be presumed was caused by the Reception of it by nine States successively, by which the Government was capable to be put in Operation, and likewise the immediate and subsequent Adoption of it by Virginia, perhaps one of the most influential and important States in the Union—The Confidence of those who were of these Sentiments, was excited because many of the most important States had acknowledged it by small Majorities, and almost all in such a Way as was expressive of its Defects, and hence they considered Amendments as certain, subsequent as precedent—Thus, unsupported by any of the States in the Prospect of a conditional Adoption, and for these Reasons, it became a political Calculation with them, whether it was not most for the Interest of this State, under all Circumstances, to continue in the Union, and trust, for the Reasons aforesaid, for Amendments: Unhappily this occasioned a Diversity of Opinion among our Friends in the Convention, who were for a conditional Adoption only—however, the Question, as you well know, was at last carried in the way it now Stands. Altho' a Division took place, both within, and without the Convention, on this Point, and for these Reasons, yet we hope that a Confidence remains on the Minds of all, that each was governed by the Principles of Rectitude, and that the Efforts and Exertions of each other collectively, as well as individually, will be considered as a Duty in future, and made use of to obtain the great Objects we have all had, and still have in View, to wit, the requisite Amendments, by having a general Convention called immediately, or as soon as possible after the Organization of the New Government.

With this design we conceive it will be very necessary to advert to the ensuing Election of Members to represent this State in the Assembly of the General Government, and to endeavour to elect such Characters who are in sentiment with us on the Subject of Amendments; nor is the Mode of Election a Matter of small Importance, when it is considered that one Mode may throw the Balance in the Hands of the Advocates of an arbitrary Government, while another may be favourable to equal Liberty.

The Activity and Duplicity of the principal of those who have contended for an unequivocal Adoption, and an uncontrouled Exercise of the New Constitution, notwithstanding their Promises to assist in procuring a Convention for the Purposes already mentioned, have given us just Causes of Suspicion, that those Promises were made with a View to deceive.

To facilitate a Communication of Sentiment and free Discussion on this Subject with you and our Friends in the other Counties, and thereby further the great Objects of our Pursuit, and oppose with success the subtle Practices of the Adversaries of constitutional Liberty, have induced us to form ourselves into a Society for the purpose of procuring a general Convention. Agreeable to the circular Letter of the late Convention of this State, and we beg leave to recommend to your Consideration the propriety of your joining together, without Delay, for the like Design.

We have only to add, that whatever diversity of sentiment may have taken place among the friends of equal Liberty in our late Convention, we are fully persuaded, that they will unite their utmost Exertions in the only mode that is now left, and should the present Opportunity which is now offered at the organization of the Government not be properly improved, it is highly probable such a favourable one will not be again presented, and the liberties of the People will then depend on the arbitrary Decrees of their Rulers.

In behalf of the Society &c

To Republican Committe[e] of Ulster ——— County &c }

(To the several states)

New York Novr. 4. 1788

Previous to the adoption of the new Constitution, a committee was formed in this place, of those who disapproved of it without essential amendments, to open a correspondence with those of the sister states who concurred with them in sentiment, to invite them to open a communication with us and concert an union of measures.[2] From the characters of a large majority of those who composed our conventions, we had reason to expect they would not have adopted the Constitution without stipulating for such previous amendments; and of this we advised our friends. Their proceedings, containing the amendments proposed, which we do ourselves the honor to inclose you, will justify this sentiment. A small majority, however, was found who were induced from ideas of political expediency to assent to a qualified adoption, in such a manner, as would admit this state into a participation of the government. It is not necessary to detail the reasons at large, nor whether they were well grounded, that influenced this measure. They may be briefly comprised in the following: A sufficient number of states had acceded to the government to authorize its going into operation; this being the case, it seems it was apprehended that the states who had adopted could not easily be prevailed upon to concur in any other mode to effect the requisite alterations, but the one pointed out in the Constitution itself. That if the state remained out of the Union, they might lose the opportunity of employing their influence in bringing them about. And from the dissatisfaction manifested by many of the states to the system as it stands, and from the spirit of accommodation which it was hoped would prevail among those who approved of it, they were induced to believe that a general agreement would take place to call another convention to consider and recommend amendments to the objectionable parts. Though these and similar reasons, we believe, influenced a majority to accede to the system with certain declarations and explanations; yet even this could not be obtained without an express declaration of their disapprobation of it, and agreeing to a circular letter,[3] inviting the other states to unite with ours in requiring a convention. In this both parties concurred unanimously.

We can with confidence assure you that the opposition to the Constitution without amendments has not decreased; but on the contrary, many of those who were zealous for its adoption declare they will unite their efforts in endeavoring to have it reconsidered. But we have reason, at the same time, to believe many of its most ardent advocates will use their influence and address to prevent this. It is, therefore, the more necessary that the friends of equal republican government should firmly unite in pursuing such measures, as will have a tendency to effect amendments.

For this purpose, a number of gentlemen in this city, influenced by a sincere regard for constitutional liberty and the public good, have associated under the name of a society for the purpose of procuring a general convention, agreeable to the circular letter of the late convention of this state; and have opened a correspondence with the several states, and with different parts of this state.

Notwithstanding so large a part of the citizens of the United States appear to be in sentiment, that it is necessary the Constitution should be altered in order to render the people happy, and their liberties secure under it; yet it is now too evident these alterations will not be obtained without great exertions and pains to awaken the attention of the people to their interests and safety. Associations of the well informed and patriotic gentlemen in the different parts of the country, we apprehend, will have the most salutary influence to effect so desirable an event; we therefore earnestly invite you to set this on foot and to open a correspondence with us.

We have only to add that whatever diversity of sentiment may have taken place among the friends of equal liberty in our late convention, we are fully persuaded that they will unite their utmost exertions to procure the amendments in the only mode that is now left. And should the present, opportunity, which is now offered at the organization of the government, not be properly improved, it is highly probable such a favorable one will not be again presented; and the liberties of the people will then depend on the arbitrary decrees of their rulers.

In behalf &c

1. MS, John Lamb Papers, NHi. For the full meeting and proceedings of the Society from 30 October to 13 November, see RCS:N.Y., 2475–80.
2. See the headnote to George Mason to John Lamb, 9 June (BoR, III, 51n–53n).
3. For the New York Convention's circular letter of 26 July 1788, see BoR, I, 153–58.

Foreign Spectator V
Philadelphia Federal Gazette, 4 November 1788[1]

REMARKS *on the Amendments to the Federal Constitution, proposed by the Conventions of Massachusetts, New-Hampshire, New-York, Virginia, South and North-Carolina, with the minorities of Pennsylvania and Maryland, by a* FOREIGN SPECTATOR.

NUMBER V.

It remains to prove, that a discretionary power to make use of direct taxation, will enable Congress to do justice to the respective states, by dividing the total federal expence among them in the most equitable manner that is practicable. The new federal government is in some degree national, and its energy depends on this very quality, as I observed in the second number.[2] Accordingly the federal revenue is partly raised from individuals, and partly from the states. What is collected in the first way, goes into the federal treasury without any enquiry how much was gathered in this or that state. What is obtained in the second mode by direct taxes, whether by requisition or otherwise, is placed to the credit of the respective states; so that if any state pays more or less than its quota determined by the number of representatives, it draws back the surplus, or makes up the deficiency. The great object of the union, which nearly concerns every individual, is defence against foreign and internal enemies. On this depend greatly all the enjoyments of domestic and civil life. Perpetual peace, or protection in case of an inevitable war, is merely with regard to property, an eminent blessing, which every wise man would gladly purchase by six per cent. of all his yearly revenue. In this view, every federal citizen will cheerfully, by a direct personal contribution, support that federal government by which alone he can be protected. The various modes of *impost, excise and other duties,* will also, if well contrived, affect individuals in a pretty equitable proportion. Those who buy foreign articles of luxury, on which the impost is high, are comparatively rich. They pay also a sort of fine for sending their money abroad, when they might benefit their fellow-citizens by a domestic expenditure. Great consumers of domestic luxuries are also more wealthy than others who must be contented with necessaries: If those commodities are noxious by excess, as spirituous liquors, or otherwise less useful to the community, the higher excise operates likewise as a satisfaction for what in some degree is wrong. The same reasoning is applicable to other duties.

By these means, the wealthier part of the federal citizens throughout the continent pay more than an equal number of others; and so far as any state has a proportionably greater number of those, it contributes more than a less wealthy sister state. This is also reasonable, because the defence of the confederacy depends not only on property, but on the number of fighting men, which may be equal in less opulent states; and because these have less property to defend.

But on the other hand, it may also be equitable, that the states should pay a part of the federal revenue by quotas proportioned to the number of people; a standard preferable to extent of territory, or any other valuation of property. First, the wealth of a state cannot, without some limitation and exception, be estimated by its quota of the impost, excise, and other duties. The United States are all agricultural: some are also in a higher degree commercial and manufacturing; and these consume articles that pay duties much beyond their proportion of real wealth. Compare a tradesman in Philadelphia with a farmer in some remote county, who upon the whole makes an equal annual expence. The one buys almost every thing, the other very little. As to foreign goods, the citizen really wants several things for his trade: he makes more use of those articles of dress, which, at least at present, must be imported, because the general ideas of decency forbid a reputable person to appear in a croud with a ragged coat or in too light a dishabille:[3] he sups and breakfasts on tea, coffee, or chocolate, partly because mush and milk, &c. would cost nearly as much, and partly from custom, which, though perhaps blameable, yet cannot soon be laid aside, and certainly is not an object of an immoderate impost, that would be a real penalty. If an excise is laid on beer, cyder, meat, and other native commodities, it falls much heavier on the citizen, than on the farmer; who, tho' he may pay a part of it on what he sells, by the consequential fall of the price, yet pays nothing for the great consumption of his family. Drawing this comparison on the great scale of cities and counties, we see clearly that a state of landed wealth contributes below its proportion in the impost, excise, and some other duties.

Secondly. As by the constitution, all duties, imposts, and excises must be uniform through the United States, and as commodities but little used in one state may be of general use in another, this condition, though very equitable, will yet limit this resource of Congress, by obliging them to select such duties, imposts, and excises, which jointly may produce the most equitable contribution. If these are not sufficient, it is much better to employ direct taxes, than by straining the others to lay the burden very unequal. Without going into a detail, this reasoning seems well founded on the known difference of the states in climate, productions and manners.

A perfect system of taxation is a work of the greatest difficulty in any country, because an hundred different things are so interwoven, as to act and re-act upon each other in all directions, and with degrees of force that elude all nice calculation. This difficulty is encreased in the federal system, partly from its double action on individuals, and on the states; and partly from the novel and unsettled finance of the United States. But this system is formed on great and reciprocal concessions between the sister states for the common welfare, and it grants the Congress this great variety of resources, in order to choose those which are most equitable and beneficial. By a proper management, the resources of an extensive and fertile country, are amply sufficient to all the exigencies of the union and of the states. The same persons who, as members of Congress, lay federal taxes, have, as individuals and citizens of the respective states, great and permanent interests to guard. It is therefore an excellent quality in the federal system of revenue, that it can be lightened or loosened, so as to embrace every part, and not press hard upon any one. At the same time, this very quality requires a disinterestedness, equity, mildness and generosity, from all the parties concerned, without which it would be a source of constant embarrassment. May then the federal people be good and wise! If by an effectual, yet easy revenue, national independence, liberty, and property can be secured, how unreasonable must it be, to dispute about paying a trifle more or less.

1. Reprinted: *New York Daily Gazette*, 8 June 1789; North Carolina *Fayetteville Gazette*, 5 October; and in the March issue of the Philadelphia *American Museum*. For the authorship of the "Foreign Spectator" series, see Essay No. I (21 October, BoR, III, 264n).
2. See BoR, III, 285–89.
3. "A garment worn in undress; a dress or costume of a negligent style" (OED).

From Collin McGregor
New York, 5 November 1788 (excerpt)[1]

... I find you wish to have my opinion respecting the New Constitution.—I am clearly of the mind that it will be the means of ensuring a general Confidence in the people, give Security to Property & enhance its' value, afford protection to Trade & fix it on a permanent footing; prove an effectual barrier agt. all ex post facto, & other dishonest Laws; And in short, I think it is Calculated in every Sense to promote the welfare & Secure the Interests of those under its' Dominion. Much however depends on the temperate Zeal & prudent Conduct of the first Congress; for should divisions take place at the outset, many are they who will avail themselves of every seeming inconsistency in order to weaken & in fact destroy the fabric which has been so lately raised with so much difficulty, for their intended Government.—By these people I mean those who were opposed to the New System, and who are now busying themselves, to obtain Amendments at the first meeting of Congress.—These amendments no doubt will be taken up; but few if any will be Seriously attended to, as most of them have *local views* towards the partial Interest of the States which propose them.— To appease the clamour of opposition something will be done; But not to injure the founding principles of the Constitution.—

When I give so flattering an opinion of the New Constitution, I cannot allow myself to think but that ample justice will be rendered betwixt of every denomination Debtor & Creditor.—There will be a head power sufficient to enforce Laws, and prevent the Individual States from doing any thing derogatory to the principles of justice & Equity.—indeed, the Powers left wt the States will be so trifling that there is really nothing to fear from them. . . .

1. FC, Collin McGregor Letterbook, 1788–1789, NN.

Massachusetts Centinel, 5 November 1788[1]

The ANTIFEDERALISTS, alias AMENDMENTITES, may fitly be compared to the Israelitish Spies, who brought up an evil report of the land of Canaan[2]—The VIGOUR and ENERGY of the System, which will undoubtedly destroy the spirit of Anarchy and Confusion, Roguery, Paper Money, and Tender Laws, are the GIANTS, the sons of Anak, which these traitors saw.

The Continental system being adopted, the friends of America anticipate the blessings of GOOD GOVERNMENT from its administration— pray Heaven, they may not be disappointed—but the *leaven* of antifederalism is still fermenting, and under the cloak of amendments, there may be danger of introducing characters into the Federal Legislature, who may by their incompetency to *great objects*, and their *little, mischievous* talents at embarrassing what they do not understand, so far defeat our just expectations, as to sanction the declamations of the enemies to the system.—For, reasoning from *experience*, the people may very easily be persuaded to think the Constitution a bad one, should they fail to realize the advantages from it, which its advocates, have so sanguinely predicted.

1. Reprinted: *Pennsylvania Packet*, 18 November; and *Pennsylvania Journal*, 19 November.
2. For the twelve Israelite spies sent to Canaan, see Numbers 13:1–33 and Deuteronomy 1:22–40.

Lucullus
Pennsylvania Gazette, 5 November 1788 (excerpts)[1]

To the FREEMEN *of* PENNSYLVANIA.

FRIENDS *and* COUNTRYMEN,
You will be called upon, on the last Wednesday of the present month, to give your votes for *eight* persons to represent you in the legislature of the United States.
You never were called upon to exercise the privilege of electing rulers upon a more important occasion. Two tickets will be offered to you. The one will contain men, who will support the new constitution in its present form; the other ticket will contain men, who will overset the government under the specious idea of *amending* it. . . .
. . . Remember, friends and countrymen, that on your success in the ensuing election will depend the liberties of America. Be wise—be active—and you cannot fail of being free and happy. . . .

1. Reprinted: Philadelphia *Federal Gazette*, 6 November; New York *Independent Journal*, 8 November; *Neue Unpartheyische Lancaster Zeitung*, 19 November. "Lucullus" was probably written by Benjamin Rush. For a response to "Lucullus," see "Centinel" XXII, Philadelphia *Independent Gazetteer*, 14 November (BoR, III, 348–49).

Virginia Independent Chronicle, 5 November 1788

Extract of a letter from a Correspondent.
"The circular letter from Poughkeepsie[1] has, at last taken a turn this way—It tells us many incredible things; but allowing many to be against the Fœderal Constitution in the state of New-York—Let us enquire into the cause—There are in that state many men in high stations, possessed of great salaries, from £. 2000 and downward—Their connexions, and other expectants of such places, have exerted their utmost diligence to mislead many honest, well-meaning men, though little acquainted with matters of government and politics, and to prejudice them against the Fœderal Constitution.
"It is their invincible reluctance to separate from, or part with their pre-eminence and salaries, which has brought on those men, their apprehensions, their disapprobation, and their want of inclination to support the Fœdral Constitution—Had the Constitution come from Heaven, the case would have been the same, as it operates so much against the private interest of men of dignity and great salaries.
"Under pretence of obtaining the confidence, the approbation and support of these good men, whom they have misled, they have the modesty to dictate to the rest of the American States, and aver that nothing but calling another general convention, with the greatest pre-

cipitation, will quiet the apprehensions of those worthy men whose principles they have poisoned.

"Now, Sir, with submission to the public, I will take upon me to point out a way, by which the apprehensions of these men may be removed, and their confidence obtained with more certainty than by calling a convention at present, which appears to me to be premature—that is only to have the government organized—the wheels put in motion—the Constitution will then recommend itself; if we are so happy as to have men of tolerable capacity, great integrity, and firmly attached to the general interests of America, in the administration.

"The Gentlemen misled, will be agreeably surprised to see the matters of government proceed so easily and equitably under the constitution, and will hold the persons in great contempt who had misled them.

"There are Gentlemen in the state of New-York of great political talents, and of great worth, who can be as serviceable in the general government, as any men in America—It is impossible they could have a hand in forming that farrago ushered into the world under the name of amendments—satisfied with having obtained the ratification of the Constitution—they have indulged the gentlemen in opposition with an opportunity of displaying their political abilities; and lo! *Parturiuns mantes I.*[2]

"If the circular letter came out with a good intention, there is great room to suspect it.

"It is calculated to throw obstacles in the way of government, to raise the passions of male-contents, which had subsided:—To revive the hopes of men in desperate circumstances, who would rather choose anarchy, than to live under a well regulated government.

"It is to be hoped that Gentlemen in the administration, will have the firmness enough to give the Constitution fair play.

"Experience is the mistress of things; during administration. The defects, if any, will after a short time plainly appear. The remedy can then be applied with more certainty, and when they do appear is the proper time to incorporate and establish amendments in a constitutional manner.

"Some men suspect that want of energy is one of the greatest defects in the Constitution: But speculative opinions in government avail little.—What politician, or what statesman, could have believed that the Romans would have prospered, under such a medley of a Constitution—Their Leges, or acts of the Centurians, their plebesula, or votes of the Tribes—Their Senators, Consuls or decrees of the Senate, interfered with one another, and the conduct of each to the other would have arrested the wheels of government. But they were so happy in almost continued succession of great statesmen, and great warriors, firmly attached to the interest of their country, that this seldom or ever happened, but once, during the time that the Plebeians contended for a share in the Consulship. There happened then an enterregnum or suspension of government for five years; which at last the Plebeians carried their point, chiefly by the interest of a Patrician lady."

1. For the New York circular letter, see BoR, I, 153–58.
2. Latin: "the mountains are in labor." It can be found in Horace, *Ars Poetica or Epistle to the Pisos*, line 139 (H. Rushton Fairclough, ed. and trans., *Horace: Satires, Epistles and Ars Poetica* [Cambridge, Mass., and London, 1956], 462, 463).

Coxe and Frazier to Wilson and Boyd
Philadelphia, 6 November 1788 (excerpt)[1]

... We learn the Legislature of Virginia appear very unfriendly, but as there will be a new house in the Spring, we hope this do not express the Sentiments of the people. They will give us probably two antifl. Senators We are not yet quite out of Danger yet it is to be feared—

1. FC, Coxe Paper, Series I, Volumes and Printed Material, Coxe and Frazier American Letterbook, PHi.

Honestus
Boston Independent Chronicle, 6 November 1788 (excerpt)[1]

Mess'rs. ADAMS & NOURSE, Every friend to America must contemplate with the highest satisfaction, the present favourable moment, which affords these States an opportunity to work out their political salvation. If ever a people were blessed with a prospect of establishing their national happiness, the inhabitants of these States may justly claim this peculiar indulgence. The hearty union of sentiment which has prevailed throughout the whole Confederacy, during the decision of a question of the greatest importance, is a pleasing presage of those blessings so eagerly expected from the adoption of the new system of government. It is an event, but little short of miraculous, that so great a spirit of harmony, should prevail throughout the several States, on the promulgation of the Constitution;—that the Conventions, should so nearly join in sentiment in the essentials of their propositions; and the pleasure is doubly heightened, when we reflect, that the government of so extensive a country, is originally founded on the basis of PEACE and GOOD WILL towards all mankind!

Thank Heaven, this is our highly favoured state! We have every happiness to hope for, from these pleasing circumstances. In this situation, when every measure has been thus far conducted with harmony; when the northern and southern States are uniting in interest and connection; when the prospect of extending our commerce is enlivening—amidst such a multiplicity of favourable occurrences, what says the voice of prudence and concord? Does it not urge us to cement every tie of friendship?—To enlarge the bonds of amity, and by every means in our power, to strengthen that chain of union, which has hitherto held us together?

If the propositions made by the States, would have the most distant tendency to weaken the energy of our government, we might have reason to contemn them; but as they cannot by any construction whatever, destroy its efficiency—the ill-policy of not attending to them, must therefore be evident to every rational mind. On the contrary, they serve to give strength and stability to the whole system, by explaining those parts which are ambiguous, and which may occasion (unless thus explained) some future litigations by their construction, which can be of no real advantage to the body of the people, however it may help a few individuals. The objects aimed at by them are general, no State or individual is particularly benefited; but every part of the Constitution stands equally permanent in every essential, requisite to the important purposes of its establishment.

This being the case, why is this hesitancy with respect to complying with them? Why this backwardness in attending to them? Are not the objects of our *union*, when they can be obtained on such easy terms, worthy of our attention? Is not our *commerce* with the southern States of such importance, as to urge us into such measures as will have a tendency to establish it on a lasting basis? If it is probable, that these amendments so earnestly urged by the several Conventions, will have this effect; and if at the same time, the vigor and energy of our government remain *more secure,* than in its present state—is it not the height of ill-policy, to neglect such important considerations? Do not such *over zealous* persons betray a want of federal sentiments? Are they not inimical to our real interest? Or rather do they not by such *obstinate* conduct, endanger that cordial disposition, which now so happily prevails throughout the Continent? *The preservation of our present union, is of more benefit to the commerce of these States, than the adopting of ten times the number of similar amendments could operate to the injury of the government.*

We are told that the amendments are of no consequence; but whether they are or not, the most important States in the whole Confederacy have by their resolves represented them as essential. If they are of no importance, we certainly act a most inconsistent part to reject them, when such valuable purposes may be answered by adopting them; every thing receives its value from opinion; it is the opinion of the people that they are of importance, consequently they ought to be attended to with the greatest impartiality.

Notwithstanding the union which prevails among the body of the people, yet it is our misfortune to be hampered by individuals, in the several States, who are acting altogether in the extremes:—One side is for carrying their measures, without any attention whatever to the disposition of the people; while the other seems anxious to level all distinctions, and reduce the government to a state of anarchy and confusion.—Either of these violent parties are dangerous to be trusted; as both of them, if permitted to pursue their plans, would ever keep these States in a violent agitation. But at this important period, when every thing depends on our prudence—we require men who are cool in their deliberations, and firm in their decisions; who will pay a regard to the just representations of the people—and at the same time will be resolute to suppress every measure which may tend to weaken the laws of the country. This happy medium of conduct is now requisite; the high partizan of either side ought to be avoided; by this means we should give vigor to our government, as the interest of the people would then be the sole object of our legislators. Party views and measure would have no influence in our national concerns, but every proceeding would be the result of the most candid and unbiased deliberations....

1. Reprinted: Philadelphia *Independent Gazetteer*, 11 December. For the authorship of the "Honestus" essays, see BoR, III, 302n–3n, note 1.

Foreign Spectator VI
Philadelphia Federal Gazette, 7 November 1788[1]

REMARKS *on the Amendments to the Federal Constitution, proposed by the Conventions of Massachusetts, New-Hampshire, New-York, Virginia, South and North-Carolina, with the minorities of Pennsylvania and Maryland, by a* FOREIGN SPECTATOR.

NUMBER VI.

We proceed to consider the amendments that regard the military power of the federal government. It is pleasing to find that the states of Massachusetts and South-Carolina are entirely silent on this important subject:—They having wisely reflected, that although a friend may possibly point that weapon to my breast, which I give him to defend me against an assassin, yet it would be absurd either to tye his right arm, or to give him only half a sword; especially when I am well armed myself. The conventions of Virginia, New-York and North-Carolina, request by the 9th, 7th, and 9th amendment respectively, "*that no standing army or regular troops shall be raised or kept up in time of peace, without the consent of two-thirds of the members present in both houses.*" The convention of New-Hampshire requires, the "*consent of three quarters of the members of each branch of Congress,*" am. 10. The minority of Pennsylvania declare in the 7th part, that "*as standing armies in time of peace are dangerous to liberty, they ought not to be kept up;*" that of Maryland will allow it on the same condition with the three first mentioned conventions, 4th am.

The expression '*time of peace,*' is very equivocal: Does it mean any time previous to a declaration of war? that whatever hostile intentions any powers may betray, or whatever formidable preparations they may carry on by sea and land, Congress must not raise a single battalion, until the enemy falls like a thunder-storm on some part of the union? It would be an unpardonable affront to suppose any American of common sense capable of such irrational language; to make him say it is time enough to raise troops, when Philadelphia, New-York, Charleston is taken—when two or three thousand of the militia, who made head against a superior force, are cut to pieces—when the enemy has laid the country under contribution, and committed ravages far and near—when my father or brother is killed or taken. I repeat again, it would be the grossest insult to deem any federal citizen capable of such sentiments. The restriction, then, only means that when there is no danger of war, no regular troops shall be kept up. But who shall be a judge of this? what symptoms of danger shall be prescribed? Is it expected that any foreign power will give us notice, that next year, or in six months, they intend to come with fifty thousand men to cut our throats, and waste our country with fire and sword? So much politeness is not yet fashionable. It is rather esteemed very clever to dart upon you like a tyger, when you least expect it; and ten to one but you receive extraordinary caresses, assurances of eternal friendship, &c. &c. just before your property and blood is demanded. If you complain of unfair dealing, they will laugh in your face, and call you a fool for not *knowing mankind better.* You think I speak of the savages? No; I mean all your good brethren of Adam's race, including the most polite nations of Europe. As for those blood-hounds of the wilderness, that have scalped and burnt so many families, I hope to God there is none among us so base and cruel as hereafter to begrudge the defenceless women and children a protection from the horrid tomahawk and the lingering fire.

The words *army or regular troops* being applicable to small numbers, extend the restriction even to the necessary garrisons, and to any military corps which may be wanted on the frontiers.

As America is happily situated so far from Europe, and will hopefully be wise enough not to involve herself in the vortex of European politics, she cannot often have occasion for a great body of regular troops, provided the militia is under good regulations; at the same time, as the congress may be under necessity of making considerable preparations of defence some time before an inimical power has taken off the mask, and unsheathed the sword, a restriction, *when or in what degree to arm,* would be pernicious. The constitution has already enacted, that *no appropriation of money for the raising and supporting of an army shall be for a longer time than two* years, 1st art. 8th sec. 12, a limatation in fact very strict, because if ever a formidable enemy should invade the United States, he may not be expelled in that time; especially as the federal army must be supported some time before it can begin to act.

On every important affair the national council ought to be nearly unanimous, because the want of wisdom or virtue is unpardonable; a minority of one fourth itself should not exist. But how far something more than a bare majority may be constitutionally required, is a delicate question. In all cases when precipitancy is more dangerous than delay, it is prudent to fix a surplus of majority according to circumstances. The present case I apprehend is quite the reverse—If the country is not in a proper state of defence, it will the sooner invite an enemy, opens its bosom to him, and may receive a dangerous wound before the arms can ward off the stroke; but all the disadvantage of collecting an army of perhaps 10 or 15,000 men without eminent necessity, is to impose some new taxes, which can never be oppressive, as the greatest part of the money is directly laid out in the country. As to any danger to liberty from such an army, it is altogether visionary; and it is needless to repeat what has been so often said on that subject. While the people have property, arms in their hands, and only a spark of a noble spirit, the most corrupt congress must be mad to form any project of tyranny.

This fair statement of the matter might dispense me from answering the question, why should not two-thirds of the congress agree in raising regular troops, if it really is necessary? Why do you surmise that a bare majority of congress would form the wicked absurd scheme of enslaving the country? Is not this much more improbable? But as the subject will bear a full examination, I shall take it up with a candid freedom. Two-thirds of both houses may not agree in timely measures of defence for these reasons—First, the natural indolence of individuals and public bodies is averse from any troublesome enterprise while it possibly can be avoided. The national character of America is also rather too easy than rash, and besides much influenced by the peaceable spirit of a republic, intent on agriculture and trade. The apparant security of local situation, the plausible reasonings of the minority, and the fear of displeasing a part of the people by a demand of supplies, will co-operate with this indolence in many well disposed minds. Secondly. As property and pecuniary interest is rather over-valued by too many, perhaps even some delegates in congress may not consider, that gold must be defended by steel; that honor and humanity forbid a true American to expose his country to disgrace, and his fellow-citizens to danger; that a single drop of patriotic blood should not be sold to keep a dollar more in all the pockets through the United States. Thirdly. A numerous and in many respects estimable denomination is religiously prejudiced against even defensive war; some of these may be members of congress, or influence its decisions in critical times. Fourthly. If corruption should ever taint any members of the federal council, it will be most dangerous under the venerable form of public spirit. The man, who in flaming colours paints a small American army as the execrable tools of traiterous tyrants, may be the very person who lets loose an host of enemies on the vitals of his native land. A time may come when some hostile power will pay a vote against raising an army with 10,000 *l.* Fifthly. As by the advantage of local situation and domestic resources, some of the states may suffer less from the eventual calamities of war, they may be less affected by the real magnitude of danger. Such a selfish disposition of only one or two may prevent the consent of two-thirds in both houses, and is more probable than treason in more than one half of congress.

1. Reprinted: *New York Daily Gazette*, 9 June 1789; North Carolina *Fayetteville Gazette*, 12 October; and in the April issue of the Philadelphia *American Museum.* For the authorship of the "Foreign Spectator" series, see Essay No. I (21 October, BoR, III, 264n).

A Friend to Liberty and Union
Philadelphia Federal Gazette, 7 November 1788[1]

Mr. BROWN. The clandestine manner, in which the enclosed address has been communicated to the inhabitants of the interior counties, furnishes proof, beyond contradiction, that this political poison was intended to operate its baneful effects, in places where the antidotes of truth and information could not be administered. It is the nature of falshood to shrink from enquiry, and it has been the unvaried practice of the *designing few,* in Pennsylvania, who are opposed to the happiness of CONFEDERATED AMERICA, to conduct their schemes of political rapine and murder, with the secrecy of thieves and assassins. The dark lanthorn, and the *dagger,* are the means best suited to effect their purpose. But the light of truth, and the arm of freedom, shall watch over and defend the FEDERAL CONSTITUTION, against all the attacks of either open or insidious enemies; nor, until the name of *Bryan* shall be more grateful to the ear of a Pennsylvanian than that of the illustrious WASHINGTON, will the specious deceptions, set forth in the following address, be permitted to prevail against the moral and political truths contained in the FEDERAL CONSTITUTION.

No American, who wishes the prosperity of his country, can think of sending men into the federal house of representatives, who are the *avowed enemies* of that system on which the duration, dignity, and happiness of the union, essentially depend. Let no such men be trusted.

A Friend to Truth and Freedom.

To the FREEMEN of PENNSYLVANIA.

Friends and Countrymen,

A FELLOW-CITIZEN, who is impressed with real anxiety at the approaching crisis of our public affairs, begs leave to address a few words to you.

Whilst the enterprising and ambitious are pressing forward to the harvest of office and emolument, which they promise themselves under the new constitution, he freely resigns all hopes of private advantage from the government, and feels no other interest than that which every citizen ought to feel, in the misfortunes or prosperity of his country. He expects no benefit from the administration of public affairs; but that which every individual will share in common with himself: he fears no misfortunes but those, which will equally affect every member of the community. With these views and motives which are alike interesting to every good citizen, he flatters himself he shall be heard with attention.

⟨Liberty was the avowed object of the late glorious revolution, in search of which we waded with patience and resolution, through all horrors of a civil war; and the constitutions of the several states were framed with admirable wisdom, according to the best models, and upon the noblest principles of civil liberty. One only defect remained. The general government of the continent, under the late articles of confederation, was too feeble to secure the safety of the people. Its defects were evident; and yet, as if by a studied contrivance, they were suffered to remain, with hardly an attempt to remedy them, until the public affairs of the continent had sunk into utter imbecility and ruin. The cry, at length, for a new form of continental government, became loud and universal.

A continental convention was called; the hopes of the people were raised to the highest pitch of expectation, and the sun never beheld a more glorious opportunity of establishing a happy form of government.

Nothing short of the most glaring defects could have excited any shadow of opposition. But it is to be feared, some selfish and artful men amongst us were but too willing to avail themselves of so favourable an opportunity of consulting the profit and power of the future governors of the continent, at the expence of the liberties of the people. Whether, however, it was the effect of accident or design, most glaring defects appear in the constitution which they have proposed to the people. These defects have been freely stated by writers in the public papers, throughout the continent, as well as in the debates of the several state-conventions. Indeed many of these defects seem now to be generally acknowledged, even by those men who, there is to much reason to fear, would still wish to evade their amendment and to retain them in the system. Some of these defects are very glaring and import: others perhaps, in the heat of contention have been exaggerated. One or two of the most considerable, I shall attempt briefly to lay before you.

The future congress, if the new constitution be not amended, will be vested with unlimited powers: the state governments which have been founded on the most excellent constitutions in the world, will crumble into ruin or dwindle into shadows, and, in their stead, an enormous unwieldy government will be erected, which must speedily fall to pieces by its own weight, and leave us to the wretched alternative of anarchy or tyranny: whereas by a due temperature, the continental government may be cloathed with all necessary powers, for the management of foreign affairs, and leave the state governments in possession of such powers, as will enable them to regulate our internal concerns, which a continental government can never effectually reach. It is just as absurd to suppose, that the general government of the whole empire can regulate the internal police of the several states, as to believe that the several states could regulate our foreign trade, and protect us in our intercourse with foreign nations. The latter we have already tried without success: the former will be found equally impracticable.

Another defect in the federal constitution is equally alarming. No security is provided for the rights of individuals; no bill of rights is framed, nor is any privilege of free men secured from the invasion of the governors. Trust me, my fellow citizens! we shall not be more powerful or more respected abroad, for being liable to oppression at home; but on the contrary, the freest states have been ever the most powerful. Yet with us no barriers will remain against slavery, under the new continental government, if it be not amended: the state governments, by the express terms of the constitution, can afford no protection to their citizens, and not even a single right is defined or stipulated, which the subject may appeal to against the will and pleasure of the moment.)

These circumstances and others of a like tendency, have excited great opposition; but the absolute necessity of a continental government of some sort, has silenced the opposition of those, who were dissatisfied with the present constitution, first in the continental convention, and afterwards in most of the conventions of the states. The wiser, if not the major part of the continental convention, would have produced to us a much better form of continental union, had it been in their power; but they preferred this to none, and, in the different states, the wisest and best of the people have acquiesced in the scheme of adopting it in its present form, from the hope of obtaining those amendments, which the constitution itself has provided for the attaining: provided two-thirds of congress, or two-thirds of the state legislatures, shall concur in requiring them. Without such a clause of obtaining amendments, there is little doubt but a majority of the freemen of America, would have spurned at the idea of subjecting themselves to the other terms of the new constitution: with this clause of obtaining amendments, it has become the duty of good citizens to make a beginning with the constitution as it is, confiding in the hope of obtaining all essential amendments in a constitutional mode. In this mode which is provided, it is certainly more eligible to reform the constitution, than by any violent or irregular opposition to attempt to overthrow it. We must have a continental government, or we are an undone people: at the same time, we ought to preserve our liberties, if possible, so far as they may consist with our essential protection. If these two points can be attained, and this extensive continent held together, in the course of a few years, we may, at once, be the greatest and happiest people on earth.[2]

Impressed with these sentiments, and in the hope of reconciling the wishes of all parties, which, on the present question, we trust, when fairly explained, are more nearly the same, than possibly were those of any people, who, by the arts of intriguing men, were ever set at variance, a large number of the freemen of Pennsylvania have, without noise or disturbance, resolved to invite their fellow-citizens to accord with their inclinations, which they trust are the inclinations of a great majority of the freemen of this state. They wish most ardently for a continental union and a continental government, upon free principles.—They wish to set the proposed government in motion: but they wish for amendments. They think that the strength of this great continent may be exerted, without impairing the private and essential rights of the meanest individual. They have therefore opened a communication with the different parts of the state; they have conferred freely together; they have corresponded: and the purpose of their investigation has been to discover men to represent them in congress, who will give their aid to the effectuating the great object of the late continental convention, that of promoting a continental government for the purpose of uniting our strength, and at the same time of securing the liberties of the subject. In a word, of carrying into execution the new government, and at the same time amending it.

In consequence of this communication, it became necessary to think of forming a ticket, to represent this state in Congress, of such men as would concur in carrying these views into effect; and great care has been taken in the choice of such men, as it was supposed, would at once concur in federal measures and accord with the different particular interests of which this state is composed. However frivolous this latter idea may appear, and however plausibly it may sound, to talk of choosing the best men, without regard to nation or distinction, yet to Pennsylvanians the precaution will appear to be far from being unnecessary. We have great confidence in their abilities and integrity, and we trust that they will all concur in promoting the real interests of this state and the United States. Such as are friends to the new constitution, and at the same time wish for amendments, it is hoped will unite their suffrages with ours.

The following are the gentlemen whose names will be run in our ticket.

WILLIAM FINDLEY,
CHARLES PETTIT,
Gen. WILLIAM IRVINE,
ROBERT WHITEHILL,

WILLIAM MONTGOMERY,
BLAIR M'CLENACHAN,
DANIEL HIESTER,
PETER MUHLENBERG.

The friends of this ticket are desired to remember that this election is for the whole state, and that however numerous or few may be its friends in particular districts, every vote will count one, and not one should omit voting who can possibly attend.—The liberties of our country are at stake.

A FRIEND TO LIBERTY AND UNION.

1. Reprinted: Philadelphia *Independent Gazetteer,* 12 November; Philadelphia *Freeman's Journal,* 12 November; *Pennsylvania Packet,* 14 November; Pennsylvania *Carlisle Gazette,* 19 November; *Neue Unpartheyische Lancaster Zeitung,* 19 November; *Boston Gazette,* 8 December (excerpt). None of the reprintings included the prefatory statement. The text in angle brackets was also reprinted in the Philadelphia *Independent Gazetteer* on 19 December with the following after the word "Liberty": "(see a writer in a late Boston paper)." The paper was the *Boston Gazette,* 8 December (see note 2 immediately below).

2. "E." transformed this Pennsylvania item through this paragraph into an election piece addressed "To the FREEMEN of MASSACHUSETTS" by replacing the introduction by "A Friend to Truth and Freedom" with

Messieurs EDES, As the Choice of Federal Representatives is soon to take place, it is essentially necessary for the good of the Union, that those Men be chosen who are most likely to promote the general desire of the People at large—Men who are of the Persuasion that Amendments to the new proposed Constitution are absolutely Requisite and Necessary to secure the Freedom, Security and perfect Confidence of every Individual throughout the Union—That Amendments are Necessary you are requested to submit the following to the candid observation of your Readers.   E.

Friend to Amendments
Exeter, N.H., Freeman's Oracle, 8 November 1788

Mess'rs Printers, I am but a plain simple man, but call myself an honest one—and therefore hope for the indulgence of the public tho' I shall cut no figure in print. I am one of those who had objections to the new constitution and wished for amendments—I don't think so badly of it as I did at first, but I think it wants mending—So I believe do most of those who voted for it—But I cannot fall in with the notions of the *friend to the people* in your last with regard to the unfitness of our worthy president [John Langdon] and chief Justice [Samuel Livermore] for Senator in the new Congress.[1] As to the latter I know he holds an office of importance and fills it as nicely as a man can do, for I have been on the jury and heard him talk as glibly as ever I heard a minister read a sermon in the pulpit without having a word writ—But if there is another office of greater importance that he is better qualified to fill than any other man, it seems to me good policy would not oppose his being hoisted into it—And such an office is that for which he is a candidate—This writer says that amendments to the new constitution *is the most important object to be looked at in settling the new congress*—in this I cannot agree with him—I think there is a number of much greater importance—but will mention only two of them—viz. the *establishing a system of revenue and revenue laws*—which will require the very wisest heads we have among us—and the *appointment of a number of very important officers*—which will demand not only an extensive acquaintance with characters but the most disinterested views. The only objection to his excellency's having a seat in the senate is his having assisted in making the constitution, and his declaring in convention as well as the chief justice that *it was already complete.* Supposing that should continue to be their opinion after they get to Congress, I don't believe they will be against the people's trying to amend it—because they would not injure it if they did not succeed—and if the people should really amend it, I would stake a yoke of oxen, that those gentlemen would acknowledge it better for it—But I am no stickler for these particular characters—we have other men I hope fit to go to congress or any where else.—There is the late president [John Sullivan] and Judge [Josiah] Bartlet and several others, fit for any business however important and difficult. I only mean to shew that those two gentlemen supposing they have the other qualifications for congress men, ought not to be set aside for their attachment to the constitution in its present form. The business that must be done by the first congress requires longer heads and honester hearts than we can find united in the same person among the opposers of the constitution, I am afraid—I must here speak freely. Mesieurs Printers, tho' perhaps I may give offence—I opposed the constitution in my own mind from my first reading it, without knowing whether others of better judgment liked it or not—As I am but a plain man with no other education than what I pick'd up by my own industry, I thought I would keep my thoughts to myself and wait to see how it was relished by others—in this state I soon found out who and who were of a state—and what I knew of the characters of all the leaders of the opposition served to make me shut my mouth the closer, for really I did not like the company I must have kept had I publickly acknowledged my dislike of the constitution—I have also endeavoured to inform myself of the characters of the two parties in the neighbouring states with pretty good success—By this enquiry I have discover'd that almost every man of abilities and established reputation is in favor of the constitution—and that its opposers consist principally of *honest uninformed yeomanry* like myself, headed by men of shatter'd fortunes, blasted reputations or inveterate tories—or in other words *men who had something to gain by living under a bad government, or some thing to loose by the establishment of a good one*—If there is in some of the neighbouring states here and there a man of good abilities, a fair reputation, and a clear estate in the opposition, I believe it will be found that he is more fam'd for his obstinacy than candour—In short it must be confessed that in N. England we have but a very small number of men who would not equally disgrace the states and the antifederal party were they sent to congress—If then *the friend to the People* would exclude all those who are friendly to this constitution as it is, or enemies to any good one at all, from a seat in congress, I fear we shall be poorly represented at best, for as to such men as he describes, *men whose acquaintance and extensive knowledge may be serviceable in bringing about amendments,* it is a lamentable truth that they are not to be found among that part of us who wish for a good government—If there are any such for God's sake let them discover themselves and rid us of the disgrace we now lie under—In a word, my honest brethren in the opposition, as the federalists have got all the men of character and abilities among them, and as we have none in our number who would not disgrace us by their want of knowledge or principle. (I mean not even except myself) I don't see but we must for our own honor and that of our state, join with the other party in giving our voices for federal members and leave the rest to Providence. They shall certainly have the influence of one honest and unfeigned

FRIEND TO AMENDMENTS.

1. See "A Friend to the People," Exeter, N.H., *Freeman's Oracle*, 1 November 1788 (BoR, III, 310–11).

Theodorick Bland to Richard Henry Lee
Richmond, Va., 9 November 1788[1]

It is with real pleasure that I congratulate you on your appointment to the Senate, to prevent which not a few manoeuvres were played off—the Gentlemen of the fœderal Side of the Question—I mean the non *Emendatorys* finding themselves Stript of the Lions Skin with great dexterity put on the *Foxes* tail but neither art or strength would avail them & the Ballots stood for Mr. R: H: Lee 98—for Mr. Willm. Grayson 86 for Mr. James Madison 77 and the two first having the majority of both houses were declared duely Elected—In you Sr. does the Majority of your Country expect an able, a Strenuous & a Steady Advocate for those Amendments without which little good and much evil I fear will be its portion—

You no doubt will have seen the artfull substitute (for the proposed application to Congress) Calculated to affront & Irritate, our Sister States, in requiring peremptorily the adoption of our Ideas in toto and an absolute conformity in all their acts untill such adoption shd take place, which altho it was in the teeth of their own Arguments against previous Amendments was Supported strongly in opposition to those which were adopted for calling a Convention[2]—The Application formed on those resolutions for calling a Convention will probably be brought forward this day, and will I think speak the clear and decided Language of this state[.] the Bill for choosing a President has passed the Delegates and that for choosing representatives is in great forwardness—much pains is taken to lay off the districts so as to include the most consequential non Emendatorys but I expect that this Bill which is almost entirely of their carving—will be hashd up and served out to the Public in a more Palatable form than it at present appears in—as you have once more honord me with your Correspondence I shall presume on a continuance of it whenever any event worth communicating shall come under your Cognizance in yr. Public Character assuring you at the same time of a reciprocity, and that in your Private one it will ever afford much pleasure to hear from you to one who is with the greatest Esteem Dr. Sr. Yr. Friend & obedt. Svt.

1. RC, Lee Family Papers, ViU.

2. For the Virginia resolution requesting Congress to call a general convention to amend the Constitution, see BoR, I, 158–80. The substitute resolution lost by a vote of 39 to 85.

Alexander Hamilton to Theodore Sedgwick
New York, 9 November 1788 (excerpt)[1]

... I am very sorry for the scism you hint at among the Foederalists; but I have so much confidence in the good management of the fast friends of the constitution that I hope no ill consequences will ensue from that disagreement.—It will however be worthy of great care to avoid suffering a difference of opinion on collateral points to produce any serious division between those who have hitherto drawn together on the great national question—Permit me to add that I do not think you should allow any line to be run between those who wish to trust alterations to future experience and those who are desirous of them at the present juncture. The rage for amendments is in my *opinion* rather to be parried by address than encountered with open force. And I should therefore be loth to learn that your parties have been arranged professedly upon the distinction I have mentioned. The *mode* in which amendments may best be made and twenty other matters may serve as pretexts for avoiding the evil and securing the good....

1. RC, Hamilton Papers, DLC. For the entire letter, see Syrett, V, 230–32n.

George Lee Turberville to James Madison
Richmond, Va., 10 November 1788 (excerpt)[1]

I have forborne my pen for some posts—flattering myself that *it* wou'd have been the harbinger of good news. but alas! I am about to detail to you some occurrences which I assure you have operated upon my feelings as sensibly and in a manner more distressing than I trust they will upon your own—

The triumph of Antifederalism is compleat—The resolution & preamble which I enclosed to you have passed by a majority of 85, to 39.[2] a resolution for a self denying ordinance has passed nemine contradicente (but myself) to vacate the seats of such Executive Legislative & Judiciary Officers of this Government as shall accept an Office under the United States—& to Crown the whole. R. H. Lee & William Grayson were yesterday elected to the Senate—the Ballot for the first was 98. the second 86. & for you 77. 63 single Votes were given to you & if the Election had been delayed untill tomorrow—I do religiously believe You wou'd have been elected. Let it not be supposed from this, that Virginia is verging toward Antifederalism even—Let it be remember'd that the Phalanx of Opposition that appeared in Convention are still alive & embodied—whilst the good Citizens who composed the Majority in the convention are disbanded—The last relying *in the true Spirit of Democracy* on the implicit obedience of every good Citizen to the voice of a majority so fairly & so deliberately obtained—were inattentive to the possible attempts of the designing—whilst their opponents have profitted from their unsuspicious inattention, & have endeavor'd to obtain by finesse—what they cou'd not accomplish by fair & argumentative discussion. . . .

1. RC, Madison Collection, NN. For the entire letter, see Rutland, *Madison*, XI, 339–41.

2. Turberville had enclosed copies of the second convention resolutions in one of his letters of 27 October to Madison (BoR, III, 290–91; Rutland, *Madison*, XI, 323–24). The resolutions were approved on 30 October, by a vote of 85–39 (the vote was to defeat the Federalist substitute resolutions; the Antifederalist resolutions were passed on an unrecorded vote, presumably very close to the 85–39 margin). See BoR, I, 158–80, especially pp. 163–66.

Foreign Spectator VII
Philadelphia Federal Gazette, 11 November 1788[1]

REMARKS *on the Amendments to the Federal Constitution, proposed by the Conventions of Massachusetts, New-Hampshire, New-York, Virginia, South and North-Carolina, with the minorities of Pennsylvania and Maryland, by a* FOREIGN SPECTATOR.

NUMBER VII.

The convention of New-York proposes, *That the Congress shall not declare war without the concurrence of two-thirds of the senators and representatives present in each house.* This restriction might be applicable to offensive war, but certainly is not to defensive, for the reasons given in the last number. It must also be observed, that a war, in reality just and necessary, sometimes may appear offensive. It is just to compel another nation to compliance with an important treaty, to the delivery of a frontier place, or to the forbearance of many indirect injuries, which may be in their effects equal to pointed violence. It is also a self-defence to prevent an enemy, when he manifestly intends to attack us, as we snatch a pistol from a robber before he can fire it. Without a detail of circumstances very prolix, and yet incompetent to every emergency, the supreme power cannot be limited on this matter; and must therefore be left to its own wisdom, public virtue, and humanity.

The convention of North-Carolina thinks proper to move a question, which we hope may never be wanted: they request, *That the Congress shall not declare any state to be in rebellion, without the consent of at least two-thirds of all the members present of both houses,* 12 am. The constitution does not explicitly treat of such a case—but is contented with defining in 3d sect. of 3d art. that *"treason against the United States shall consist only in levying war against them, or adhering to their enemies, giving them aid and comfort*; and stipulating in 4th sect. of 4th art. *that the United States shall protect each state in the union against domestic violence, on application of the legislature, or of the executive council when the legislature cannot be convened.* In this, as in other things, the new government will by a direct operation on individuals, preserve national safety and prevent dreadful calamities. If the states were only connected by a simple reciprocal contract, the violation of it by any state could not otherwise be remedied than by the united force of all the rest. Here is then an appeal to arms, and a civil war in the first instance! Therefore the anarchy of the old constitution became so alarming, that a dissolution of the union, or a union by force, was the dreadful alternative. But in the new confederacy, the necessity of declaring any state to be in rebellion, can hardly ever exist, because traitors are disarmed before they can raise any dangerous insurrections; and if such should happen in any state, they will be quelled by federal arms on the request of the legislature, or executive of that state.

While the federal government is just and mild, yet firm and vigilant, it is hardly possible that disaffection should be so general and violent in any state, as to fill both the legislative and executive departments with traitors. But suppose this extraordinary event to happen from some rapid epidemic phrenzy, the minority will then be considered as true members of the union, and the majority as a faction that must be suppressed, and the leaders of which have incurred the punishment of treason. Even in this case, there is no necessity of declaring the state to be in rebellion. During the tumult, some general regulations must be made, by which the people at large must necessarily suffer; but no punishment can be inflicted upon the state, without depriving it of those rights and benefits which are common to all the states of the union, and consequently changing the federal constitution itself. Yet without such declaration, a speedy and powerful remedy must be applied in the alarming crisis, when a strong faction has seized upon the government and resources of a state, to levy war against the federal head: the federal arm should certainly in time crush those double traitors, who, by a cruel separation would maim the body and mortify the limb. During a slow deliberation, the fire may spread with such a rage, as not to be quenched without torrents of federal blood. It is true, that a unanimous vote would be desirable in this case; but we must allow a proportion to selfish, timid, and erroneous opinions. Perhaps it will be difficult to get a bare majority in a very upright and enlightened Congress, from an indulgence to revolution principles carried to extremes by many well-disposed minds, and from the natural reluctance against violent means, while there is any hope in gentle proceedings.

The same convention does also request, *that congress shall not introduce foreign troops into the United States without the consent of two-thirds of the members present of both houses*, 26th am. America well united, has nothing to fear from any power that will probably ever attack her, while she acts towards other nations with integrity and wisdom. At the same time as she may in some emergency act in concert with an ally, his troops may with propriety be admitted. If this caution implies a suspicion of Congress, is it not more reasonable to surmise that one or two states may be inveigled by a foreign power, and supported by a formidable army? In such a wo[e]ful situation, an ally may be very acceptable, nor should it be in the power of the disaffected in Congress to refuse his admittance.

Tho' I cannot see the propriety of requiring the consent of two-thirds of congress on the matters now discussed; yet I must observe, that if the word *present* implies a fear of absentees, I heartily agree to the necessity of very full houses when such capital resolves are to be made. A legislator who then is kept away by gain, pleasure, or idleness, is, with all his abilities or domestic virtues, a mean wretch, who ought to be severely punished for being such a slovenly faithless guardian of his country's dearest interests. This remark is the more essential, as a traitor may, by an insidious absence, injure his country both by carrying and loosing an important motion.

The conventions of Virginia and North-Carolina in the 10th am. and the minority of Maryland, desire, *that no soldier shall be enlisted for any longer term than four years, except in time of war, and then for no longer term than the continuance of the war.* This amendment is superfluous, because money for the support of troops is appropriated only for two years: If a new appropriation is made, troops can be kept, if not they must be disbanded.

The above minority, and the convention of New-Hampshire 10th am. request, *that soldiers in time of peace may not be quartered upon private houses without the consent of the owners.* If barracks and public houses can be had, this inconvenience will certainly be avoided; but otherwise, if regular troops are requisite, they must be provided with necessaries. Suppose a regiment on a march in the dead of winter; must the brave fellows lye in the field, because churlish people will not let them sleep on their floors? Federal soldiers deserve the affection of their country as well as the militia, being its defenders, and not oppressors; unreasonable prejudices against them are illiberal and inconsistent with federal sentiments. To render those troops more agreeable to the people and more useful to the United States, they should be chosen with discretion; a man of principle will die for his country, a villain will stab it for good pay.

1. Reprinted: *New York Daily Gazette*, 10 June 1789; North Carolina *Fayetteville Gazette*, 19 October; and in the April issue of the Philadelphia *American Museum*. For the authorship of the "Foreign Spectator" series, see the headnote to Essay No. I (21 October, BoR, III, 264n).

Francis Corbin to James Madison
Richmond, Va., 12 November 1788 (excerpt)[1]

... You will find in the Journals Mr. Henry's Resolutions upon the business of a second Convention and an answer to the Inflammatory Governor of Newyork.—You will also see the Amendment which I offered to them. I hope they will meet your approbation. Mr. John Page & Carrington are with me at this moment drawing an Address to Congress in conformity to the Resoñs proposed by me as a Substitute for the one drawn agreably to Mr. Henry's. This will appear upon our Journals & will tend to justify our Conduct and to operate as a Protest against theirs.[2]

1. RC, Madison Papers, DLC. For the entire letter, see Rutland, *Madison*, XI, 341–43.
2. The substitute address was defeated by a vote of 71 to 50 (the clerk mistakenly gave the total as 72 nays) on 14 November. See BoR, I, 158–80, especially pp. 171–72.

Pennsylvania Carlisle Gazette, 12 November 1788

To the PUBLIC

The last Wednesday in this month is appointed by the General Assembly of the state of Pennsylvania, for the purpose of choosing eight members to represent us in the new Congress. As amendments in the proposed plan are thought necessary, it therefore behoves every Freeman to attend at his respective district, and give his vote to such men as will use their endeavour to procure the same.—The following Gentlemen are approved of by the friends of Equal Liberty; and will be run in our ticket. Robert Whitehill, William Montgomery, Daniel Heister, Peter Muhlenberg, William Findley, Charles Petitt, Blair M'Clanahan, Gen. William Irvine.

Philadelphia Federal Gazette, 12 November 1788[1]

PHILADELPHIA, NOV. 6

The dispositions discovered by the legislature of Virginia are recommended to the notice of the friends of the federal constitution in this state and elsewhere. There appears a warm unfriendly spirit against the constitution in a considerable part of that honorable body. The propriety of a firm, steady conduct on the part of the federal interest, and a conciliating temper among one another, with a disposition to put by every consideration that may possibly interrupt the present harmony, is obviously necessary to our political salvation. This caution seems the more necessary, as it is said that overtures (with insidious intentions) have been made by the opponents of the constitution to a numerous and respectable body of its friends, with a view to distract and divide. It is not doubted, however, that the prudence and good sense of that valuable body of men, to whom this matter has been thrown out, will be sufficient to save them and the constitution from the dangers of these artful contrivances.

1. The *Pennsylvania Gazette* also printed this item on 12 November. Reprinted seven times by 30 December: N.H. (2), Mass. (1), R.I. (1), N.Y. (1), Pa. (1), Md. (1).

Virginia Centinel, 12 November 1788[1]

Should a majority of the states approve the Letter sent for their consideration by Governor Clinton, of New-York, another Convention to revise the Constitution will inevitably be the result.

1. Reprinted: *Kentucky Gazette*, 13 December.

George Lee Turberville to James Madison
Richmond, Va., 13 November 1788 (excerpt)[1]

... Wou'd to heaven that I had it in my power to lay open my heart to you, that you might perceive my sincerity & observe my anxiety—I am so afflicted with our present misreable—nay despicable [suite?] of politics—that I am almost brought, to lament that we are in a republican situation.

The Man who leads a *mob* majority in such a governt. is the most cruelly oppressive of all possible Tyrants—to a prostrate Minority—had I not a hope that a little year might—may possibly eventuate in a salutary change I shou'd in a fit of dispair—give up all idea of ever seeing a Government rising from deliberate Ratiocination—

Some of yr. arguments against *Convention's* arose in my mind—& were enforced with all the little Energy I was master of—but in Vain: the enclosed paper will shew you the result[2]—Tomorrow come on the Letter to Congress—to Genl. Clinton & to our sister states—pregnant with all the insidious Art base misrepresentation—& unfounded Visionary apprehensions that are so apparently characteristic in the thinking ones of the Majority—Pass they will but not without the Ayes—& Nays that the world in reading the names of their advocates may form such a judgement upon them as they merit.—

Mr. Randolph has this day resigned [as governor] & will be in our house in a few days it is said—

You shall have the Letters by next post if I can get them copied if not by the next post—they shall be forwarded as soon as they can be had—I shall continue to write to you—if you leave New York pray desire some friend of yrs. to enquire for letters directed to you & forward them to you.

1. RC, Madison Collection, NN. For the entire letter, see Rutland, *Madison,* XI, 343–45.

2. The enclosed paper was the *Virginia Independent Chronicle* of 12 November, which printed the resolutions and vote of 30 October in the House of Delegates on the subject of a second convention. For Virginia's call of a second general convention, see BoR, I, 158–80.

Annapolis Maryland Gazette, 13 November 1788[1]

Extract of a letter from a gentleman in Fredericksburg to his friend in this city, dated November 4, 1788.

On the other side is a resolution, carried ayes 85, noes 39, which will shew that we repent of our folly in adopting a constitution without previous amendment—But, since it is done, the assembly are proceeding to organize it agreeably to the constitution, at least as they understand it, that is, to have the electors, and the delegates chosen by the people, by districts, the elected to be residentees; this was nearly the unanimous vote; but, by what rule the districts are to be measured, is yet in doubt—The delegates have at present adopted the rule by that of the militia—But, as they had but a majority of 6, and the senate are opposed to it, I expect the rule of tythes will be their guide—that is, to take in three fifths of the blacks, the which, I conceive to be right, as our delegation is increased by that rule, and we are also to be taxed accordingly.

Whereas the convention of this state did, &c. ratify a constitution for the United States, and did also declare that sundry amendments to exceptionable parts of the same ought to be adopted: And whereas the subject matter of the amendments agreed to by the said convention *involves all the great unalienable and essential rights, liberties and privileges, of freemen,* many of which, if *not cancelled,* are rendered *insecure* under the *said constitution* until they shall be altered and amended: RESOLVED, *as the opinion of this committee,* That, for quieting the minds of the good citizens of this commonwealth, and securing their dearest rights and privileges, and preventing those disorders which must arise under a government not founded in the confidence of the people, application be made to the congress of the United States, so soon as they shall assemble under the said constitution, to call a convention for proposing amendments to the same according to the mode therein directed,

RESOLVED, *also,* That a circular letter be written to the different legislatures, &c. on the foregoing subject.[2]

Ayes 85
Noes 39
46 Majority.[3]

These resolutions were introduced by Mr. Henry—opposed by F. Corbin—an amendment offered to *recommend* it to the *delegates in congress* to have the amendments offered by the states considered by congress, and, when amended, to be submitted to the consideration of the legislatures, as in the alternative mentioned in the 5th article.

You are not to suppose that thirty-nine members approved of this—but that number divided for the amendment—because many thought Henry's resolution contained reflections on the late Virginia and continental conventions—but I do not think six members would have voted for amendments by congress instead of a convention.—I was in the house and heard the great ground of objection applied to the language.

1. Reprinted: Philadelphia *Independent Gazetteer,* 21 November; Philadelphia *Pennsylvania Journal,* 22 November; Philadelphia *Pennsylvania Gazette,* 26 November; Winchester *Virginia Gazette,* 26 November; and *Boston Gazette,* 15 December.
2. For the official wording of the preamble and resolutions reported to the House of Delegates on 30 October by the Committee of the Whole on the State of the Commonwealth, see BoR, I, 163–64.
3. The roll-call vote is actually to reject the substitute preamble and resolutions. The original preamble and resolutions passed without a recorded roll-call vote (*ibid.,* 164–65).

Centinel XXII
Philadelphia Independent Gazetteer, 14 November 1788 (excerpt)[1]

To the PEOPLE of PENNSYLVANIA.

Friends and Fellow Citizens, It was my intention to appropriate this number to the consideration of the enormous sums of public money unaccounted for by individuals, now ascertained by a late investigation of Congress; but accidentally meeting with an address to the freemen of Pennsylvania, signed *Lucullus,* published in the *Federal* Gazette of November the 6th,[2] I thought no time should be lost in detecting the attrocious falsehoods, and counteracting the baneful poison contained in that address. In a former number I noticed the base policy practiced by the *republicans,* as they stiled themselves, of imitating and prejudicing that part of the community who were disaffected to our cause in the late war, against the constitutional whigs, by the grossest calumny and misrepresentation of their conduct and principles, and thereby duping the disaffected into the support of measures, which their dispassionate judgement would have reprobated, as highly injurious to the common welfare. That address is a continuation of the same policy, and from characteristic features, is known to be the production of *Galen,*[3] who has done more to destroy the harmony of Pennsylvania, and forward the vassalage of her citizens to the *rich and aspiring,* than all the other firebrands of party and instruments of ambition.

We are now hastening to a crisis that will determine the fate of this great country, that will decide whether the United States is to be ruled by a free government, or subjected to the supremacy of *a lordly and profligate few.* Hitherto the gratification of party spirit and prejudice was attended with the ruin of the honest whigs and the emolument and aggrandisement of the *republicans* at the common expence; but now it would be attended with the loss of all liberty and the establishment of a general thraldom—men of all descriptions, except our rulers, would equally wear the fetters, and experience the evils of despotism; it therefore behoves every man who has any regard for the welfare and happiness of his country, of himself, or his posterity, to endeavor to divest himself of all prejudices that may bias or blind his judgement on this great occasion. In confidence of a dispassionate perusal and consideration, I will now take up the address and expose its falacy. It begins "You will be called upon, on the last Wednesday of the present month, to give your votes for *eight* persons to represent you in the Legislature of the United States. You never were called upon to exercise the privilege of electing rulers upon a more important occasion. Two tickets will be offered you. The one will contain men who will support the new constitution *in its present form*; the other ticket will contain men, who will overset the government under the specious pretext of amending it." Here is a plain, explicit avowal that the new constitution is to be supported in its *present form*; I hope this declaration will open the eyes of those people who have been deluded by the deceitful promises of amendments, and, that being thereby convinced of the fallacy of the reiterated assurances of amendments, they will now embrace the only method left of obtaining them, by giving their suffrages and influence to the other ticket. The bugbear raised to intimidate the people from voting for this ticket, viz. "That the design is to destroy the government under the specious pretext of amending it," I trust will be treated with the deserved contempt, and that this low device will only confirm the people the more in their determination to support men favorable to amendments....

Philadelphia, 12 November.

1. Reprinted: *New York Journal*, 27 November. For the entire essay, see DHFFE, I, 341–45. For the authorship, circulation, and responses to the "Centinel" essays, see the headnote to "Centinel" I, 5 October 1787 (BoR, II, 21–23).
2. "Lucullus," which was first printed in the *Pennsylvania Gazette* on 5 November (BoR, III, 324), was reprinted in the Philadelphia *Federal Gazette* on 6 November.
3. Benjamin Rush.

Foreign Spectator VIII
Philadelphia Federal Gazette, 14 November 1788[1]

REMARKS *on the Amendments to the Federal Constitution, proposed by the Conventions of Massachusetts, New-Hampshire, New-York, Virginia, South and North-Carolina, with the minorities of Pennsylvania and Maryland, by a* FOREIGN SPECTATOR.

NUMBER VIII.

A Good militia is the natural, easy, powerful and honorable defence of a country. Even those nations which are surrounded with formidable neighbours, need not altogether depend on great standing armies, which are not favourable to liberty, and create an enormous expence. Indeed regular troops are more excellent, as they resemble a militia; which is evidently seen in the Swedish army, and acknowledged by the best military writers of different nations. America will be well defended against any attack by the united strength of a small but well appointed army, and a numerous well ordered militia. The federal government is empowered to provide for the organizing and calling forth this principal branch of national defence, by the 15th and 16th par. in 8th sect. of 1st art.[2] on which the following amendments are proposed. *That each state respectively shall have the power to provide for organizing, arming and disciplining its own militia, whensoever congress shall omit or neglect to provide for the same. That the militia shall not be subject to martial law, except when in actual service, in time of war, invasion, or rebellion: and when not in the actual service of the United States, shall be subject only to such fines, penalties, and punishments as shall be directed or inflicted by the laws of its own state.* Convent. of Virginia and N. Carol. 11 am. *That the power of organizing, arming, and disciplining the militia (the manner of disciplining the militia to be prescribed by Congress) remain with the individual states; and that Congress shall not have authority to call or march any of the militia out of their own state, without the consent of such state, and for such length of time only as such state shall agree.* Minor. of Pennsylvania, 11 am. *That the militia shall not be subject to martial law, except in time of war, invasion, or rebellion; and that it shall not, unless selected by lot, or voluntarily enlisted, be marched beyond the limits of an adjoining state, without the consent of their legislature or executive.* Min. of Maryl. 11 and 1 am.⁽ᵃ⁾ *That the militia of any state shall not be compelled to serve without the limits of the state for a longer term than six weeks, without the consent of the legislature thereof.* Conv. of New-York, 29 am. Before I enter on the discussion of these amendments, I beg leave to observe the want of agreement, and the silence of the New-Hampshire convention with those of South-Carolina and Massachusetts, who, as was remarked above, are satisfied with the military powers of the new constitution. The request, that each state respectively may provide for organizing, &c. its own militia, whensoever Congress shall omit or neglect to provide for the same, I humbly presume to be a mere suggestion of jealousy. Congress never can omit such an important and general duty without a treasonable design, which supposes many preceding degrees of corruption; but this corruption cannot continue and accumulate in a body formed and frequently changed by the people, except the people themselves are thoroughly corrupted.

The proposition, that a state-government may controul the power of Congress to call the militia out of the state, must be regarded as hastily formed in the fermentation of party, and now disavowed by every American, who regards the safety and honor of the union and of his own state. If a powerful enemy invades any part of the United States, he must be opposed with all possible expedition, before he gets possession of any important passes, lays the country under contributions, defeats the weak forces that fall in his way, and creates the usual calamities of war. Sympathy with a sister state, and the assurance that she will in time of need repay the obligation, are sufficient motives to lend what aid the common guardian requires. The federal power watches for the whole union, views the magnitude of the danger, knows the resources of every state, and feels impartially for all; it is therefore the best judge of what they should in every emergency do and suffer for each other. That the militia should not be called to a further distance, and in greater numbers, or kept in the field for a longer time than is necessary, every person of sense will readily grant; that a select body is in real danger, much preferable to a multitude of ordinary militia, every military man well knows; but every regulation on this important matter should be left to the general government. It will certainly not be so liable to an abuse of such power as a state-government, which, with all its generosity, cannot in the same manner think and feel for the United States. What may be the consequence of recalling the militia on the eve of a decisive battle? Perhaps the conquest of two or three states, and the miseries of war for several years!

The constitution *reserves to the states respectively the appointment of the officers, and the authority of training the militia according to the discipline prescribed by Congress.* This surely is a perfect security to any state against an encroachment of the federal power. The safety of the union requires that the militia of every state should be well armed, and in every respect qualified for the defence of the country, consequently general and effectual regulations must be made by Congress. Fines, penalties, and punishments of a proper kind are a necessary part of discipline; if these are to be exercised by the several states, it is needless to compliment the Congress with the ridiculous power of organizing the militia.

A citizen, as a militia man is to perform duties which are different from the usual transactions of civil society; and which consequently must be enforced by congenial laws and regulations. These military duties have in time of peace no other object than a compleat preparation for war, and therefore do not require that rigour of martial law, which is indispensible in actual service;—yet when we consider the extreme importance of every military duty in time of war, and the necessity of acquiring an habitual exercise of them in time of peace; it would be childish to enervate by a scrupulous delicacy that manly discipline, which is the bulwark of the country—Give us then, for heaven's sake, martial law enough to be truly martial when we are to face the veterans of a powerful enemy.

Fines alone are very insufficient to prevent the various kinds of neglect and misdemeanor in the militia service, because they will not affect the rich, and at the best only produce a mechanical compliance without life and spirit. Disgrace in different and just degrees is the most effectual penalty; and it will keep alive that high sense of military honor, without which a militia is only a disorderly populace, or a mass of animal machines. With an equitable allowance for age, bodily infirmities, religious opinions, and pressing avocations, absence and the hiring of substitutes should be held dishonorable. Not to join your company, because you can earn more than the fine in your shop or your field; or because you had rather loll in an easy chair; or because you like the gambling table better than the drum; oh, for shame! not to learn that noble art, by which you can defend your life, liberty and property; your parents, wife and children! in a day of danger to be defended by others like a weak woman and a helpless child! A man of spirit will be delighted with the play of arms in all the manœuvres that present the image of real war. Though worth 10,000 *l.* a year he chearfully takes his place in the rank with a day laborer, who is his brother-citizen, and defender of the common country—His fortune only inspires the noble pride of a greater application to the theory and practice of the military art, that by superior abilities he may deserve the honor to command a band of patriots.

As the constitution makes no mention of martial law, it is not my business to enter further into this subject; only observing that the only means to render a standing army useless, is to form a truly warlike militia.

(a) *This minority has two sets of amendments; the latter negatived by a majority of the committee.*[3]

1. Reprinted: *New York Daily Gazette,* 11 June 1789; and in the June issue of the Philadelphia *American Museum.* For the authorship of the "Foreign Spectator" series, see the headnote to Essay No. I (21 October, BoR, III, 264n).
2. For these two paragraphs, see BoR, I, 611.
3. For these two sets of amendments, see Appendix I (BoR, III, 472–76).

Edward Carrington to James Madison
Richmond, Va., 15 November 1788[1]

I had the pleasure to write you on the 9th. or 10th.[2] Inst. and inclosed the Journals to the 6th. in these you had the Resolutions which had been agreed to upon the subject of a Convention—and you must also have seen that these resolutions were refered to a committee for the purpose of having letters drawn according to the matter of them. the letters were reported last tuesday, and have today been under the consideration of a Committee of the whole—they are agreed to but we have lessened the Majority considerably by proposing drafts conforming to the resolutions of the Convention in June, and insisting that the people in that Convention had pointed out the mode in which amendments should be sought, and that the Assembly ought not to divert the course of their pursuit. the drafts which we proposed are accompanied with reasons addressed to the people with a view that they may see that the Minority were for the most speedy & safe mode of gaining the desired object. for our amendments there were 49 Yeas & 71 Nays. the drafts that are agreed to are drawn in a Stile which, I think, would of itself alone place the authors of the measure in a disadvantageous light.[3] the journals will be printed by the next post, when I will transmit them. it has hitherto been unfortunate that the federalists in the House have not acted in proper Concert—we are however getting Martialed and I hope we shall, at least, upon every occasion be able to shew a respectable Minority.

The Bill for district Elections of Representatives passed our House yesterday—the antis have levelled every effort at you—the point of residence in the district is carried by some of the Feds having at an early period committed themselves upon that side. Your district is composed of the Counties of Amherst, Albemarle, Louisa, Orange Culpepper, Spotsylvania Goochland & Fluvanna—we wished to get Fauquier but the powers of the Antis were too strong for us. You will have active Friends in Culpepper Spotsylvania Albemarle & Fluvanna—Orange & Louisa will, it is supposed require no prompting—your Friends wish you however to come into this district at an early period, in order to Counteract a number of reports which may take hold upon the Minds of the people—it is busily circulated that you declared in Convention that the Constitution required no alteration whatever—it is as yet doubted whether Mr. Strother, or Mr. W. Cabel the Elder,[4] will be your opponent—the latter however will not, unless upon the principle of having the strongest Interest of the two, and having reason to doubt whether the other will be able to exclude you—no effort will be left untried for effecting their purpose.

I have seen a letter of yours to Mr. Turberville[5] which I think you ought to permit to be published as yours—it is calculated at once to give the lye to the reports I have mentioned, & to condemn the measure of a Convention. I wish you would consider this Matter, and should you not disapprove, permit the publication to take place—even Mr. Henry has asserted in the House that you was against, or unfriendly, to amendments. Your Friends from the district will write you & therefore I will not say more on the point of yr. Election—you may however depend on meeting with all the opposition that can be brought into practice against you.

Present me to the President[6] and believe me to be, my dr sir with great sincerity yr. Affe. Friend & Hl St.

P.S. The Govr. [Edmund Randolph] will take his seat in the House tomorrow.

1. RC, Madison Papers, DLC.
2. For the 10 November letter, see BoR, III, 340–41.

3. For the opposing letters and the roll-call vote, see BoR, I, 170–72.
4. French Strother and William Cabell, Sr. (1730–1798). For the election in Virginia Congressional District 5, see DHFFE, II, 317–49.
5. For this 2 November letter, see BoR, III, 312–14.
6. Cyrus Griffin of Virginia was serving as president of the Confederation Congress.

Patrick Henry to Richard Henry Lee
Richmond, Va., 15 November 1788 (excerpt)[1]

I postponed answering your Favor until I could have the pleasure of congratulating you on your Election to the Office of Senator for Virga. in the new Congress, which I now do. The Friends of the System are much displeased that Mr. Madison was left out of the Choice. They urged his Election most warmly, claiming as a sort of Right The Admission of one federal Member; but in vain—For to no Purpose must the Efforts of Virga. have been expected to procure Amendments, if one of her Senators had been found adverse to that Scheme—The universal Cry is for Amendments, & the federals are obliged to join in it; but whether to amuse, or conceal other Views seems dubious—You have been too long used to political Measures not to see the Grounds of this Doubt, & how little Dependance can be placed on such occasional conformity—And you know too well the Value of the Matters in Contest to trust their Safety to those whose late Proceedings, if they do not manifest Enmity to public Liberty, yet shew too little Sollicitude or Zeal for its Preservation—

Your Age & mine seems to exempt us from the Task of stepping forth again into the busy Scenes which now present themselves—I am glad to know that you have Health & Spirits enough to accede to every Exertion—I shall not claim it further than it will extend to distant Operations—I mean not to take any Part in Deliberations held out of this State—unless in Carolina from which I am not very distant & to whose Politics I wish to be attentive—If Congress do not give us substantial Amendments, I will turn my Eyes to that Country a Connection with which may become necessary for me as an Individual. I am indeed happy where I now live in the Unanimity which prevails on this Subject; for in near 20 adjoining Countys I think at least 19/20ths are antifederal,[2] & this great Extent of Country in Virga. lays adjoining to No. Carolina, & with her forms a great Mass of Opposition not easy to surmount. This Opposition it is the Wish of my Soul so see wise, firm, temperate. It will scarcely Preserve the latter Epithet longer than Congress shall hold out the Hope of forwarding Amendmts—I really dread the Consequences following from a Conduct manifesting in that body, an Aversion to that System—I firmly believe the American Union de-

COMMENTARIES, 15 NOVEMBER 1788 355

pends on the Success of Amendments—God grant I may never see the Day when it shall be the Duty of Whiggish Americans to seek for Shelter under any other Government than that of the united States—The old Charges of Turbulence & Ambition have been plentifully bestowed on me. You have not escaped; but as to us who have so long been accustomed to despise these Attempts, they will have little Effect further than to excite Pity—

I have no Correspondence at present on the Subject of Politics—For that Reason I beg you will now & then drop me a Line when you may find Leisure. The progress of Things under the new Governt. in its Commencement, will be highly interesting & important to be known. Letters addressed to the Care of George Fleming Esqr. in this City, Will reach me. . . .

1. RC, Henry Papers, DLC. Printed: DHFFE, II, 374–75.
2. Henry represented Prince Edward County in the state Convention. See the endpaper map in RCS:Va. for how the delegates from this part of Virginia voted on the ratification of the Constitution.

Massachusetts Centinel, 15 November 1788[1]

MISCELLANY.
SHIP NEWS.

The SHIP CONSTITUTION, the property of the United States, being now completely fitted for her voyage, is taking in her complement of hands. The crew is ordered to consist of *picked men* from all the States—and we hear some have been entered on the ship's books, as in the States of Pennsylvania, Delaware and Connecticut—Several others are now debating upon the best methods of selecting their quota—and it is said the business meets with opposition from certain *fresh water sailors*—who pretending to be dissatisfied with her workmanship, are strenuous for having her overhauled before sailing. Some of these are your *cabin-window gentry*, who without the smallest pretensions to seamanship are pushing for appointments on board.

These fellows pretend to great concern for the FREIGHT, which the people mean to risk on the voyage—but it is hoped that they will be disappointed in their schemes of *procrastination*—as the owners are fully satisfied that success depends *as much* upon her sailing in good season, as in the qualifications of the crew.

One of the EASTERN STATES, which has always been distinguished for its nautical abilities—and abounding in *able seamen*—and which is very hearty in prosecuting the voyage, having as much, or more than any other State depending—has been greatly *thwarted* in her attempts to turn out her proportion of sailors.—But the *embarrassments* are nearly surmounted, and as this opposition may be considered as "the struggles of an expiring faction" of *luke-warm federalists* and *seekers*, it is not so much to be wondered at.

The CAPTAIN who is already elected in the resolution of every well-wisher to the voyage, possesses such professional talents as (under Providence) will render all insurance unnecessary; especially, as to *his* abilities—the owners are *determined* to add as Chief Mate, those of another *experienced* navigator—who when commanding the PEACE, a FIRST-RATE SHIP, piloted her with consummate skill and address, through obstacles insurmountable to common minds, into a safe and secure harbour.[2]

The crew in general, from the specimens in those already entered, there is every reason to suppose, will consist of a complete *set* of *staunch* and *federal seamen.* (*Tom Bowline's Marine-List.*)

1. Reprinted: *Virginia Independent Chronicle,* 17 December; Philadelphia *Federal Gazette,* 29 December; *Virginia Centinel,* 7 January 1789; Pennsylvania *Carlisle Gazette,* 28 January.
2. Chief Mate refers to John Adams alluding to his role in negotiating the peace ending the Revolutionary War.

George Lee Turberville to James Madison
Richmond, Va., 16 November 1788[1]

Yrs of the 6th has just reach'd me—wou'd to heaven that that of November 2d. had arrived four days sooner[2]—Mr. Henry on yr. being nominated for the senate publicly declared in the house that you were not to be trusted with *amendments* since you had declared, that not a letter of the Constitution cou'd be spared—in Convention—

This was denied by many & a very respectable testimonial of abhorrence at such Conduct & of Justification for you was manifested—I am sollicited by Carrington—R. B. Lee—Doctor Stuart, Mr. J. Page & General Weedon[3] to publish yr. Letter as it will give the Lie to all the flagitious assertions of a party who have nothing more at heart than to keep you out of the Representation—I have been induced from a desire to do you justice to shew that Clause wherein you say that you never thought the system a faultless one to Mr. Henry or rather to read it to him amid a group of his friends but I never can agree to commit yr. Letter (altho conscious of its producing nothing but acknowlegements in yr. favor) to the Public without yr. concurrence—

The Letters upon the Resolutions I enclosed to you[4] are entirely of a peice with them—or rather they are more inflammatory—stamped with direct falshood in themselves (insomuch as they mention that the

Assembly are entirely concurrent in their passage—when the Yeas & Nays on our Journal will shew that they passed by a majority of 71 to 50)—and altered by the Amendments of the minority 'tis to be hoped for the sake of poor Virginia & the Union—that they will be received as the Child of temporaryly triumphant faction—& Ultimately that they will rather be ridiculous & Dangerous—

So soon as the District (or the organizing) Bill comes from the Senate I will enclose you the Districts & the Journals (as soon as they are printed) with the pretty Circular & other Letters with our *rejected* amendments to them—shall be forwarded

In the mean time with the utmost sincerity of Friendship regard & respect I remain my dear sir yrs

1. RC, Madison Collection, NN.
2. Madison's letter to Turberville of 6 November has not been located. For Madison's letter of 2 November, see BoR, III, 312–14.
3. Edward Carrington, Richard Bland Lee, David Stuart, John Page, and General George Weeden.
4. For the Virginia legislature's resolution requesting Congress to call a second convention to propose amendments and the circular letters to New York Governor George Clinton and the other state executives, see BoR, I, 158–80.

Peter S. Du Ponceau to Edward Jones
Philadelphia, 17 November 1788 (excerpt)[1]

My Dear Friend:

... The observations you make on my politics are just in a great measure. My zeal, I own, has carried me farther than my interest justified. But my principles have [- - -] as pure as they are solid, and as they are fixed and invariable, I have ever thought a Democratical government the most suited to the dignity of the human species, and the suggestions of pride, interest or ambition have no weight with me. A gentleman, according to the idea I have of the world, can be found among all classes of people, and the childish pomp of human greatness appears to my eyes in the most pitiful light. Merit, education and riches will always create sufficiently high positions among mankind without the help of the paltry splendor of titles, crowns, and coronets. The efficiency of Government ought to consist in dealing out power to great men without [- - -].

The people may be well governed without being restrained too much, and the simpler is the machine of government, the more easily it is put in motion.

Of all the nations that I have seen, there is none more easily governed than the American. They may be led by gentleness, but like the generous horse, they will kick against the lash. At the same time that I profess these sentiments, I esteem a man who adopts different ones, and particularly when that man is known to me to be possessed of strict honor, justice and integrity. For this reason I rejoice to see you called to the important duty of a legislator of your State.—I hope you will think seriously of the important trust committed to you, and remember that now you are answerable for all your steps, to God and your country. I hope your State[2] will adopt the new Federal Constitution. I wonder how they can be so blind as not to see that, if they do not adopt it, their vote will be lost on the question of amendments. Opposed (as I might be) to the system, had I the honor to be in your place, I would, without hesitation, give my vote for it. "Let the will of the people be done," has always been my constant motto. The man who will do them good against their will, paves the way for him who will do them an injury. They have an undoubted right to be, [- - -] if they choose; and the true patriot at present, is he who will yield to the torrent, and reserves his strength for another opportunity. I shall thank you for your [- - -] of the constitution, which you have promised to send me. No doubt it will be an able, and what is still better, an honest one. Who knows but that you may make a convert of me to your principles? . . .

1. Printed: W. Hooper, "Biographical Sketch of Edward Jones Esq., Late Solicitor General of the State of North Carolina," *North Carolina University Magazine*, V (1856), 349–51. The author of the sketch indicated that the manuscript was mutilated.
2. North Carolina.

Richard Bland Lee to James Madison
Richmond, Va., 17 November 1788[1]

I was honored with your favor of the 6th Instant and am happy to find my opinion corroborated by your authority. I flattered myself that we should have been able notwithstanding the party spirit prevalent in our councils to have placed you in the Senate from this state; but faction has prevailed over gratitude and propriety;—and without a reason you have been left out of the appointment. However considering all circumstances the ballot was honorable. The Country will be divided into districts for the election of representatives—We have it in contemplation to publish the proceedings of the assembly touching the calling of another General Convention together with your letter to Mr: Turberville which will amply justify the principles of the friends of the Government and remove the slanderous imputation on you—as an enemy to all amendments and in every form.[2]

You will recollect by Mr: Henry's resolutions—an application was to be made to Congress to call another convention—an answer to be written to Governor Clinton's letter; and a circular to all the states on this subject. When these papers were introduced—we moved a set of papers in amendment—expressing our disapprobation of a Convention provided Congress at their first meeting, will consider the necessary amendments and forward them to the state Legislatures for their adoption—these were negatived by 70 to 50.[3] They are couched in such terms and the minority is so respectable, as in my opinion, will not only turn the tide of sentiment in our favor in this state, but will destroy the effect of our measures in the other states. These will form the material papers which we mean to publish, except your letter, which is all-important to be known—as it will remove the present ill impressions concerning you and consequently secure your election into the house of Representatives—and as it in the most able manner justifies the conduct of the minority.

As soon as this little pamplet comes from the press—it shall be forwarded to you—and I hope you will take no offence at the Liberty we mean to take with your letter.

I received yr letter very late to night therefore excuse this hasty scrawl—and believe me to be with every sentiment of respect and esteem

1. RC, Richard Bland Lee Papers, DLC.
2. For Madison's 2 November letter to George Lee Turberville expressing his sentiments on a second general convention and amending the Constitution, see BoR, III, 312–14. Turberville decided not to publish the letter (to Madison, 12 December, *ibid.*, 415). No pamphlet has been located, but see "A True Federalist," New York *Daily Advertiser*, 7 January 1789, for what might have been in the pamphlet (BoR, IV).
3. For the original draft letters and the Federalist substitute, see BoR, I, 168–73. The vote was actually 72 to 50 to defeat the substitute letter.

George Washington to James Madison
Mount Vernon, Fairfax County, Va., 17 November 1788 (excerpt)[1]

... The Accts. from Richmond are indeed, very unpropitious to fœderal measures.—The whole proceedings of the Assembly,[2] *it is said* may be summed up in one word—to wit—that the Edicts of Mr. H—— are enregistered with less opposition by the Majority of that body, than those of the Grand Monarch are in the Parliaments of France.—He has only to say let this be Law—and it is Law.

1. RC, Misc. Collection, Henry E. Huntington Library, San Marino, Calif. For the entire letter, see Abbot, *Washington, Presidential Series*, I, 112–16n.
2. For the proceedings, see BoR, I, 158–80.

Edward Carrington to James Madison
Richmond, Va., 18 November 1788 (excerpt)[1]

I have been favoured with yours of the 4th & 6th. Inst. in my last[2] I inclosed the Journals to the 6th. and now send the continuation to the 15th. here you will see at large the drafts of letters upon the subject of a Convention which I mentioned in the letter alluded to above, and those which were proposed by the Minority in place of them. It is to be exceedingly regretted that the Feds had not acted from the first of the session, in concert—I verily believe that had such an union taken place at an early period, Mr. Henry might, upon such propositions as these, have been left in a Minority, by the day that his drafts of letters passed[3]—as that subject upon the whole is now placed, I think the Feds have exhibitted themselves in a light before the Eyes of the people, which will be more satisfactory even to Antis, than the measures of the Majority; indeed the palpable untruths contained in the drafts ought to fix the condemnation of the people in the State, & upon them. . . .

1. RC, Madison Papers, DLC. For the entire letter, see Rutland, *Madison*, XI, 351–53.
2. See Carrington's letter of 15 November (BoR, III, 352–54n).
3. For the majority and minority draft letters and the vote to reject the minority draft letter, see BoR, I, 170–72.

Thomas Jefferson to James Madison
Paris, 18 November 1788 (excerpt)[1]

. . . Mr. Carrington was so kind as to send me the 2d. vol. of the Amer. phil. transactions, the federalist, and some other interesting pamphlets; and I am to thank you for another copy of the federalist and the report of the instrns to the ministers for negotiating peace. the latter unluckily omitted exactly the passage I wanted, which was what related to the navigation of the Missisipi. with respect to the Federalist, the three authors[2] had been named to me. I read it with care, pleasure & improvement, and was satisfied there was nothing in it by one of those hands, & not a great deal by a second. it does the highest honor to the third, as being, in my opinion, the best commentary on the principles of government which ever was written. in some parts it is discoverable that the author means only to say what may be best said in defence of opinions in which he did not concur, but in general it establishes firmly the plan of government. I confess it has rectified me in several points. as to the the bill of rights[3] however I still think it should be added, and I am glad to see that three states have at length considered the perpetual re-eligibility of the president as an article which should be amended. I should deprecate with you indeed the meeting of a new convention. I hope they will adopt the mode of amendment by Congress & the Assemblies, in which case I should not fear any dangerous innovation in the plan. but the minorities are too respectable not to be entitled to some sacrifice of opinion in the majority. especially when a great proportion of them would be contented with a bill of rights. . . .

 1. RC, Madison Papers, DLC. For the entire letter, see Rutland, *Madison*, XI, 353–55.
 2. Alexander Hamilton, James Madison, and John Jay wrote *The Federalist* essays. See the headnote to CC:201.
 3. Essays 38, 84, and 85 of *The Federalist* specifically address the bill of rights issue. See BoR, II, 252–53, 482–88.

William Shippen, Jr., to Thomas Lee Shippen
Philadelphia, 18 November 1788 (excerpt)[1]

. . . We hear to day that R.H. Lee & Col. Grayson are chosen Senators for Virginia both fond of Amendments to the new Constitution—therefore very disagreable to Bobby[2] & our warm Fœderalists—Your Uncle[3] in his last Letter to me says "As so many great men are fond of this Bantling I suppose we must adopt it—but dont you think he will look better when newly dress'd?"—I believe a good half of the people of America if not more are of his Opinion. . . .

 1. RC, Thomas Lee Shippen Family Papers, DLC.
 2. Robert Morris.
 3. Either Richard Henry Lee or Arthur Lee, both Antifederalists, whose sister Alice had married William Shippen, Jr., the father of Thomas Lee Shippen.

Foreign Spectator IX
Philadelphia Federal Gazette, 18 November 1788[1]

REMARKS *on the Amendments to the Federal Constitution, proposed by the Conventions of Massachusetts, New-Hampshire, New-York, Virginia, South and North-Carolina, with the minorities of Pennsylvania and Maryland, by a* FOREIGN SPECTATOR.

NUMBER IX.

The deep silence of the federal constitution on matters of religion is blamed by some religious persons; yet the two minorities of Pennsylvania and Maryland, with the convention of New-Hampshire, are dissatisfied because express stipulations are not made for liberty of conscience, and request the following amendments. *The right of conscience shall be held inviolable, and neither the legislative, executive, nor judicial powers of the United States, shall have authority to alter, abrogate, or infringe any part of the constitutions of the several states, which provide for the preservation of liberty in matters of religion,* 1st prop. of the min. of Penns. *That no person conscientiously scrupulous of bearing arms in any case, shall be compelled personally to serve as a soldier. That there be no national religion established by law; but that all persons be equally entitled to protection in their religious liberty,* 11th and 12th am. by the min. of Mar. *Congress shall make no laws touching religion, or to infringe the rights of conscience,* 11th am. by the conv. of N. H.

It would be very unjust and pernicious, to establish any religious system in the United States; but it is needless to guard against such a visionary evil. Congress cannot, by any construction, claim such a power; nor will they have any inclination for it. But if, by a very wonderful chance, a majority of Congress were so bigotted, their project would not have the least probability of success, while the several great denominations are a check upon each other, and while sound philosophy makes a rapid progress in the train of civilization. Besides, the people of America will hardly submit to the payment of necessary taxes; is it then likely they would pay tithe to the clergy?

Partiality to any sect, or ill treatment of any, is neither in the least warranted by the constitution, nor compatible with the general spirit of toleration; an equal security of civil and religious rights, is therefore given to all denominations, without any formal stipulations; which, indeed, might suggest an idea, that such an equality was doubtful. If the constitution must at all have any amendment on this subject, it should be to guarantee to every state in the union perfect liberty of conscience; because it is much more probable that superstition, mingled with political faction, might corrupt a single state, than that bigotry should infect a majority of the states in Congress.

At the same time, rights of conscience should be properly understood. Religion, as such, is a transaction between man and his maker, and is above the cognizance of any human tribunal; however unreasonable, or even prophane, it may appear, God alone is the judge. But when any person claims, from a religious principle, the right of injuring his fellow-citizens, or the community at large, he must be restrained, and, in attrocious cases, punished. If he is a fool, or a madman, he must not be a tyrant. It is impossible that God could order him to be unjust, because he commands us all to be just and good. Frantic devotees murdered Henry IV. of France, William first Prince of Orange, and other benefactors of mankind. Superstition has destroyed many hundred thousands of mankind, and, in different periods, laid waste the four quarters of the globe.

A wise government will therefore keep a watchful eye on any form of superstition which is baneful to morality, and full of danger to society; if not timely checked, it may soon spread like a plague, distress individuals, and even embarrass the government. False religions had never been established in the world, if legislators had seen their fatal tendency, and nipt them in the bud. We happily live in a civilized æra; but the human heart is very wandering, and the fancy of mortals very whimsical. Whenever a religion morally and politically bad attacks the United States, it should as a general evil be restrained by the federal government. Suppose that some bold and artful prophet should pretend to have a commission from heaven to erect an earthly dominion, and inspire a multitude of his votaries with a blind intrepid enthusiasm; such a gentleman must not, from his tender conscience, cut our throats, and plunder our property. Again, if great numbers from a mistaken devotion, should renounce civil and political duties, and merely by compulsion, contribute to the support and preservation of the society, half a million of such Christians would be a very heavy clog on the arms of active citizens. The moral virtues are more necessary for the peace of this country, than any other, because the people are extremely free; consequently rational religion is of the highest importance, as in many respects the security and perfection of virtue. The foundation of both should be laid in a good education. This ought to be a great object in the government of every state, and with the federal government in the territory belonging to the United States, for which (by the 2d par. 3 sect. 4 art.) *it is to make all needful rules and regulations.* Schools ought to be formed with the gradual settlement of this country, and provided with sensible teachers, who shall instruct their pupils in those capital principles of religion which are generally received, such as the being and attributes of God, his rewards and judgments, a future state, &c.

There is not the least danger of the federal government compelling persons of a scrupulous conscience to bear arms, as the United States would be poorly defended by such; besides, troops can, if necessary, be hired for their money.

The convention of South-Carolina would amend the 3d sect. of the 6th art. by inserting the word *other* between the words *no* and religious. This section, after requiring from all concerned an oath or affirmation to support the constitution, adds, *but no religious test shall ever be required as a qualification to any office or public trust under the United States.* If this amendment points out a mere inaccuracy of stile, it is so far proper— an oath or affirmation being a religious test; if it means to guard against religious establishments, it is, by what has been said, superfluous.

1. Reprinted: *New York Daily Gazette,* 12 June 1789; and in the September issue of the Philadelphia *American Museum.* For the authorship of the "Foreign Spectator" series, see the headnote to Essay No. I (21 October, BoR, III, 264n).

Joseph Willard to Richard Price
Cambridge, Mass., 19 November 1788 (excerpt)[1]

... I am pleased to find that you are so far satisfied with our new federal Constitution. Eleven of the States have adopted it and the general Government is to be organized the next March. It is to be hoped that this new Government will have more energy than the old; and indeed it is so constituted that I think it must necessarily be the case. It is impossible that we should be a flourishing people or have national distinction if we should continue to go on as we have done since the conclusion of the war which established our independence. Recommendations may do in times of danger; but seldom is it that they will have the efficacy of laws in a time of peace.—Several of the State Conventions have recommended alterations. Some of them, if adopted, would, it is probable, improve the Constitution; and I think it likely that this will after a while take place....

1. RC, Price Papers, American Philosophical Society Library, Philadelphia.

A Federalist
Pennsylvania Carlisle Gazette, 19 November 1788

To the Freeman of Pennsylvania.

You are addressed upon the subject of the ensuing Election, by an author who stiles himself "A Friend to Liberty and Union."[1] A plain countryman equally remote from the guilded prospects of "office and emolument," begs your attention a few moments to the same subject.

That "Liberty was the avowed object of the late glorious revolution," is fully acquiesed in; but at the same time 'tis contended that this object was not wholly attained, until not only each individual became fully secured in the possession of that valuable acquisition, by adequate state governments; but that those governments being the basis upon which the rights of individuals are founded, were in like manner shielded from the inroads of each other—for there is not any thing, the duration of which, can be more than coeval with the basis upon which it is erected.

The defects of the confederation were evident, and yet we are told, that, "As if by studied contrivance, they were suffered to remain with hardly any attempt to remedy them until the public affairs of the continent had sunk into utter imbecility and ruin."

"As if by studied contrivance"—ungenerous reflection upon the citizens of America! Is the spirit of the Centinal to be revived, and we again to have the language of "conspiracy" founded in our ears?[2]—

Trust me, this trick will not bear repetition—the passions of the people inflamed by falsehood and declamation, have measureably subsided; and the gentle language of truth begins to be heard. It is alledged that "Congress under the new government will be vested with unlimited powers."—That the state governments "will crumble into ruins, or dwindle into shadows, and in their stead an enormous and unwieldy government be erected."

"That the powers of the new Congress are unlimited," is an assertion very foreign from truth: 'tis well known that previous to the formation of the new constitution, all the powers communicated to man, by the author of his existence, were either lodged in the state constitution, or retained in the breast of individuals. 'Tis an axiom as plain as any laid down by Euclid, that nothing is granted but what are either expressed or implied in the grant, and 'tis equally plain.

That many of the most valuable rights of individuals, as well as of states are not given up to the rulers of the new government, either by expression or implication. Of this number is liberty of conscience and of the press, and the right of defining and punishing all crimes, except piracies committed on the high seas, high treason, counterfeiting the currency of the United States, and offences against the law of nations. These circumstances properly averted to, all the assertions of this "Friend to Liberty and Union," on this subject fall to the ground; notwithstanding he has enforced the same idea in varied language, six or seven times over without a single reason to support his declamation.

If it were probable that any person who would give himself liesure to reflect on the subject of a bill of rights for the new government, could entertain a doubt of the foregoing axiom—let him reflect that the nature of all grants are such as in the first instance, to require no reservations; and that where provisions or exceptions are made use of, it is only to qualify general expressions that otherwise may be misunderstood; of this kind are some exceptions or limitations in the new frame of government, but that in a plain deed for a part of a tract of land, regularly described by courses and distances, it would be altogether as unnecessary as rediculous to reserve any thing which was manifestly not within those courses and distances;—and he will easily discern that in the question now before us, it is equally manifest that those powers not contained in the grant, remains yet in the sources from whence they were derived.

One part of the imbecility of the confederation has been owing to a cause very little attended to, and which has contributed more towards the ruin of confederacies than perhaps any other, I mean the powerfulness of the object upon which the laws operated,—for it is a truth well known in mechanicks, that the power propeled must be less than that propeling. Hence the enforcing the obedience of a state to the laws of the union, requires exertions too great, and is attended with consequences too alarming to the peace of society, to be performed with an ease bearing any proportion to the frequency with which the necessity will occur.—Hence the energy of government as well as the peace and order of society, render it necessary that the laws of the union should operate upon individuals and not upon states.

As to 13 august the idea of the general government encroaching on that of the several states, must be confessed to be one of those events which lie hid in the bosom of time; but as far as we can judge from reason on this subject, the direct contrary seems most likely to be the case. The principles upon which this conjecture is founded, is, that all popular governments take their bias from that of the people.—That the people of the United States will generally possess a greater confidence in their states governments, than in the general government—that the legislative and executive branches of the state governments, will feel their dignities deminished in proportion as the prerogatives of the states are lessened, and will add their extensive influence to procure persons elected in the Representative branch of Congress, who will favour the state prerogatives.—To this we may add the influence of the Senatorial branch, who being the immediate representatives of the state legislatures, & from whom they may exact an oath previous to their election, if they see cause; and who being the most dignified branch will in proportion to the consequence with which they feel themselves surrounded, be inclined to pursue those paths which lead on in a continuance in office, and that as no way will more effectually promote this view than that of strictly conforming to the instructions of those bodies from whence they derive their power, the most natural conclusion is, that they will do so. Upon the plausible subject of amendments; It may just be remarked, that the gentlemen in the ticket agreed on in the conference at Lancaster,[3] will from their manifest attachment to, and interest in the welfare of their country, be as likely as those now recommended by "A Friend to Liberty and Union," to promote amendments whenever they are found necessary from experiment;—and the idea of amending a system approaching so near to the standard of human perfection before it is tried, ought to be reprobated by every friend to the union.

As it is not to be expected that those opposed to the new system will strike a single man out of their ticket, it will be the duty of its supporters to observe the like caution; and although a preference may be felt by a few individuals to some persons in that ticket, yet as there can be no concert who to strike out, some may strike one and some another, by which means the whole may be lost.

York county, 15th Nov. 1788.

1. See "A Friend to Liberty and Union," Philadelphia *Federal Gazette*, 7 November (BoR, III, 332–37n).
2. For example, "Centinel" XII asserted that "The term *conspirators* was not, as has been alledged, rashly or inconsiderately adopted; it is the language of dispassionate and deliberate reason, influenced by the purest patriotism" (CC:470).
3. The Lancaster conference met on 3 November 1788 and recommended a ticket of eight Federalist candidates for the U.S. House of Representatives. The proceedings and ticket of the conference were first printed in the *Pennsylvania Packet* on 8 November. See DHFFE, I, 323–29.

A Federalist
Pennsylvania Packet, 19 November 1788

To the PUBLIC.

The time is approaching in which you are to exercise one of the greatest privileges of free men, that of electing representatives to serve you in Congress. The importance of this appointment ought to induce your greatest deliberation and most dispassionate reasoning. The question is not whether you will have this or that man in Congress who will serve the purposes of party, but who will consider the state as a family of which he is the guardian and protector.—The passions and prejudices of a party-man ought not to find entrance in the breast of him to whom thousands look up for safety. Let the patriot and honest man meet your appointment, whether he be stigmatised with the odious and party appellation of an anti federalist, or called by the popular and delusive name of a federalist. These distinctions are only intended to biass your minds and excite your passions against men who have every claim upon you, and whose bosoms glow with as much patriotic warmth as the most republican spirit could desire.—The most zealous advocates for the federal government will admit that it has defects which ought to be remedied, and as it has a remedy in itself, why shall the man who wishes to avail himself of this constitutional redress, be rejected? If it is a perfect system of government (and that it is not no one will deny) I would lead the man with the bitterest execrations who attempted an alteration; but if it is not, would it not be consistent with reason and prudence to make such men our choice who would give us the security we desire? None but he who would wade through the filth of party to serve his purposes, would deny the propriety and justice of the measure. No doubt these opinions will be considered by some as flowing from anti-federal principles, but I can declare, with the honesty and sincerity of a man of honor, that I feel as much interest in obtaining the operation of the federal constitution, as the most zealous advocate for it; but under the impression of the necessity of amendments, I should be glad to see our representatives in Congress men of moderation, abilities, and zeal for the liberty and happiness of our country.—With this view I have suggested the following ticket for your consideration, as being in my estimation superior to any that has hitherto been offered to you

>William Bingham,
>Charles Pettit,
>John Armstrong,
>William Findley,
>Peter Muhlenberg,
>General William Irvine,
>William Montgomery,
>Edward Hand.

In the formation of this ticket, party has not had the smallest influence. I disclaim every connexion with party, but in common with my fellow citizens I have something to lose; this something I should wish to entrust with such as knew the full value of it, and I conceive none more proper than the above mentioned gentlemen, many of whom afforded their personal services for the security and happiness of our country.

Joseph Jones to James Madison
Richmond, Va., 21 November 1788 (excerpt)[1]

... The parties feds and anti have in most transactions been pretty distinguished. Your case is one among others where the spirit of party operated strongly. Being among the number of those who wish to see some amendments in the plan I have been pressed to come forward and be of the new Congress but it is too late in the day for me to involve myself in troublesome business and have declared agt. it....

1. RC, Madison Papers, DLC. For the entire letter, see Rutland, *Madison,* XI, 358–59.

Foreign Spectator X
Philadelphia Federal Gazette, 21 November 1788[1]

REMARKS *on the Amendments to the Federal Constitution, proposed by the Conventions of Massachusetts, New-Hampshire, New-York, Virginia, South and North-Carolina, with the minorities of Pennsylvania and Maryland, by a* FOREIGN SPECTATOR.

NUMBER X.

We shall now consider the amendments relative to the regulation of commerce. The conventions of Massachusetts, New-Hampshire, and North-Carolina, request *that Congress erect no company of merchants with exclusive advantages of commerce*, 5th, 5th and 22d am. respectively; that of New-York extends the restriction, by the 6th am. *that Congress do not grant monopolies, or erect any company with exclusive advantages of commerce.*

Monopolies are in general pernicious, and therefore adopted but in extraordinary cases by the politicians of the present enlightened æra. In this, as in many other political maxims, exceptions must be admitted. It is not my business to show when or how they may be useful in America; but only to prove that an absolute prohibition should not fetter our commercial operations. I beg leave then to quote a celebrated author on this subject, as his reasoning is very plain and sensible: "When a company of merchants undertake, at their own risk and expence, to establish a new trade with some remote and barbarous nation, it may not be unreasonable to incorporate them into a joint stock company, and to grant them, in case of their success, a monopoly of the trade for a certain number of years. It is the easiest and most natural way to which the state can recompence them for hazarding a dangerous and expensive experiment, of which the public is afterwards to reap the benefit. A temporary monopoly of this kind may be vindicated upon the same principles upon which a like monopoly of a new machine is granted to its inventor, and that of a new book to its author. But upon the expiration of the term, the monopoly ought certainly to terminate, &c."⁽ᵃ⁾ "To render the establishment of a joint stock company perfectly reasonable, with the circumstance of being reducible to strict rule and method, two other circumstances ought to concur. First, it ought to appear with the clearest evidence, that the undertaking is of greater and more general utility, than the greater part of common trades. And secondly, that it requires a greater capital than can easily be collected into a private co-partnery."⁽ᵇ⁾ He then applies this theory to four particular trades—banks, insurance from fire, sea risk and capture in time of war; making and maintaining a navigable canal; bringing water for the supply of a great city. At the same time he disapproves of granting any other privileges to such companies than what are indispensible for the undertaking. In this young and extensive country, few individuals have large capitals; yet many great sources of industry may be opened by a joint stock, as manufactures, public roads, and canals, mines, fisheries, trade with the interior and still unexplored regions. As to those monopolies, which by way of premiums, are granted for certain years to ingenious discoveries in medicine, machines and useful arts; they are common in all countries, and more necessary in this, as the government has no resources to reward extraordinary merit.

The convention of New-York desires, *that the power of Congress to pass uniform laws concerning bankruptcy, shall only extend to merchants and other traders; and that the states respectively may pass laws for the relief of other insolvent debtors,* 19th am. It is difficult to describe with accuracy the class of traders; every man that buys and sells may be so called. Besides, if a general distinction between citizens and landed proprietors is necessary, it may be drawn by Congress, which represents all the states, and all the different classes of society. Uniform laws of this kind are certainly very necessary, because the people of the United States will have as much intercourse as if they formed only one empire; and by 2d sect. 4th art. *the citizens of each state shall be entitled to all the privileges and immunities of citizens in the several states.* The evils of tender-laws will in a great measure remain, while a debt due in another state may be cancelled, reduced, or suspended by a fluctuating local system. Foreigners have a claim to equal justice with domestic creditors, and without it we can expect no beneficial intercourse with them.

The 24th am. of the North Carolina convention, concerning the latter part of the 5th par. of 9th sect. of 1st art. seems to be only an explanation; as the expression in that place is too concise to be clear.[2] If it means to guard against duties on exportation, it is needless, because by the first part of that par. no tax or duty shall be laid on articles exported from any state.

The same convention proposes by the 25th am. *that congress shall not directly or indirectly either by themselves or through the judiciary, interfere with any one of the states in the redemption of paper money already emitted, and now in circulation, or in liquidating and discharging the public securities of any one of the states: but each and every state shall have the exclusive right of making such laws and regulations for the above purposes, as they will think proper.* The perplexed finances of some states will not permit them to cancel the paper money before the new government commences. Indeed this inveterate and extensive evil must be abolished with such a discretion, as the public good and justice to individuals require. At the same time it is necessary for the general prosperity of the union, that it should be done with all public expedition; and that the laws and regulations made in any state should not injure other states, nor even a part of the people in that state. I have no doubt but this business may be settled with a moderation and prudence that shall please all parties.

The convention of New-York proposes by the 8th amend. *That no money be borrowed on the credit of the United States, without the assent of two-thirds of the senators and representatives present in each house.* Borrowing is not a more important trust, than many others, which must be given to the federal government. Very probable this resource will not be considerable for several years; neither foreign nations nor the people of this country will, lend until they see the confederacy well established; an extraordinary majority is not therefore necessary in this case.

The conventions of Virginia and North-Carolina request *that no navigation laws, or law regulating commerce shall be passed without the consent of two-thirds of the members present in both houses,* 8th amend. respectively. The minority of Maryland, in the 1st am. signifies the same in words a little different.³ Systematic regulations of commerce embrace many objects, and if they prove wrong in the course of operations, cannot be changed without confusion, and various disadvantages; they should therefore be made with mature deliberation; especially as they do not require a pressing expedition. It appears therefore reasonable to stipulate a greater majority in this case. Yet although this condition is not expressed, there is no danger that any navigation act will be passed without a large majority, because it will affect the states in a sensible and permanent manner. A bare majority will certainly never dare to make an act of oppression against nearly one half! no, three-fourths would not attack the other fourth. The federal government with all the parade of powers has no real strength without a very great unanimity. Any twelve would never presume to affront one of the great states. As for the small ones, they are blended with the others from north to south, and have respectively the same commercial interest with a powerful neighbour; from which they drive an additional security.

Finally, any partiality that might disgrace congress is considerably checked by the express declaration in the 5th par. 9th sect. 1st art. that *no preference shall be given by any regulation of commerce or revenue, to the ports of one state over those of another.*

Commercial treaties will be considered under the amendment that respects the senate.

(a) *Smith on the wealth of nations,* 3d vol. p. 143–4.
(b) *Ditto,* 147–8.

1. Reprinted: *New York Daily Gazette,* 13 June 1789; and in the October issue of the Philadelphia *American Museum.* For the authorship of the "Foreign Spectator" series, see the headnote to Essay No. I (21 October, BoR, III, 264n).
2. For Article XXIV, see BoR, I, 269.

3. This is actually the seventh amendment in the list of amendments not agreed to by the committee (Appendix I, BoR, III, 476).

A Federalist who is for Amendments
New York Daily Advertiser, 22 November 1788[1]

Sir, I Observed, in your paper of the 17th, an extract of a letter from a gentleman at Newport, to the printers of the Hartford paper, with some remarks on the proceedings of the legislature of the state of Rhode-Island, in their late sessions.[2]

It is not my design to vindicate the conduct of that state with respect to their paper money system; I believe it to be impolitic in the highest degree, at the same time I consider such scurrilous reflections on the conduct of a sovereign state, as indecent and scandalous, and calculated to inflame the passions and fix them in error, rather than to lead them to abandon them. But what is very extraordinary in this publication is, that it is said '*the assembly of Rhode-Island seem at present to be established in their proceedings by receiving governor Clinton's letter.*' At first view, one would suppose, from this writer's mode of expression, that governor Clinton had written to the legislature of Rhode-Island, advising and encouraging them to persist in their paper money system. But from what follows, it appears that he alluded to the circular letter agreed to by the convention of this state, inviting their sister states to unite in calling another general convention, to consider of and recommend amendments to the new constitution.—Why is this called governor Clinton's letter? It is true he signed it, but not in his private character, nor yet as governor, but by order of the convention.—I ask again, what tendency had this letter to *establish and comfort* the legislature in their proceedings respecting the paper money, when it did not contain one word relating to it, nor do any of the amendments recommended, hold out the most distant idea in its favor?[3]

This writer's reasoning upon the constitution, and amendments to it, is as extraordinary as what he says respecting governor Clinton's letter. He says that *the arguments in its favor, drawn from the proceedings of Rhode-Island are the most powerful and uncontradictory of any that have yet been suggested*—It is this, Rhode-Island is against the constitution, therefore it is a good one, because Rhode-Island has done wrong in making paper money. Rhode-Island is in favor of amendments to the new constitution, therefore none ought to be made, because she has acted unjustly and impolitically in her paper system. If this writer has no better arguments to support his opinion in favor of the new government, very little dependence is to be placed upon him. Is it true, that because a man is wrong in one measure, or even in many, that he is wrong in all?

at this rate any government might be proved good. No one can doubt but that Rhode-Island would oppose a hereditary despotism: but would it thence follow that it would be a good government? But my principal aim in taking notice of this publication, is to point out the conduct of a few individuals in different parts of the union, who are using all the means in their power to divert the minds of the good people of America from the subject of amendments. Most of those who were for adopting the new constitution in this state, declared in the most explicit terms that they wished for amendments; but they differed with a number of their fellow citizens who were opposed to its adoption with respect to the mode of obtaining them. They said, we will adopt it first, and procure the alterations in the mode prescribed in the constitution.—I was among those who were of this opinion, and it is evident that great part of the people of America were in this sentiment. This appears from the proceedings of the different conventions, as well as from other evidence. The convention of this state, though divided upon the question, whether they should adopt the constitution or not, a great majority were in favor of the amendments they recommended; and they were unanimously of opinion that some amendments were proper; and with one voice united that a revision of the system was necessary to recommend it to the approbation and support of a numerous body of their constituents, and earnestly exhort and request the legislature of the several states to take the earliest opportunity of making application for another convention, to meet at a period not far remote.

Similar language was held by the most of those who were in favor of the system previous to its adoption.

It is therefore an insult, not only upon the people of this state, but to a majority of the people of the United States, to treat the proposal of calling another convention with the contempt that this writer and some others have done.

Wisdom and sound policy dictate that the constitution should be revised, that it should be made conformable, as far as may be, to the wishes of all. It is impossible to support a free government, against which the sentiments of a great part of the people are opposed, and those who would attempt to do it, manifest a disposition unfriendly to equal liberty.

The constitution is adopted by small majorities in a number of the most important states; in several of them a confidence that their sister states would consent to unite in a revision of the system, and alter the exceptionable parts, was the prevailing inducement with a number to accede to it. This confidence was cherished by the express declaration of many of the advocates for its adoption, that they would cordially concur in endeavoring to procure a revision of the system. I hope none of those who made such professions will be guilty of such duplicity of conduct as to oppose the calling a convention to propose amendments.

I consider the man who pursues this conduct as promoting a measure that will produce discord, and perhaps convulsions, in the United States, and therefore, as acting the part of an enemy to his country.

1. On 21 November the *Daily Advertiser* promised that this essay "will appear in our paper to-morrow."
2. "Extract of a letter from a gentleman at Newport to the Printers of this Paper, dated Nov. 4," *Connecticut Courant*, 10 November 1788 (RCS:R.I., 428–29).
3. For the New York Convention's circular letter and amendments, see BoR, I, 153–58, 256–64.

A Real Patriot
Philadelphia Federal Gazette, 22 November 1788

To ALL TRUE FEDERALISTS.

Friends and Fellow-Citizens,

Once more your country calls upon you, to step forth and rescue her from impending ruin—you have already done much you have waded thro' deluges of blood, to stem the torrent of tyranny and purchase freedom to yourselves, and your posterity—you have formed and adopted a constitution to preserve the blessings of liberty and independence, which you had so dearly purchased. These atchievements, my fellow-citizens, will be gratefuly remembered by millions yet unborn who will revere the memory of the men, who established their rights on a firm basis, and whose pride it will be, that such were their forefathers.

The cause of virtue, of liberty and your country, again summons you to the field, to complete the great work, and by one generous effort to crown all your past success with happiness and glory: I need not tell you that the enemies to the federal constitution in this state, having failed in their base attempts to prevent its adoption, are endeavouring under the show of *amendments*, to debilitate and destroy its energy, and to make it as wretched a system as that by which we are at present exposed to misery at home, and contempt abroad.

With this view, a ticket formed by the junto at Harrisburg has been industriously circulated through the back counties, with that secrecy and silence, which are ever the concomitants of dark and villainous designs, and which have always characterized the party.

With this ticket, they hope for success, in some of the back counties; but as this alone would be insufficient, they have fallen upon another grand project, to effect a division of the federal interest, in this part of the state; and to effect this infamous purpose, have dared to place some worthy federal gentlemen on the ticket, with three members of the Harrisburg ticket.

It requires but a very small share of penetration, to perceive that the federal gentlemen on this last ticket, are only intended as mere machines to serve their purpose; they will not be run in the back part of the state, but they will be run here, to divide the federal interest, so that if they should fail of success with the members of the Harrisburg ticket, *in toto,* they may at least ensure the election of such of them as are on both their tickets.

Never was a more artful plan projected than this: but their dark contrivances are now exposed to public view, and it remains with you, to say, whether you are weak enough to be duped, by such base artifices, and thus be led to overthrow that constitution which you have strenuously endeavoured to establish; or whether you will not rather vote for those men, who are firm friends to your cause, and have been nominated by conferrees elected by the people at large, throughout the state, and convened for the purpose at Lancaster.—I will not, my friends, suppose you mean enough to desert the great cause of America, at this critical juncture; when her fate is to be determined, as it were by one throw. Forbid it heaven, that ever my fellow-citizens should be so lost to all sense of their own, and their country's happiness.

Philadelphia Independent Gazetteer, 22 November 1788[1]

MR. PRINTER, I see a number of tickets published, containing the names of candidates for seats in Congress, to be run at the approaching election. Different persons have different friends to serve; but the PEOPLE have but one interest. Under the new constitution, properly AMENDED, in all probability, we shall be very happy; but without AMENDMENTS, we shall be miserable slaves. Under this view, it is the interest and duty of every freemen, to vote for such men as will vote for AMENDMENTS. The following ticket is that, which has been fixed upon by the FRIENDS OF AMENDMENTS; and the members, if chosen, will do every thing in their power, as soon as the new government is organized and set in motion, to procure AMENDMENTS in a constitutional way. Every FRIEND TO AMENDMENTS, which is but another name for a FRIEND TO HIS COUNTRY, it is hoped will vote for it. The only way to obtain AMENDMENTS is to vote for the FRIENDS OF AMENDMENTS. The TOOLS AND MINIONS OF POWER will oppose AMENDMENTS, and will enslave us if they can.

The following is the ticket:—

WILLIAM FINDLEY,	WILLIAM MONTGOMERY,
CHARLES PETTIT,	BLAIR M'CLENACHAN,
Gen. WILLIAM IRVINE,	DANIEL HIESTER,
ROBERT WHITEHILL,	PETER MUHLENBERG.

1. Two days later, the Philadelphia *Independent Gazetteer* again printed the Antifederalist ticket followed by a ticket of ten candidates for presidential electors. The tickets were prefaced: "The real friends of American liberty, who wish to carry the Constitution of the United States into execution, and at the same time to procure such amendments, as will secure the liberties of the people, have determined to vote for the following Gentlemen as Representatives and Electors."

Philadelphia Independent Gazetteer, 22 November 1788 (excerpts)

Extract of a letter from a gentleman of information in New-York to his friend in this city.

... "All good *feds* as well as *antis* in this state call for amendments, and are astonished at some paragraphs against amendments published from your papers; certainly their must be some among you, who would go to any length to carry the new government in its present form, would involve America in all the horrors of a civil war and dissolve the union, if the people would be led by them into such measures. You know the office hunters would be much narrowed in their prospects when amendments take place.

"None go into Congress from this state except they promise to secure the rights of the people by amendments—and we will admit no lawyers into the house of representatives or popular part of Congress. How careful should the people be to appoint good men to hold *their purse strings*, when the great men are always watching to *peculate!*

"Our Legislature will take up the business of the union the first in order, and will, I have no doubt, adopt amendments."[1]

1. In early October 1788 the Federalist-dominated Pennsylvania Assembly, by a vote of 38 to 24, defeated an Antifederalist motion to recommend the New York Convention's circular letter to the next General Assembly. On 5 March 1789, the Pennsylvania Assembly voted 41 to 20 not to agree with Virginia's call for a second general convention to amend the Constitution (BoR, I, 191–92).

Abraham Baldwin to Joel Barlow
New York, 23 November 1788 (excerpt)[1]

... I have now told you all the politicks, nothing else has been talked of, nothing else has been done, since you left us. the great prospect has hushed us all into silent expectation; fed and antifed has scarcely been mentioned for several months. some few begin now to scratch away a little about amendments, I believe it to be merely an electioneering tool....

1. RC, Misc. Manuscripts, Abraham Baldwin Folder, CtY.

Alexander Hamilton to James Madison
New York, 23 November 1788 (excerpt)[1]

... On the whole I have concluded to support Adams [for vice president]; though I am not without apprehensions on the score we have conversed about. My principal reasons are these—First He is a declared partisan of referring to future experience the expediency of amendments in the system (and though I do not *altogether* adopt this sentiment) it is much nearer my own than certain other doctrines. Secondly As he is certainly a character of importance in the Eastern states, if he is not Vice President, one of two worse things will be likely to happen— Either he must be nominated to some important office for which he is less proper, or will become a malcontent and possibly expouse and give additional weight to the opposition to the Government....

1. RC, Madison Papers, DLC. For the entire letter, see Rutland, *Madison*, XI, 365–67.

William Duer to James Madison
post-23 November 1788 (excerpt)[1]

... You may remember some Conversation I once had with you on the Subject of Electing Mr. John Adams as Vice President. I have ascertained it in a Mode perfectly satisfactory, that this Gentleman if chosen, will be a Strenuous Opposer against calling a Convention; which in the present State of Parties, I consider as a vital Stab to the Constitution; and not only that; but that he and his old Coadjuter R H Lee, will be perfectly opposite in all measures, relative to the Establishment of the Character and Credit of the Government. I am therefore anxious, that the Fœderalists to the Southward may join in supporting his Nomination as Vice President. A Greater Knowledge of the World has cured him of his old Party Prejudice.—and I am satisfy'd nothing is to be feard from that Quarter. On the Contrary, should he not be Elected to this Station (which I am fully convinced is his Wish) his Lukewarmness (should nothing Else be the Consequence,) will throw a pernicious Weight into the Antifederal Scale....

1. RC, Madison Papers, DLC. For the entire letter, see Rutland, *Madison*, XI, 367–68. In the omitted portion of the letter, Duer refers to Madison's 20 November letter to Hamilton, which Hamilton answered on 23 November (immediately above). Duer probably wrote this letter slightly thereafter.

De Witt Clinton to Charles Clinton, Jr.
New York, 25 November 1788 (excerpt)[1]

... The Legislature of Virginia have chosen Richard Henry Lee and William Grayson Esquires (decided antifederalists) senators to the new Congress—I am informed that Mr. P. Henry would not accept of the office of Senator—probably he prefers staying at home in order to keep the coals of *Antifederalism* alive—They have also censured the Constitution in high terms, declared the necessity of immediate amendments, & appointed Committees to draw up their reasons, to write an Answer to the circular letter of our late Convention, and to write circular letters to all the States in the Union urging the necessity of cooperating with them in the obtainment of alterations.[2] R. Island would have nothing to do with the Constitution, but recommended our Circular Letter to the consideration of all the townships in their state.[3] ...

1. RC, Personal Misc. Papers, Box Cle–Cord, Folder: Clinton, De Witt, DLC.
2. For Virginia's call of a general convention to consider amendments and letters to New York governor George Clinton and a circular letter to the other governors, see BoR, I, 158–80.
3. Reacting to the New York circular letter, the Rhode Island General Assembly, dominated by Antifederalists, overwhelmingly adopted on 1 November 1788 a resolution calling upon the state's thirty towns to consider if delegates should be appointed to a general convention and to instruct their representatives to the legislature on what to do if such delegates were appointed. Such advisory referenda were common in Rhode Island. Only nine towns voted for a general convention. See RCS:R.I., 425–27n, 435–49.

Edward Carrington to James Madison
Richmond, Va., 26 November 1788 (excerpt)[1]

Since my last[2] it is decided that [James] Monroe is to be your opponent. the Interest of both Cabel & Strother will be combined in his favor. I wish you could be in the district as no pains will be spared to impress the minds of the people with prejudice against you—the ground taken is that you are utterly against any kind of alteration in the Govt.— the Election throughout the state is to be on the second of February— so it went from the lower House—I was told this evning that an alteration to sometime about the last of January took place in the Senate,— if such is the case it escaped me when the bill was returned. I have already apprised you of the *political* Hostility of Monroe, and it will be well for you to pay some regard to it....

1. RC, Madison Papers, DLC. For the entire letter, see Rutland, *Madison*, XI, 369–70.
2. For Carrington's letter of 18 November, see BoR, III, 360.

Foreign Spectator XI
Philadelphia Federal Gazette, 28 November 1788[1]

REMARKS *on the Amendments to the Federal Constitution, proposed by the Conventions of Massachusetts, New-Hampshire, New-York, Virginia, South and North-Carolina, with the minorities of Pennsylvania and Maryland, by a* FOREIGN SPECTATOR.

NUMBER XI.

We shall now proceed to view those amendments which particularly concern several personal rights and liberties.

Arbitrary imprisonment has in all ages and countries been a favourite and formidable instrument of tyranny. "To bereave a man of life (says a well-known author) or by violence to confiscate his estate, without accusation or trial, would be so gross and notorious an act of despotism, as must at once convey the alarm of tyranny throughout the whole nation; but confinement of the person, by secretly hurrying him to gaol, where his sufferings are unknown or forgotten, is a less public, a less striking, and therefore *a more dangerous engine* of arbitrary government.[a]" A provision must then be made, that if any person should, without a legal cause, be committed or detained in prison, or otherwise restrained by any authority whatever, he shall be discharged, bailed, or brought to a speedy trial according to circumstances. This is done by that excellent law, called the writ of habeas corpus, which is deservedly extolled as one of the principal balwarks of a free constitution. Yet when the state is in real danger, even this valuable privilege must be suspended. A person who may injure the life, property and liberty of many fellow-citizens, and stab his country in the most sensible part, must be secured without formal delay; no bail can be responsible for his good behaviour; a legal trial may for some time be impracticable; in some cases his punishment may even encrease the fury of rebellion. It is not common that innocent people incur such strong suspicion, as to be long deprived of liberty; but if, by some extraordinary causes, it was to be the lot of a faithful citizen, would he not freely submit to a general regulation so necessary for the safety of his country, and all his dear connexions! In Great-Britain, the parliament can, whenever it sees proper, by suspending the habeas corpus act for a limited time, authorise the executive to imprison suspected persons, without giving any reason for so doing.—"The nation parts with its liberty for a while, in order to preserve it for ever," as the above judicious author expresses it.[b]

The federal constitution, on the true principles of liberty and patriotism, enacts by the 2d part 9th sect. 1st art. *that the privilege of the writ of habeas corpus shall not be suspended, unless when in cases of rebellion or invasion the public safety may require it.* The convention of New-York would add this limitation: *that the privilege of the habeas corpus shall not by any law be suspended for a longer term than six months, or until twenty days after the meeting of the Congress next following the passing the act for such suspension,* 10 am. As the safety, perhaps the preservation of the country, renders this act necessary, it must also determine its duration. It would be folly, nay, cruelty, to repeal it in the height of rebellion, or when a powerful enemy, assisted by a band of traitors, spills the best blood of America, and murders her patriots in dungeons or prison-ships. No! by the sacred name of liberty, by the honor of the union, by every faithful American heart! if my father, son, or brother has forfeited his liberty to an injured country, let his worthless body be secured by walls, and if necessary, by chains. I remark again, that innocence can scarcely ever, for a long time, suffer from suspicion. The more vigorous efforts we make in such public disasters, the sooner will the mild laws and all the blessings of civil government be restored.

What is said on this matter, is a sufficient reply to the 12th amend. of the New-Hampshire convention, *that congress shall never disarm any citizen, unless such as are or have been in actual rebellion.* If, by the acknowledged necessity of suspending the privilege of *habeas corpus,* a suspected person may be secured, he may much more be disarmed. In such unhappy times it may be very expedient to disarm those, who cannot conveniently be guarded, or whose conduct has been less obnoxious. Indeed to prevent by such a gentle measure, crimes and misery, is at once justice to the nation, and mercy to deluded wretches, who may otherwise, by the instigation of a dark and bloody ringleader, commit many horrid murders, for which they must suffer condign punishments.

The minority of Pennsylvania seems to have been desirous of limiting the federal power in these cases; but their conviction of its necessity appears by those very parts of the 3d and 7th amendments framed in this view, to wit, *that no man be deprived of his liberty except by the law of the land, or the judgment of his peers—and that no law shall be passed for disarming the people, or any of them, unless for crimes committed, or real danger of public injury from individuals.* The occasional suspension of the above privilege becomes pro tempore the law of the land, and by virtue of it dangerous persons are secured. Insurrections against the federal government are undoubtedly real dangers of public injury, not only from individuals, but great bodies; consequently the laws of the union should be competent for the disarming of both.

Not to be misunderstood, I shall add, that the suspension of *habeas corpus* is by no means requisite in commotions that may be quelled by the ordinary resources of public justice;—neither do I wish for any such rigorous riot acts, by which human lives are destroyed merely to prevent moderate damage to property, or some other not very grievous disorders. Indeed the spirit of republican liberty will be a sufficient guard against such; and of the two evils, extreme lenity is most to be apprehended.

(a) *Blackstone's Commentaries*, vol. 1, page 156.[2]
(b) *Ditto*, page 126.[3]

1. Reprinted: *New York Daily Gazette*, 15 June 1789. For the authorship of the "Foreign Spectator" series, see the headnote to Essay No. I (21 October, BoR, III, 264n).
2. Blackstone, *Commentaries*, Book I, chapter 1, p. 136. *The Federalist* 84 also quotes this passage (BoR, II, 484).
3. Blackstone, *Commentaries*, Book I, chapter 1, p. 132.

David Humphreys to Thomas Jefferson
Mount Vernon, Fairfax County, Va., 29 November 1788 (excerpt)[1]

... There has been an extraordinary revolution in the sentiments of men, respecting political affairs, since I came to America;[2] & much more favorable in the result than could then have been reasonably expected. At the close of the war, after the little season of unlimited credit was passed, the people in moderate circumstances found themselves very much embarrassed by the scarcity of money, by debts & taxes. They affected to think that the part of Society composed of men in the liberal professions & those who had considerable property, were in combination to distress them, & to establish an Aristocracy. Demagogues made use of these impressions to procure their own elections & to carry their own schemes into execution. Lawyers, in some States, by these artifices, became indiscriminately odious. In others men of the strongest local prejudices & narrowest principles had the whole direction of the affairs of their States. You will feel the force of this assertion the more readily, when you shall have been informed that the same Genl [James] Wadsworth, who was in Congress with you at Annapolis became, in conjunction with two or three of his Subalterns, the director of every political measure in Connecticut; and prevented, in almost every instance, a compliance with the Requisitions of Congress. On the other part, great numbers of those who wished to see an efficient fœderal government prevail, began to fear that the bulk of the people would never submit to it. In short some of them, who had been utterly averse to Royalty, began to imagine that hardly any thing but a king could cure the evil. It was truly astonishing to have been witness to some conversations, which I have heard. Still all the more reasonable men saw that the remedy would be infinitely worse than the disease. In this fluctuating & irritable situation the public mind continued, for some time. The insurrection in Massachusetts[3] was not without its benefits. From a view of the impotence of the general government, of the contempt in which we were held abroad & of the want of happiness at home, the Public was thus gradually wrought to a disposition for receiving a government possessed of sufficient energy to prevent the calamities of Anarchy & civil war; & yet guarded, as well as the nature of circumstances will admit, so as to prevent it from degenerating into Aristocracy, Oligarchy or Monarchy. True it is, that honest & wise men have differed in sentiment about the kind of checks & balances which are necessary for this purpose: but equally true it is, that there is not an honest & wise man who does not see & feel the indispensable necessity of preserving the Union. You will have been informed, long since, that all the States, Rhode Island & North Carolina excepted, have acceded to the proposed form of government. In the former paper-money & dishonesty are the sole causes of their perseverance in opposition—the same reasons are also assigned for the conduct of North Carolina; how justly, or unjustly, I know not. It is believed, however that the latter will come into the pale of the new Union at the eleventh hour.

The general opinion of the Advocates for the Government is, that some explanations & amendments are highly necessary. They conceive, however, that it might be dangerous to put every thing afloat, in seeking that object, before some degree of stability shall have been given to the System, by its being carried into effect. But it is thought that some, who push for premature amendments, wish to sap its very existance. That is to say, its opponents in the State of New York. Be that as it may, the probability amounts almost to a certainty, that it will be quietly carried into effect in March next. . . .

1. RC, Jefferson Papers, DLC. For the entire letter, see Boyd, XIV, 300–304.
2. Humphreys served as secretary to the American commission to negotiate commercial treaties in Paris from 1784 to 1786 when he returned to his home in Derby, Conn.
3. Shays's Rebellion. See CC:18 on this and other agrarian unrest.

James Madison to Henry Lee
Philadelphia, 30 November 1788 (excerpt)[1]

. . . The measures pursued at Richmond are as impolitic as they are otherwise exceptionable—if alterations of a reasonable sort are really in view, they are much more attainable from Congress than from attempts to bring about another Convention—It is already decided that the latter mode is a hopeless pursuit. . . .

1. RC (copy), Madison Papers, DLC. The letter is not in Madison's hand and is probably a copy of the recipient's copy supplied by the sons of Henry Lee in the 1830s. Madison had requested copies of his letters to their father. For the entire letter, see Rutland, *Madison*, XI, 371–72.

James Madison to George Washington
Philadelphia, 2 December 1788 (excerpt)[1]

... This prospect[2] is on the whole auspicious, and shews the folly of Virga if the measures of the legislature are to be taken for the sense of the State in urging another Convention at this time.[3] The real friends to the object professed by the leaders at Richmond ought to see that the only hope of obtaining alterations lies in not aiming at too many, and in being conciliatory as to the mode....

1. RC, Washington Papers, DLC. For the entire letter, see Abbot, *Washington, Presidential Series*, I, 145–47.
2. "This prospect" is that seven out of eight or all eight U.S. representatives from Pennsylvania probably would be Federalists.
3. For the legislative "measures," see BoR, I, 158–80.

Foreign Spectator XII
Philadelphia Federal Gazette, 2 December 1788[1]

REMARKS *on the Amendments to the Federal Constitution, proposed by the Conventions of Massachusetts, New-Hampshire, New-York, Virginia, South and North-Carolina, with the minorities of Pennsylvania and Maryland, by a* FOREIGN SPECTATOR.

NUMBER XII.

The important right of trial by jury in all criminal cases, is insured by the constitution in the clearest and most ample expressions.—*The trial of all crimes, except in cases of impeachment, shall be by jury; and such trial shall be held in the state where the said crimes shall have been committed; but when not committed within any state, the trial shall be at such place or places as the Congress may by law have directed,* 3d par. 2d sect. 3d art. Even the critical accusation of treason is to be judged by *double-fellow-citizens* (if I may coin a new word) by which the prisoner will receive not only full justice, but even some degree of partiality from his own state; indeed probably too much in every case when he has acted as member of a faction. If the crime is committed on the sea, rivers, or the common territory of the union, he is tried in a place previously nominated as a general seat of justice, lest the government, by a special appointment, should take a local advantage against him. The amendments proposed on this subject, appear therefore to be quite useless. *That no person shall be tried for any crime by which he may incur an infamous punishment or loss of life, until he be first indicted by a grand jury,* 6 am. by the conventions of Massachusetts and New-Hampshire, it is clearly stipulated. *That in criminal prosecutions, no man shall be restrained in the exercise of the usual and accustomed right of challenging or excepting to the jury,* 15 and 16 am. of the Virginia and North-Carolina conventions respectively. It is all implied in the above declaration. I shall only observe on this, that although in criminal or at least capital cases it is reasonable to allow an arbitrary challenge to a certain number of jurors, without shewing any cause at all, yet a boundary must be set to this privilege, otherwise the worst malefactors might elude all trial; and it is accordingly by the common law settled at 35, being nearly three full juries.[a] *That in all capital and criminal prosecutions, a man has a right to demand the cause and nature of his accusation; to be heard by himself and his council; to be confronted with his accusers and witnesses; to call for evidence in his favour, and a speedy trial by an impartial jury of his vicinage, without whose unanimous consent he cannot be found guilty; nor can he be compelled to give evidence against himself,* 3d am. by the min. of Pennsylvania. All these particulars are included in the usual trial by jury. By the general regulations, every action will be tried in the federal court of the district. *As to treason, no person shall be convicted of it, unless on the testimony of two witnesses to the same open act, or on confession in open court,* 3d sect. 3d art. Consider how many treasonable acts a person may commit, and still in neither one be discovered by two witnesses, and what a jury can do even against this united testimony!

The minority of Pennsylvania would explicitly enact, *that excessive bail ought not to be required, nor excessive fines imposed, nor cruel nor unusual punishments inflicted.* All this is universally acknowledged to be necessary for civil freedom and happiness. Nothing to the contrary is even indirectly hinted at in the federal constitution. As to particular laws, we must expect a wisdom, equity, and mildness, which ought to distinguish the chosen representatives of a people fond of liberty even to enthusiasm. No stiff rules can possibly be previously contrived; who will pretend to specify the proper amount of bail, or fines in every case?[b] As to treason, Congress will determine its punishment by a general act in the calm of domestic peace; which cannot be altered by any sanguinary party-rage, that unfortunately may arise hereafter. By the 9th sect. 1st art. *all ex post facto laws* are expressly forbidden; thus no person can ever be punished for things, which, when done, were breaches of no law; nor suffer a greater penalty for any transgression than was fixed prior to the commission of it.

The two minorities of Pennsylvania and Maryland, by the 5th and 8th amendments respectively, anxiously guard against the oppression of general warrants, and special warrants unsupported by evidence. The latter enforces the reasons for this express declaration in the language of a pompous severity: *Congress having the power of laying excises, the horror of a free people, by which our dwelling-houses, those castles considered so sacred by the English law, will be laid open to the insolence and oppression of office; there could be no constitutional check provided, that would prove so effectual a safeguard to our citizens. General warrants, too, the great engine by which power may destroy those individuals who resist usurpation, are also hereby forbid to those magistrates, who are to administer the general government.* I began this essay with a firm resolution against a single touch of satire; but in this place, the image of Don Quixot fighting the windmill forces itself irresistably on my fancy. We must be knight-errants in liberty, to imagine the dreadful giant Congress storming our domestic castles by warrants both general and special, and searching our cellars, garrets, bed-chambers and closets by a cursed host of excise-men worse than the Prussian Death-Heads, or the Emperor's Pandours. But don't be alarmed good Americans! If I know any thing at all about you after eighteen years acquaintance, you are not such gentle doves, as to let any cormorants rifle your nests, snatch the victuals from your little ones, and tear the feathers of your beloved mates. Mercy on the Congress that would attempt it. You may safely laugh (if you don't resent the degrading affront) at the ominous contrast between the mildness of English government, and the tyranny of Congress! If English law holds the dwelling of a Wilkes sacred,[2] the federal constitution will equally consecrate yours from any violation whether English, American, or any other.

This minority [i.e., Maryland] requests by the 12th am. *that the freedom of the press be inviolably preserved, adding, in prosecutions in the federal courts for libels, the constitutional preservation of this great and fundamental right, may prove invaluable.* The minority of Pennsylvania declare by the 6th am. *that the people have a right to the freedom of speech, and of writing and publishing their sentiments; therefore the freedom of the press shall not be restrained by any law of the United States.*

As the constitution is entirely silent on this matter, no vindication is necessary; I shall, however, freely express my opinion. Freedom of the press is not only a noble right of individual citizens, but also an excellent means to enlighten, refrain, animate, and improve the government. I would rather see the press licentious than fettered; yet an absolute permission to write any thing whatever, would be very pernicious. Without going into a subject, on which a volume might be written, let me only ask these questions: In case of a dangerous invasion, may a traitor, by seditious pamphlets, inveigle numbers to join the enemy? As to personal wrongs, shall a member of Congress be given up to the poison and poignard of scribbling assassins? When every fellow-citizen may sue for defamation, shall he be held up, as a paricide who is in foreign pay, ready on the first occasion to sell the blood of his country? *The liberty of the press must then be inviolable, but not violate the dearest interests of society.* If the first part is to be inserted in the federal constitution, the other also must. Whatever laws may be enacted on this subject, either by Congress or the state governments, cannot fail of being proper, if dictated by a spirit of rational liberty: and this spirit is the ultimate safety of every republic.

(a) *Blackstone's Commentaries*, 4 vol. page 346–7.[3]
(b) See *Blackstone*, 295–6, 4 vol.[4]

1. Reprinted: *New York Daily Gazette*, 16 June 1789. For the authorship of the "Foreign Spectator" series, see the headnote to Essay No. I (21 October, BoR, III, 264n).
2. A reference to John Wilkes's 1763 trial against the use of general warrants.
3. Blackstone, *Commentaries*, Book IV, chapter 27, pp. 347–48.
4. *Ibid.*, chapter 22 ("Of Commitment and Bail"), especially pp. 296–97.

Massachusetts Salem Mercury, 2 December 1788[1]

We hear that the Legislature of Virginia have passed some resolutions concurring with the recommendation in the circular letter of the late Convention of Newyork, for taking measures for procuring another General Convention, in order to revise and AMEND the new Constitution of the United States.

1. Reprinted: Philadelphia *Independent Gazetteer*, 4 December; Portland, Maine, *Cumberland Gazette*, 11 December; *New Jersey Journal*, 17 December; *New Hampshire Recorder*, 23 December.

Thomas Jefferson to George Washington
Paris, 4 December 1788 (excerpt)[1]

... I have seen, with infinite pleasure, our new constitution accepted by 11. states, not rejected by the 12th. and that the 13th. happens to be a state of the least importance.[2] it is true that the minorities in most of the accepting states have been very respectable, so much so as to render it prudent, were it not otherwise reasonable, to make some sacrifices to them. I am in hopes that the annexation of a bill of rights to the constitution will alone draw over so great a proportion of the minorities, as to leave little danger in the opposition of the residue; and that this annexation may be made by Congress and the assemblies, without calling a convention which might endanger the most valuable parts of the system. ...

COMMENTARIES, 4 DECEMBER 1788   387

1. RC, Washington Papers, DLC. For the entire letter, see Abbot, *Washington, Presidential Series,* I, 152–58n.
2. North Carolina and Rhode Island, respectively.

George Washington to Jonathan Trumbull, Jr.
Mount Vernon, Fairfax County, Va., 4 December 1788 (excerpt)[1]

... In general the appointments to the Senate seem to have been very happy. Much will depend upon having disinterested and respectable characters in both Houses. For if the new Congress should be composed of characters in whom the citizens will naturally place a confidence, it will be a most fortunate circumstance for conciliating their good will to the government—and then, if the government can be carried on without touching the purses of the people too deeply, I think it will not be in the power of its adversaries to throw every thing into confusion, by effecting premature amendments. A few months will, however, shew what we are to expect. ...

1. RC (photocopy), Mount Vernon Ladies' Association of the Union. For the entire letter, see Abbot, *Washington, Presidential Series,* I, 158–59.

Alexander White to James Madison
Richmond, Va., 4 December 1788 (excerpt)[1]

Your obliging letter of 5 October reached me before I left Woodville—I was detained some days by an indisposition so that the Resolutions on which the Address to Congress and letter to Clinton were founded, had passed before my arrival; I had however the pleasure of giving my negative to the Address and Letters themselves, and of contributing somewhat towards forming those which were offered as Amendments[2]

But of these matters I understand you have been informed by your other Friends. ...

1. RC, Madison Papers, DLC. For the entire letter, see Rutland, *Madison,* XI, 379–80.
2. For the competing letters and White's vote, see BoR, I, 170–72.

A True Federalist
Worcester, Mass., *American Herald,* 4 December 1788

To the FREE Electors of the County of Worcester.
We have now arrived to a critical period of our political existence; and we are soon to determine (and we must determine for ourselves) whether we are to be a free, happy people under our Government, or not: Whether the New System has been sent directly from Heaven, as has been represented, and is, in its nature, perfect; or, whether it would

possibly admit of some amendments; whether the *balance* of Government is fixed on its proper basis; and whether the powers delegated are properly *checked*, &c.—These are questions important for us to determine; and as the time for electing a Federal Representative and Electors for this district is at hand, we shall naturally form our choice according as we determine upon the questions above.

It is hoped, however, that every person will have an opinion of his own upon the subject, and act accordingly, now the System is in embryo, and all depends upon the first impressions.—In fact, the great and ultimate question is, shall we preserve our *Republican Government*, or shall we suffer it to deg[en]erate into a *baleful Aristocracy!* Upon the determination of this one question, depends our political salvation and happiness; and much therefore depends on our first impressions:—It is therefore wished, that those who are better qualified for the task, would give information of such characters as they suppose would be well calculated for the present important exigences of our political affairs.

The following characters have already been recommended, viz.

The Hon. ARTEMAS WARD, Esq.   MARTIN KINGSLEY, Esq.
The Hon. JONATHAN GROUT, Esq.   JOHN SPRAGUE, Esq.
The Hon. TIMOTHY PAINE, Esq.   Doctor SAMUEL WILLIARD.

François de la E——.
Boston Herald of Freedom, 4 December 1788 (excerpt)[1]

LETTER XIX.

Dear Pierre, Ever attentive to the calls of friendship, again I resume the pen, for the purpose of transmitting to you an account of every thing remarkable, which occurs in this land of Liberty and plenty.

The Americans, bid fair to become an example to the rest of mankind, not only in matters of a political, but also of a religious nature; their sentiments, in regard to religion, are such as do honour to the age, and will be lasting monuments of their wisdom, when the present generation shall be no more; and lie down to sleep with their fathers.

In their darling Constitution, (the progress of which is still the general topick here, and to the administration of which the industrious and honourable MECHANICK, the enterprizing and persevering MERCHANT, the upright and judicious LAWYER, and every class of citizens which a nation contains, look forward to with rapture) no religious test is required as a qualification for any office whatever, but the truly good man, whether a Protestant, a Papist, a Mahometan or a Jew, is equally alike eligible to any post in government. On reflecting on such unexampled liberality, displayed by these god-like offspring of FREEDOM, the heart of every one, "*who looks through nature up to nature's God,*"[2] must expand with rapture inexpressible. "Happy, happy country, may thy happiness be perpetual."[3] . . .

1. Reprinted: Philadelphia *Federal Gazette,* 16 December; *Pennsylvania Packet,* 16 January 1789; *Pennsylvania Mercury,* 17 January; *Maryland Journal,* 29 January; Baltimore *Maryland Gazette,* 29 January.
2. Alexander Pope, *An Essay on Man, In Epistles to a Friend, Epistle IV* (London, 1734), 16, lines 326–27: "Slave to no Sect, who takes no private road,/But looks thro' *Nature* up to *Nature*'s GOD."
3. Quoted from James Wilson's Fourth of July oration printed in *Account of the Grand Federal Procession, Philadelphia, July 4, 1788* . . . (Philadelphia, 1788) (Evans 21149), 18.

Sidney
New York Journal, 4 December 1788[1]

To the Members of the Legislature of the STATE *of* NEW-YORK.

The arguments heretofore urged in favor of the new constitution have been progressive. Its advocates, at first, asserted it to be an excellent and a complete form of government, amply sufficient to secure the rights and liberties of the people; that a bill of rights was unnecessary; that the rulers ought to have the power to keep a standing army, build a navy, command the militia, and order them when and where they pleased, and to raise a revenue by direct taxes, poll taxes, and such excises as they might think proper: in a word, it was represented to be perfect, and that it was not in the power of human wisdom to devise a better.

Then again they admitted, that the constitution was imperfect, and that amendments were absolutely necessary, but strenuously advocated an adoption in its present form; trusting to subsequent amendments, because it could not be supposed that all the states would agree upon the same set of amendments.

It seems, however, to be now the general and prevailing opinion, that the amendments agreed to by the convention of this state, will be necessary and extensively beneficial.[2]

I shall enquire no farther into the motives which induced the convention to ratify this very imperfect constitution without a previous stipulation for all the amendments, than that it is said, on the one hand, that they were seduced and deceived by fears of convulsion, anarchy, and confusion, and that Congress would remove from the state in case of its non-adoption; and, on the other, that they adopted it from an invincible reluctance to a seperation from our sister states. It is sufficient to know, that it has been adopted in full confidence that amendments should take place, and that there were gentlemen strenuously for and against the measure; which of them were right and which wrong, time and experience will determine. Should the amendments be obtained without much opposition, trouble, and difficulty, it may be said, that those who were for the present adoption of it, have done well; but if, on the contrary, the amendments are opposed, and the means of obtaining them should throw the state into convulsions, I suppose it will not only be said, that they have done ill, but that they have acted against the experience of all ages.

By this adoption, we are placed in a most dangerous situation; and unless we proceed with the utmost caution and circumspection, and use all the means in our power to obtain the proposed amendments, we may be frustrated in our hopes and expectations; and the consequence will be, that we and our posterity must submit to the constitution in its present defective form; the greatest curse that ever befel a free people, since the fall of Adam. Our continental rulers will no doubt be prudent and cautious enough for a time and not exert all the powers delegated to them—and thus afford a temporary ease and relief to the minds and purses of the people: but although it may not effect an immediate slavery, yet it will hang like a mill-stone about us, until at last it must unavoidably settle us into hewers of wood and drawers of water.[3] Before its adoption, it was in our power to prevent, and we could have prevented, its operation, until its radical and dangerous defects were amended; whereas it now requires two thirds of the states to call a convention, the like number to agree to the amendments, and three fourths of the legislatures to ratify them.

From this train the difficulty of effecting any material amendments may be easily observed. It lately took Congress ten weeks, before seven states could be prevailed on, to agree upon the place, where the new government was to meet.[4] And this is not all, for (unless prevented) it becomes the duty "of the members of the several legislatures, and all the executive and judicial officers, both of the United States and of the several states, to be bound by oath or affirmation to support this constitution." Observe the constitution in its present form!

In this dangerous situation, where our all is at stake, I beg leave to suggest the propriety of passing an act as soon as possible, to inhibit your federal officers from taking that oath, until agreeable to our amendments. "The senators, and representatives and all the executive and judicial officers of the United States, shall be bound by oath or affirmation, not to infringe or violate the constitutions or the rights of the respective states." And the state officers, until the amendments have been previously agreed to, and confirmed by three fourths of the several legislatures.

Also to convert the following instruction into an oath of office. "And your representatives do swear, that they will exert all their influence and use all reasonable means to obtain a ratification of all the amendments; and in all laws to be passed by the Congress, in the mean time, to conform to the spirit of the said amendments."

This will undoubtedly be opposed and especially out of doors; for some of the most zealous advocates for the new government do not wish or desire any amendments (unless it should be to make it still stronger) and will exert every faculty of mind and body to oppose them; as if it was not enough, that we have transferred "the power of determining whether that government shall be rendered perpetual in its present form, or altered agreeable to our wishes on a minority of the states with whom we unite." They will wish to see the public officers embarrassed under this oath, and become even involuntary abettors in frustrating the accomplishment of the amendments; or at least secure their silence when their constituents shall be reduced to the dire necessity of calling out, stand fast in your liberty, be not again entangled with the yoke of bondage.[5]

Suppose Congress should interfere in your elections, attempt to violate the trial by jury, call out the militia, lay poll taxes and excises, or exercise other powers, contrary to the letter and spirit of your amendments, with what face could your legislative, executive or judicial officers (having taken that oath) oppose such proceedings? A conscientious man can have no idea of a mental evasion or a secret reservation, when under an oath; for though he sweareth to his own hurt he changeth not:[6] will it afford any consolation to you, or to your constituents, or give relief, when thus expressed, that the convention adopted in full confidence of future amendments.

What arguments may be used, or what measures will be taken by those who are opposed to the amendments in this state; in order to frustrate the measure, is difficult to predict. Their coadjutors in Massachusetts, it seems, at first attempted to persuade the people that it would be best to postpone calling a convention and to let experience dictate the defects, and then the necessary amendments would be immediately adopted.

When they found the bait would not take[(a)] they came out more openly. (Boston Gazette, 21st of October 1788.) He is now called "an enemy to his country, who would attempt amendments, and told, that the propositions for that purpose in the convention, were only conciliatory, and the constitution being adopted there can be no need of them."⁷

Perhaps those in this state will pursue their former delusive manœuvres, and inform you, that the more confidence you place in your rulers, the more good they will do; that Americans are an enlightened people—that they will make choice of good representatives, so that there will be no danger of procuring a convention, an agreement to the amendments, and three fourths of the states to confirm them; that the rulers will not dare, nor would a people so enlightened suffer them, to abuse their powers—Or perhaps (preposterous as it may appear, considering the conduct of our legislature, of Congress, and of the general convention in Philadelphia) they may say, that you have no right or power to make such a law, and that by the adoption you are obliged to implicit acquiescence, though it should be at the risk of all the rights and privileges of your constituents.

That the advocates for this new constitution have had the advantage in starting, is no new thing. I suppose it ever was, and always will be the case, that those who are for subverting the government (their movements being preconcerted⁽ᵇ⁾) have at first the advantage of those who are for supporting it. They choose their epithets, or ketch-words—the confederation is a rope of sand—trade and credit abroad—the worse the better: of late they have covered themselves under the term federal, while they were undermining and annihilating the confederation. But that these circumstances should be adduced to prove that we are distanced, and not warranted to proceed, and that we ought cheerfully to submit, is so great a perversion of reason, and so entirely unwarranted by the real state of things, that common sense stands aghast at the idea.

You are the representatives, the guardians of the rights and liberties of the people, and invested with every power necessary for their preservation and happiness. The words of Vattel are, "A nation is under an obligation to preserve itself, and has (not only) a right to every thing necessary for its preservation, but to avoid every thing that might occasion its destruction; and, as the pact may be dissolved by common consent of the parties, if the individuals that compose the nation, unanimously consent to break the knot that binds them, they may be permitted to do it,⁽ᶜ⁾ and thus to destroy the state or nation; but they doubtless cannot innocently do it, if they take this step without just and weighty reasons—and, as it is impossible that the nation should ever permit the use of such means, if on a particular occasion no other present themselves for fulfilling a general obligation, the obligation ought to cease in that particular instance as impossible, and consequently void—By an evident consequence from what has been said, a nation ought carefully to avoid, as much as possible, whatever may cause its destruction, or that of the state which is the same thing—A nation or state has a right to every thing that can secure it from such a threatening danger, and to keep at a distance whatever is capable of causing its ruin; and that from the very reasons that establish its right to the things necessary to its preservation." Vattel, 12, 13.[8]

By the laws of Moses, although a man might, if he pleased, become a slave, yet no one had a right to use delusive arguments to induce him to submit to a state of bondage; and that it might evidently appear that he had not been imposed upon, he was, after having expressed his inclination, taken by his master before the judges to be interrogated, and if he persisted before the judge, if the voice of reason did not influence him, the judge directed him to be put to the shameful and painful operation of having his ear nailed to the door post; and if he still persisted was then, and not till then, deemed a complete and voluntary slave.[9]

That honorable body (of blessed memory) the Congress of 1776 appear to have been of the same opinion; "We hold these things (said they) to be self-evident, that all men are created equal; that they are endowed by their creator with certain unalienable rights, that among these are life liberty and the pursuit of happiness."[10] But supposing an individual had, in a fit of delusion, submitted to become a voluntary slave, would he not have a right, when his mind acquired its wonted tone, to extricate himself? He certainly would.

Is it not notorious that even some members of the convention at Poughkeepsie were intimidated and deluded by threats and promises? Was it not asserted in the convention, that they had no right to amend, that they could only approve or reject? Were they not threatened, that unless they adopted the constitution in its present form, the southern part of the state would secede from the northern and join with the adopting states to subdue it? That it would throw the state into convulsions, and a scene of blood and devastation would ensue? and besides, that Congress would remove from the state and, were they not induced to believe, that if they did adopt it in its present form, Congress would remain in the city of New York? Is it not notorious that these threats and promises influenced some of the members to agree to the adoption, who would otherwise have spurned at it? to use their own words, "several articles in it appear so exceptionable to a majority of us, that nothing but the fullest confidence of obtaining a revision of them by a general convention and an invincible reluctance to seperating from our sister states, would have prevailed upon a sufficient number to ratify it without stipulating for previous amendments."[11]

Every man in his private capacity in such a case, might, in a court of justice, avail himself of the plea of duress, and avoid the contract. Would it be just or expedient, that the legislative, executive, and judicial officers should be bound and fettered by an oath to support a constitution thus adopted, and which your convention declares to be so very exceptionable; and which, if not amended, will produce the most direful effects.

I apprehend the time is not far distant, when the propriety of these observations will be more fully evinced: even now there are but few who do not consider the bill and declaration of rights as incorporated with and making part of the adoption, although they are not so expressed: it seems state policy has not yet rendered it expedient.

Be that as it may, the present legislature are under no restraint, and therefore have only to consider whether the law proposed will have the effect intended, viz. to secure the amendments, and consequently the rights and liberties of the people.

November 29, 1788.

> (a) "It was compared to the loaning a man's money untold and without proper security for the payment thereof, in order to ascertain his honor; or to neglect to repair a breach in the walls of a city, liable to be besieged, in order to discover whether the assailants would avail themselves of the advantage offered them; the loss of property, however, in the one case, and a lodgement gained behind the breech in the other, would tender after precaution unavailable." (See New-York Journal of the 25 of Sept. 1788.)[12]
>
> (b) "The dark councils of the Cabal, though from the first they gave anxiety to all men of reflection; were not thoroughly known but by the event," 7 Hume, 471.[13] Absalom, under the cloak of serving the Lord, attempted to dethrone his father David."[14]
>
> (c) The notions of mankind are sometimes very unaccountable, and their desires equally absurd and importunate, "Nay, but we will have a King over us," was the cry in the days of Samuel;[15] and John the divine foretels, that all the world will worship the beast—saying, "who is like unto the beast! who is able to make war with him."[16]

1. The manuscript draft of this essay is in the Abraham Yates, Jr., Papers at the New York Public Library.

2. For the amendments proposed by the New York Convention on 26 July 1788, see BoR, I, 256–64.

COMMENTARIES, 5 DECEMBER 1788 395

3. Joshua 9:21.
4. For the debate in the Confederation Congress on the temporary location of the federal capital, see RCS:Congress, passim.
5. Galatians 5:1.
6. Psalms 15:4. Yates himself refused to take the oath to support the new Constitution when voting in elections.
7. A reference to "Alfred" II, *Massachusetts Spy*, 16 October 1788, which was reprinted in the *Massachusetts Gazette*, 21 October (BoR, III, 255–56).
8. Emmerich de Vattel, *The Law of Nations; or, Principles of the Law of Nature: Applied to the Conduct and Affairs of Nations and Sovereigns* (Dublin, 1787), Book I, chapter II, sections 16, 18–20, pp. 20–22. The *Law of Nations* was first published in 1758 in London in a two-volume French edition. These volumes were translated into English and published in London in 1759 and again in 1759–60.
9. Deuteronomy 15:17.
10. See the Declaration of Independence, 4 July 1776 (CDR, 73).
11. See the first paragraph of the New York Convention's circular letter (BoR, I, 187).
12. "Sidney" refers to an item first printed in the Boston *Independent Chronicle* on 11 September 1788 (BoR, III, 206–8n) that was reprinted in the *New York Journal* on 25 September. The article supported amending the Constitution before it was ratified.
13. David Hume, *The History of England* . . . (8 vols., London, 1767), VII, 471. Hume was referring to the ministers under Charles II known as the "Cabal"—Clifford, Ashley, Buckingham, Arlington, and Lauderdale—"a word which the initial letters of their names happened to compose" (*ibid.*).
14. Absalom's relationship to his father, King David, is found in 2 Samuel 13–20.
15. 1 Samuel 8:19.
16. Revelation 13:4.

New York Journal, 4 December 1788[1]

From a CORRESPONDENT.

I find, by conversing with a number of gentlemen from the southward, that the present state of politics in several of the states on that course is far from being so favorable to (what the antis call) the aristocratic plan as it at first was. As for Pennsylvania, there will, it seems, be a warm contest. The inhabitants of Virginia are almost universally in favor of amendments to the constitution; of course members will be sent from that state to the Congress under the new constitution, who will adhere to the spirit of their form of ratification.—Their general wish now is, that amendments might constitutionally take place; and, Mr. Printer, however zealous a federal I may have been hitherto, I cannot help wishing it also, that unanimity may be re-established.

1. Reprinted: Poughkeepsie, N.Y., *Country Journal*, 9 December.

St. John de Crevecoeur to William Short
New York, 5 December 1788 (excerpt)[1]

. . . If the new Constitution is adopted the Congress must assemble itself in the beginning of March. I did not see the resolutions of your assembly made by P[atrick] Henry which were entirely antifederalist.[2] We must hope that everything will be tempered when the Congress is united and presided over by G[enera]l Washington who has great Talents as a conciliator. The Governor of this state [George Clinton] is also preparing the roll of his assembly to be opposed with all his power to the measures of the Convention, because he is a Violent *anti*.[3] . . .

1. RC (Tr), Short Papers, DLC.
2. For the Virginia legislature's resolutions of 20 November 1788 requesting that Congress call a general convention to amend the Constitution, see BoR, I, 175–78.
3. For the New York General Assembly's resolution of 7 February 1789 requesting that Congress call a general convention to amend the Constitution, see BoR, I, 195–230.

Foreign Spectator XIII
Philadelphia Federal Gazette, 5 December 1788[1]

REMARKS *on the Amendments to the Federal Constitution, proposed by the Conventions of Massachusetts, New-Hampshire, New-York, Virginia, South and North-Carolina, with the minorities of Pennsylvania and Maryland, by a* FOREIGN SPECTATOR.

NUMBER XIII.

Having viewed those amendments which concern the general powers of Congress with respect to the states and individual citizens, we shall in this paper consider the objections against two particular clauses. The conventions of Virginia and North-Carolina, by the 12th and 13th amendments respectively, would stipulate, *that the exclusive power of legislation given to Congress over the federal town and its adjacent district, and other places, purchased or to be purchased by Congress, of any of the states, shall extend only to such regulations, as respect the police and good government thereof.* The convention of New-York requests by the 11th and 12th amendment, *That the right of the Congress to exercise exclusive legislation over such district, not exceeding ten miles square, as may by cession of a particular state, and the acceptance of Congress, become the seat of the government of the United States, shall not be so exercised, as to exempt the inhabitants of such district from paying the like taxes, imposts, duties, and excises, as shall be imposed on the other inhabitants of the state, in which such district may be; and that no person shall be privileged within the said district, from arrest for crimes committed, or debts contracted out of the said district. That the right of exclusive legislation with respect to such places, as may be purchased for the erection of forts, magazines, arsenals, dock-yards, and other needful buildings, shall not authorise the Congress to make any law to prevent the laws of the states respectively in which they may be, from extending to such places in all civil and criminal matters, except as to such persons as shall be in the service of the United States; nor to them, with respect to crimes committed without such places.*

On this matter this observation is first obvious, that the last mentioned body differs materially from the two others in regard to the federal town, permitting exclusive legislation with some exceptions; whereas they allow only regulations necessary for the police and good government. Secondly, I beg leave to remark that the amendments of both are not so definitive, as to prevent uncertainty and disputes. *Police and good government* implies a great deal, and extends to persons, manners, property, &c. The general clause that *no person shall be privileged within the ten mile district from arrest for debts contracted out of it,* cannot be meant to include the federal senators and representatives, who, by the 6th sect. 1st art. of the constitution, are entitled to this privilege; which is necessary for the due administration of government, and granted in all free countries.

The supposition, that the federal districts may become assylums for malefactors, is the more groundless, as a practice so dishonorable to the federal government would be an open infringement of the 2d par. of 2d sect. in 4th art. by virtue of which *a person charged in any state with treason, felony, or other crime, who shall flee from justice, and be found in another state, shall, on demand of the executive authority of the state from which he fled, be delivered up, to be removed to the state having jurisdiction of the crime.* It is also explicitly declared in 3d sect. of 3d art. *that the trial of all crimes shall be held in the state where they have been committed.* As to debts, and any civil actions arising out of such districts, common sense dictates, that the federal government must observe the injunction laid on every state in the union, *not to pass any law impairing the obligation of contracts*—1st par. 10th sect. 1st art. Could it possibly be so foolish or wicked as to shelter the spendthrifts, knaves, and vagabonds, from every part of the union, such injury would create a general resentment from the states.

As all duties, imposts, and excises, shall be uniform throughout the United States, by 1st par, 8th sect. 1st art. the federal districts cannot claim any immunity in this respect; which, indeed, might be very prejudicial to neighbouring places, especially commercial towns. I apprehend, likewise, that all other laws which, by the constitution, must be uniform throughout the union, will extend to these places, as those on the subjects of bankruptcies, the privilege of the habeas corpus writ, trial by jury in criminal cases, &c.

In the progress of the federal empire, the seat of Congress, and the other districts in question, will be very important, by valuable magazines, naval and military stores, buildings and fortifications, with the archives and treasury of the confederacy. They should therefore be under the immediate management of the federal government, in every respect that may affect their security; and, though this may not strictly amount to exclusive legislation in all cases whatever, yet it would otherwise, in so many instances, jar with the authority of the state in which they are situate, and require so many exceptions from its general regulations, as to create great inconveniencies, if not contentions, between the parties. The federal town will, no doubt, in time, become very populous; there will, at all times, be a great concourse of people from foreign countries, and every part of the United States; this must require a peculiar legislation in many instances, and modes of administering justice different from the general rules of the state. This heterogeneous conflux of people, the importance of the place, and the accommodation of Congress, point out the necessity of a police very different from that in other American towns, and which, however just, may be less consistent with the general ideas of personal rights. An immediate command of the militia in this place, especially, is highly necessary; and it will save the expence of a considerable garrison. Without this, a mob may insult the Congress, rob the treasury, and burn the town. The federal government, and such valuable property of the union, should not depend on the protection of a particular state, which, with the best intention, is not sufficiently energetic in sudden emergencies; and which, from the fluctuation of human affairs, may on particular occasions be denied.

As several states are competitors for the seat of Congress, it is evidently regarded as a great advantage. Wherever it may be chosen, the state concerned will no doubt stipulate an adequate compensation; nor can the people of that district be disposed of without their free consent; as to any undue influence of the federal government, from these little domains, it cannot be very considerable. It must however be granted that the peculiar situation of the people in such districts will raise the question, how are they to be represented in Congress? or shall they have no vote, even when their number may be 40 or 50,000? Probably the constitution may require some change before this happens; therefore I only start the subject, as the result of a novel institution, which yet, for very cogent reasons, appears indispensible.

The conventions of Massachusetts and New-Hampshire request *that Congress shall at no time consent, that any person, holding an office of trust or profit under the United States, shall accept of a title of nobility, or any other title or office, from any king, prince, or foreign state,* 9th am. resp. That of New-York expresses the same in the 30th am. *That the words,* without the consent of Congress, *in the second clause of the ninth section of the first article of the constitution be expunged.*[a] It is a general custom among all civilized nations to reward the distinguished citizens of each other by various marks of honour. Such liberality is the fruit of cultivated humanity, and happily promotes general civilization by eradicating national prejudices, stamping a general value on the talents and virtues that exalt human nature, and forming a connexion among all the eminent citizens of the world, pleasing to themselves, and highly beneficial to mankind. If all the great characters that are scattered over the globe, could be brought into a circle of correspondence, what an excellent improvement in knowledge, manners, laws, government, religion, arts, and all the great concerns of men, would result from this contraction of goodness and wisdom! I should therefore be very sorry to see this prohibition fixing a mark of illiberality on the people of the United States, who are the offspring of several great European nations, and have from them originally inherited all the useful, great and elegant arts of life. Shall an American ambassador be forbid to receive a ring, a portrait, or a book from any prince whatever? Why, because he ought to despise all princes and their presents? or because he may be corrupted by any toy whatever? Softly, let us not give the world such an opinion of our vanity or meanness! An excellent author, the inventor of useful machinery, or a superior medicine, are benefactors to all mankind; why should we then begrudge them a generous reward from any nation whatever! No, I wish the American philosophers, poets and artists may be rewarded, if possible, by the Grand Signior, the Great Mogul, and the Emperor of Japan.

A title of nobility may be received on the general principle, as an honorary distinction adopted in some countries, and really often conferred on great personal merit. It will be so rarely offered by any foreign power, that the example cannot create any improper ambition; but should it from any unexpected causes, produce a lust after domestic nobility, it must be absolutely prohibited.

In some particular cases persons may hold offices under two different governments: in some sea ports, for example, the same person is consul for two nations. Such a trust from another country is compatible with true allegiance to our own, when they have no opposite interests.

When two nations are in strict active alliance, a great character is frequently intrusted from both with the most important offices: how often does a general command a great body of allied troops? and how often do the public ministers of allies act in concert at a treaty of peace? I would by no means wish America to be intimately connected with any foreign power whatever; yet the general government should be authorized to do whatever is necessary and honorable for the United States. The amendments are meant to guard against foreign influence; but this can never be dangerous in such an open manner: whereas a man whom you forbid to receive a snuff-box, may, if he is a knave, take 10,000 pounds without the knowledge of a single fellow-citizen.

(a) *This clause runs thus: "no title of nobility shall be granted by the United States: and no person holding any office of profit, or trust, under them, shall,* without the consent of Congress, accept of any present, emolument, office, or title of any kind whatever, from any king, prince or foreign state."[2]

1. Reprinted: *New York Daily Gazette,* 17 June 1789. For the authorship of the "Foreign Spectator" series, see the headnote to Essay No. I (21 October, BoR, III, 264n).
2. Article I, Section 9, clause 8.

Massachusetts Centinel, 6 December 1788[1]

The subject of dispute, between the JUNTO and the friends to government, the Federalists, is merely this—Whether the "TOP STONE" of the New Constitution, "shall be brought forth with shouting," by its complete organization in a truly federal and independent Representation—Or, whether the publick expectations shall be completely disappointed by mixing the *"wood, hay, stubble, &c."* of *antifederalism* and *amendmentism* in the formation of the Federal Legislature.—The FRIENDS OF THE UNION, suppose that an unequivocal federal Representation will consummate the wishes of the people: that on the other hand, should *some characters* be successful in their MANŒUVRING, the hopes of the people will be *blasted,* while the LOAVES AND THE FISHES will be found insufficient to satisfy a numerous and hungry train of dependents, expectants and seekers.

1. Reprinted: Philadelphia *Federal Gazette,* 17 December; *Pennsylvania Gazette,* 17 December.

Thomas Jefferson to William Short
Paris, 8 December 1788 (excerpt)[1]

... it seems agreed that some amendments will be made to the new constitution. all are willing to add a bill of rights; but they fear the power of internal taxation will be abridged. the friends of the new government will oppose the method of amendment by a federal convention which would subject the whole instrument to change, and they will support the other method which admits Congress by a vote of ⅔ to submit specific changes to the assemblies, ¾ of whom must concur to establish them....

1. FC, Jefferson Papers, DLC. For the entire letter, see Boyd, XIV, 343–44.

COMMENTARIES, 8 DECEMBER 1788   401

Henry Lee to James Madison
Alexandria, Va., 8 December 1788 (excerpt)[1]

... The phrenzy in Richmond seems not yet to have abated, the circular letters[2] afford new testimony of Henrys influence & venom. It is farther said that this gentlemans efforts on the late occasion have been concluded by instructing the representatives to the new Congress to act only in cases where the spirit of the Virga. amendments shall govern—If the tale is true our delegates will be expressly limited in their powers. This is only a rumour & for the reputation of our country, I hope will turn out nothing more. . . .

1. RC, Madison Papers, DLC. For the entire letter, see Rutland, *Madison*, XI, 387–88.
2. For the Virginia legislature's letters to New York Governor George Clinton and to the other state executives of 20 November, see BoR, I, 177–78.

James Madison to Thomas Jefferson
Philadelphia, 8 December 1788 (excerpts)[1]

... Notwithstanding the formidable opposition made to the New federal Government, first in order to prevent its adoption, and since in order to place its administration in the hands of disaffected men, there is a flattering prospect not only a certainty now both a certainty of its peaceable commencement in March next, and a flattering prospect that it will be administred by men who will give it a fair trial. . . .

The questions which divide the public at present relate 1. to the extent of the amendments that ought to be made to the Constitution. 2. to the mode in which they ought to be made. The friends of the Constitution, some from an approbation of particular amendments, others from a spirit of conciliation, are generally agreed that the system should be revised. But they wish the revisal to be carried no farther than to supply additional guards for liberty, without abridging the sum of power transferred from the States to the general Government or altering previous to trial, the particular structure of the latter and are fixed in opposition to the risk of another Convention, whilst the purpose can be as well answered, by the other mode provided for introducing amendments. Those who have opposed the Constitution, are on the other hand, zealous for a second Convention, and for a revisal which may either not be restrained at all, or extend at least as far as alterations have been proposed by any State. Some of this class, are, no doubt, friends to an effective Government, and even to the substance of the particular Government in question. It is equally certain that there are others who urge a second Convention with the insidious hope, of throwing all things into Confusion, and of subverting the fabric just established, if not the Union itself.—If the first Congress embrace the policy which circumstances mark out, they will not fail to propose of themselves, every desireable safeguard for popular rights; and by thus separating the well meaning from the designing opponents, fix on the latter their true character, and give to the Government its due popularity and stability....

1. RC, Madison Papers, DLC. For the entire letter, see Rutland, *Madison*, XI, 381–85n.

Foreign Spectator XIV
Philadelphia Federal Gazette, 9 December 1788[1]

REMARKS *on the Amendments to the Federal Constitution, proposed by the Conventions of Massachusetts, New-Hampshire, New-York, Virginia, South and North-Carolina, with the minorities of Pennsylvania and Maryland, by a* FOREIGN SPECTATOR.

NUMBER XIV.

We proceed to view the amendments that respect the executive powers of the federal government. The minority of Maryland request, *that the president shall not command the army in person, without the consent of Congress*—5th am. The convention of New-York lays the same condition on him, *or the person exercising his powers for the time being*—22d am. It also proposes, *that the executive shall not grant pardons for treason, unless with the consent of Congress; but may, at his discretion, grant reprieves to persons convicted of treason, until their cases can be laid before the Congress*—21st am. Before a particular discussion of these amendments, which are meant to guard against dangerous misconduct of the executive, let us examine what degree of probability this supposition may have. The constitution has provided a truly excellent mode of electing this first officer of the United States. He is chosen by the whole people, through the refined medium of electors, on whom the people devolve this confidential trust. A number of electors, equal to the collective body of Congress, many of whom have no doubt equal abilities with the senators and representatives, must be competent judges of the talents and virtues requisite for this august office, and, either by personal acquaintance or authentic information, have an extensive knowledge of the most distinguished citizens of the union; consequently a sufficient choice of candidates. To prevent any influence of personal interest, party, or local prejudices, *the electors shall meet in their respective states, and vote by ballot for two persons, of whom one at least shall not be an inhabitant of the same state with themselves. No senator or representative, or person holding an office of trust or profit under the United States, shall be appointed an elector.* A majority of the whole number of electors is required. *If there be more than one who have such majority, and have an equal number of votes, then the house of representatives shall immediately choose by ballot one of them for president; and if no person has a majority, then from the five highest on the list the said house shall in like manner choose the president. But in choosing the president, the votes shall be taken by states, the representatives from each state having one vote*—1st sect. 2d art. The transient existence and distant situation of the electors, is a very great security from corruption; the most artful and powerful candidate has not time for operations of intrigue on a great number of men, dispersed over thirteen states, of different characters and situations in life, many of whom must be strangers to him; nor can the electors themselves enter into any combinations inconsistent with their duty. If the votes are divided, the house of representatives, which by its constitution is the immediate offspring of the people, decides in a mode which prevents all undue influence of the greater states.

By these proceedings, there is a moral certainty that the first magistrate of the union will always be one of the most illustrious citizens, whose wisdom, integrity, and honour are universally respected. If, after all, it should happen, by that imbecility incident to human affairs, that Congress entertain an unfavourable opinion of his heart or understanding, it is very uncertain how far their judgment is to be esteemed in this case, when opposed to the sentiments of that respectable body of electors, who, like themselves, were delegated by the people. As it is scarce possible that this voice of Congress is unanimous, the minority must be added in the opposite scale, which may then greatly preponderate in the estimation of impartial spectators, and suggest a belief that only a party in Congress disapproved of the president.

As to military talents, they are very valuable in the first confidential office of the union, and judicious electors will no doubt pay a due regard to them without lessening their estimation of the civil acquirements. Happily, a long and profound peace may deny the opportunity of military exploits; but a just and extensive theory of war, is a principal branch of that political science which should be the favourite study of every person who aspires to the highest offices of government. This theory, improved by all the practice, which, in time of peace is attainable, will qualify a president of Congress for the command of the army and militia in time of danger. But if, with other estimable qualities, he is not a general, it is to be hoped that vanity would not make him hazard his own reputation, and the welfare of his country; at least, he will not without a sense of personal courage, take upon him a dangerous office.

Supposing an occasional necessity for the interference of Congress, it would very little mend the evil, because the president will still by his official authority direct the operation of war; he can not only check and thwart the actions of the federal general, but also, by positive orders, force him into very bad measures.

The principal benefit intended by this prohibition is, perhaps, to prevent a traiterous president from turning the military force against his country. Such a desperate act of treason supposes him to be the head of a powerful faction, and to have many friends in both houses of Congress. It is then very probable that he may gain a majority in the senate to concur with him in the appointment of a general fit for his purpose; and he may by such a tool effect more mischief than he could in person: because between two traitors the guilt is not easily fixed. Many preparatory steps may be taken towards an effectual rebellion, which yet afford not a full proof of treason. At all events the president may wait till his associate has tried a capital stroke, and, if it miscarries, send him off to a foreign country.

The second amendment of the New-York convention, by which the executive shall not grant pardons for treason without the consent of Congress, is a necessary appendage to the one we have now considered; and the omission of it by the minority of Maryland is an inconsistency. Except the correspondence of individuals with a foreign enemy in time of war, treason against the United States will be carried on by leaders of a strong party, and therefore in various degrees involve a considerable number of persons. Such epidemic madness will probably, in part, affect the representatives of the people, and consequently disqualify them for impartial judgment. The sympathy of those who favour the condemned, with the good-natured weakness of others, may procure impunity, where the terror of example is necessary.

Again, when the victorious party, inflamed by a severe contest, has got full possession of legislative powers, they may stain the annals of the empire with acts of barbarity, which their children cannot blot out with tears of shame and sorrow. I appeal to every man of information, if this reasoning is not founded on the history of all republics. The president of the union may from the mode of his election and the dignity of his office, be supposed, if not entirely sound, at least far less tainted by the fever of such dreadful times. The solicitations of the condemned and their friends, the consciousness that the lives of fellow-creatures, and all the future happiness of their families depend on him, the reflection that a whole nation, nay, a great part of the world, critically observe his conduct: all this must awaken every feeling of humanity, and the most scrupulous caution; whereas a band of judges often exercise cruelty, because they divide the guilt among them, or lay the blame on some principal agents. It is moreover, a weighty consideration, that the appointment of the president, being for four years, may probably be previous to the commencement of a rebellion; but a house of representatives may be formed in the height of it, or what is worse, at the conclusion. Such a number of men, under the impulse of revenge, mingling, after two years, with the general mass, are eligible judges[2] on the lives and fortunes of their fellow-citizens.

Another great argument for granting this power to the chief magistrate is, that in times of civil tumults, a well-timed offer of pardon to the insurgents, may restore the tranquility of the commonwealth. If the convening of the legislature is necessary for this measure, the opportunity may be irreparably lost; every person knows the amazing effect of transient symptoms in such political convulsions.

We may then conclude, that although it is possible that the first confidential officer of the confederacy may prove a traitor, yet those events are far more probable, in which his power of granting pardon for treason will be useful to the republic.

1. Reprinted: *New York Daily Gazette*, 18 June 1789. For the authorship of the "Foreign Spectator" series, see the headnote to Essay No. I (21 October, BoR, III, 264n).

2. In its 12 December 1788 issue, the Philadelphia *Federal Gazette* printed the following errata:

☞ *In the 14th number of the remarks on the amendments, &c. in last Tuesday's paper—12th line from the bottom of the 2d column, for "are eligible judges" read "are not eligible judges."*

James Madison to Philip Mazzei
Philadelphia, 10 December 1788 (excerpt)[1]

... All the States except N. Carolina & Rh. Island have ratified the proposed Constitution. Seven of them have appointed their Senators, of whom those of Virga. R. H. Lee & Col. Grayson alone, are among the opponents of the system. The appointments of Maryld. S. Carolina & Georgia, will pretty certainly be of the same stamp with the majority. The H. of Representatives is yet to be chosen every where except in Penna. From the partial returns recd., the election will wear a federal aspect, unless the event in one or two particular Counties should contradict every calculation. If the eight members from this State be on the side of the Constitution, it will in a manner secure the majority in that branch of the Congress also. The object of the antifederalists is to bring about another General Convention, which would either agree on nothing as would be agreeable to some, and throw every thing into confusion; or expunge from the Constitution parts which are held by its friends to be essential to it. The latter party are willing to gratify their opponents with every supplemental provision for guaranteeing their rights, but insist that this can be better done in the [congressional?] mode provided for amendments.

1. RC, Dartmouth College Library. For the entire letter, see Rutland, *Madison*, XI, 388–90n.

The Conversion
Massachusetts Centinel, 10 December 1788[1]

Mr. RUSSELL, *Is requested to insert in the Centinel, the following—the fact cannot be denied—however the relation of it may be condemned—it is the child of a* RAINY DAY.

THE CONVERSION.—A FRAGMENT.
"From trivial causes, great events arise."[2]

Avonius was a confident, decided malcontent.—With him, a thing to be hated, need not but meet with general admiration.

When the new Constitution was first promulged, AVONIUS was *silent* on the subject: But when its merits were generally known—and its excellence universally acknowledged, AVONIUS zealously condemned it—*It wore, he said, the marks of despotism—and the features of tyranny shewed themselves in every line*; In short, with AVONIUS, *it was the worst system ever formed by man.*

After it had been ratified by Nine States—and THE PEOPLE no longer found a necessity in warmly espousing it, AVONIUS became less its opposer; and at length, softened down to a *warm* Amendmentite:—Then amendments and alterations of *some parts* were the burden of his song—his morning and evening meditation.

At this time, AVONIUS had occasion to travel into a neighbouring State—on the road lived an old classmate—and AVONIUS having promised never to "pass without calling," made his house his noonday stage. It was somewhat late, but his friends had a fine Turkey roasting at the fire—which, with other country cheer, seemed to promise to AVONIUS a good dinner.

Being seated, the favourite topick was broached.—But, alas, the friend of AVONIUS was a staunch Federalist: The discussion therefore was *wordy*, and, on the part of AVONIUS, warm—The summons to dinner, however, put an end to it.

Instructions had previously been given—*"Take away that Turkey, it is not a good one"*—said the host. *"But, my dear."* answered his lady, *"had you not better* TRY *it before you condemn it—you may be deceived—Besides, I have taken much pains in the cooking—and to say the least, it looks like a good one."* "No, no, my dear, it will not do, my friend AVONIUS has convinced me, that a thing ought not be TRIED to be PROVED—*it is not good—so John take it away."* AVONIUS felt the force of his friends wit, but was surprised to see the servant, with all imaginable *sang froid*,[3] carrying off the Turkey. He said nothing; but partaking of the other things of the table, he made out to *dampen* his appetite a little: His friend pledged him in a glass of good wine, but not a word about the Turkey, or the Constitution. Dinner being over, AVONIUS bid his friend farewell, and the tavern being then several miles distant—the hour for meals being passed—and he intolerably hungry, the scales fell from his eyes—he saw and cursed the absurdity of his political tenets, and has since returned, a warm advocate for the Constitution's having a fair trial before it is *altered.*

1. Reprinted: Rhode Island *Newport Herald,* 25 December; and North Carolina *Wilmington Centinel,* 29 January 1789.
2. Perhaps inspired by Alexander Pope, *The Rape of Lock. An Heroi-comical Poem. In Five Canto's* (London, 1714), Canto I, line 2: "What mighty Quarrels rise from trivial things."
3. "Coolness, indifference, absence of excitement or agitation" (OED).

An American Citizen
Philadelphia Federal Gazette, 10 December 1788[1]

Thoughts on the Subject of Amendments *to the* Federal Constitution.

To moderate the ardor and diminish the fears of the friends of *amendment,* we took a cursory view, in the last paper, of the ground upon which liberty is fixed in this enlightened time, and particularly in the United States. It clearly appeared, that the dangers to property, peace, liberty and life, so far as they have heretofore proceeded from the abuse of ecclesiastical power, are now done away by the total suppression of that species of authority. It was also evident, that instead of *general feeling* and *opinion,* on which the liberties of the ancient republics precariously rested, the progress of political knowledge had given us the more certain basis of *the acknowledged rights* of man, and *the established principles* of freedom. Being possessed of constitutions formed out of these *rights and principles,* it was argued, that no sudden inroads upon the liberties of the people could be made, no insidious encroachments could be effected. Wherefore, it was further observed, the business of amendment, equally important to *liberty* and *government,* need not be precipitated, from any dangerous circumstances in our present situation.

In considering those amendments which immediately relate to the rights of individuals, we must call to mind that the United States have successfully concluded an important contest, the grounds of which principally were, their assertion of their general and common rights, in the utmost extent to which the theory of a free government could carry them. We must remember also, that our federal and state governments are and will be, so far as a very large majority goes, in the hands of those men who *originated* that contest, or *maintained* it to an happy issue. If we give ourselves a moment's time for reflection, we shall be satisfied that the leaders of the general and state councils from 1775 to 1787, both civil and military characters, who are now entering upon the duties of the new government, will not betray that liberty they then asserted, nor be silent spectators of its destruction by the plans of their fellow citizens. When the body of the new Congress shall be assembled; when the state legislatures shall see in the senate the representatives of their various interests, *created by a deliberate exercise of their own powers*— when the people at large shall behold in the house of representatives *the men of their freest choice*, and in their chief magistrates, *the creature of their breath* and *the venerated object of their warmest affections*; they will not unreasonably and ungenerously suppose that such a body, formed at a juncture so important and by means so just, will be inattentive to any consideration, which may affect the happiness of a country on whose fortunes hang all their joys and sorrows. Shall we not then *calmly wait* the short period of their meeting? shall we formally elect them for the most important duties, and immediately withdraw from them the confidence their station demands? 'Till their conduct gives us some shadow of cause to censure them let us rationally expect that they will examine with becoming anxiety and care, what further checks in favour of liberty can be introduced, what further explanations of the constitution time and reflection prove to be necessary. Should they discover that the preservation of freedom, or *even the restoration of general harmony*, renders it necessary that a declaration of the rights of conscience, the freedom of the press, and other articles, should be expressed as fully in the constitution of the union as they are in those of the states, we should be wanting to ourselves, and cruelly unjust to them, to suppose they will neglect to propose them.

If we consider the manner in which a general convention will be created, *by the election of the state legislatures*—if we remember at the same time, that one branch of the new Congress are to be chosen by those bodies and the other by the people at large; if we bear in mind also, that *the rights of the states*, as well as those of *the people*, are involved in the proposed amendments; we shall see that a general convention would not be as competent to decide on alterations, as the new Congress, from the nature of its two branches, will be to propose them for the determination of the legislatures or people of the states. Considering the mixed nature of the new constitution, made up as it is of the rights of the people and the rights of the states, a mixed body only, created *by both the parties concerned*, can safely and equitably amend it. The contracting parties in the federal compact are *the people of the several states*, and *the several state governments.* Amendments originated by the representatives of either, alone, cannot be just, and may be dangerous to the other.

Considering, then, that the present situation of the United States is peculiarly free from those rocks on which the liberties of the people have formerly been lost—that we may place our affairs, both in the state and general governments, under the guidance of our most enlightened citizens—that there is every reason to believe the interest, the wisdom, and the virtue of those, whom the people and the legislatures shall elect, will ensure a due attention to the peace and safety of our country—that precipitation, warmth, and unreasonable prejudices may possibly mar the constitution, but cannot amend it—we must deem it at once our interest and duty, calmly to wait the first operations of the federal legislature. Impatience under assumed powers has been the just characteristic of Americans. Let not our enemies, in this our political infancy, be able to charge us with the same temper towards the just authority, *which we ourselves have deliberately created.*

1. Also printed in the *Pennsylvania Gazette* on 10 December 1788. Tench Coxe was the author of the "American Citizen" essays. On 17 December Coxe informed Timothy Pickering that "You will see in the late papers 2 or 3 publications of mine calculated to give temper & patience to the friends of Amendment—They are short and may be of use— I can only find one of them which I enclose you" (Pickering Papers, MHi).

For the other "American Citizen" essays in this volume published on 4 June and 24, 31 December, see BoR III, 7–8, 442–45, 456–57.

An American
Boston Independent Chronicle, 11 December 1788

Messieurs ADAMS & NOURSE, I wish you to republish the Resolutions of the House of Delegates of Virginia, respecting amendments to the Constitution of the United States.

Amendments to that system have now become of serious consequence; the greater part of the people of the United States, demand attention on this point; the object is too dear to them to be detered from its pursuit by any abusive and injudicious scribblings.

The essential interest of the United States, depend upon the new Congress attending to and discussing this matter immediately after they are organized; unless this is done, and amendments proposed to the several Legislatures, the people will have a new Convention; this will be a troublesome, if not a dangerous measure. The object is of consequence enough to urge the several towns to instruct their Representatives to take measures in their next session, as the Delegates of Virginia have done.

[Here follows the preamble and resolutions of the Virginia House of Delegates of 30 October 1788 appointing a committee to apply to Congress to call a convention to amend the Constitution and prepare a letter to the other states in response to the New York Convention's circular letter. See BoR, I, 163–64.]

A Federal Republican II
New York Journal, 11 December 1788[1]

When men divide in sentiments on a political question, it frequently happens that they really pursue the same end by different means, or (if this is not the case) that they possess to have the same object in view, though they follow different courses to attain it. In the first case the two opposing parties will ultimately unite when they come to understand each others views and designs, unless in the progress of the controversy passion gains the ascendancy of reason, or an attachment to a party supplies the place of a regard to the public good. In the latter case it generally falls out that the possessions of one party, or possibly of both, appear to have been adopted merely as a blind to conceal their real designs—When a favorite point is gained the cloak is cast off, and their true end is avowed.

Men of integrity, and who act from principle, ought to be on their guard, to take care that they do not suffer themselves to be actuated by party spirit in the room of a regard for the public good—It is extremely natural for mankind to wish to gain victory to the party to which they unite—Men may, and often do, take a side from a conviction that it is right; they advocate a cause in the first instance, because they are convinced truth and the public good is on its side—But it is not uncommon, that when parties run high, in the course of the controversy, they abandon the principles upon which they set out, and adhere to their party in the pursuit of measures which they reprobated as much as their opposers. What serves as a mean to promote this is, that in almost all parties, there are individuals, and frequently the leaders of the party who have in view something different from what they profess—They pretend one thing, but aim at another—They commence with fair and plausible professions, and under these form their party. In the course of the contests the passions of their adherents get inflamed prejudices are excited, and taking advantage of these, they carry their party with them to an object, which at first a great part with them would have rejected as much as their opposers.—The truth of these remarks might be confirmed by instances adduced from the history of the greatest revolutions that have happened in the world—The annals of the English history record a notable one in the case of Cromwell. No period of the world produced men of greater abilities, or more disinterested patriots than those who were concerned in effecting that revolution. Charles the first was a tyrant—The opposition made to him was justifiable upon every principle of justice and right reason. It was right to deprive him of that sovereign power, which he received to exercise for the benefit of the people, but which he employed for his own interest and their injury—But the leaders who were concerned in effecting this, after accomplishing it by the power of the people, instead of establishing a free government, partly by force, and partly by fraud, they set up one more tyranical than that from which they had been delivered. It cannot be doubted, but that Cromwell, and a number of others who were attached to him, were influenced by as bad principles as those of Charles—they were enemies to equal liberty, though they did not like Charles for a master and a tyrant, they sought to be masters and tyrants themselves. Many very honest men were either seduced to favor his scheme, persuaded to acquiesce in it, or detered from fear of his power from opposing it.

The present condition of our own country, ought to excite our apprehensions, and put us upon our guard, lest similar events should take place among us—No revolution ever took place, that could more truly be said to be for the people, than the one which we have seen in this country—Power was in great measure opposed to it through the whole union.—It originated in the purest whig principles—was supported on the broad basis of the equal rights of mankind—and the form of government which were agreed to, recognized these principles, and the administration has moved upon them. In the progress of the general government, it has appeared to the conviction of almost every man, that the powers under the confederation were not adequate to the management of the general concerns of the union. A very general concurrence of sentiment therefore took place to revise the system—For this purpose a convention of the states by their delegates assembled, and the result of their deliberations was not merely an extension of the powers, but a change of the form of government, this has been submitted to all the states, and acceded to by eleven of them. The officers are now choosing, and the system will soon be in operation. An entire revolution is about taking place without war or bloodshed. In the discussion of this great question there has been a great division of sentiments with regard to the merits of the plan proposed—It has been urged by those who were opposed to it, that the great principles of the revolution has been too little attended to in its formation—that it embraces objects not necessary to be committed to the care of a general government—that sufficient checks are not placed in it to restrain the rulers from an abuse of power—that it will annihilate the state governments on whom we must depend for the preservation of our liberties; and, that it will operate to deprive the people of those rights, which they have so dearly earned—On the other side, it has been said, that these apprehensions are imaginary—that although there are imperfections in the plan, yet, on the whole, it is a well ballanced government, and that sufficient security is afforded against every abuse by committing the power of electing their rulers to the people. To this it is replied, that very little safety will be derived from the right of the people to elect—For that this power will be rather nominal than real—that the number of representatives will be so small, and so great a number concerned in chusing them, that the influence of a few will always predominate.—It is not my design to investigate this subject, as to repeat all that has been said upon it—It is not necessary for my purpose—It has been the general opinion in this state, of both parties, if we may judge from their professions that there are defects in the plan—the same sentiment has prevailed throughout the union. And hence it is, that the most prevailing arguments that the advocates for the system have used, have been drawn, not from its merits, but from the expediency of adopting it, considering the actual situation in which the country was. The language has been, if we must have a government adopt this, and we will cordially unite in making amendments. No inducement whatever would have prevailed upon the convention of this state to have ratified the constitution, had they not had confidence that a general union would have prevailed to submit it to the revision of another general convention. It is manifest from the proceedings of the conventions of many of the other states, that the same motives influenced them. In our own state, almost every sober thinking man declared, without reserve, their wishes to have the system revised—But what is the present language of many of the leading men who advocated the adoption of the constitution. Do they now urge the necessity and propriety of another convention? Nothing is further from their present persuit. They now say, it is wise and proper to give the government a trial. The goodness or badness of the scheme will be proved from experiment—If it should prove defective on a trial of ten or twenty years, then we shall be better able to amend it—But if it be true that the liberties of the people are not well secured under it, in twenty years it may, and probably will be too late to secure them. What are we to think of men who hold this language after they have pledged themselves to unite in procuring another convention? Can we refrain from suspecting that they are unfriendly to equal liberty,—that they have in view a system of government which they dare not avow, and which they mean to fix over the people of this country by insensible degrees, and without their perceiving it until it is accomplished? It is time for every disinterested man and real friend to his country to open his eyes, and act with decision.

All who were sincere in declaring that they wished for a re-consideration and amendments to the system will do so, and will give their voices decidedly in favor of such men to represent them as will firmly pursue the plan recommended by the convention of this state. A variety of unanswerable arguments, beside the defects in the constitution itself, point this out as the wise, prudent, and patriotic line of conduct which ought to be pursued.

1. For the suggestion that "A Federal Republican" was written by Melancton Smith, see Alfred F. Young, *The Democratic-Republicans of New York: The Origins, 1763–1797* (Chapel Hill, N.C., 1967), 123. Young bases his supposition on the similarity of ideas expressed in "A Federal Republican" *New York Journal*, 1 January 1789, and Melancton Smith to John Smith, 10 January 1789 (DHFFE, III, 261–64, 315–16).

George Clinton to John Dawson
New York, 12 December 1788 (excerpt)[1]

... The letter of the legislature of Virginia is not yet received,[2] and I am not without apprehensions that measures may be taken to retard the delivery of it so as to defeat its utility. You will not, I am persuaded, ascribe my suspicions on this occasion to an undue degree of jealousy when you recollect the circumstance respecting my letter which was laid before your convention.[3] ...

1. Printed: Moncure Daniel Conway, *Omitted Chapters of History Disclosed in the Life and Papers of Edmund Randolph* ... (New York and London, 1888), 114–15.
2. For the Virginia legislature's 20 November letter, see BoR, I, 177. It was forwarded to Clinton by Virginia Governor Beverley Randolph on 2 December. See *ibid.*, 179–80.
3. A reference to the delay surrounding Clinton's letter to Virginia Governor Edmund Randolph, 8 May 1788 (RCS:Va., 788–93n).

Richard Bland Lee to James Madison
Richmond, Va., 12 December 1788[1]

Your favor of the 1st. Instant arrived here yesterday—The intended publication was not struck off—it being unnecessary to have it done till near the close of the session—and we being anxious if possible to have yr. approbation to the insertion of certain extracts from your letter to Mr: Turberville.[2] The inclosed which was taken from the proof sheet and is the only printed copy in existence will shew you how cautious we had been with regard to the parts intended to be submitted to the public eye. Such only were selected as would counteract the report industriously circulated in the Assembly and consequently in the state that you were opposed to every amendment to the new government; and in every mode, and such as shewed the happy effects the adoption of it had already produced in relation to our character in Europe. Tho' your friends and the friends of the new system thought the insertion of this extract would have promoted your election and the federal interests thro'out the state, yet from the delicacy you express on the subject we did not hesitate a moment in erasing it—and perhaps it was prudent to omit it. Your name is not mentioned in the publication, a copy of which shall be herewith sent,[3] and only a general allusion made to the impropriety of making a faithful and conspicuous public servant the victim of Party rage for no other reason, but that he had intrepidly delivered his opinion on a subject on which silence would have been in the highest degree criminal. Where base and unworthy means are used to promote measures, contrary to candor, reason, and the public good, it can never in my opinion be improper to counteract them by a true narration of facts.—The People are easily imposed on both with regard to men and measures by the enemies of Virtue and order. And as they are generally governed by Passion and not by reason, a fair representation of facts is necessary, to rouse the latent generosity of the human mind and rekindle their affection for the character or the measure which has been so falsely traduced—But whether the publication of the extract was proper or improper you may be assured that the intention arose from a desire to secure your election, which, tho' an honor from all considerations you are entitled to, we considered as essentially important to the interests of America and our own Country—tho' by no means important as you yourself were concerned—personal aggrandizement having never been your object—and your reputation being too high to stand in need of such partial aids. You may be also assured of Mr. Turberville's delicacy on the occasion.— Nothing but the strongest conviction of the propriety of the measure induced him to suffer the extract to be made.

From what I can hear your interest seems to be gaining ground tho every effort will be made by the Party, which precluded you from the Senate to prevent your election. It may not therefore be improper for you to hasten your return to Virginia, as your very presence probably would contribute much to dissipate the little plots which may be forming agt. you. If you were to visit the Counties previous to the election and attend the Culpepper election yourself—I think there would be little doubt of your success. I suppose you know that Mr: Monroe is to be your Competitor.

I am pleased to hear that moderation prevails in the Councils of the east. And I flatter myself that another year will restore perfect harmony & concord to *us.*

We shall probably model our district court system so as to render it practicable—which next to the ratification of the Constitution will be the most salutory measure for our native Country.

1. RC, Richard Bland Lee Papers, DLC.
2. For this 2 November letter, see BoR, III, 212–14. For earlier efforts to publish a portion of this letter, see Edward Carrington to Madison, 15 November, and Lee to Madison, 17 November (*ibid.*, 333, 358).
3. No pamphlet has been located, but see "A True Federalist," New York *Daily Advertiser*, 7 January 1789 (BoR, IV).

James Madison to Thomas Jefferson
Philadelphia, 12 December 1788 (excerpt)[1]

The inclosed letter has been just sent me by Miss Rittenhouse and I avail myself of the delay of Mr. Morris to give it a conveyance. Since mine already in the hands of Mr. Morris further returns have been recd. from the Western Counties of this state, which tho' not the entire residue, reduces the final result to certainty. There will be seven representatives of the federal party, and one a moderate antifederalist. I consider this choice as ensuring a majority of friends to the federal Constitution, in both branches of the Congress; as securing the Constitution agst the hazardous experiment of a second Convention; and if prudence should be the character of the first Congress, as leading to measures which will conciliate the well-meaning of all parties, and putting our affairs into an auspicious train. . . .

1. RC, Madison Papers, DLC. For the entire letter, see Rutland, *Madison*, XI, 390.

George Lee Turberville to James Madison
Richmond, Va., 12 December 1788 (excerpt)[1]

The moment of sympathetic fervor that prevails amongst a set of Friends, when they are distressed at the success of opposing Party, is very seldom the period for prudence to be attended to in—fortunately I have withstood all temptation and importunity so far as to save your letter from the press.[2] The illicit & misrepresented use that might—(& most certainly wou'd be) made of it by those who are determined to extract mischief from the essence itself of perfection & honesty if it wou'd serve their turns is too apparent—& that they wou'd have construed it into an endeavor to obtain an interest in yr. district wou'd I believe have been the inevitable consequence of its publication—

Wou'd to God I cou'd promise myself so much gratification as to suppose that there was a certainty of yr. Election in yr. district—your friends are sanguine in yr. favor, yr. opponents as sanguine on the contrary—the Utmost that I can from cool deliberation, extract from the opinions of both is that there is a probability in yr. favor—the great exertions made in Mr. Munro's favor will most probably be greatly assistant towards his Election—altho I have heard that some *few* have been disgusted by the assiduity & importunity of his friends & thrown thereby into the opposite scale—There is a strong probability in favor of six federal Representatives out of this state—as far as I am inabled to judge at present—

Shou'd you have leizure to answer my letters after this Date a direction to me in Richmond County by the way of Hobbs Hole will reach me. . . .

1. RC, Madison Collection, NN. For the entire letter, see Rutland, Madison, XI, 392–93.

2. For Madison's letter of 2 November to Turberville, which the Federalists wanted to publish, see BoR, 212–14.

New Hampshire Spy, 12 December 1788

MR. OSBORNE, Among the several tickets for Federal Representatives, which you have mentioned in the Spy, I have not observed one, which, from the disposition of the people to *a general coalition*, I think the most likely to succeed, I mean that for WOODBURY LANGDON, NATH'l. PEABODY, and BENJAMIN WEST, esquires. This ticket is founded on principles of reciprocal *accession*, and is calculated to embrace all parties. As there are two classes, one for, and one against Amendments, an attempt to force a ticket composed entirely of gentlemen from either class, would have a direct tendency to destroy that confidence and mutual goodwill, which, in the commencement of the new government, is so essential to ensure success. If a large number of respectable citizens yet wish for amendments, they undoubtedly are entitled to have their proposals duly discussed in the Federal Legislature; but if the Representatives consist of those only who are decidedly against any amendments, such a discussion will never, probably, take place. Therefore, to remove all complaints, and to give satisfaction, and a fair chance, even to those that differ from us in sentiment, prudence and good policy will dictate an adoption of the foregoing, or a similar ticket.—Mr. Langdon, being intended as the representative of commerce, and his influence and abilities, in that line, being universally acknowledged, *he* probably, will have the general suffrage in his favour.

Foreign Spectator XV
Philadelphia Federal Gazette, 12 December 1788[1]

REMARKS *on the Amendments to the Federal Constitution, proposed by the Conventions of Massachusetts, New-Hampshire, New-York, Virginia, South and North-Carolina, with the minorities of Pennsylvania and Maryland, by a* FOREIGN SPECTATOR.

NUMBER XV.

The minority of Pennsylvania project, by the 12th am. *that a constitutional council be appointed to advise and assist the president, who shall be responsible for the advice they give.* This alteration they deem necessary, *to the end that the legislative, executive, and judiciary powers, may be kept separate*; and think it advantageous, *as thereby the senators would be relieved from almost constant attendance.* The minority of Maryland, in the 11th am. has the short expression, *that there be a responsible council to the president.* Such a material subject required a more clear and ample explanation. The sense of both must, however, be to invest the president alone with all the powers, which the constitution gives to him and the senate jointly, under the simple restriction of hearing the advice of the constitutional council.

It would avail very little to make the council responsible, when the president may reject their advice at pleasure. At the same time his responsibility would be considerably diminished, when divided between him and them; their unanimity or disagreement affording him an equal excuse for bad measures. The example of the British constitution is not at all applicable here. In a monarchy, the maxim, "that the king can do no wrong,"[2] must, for the sake of public peace, be admitted even in cases really criminal. To restrain an executive so formidable, his necessary instruments must, so far as possible, be disabled for doing mischief, by the dread of an awful account; the privy council is therefore a substitute for the responsibility of the first magistrate. But in a republic, no such distinction is necessary; and accordingly the president himself is, by the 4th sect. 4th art. liable to *impeachment*, and, even after conviction and removal from office, *to indictment, trial, judgment and punishment, according to law*, by the last par. 3d sect. 1st art.

If this argument against a constitutional council has due weight, a consideration of œconomy can do little in its favour. But this itself is on the other side, because all the expence saved by lessening the business of the senate, would be greatly exceeded by the salaries of a dozen counsellors, who must constantly reside at the seat of government, and be supported according to their official dignity.

It certainly is not reasonable to give the president, exclusively, the great powers of making treaties, and appointment to all the important offices under the United States. Such monarchial greatness is too much for any citizen of a republic, who can never personally be so deeply interested in the honor and prosperity of the empire, as an hereditary king; who may be influenced not only by favourites, but numerous friends and relations; who may himself want patrons when he returns to a private station; who may also be liable to the pernicious biass of party. The exercise of those powers partake more of the legislative than executive department, and requires not that degree of secrecy, decision and dispatch, which makes the military command so indivisible. This part of the government must then be vested in a body, of which the president is the head. The mode of his election, and the magnitude of his other constitutional prerogatives, fully justify this confidence, which will unite activity and great responsibility with deliberate wisdom, in this important department. The only question is, whether the federal senate may not form the body.

It is indeed an excellent principle, to keep the legislative, executive, and judicial powers of government, separate from and independent of each other; but it should be applied with this judicious sentiment in the constitution of New-Hampshire,[a] "so far as the nature of a free government will admit, or as is consistent with that chain of connection that binds the whole fabric of the constitution in one indissoluble bond of unity and amity." The above minorities do not criticize the negative power of legislation conferred on the executive, which may counteract any majority less than two thirds of both houses. With all their amendments of the judicial powers, they still acquiesce in the right of Congress to establish federal courts, and in the appointment of the judges by the executive. The democratic constitution of Pennsylvania yet found it necessary to appoint the judges by the president and council; and in Maryland, even justices of the peace are commissioned by the governor and council. In Pennsylvania all impeachments brought by the assembly against any officer of the state, whether judicial or executive, are also heard and determined by the president and council.

The legislative authority of the senate could only indirectly and feebly assist them in the abuse of this portion of executive power, and not at all without corrupting the house of representatives: but their judicial right of trying impeachments creates an apprehension of partiality to members of their own body, or the officers of their appointment. Jealousy between colleagues is perhaps more common than indulgence. The mere appointment to an office cannot produce an attachment that will connive at capital faults; it must rather, with a sense of responsibility and public blame, provoke a resentment: on this principle is founded the general practice in the present state-governments, and other nations, to render the continuance in many offices dependent on the pleasure of those who bestow them.

In the great diversity of connexions, it is not probable that many persons could have a majority of zealous friends in the senate, and less probable that any would find them willing to hazard their own reputation in defence of his crimes, when he stands accused by the national representatives. It is also evident that in general the officers jointly appointed by the president and senate must rather be his choice than theirs, because they can only reject his nomination; and in many cases by repeated dissent only procure a less disagreeable person.

A corrupt junto in the senate will indeed commit great mischief: if it forms a majority, it may often force the president into less eligible appointments: if it only exceeds one-third at a critical time, it can prevent the formation of a beneficial treaty. The same number can also defeat an impeachment, and consequently in case of extremity protect each other. The worst effect, however, of any corruption in the senate are of a negative kind, and small in comparison to the evils of a collusion between them and the president. With a majority, he could place worthless men in the first offices of the union; and with two-thirds he may conclude a shameful and pernicious treaty. The depravity of human nature justifies indeed any supposition, and no practicable tie should be neglected; yet, as the senators will be chosen by great bodies of what should be the best and wisest men in the respective states, and as every means is taken to elect the president from the circle of the most illustrious citizens, I must confess that a nefarious corruption in the head would be a lamentable sym[p]tom of disease in the whole body, and that any other tribunal which may be devised for judging them, could merit no confidence. We shall, however, consider the amendments proposed for this purpose.

(a) *Constitution of New-Hampshire*, 1st part, 37th par.

1. Reprinted: *New York Daily Gazette*, 19 June 1789. For the authorship of the "Foreign Spectator" series, see the headnote to Essay No. I (21 October, BoR, III, 264n).

2. Latin: *Rex non potest peccare* ("the king can do no wrong"). William Blackstone wrote: "That the king can do no wrong, is a necessary and fundamental principle of the English constitution: meaning only ... that, in the first place, whatever may be amiss in the conduct of public affairs is not chargeable personally on the king; nor is he, but his ministers, accountable for it to the people: and, secondly, that the prerogative of the crown extends not to do any injury; for, being created for the benefit of the people, it cannot be exerted to their prejudice" (*Commentaries*, Book III, chapter XVII, 254–55).

Nobody
Massachusetts Centinel, 13 December 1788

Of SPOTS.

What is there without a SPOT?—If we confine our views to this world, shall we not find SPOTS even in the *fairest* works of creation.

Let us ascend, and even *"eye the solar ray"*—shall we there escape SPOTS?—No, they abound in the *"source of day."*

Are the works of poets, philosophers and statesmen without SPOTS? Or are their characters without them? Those who have read the first will readily answer, *No*—and to the latter, a negative answer has always been given.

Pope exceeded in "tuneful numbers"—but are Pope's *tuneful numbers* without a SPOT—Let us see his complimentary address to Lord MANSFIELD:

> *"Blest as thou art, with all the power of words,*
> *So known, so honoured in the House of Lords."*[1]

Excellent harmony! To parodize them, one might add,

> *"Persuasion tips his tongue whene'er he talks,*
> *And he has chambers in the King's Bench walks."*[2]

The Constitution was deemed excellent—but is it without a SPOT? Indeed the Antifederalists say, No, verily, it is full—But, Mr. Printer, I do not believe there are half so many as they pretend there are.

1. Alexander Pope, *The Sixth Epistle of the First Book of Horace* (Dublin, 1738), p. 7, lines 48–49.
2. A parody on the above lines by Pope by Colley Cibber (1671–1757) according to John Bartlett, *Familiar Quotations* (10th edition, New York, 1919).

George Lee Turberville to James Madison
Richmond, Va., 14 December 1788 (excerpt)[1]

Yes we had almost supposed from your silence that you had assented to the publication of a part of your favor to me—the type was set—but only one single copy was struck—that copy Mr. R. B. Lee[2] informs me has been transmitted to you—My fortunate stars steel'd me agt. importunities when my conscience almost condemn'd my obstinacy—A Copy of the publication is transmitted to you—in which the clauses of yr. Letter were inserted.—

In my hurry last post[3] I neglected to inform you that the District in which Orange is placed—is composed of the Counties of Amherst—Albemarle—Goochland—Louisa—Fluvanna Orange—& Culpepper—

Mr. Munroe is writing Myriads of Letters to the different Counties their contents I know not—but the direction in his hand-writing I have seen—lodged with Colo. William Cabell for their conveyance to Amherst—every possible exertion is making against you—& Mr. Henry's insinuations agt. you are held forth to the people as sacred incontrovertable facts—They were—That you had said in Convention not a letter of the Constitution cou'd be spared—and you were a Friend to direct Taxation which was the most oppressive part of the whole Constitution—Yr. Friends are not less Active, (as the enclosed publication will shew you)—and find their hopes more & more elevated every day—The violence of the Antifederals has begun to arrouse suspicion—& so soon as the people become acquainted with the Conduct of their *great high preist* I have not a doubt, but that they will take that direction which reason & moderation point out to them—Great Temper & deliberation is still the Characteristic of the Federals, who are at this period the most popular side of the house—that is upon questions not connected with the grand subject—We are all greatly pleased at the prospect of a Majority of the Friends to the new Government being appointed in the first instance to administer it—since it is a warrantable supposition that those who have been inveterately opposed to it will be very anxious to prove the clearness of their foresight & will therefore endeavor to present it to the people in the most disgusting & terrifying form....

1. RC, Madison Collection, NN. For the entire letter, see Rutland, *Madison*, XI, 396–98.
2. Richard Bland Lee. No copy of the pamphlet has been found, but see "A True Federalist," New York *Daily Advertiser*, 7 January 1789 (BoR, IV).
3. For the 12 December letter, see BoR, III, 415–16.

Consistency
Boston Herald of Freedom, 15 December 1788

To the FREE ELECTORS.

The day approaches, my fellow citizens, upon which you are either to confirm your uniform professions of love to your country, and of your attachment to the blessings of good government; or to exhibit a melancholy and fatal instance of the utter instability of popular sentiment.—If you, my friends, allow your reason to operate, unwarped by the influence of your passions and affections, you must be convinced that upon the unanimity of your suffrages in favour of a federal candidate, depends not only the prosperity, but the peace and salvation of this Union.—This Commonwealth was among the foremost of the States to ratify the present Constitution; and, unaided by the influence of this metropolis, this great and interesting event would not probably have happened. With what anxiety did you, my friends, throng the galleries of the honourable Convention! What fear and agitation did you experience concerning the event! Have you forgotten how sincerely and how justly you considered that all your hearts held dear, your liberties, lives and fortunes, the revival of commerce, the encouragement of manufactures, the welfare and honour of the Republick, depended upon the issue of their debates! Do you not recollect the indignation and chagrin which affected every bosom, upon the appearance of a bigoted opposition, arising from the pride and obstinacy of some, and from the mischievous policy of others!—If these suggestions remind you of the ideas and principles which you then entertained, let me intreat you to consult your dignity and happiness, by a consistent and patriotick conduct—by the deputation of a man to serve you, whose federalism is unsuspected, and whose commercial abilities may be equal to his station, and to your purposes.—Upon this measure, I may venture to assert, the happiness of this continent depends. In the ancient dominion of Virginia, popular art and intrigue have gained the ascendant: and their delegation principally consists of men who are warm advocates for *a new Convention,* or at least for *numerous amendments.* From several other States a similar deputation may be expected. This party consists of men who are conspicuous; and who, having espoused the antifederal cause, must rise or fall by its success: their pride cannot suffer them to recede. It is notorious that great efforts will be attempted in favour of a new Convention. The *sanguine Virginians* declare it openly. And if these efforts are successful, the Union will be immediately involved in anarchy, uproar, and civil war!—Massachusetts must, as she has ever done, hold the balance. The men of true and federal principles throughout the continent, depend upon a delegation of calm and steady adherents to the Constitution, from this Commonwealth. We have reason to fear they may be disappointed; and all the promised advantages of this system will in that case vanish like a dream.—Three or four of our districts will probably elect antifederal men. From Bristol, Worcester, and even from the upper counties, much is to be feared. And should the delegate from this district, supported by the influence which he will naturally acquire, be even lukewarm in the cause, the federal scale will kick the beam; a thousand systems of amendments will arise; and God only knows what fate will attend this once happy country.—I conjure you, therefore, my friends, to consider the importance of the approaching crisis. If a man who *was* professedly antifederal, and who is remarkable for the obstinacy of his temper, appears a candidate, will you think upon him a moment! If he declares he has changed his opinions, will you believe him? or if you believe him, can you approve his motives, or confide that he will not alter his sentiments whenever interest shall prompt? No, my friends! Such a man may have great merit, and may be entitled to an honourable provision at home; but if trusted abroad, persevering, disappointed and ambitious, connected with the warmest antifederalists in all the States, he will pull down the pillars of the government in attempting to prop it, and expire in the ruins.

North End
Boston Herald of Freedom, 15 December 1788

FEDERALISTS, HO!

The citizens of this town can be at no loss what line of conduct to adopt at the ensuing election.—Look through the town, and see what a gloom overspreads the face of our affairs! As a town, we are sinking under the pressure of debt and taxes; our trade in a languid condition—our mechanicks and artizans out of business—and multitudes of them obliged to seek employ, or a grave, in the sickly regions of the south; poverty and distress staring us in the face!—Is this an exaggerated description? Let the voice of cruel experience declare.—And what are our prospects?—Some have supposed that a revolution in the police of the town, by an act of incorporation, would mend our situation: but the slightest attention to a few considerations, would prove the futility of such an idea. Will incorporation place our trade upon a more respectable footing?[1] Will it command the reception of our *lumber, fish*, and the *labours of our mechanicks*, upon reciprocal terms in foreign markets? Will an incorporation fill our harbour with *ships, brigs*, and *snows*,[2] from all nations, as we see the case is at Philadelphia and New-York? No. What will any alterations signify, that affect merely our local circumstances?—'Tis the operation of the federal government alone, to which we must turn our eyes and expectations; 'tis that alone, that opens any rational prospect upon us. When we begin to feel its blessed influences, then will be the time to rip up old rotten foundations, and lay a new one. The citizens of this town have justly anticipated a revival of their business, and mechanical arts, from *this cause*; and so far as in them lies, they will take care that no considerations shall divert them from doing their part, by electing such FEDERAL CHARACTERS for the new government, as will be abundantly competent to doing justice to the TRADE and COMMERCE of this great Commonwealth.

And shall we be restricted by a "newspaper necessity," or by any other cause, from chusing such a real federal character as will realize to us all the blessings which can result only from a *full* and *speedy* operation of the new government?—Our brethren of Philadelphia have set us a noble example, in excluding every *amendment-stickler* from their suffrages—justly considering the plan of amendments, *before a trial of the Constitution*, AS A DAGGER AIMED AT ITS VITALS. For, in the words of Mr. Wilson, "Who is most likely to improve the Constitution, its friends, or its opposers?" This question is easily answered; and upon that answer our votes should be formed. Every candid elector will say, "*Let the Constitution be fairly carried into execution, by those who are* NOT ITS ENEMIES— *then such amendments as* EXPERIENCE *may discover to be necessary, can be made*, WITHOUT TEARING THE WHOLE TO PIECES."—OUR ALL, as men, as merchants, traders, mechanicks and farmers, is suspended on our electing a *firm, decided, able,* and *efficient* member of the federal House of Representatives.

1. Probably a reference to the attempts in 1784 and 1785 by merchants and other prominent citizens to persuade the town meeting to seek incorporation of Boston, thereby abandoning town-meeting government in favor of city government. Samuel Adams, backed by Boston's mechanics, opposed incorporation. "An American" in the *Massachusetts Centinel*, 26 May 1784, stated that incorporation of Boston would benefit the mechanics who were suffering from competition from country people. The latter could afford to manufacture goods more cheaply, and they paid lower taxes.

2. "A small sailing-vessel resembling a brig, carrying a main and fore mast and a supplementary trysail mast close behind the mainmast; formerly employed as a warship" (OED).

An Elector
Boston Herald of Freedom, 15 December 1788

To the FEDERAL ELECTORS *of the Suffolk District.*

Amidst the various opinions and characters now sported upon the publick, the FEDERAL ELECTORS of this district, and of this metropolis in *particular*, cannot lose sight of the noble principles, that actuated them, upon the RATIFICATION of the new Constitution. Through many struggles, perils and dangers, was the adoption of the system effected. We *then* justly considered our ALL AT STAKE: and can we be less solicitous at the PRESENT CRISIS? especially when we consider that a *Constitution is nothing,* if we are not favoured with a *wise, honest* and *federal* administration. Let us then, *one and all,* SOLEMNLY SWEAR that we will not give a vote in favour of any man who has a TRAIT OF ANTIFEDERALISM in his character. Upon the principles and abilities of the delegation from this Commonwealth, much more may depend than we may be aware of. The federal characters in the new government, will have an HERCULEAN TASK to perform, in encountering the wit, arts and arguments of the anti-federalists which will be in the federal legislature:

Therefore, men of moderate capacities will be found incompetent; we must therefore look for CONSUMMATE ABILITIES—men THOROUGHLY VERSED in the Constitution, FULLY ACQUAINTED with the circumstances of the United States, and ABUNDANTLY ABLE to advocate and support the federal Union. Can there be any safety in trusting *equivocal, slippery, doubting, narrative amendment, antifederal* characters? surely not.

Boston Gazette, 15 December 1788[1]

" 'Tis from EXPERIENCE that we reason best."[2] The glorious system of Federal Government, which the wisdom of these rising States has led them to adopt, has grown out of that EXPERIENCE which we have had of the weakness and inefficiency of the old Confederation; and shall we now marr the work of our own hand, by pretended amendments and alterations, without bringing it to the touch-stone of EXPERIENCE? The great Mr. [Samuel] Adams has very judiciously observed, to this effect, "That the wisdom and magnanimity which led this great people, to devise, and frame, in a peaceable manner, a form of government, calculated to embrace so many apparently discordant interests, will doubtless lead them to make such alterations and amendments as EXPERIENCE shall dictate to be necessary"—and before we have had this EXPERIENCE, to set the whole business afloat, under the idea of making the Constitution more perfect, is quitting the SHEET ANCHOR of our hope as a people, and trusting to the most uncertain of all contingencies, the caprice and local prejudices of interested individuals, whether this country shall ever be blessed with any settled form of Government, or not. It is therefore, devoutly to be wished, that the FEDERALISTS, which doubtless for the honour of Massachusetts, compose a decided majority, would hold fast their integrity, and steer clear of all antifederal amendments and suspicious characters, at the ensuing election.

1. Reprinted: New York *Daily Advertiser*, 25 December; Philadelphia *Federal Gazette*, 31 December; *Pennsylvania Packet*, 1 January 1789; *Maryland Journal*, 6 January.
2. Quoted from *The Poem Which the Committee of the Town of Boston Had Voted Unanimously with the Late Oration* . . . (Boston, 1777), 11.

Hardin Burnley to James Madison
Richmond, Va., 16 December 1788 (excerpt)[1]

I suppose that you have been made acquainted before this with the several acts which have passed the legislature of Virga. for the purpose of organizing the new Government. You have no doubt been informed that this State is divided into ten districts, each to choose a representative in the new Congress, on the second day of February next. The district in which Orange is included, consists of the counties of Albermarle Amherst Orange Culpeper Spotsylvania Louisa Goochland & Fluvanna. Your friends in this district have taken the liberty of assuring the people that your services may be commanded in the house of representatives if they will confer the appointment on you. With many this is sufficient, but with all it is not. Col: Monroe is also nominated & the most active unceasing endeavours will not be wanting among his friends to secure his election. It therefore becomes indispensably necessary that your return to Virga. should be hastened as much as possible. If you could return before Culpeper Jany. Court which is on the third Monday & make it convenient to see the people of that county on that day I am satisfied it would have a decided influence on the election. I know that this has not been your usual practice, and am certain that it will be very irksome to you, but your friends hope that you will make some sacrifices of this sort however disagreable they may be in order to secure a measure to which the views of all the friends to the Govt. are pointed with the most earnest Sollicitude. Every Subject which has been introduced into the legislature & which has had the most distant relation to the new Constitution has before its determination been made a federal & antefederal question. Great endeavours are making to give the Elections the same turn & to propogate an idea that you are wholly opposed to any alteration in the Govt. having declared that you did not think that a single letter in it would admit of a change. This circumstance alone would render your presence necessary for let these reports be denied as often as they may by your friends there are others among those who oppose you who will as repeatedly revive them and nothing can give them an effectual check but a Denial of them in the face of the people and an avowal of your real sentiments on the subject of amendments. If you approve my ideas on this subject & should have it in your power, perhaps a day spent at Louisa court on the second Monday in Jany. would not be time lost. . . .

1. RC, Madison Papers, DLC. For the entire letter, see Rutland, *Madison,* XI, 398–99.

Foreign Spectator XVI
Philadelphia Federal Gazette, 16 December 1788[1]

REMARKS *on the Amendments to the Federal Constitution, proposed by the Conventions of Massachusetts, New-Hampshire, New-York, Virginia, South and North-Carolina, with the minorities of Pennsylvania and Maryland, by a* FOREIGN SPECTATOR.

NUMBER XVI.

The conventions of Virginia and North-Carolina, by the 19th and 20th ams. respectively, demand, *that some tribunal other than the senate, be*

COMMENTARIES, 16 DECEMBER 1788   427

provided for trying impeachments of senators. The convention of New-York proposes, that all impeachments whatever may be tried by a temporary court, of which the senate shall be a part, in the following manner: *That the court for the trial of impeachments shall consist of the senate, the judges of the supreme court of the United States, and the first or senior judge, for the time being, of the highest court of general and ordinary common law jurisdiction in each state; that the Congress shall, by standing laws, designate the courts in the respective states, answering this description, and in the states having no courts exactly answering this description, shall designate some other court; preferring such, if any there be, whose judge or judges may hold their places during good behaviour: provided that no more than one judge other than judges of the supreme court of the United States, shall come from one state. That the Congress be authorised to pass laws for compensating the said judges for such services, and for compelling their attendance; and that a majority at least of the said judges shall be requisite to constitute the said court. That no person impeached, shall sit as a member thereof: that each member shall, previous to the entering upon any trial, take an oath or affirmation, honestly and impartially to hear and determine the cause; and that a majority of the members present shall be necessary to a conviction,* 25th am.

We have just seen that the most dangerous parts of mal-administration, are those which require a collusion between the president and a majority of the senate: let us then candidly examine what security against this may be expected from the suggested provision. The members of this constitution will be 26 senators, 13 judges from the respective states, and those of the supreme federal court, which I shall suppose 7; in all 46. From this number must be deducted the majority of impeached senators, at least 14; and no doubt, on the smallest computation, 4 of the other members, by reason of vacancies, sickness, or other impediments; which makes the remainder 28. A majority of this viz. 15, is necessary for conviction; consequently if 13 can be gained by the president and his colleagues, those high criminals will come off with impunity. I leave it to the reflection of every thinking man, whether any 13 persons in the most respectable stations can be depended on, when 15, the most confidential persons in the United States, have basely betrayed their trust! Possibly the senators may have brothers or near relations among the federal judges, and those sent from the different states. They and the president will certainly spare no means of corruption to save themselves from infamy, confiscation and other penalties; and by distributing only a part of the nefarious emoluments of their offices, they may still retain some wages of iniquity, and a half tarnished reputation.

This reasoning applies, with still greater force, to the case when a pernicious treaty is the object of impeachment. By corrupting only twelve members of the court, the president, with his eighteen fellow-traitors, will then be acquitted; and they will have more ample means of corruption, by that foreign gold which is the price of their guilt. It is also less probable that the virtue of these twelve judges will be invincible, when nineteen of those who were deemed the best men in the country, have acted so basely.

It is then, at best, very doubtful, if the remedy proposed by this amendment, or any other of the kind, would have the desired effect. If any particular court, for the trial of impeachments, must be erected, the senate ought not to make a part of it. It would also be necessary to exclude the judges of the supreme court, as they must again sit in judgment on the same offenders, if, after the impeachment, they should be indicted to take their trial in the course of criminal law. This court ought, also, to be equally numerous with the one proposed, in order to compensate, if possible, by numbers, the lamentable scarcity of public virtue, too visible from the depravity of so many high offenders. The trouble and expence of collecting such a number of persons, from the distant parts of the continent, will be so great, that the more common impeachment of an officer, or a senator, would not be an adequate object; yet it will not be easy to determine the cases in which the senate may be empowered to try an impeachment, and in which it should be reserved for such a court. Probably, however, such an extraordinary expedient may seem only proper when the president and a majority of the senate are impeached; and the importance of the matter demands the discussion of such a plan.

As, on the one hand, we suppose the executive department capable of very criminal conduct, so we must, on the other, admit the possibility of guilt in the house of representatives. Forty persons, or less, may combine in a false, or, at least, highly aggravated accusation against the president and fourteen senators. The weight of a superior number is here balanced by the greatness of confidence reposed in these men by those who chose them.

Party is the species of corruption most likely to happen in this, as all other free states; and this may infect the house of representatives not less than the senate; indeed, probably with more feverish symptoms, from their immediate and frequent delegation by the people. When a nation is unhappily divided by two parties, they generally prevail by turns, and persecute each other. The minority may, by a sudden change of the public mind, or by extraordinary exertions, carry an election, and form a majority in the house of representatives; and animated by the true spirit of party, immediately bring an impeachment against the president and the senate. This they may do merely to turn them out, in order to get their friends into these consequential departments, and all the appointments thereon depending. It is even well if nothing worse happens, as frequently the most faithful discharge of their trust may be construed into treason and attrocious crimes, because in opposition to a favourite system. Can we reasonably expect that any court, though previously constituted in the best manner, would be free from prejudices, or firm enough against popular clamours!

In the present mode, the executive is protected from this fury of party; for though the one-third of new senators that come in with the new house of representatives, and even some of those that remain, may be violent partisans, yet they cannot easily make up two-thirds of the whole, as a majority of the senate has by the supposition sided with the president. At the same time, the president is not safe from condign punishments, except he has indeed a very strong party in the senate; because, by the rotation, that happens every second year, he may exchange some of his best friends for severe judges. If the chief-justice, who presides on the impeachment of the president, will do his duty, he can expose his guilt to public view in a manner that will nearly answer the purpose, although a proper judgment cannot be obtained for the want of integrity in two-thirds of the members.

Every honest man will heartily wish for all practicable checks on the abuse of power; but there is a limit, beyond which they cannot be strained. A majority of a legislature may pass very unjust and pernicious laws; yet the only remedy is to repeal them by a new representation. What constitutional courts can be formed for judging and punishing a depraved legislative body? Such proceedings would subvert all regular government, and introduce the dominion of anarchy. What cruel tender-laws have been enacted by our state governments; yet we have not seen any impeachments brought against them. It is only in extreme cases that the people can punish such abuse of their trust, by erecting temporary and very extraordinary courts for the purpose—a remedy worse than the evil.

An attrocious collusion, between the president and senate, may be impeached, by the house of representatives, before the next senate, when all the old members shall be changed; but even this would require a nice attention to public justice on one side, and personal rights on the other; because a fearful suspence is itself a severe punishment.

1. Reprinted: *New York Daily Gazette,* 20 June 1789. For the authorship of the "Foreign Spectator" series, see the headnote to Essay No. I (21 October, BoR, III, 264n).

Massachusetts Centinel, 17 December 1788

Since it has been ascertained, that the Citizens of this Federal Metropolis [i.e., Boston], are in favour of a fair trial of the Constitution previous to amendments, the *junto*, to suit their plans to the *popular opinion*, now *shamelessly* assert, that those who are known to be decidedly *against* the Constitution, are in favour of a previous trial. But, until within *two or three days*, those who were opposed to previous amendments, have been abused with every opprob[r]ious epithet.

The people of this *federal* metropolis, cannot have forgotten with what *anxiety* they waited through the *long* session of the Convention, to hear from the Hon. Mr. A. his voice in support of the Constitution—and when at the *close* of the session, he did *come out*, what a CONSTERNATION they were then thrown into, by the extraordinary propositions he *then* brought forward[1]—truly "the die" with respect to the RATIFICATION, "spun doubtful."

If this gentleman really possesses all that federalism and love to his country, which his advocates pretend, how can they reconcile his *silence* at so interesting a period with an independent noble spirit of patriotism—especially when it is known that much was expected from his age and abilities.

The *consistency* of the junto is strikingly exemplified in their eulogium upon *some* deserving characters of 1775—and that torrent of abuse which they pour out upon others *equally deserving*. But it is remarkable, that the *same spirit* which actuates the *antifederalists* at the *southward*, is predominant in the *scurrilities* of their coadjutors at the eastward—not a *veteran* of 1775, even General WASHINGTON himself, has escaped the gall and venom of these harpies.

In Edes's paper of Monday last,[2] the antifederalists have fairly "*let the cat out of the bag*" as the saying is.—Hear, their whole plan in this precious antifederal paragraph, viz. "Mr. Adams was in our first Congress, *previous* to the war, he then became acquainted with many of those leading characters, who will probably compose the present Government—HE KNOWS THEM, AND THEY KNOW HIM—they are conversant with each others politicks.—Such a body of men meeting in our first Congress, will give decision to the publick business; AS THEY ARE ONLY TO BEGIN, WHERE THEY BEFORE LEFT OFF."[3]—That is, in plain English, by first deciding upon the NEW CONSTITUTION, which it is very generally believed, the amendment stickler would very soon *annihilate*—and then "*begin where they left off*," that is, with that wretched *sand-rope*, the OLD CONFEDERATION. FEDERALISTS! If this does not open your eyes, it is because judicial blindness hath fallen upon you.

1. A reference to the additional amendments proposed (and withdrawn) by Samuel Adams in the Massachusetts Convention on 6 February 1788 (RCS:Mass., 1452n–54n, 1598).

2. See "An Elector," *Boston Gazette,* 15 December (DHFFE, I, 558–59).
3. *Ibid.*

George Mason to John Mason
Gunston Hall, Fairfax County, Va., 18 December 1788 (excerpts)[1]

... North Carolina has rejected the new Government, unless previous Amendments, almost the same with the subsequent Amendments proposed by Virginia, can be obtained; Rhode Island has yet done nothing decisive on the Subject. New York, discouraged by the Adoption in Virginia, with a Majority in their Convention of two to one against the new Form of Government, received it; upon the Minority's agreeing to recommend unanimously, Amendments similar to those of Virginia, & voting a circular Letter, from their President, Governor Clinton, to invite the Concurrence of the other States, in an immediate Application to the new Congress for calling another federal Convention, to consider them—the other States have all adopted. Connecticut, Jersey, Pensylvania, Delaware, & Maryland without recommending any Amendments—New Hampshire, Massachusetts, South Carolina, and (I think) Georgia,[2] with a Recommendation of Amendments. The Virginia Legislature now sitting have taken up the Subject, upon the Ground of the New York Circular Letter, & by a large Majority, have voted an Application to Congress for immediately calling a federal Convention, to consider the amendments proposed by this & the other States; their Address to Congress for this purpose is a very firm, & in my opinion, proper one; they have also wrote a Circular to the other States, desiring their Concurrence.[3] Your Brother George will send You a Collection of American Papers, in which you will see the particulars....

it is thought the Elections [for U.S. Representatives from Virginia] will go, very generally in favour of Men, who are for calling a federal Convention, to make Amendments. [In] Our District ... The Gentlemen for amendments have not yet fixed upon a Candidate, & I doubt we shall be at a Loss for one. Several who have been applied to having refused; if we can prevail upon a proper person to offer, I think there will be little Doubt of his Succeeding.—Jas. Monroe of Fredericksburg (late Member of Congress) opposes Mr. Maddison in the Spotsylvania & Orange District, & it's thought will carry his Election.

Beverley Randolph is chosen Govr: of Virginia, in the Room of Young A——ld.[4]

1. RC, George Mason Papers, DLC. For the entire letter, see Rutland, *Mason,* III, 1135–40.
2. The Georgia Convention did not propose amendments.

3. For the Virginia legislature's call for another general convention, see BoR, I, 158–80.

4. Many Antifederalists considered Edmund Randolph, the retiring governor, a traitor, i.e., Benedict Arnold.

A Bostonian
Boston Herald of Freedom, 18 December 1788

Messrs. PRINTERS, A writer in the Centinel of Saturday last [13 December], under the signature of *Constitutionalist*, after declaring that Mr. [Samuel] Adams, "was firm and intrepid in the hour of danger:" "That he has been steady, consistent and persevering;" "That he was a distinguished Patriot of 75."—concludes his remarks with these ungenerous queries; "*But what of all this.*" "What was *the state of facts in 87, and how is it in 88?*"[1]

Provided this writer really wishes to know the *present* character of Mr. Adams, I would inform him, that he *remains* the same intrepid, steady, consistent, persevering and distinguished Patriot.—It became the writer to prove the instances wherein this gentleman had *faultered*, and not after admitting him to possess the most exalted virtues *formerly*, ungenerously reflect on him as now being destitute of every quality requisite for a member of our federal legislature.—we cannot suppose that Mr. Adams means to sully his character at this period of his life, by acting contrary to those sentiments of patriotism which have hitherto endeared him to his countrymen, after spending so many years in promoting the interest of his country; after standing forth in vindication of its rights and liberties *in the hour of danger*! If his very opponents, are obliged to acknowledge his many tried virtues, surely his friends have the greatest reason still to confide in his integrity and unshaken patriotism.

But, says this writer, "how is he affected to the new Constitution?" Let the debates determine.—In the convention his speeches were warm in its support. He advocated the necessity of a uniform *commercial system*; and endeavoured to inculcate the spirit of harmony throughout the debates.—How ungenerous then for a writer to insinuate that this venerable gentleman, after acting with the greatest "firmness, steadiness and consistency" for a series of years in the service of his country, should, just *at the close of life*, become the greatest hypocrite; the vilest traitor; and would *now*, if in his power, plunge his country into all the horrors of a civil war?—How cruel and unkind to reflect on the man, who stood forth in the "*hour of danger,*" as if he was now become an enemy to that country which he hazarded his life to defend?

The amendment proposed respecting the *fire arms, &c.* has been unjustly reckoned, as *intended* by him to overthrow the constitution.—

These propositions were introduced after those proposed by his Excellency; they were approved by many of the warmest advocates for the constitution. But when Mr. A. found that there was danger of introducing a debate, which might retard an immediate adoption of the constitution, he prudently withdrew his motion.[2]—If he was desirous of doing that mischief so ungenerously suggested, it was then in his power to have accomplished his purposes.

The *people of Boston* however, ought to consider this motion with the greatest candour—this town had experienced but a few years since, the demands of an arbitrary power to surrender *their arms.*—This *precaution* therefore, coming from a citizen, who had all the delicate feelings of a freeman, should not be urged to *condemn him*, but should rather be considered as the earnest *solicitude* of a faithful patriot, to secure his townsmen from being again exposed to so humiliating a situation.

Upon the whole Mr. ADAMS has some enemies, but we trust he has yet MANY FRIENDS.

1. See "Constitutionalist," *Massachusetts Centinel*, 13 December 1788 (DHFFE, I, 554–55).

2. For the amendments proposed by Samuel Adams in the Massachusetts Convention on 6 February 1788, see RCS:Mass., 1452–54n, 1598.

A Citizen of New-Haven
Connecticut New Haven Gazette, 18 December 1788[1]

OBSERVATIONS.

On the ALTERATIONS proposed as AMENDMENTS to the new Federal Constitution.

Six of the states have adopted the new constitution without proposing any alterations, and the most of those proposed by the conventions of other states may be provided for by congress in a code of laws without altering the constitution. If congress may be safely trusted with the affairs of the Union, and have sufficient powers for that purpose, and possess no powers but such as respect the common interest of the states (as I have endeavoured to shew in a former piece)[2] then all the matters that can be regulated by law may safely be left to their direction, and those will include all that I have noticed, except the following, which I think on due consideration will appear to be improper or unnecessary.

1. It is proposed that the consent of two thirds or three fourths of the members present in each branch of the congress shall be required for passing certain acts.

On which I would observe, that this would give a minority in congress power to controul the majority, joined with the concurrent voice of the president, for if the president dissents no act can pass without the consent of two thirds of the members in each branch of congress; and would not that be contrary to the general principles of republican government?

2. That impeachments ought not to be tried by the senate, or not by the senate alone.

But what good reason can be assigned why the senate is not the most proper tribunal for that purpose.—The members are to be chosen by the legislatures of the several states, who will doubtless appoint persons of wisdom and probity, and from their office can have no interested motives to partiality. The house of peers in Great Britain try impeachments and are also a branch of the legislature.

3. It is said that the president ought not to have power to grant pardons in cases of high treason, but the congress.

It does not appear that any great mischief can arise from the exercise of this power by the president (though perhaps it might as well have been lodged in congress). The president cannot pardon in case of impeachment, so that such offenders may be excluded from office notwithstanding his pardon.

4. It is proposed that members of congress be rendered inelegible to any other office during the time for which they are elected members of that body.

This is an objection that will admit of something plausible to be said on both sides, and it was settled in convention on full discussion and deliberation, there are some offices which a member of congress may be best qualified to fill, from his knowledge of public affairs acquired by being a member. Such as minister to foreign courts, &c. and on accepting any other office his seat in congress will be vacated, and no member is elegible to any office that shall have been instituted or the emoluments increased while he was a member.

5. It is proposed to make the president and senators inelegible after certain periods.

But this would abridge the privilege of the people, and remove one great motive to fidelity in office, and render persons incapable of serving in offices, on account of their experience, which would best qualify them for usefulness in office—but if their services are not acceptable they may be left out at any new election.

6. It is proposed that no commercial treaty should be made without the consent of two thirds of the senators, nor any cession of territory, right of navigation or fishery, without the consent of three fourths of the members present in each branch of congress.

It is provided by the constitution that no commercial treaty shall be made by the president without the consent of two thirds of the senators present, and as each state has an equal representation and suffrage in the senate, the rights of the states will be as well secured under the new constitution as under the old;[3] and it is not probable that they would ever make a cession of territory or any important national right without the consent of congress. The king of Great Britain has by the constitution a power to make treaties, yet in matters of great importance he consults the parliament.

7. There is one amendment proposed by the convention of South Carolina respecting religious tests, by inserting the word *other*, between the words *no* and *religious* in that article, which is an ingenious thought, and had that word been inserted, it would probably have prevented any objection on that head.[4] But it may be considered as a clerical omission and be inserted without calling a convention, as it now stands the effect will be the same.

On the whole it is hoped that all the states will consent to make a fair trial of the constitution before they attempt to alter it, experience will best shew whether it is deficient or not, on trial it may appear that the alterations that have been proposed are not necessary, or that others not yet thought of may be necessary, every thing that tends to disunion ought to be avoided. Instability in government and laws, tends to weaken a state and render the rights of the people precarious.

If another convention should be called to revise the constitution, tis not likely they would be more unanimous than the former, they might judge differently in some things, but is it certain that they would judge better? When experience has convinced the states and people in general, that alterations are necessary they may be easily made, but attempting it at present may be detrimental if not fatal to the union of the states.

The judiciary department is perhaps the most difficult to be precisely limited by the constitution, but congress have full power to regulate it by law, and it may be found necessary to vary the regulations at different times as circumstances may differ.

Congress may make requisitions for supplies previous to direct taxation, if it should be thought expedient, but if requisitions be made and some states comply and others not, the non complying states must be considered and treated as delinquents, which will tend to excite disaffection and disunion among the states, besides occasioning delay; but if congress lay the taxes in the first instance these evils will be prevented, and they will doubtless accommodate the taxes to the customs and convenience of the several states.

Some suppose that the representation will be too small, but I think it is in the power of congress to make it too large, but I believe that it may be safely trusted with them, Great Britain contains about three times the number of the inhabitants in the United States, and according to Burgh's account in his political disquisitions, the members of parliament in that kingdom do not exceed 131,[5] and if 69 more be added from the principal cities and towns the number would be 200, and strike off those who are elected by the small boroughs, which are called the rotten part of the constitution by their best patriots and politicians, that nation would be more equally and better represented than at present, and if that would be a sufficient number for their national legislature, one third of that number will be more than sufficient for our federal legislature who will have a few general matters to transact. But these and other objections have been considered in a former paper, before referred to. I shall therefore conclude this with my best wishes for the continuance of the peace, liberty and union of these states.

N.B. The piece above referred to has not been published in this Gazette, but will be in our next.[6]

1. Reprinted with revisions: *New York Packet*, 24 March 1789. Roger Sherman was probably the author of this item. He had previously written under that pseudonym during Connecticut's debate over ratifying the Constitution (RCS:Conn., 524–27). James Madison identified Sherman as "a Citizen of New Haven" in a letter to Edmund Randolph of 12 April 1789 (Rutland, *Madison*, XII, 76).

2. The "A Citizen of New-Haven" essay alluded to here appeared in the *New Haven Gazette*, 25 December 1788. See CC:421 and *New York Packet*, 20, 24 March 1789 (BoR, IV).

3. Under the Articles of Confederation, the approval of nine of the thirteen states was necessary to ratify treaties.

4. For South Carolina's proposed amendment concerning religious tests, see BoR, I, 248.

5. James Burgh, *Political Disquisitions: or, An Enquiry into Public Errors, Defects, and Abuses* . . . (3 vols., London, 1774–1775), I, Book II, chapter IV, 45–48.

6. See note 2 (above).

Massachusetts Spy, 18 December 1788

A correspondent observes, that many of "the opposers of the New Federal Government, at the southward, are using their endeavours to put the States to the expense of another General Convention, in order to alter, or amend the Constitution. If amendments are necessary, surely they can be effected without the expense of another Convention."

John Francis Mercer Declares His Candidacy
Annapolis, Md., 20 December 1788[1]

The organization of the new federal government has presented a very awful crisis to these States—Individual happiness and national prosperity are deeply involved in its first movements—The contrariety of opinion discovered throughout the continent with respect to its leading features—splendid expectations on one part—fears and disquietude on the other—the existing separation of two states heretofore united by the ties of blood, common interest, sufferings and success—the terms and instructions which five others have annexed to their ratifications, must satisfy every dispassionate mind, that mutual concession can alone produce that harmony and concord, without which the government will be neither happy in its operations, or of lasting duration—They must also prove, that to elect men to administer this government, who are altogether the enthusiastic admirers of this constitution without any amendments, will not produce a real representation of the interests and wishes of the people, but tend to establish that violent adherence to party spirit and views, which destroys the mild influence of reason, the only true principle of republican government.

With these sentiments, I offer myself to represent the third district of this state in the new congress.

The conduct I have hitherto pursued in this state, however ineffectual it has been, still affords strong evidence that I am the decided friend to those declaratory acts and amendments, which will effectually guard the great and fundamental rights of the people.—These can admit of no delay.

I am also persuaded that several alterations in its form are highly necessary; but the government being adopted, and the necessities of the union requiring its immediate and energetic execution, all changes that might tend to retard its operations, should be gradually and cautiously effected, and the general sense of the continent previously consulted.

If under these impressions I should meet your approbation, I shall hope your assistance at the ensuing election, in confidence that my conduct will so far correspond with your expectations.

I am, with respect and esteem, Your Obedient Servt

1. Broadside, James Thomas Letters, Maryland State Archives, Annapolis. The broadside was printed in script, while the closing (including signature) is in Mercer's hand. It was addressed to William Thomas, Jr., St. Marys County. (Another copy of this letter/broadside (unaddressed) is in the Virginia Historical Society. In this copy the closing and signature are in printed script.) Mercer was not elected as a U.S. representative.

John Wright Stanly to Joseph Clay
New Bern, N.C., 20 December 1788 (excerpt)[1]

... Our State has indeed Rejected the proposed Constitution—but having Called a Convention to Meet in Octr. next, will readily, I believe, adopt it, if in the intrim amendments should be made—without them,

Our leaders seem determin'd that our State shall stand or fall by itself—

My private Opinion however is, that we cannot long stand unsupported, & that it would have been good policy to have concurred with our Sister States in endeavouring to bring about the desired amendments & in the mean time to have been represented in the New Congress & had a Share in the formation of the Commercial System & Laws of the Union. . . .

1. RC, Unbound Manuscript Collections, Connecticut State Library. The letter was addressed to "Joseph Clay esquire" in Savannah. It was endorsed as "Favour'd by Jas. Bryson esqr," of Philadelphia who Stanly identified as surveyor general of post roads toward the end of the letter.

Massachusetts Centinel, 20 December 1788[1]

Notwithstanding what has been said relative to the disposition of the two Senators elected by Virginia, that they wished for amendments to the Constitution, previous to its being put into operation; we are authorized, from the best authority, to say, that they both wish to see the Government fully carried into execution; and that they wish that such alterations only should be adopted, as may be found necessary from its errours and defects.

This information, authentick and indubitable, must be highly pleasing to every friend to the happiness of the United States, as it augurs a greater degree of unanimity in our federal councils, than what we have been led to expect.—It is the opinion of the "wise and learned of the land," that the Constitution need only to be *tried* to be found *good*—and as it is now determined, that that trial shall be had, the fears of those who dreaded lest it should be mutilated and destroyed, are consequently done away.

1. Reprinted: *New Hampshire Gazette*, 23 December; Portland, Maine, *Cumberland Gazette*, 25 December (first paragraph only); Rhode Island *Newport Herald*, 25 December; Providence, R.I., *United States Chronicle*, 25 December.

Thomas Jefferson to Francis Hopkinson
Paris, 21 December 1788 (excerpt)[1]

. . . I am happy to find that our new constitution is accepted and our government likely to answer it's purposes better. I hope that the addition of a bill of rights will bring over to it the greater part of those now opposed to it: and that this may be added without submitting the whole to the risk of a new convention. it would still have one fault in my eye, that of the perpetual reeligibility of the president. but if my fears on that should be verified in the experiment, I trust to the good sense of our children that they will apply the remedy which shall suit the circumstances then existing. . . .

1. FC, Jefferson Papers, DLC. Jefferson added a P.S. to this letter on 11 and 12 January 1789. For the entire letter, see Boyd, XIV, 369–71.

Meriwether Smith: Campaign Address, c. 21 December 1788 (excerpt)

This undated, signed manuscript is located in the Mercer Papers in the Virginia Historical Society. It, or a similar address, was probably enclosed in a letter that Smith wrote to Robert Carter, a Westmoreland County, Va., planter, on 21 December 1788 requesting support for Smith's candidacy for the U.S. House of Representatives (Charles Francis Jenkins Collection, PHi). No enclosure is filed with the manuscript letter nor has a printed copy of Smith's address been located. The right margin of the manuscript is damaged. In his letter to Carter, Smith wrote: "Whatever may be your Sentiments of the Author of the inclosed Address, permit me to commit it to your patronage, & to request that you will make it public within your County.

To the Freeholders of the County of ─────────
Friends and Fellow-Citizens! . . . The establishing a Constitution of Government as the result of cool [deliberation?] [– – –] Discussion, is an Advantage which the Americans [have?] Experienced in an eminent Degree. [– – –] the Present moment should be well improved. To rest satisfied with the adoption of the new Constitution Proceeding from a supposed necessity of changing the old form of Government, may be fatal to you. It should secure in its operation your Rights & Interests against Ambition & Avarice, [the?] constant Enemies of both civil and religious Liberty. It should be critically examined [and?] not suffered by Precedents founded on the Construction of loose and inaccurate Expressions, to speak a Language and assume a Principle, neither understood nor foreseen by the People, when they adopted it.

Although I am sensible of the necessity of Reformation in Government, I own I [do not like?] the Constitution in its present Dress. I fear it is a wolf in Sheep's clothing, that will seek a fi[rst?] opportunity to devour us. But whatever may be my Sentiments, I hold it the duty of every good Citizen to submit to the Determination of the Majority, as the only rule by which free Societies can be supported. Time may better inform the Judgment and Experience correct the Errors that may be found in it.—

    I am, with unfeigned Respect, my Fellow Citizens
     Your most obedt. & hble. servant
     [Signed] M. Smith

Foreign Spectator XVII
Philadelphia Federal Gazette, 23 December 1788[1]

REMARKS *on the Amendments to the Federal Constitution, proposed by the Conventions of Massachusetts, New-Hampshire, New-York, Virginia, South and North-Carolina, with the minorities of Pennsylvania and Maryland, by a* FOREIGN SPECTATOR.

NUMBER XVII.

The following amendments relate to the power of making treaties, which, by the constitution, is lodged with the president and senate. *That no treaty shall be effectual to repeal or abrogate the constitutions or bills of rights of the states, or any part of them,* 6th am. by the min. of Maryland. *That no treaty which shall be directly opposed to the existing laws of the United States in Congress assembled, shall be valid until such laws shall be repealed or made conformable to such treaty; neither shall any treaties be valid which are contradictory to the constitution of the United States, or the constitutions of the individual states,* 13th am. by the minority of Pennsylvania. *That no commercial treaty shall be ratified without the concurrence of two-thirds of the whole number of the members of the senate; and no treaty, ceding, contracting, or restraining, or suspending the territorial rights or claims of the United States, or any of them—or their, or any of their rights or claims to fishing in the American seas, or navigating the American rivers, shall be made, but in cases of the most urgent and extreme necessity; nor shall any such treaty be ratified, without the concurrence of three-fourths of the whole number of members of both houses respectively,* 7th am. by Virginia and North-Carolina. It is self-evident that the executive can have no power to infringe the constitution of the United States by any treaty, however beneficial it might appear. The whole federal government had no such authority. It is also granted that the constitutions of the several states cannot be repealed or abrogated by any acts of the federal power: besides, treaties concern the general affairs of the union, and cannot affect the forms of the several state-governments.

The power of legislation is vested in both houses of Congress with the president so far as his negative extends. Treaties, which must necessarily have the full energy of laws, are to be made by the president and the senate. Consequently, as two co-equal separate powers are a solecism in politics, it would seem reasonable to require a concert between the two parties, and to enact that no treaty, which shall be directly opposed to the existing laws of the United States, shall be valid until such laws shall be repealed, or made conformable to it. But, on the other hand, very momentous reasons justify the delegation of this power to the executive and senators exclusively. First, these persons will, from their long continuance in office, derive a more ample, exact and systematic knowledge of those great national affairs which are the objects of treaties, than can be generally expected from a popular assembly that is changed every second year. Secondly, negociations often require secrecy and expedition. It may be imprudent to lay open our whole situation to the nation with whom we treat. It may also be proper to conceal many things from another which is a rival in such treaty. In the cabinet, as in the field, the moments are sometimes precious, and must be caught as they pass. Every person who is versed in history must know, that a battle, the death of a prince, the change of a ministry, and many other circumstances, have often caused great alterations; and that able politicians have made an excellent use of such events. Thirdly, if a treaty is advantageous, there is no doubt but Congress will repeal or alter such laws as are in opposition to it. Fourthly, the president and senate will certainly confer with some of the principal members in the house of representatives in all difficult cases, when the treaty in agitation demands a change of some important laws.

The concurrence of two thirds of the whole senate is, undoubtedly, very desirable, when a commercial treaty or any other is to be ratified. But what must be done, when so great a majority of those present cannot be obtained, and a delay would have bad consequences? I have before observed the pernicious tendency of indolence, and other private avocations, and repeat again, that such conduct is peculiarly disgraceful and criminal in offices of high trust. The constitution might have fixed a quorum of the senate for transacting the more important business; but it supposed a sense of duty and honor that wants no coercion. Indeed, what can be a substitute for this? May not the plea of sickness, alone, elude any compulsive measures?

That no detrimental treaties ought to be made, but from necessity, is clear. The magnitude of the sacrifice must not exceed the greatness of this necessity; but it is difficult to determine this proportion, previous to such deplorable events. The cases expressed by the conventions of Virginia and North-Carolina, are all very alarming, yet not in the same degree; the cession of territorial, or other, rights, is worse than a temporary suspension; positive rights are less alienable than mere claims. A part of the federal territory, or any other common advantages, may also, *ceteris peribus*,[2] be given up sooner than the appurtenance of any particular state. The federal constitution expressly declares, *that nothing in the same shall be so construed as to prejudice any claims of the United States, or of any particular state,* 4th art. 3d sect. 2d par. In strict compliance with this clause, neither the executive nor the congress have the power to abalienate[3] any possessions or rights of the United States, or any of them. Such unhappy necessity may, however, exist, and the general government must then concert what remedy is practicable. The house of representatives may, in this case, have a salutary co-operation with the president and senate, especially as secrecy and dispatch are less requisite. Unanimity is devoutly to be wished for in such critical resolves; but it is extremely difficult to fix the degree of it. It is doubtful whether even two thirds of both houses would agree on a measure, that must affect some states very deeply. Necessity has no law; when a victorious army can inforce hard conditions, there is no choice.

It is a consolation, that this kind of amendments will, probably, never be wanted, while a solid confederation is an impregnable bulwark to every state in the union.

An explanation on this important subject, will be an improvement of the constitution, but, at the same time, a very arduous task. In the vicissitude of human affairs, the cession of a frontier state may become indispensible; yet what constitutional act can be framed for such a melancholy event, which is, in fact, a partial dissolution of the union, and, consequently, of the constitution itself? Human prudence cannot pass certain limits; let us trust something to Divine Providence, and the means of security he has graciously given.

1. Reprinted: *New York Daily Gazette*, 22 June 1789. For the authorship of the "Foreign Spectator" series, see the headnote to Essay No. I (21 October, BoR, III, 264n).
2. Latin: All other things being equal.
3. Obsolete. "To transfer or make over (property) to another" (OED).

An American Citizen
Philadelphia Federal Gazette, 24 December 1788[1]

THOUGHTS on the SUBJECT of AMENDMENTS
of the FEDERAL CONSTITUTION.

In examining those amendments which relate to *the powers* vested in Congress by the new constitution, we find the principal ground of objection to be, the effect which the general government will have upon the governments of the states. And here it may be well for us briefly to notice the principal causes of opposition throughout the United States, which unhappily can be too easily ascertained. Considerations with regard to personal rights no doubt have affected many worthy men, but we trust we have already shewn, that every amendment really affecting liberty may be expected of the new Congress. The event must very soon prove the prediction to be true or false, and in the mean time it must be evident that there is no danger from an unorganized government, from a constitution yet on paper.

The first great cause of objection which presents itself is, that the federal constitution will prevent those legal invasions of *the rights of property*, which have shewn themselves in *paper emissions, lawful tenders, instalment laws,* and *valuation laws.* To all arguments drawn from *such* considerations, it would be an insult to the integrity of an honest opponent to the constitution to offer an answer. He will reject them of his own accord. Only to remind him of the facts will be sufficient. He will find, on examination, that a majority of the state legislatures had committed trespasses of this kind, *prior* to the meeting of the late general convention, and that attempts were making in some one of the remaining states at every session.

The second objection to the constitution of the United States which occurs, and which is of too general influence, is, that it aims to restore *energy*, and to give *effect* to government. The delay of justice, and in the collection of taxes and debts, in the interior parts of some, and every part of other states, is too convenient, too agreeable to many. To all arguments drawn from *such* considerations, also, it would be an insult to the integrity of an honest opponent of the constitution to offer an answer. Measures, which will remedy these two evils, must be acceptable to good men of both parties, and are indispensibly necessary to the prosperity and honor of the United States.

The third objection to the powers of the federal government, which creates a strong and warm body of opponents, is the influence, 'tis said, it will have on the powers of the state governments.

Let us examine briefly a few points in the constitutions of the states, and the administration of them since the peace.

The constitutions of a majority of the states establish, in many important particulars, an equality among their respective counties, though they differ in their number of freemen in the proportion of ten to one, and in their contributions to government much more. This is surely a violation of justice and the equal rights of man. Such constitutions are not *the codes of liberty*, nor can a just and safe administration take place under them.

Several of the state constitutions impose religious tests. One of them disfranchises the whole body of the clergy of all denominations[2]—another disfranchises all Christian sects but one. Would not the friends of religious men, and the meritorious advocates of religious liberty, be well employed in obtaining amendments of these articles?

If the state constitutions thus violate the rights of man, both *temporal* and *spiritual*, the administration under them must always be precarious, and has been already extremely unjust. Foreigners, and the merchants and tradesmen of New-Hampshire, Massachusetts, Connecticut,

Pennsylvania and Maryland (where special payments can be compelled) have placed large properties in goods in the hands of the merchants, traders, planters and farmers in Georgia, the Carolinas, Virginia, New-Jersey and Rhode-Island. The *legal* impediments, which the several legislatures of the latter states have thrown in the way, or which they have purposely omitted to remove, though within their powers, have long detained, and yet continue to keep the rightful property of the former out of their hands. The consequence to the unhappy creditor, who is within the reach of a just and efficient government, is a loss of those profits, which would maintain his family and educate his children, injurious sales of his landed property to make his payments, too often forced by legal executions, or even a distressful bankruptcy. The public debts and the public revenues might be enlarged on; but the picture of our country, as it stood at the time of the establishment of the federal constitution, arising principally from the defects and faults in the state constitutions, or the mal-administration of them, would be too painful. Let our own reflection, and these facts, which are *as true* as they are *deplorable,* suffice. Let us, however, deduce from these observations the conclusion to which they were meant to lead, that *a diminution of the powers of the state governments, and a transfer of a due portion of them to a national body, was necessary to the salvation of our country.*

In the formation of this national body, a careful examination was previously made. It was seen, that the United States were made up of *the people at large,* and of *thirteen local governments,* and that both must be completely represented in the general government. Hence an entire body was assigned to the people, called *the house of representatives,* without whose consent *nothing* can be done, and whose election is always to be made in a manner as consistent with equality and liberty, as that of any body upon earth. Hence, also, an entire representative body was assigned to the state legislatures, called *the senate,* in which the thirteen governments are completely represented, and their equal rights are duly maintained. To preserve unimpaired the independency of *the freemen* of the United States, no inequality was permitted to be introduced, to the prejudice of any man, in the election of the federal representatives; so also, to preserve inviolate the independency of *the states,* no inequality was allowed, to the injury of any one of them, in the election of their representatives, *the federal senators.* How just and safe to both *is this* arrangement.

We are now electing the *men of our choice* to represent us in the two houses of the general government. Let us, 'till the short period of their meeting, give them a generous credit for the amendments they will propose, affecting the rights of conscience, the liberty of the press, and other topics, concerning which our apprehensions have been sometimes honestly, and at other times dishonestly, excited. Let us remember, what we will all admit, that they love virtue and freedom no less than ourselves.

1. Also printed in the *Pennsylvania Gazette* on 24 December, and reprinted in the *New York Packet*, 2 January 1789; Boston *Herald of Freedom*, 13 January; Rhode Island *Newport Herald*, 22 January; *Virginia Centinel*, 4 February. This essay was written by Tench Coxe. For other "American Citizen" essays in this volume published on 4 June and 10, 31 December, see BoR, III, 7–8, 407–9, 456–57.
2. The constitutions of Georgia, New York, North Carolina and South Carolina restricted the holding of all or some public offices by clergymen. (See BoR, I, 68, 88, 99–100.)

Thomas Jefferson to William Carmichael
Paris, 25 December 1788 (excerpt)[1]

... You have long ago known that 11. states have ratified our new constitution, and that N. Carolina, contrary to all expectation, has declined either accepting or refusing, but has proposed amendments copied verbatim from those of Virginia. Virginia & Massachusets had preferred this method of amendment that is to say, desiring Congress to propose specific amendments to the several legislatures, which is one of the modes of amendment provided in the new constitution. in this way nothing can be touched but the parts specifically pointed out. New York has written circular letters to the legislatures to adopt the other mode of amendment, provided also by the constitution, that is to say to assemble another federal convention. in this way the whole fabric would be submitted to alteration. it's friends therefore unite in endeavoring to have the first method adopted, and they seem agreed to concur in adding a bill of rights to the Constitution. this measure will bring over so great a part of the Opposition that what will remain after that will have no other than the good effect of watching, as centinels, the conduct of government, and laying it before the public. many of the opposition wish to take from Congress the power of internal taxation. calculation has convinced me this would be very mischievous....

1. FC, Jefferson Papers, DLC. For the entire letter, see Boyd, XIV, 385–88n.

An Inhabitant
Maryland Journal, 26 December 1788 (excerpt)[1]

To the INHABITANTS of FREDERICK, WASHINGTON, and MONTGOMERY COUNTIES.

You are called upon, by a law passed this session of Assembly, to attend at your respective Court-Houses on the first Wednesday in January, to vote for Six Representatives, who are to serve in Congress two years, one of whom is to be a resident of each of the six districts, into which the state is divided, and these three counties make one district.

You are at the same time to vote for Eight Electors of the President and Vice-President of the United States, agreeably to the direction of the new Federal Government.

⟨After a fair examination, and full discussion, the people of eleven states have agreed to put this excellent form of government in motion, and the several states are now taking the necessary steps for that purpose. The wisest and best men of the nation, supported by a large majority of the people, have hitherto nobly stood forth, and have effectually counteracted the opponents of the constitution. One step more and the business, I trust, will be happily completed; but this *one* step requires all your vigilance, activity, and firmness. The enemies of the government, in this state, having been frustrated in their attempts to prevent its adoption, are now making their last efforts to render it abortive, in which they must infallibly fail, if the friends of the constitution will stand guarded against deception, and prevent them from *creeping* into power.

Their leaders will employ all their *tools*, and will intrigue deeply to obtain seats in the new Congress, where they would exert all their influence to clog the wheels in such a manner as to prevent the government from acquiring any efficient motion; or, if it was permitted to operate, they would, most probably, contrive (if they found themselves *in force*) to render it subservient to the selfish, I will not say sinister, views of the party. If the friends of federalism, will now unite, in refusing them their suffrages, their hopes are blasted, and they must retire. They have now like the tories at the revolution, changed their ground, but not their principles, which are precisely the same as they were in the beginning. They would, if indulged in their plan of *amendments*, aim as deadly a blow at the vitals of the constitution, as the tories aimed at the liberties of our country by their *conciliatory propositions* after the declaration of independence. Those who opposed the ratification of the government, have *all at once* become federal!—When they have proved their faith by *good works*, they may be let into favour! but their conversion has been rather sudden; and their term of probation too short, for them to be trusted in the councils of federal government, at the present critical period, without danger.

He who is an advocate for going into a consideration of amendments, *before experience has given the government a fair trial*, is in my apprehension as much an antifederalist, to all intents and purposes, as him who voted against the ratification. Trust not to the federal declarations of any man whose *actions* are antifederal.⟩ I mean those who league with, and support the antifederal party in, and out of the H—— of D——,[2] while they, at the same time, declare themselves to be federal. The character of a *trimmer* in politicks is every way contemptible, and ought never to be trusted. He will certainly *always* be ready to betray you when he conceives that he can serve himself by so doing. If you wish to see the government properly organized, and happily executed, give your votes in favour of such men only whose words and actions have been, and still are, uniformly in favour of the proposed plan of government, and whose abilities and experience bid fair to enable them to support the honour and dignity of the State, *and* to protect your freedom and independence, as well as to promote a wise and beneficial administration of the government on true federal principles. . . .

Frederick, December 22, 1788.

1. The text in angle brackets was reprinted in the Philadelphia *Federal Gazette,* 1 January 1789.
2. The Maryland House of Delegates.

Samuel Sterett: Circular letter and Address on His Candidacy 27 December 1788[1]

BALTIMORE, December 27, 1788

SIR,

Encouraged by the Patronage and promised Support of a Number of very respectable Characters, I take the Liberty of offering myself a Candidate to represent this State in Congress, and soliciting your Vote and Interest to place me on the Return, at the ensuing Election for the Fourth District.

To see immediate energetic Operation given to the New-Government, is the great Object of my Wishes. I should then be happy to promote such Amendments as will produce Union and Harmony among the States, and guard the great and fundamental Rights of the People, without impairing or injuring, in the smallest Degree, the real Vigour or true Beauty of the System. The Trial by Jury ought to be unequivocally secured, and a Bill of Rights would quiet the Apprehensions of many Citizens, and ought to be granted.

Under this Impression, and with these Sentiments, I offer my humble Services to my Country, and shall consider myself very happy in having your Approbation, and the Honour of your Suffrage and Interest.

With Sentiments of Respect, I am, Sir, Your obedient Servant,

SAMUEL STERETT.

1. Printed in the *Maryland Journal,* 2 January 1789. Sterett, a merchant in Baltimore, was not elected as a U.S. representative.

Antilocalis
Massachusetts Centinel, 27 December 1788

MR. RUSSELL, It appears by the speech of Gov. CLINTON, that a suspension to the exercise of "different powers," under the Federal Constitution is expected by the Antifederalists of that State, until it undergoes a REVISION by a new general Convention.[1]—This Speech, among a thousand other evidences of a similar nature, sufficiently developes the latent hopes and designs of the antifederal sticklers for amendments: It now fully appears, that a continuance of our present deranged, humiliated situation, is their object; for if the Constitution, through their artifices, can be set afloat upon the boundless sea of a DIVIDED, ANTIFEDERAL CONVENTION, they know it will be totally wrecked and lost.—A loud call to this federal Commonwealth, to be particularly attentive to the characters they may send to the Federal Legislature, at this truly important crisis! and as there is a certainty, that the elections will not be completed in several of the districts in the first instance[2]—if any antifederal, or suspicious characters, have obtained a plurality of votes, their country, and every thing they hold dear, call upon the Federal Electors, to "TURN OUT" and exert themselves, to prevent such candidates from obtaining a final election.

The LOCAL and SELFISH ideas contained in the above speech, betray its motives most glaringly—and evince that the "LOAVES AND FISHES" of that State, are of more consequence to those who are fattening upon them, than the peace, honour, and happiness of all America beside.

The Federal Constitution is our polar Star—by that let us shape our course: Its free operation alone, can enable us to form a true estimate of its worth—"THE CONFIDENCE AND GOOD WILL OF THE PEOPLE" cannot in the nature of things, be *antecedent* to a fair experiment—*that* will ascertain its congeniality to our ideas and habits—and in that way only can we rationally determine its pernicious or salutary nature and influence.

1. For Governor George Clinton's speech to the New York General Assembly on 11 December 1788, see BoR, I, 202–3.
2. On 20 November 1788, the Massachusetts legislature adopted resolutions providing for the election of federal representatives in eight districts. To win election, a candidate had to obtain a majority of votes cast. Without a majority, another election was to be held, to be repeated until a candidate received a majority of the votes (DHFFE, I, 508–11).

Kentucky Gazette, 27 December 1788

Extract of a letter from one of the Members from the District of Kentucky now in Assembly: dated Richmond Nov. 13, 1788

Enclosed I have sent you one of our late papers; it contains some of the resolutions of Congress [and] of the House of Delegates, you will find by it that the Assembly have come to the resolution to request the Federal Congress when they meet, to call a Federal Convention for the purpose of amending the Constitution, and have invited the Sister States to take like measures.[1] A very large majority is for amendments to the Constitution. We have been seven days employed in organizing the New Government. Richard Henry Lee, and William Grayson, are elected Senators to the New Congress. Mr. Madison lost it by nine votes, which has much alarmed the friends to the New Constitution. The Election for Representatives to Congress will, I expect, be on the first Monday in February next. The Counties in Kentucky, is to elect one Member: he must be a Resident for one year in the District. The New Congress is to meet on the first Wednesday in March next.

1. For these resolutions and letters to the state executives, see BoR, I, 168–70, 175–76.

John Adams to Abigail Adams
Braintree, Mass., 28 December 1788 (excerpt)[1]

... You will not expect from me, much upon Public affairs. I shall only Say that the fœderal or more properly national Spirit runs high and bids fair to defeat every insidious as well as open Attempt of its Adversaries. This gives us a comfortable Prospect of a good Government, which is all that will be necessary to our Happiness. Yet I fear that confused and ill digested Efforts at Amendments will perplex for sometime....

1. RC, Adams Papers, MHi. For the entire letter, see *Adams Family Correspondence*, VIII, 323–24.

Edward Carrington to Henry Knox
Richmond, Va., 30 December 1788 (excerpt)[1]

... [On favorable news of the election of Federalist U.S. senators and representatives] enough is discovered to give me the most flattering expectations that the destructive policy of another convention will not be adopted....

1. RC, GLC 02437.04057, The Gilder Lehrman Collection, The Gilder Lehrman Institute of American History, at the New-York Historical Society.

Foreign Spectator XVIII
Philadelphia Federal Gazette, 30 December 1788[1]

REMARKS *on the Amendments to the Federal Constitution, proposed by the Conventions of Massachusetts, New-Hampshire, New-York, Virginia, South and*

North-Carolina, with the minorities of Pennsylvania and Maryland, by a FOREIGN SPECTATOR.
NUMBER XVIII.
The judicial power of the federal government is criticized by various discordant amendments. We shall begin with those that limit its extent. *The judicial power shall extend to all cases in law and equity, arising under treaties, made, or which shall be made, under the authority of the United States; to all cases affecting ambassadors, other foreign ministers, or consuls; to all cases of admiralty and maritime jurisdiction; to controversies to which the United States shall be a party; to controversies between two or more states, and between parties claiming lands under grants of different states*—14th and 15th ams. by the conventions of Virginia and North-Carolina respectively. This excludes from the federal jurisdiction, "controversies between a state and citizens of another state, between citizens of different states (except in the case of claiming lands, &c.) and between a state, or the citizens thereof, and foreign states, citizens or subjects," 3d art. 2d sec. 1st par. *That the judicial power of the United States shall extend to no controversies respecting land, unless it relate to claims of territory or jurisdiction between states, or to claims of land between individuals, or between states and individuals under the grants of different states,* 28th am. by the convention of New-York. This excludes all controversies about land, between the United States and a state or individual, and between individuals and states, or citizens of different states, except claims of the above description. The minority of Pennsylvania, enumerating, in the 14th am. the objects of the federal judiciary power, omits "controversies between the citizens of a state and those of foreign states (public ministers excepted) and between citizens of different states, except when claiming land under grants of different states."

That the federal judiciary should take cognizance of every controversy, between any of the states and a foreign power, is an axiom in politics. Foreign nations know the United States only as *one nation,* and regard each particular state only as a province of one empire. Had the constitution bereft the federal government of this important power, it would have loosened a principal tye of the union, by laying the several states open to intrigues and wars with foreign nations.

Controversies between a foreign nation and an American citizen are also, with respect to the first party, national affairs, and consequently must be so with regard to the other. Foreign nations view us, not as Pennsylvanians, Virginians, &c. but as citizens of the United States; just as America regards a Spaniard or a Frenchman, not as inhabitants of Paris and Cadiz, but as subjects of Spain and France, and looks to these governments for satisfaction, if any of their people transgress against the laws of nations, whether a treaty has taken place or not. The propriety of giving the federal judiciary the decision of such causes is therefore evident from the nature of things, and general usage of nations; it was moreover inforced by a regard to the public peace, because powerful ambitious leaders in the frontier-states might otherwise, by trespassing on the neighbouring countries, involve their own state, and eventually the union in contention and bloodshed.

Causes between a state or its citizens and foreign subjects are also in a degree national. When they arise under the laws of the Union, they are undoubtedly proper objects of the federal jurisdiction, which must be co-extensive with federal legislation. If they originate within the sphere of state legislation, plausible doubts may indeed be raised. It may be said, that foreigners are at liberty to deal or not with the people of the several states, as they are more or less pleased with the laws; and that justice will be administered as well in the state courts as by federal judges. But again it merits consideration, that every nation in Europe will most certainly, for many years, place more confidence in the federal government than in those of the states; that we should regard this opinion, if we mean to have a great and beneficial intercourse with them, and to draw large foreign capitals into the channels of our agriculture, commerce and manufactures.

It is certainly reasonable to make the federal judiciary an umpire in controversies between a state and the citizens of another state. Whether a state is plaintiff or defendant, its dignity will not permit subjection to the tribunals of a sister state. Sometimes it may not find justice against a powerful individual in his own state. Again, the pride of state, and anxious regard to personal rights, will certainly not give up a citizen to the judicial power of the other party.

In controversies between citizens of different states, federal courts are also the proper forum, with those limitations that convenience may require.

The distinction between matters of federal and state legislation might again be alledged in both these cases; but as many causes will probably be of a mixed nature, it is best to go by general rules merely to avoid confusion and contention. Besides, as by 2d sect. 4th article, "the citizens of each state shall be entitled to all the privileges and immunities of citizens in the federal[2] states," the interposition of the federal judiciary seems necessary to carry this provision into execution; otherwise this reciprocal stipulation of the states must ultimately depend on the good disposition of each. This federal arbitration is no doubt promotive of pubic peace, as without it disagreeable and serious contentions may be fomented between the states by artful and turbulent individuals, or by momentous but dubious questions of personal right. Whether federal justice may always be the best is not the principal question; but to judge from the sad experience of many years it will be preferable to that of some state governments. I mean no reflection on men, but reason only from the natural effects of systems. Is it not acknowledged by every *thinking person, that nothing but a general system* can restore a sense of general justice?

The exception against federal jurisdiction in causes respecting lands, appears unsupported by any peculiar arguments; besides, it would be very extensive, as so many claims and titles to lands on the frontiers are yet undecided.

The minority of Pennsylvania desire, that the federal judiciary *shall in criminal cases be confined only to such as are expressly enumerated in the constitution; and that the United States in Congress assembled shall not have power to exact [i.e., enact] laws which shall alter the laws of descents and distributions of the effects of deceased persons, the titles of lands or goods, or the regulation of contracts in the individual states,* 14th am.

Causes of the most important federal consequence may be of a criminal nature: if a party of individuals should by arms, pursue a claim of lands in a neighbouring state, burn houses and commit murders, this case is neither treason against the United States, nor felony on the high seas, nor counterfeiting of the coin, nor offence against the laws of nations (not being an injury to foreigners) yet it is an atrocious breach of public peace. Many actions may, in a similar manner, be either purely criminal or of a mixed quality not easily separable. To disarm the federal power of criminal jurisdiction, when really just and necessary, is a jealousy the more improper as trial of jury is insured in all those cases.

The federal government assumes no power to regulate contracts in the individual states, while they, in conformity to the 10th sect. 1st art. "do not pass any law impairing the obligation of contracts;" nor can it meddle with titles of goods or lands, except in the controversies above-mentioned: even in these possession for a certain term of years will, no doubt, by law, be a valid title. As to laws of descents and distributions of the effects of deceased persons, Congress must, with regard to foreigners, observe treaties, and the general laws of nations.

The conventions of Virginia and North-Carolina in the above 14th & 15th ams. demand, "that the judicial power of the united states shall extend to no case where the cause of action shall have originated before the ratification of this constitution; except in disputes between states about their territory; disputes between persons claiming lands under the grants of different states; and suits for debts due to the United States." Whatever just demands foreign nations may have on the citizens of any state, by virtue of treaties previous to the ratification of the new constitution; the general government is responsible for their satisfaction, as it has been all the time: no contracts with other powers can be impaired by any change of the constitution; the nation is the party, and its mode of government is in this respect as immaterial as a fashion in dress. But if the subjects of a foreign power have merely by the general laws of nations acquired claims on the citizens of any state, they must look to this for justice, and cannot demand it from the United States, because they had hitherto no constitutional power to inforce compliance with contracts. This state remains however under such obligation in the new confederation, and is liable to prosecution from that foreign power, whose subjects it has injured; nor can it in that case be protected by the union. This event is not indeed very probable. Nevertheless it is necessary for the honour and credit of the federal empire, that all its members should fulfil former engagements.

The reciprocal claims of the states and their citizens cannot be annulled by a change of the constitution. The states might indeed have reserved the right of settling them in the old way; but this not having proved good, the new mode was thought more eligible; and will no doubt, by a proper conduct, give satisfaction to all parties. This expedient is the more reasonable as even by the old constitution "the United States in congress assembled are the last resort, on appeal of all disputes between the states in any cause whatever; and the citizens of each are reciprocally entitled to all immunities and privileges of free citizens."

1. Reprinted: *New York Daily Gazette*, 23 June 1789. For the authorship of the "Foreign Spectator" series, see the headnote to Essay No. I (21 October, BoR, III, 264n).

2. Both the *Federal Gazette* and the reprinting has "federal," but in the Constitution the word is "several."

A Marylander
Baltimore Maryland Gazette, 30 December 1788 (excerpt)

Mr. HAYES, . . . Firm friends to the new government, are of course recommended in the fœderal ticket. In the other, three known to be of the same description are also recommended—For my own part, I could have wished to see a compromise take place, and the ablest men called forth, particularly that Mr. *Paca* should have been run by general consent for the third district, because an able and honest man, although some of the amendments, proposed by him in convention,[1] were subversive of the union, and an energetic government.

I never could agree, that every man, who wished an alteration of particular parts of the new constitution, could be called *antifederal*, if

he was only for having them in the regular way by the congress, after the adoption of the government—When a man advocates a new general convention, to which the members from the different states would come, bound down by instructions of a local nature, and thereby prevent any agreement, which can only take place from a spirit of mutual conciliation and concession; such a man may safely be termed antifederal—For that reason I am pointedly opposed to Mr. *Mercer's* election, who may justly be termed a *rigid anti*—If Col. *Forrest* could have been approved of, I should have been pleased, on account of his commercial knowledge, address and genius for intrigue, but as he is in neither ticket, I am for Mr. *William Smith,* because we ought to have *one commercial character* in the house of representatives; he served in congress with reputation, and was a very useful member in the commercial and marine committees, and at the treasury board, besides which his character and fœderalism are irreproachable—Mr. *Sterett,* is a man of abilities and merit, and having been secretary to two presidents of congress, must be well acquainted with continental affairs, and therefore a proper man to represent us, if he would boldly come forth, and say *where he would stop* with his amendments—the great misfortune is, that if he is chosen, we must lose the only *experienced* commercial character, nominated in either ticket. One comfort is, they are both Americans by birth, and Presbyterians, so no divisions respecting religion or country can take place among us in the *present instance.* . . .
Baltimore, Dec. 26, 1788.

1. For the amendments proposed by William Paca in the Maryland Convention, see BoR, I, 245–47.

An American Citizen
Philadelphia Federal Gazette, 31 December 1788[1]

Thoughts on the subject of Amendments *of the Federal Constitution.*
NUMBER IV.[a]

When we consider the nature of our affairs, and compare the business of amending the constitution with the same measure in any other country, we discover at once, that a general convention will not be a proper body to effect the proposed alterations. Were the state legislatures to elect the members of a federal convention, it is evident that the people would have *no representatives* therein; on the other hand, were the people at large to elect them, the state governments would have *no representatives*; and thus *the federal qualities* of the constitution would be endangered, and that *consolidation,* about which so much apprehension has been expressed, would certainly ensue. But these objections do not exist against *proposing* amendments by the *two houses* of Congress; for the house of representatives will consent to none, that will affect the liberties of the people at large, by whom they are chosen; and the senate will consent to none that will diminish the rights of the state governments, by whose legislatures they are elected; nor will they agree to any thing that will change the federal qualities of the constitution.

Were any alterations in the government of Great-Britain proposed, we cannot suppose a general convention, chosen by the people alone, would have that duty assigned to them; for the constitutional powers of the two other branches would probably be diminished by them. Less probable is it that the people could acquiesce in an election by the upper house. *No one* estate of Parliament would be permitted to form alterations affecting the other two. All three must consent. In short, whether we consider what equity and policy suggest as proper here, or reason from a comparison with the necessary and rational proceedings under other forms of government, we must prefer the measure of proposing amendments by the new Congress, as the only one that is strictly proper. A trial of that mode first will not preclude the other, which will be as practicable then as now. Whatever amendments the mode by Congress shall give will be more immediate, less expensive and inconvenient, and less disagreeable in their effects upon the minds of the people, who are prevented by political agitations from attending to their private duties. A resort to a general convention should never be used, but upon extraordinary occasions, and for cogent reasons. The ferment that attends them must ever give an unfavourable impression abroad, and must produce injurious effects at home. Cool reason is best exercised, when the measures in discussion have the complexion of ordinary acts of legislation. Passion naturally rises high in extraordinary assemblies.

The number of persons qualified to discharge important public trusts are not very many in any country. America has certainly her share of them, but many are prevented from undertaking them by the necessary attention to their professions and private affairs. From this, and other causes, it is highly probable a new convention would contain many members of the new Congress. In confirmation of this, we see, that of the federal Representatives and Senators already chosen, thirteen were members of the late general convention, and the remainder who were not of that body, are only eleven. Of the whole twenty-four now elected, two thirds were chosen by the people to represent them in their respective state conventions. 'Tis really unreasonable to doubt the conduct of men thus repeatedly selected for public service, and it were preposterous to suppose they do not possess and deserve the confidence of the people.

(a) *For the three preceding numbers, see the Federal Gazette of the 4th, 10th, and 24th instant.*

1. Also printed in the *Pennsylvania Gazette* on 31 December. Reprinted: *Maryland Journal*, 6 January 1789; *New York Packet*, 13 January; *Boston Gazette*, 19 January; *New Hampshire Gazette*, 28 January. Tench Coxe was the author of the "American Citizen" essays, which also appeared on 4 June and 10, 24 December 1788 (BoR III, 7–8, 407–9, 442–45).

Address Supporting the Election of James Monroe to the U.S. House of Representatives, c. 31 December 1788[1]

Gent.

My Solicitude for the liberty of my Country constrains me to Call your attention to the Subject of Electing a Representative for this District to Congress, under the General Government you are Sensible that the Constitution in its present form has not the hearts and affections of the people: Their fears and apprehensions are greatly alarmed and in my opinion Very justly: the Convention in June last at the same time they Ratified it, agreed it was so far defective as to Require a Bill of Rights and a number of Amendments which you Cannot be Strangers to: also enjoined it on their Representatives in Congress to exert all their influence and use all reasonable and Legal methods to obtain the Same and Even went so far as to Recommend that all Congressional laws which Should be passed in the mean time Should Conform to the Spirit of the Amendments as far as the Said Constitution would admit.[2] the late Assembly has taken Great pains to Clear the way for this Great and desirable object, by making application to Congress, at their first meeting to Call a General Convention of the States to Consider of the amendments and have at the same time written a Circular letter to the Different States to join them in Similar application,[3] which is agreeable to the fifth article of the Constitution and thare Remains little doubt, if proper men are Elected but the Amendments will take place and thereby the minds of the people quieted and I hope peace safety and happiness Secured, when you Consider thare are at least nine tenths of the Habitable Globe are immersed in & Groaning under the mode [i.e., most] Dreadful oppressions of Tyrany: and that it never was the Design of Providence in forming Such an order of Beings that they Should be thus Circumstanced and that it is only by a strange and unaccountable perversion of his Benevolent intensions to mankind that they ware Ever Deprived of liberty. I hope you will Consider the necessity of uniting in favor of a Gent. who has been uniformly in favour of

Amendments I mean James Munroe Esq. a man who possesses great abilities integrity and a most amiable Character who has been many years a member of Congress of the House of Delegats and of the Privy Council and whome I have Prevaled on to offer in our District: Considering him as being able to Render his Country Great Servises on this important occasion. it is now Submitted to your Consideration whether you wish for Amendments or not, and if you do who is the most likely to obtain them, the man who has been uniformly in favor of them, or one who has been uniformly against them. This is so clear that I am persuaded you will all Join with me in opinion, that the object of amendments Can alone be Promoted by one who feels a desire for their introduction. if the people at large had always united against Tyranny and oppression, thare would have been no Such Monsters in the world. but from some fratality or other, we Generally get Devided by men who are fond of Power and thus the liberty of the people has always been Endangered if not Snatched away. when we Consider that the human Mind is not to be Satisfied with Power, and that Powers once parted with, are Seldom if Ever Recovered, it Shews how necessary it is to Elect the Gent. I have taken the liberty to Mention, whose heart and mind is bent on obtaining the amendments it is not my wish or Design to influence the Suffrage of any person, but have stated the above Observations for the free Exercise of your best judgments. I have thus Spoke to you the language of my heart, which if you approve I shall be happy, if not, Shall be Content, having done what I conceive to be my Duty, and hope if by a Contrary Conduct you Should Entale misery on your Selves and posterity that I shall Stand acquitted from haveing had any hand in it.

I am Gent. with Sincear Respect Your Friend and Sert: W: Cabell.

1. MS, Surveys/Amherst County/1781–1802, Virginia State Library. This manuscript is undated and unsigned. Another copy of the manuscript printed in the *William and Mary Quarterly*, 2nd series, IX (1929), 124–25, is signed by William Cabell, Sr., and addressed to James Higginbotham. No newspaper version of the address has been located.

2. For the bill of rights and amendments to the constitution proposed by the Virginia Convention on 27 June 1788, see BoR, I, 251–56. For the injunction, see RCS:Va., 1556.

3. For the Virginia legislature's call for a general convention to amend the Constitution, see BoR, I, 158–80.

Biographical Gazetteer

The following sketches outline the political careers of those people in the Bill of Rights volume three who either wrote letters, newspaper essays, or pamphlets, or delivered speeches concerning amendments to the Constitution.

HENRY ABBOT (c. 1740–1791), a Baptist minister, was born in London, England. He migrated to America without the consent or knowledge of his parents. As a minister, he supported and endorsed American independence. He contributed in drafting the constitution and declaration of rights for North Carolina and is recognized as the author of its nineteenth article acknowledging a broad freedom of conscience. He represented Camden in the both the Hillsborough and Fayetteville conventions of 1788 and 1789, where he supported the ratification of the Constitution.

JOHN ADAMS (1735–1826). See BoR, II, 490.

PELEG ARNOLD (1752–1820), a Smithfield, Rhode Island, lawyer and tavern keeper, was a deputy in the General Assembly, 1777–78, 1782–83; member of the Confederation Congress, 1787–88; and town meeting moderator, 1787, 1796, 1798, 1801–7, 1809–16. He was an assistant in the General Assembly, 1790–95; a twice-failed candidate for U.S. Congress, 1794, 1796; and chief justice of the Superior Court of Judicature, 1796–1809, 1810–12.

JOSHUA ATHERTON (1737–1809), a lawyer originally from Massachusetts, moved to New Hampshire in 1765. An early sympathizer with the British, he was jailed in 1777 as a "disaffected person," but took the oath of allegiance in October 1778 and was re-admitted to the bar by the N.H. Supreme Court. He served in the state constitutional conventions, 1781–83, 1791. In the state Convention, he voted against ratification of the Constitution in June 1788. He served in the state Senate, 1792–93, and as state attorney general, 1793–1800. He became a Federalist in the 1790s and lost his popularity.

BENJAMIN AUSTIN, JR. (1752–1820), a Boston merchant, revolutionary publicist, and follower of Samuel Adams, wrote influential and controversial newspaper essays attacking the legal profession under the pseudonym "Honestus" in 1786. He served in the state Senate, 1787–88, 1789–97; wrote the Antifederalist "Candidus" essays, 1787–88; and was an active Republican agitator and publicist in the 1790s.

ABRAHAM BALDWIN (1754–1807), the son of a Connecticut blacksmith, Baldwin graduated from Yale College in 1772. He became a minister and was a tutor at Yale from 1775 to 1779, when he left to become an army chaplain. In 1781 he was offered the professorship of divinity at Yale but rejected it to study law. He had moved to Georgia by 1784. In January of that year the Assembly admitted him to practice law and in December Wilkes County elected him to the Assembly. During 1785 he wrote the charter for a state educational system and the future University of Georgia. He was also elected to Congress, where he served until 1788. In 1787 he was a delegate to the Constitutional Convention, and in 1789 he was elected to the U.S. House of Representatives, serving until 1799, when he was elected to the U.S. Senate where he served until his death in 1807.

BIOGRAPHICAL GAZETTEER   459

ABRAHAM B. BANCKER (1754–1806), a resident of Kingston, Ulster County, New York, was from 1784 to 1802 clerk of the state Senate. He was a lieutenant in the Continental Army and a commissary of prisoners during the Revolutionary War. He was one of the two secretaries of the state Convention in 1788.

THEODORICK BLAND (1741–1790). See BoR, II, 490.

TIMOTHY BLOODWORTH (1736–1814) practiced a variety of artisanal occupations before entering politics. He represented New Hanover in the North Carolina House of Commons, 1778–81, 1783–85, 1787, 1791–92, 1794–95 (speaker), 1801 and the state Senate, 1788–89. He was a delegate to the Confederation Congress, 1786–87. In both the Hillsborough and Fayetteville conventions of 1788 and 1789, he opposed ratifying the Constitution. He was a U.S. representative, 1790–91; a U.S. senator, 1795–1801; and collector of the Port of Wilmington, N.C., 1801–7.

BENJAMIN BLYTH (c. 1724–1807?), was a colonel in the Cumberland County militia during the Revolution and commissioned a county sub-lieutenant in 1777 and 1780. He owned 408 acres and two slaves in 1785.

THOMAS BRAND-HOLLIS (1719–1804), a resident of Ingatestone, Essex County, England, studied at the University of Glasgow and the Inns of Court (Inner Temple) in London, but never practiced law. He took the name of Hollis in 1774, when he inherited the substantial estate of his friend Thomas Hollis. In the mid-1780s John Adams and Brand-Hollis—dissenter, Whig, and strong supporter of America—became friends.

HARDIN BURNLEY (1761–1809), an Orange County, Virginia, lawyer-planter, served in the House of Delegates, 1787–91, and on the Council of State, 1791–99. He then retired from public life.

WILLIAM CABELL, SR. (1730–1798), a Virginia planter, represented Albemarle and then Amherst in the House of Burgesses, in all five revolutionary conventions, and in both houses of the state legislature almost continuously from 1756 to 1789. In the state Convention, he voted against ratification of the Constitution in June 1788. After serving as a presidential elector in 1789, he retired from public service.

DAVID CALDWELL (1725–1824), born in Lancaster, Pennsylvania, was a Presbyterian minister and educator. He moved to Guilford County, North Carolina, as a missionary in 1765, serving as minister to several congregations in the Greensboro area until his death. Caldwell represented Guilford County in the Fifth Provincial Congress, 1776, and supported the Patriot cause during the Revolutionary War. He had his property burned by the British in retribution. In the Hillsborough Convention, he opposed ratification of the Constitution in August 1788.

ARTHUR CAMPBELL (1743–1811), a planter, was a Washington County justice of the peace and county lieutenant. He represented Fincastle in Virginia's fifth revolutionary convention, 1776, and in the House of Delegates, 1776–77. In 1777 Fincastle became Washington County and Campbell continued to represent the county in 1778–79, 1782–84, 1786–88. In 1784–85 Campbell was a leader of the movement to separate southwestern Virginia and place it in the State of Franklin.

EDWARD CARRINGTON (1749-1810). See BoR, II, 491.

SAMUEL CHASE (1741-1811), a Baltimore lawyer, represented Annapolis in the Lower House, 1765-66, 1777, 1779-83, 1784-85; Anne Arundel County, 1768-71, 1773-74, 1786-87; and Baltimore Town, 1787-88. He was a delegate to the Continental Congress, 1774-78, where he signed the Declaration of Independence. With Benjamin Franklin, Charles Carroll of Carrollton, and the Rev. John Carroll, he travelled to Canada to seek Canadian support for the revolutionary cause, 1776. He was an Anne Arundel County delegate to the state Convention, where he voted against ratification in April 1788; a judge of the state General Court, 1791-96 (resigned); and an associate justice of the U.S. Supreme Court, 1796-1811. He was impeached by the U.S. House of Representatives for alleged judicial improprieties in 1804 but the Senate acquitted him in 1805.

ABRAHAM CLARK (1726-1794), a lawyer and the leader of the East Jersey party, was born in Elizabethtown, New Jersey. Before the Revolutionary War, he was sheriff and clerk of the Assembly. He was a member of the committee of safety, 1775-76; a delegate to the three provincial congresses, 1775-76; a member of the state Council, 1778-79; and an assemblyman, 1783-86. He was a delegate to Congress, 1776-78, 1780-83, 1786-88 (signed the Declaration of Independence) and served as a commissioner to the Annapolis Convention, 1786. He was elected to the Constitutional Convention but declined to serve. He was a defeated candidate for the U.S. House of Representatives, 1789. He served as commissioner to settle New Jersey's accounts with the U.S., 1789-90, and as a U.S. representative, 1791-94.

JOSEPH CLAY (1741-1804), a Savannah, Georgia, merchant, served as an assemblyman, 1782-83, 1787-88; as state treasurer, 1782; and as U.S. district judge, 1796-1801.

DE WITT CLINTON (1769-1828), a native of Little Britain, Orange County, New York, and a graduate of Columbia College (1786), was studying law in New York City with Antifederalist leader Samuel Jones of Queens County. Not long after New York ratified the Constitution, Clinton became private secretary to his uncle Governor George Clinton. De Witt Clinton served in the state Assembly, 1798; state Senate, 1798-1802, 1806-11; and U.S. Senate, 1802-3. He was also mayor of New York City almost continuously between 1803 and 1815 and was governor of New York from 1817 to 1822 and from 1825 until his death.

GEORGE CLINTON (1739-1812). See BoR, II, 492.

THOMAS COGSWELL (1746-1810). See BoR, II, 492.

NICHOLAS COLLIN (1746-1851) came to America in 1770 to become a pastor of the Swedish mission Trinity Church in Swedesboro, New Jersey, where he served until 1786. In that year he became the first pastor of Gloria Dei "Old Swedes" Church in Philadelphia, serving there until his death. He was an *ex officio* member (as senior Lutheran pastor in Philadelphia) of the Board of Trustees of the University of the State of Pennsylvania (now the University of Pennsylvania), 1784-91, and became a member of the American Philosophical Society in 1789. He was the author of two series of essays signed "Foreign Spectator" in 1787 and 1788-89.

BIOGRAPHICAL GAZETTEER 461

FRANCIS CORBIN (1759-1821) was born in Caroline County, Virginia, of wealthy Loyalist parents. He attended Cambridge University and Inner Temple, before returning to Virginia after the Revolutionary War. He represented Middlesex in the House of Delegates, 1784-95, and in the state Convention, 1788, where he voted to ratify the Constitution. He was rector of the College of William and Mary in 1790, and was elected a U.S. representative in 1792, but declined to serve.

TENCH COXE (1755-1824). See BoR, II, 492.

COXE AND FRAZIER was a Philadelphia mercantile firm formed by Tench Coxe and Nalbro Frazier in 1783. Most of their trade was with the British West Indies.

ST. JOHN DE CREVECOEUR (1735-1813), a native of France, immigrated to Canada and served as a scout in the French army and as a mapmaker during the French and Indian War. From 1759 to 1769 he traveled extensively throughout the American colonies. He became a naturalized citizen in 1765 and four years later settled on a farm in Orange County, N.Y. He visited France in 1780 and returned to the United States in 1783 as French consul for New York, New Jersey, and Connecticut.

JOHN BROWN CUTTING (c. 1755-1831), an apothecary during the Revolutionary War, studied law with John Lowell of Boston in 1783 and was in England to complete his legal studies. In June 1787 he was "a ministerial amanuensis" to John Adams. He visited Paris in September and October and was hired as an attorney by a group with claims against South Carolina.

WILLIAM R. DAVIE (1756-1820), born in County Cumberland, England, was a Halifax, North Carolina, lawyer and planter. He immigrated to America in 1763. He was an officer in the Revolutionary War and was wounded in the Battle of Stono Ferry in 1779. He served as a delegate to the Constitutional Convention, 1787, and to both the Hillsborough and Fayetteville conventions of 1788 and 1789, where he supported ratification. Davie served in the North Carolina House of Commons, 1784-85, 1786-87, 1789, 1791-92, 1793-96, 1798; as governor, 1798-99; and as a U.S. diplomatic envoy to France, 1799-1800. He was influential in founding the University of North Carolina, 1789.

JOHN DAWSON (1762-1814), a graduate of Harvard College (1782) and a planter-lawyer, represented Spotsylvania County in the Virginia House of Delegates, 1786-90, and in the state Convention, where he voted against ratification of the Constitution.

PETER STEPHEN DU PONCEAU (1760-1844) was a French-American linguist. He emigrated from France in 1777 and during the Revolutionary War served as Baron von Stueben's secretary. After the war Du Ponceau moved to Philadelphia where he studied Native American languages and written Chinese. He was admitted to the American Philosophical Society in 1791.

WILLIAM DUER (1747-1799), a native of England and a wealthy New York City merchant and speculator in land and public securities, immigrated to America in 1769 and represented Washington County in the Fourth Provincial Congress, 1776-77, where he was a member of the committee that drafted the state constitution. He was a delegate to Congress, 1777-78; served as secretary of the Confederation Board of Treasury, 1785-89; represented New York County in the state Assembly, 1786; and served as Assistant to the

Secretary of the U.S. Treasury, 1789–90. His insolvency, brought about by his financial and land speculations, helped to precipitate a financial crisis in New York in 1792. Duer was arrested for debt and spent most of the remainder of his life in prison.

BENJAMIN ELLIOT (1752–1835), a resident of Huntingdon, Pennsylvania, was a member of the state constitutional convention and Assembly, 1776–77; and was commissioned sheriff of Bedford County in October 1785, and newly created Huntingdon County in October 1787. He was Huntingdon County's only representative in the state Convention, where he voted to ratify the Constitution in December 1787. He was appointed one of the county lieutenants in 1787 and again in 1789; and joined the Supreme Executive Council on 29 December 1789.

BENJAMIN FRANKLIN (1706–1790). See BoR, II, 494.

ALBERT GALLATIN (1761–1849) was born in Geneva, Switzerland, and immigrated to the United States in 1780. After several unsuccessful business ventures, brief militia service in the Revolutionary War, and being an instructor of French at Harvard in 1782, he settled on 400 acres in Fayette County, Pa., in 1786. He was a member of the Harrisburg Convention, 1788; the state constitutional convention, 1789; and the state House of Representatives, 1790–92. His marriage to Hannah Nicholson in 1793 secured him financially and he spent most of the rest of his life living in east coast cities. He served in the U.S. Senate for three months (December 1793 through February 1794) but was removed on a party vote for not meeting the citizenship requirement. He was a U.S. representative, 1795–1801; U.S. Secretary of the Treasury, 1801–14; and a U.S. diplomat.

JAMES GALLAWAY (c. 1743–1798), a native of Scotland, was a Rockingham County, North Carolina, merchant and planter. He served in the state House of Commons, 1783–84, and in the state Senate, 1784–89, where, in November 1787 he opposed calling a convention to ratify the Constitution. In the Hillsborough and Fayetteville conventions of 1788 and 1789, he voted against ratifying the Constitution.

JAMES GORDON, JR. (1759–1799), an Orange County, Virginia, planter, represented Richmond County in the House of Delegates, 1782–84, and Orange County, 1788–89. He also represented Orange County in the state Convention, where he voted to ratify the Constitution.

ALEXANDER GRAYDON (1752–1818) served in the Continental Army during the Revolutionary War; was elected prothonotary of newly created Dauphin County, Pennsylvania, in 1785, and moved to Harrisburg. He was a strong supporter of the ratification of the Constitution. After being dismissed from his prothonotary office in 1799, he retired to a small farm near Harrisburg. In 1811 he published his *Memoirs of a Life, Chiefly Passed in Pennsylvania Within the Last Sixty Years* . . . .

WILLIAM GRAYSON (c. 1736–1790). See BoR, II, 495.

ALEXANDER HAMILTON (1757–1804). See BoR, II, 495.

JOHN HANCOCK (1737–1793). See BoR, II, 495.

JOHN A. HANNA (1762–1805) was a native of New Jersey, a 1782 graduate of the College of New Jersey (Princeton), and Harrisburg, Pa., lawyer. He voted against ratification of the Constitution in the state Convention in December 1787; was secretary of the Harrisburg Convention, 1788; was a member of the state House of Representatives, 1791; commanded the Dauphin County militia brigade as brigadier general during the Whiskey Rebellion, 1793; and was a U.S. representative, 1797–1805.

JOHN HARRIS (1723–1794), a native of Ireland and a Cumberland County, Pennsylvania, farmer, was a member of the state constitutional convention, 1776; was a member of the state Assembly, 1777–81, where even as a slaveowner he voted for gradual emancipation in 1780; and was appointed a justice of the peace in February 1779. He voted against ratification of the Constitution in the state Convention in December 1787. About 1790 he donated land for public buildings in the town of Milton which he laid out.

THOMAS HARTLEY (1748–1800). See BoR, II, 495.

EBENEZER HAZARD (1744–1817), born in Philadelphia and a 1762 graduate of the College of New Jersey (Princeton), ran a publishing business in New York City, 1770–75. He was postmaster of New York City, 1775; surveyor general of the Continental Post Office, 1776–82; and postmaster general of the United States, 1782–89. Criticized for partisanship in administering the post office during the ratification debate, he was not reappointed by President Washington. He became a member of the American Philosophical Society and the American Academy of Arts and Sciences in 1781 and published his two-volume *Historical Collections; Consisting of State Papers, and Other Authentic Documents* . . . in Philadelphia in 1792 and 1794.

WILLIAM HEATH (1737–1814). See BoR, II, 496.

PATRICK HENRY (1736–1799), a Prince Edward County lawyer, was admitted to the bar in 1760. He served in the House of Burgesses, 1765–76; in the revolutionary conventions, 1774–76; and the House of Delegates, 1780–84, 1787–91. He was a delegate to Congress, 1774–75; commander of the Virginia forces, 1775–76; and governor of Virginia, 1776–79, 1784–86. He refused appointment to the Constitutional Convention in 1787. In the state Convention, he led the Antifederalists and voted against ratification of the Constitution in June 1788. He declined appointments as U.S. senator, 1794, U.S. Secretary of State, 1795, and Chief Justice of the U.S., 1796.

FRANCIS HOPKINSON (1737–1791). See BoR, II, 496.

DAVID HOWELL (1747–1824), a native of New Jersey, a 1766 graduate of the College of New Jersey (Princeton), and a Providence, R.I., lawyer, was a delegate to Congress, 1782–85; judge of the state Superior Court, 1786–87; state attorney general, 1789–90; a member of the commission to settle the border between the U.S. and Canada, 1796; and U.S. District Judge for Rhode Island, 1812–24. He vigorously opposed Rhode Island's paper money policies.

DAVID HUMPHREYS (1752–1818), a native of Derby, Connecticut, and Harvard graduate (1771), was an aide-de-camp to George Washington during the Revolutionary War. He was the secretary to the U.S. commission to negotiate commercial treaties in Paris, 1784–86. In 1786–87 he served as a lieutenant colonel in the Connecticut militia raised to help suppress Shays's Rebellion. He was a delegate from the Connecticut chapter of the Society of the Cincinnati to a national meeting of the Cincinnati in Philadelphia in May 1787. He lived at Mount Vernon from 18 November, serving for a time as Washington's secretary, until he accompanied the newly elected President Washington to New York City in April 1789. He was a member of a group of poets known as the "Connecticut Wits" and co-authored "The Anarchiad."

SAMUEL HUNTINGTON (1731-1796), a lawyer, was born in Windham, Conn. Admitted to bar in 1754, he moved to Norwich in 1760. He served as king's attorney for New London County, 1765-74; New London County justice of peace, 1765-75; Norwich delegate to the assembly, 1765, 1775; judge of the Superior Court, 1773-85 (chief judge, 1784-85); member of the Council, 1775-84; member of the council of safety, 1775-76, 1782-83; delegate to Congress, 1776-81, 1783 (president, 1779-81; signed the Declaration of Independence and Articles of Confederation); lieutenant governor, 1784-86; and governor, 1786-96. As president of the state Convention, he voted to ratify the Constitution in January 1788.

JAMES IREDELL (1751-1799). See BoR, II, 496.

JOHN JAY (1745-1829). See BoR, II, 497.

THOMAS JEFFERSON (1743-1826). See BoR, II, 497.

THOMAS JOHNSON (1732-1819), a Frederick County, Maryland, lawyer and ironworks owner in partnership with his brothers, frequently served in the colonial lower house of the legislature between 1762 and 1774; was a member of all nine revolutionary conventions, 1774-76; and was a delegate to Congress, 1774-76. He was a militia brigadier general, 1776-77; state senator, 1777; governor, 1777-79; and member of the state House of Delegates, 1786-88. In the state Convention, 1788, he voted to ratify the Constitution. He was elected governor, 1788, but declined to serve. He was chief judge of the state General Court, 1790-91; associate justice of the U.S. Supreme Court, 1791-93 (resigned); and member of the Board of Commissioners of the District of Columbia, 1791-94.

WILLIAM SAMUEL JOHNSON (1727-1819). See BoR, II, 497.

SAMUEL JOHNSTON (1733-1816), born in Dundee, Scotland, was a Perquimans County, North Carolina, lawyer and planter. In 1735, Johnston's family immigrated to North Carolina, where his paternal uncle was the royal governor. He represented Chowan County or Edenton in colonial assemblies, 1759-75. Johnston was sympathetic to the cause of independence but opposed radicalism. He served in the North Carolina committee of correspondence, 1773; the first four provincial congresses, 1774-76; the state Senate, 1779, 1783-84; and the Continental Congress, 1780. In 1781 he was chosen as president of the Confederation Congress but declined to serve because of ill health. While governor (1787-89), he served as president of both the Hillsborough and Fayetteville conventions of 1788 and 1789, where he supported ratification of the Constitution. He was a U.S. senator, 1789-1793, and a judge in the state Superior Court, 1800-1803. He was James Iredell's brother-in-law.

JOSEPH JONES (1727-1805) was admitted to Inner Temple, 1749, Middle Temple, 1751, and the English bar, 1751. He practiced law in Fredericksburg, Virginia, and represented

BIOGRAPHICAL GAZETTEER 465

King George County in the House of Burgesses, 1772-76, in all five revolutionary conventions, 1774-76, and in the House of Delegates, 1776-78, 1780-81, 1783-85. He was a member of the Virginia Committee of Safety, 1775; delegate to Congress, 1777, 1780-83: a judge on the General Court, 1778-79, 1789-1805; and a member of the Council of State, 1785-89. He was James Monroe's uncle.

MARQUIS DE LAFAYETTE (1757-1834). See BoR, II, 498.

WILLIAM LANCASTER (d. 1826), was an elder who often served as interim pastor of Baptist churches. He represented Franklin County, North Carolina, in the Hillsborough Convention, where in August 1788 he voted against ratifying the Constitution, feeling bound by his instructions from his constituents. He did not vote in the Fayetteville Convention (1789).

JOHN LANGDON (1741-1819), a Portsmouth, New Hampshire, merchant and politician, attended Major Samuel Hale's Latin Grammar School; was a Clerk in Daniel Rindge's Portsmouth counting house; and a ship captain and later owner of vessels engaged in West Indian trade. He was an early opponent of British imperial policy. In December 1775 he led a raid on Fort William and Mary, Portsmouth, to seize British munitions. He was a delegate to the Second Continental Congress, 1775-76, and continental agent for New Hampshire, selling spoils of privateers for a percentage of sales. As a militia colonel, he saw action at Saratoga and in Rhode Island, 1777-78. He was a judge of the Court of Common Pleas, Rockingham County, 1776-77; a member and the speaker of the state House of Representatives, 1776-82, 1786-87; a member of the state Senate, 1784-85; a delegate to the Confederation Congress, 1787; state president, 1785-86, 1788-89; and a delegate to the Constitutional Convention, 1787, where he signed the Constitution and paid for the state's delegates to attend the Convention. He was a Federalist leader in the first and second sessions of the state Convention, where he voted to ratify the Constitution in June 1788. He was a member of the U.S. Senate, 1789-1801; became a Democratic-Republican in the mid-1790s; was a member of the state House of Representatives, 1801-4 (speaker, 1803); and state governor, 1805-11 (except for 1809).

JOHN LANSING, JR. (1754-1829), an Albany, New York, lawyer, was the brother of Abraham G. Lansing; had studied law in Albany with Robert Yates and in New York City with James Duane; and was admitted to the bar in Albany, 1775, and began practice there. He was a military secretary to Gen. Philip Schuyler, 1776-77; a member of the state Assembly, 1780-84, 1786, 1788-89 (speaker, 1786, 1788-89); a delegate to the Confederation Congress, 1785; on the commission to settle western land disputes with Massachusetts, 1786; and mayor of Albany, 1786-90. As a delegate to the Constitutional Convention, 1787, he left early and did not sign the Constitution. In the state Convention, 1788, he voted against ratification of the Constitution. He was a justice on the state Supreme Court, 1790-1801 (chief justice, 1798-1801); a commissioner to settle the boundary between New York and Vermont, 1790; and chancellor, 1801-14. He then resumed his law practice before disappearing on 12 December 1829 after leaving his New York City hotel room to mail a letter. No trace was ever found, and what happened to Lansing remains unknown.

CHARLES LEE (1758-1815), of Prince William County, Virginia, was a 1775 graduate of the College of New Jersey (Princeton), a lawyer, and brother of Henry ("Light Horse Harry") and Richard Bland Lee, was state naval officer of the South Potomac District, 1777-89; U.S. customs collector for the Port of Alexandria, Va., 1789-93; a member of the state House of Delegates, 1793–95; acting U.S. Secretary of State, 1800; and U.S. Attorney General, 1795–1801. He was a "midnight judge" appointment to a newly created U.S. Circuit Court in 1801, returning to private practice in 1802. He represented William Marbury in the 1803 Supreme Court case *Marbury v. Madison* and Aaron Burr in his treason trial in 1807.

HENRY LEE ("Light Horse Harry") (1756–1818). See BoR, II, 498.

RICHARD BLAND LEE (1761–1827). See BoR, II, 499.

RICHARD HENRY LEE (1732–1794). See BoR, II, 499.

WILLIAM LENOIR (1751–1839), a soldier, justice of the peace, state legislator, and planter-entrepreneur, was born in Brunswick County, Virginia. As a child he moved with his family to Edgecombe County, North Carolina. In 1775 he moved his family to what was to become Wilkes County. He was in the House of Commons, 1781–83, and state Senate, 1787–94. As a militia officer he was wounded at the Battle of King's Mountain (1780). He eventually obtained the rank of major-general in his eighteen years in the militia. In both the Hillsborough and Fayetteville conventions of 1788 and 1789, he voted against ratification of the Constitution. In 1789 he was designated a trustee of the newly chartered University of North Carolina and acted as president pro tem at the first meeting in 1790.

BENJAMIN LINCOLN (1733–1810), a farmer born in Hingham, Massachusetts, was a member of three provincial congresses, 1774–75 (secretary, first and second congresses) and the Committee of Supplies of Provincial Congress, 1774–75. He was appointed a major-general of the Massachusetts militia, 1776, and a major-general of the Continental Line, 1777. He was wounded at Battle of Saratoga, 1777; commanded the Southern Department, 1777–80; was captured by the British at Charleston, S.C., and exchanged, 1780. He rejoined Washington's army and accepted Cornwallis' sword at Yorktown, 1781. He was Confederation Secretary at War, 1781–83, and led the troops that suppressed Shays's Rebellion, 1786–87. As a member of the state Convention, 1788, he voted to ratify the Constitution. He was elected lieutenant governor, 1788, and served as the Collector of the Port of Boston, 1789–1809.

BLAIR M'CLENACHAN (d. 1812), a native of Ireland and a Philadelphia merchant, was allied with Robert Morris in gaining contracts and privateering during the Revolutionary War; a stockholder of the Bank of North America; and a large holder of the wartime government debt. A Constitutionalist in state politics, he was chairman of the Harrisburg Convention, 1788; an unsuccessful candidate for Congress, 1788; a member of the state legislature, 1790–95; a strong opponent of the Jay Treaty; and a U.S. representative, 1797–99. After a time in debtor's prison, President Thomas Jefferson appointed him Commissioner of Loans, an office he held until his death.

JOSEPH MCDOWALL OF QUAKER MEADOWS (SR.) (1756–1801), a planter, was born in Winchester, Virginia, and settled at Quaker Meadows in Burke County, North Carolina. He was a militia major at the Battle of King's Mountain (1780) and eventually rose in rank to brigadier-general. He served in the North Carolina House of Commons, 1780–1789, and in the state Senate, 1790–1795. In 1787 he was elected to the Council of State and to the Confederation Congress although there is no record of his attendance. In both the Hillsborough and Fayetteville conventions of 1788 and 1789, he voted against ratifying the Constitution. He also served as a U.S. representative, 1794–95, 1797–99. He is often confused with his cousin, Joseph McDowall of Pleasant Garden (Jr.).

COLLIN MCGREGOR (d. 1801), a native of Scotland who came to America in 1781, was a New York City merchant and a speculator in land and securities. He was a member of the St. Andrew's Society.

JAMES MCHENRY (c. 1752–1816), a merchant and land developer, was born in County Antrim, Ireland. He immigrated to Philadelphia in 1771 and then to Baltimore in 1781. He studied medicine with Benjamin Rush and served as Continental Army surgeon, 1776–78. He was an assistant secretary to General George Washington, 1778–80, and a major and aide-de-camp to General Lafayette, 1780–81. He served in the Maryland Senate, 1781–84, 1791–95; as a delegate to Congress, 1783–84; and as a delegate to the Constitutional Convention where he signed the Constitution, 1787. In the state Convention, he voted to ratify the Constitution in April 1788. He served in the state House of Delegates, 1788–89, and as U.S. Secretary of War, 1796–1800.

THOMAS MCKEAN (1734–1817). See BoR, II, 499.

ARCHIBALD MACLAINE (1728–1790), a lawyer-planter, had Scottish parents who immigrated to North Carolina from Ireland. Maclaine represented Brunswick County in the state Senate, 1777, 1780–82, and Wilmington in the House of Commons, 1783–87. In the Hillsborough Convention, he supported the Constitution in July and August 1788. He wrote a Federalist essay under the pseudonym "Publicola."

JAMES MCLENE (1730–1806), who settled in Cumberland County in the early 1750s, was a member of the convention that wrote the Pennsylvania constitution, 1776; of the state Assembly, 1776–77; of the Supreme Executive Council, 1778–79; and of Congress, 1780. After Franklin County was created from part of Cumberland County in 1784, he represented the new county in the Supreme Executive Council, 1784–87; in the state Assembly, 1787–89; in the state constitutional convention, 1789–90; and in the state House of Representatives, 1790–91, 1793–94.

JAMES MADISON (1751–1836). See BoR, II, 499.

JOHN MARSHALL (1755–1835), a Richmond, Virginia, lawyer, was an officer in the militia and Continental army, 1775–81 (inactive after 1779). He served in the Virginia House of Delegates, 1782, 1784–85, 1787–91, 1795–97; and the Virginia Council of State, 1782–84. In the state Convention, he voted to ratify the Constitution in June 1788. He was a diplomatic envoy to France in the XYZ Affair, 1797–98; U.S. representative, 1799–1800; U.S. Secretary of State, 1800–1801; and Chief Justice of the United States, 1801–35. He was a member of the Virginia constitutional convention, 1829–30.

GEORGE MASON (1725–1792). See BoR, II, 500.

JOHN FRANCIS MERCER (1759–1821). See BoR, II, 500.

THOMAS MIFFLIN (1744–1800). See BoR, II, 500.

JAMES MONROE (1758–1831) was a Fredericksburg, Virginia, lawyer. He served in the House of Delegates, 1782, 1787–89, 1810–11; was a member of the Council of State, 1782–83; and a delegate to Congress, 1783–86. In the state Convention, he voted not to ratify the Constitution in June 1788. He was defeated by James Madison in the 1789 election for U.S. representatives. He served as U.S. senator, 1790–94; U.S. minister to France, 1794–96; and governor, 1799–1802, 1811. As a special envoy to France, he helped negotiate the Louisiana Purchase, 1803. He was U.S. Secretary of State, 1811–17; U.S. Secretary of War, 1814–15; U.S. President, 1817–25; and president of the Virginia constitutional convention, 1829–30.

COMTE DE MOUSTIER (1751–1817), was appointed minister plenipotentiary from France to the United States in September 1787. He arrived in New York City on 18 January 1788 and presented his credentials to Congress on 26 February. He remained in America until October 1789.

CHARLES NESBIT (1736–1804), a Presbyterian minister who had studied at Divinity Hall, University of Edinburgh, migrated to Carlisle, Pennsylvania, in April 1785 to become the first president of the newly founded Dickinson College. He served in that position from 1785 until his death during which time he taught a course of 418 lectures on systematic theology and 22 on pastoral theology for students preparing for the ministry.

GEORGE NICHOLAS (c. 1754–1799). See BoR, II, 501.

EDMUND PENDLETON (1721–1803), a planter-lawyer, from Caroline County, Virginia, was a delegate to the First Continental Congress, 1774–75, and president of the provincial convention that drafted the state constitution, 1776. He was a judge on Virginia's High Court of Chancery, 1778–88, and president of the newly created Supreme Court of Appeals, 1788–1803. He was president of the state Convention, where he voted to ratify the Constitution in June 1788.

RICHARD PETERS (1744–1828), a Philadelphia lawyer, was secretary to the Continental Board of War, 1776; and was a member of the Board of War, 1777–81; of the Confederation Congress, 1782–83; and the state Assembly, 1787–90 (speaker, 1788–90). He served as the U.S. district judge for Pennsylvania, 1792–1828.

EDMUND RANDOLPH (1753–1813). See BoR, II, 503.

CALEB S. RIGGS (c. 1763–1826) was a New Jersey lawyer.

BENJAMIN RUSH (1745–1813). See BoR, II, 503.

THEODORE SEDGWICK (1746–1813). See BoR, II, 503.

ROGER SHERMAN (1721–1793). See BoR, II, 503.

WILLIAM SHIPPEN, JR. (1736–1808) was a Philadelphia physician. A 1754 graduate of the College of New Jersey (Princeton), he received his medical degree in 1761 from the University of Edinburgh Medical School. He was a professor at America's first medical school at the College of Philadelphia (now the University of Pennsylvania). He was elected to the American Philosophical Society in 1767. He served as a physician in the Continental

BIOGRAPHICAL GAZETTEER 469

Line from 1776 through 1781 ending as the director of Hospitals, 1777–81. A staunch Antifederalist, he was a brother-in-law to Richard Henry Lee and Arthur Lee. Shippen corresponded frequently with his son Thomas Lee Shippen, who was in Europe on the grand tour.

ABIGAIL ADAMS SMITH (1765–1813), the sister of John Quincy Adams, was married to William Stephens Smith, of New York, secretary to the American legation in London which was headed by her father, American minister plenipotentiary John Adams. The Smiths returned to America in May 1788.

MERIWETHER SMITH (1730–1794), a Virginia planter, was a member of Congress, 1778–79, 1781, and the Council of State, 1776–77, 1779–80, 1782–85. He also represented Essex County in the House of Burgesses, 1775–76, all five revolutionary conventions, 1774–76, and in the House of Delegates, 1776–77, 1778, 1781–82, 1785–89. A strong supporter of amendments, he voted against ratification of the Constitution in the state Convention in June 1788.

THOMAS DUNCAN SMITH (1760–1789), a 1776 graduate of Pennsylvania College and physician, was first justice, Huntingdon County, Pennsylvania, 1787–89.

RICHARD DOBBS SPAIGHT (1758–1802), a North Carolina planter, was the great-great nephew of colonial Governor Arthur Dobbs. Orphaned as a child, he was sent to Great Britain for his education, graduating from the University of Glasgow. He returned to North Carolina, 1778; served in the militia at the Battle of Camden, 1780; represented New Bern in the state House of Commons, 1779–83, 1792; and was a delegate to the Confederation Congress, 1783–85. He represented Craven County in the state House of Commons, 1785–87 (speaker, 1785), and was a delegate to the Constitutional Convention, 1787, and the Hillsborough Convention, 1788, where he spoke nearly a dozen times in favor of ratification. Ill-health forced Spaight to retire from public life, 1788–92. He returned briefly to the House of Commons, 1792, but resigned his seat to serve as governor, 1792–95. He was a presidential elector, 1793; and a member of the U.S. House of Representatives, 1798–1801. In the 1790s, his views aligned with the Jeffersonian Republicans. He represented Craven in the state Senate, 1801, and was re-elected to serve in 1802. As a leader of the New Bern Republicans, he developed a feud with John Stanly, the leader of the New Bern Federalists. Stanly killed Spaight in a duel in September 1802 on the fourth exchange of fire.

SAMUEL SPENCER (1734–1793), a jurist and planter, was born in East Haddam, Connecticut. He moved to Cheraws District, S.C., in 1758. Before 1774, he moved to Anson County, North Carolina, which he represented in the colonial Assembly, 1766–68; in the Provincial Congress, 1775–76; and was a member of the Provincial Council, 1775–76. Spencer served as a justice in the state Superior Court of Law and Equity, 1777–93. In both the Hillsborough and Fayetteville conventions of 1788 and 1789, he voted against ratification of the Constitution.

JOHN WRIGHT STANLY (1742–1789), a native of Charles City County, Virginia, came to New Bern, North Carolina, in 1773 and was a merchant, distiller, and planter who became wealthy during the Revolutionary War by investing in privateers. On 15 March 1789 Stanly was appointed to the Admiralty Court at New Bern, but he died on 1 June. He had been nominated for the Council of State.

SAMUEL STERETT (1756–1833), a native of Pennsylvania and a Baltimore merchant, was private secretary to President of Congress Elias Boudinot, 1782; a member of the Maryland House of Delegates, 1789; and a U.S. representative, 1791–93. In 1791 he was president of the Maryland Society for the Abolition of Slavery.

EZRA STILES (1727–1795) graduated from Yale College in 1746 and served as a tutor there from 1749 to 1755. He was licensed to preach in 1749 and was admitted to Connecticut's New Haven County bar in 1753. In 1755 he was ordained a Congregational minister and served as pastor of churches in Rhode Island, Massachusetts, and New Hampshire until 1778, when he accepted the presidency of Yale College, serving in that capacity until his death.

CALEB STRONG (1745–1819), a Northampton, Massachusetts, lawyer and Harvard graduate (1764), was a member of the state House of Representatives, 1776–77, 1779–80, 1797–98; state constitutional convention, 1779–80; and state Senate, 1780–81, 1782–83, 1784–89. He was a delegate to the Constitutional Convention, 1787, but left early in August. As a member of the state Convention, he voted to ratify the Constitution in February 1788. He served as a U.S. senator, 1789–96 (resigned), and Massachusetts governor, 1800–1807, 1812–16.

JAMES TILGHMAN (1716–1793), a native of Queen Anne's County, Maryland, was a wealthy planter and lawyer. He moved to Philadelphia in 1764. He was a member of the governor's council of Pennsylvania, 1767–76, and secretary of the proprietary land office, 1769–76. A Loyalist, Tilghman left Philadelphia in 1777 on parole from the patriot government and retired to Chestertown, Kent County, Maryland, where he lived quietly. He was discharged from his parole in 1778. He was a trustee of the College of Philadelphia (now the University of Pennsylvania), 1775–88.

THOMAS TREDWELL (1743–1831), a Suffolk County, New York, lawyer, was the judge of the probate court, 1778–87, and county surrogate, 1787–91. He served in the provincial convention, 1775; all four provincial congresses, 1775–77; the Assembly, 1777–83; and the state Senate, 1786–89. In the state Convention, he voted against ratification of the Constitution in July 1788. He was a U.S. representative, 1791–95.

JONATHAN TRUMBULL, JR. (1740–1809), a graduate of Harvard (B.A., 1759; M.A., 1762), was a Lebanon, Connecticut, shopkeeper, merchant, and farmer. He was a selectman, 1770–75; a delegate to the state House of Representatives, 1774–75, 1779–81, 1788–89 (speaker, 1788–89); congressional paymaster for the Northern department, 1775–78; Windham County justice of the peace, 1776–96; and comptroller of the U.S. treasury, 1778–79. He served as secretary to General George Washington, 1781–83 with the rank of lieutenant colonel, and was secretary of the Connecticut branch of the Society of the Cincinnati, 1783–93. He was a U.S. representative, 1789–94 (speaker, 1791–93); U.S. senator, 1794–96; presidential elector, 1796, 1800; lieutenant governor, 1796–97; and governor, 1797–1809.

THOMAS TUDOR TUCKER (1745–1828). See BoR, II, 505–6.

GEORGE LEE TURBERVILLE (1760–1798). See BoR, II, 506.

BIOGRAPHICAL GAZETTEER   471

JEREMIAH WADSWORTH (1743-1804). See BoR, II, 506.

THOMAS B. WAIT (1762-1830). See BoR, II, 506.

GEORGE WASHINGTON (1732-1799). See BoR, II, 506.

ALEXANDER WHITE (1738-1804). See BoR, II, 507.

WILLIAM WIDGERY (c. 1753-1822). See BoR, II, 507.

JOSEPH WILLARD (1738-1804), born in Biddeford, Maine, was a 1765 graduate of Harvard College and a minister, scientist, and mathematician. He helped form the American Academy of Arts and Sciences in 1780, serving as its corresponding secretary and contributing to its publications. He was president of Harvard, 1781-1804.

OTHO HOLLAND WILLIAMS (1749-1794), a pre-Revolutionary War merchant, was a Continental Army officer who rose from the rank of lieutenant (1775) to that of brigadier general (1782). After the war, he settled in Baltimore, where, in 1783, he was appointed state naval officer for the Baltimore district. In 1789 President George Washington appointed him collector of the Port of Baltimore.

GEORGE WYTHE (1726-1806), a Williamsburg, Virginia, lawyer, represented Williamsburg, 1754-55, College of William and Mary, 1758-61, and Elizabeth City County, 1761-68, in the Virginia House of Burgesses. He was the temporary Attorney General, 1754-55; author of the Virginia's Remonstrance against the Stamp Act, 1764; mayor of Williamsburg, 1768; and clerk of the House of Burgesses, 1768-76. As a delegate to Congress, 1775-76, he signed the Declaration of Independence. He was a member of the Commonwealth committee to revise laws, 1777-79; and represented Williamsburg in the House of Delegates, 1777-78 (speaker). He was a judge on the High Court of Chancery, 1778-88 (becoming sole Chancellor in 1788); first professor of law at the College of William and Mary, 1779-89; and a delegate to the Constitutional Convention, 1787, leaving before the Convention adjourned. He was a York County delegate to the state Convention, where he chaired the committee of whole and voted to ratify the Constitution in June 1788. He moved to Richmond in 1791.

ABRAHAM YATES, JR. (1724-1796). See BoR, II, 508.

Appendix I
Amendments Proposed by the Maryland Convention Minority As Remarked Upon by Foreign Spectator

On 24 April 1788 William Paca indicated to the Maryland Convention "that he had great objections to the constitution proposed, in its present form, and meant to propose a variety of amendments, not to prevent, but to accompany the ratification. Federalists prevented Paca from introducing his amendments until after the Convention ratified the Constitution 63 to 11 on 26 April. Paca, who had voted to ratify, was finally permitted to read his amendments. By a vote of "66 members for, and not more than 7 against," the Convention agreed to create a committee of thirteen, consisting of nine Federalists, three Antifederalists, and Paca himself, to consider amendments. Paca's amendments were referred to the committee. On 28 April the sixty-three ratifying delegates signed the Form of Ratification. After considerable wrangling among the members of the committee of thirteen, committee chairman Paca informed the Convention that the committee "could come to no Agreement to make any report." The Convention then adjourned.

Believing that the form of government proposed in the Constitution was "very defective" and "the liberties and the happiness of the people" would be endangered if the Constitution was not amended, Paca and the eleven non-ratifying delegates prepared an address to the people of Maryland for publication. They laid before the people the thirteen amendments agreed upon by the committee of thirteen and the fifteen amendments that the Federalist majority on the committee rejected. The Antifederalists indicated that they had offered "not only [to] cease to oppose the government, but [to] give all their assistance to carry it into execution as amended" if the committee of thirteen would only submit the first three rejected amendments to the Convention for a vote. The minority related how their offer was rejected 8 to 5, one Federalist voting with them. When the committee refused to make a report, all amendments were lost. In the address the Antifederalist minority presented the amendments to the public "for your consideration, that you may express your sense as to such alterations as you may think proper to be made in the new constitution."

The address of the Maryland Convention Antifederalist minority first appeared in Annapolis either in the *Maryland Gazette* of 1 May, or as a broadside published by the *Gazette*'s printers, Frederick and Samuel Green (Evans 45288). On 2 May the Baltimore *Maryland Gazette* and *Maryland Journal* announced that they would print the address in their next issues, which they did on 6 May. The address was reprinted in the *Pennsylvania Packet* and Philadelphia *Independent Gazetteer*, 8 May; *New York Journal*, 12 May; Philadelphia *Freeman's Journal*, 14 May; Boston *American Herald*, 22, 26 May; Charleston, S.C., *City Gazette*, 2 June; and Rhode Island *Providence Gazette*, 7 June; and in the May issue of the nationally circulated Philadelphia *American Museum*.

The amendments printed here are excerpted from the printing of the address that appeared in the Annapolis *Maryland Gazette*, 1 May. For the complete address, see RCS:Md., 659–69. For William Paca's proposed amendments, see

BoR, I, 245–47. Paca's amendments, not those from the Convention minority's address, appeared in the pamphlet compilation of the proposed amendments to the Constitution printed by Augustine Davis sometime after 2 August 1788 (BoR, III, 129).

The following amendments to the proposed constitution were separately agreed to by the committee, most of them by an *unanimous* vote, and all of them by a *great majority:*

1. That congress shall exercise no power but what is expressly delegated by this constitution.

By this amendment, the general powers given to congress by the first and last paragraphs of the 8th sect. of art. 1, and the second paragraph of the 6th article, would be in a great measure restrained: those dangerous expressions by which the bills of rights and constitutions of the several states may be repealed by the laws of congress, in some degree moderated, and the exercise of *constructive* powers wholly prevented.

2. That there shall be a trial by jury in all criminal cases, according to the course of proceeding in the state where the offence is committed; and that there be no appeal from matter of fact, or second trial after acquittal; but this provision shall not extend to such cases as may arise in the government of the land or naval forces.

3. That in all actions on debts or contracts, and in all other controversies respecting property, or which the inferior federal courts have jurisdiction, the trial of facts shall be by jury, if required by either party; and that it be expressly declared, that the state courts, in such cases, have a concurrent jurisdiction with the federal courts, with an appeal from either, only as to matter of law, to the supreme federal court, if the matter in dispute be of the value of _____ dollars.

4. That the inferior federal courts shall not have jurisdiction of less than _____ dollars; and there may be an appeal in all cases of revenue, as well to matter of fact as law, and congress may give the state courts jurisdiction of revenue cases, for such sums, and in such manner, as they may think proper.

5. That in all cases of trespasses done within the body of a county, and within the inferior federal jurisdiction, the party injured shall be entitled to trial by jury in the state where the injury shall be committed; and that it be expressly declared, that the state courts, in such cases, shall have concurrent jurisdiction with the federal courts; and there shall be no appeal from either, except on matter of law; and that no person be exempt from such jurisdiction and trial but ambassadors and ministers privileged by the law of nations.

6. That the federal courts shall not be entitled to jurisdiction by fictions or collusion.

7. That the federal judges do not hold any other office of profit, or receive the profits of any other office under congress, during the time they hold their commission.

The great objects of these amendments were, 1st. To secure the trial by jury in all cases, the boasted birth-right of Englishmen, and their decendants, and the palladium of civil liberty; and to prevent the *appeal from fact*, which not only destroys that trial in civil cases, but by *construction*, may also elude it in criminal cases; a mode of proceeding both expensive and burthensome, and also by blending law with fact, will destroy all check on the judiciary authority, render it almost impossible to convict judges of corruption, and may lay the foundation of that gradual and silent attack on individuals, by which the approaches of tyranny become irresistable. 2d. To give a concurrent jurisdiction to the state courts, in order that congress may not be compelled, as they will be under the present form, to establish inferior federal courts, which if not numerous will be inconvenient, and if numerous very expensive; the circumstances of the people being unequal to the increased expence of double courts, and double officers; an arrangement that will render the law so complicated and confused, that few men can know how to conduct themselves with safety to their persons or property, the great and only security of freemen. 3dly, To give such jurisdiction to the state courts, that transient foreigners, and persons from other states, committing injuries in this state, may be amenable to the state, whose laws they violate, and whose citizens they injure. 4thly, To prevent an extension of the federal jurisdiction, which may, and in all probability will, swallow up the state jurisdictions, and consequently sap those rules of descent and regulations of personal property, by which men now hold their estates; and lastly, To secure the independence of the federal judges, to whom the happiness of the people of this great continent will be so greatly committed by the extensive powers assigned them.

8. That all war[r]ants without oath, or affirmation of a person conscientiously scrupulous of taking an oath, to search suspected places, or to seize any person or his property, are grievous and oppressive; and all general warrants to search suspected places, or to apprehend any person suspected, without naming or describing the place or person in special, are dangerous, and ought not to be granted.

This amendment was considered indispensable by many of the committee, for congress having the power of laying excises, the horror of a free people, by which our dwelling-houses, those castles considered so sacred by the English law, will be laid open to the insolence and oppression of office, there could be no constitutional check provided, that would prove so effectual a safeguard to our citizens. General warrants too, the great engine by which power may destroy those individuals who resist usurpation, are also hereby forbid to those magistrates who are to administer the general government.

9. That no soldier be enlisted for a longer time than four years except in time of war, and then only during the war.

10. That soldiers be not quartered in time of peace upon private houses, without the consent of the owners.

11. That no mutiny bill continue in force longer than two years.

These were the only checks that could be obtained against the unlimitted power of raising and regulating standing armies, the natural enemies to freedom, and even with these restrictions, the new congress will not be under such constitutional restraints as the parliament of Great-Britain; restraints which our ancestors have bled to establish, and which have hitherto preserved the liberty of their posterity.

12. That the freedom of the press be inviolably preserved.

In prosecutions in the federal courts for libels, the constitutional preservation of this great and fundamental right, may prove invaluable.

13. That the militia shall not be subject to martial law, except in time of war, invasion or rebellion.

This provision to restrain the powers of congress over the militia, although, by no means so ample as that provided by magna charta, and the other fundamental and constitutional laws of Great Britain, (it being contrary to magna charta to punish a freeman by martial law in time of peace, and murder to execute him,) yet it may prove an inestimable check; for all other provisions in favour of the rights of men, would be vain and nugatory, if the power of subjecting all men able to bear arms to martial law at any moment, should remain vested in congress.

Thus far the amendments were agreed to.

The following amendments were laid before the committee, and negatived by a majority.

1. That the militia, unless selected by lot or voluntarily enlisted, shall not be marched beyond the limits of an adjoining state, without the consent of their legislature or executive.

2. That congress shall have no power to alter or change the time, place or manner, of holding elections for senators or representatives, unless a state shall neglect to make regulations, or to execute its regulations, or shall be prevented by invasion or rebellion; in which cases only congress may interfere, until the cause be removed.

3. That, in every law of congress imposing *direct* taxes, the collection thereof shall be *suspended* for a certain reasonable time therein limited,

and on payment of the sum by any state, by the time appointed, such taxes shall not be collected.

4. That no standing army shall be kept up *in time of peace*, unless with the consent of two thirds of the members present of each branch of congress.

5. That the president shall not command the army in person, without the consent of congress.

6. That no treaty shall be effectual to repeal or abrogate the *constitutions* or *bills of rights* of the states, or any part of them.

7. That no regulation of commerce, or navigation act, shall be made, unless with the consent of two thirds of the members of each branch of congress.

8. That no member of congress shall be eligible to any office of profit under congress during the time for which he shall be appointed.

9. That congress shall have no power to lay a *poll tax*.

10. That no person, conscientiously scrupulous of bearing arms in any case, shall be compelled *personally* to serve as a soldier.

11. That there be a responsible council to the president.

12. That there be no national religion established by law, but that all persons be equally entitled to protection in their religious liberty.

13. That all imposts and duties laid by congress shall be placed to the credit of the state in which the same be collected, and shall be deducted out of such state's quota of the common or general expences of government.

14. That every man hath a right to petition the legislature for the redress of grievances in a peaceable and orderly manner.

15. That it be declared, that all persons intrusted with the legislative or executive powers of government are the trustees and servants of the public, and as such accountable for their conduct. Wherefore, whenever the ends of government are perverted, and public liberty manifestly endangered, and all other means of redress are ineffectual, the people may, and of right ought, to reform the old, or establish a new government; the doctrine of non-resistance against arbitrary power and oppression, is absurd, slavish, and destructive of the good and happiness of mankind.

Index

Explanatory Note

To aid the reader, compilations of similar items have been grouped together under a common main entry in this index. Such compilations are listed below. In addition to their being grouped under "Pseudonyms," pseudonymous items printed in this volume are indexed individually. When known, the author's name is placed in parentheses after the pseudonym. Some entries in this index are so unusual that they deserve to be highlighted. The reader should be particularly aware of these entries listed below.

COMPILATIONS

Biblical References
Broadsides, Pamphlets, and Books
Celebrations
Classical Antiquity
Governments, Ancient and
  Modern

Literary References
Newspapers
Political and Legal Writers and
  Writings
Pseudonyms
Ratification, Prospects for

UNUSUAL ENTRIES

Discourse
Foreign Opinion
  of the U.S.
General Welfare
God

Government, Debate
  over Nature of
Happiness
Human Nature
Interests

Patriotism
The People
Poetry
Rich verses Poor

Sovereignty
Toasts
Union
Virtue

"A.B.": text of, 243-44
"A.B.": text of, 174
ABBOT, HENRY (Camden Co., N.C.): id., 458
—speech of in N.C. Convention, 113-14; responses to, 116, 117
ACCUSATION, CAUSE AND NATURE OF: defense of Constitution's lack of protection for, 384; included in Va. Convention amendments, 54; must provide in jury trials, 32
ADAMS, ABIGAIL (Braintree, Mass.)
—letter to, 449
ADAMS, JOHN (Braintree, Mass.; id., BoR, II, 490): as possible first U.S. Vice President, 127, 314, 356, 356n, 377; returns to U.S. from Europe, 127, 128n; favors amendments after experience warrants, 314
—*Defence of the Constitutions*: examines ancient and modern European politics, 127, 128n; praise of, 127, 128n, 220, 315
—letter from, 449
—letters to, 127-28n, 315-17n

ADAMS, JOHN QUINCY (Newburyport, Mass.)
—letter to, 144
ADAMS, SAMUEL (Boston): as candidate for U.S. House of Representatives, 201, 208; as candidate for U.S. Senate, 153, 154n, 191; compared to Thomas Hutchinson, 153, 154n, 161; criticized for his vote to ratify Constitution, 432; favors amendments when experience warrants, 425; called a patriot, 432; patriotism questioned, 430; proposed amendments in Mass. Convention, 256, 430, 430n, 432-33, 433n
ADMIRALTY LAW: different trials under, 100; no jury trials in, 34, 111-12, 279; only federal inferior courts that should be created for, 181
AFRICAN AMERICANS: number of freedmen in Va., 49n. *See also* Slave trade; Slavery
AGRICULTURE: Americans interested in, 332; Constitution would benefit, 230, 232; Hessian Fly caused damage to, 287, 289n; Union needed to restore, 302. *See also* Farmers; Planters

477

ALBANY ANTIFEDERALIST COMMITTEE: N.H. will send news to, 58
"ALBERT": text of, 211–13
"ALFRED" (Caleb Strong), 280n, 395n; text of, 255–56, 277–80; response to, 273, 274n; written by Caleb Strong, 256n
"ALFREDUS" (Samuel Tenney), 85n; identified as Samuel Tenney, 85n; response to, 83–85
AMENDMENTS TO THE ARTICLES OF CONFEDERATION: procedure for, 122n–23n; seldom attempted, 333; would be forever needed, 274
AMENDMENTS TO THE CONSTITUTION: advocated in western Pa. in combination with N.Y., 130; to allow senators to vote by proxy, 163; anarchy would occur from excessive, 135; are all deficient, 266–67; are to majesty of the people, 218; cannot precede ratification of Constitution, 122; criticism of opposition to, 155, 160; criticism of those proposed, 156; defense of those proposed as honest and praiseworthy, 161; dependent on wisdom and virtue of the states, 225; difficult process means only general ones will be adopted, 90; done two ways by states under Articles or by Constitution's procedure, 147; endanger Union, 209; favor only beneficial "federal" amendments, 128; favored in constitutional way, 212; favored previous to adoption of Constitution, 57, 59; a few will please everyone, 293; God asked to help in defeating, 219; great support for in Va., 354; has helped clarify ambiguity in Constitution, 35, 328; if adopted it will be by trickery, 146; James Madison's opinion of, 257; Jefferson's tally sheet listing state approval of, ii; majority of people support, 153–54, 200, 226–27, 409; majority of those voting for ratification of Constitution favor, 192; many people and states want, 147; Md. Convention fails to recommend, 253; Md. Convention minority amendments, 472n–76; most effort for will come from Va. and N.Y., 290; N.C. Convention will not ratify without, 129; N.C. will help obtain if it first ratifies Constitution, 122; N.C.'s are similar to Va.'s, 162–63, 431; N.H. Convention recommends, 67; N.H. looks to N.Y. for leadership on, 58; newspapers in Boston and Philadelphia oppose, 191; no hope of previous amendments after nine states ratify Constitution, 85; no objection to those ensuring rights, 222; non-ratifying states will be unable to participate in adopting, 148; none can gain support of a majority of rational men, 268; not needed, 264; not treasonous to seek, 207; only a few should be sought in a conciliatory manner, 383; only question is previous or subsequent, 35–36; opponents are guilty of treason against majesty of people, 207, 208; opposition to previous to Constitution's ratification, 11; opposition to threatens the Union, 301; pamphlet compilation of by Augustine Davis, 129; Pa. Antifederalists will seek in constitutional manner, 152; Pa. Assembly opposes premature, 5; Pa. Convention not allowed to propose, 193; listed in Dissent of Minority of Pa. Convention, 189; praise of Constitution's provision for, 10, 91–92, 141, 205, 274; premature and would cause confusion, 289, 387; premature ones will not be favored by seven states, 289; previous to implementation characterized as treasonous, 202; promise of subsequent amendments threatens Union, 47; proposed by S.C. Convention, 64n, 65; R.I. and N.C. needed in Union to obtain, 148; represents wishes of the people, 437; six state convention adopt without, 138–39; some should be adopted, 203; some should be adopted immediately, 82, 173, 200, 312–13; sought by Greensburgh, Pa., meeting, 131–34; supporters of called names, 303; supporters of called office seekers, 303; supporters of said to be enemies of their country, 391; toast in Carlisle, Pa., to speedy and unanimous adoption of, 82; Va. generally favors, 53; Washington supports most, 159; will be considered in a second constitutional convention, 92; will be favored by representatives from states that did not recommend, 140; will promote anarchy, 187
—will damage or destroy Constitution, 59, 123, 128, 138, 152, 187, 197, 218, 235, 236, 237–38, 242–43, 260–61, 269, 273–74, 276, 293, 303, 324, 325, 374, 382, 386, 405, 422, 424, 446; will damage best parts of Constitution, 228; will destroy spirit of Constitution, 219; called insidious and ruinous alterations, 260; called unnecessary and injurious abridgments of the wholesome, 260; denial they will destroy Constitution, 238–39; before experience is equivalent to opposing Constitution, 446–47; opposition to those that might destroy the Constitution, 174; previous the same as rejection of Constitution, 62, 87; proposed by N.Y. Convention would destroy

INDEX   479

Constitution, 123, 135, 138, 141; will make
Constitution inferior to Articles of Confederation, 202
—and Antifederalists: differ over, 217–18,
275, 276, 350; not willing to await experience, 273–74; many different ones proposed, 90; seek in constitutional way, 126,
142, 177–78; seek through interstate co-
operation, 126; use as means to gain their
election to U.S. House of Representatives,
199
—and Federalists: allegedly never really supported, 191; said to oppose all, 231–32;
seemingly agree to, 250; agree that a few
are needed, 123, 124; some want those
protecting individual rights, 257
—procedure for in Article V, 7, 145, 148,
211, 236, 238–39; will be used to correct
defects of Constitution, 142; ought to be
acted upon, 173, 367
—needed, 4, 65, 84–85, 103, 120, 123, 124,
128, 132, 135, 140, 150, 153, 154, 162,
164, 165, 169, 176–77, 178, 179, 224, 227,
292, 339, 378, 454; necessary ones should
be adopted, 126; after implementation of
Constitution, 41–42, 42–43, 63, 123; before adoption of Constitution, 41, 46, 57–
58, 65; for happiness and harmony, 437;
speedily, 6; to avoid civil war, 190; to explain rights of the people, 209; to make
Constitution as perfect as possible, 228; to
preserve a federal government, 155; to
preserve states under Constitution, 65
—and Congress: and a convention can propose, 232; can be required to call constitutional convention, 7; can only propose,
7; cannot adopt, 7; will propose a few,
285; only can propose, 193; should be
added via and not by convention, 3, 240,
382, 400, 454–55; should be obtained via
and state legislatures, 386; friends of
should be elected to, 336n–37n; more
likely to be obtained from than from a
convention, 408; opponents of should not
be elected to, 300; advocates of should be
elected to U.S. House of Representatives,
367–68; danger of premature if Antifederalists are elected to U.S. House of Representatives, 152; vote for supporters of for
U.S. House of Representatives, 375–76
—proposed by Harrisburg Convention, 184;
as aim of, 175; differ from Southern
States, 222; are unimportant, 196; are
similar to some state convention's, 196;
are similar to Dissent of the Minority of
the Pa. Convention, 234; are unnecessary,
194; are submitted to Pa. Assembly, 182

—recommended by Mass. Convention, 57,
59n, 64n, 65, 67, 86, 92n, 161, 218, 285,
303, 445; were merely conciliatory, 220,
256, 273, 391–91; were not merely conciliatory, 299–300; incompatible with a consolidated government, 277; reserving powers, 64, 64n; were not local, 301; not
sufficient enough, 53; as part of form of
ratification, 231, 300; instructed future
representatives to seek, 280
—recommended by N.Y. Convention, 123,
128; criticism of, 138; were needed to ratify Constitution, 148–49; expected, 87;
are similar to Va.'s, 162, 431; received by
N.H. president, 136; printed Debates said
to be biased against, 71; uncertainty of,
87; will destroy Constitution, 128, 135,
138, 141; encouraged by N.Y. circular letter, 149
—recommended by Va. Convention, 8n, 42,
53–56, 68, 69, 70, 445, 456–57; sent to
N.Y. Antifederalists, 52n; rejects previous
to ratification of Constitution, 68; are a
concerted plan, 130; will be discussed, 90;
influence N.Y. Antifederalists, 86; N.C.'s
amendments are similar to, 162–63; N.Y.'s
amendments are similar to, 162; proposed
by Patrick Henry do not change nature of
Constitution, 48
—should await experience, 62, 91, 127,
138–39, 152, 179, 199, 214, 220, 225, 238,
262, 268–69, 274, 298, 312–13, 326, 373,
377, 382, 389, 391, 401, 406–7, 412, 424,
425, 429–30, 435, 438, 439, 448; Antifederalists not willing to await experience,
273–74; hope they won't be adopted for
twelve to twenty years, 127; should not be
adopted for at least one year, 147; should
not be approved for 500 years, 311; will
take place when needed, 123, 142, 285;
would be dangerous, 207; experience will
either sanctify or repel, 246; praise of procedure for that will be used with experience, 141; opposition to waiting for experience to reveal proper, 160; safer to get
after implementation of Constitution, 36;
should be obtained before ratification of
Constitution, 47; will be needed in the future, 266
—are local or not local: are not local, 154,
301, 303, 328; most are local, 324; will not
serve the general welfare, 146; will promote Union and harmony, 447
—will be difficult or impossible to adopt after implementation of Constitution, 7, 45,
65, 70, 122, 224, 390, 449; Congress will
not propose, 281

—will be attainable after Constitution is implemented, 62, 67, 67n, 86, 139, 145, 206, 257, 400; bill of rights can be adopted after Constitution is implemented, 29; hope for from first federal Congress, 70; only a few will be approved, 324; will be the first order of business in first Congress, 139; for protection of rights will be obtained from first Congress, 262; subsequent easier to obtain than previous, 42
"An American," 424n
"An American Citizen" (Tench Coxe), 445n, 457; Tench Coxe as author of, 409n; text of, 7–8, 407–8, 442–45, 454–56
American Revolution: as a civil war, 304; Constitution will complete, 374; done for the people, 411; as extraordinary event in world history, 70; fought for liberty, 24, 32, 41, 65, 72, 98, 100, 230, 234, 250, 302, 333, 364, 374, 407; God helped Americans win, 127, 153, 154; not yet over, 246; lack of jury trial in the vicinage as a cause of, 105; British threats to jury trial in civil as a cases cause, 98, 278, 280nAmericans: admire Magna Charta, 63; are an example to the rest of the world, 388; are impatient, 409; change in mindset of, 70; diversity of, 141; diversity of requires strong government, 151; face monumental decision over Constitution, 205; favor liberty, 47; God has protected, 80, 127, 153, 154, 155, 157–58, 161, 302; half of are Antifederalists, 361; have a predilection to change their government, 129; know more about government than any other people, 106–7, 140, 304; know more about natural rights than others, 140, 281; lack patriotism, 150; majority of feel Constitution is dangerous, 65; majority of favor Constitution, 146; are the most easily governed, 357–58; referred to as ignorant peasants, 217; remarkable for good sense and discernment, 304; seek political happiness, 47; support Union, 151–52; unanimously want Constitution implemented, 213; uneasy until amendments are adopted, 175; will bear Constitution, 315. *See also* United States
Anarchy: Antifederalist amendments will promote, 187; Antifederalists called sons of anarchy, 237; Constitution will lead to, 169, 334; Constitution will protect against, 68, 288, 324; danger of if Constitution is rejected, 35, 58, 90, 145, 237, 265; fear of in postwar America, 382; God will protect America from, 127; is worst that can be expected from a bad government, 169; men in desperate circumstances prefer, 326; as reason for ratification of Constitution, 389; second convention will lead to, 214, 422; some men want, 329; U.S. is experiencing, 68, 135, 142, 197, 266, 333, 412; U.S. would be in if ratified by ten states but not put into effect, 212; will result if N.Y. rejects Constitution, 87; would occur from excessive amendments, 135; would result if people aren't virtuous enough to elect good representatives, 152
Anderson, James (Pa.): as delegate to Harrisburg Convention, 177
Annapolis Convention: Va. calls, 88
"Anti": text of, 248–49
Antifederalists: acquiesce with Constitution, 68, 123, 126, 130, 142, 152, 167, 169, 173,178, 179, 190, 203, 205, 223; acquiesce with Constitution but seek amendments in constitutional way, 126, 152, 173; attempt interstate coordination, 126; bill of rights would satisfy many, 445, 447; call second convention to destroy Constitution, 238; celebrate 4th of July in Carlisle, Pa., 82; criticized for criticizing delegates to Constitutional Convention, 143; defended against name-calling, 83; differ over amendments, 217–18, 275, 276, 350; disagree over bill of rights, 257; disappointed with Harrisburg Convention, 188, 192; divided, 401; propagate eight lies, 270–71; encouraged by N.Y. circular letter, 88n, 145, 146, 149, 158, 221–22, 262; endanger Union, 50; fear they plot to subvert Constitution, 124; four different classes of, 198–99; hard to differentiate well-meaning from dishonorable, 269; lack patriotism, 188–89, 249; literature of criticized as faulty in knowledge and grammar, 220; lost influence in Conn. Assembly, 315; majority of Virginians are, 47; in Md. work to elect cabals, 126; in N.C. will not ratify Constitution without amendments, 438; in N.H. will send news to Albany Antifederalist committee, 58; nominated for U.S. House of Representatives, 335–36; not treasonous to seek amendments, 207; officeholders more concerned about themselves, 183, 197, 448; only a few are well-meaning, 269; in Pa. affected by N.Y. ratification, 130; in Pa. have become Federalists, 188; in Philadelphia are talented and hard-working, 130; praise of for adopting Constitution first before amendments are acted on, 199–201n; seek only their election instead of amend-

INDEX   481

ments, 199; setting up committees of correspondence in every state to ruin Constitution, 217; should be wary of those who want amendments for their own benefit, 152; should drop the "anti" from name, 186–87; should not be elected to first Congress, 215, 226, 276, 290, 333, 424, 425; should be elected to U.S. House of Representatives, 284, 344; some attempt to destroy Constitution secretly, 153; sow discord and dissension, 197; still have differences with Federalists, 239–42; supported monarchy at beginning of Revolution, 248; term of denounced, 213; term of used derogatively, 301; those who support amendments are truly federal, 169; unable and unwilling to improve Constitution, 268–69; use secret and perhaps insidious means opposing Constitution, 126; vilified by Federalists, 282; want confusion, 234; want second convention, 3, 201, 448; want to destroy Constitution, 175, 284, 324, 448; want to lull people to think Constitution will be implemented, 233; in Westmoreland Co., Pa., possess federal sentiments, 132; would be satisfied with a bill of rights, 361, 386, 438, 445, 447
—in New York: in New York City want N.Y. ratification, 87; are in command of state, 130; are moderating, 221, 254; split in Convention, 318, 320; have majority in Convention of, 51n, 58–59, 59n
—in Virginia: acquiesce with Constitution, 68; are firmly attached to Union, 68; are quiet but might make violent attack, 158; strong in, 354; some in Convention remain staunchly opposed to Constitution, 68; will be encouraged by N.C.'s rejection of Constitution, 182
—strength of: are in command in N.Y., 130; are diminishing, 305; only a few discordant in Conn., 293; as formidable minority in some states, 70; gaining strength, 395; half of Americans are, 361; strong in N.C., 354; strong in Va., 354; have a majority in N.H. Convention, 58; have a majority in N.Y. Convention of, 51n, 58–59, 59n; have a majority in N.C. Convention, 92
—called: alteration mongers, 226, 238; amendmentites, 324; antifederal anarchiads, 242; antifederal sticklers for amendments, 448; cabin-window gentry, 355; deceitful, 146, 198, 204–5, 205, 206, 326, 346, 360, 374–75, 446–47; demagogues, 199; depraved, 234; enemies of their country, 58; former leaders of the Revolution, 162; Government-Menders, 174; are honest uninformed yeomen, shattered fortunes, and tories, 338; compared to Indians, 144; are intriguers, 290; mischievous, 325, 422; moonshine politicians, 220; are obstinate, 338, 442; patriots, 162, 284, 303; said to be true federalists and true patriots, 303; said to have patriotism, 162; political serpents, 236; selfish state officeholders, 325; Shaysites, 161; sons of anarchy, 237; sticklers for amendments, 156; likened to tories, 446; trimmers never to be trusted, 446–47; described as wicked and evil disposed persons, 171

See also Constitutional convention, second; Harrisburg Convention

"ANTILOCALIS": text of, 448

APPROPRIATIONS: may not provide sufficient funds for military, 331; for military limited to two years in Md. minority amendments, 475; for military limited to two years in Va. Convention amendments, 56; praise of two-year limit for military, 15, 50, 241, 343

ARISTOCRACY: Americans must choose between a republic and, 387–88; Constitution has features of, 119; Constitution will create, 119, 120, 164, 282–84, 348; danger of, 76; fear of in postwar America, 381; House of Representatives will be aristocratic, 252; Senate will be aristocratic, 251

ARMS, RIGHT TO BEAR: Constitution endangers, 120; defense of federal government's power to disarm people, 380; protected in Va. Convention amendments, 55; Samuel Adams proposes amendment to protect, 432–33; will prevent tyranny, 331

ARMSTRONG, JOHN (Carlisle, Pa.): nominated for U.S. House of Representatives, 368

ARMY: Congress should have power to raise and maintain, 132; praise of Constitution's two-year limit of appropriations for, 15, 50, 241, 343; soldiers limited to four-year terms in Md. minority amendments, 475; soldiers limited to four-year terms in Va. Convention amendments, 56. See also Army, standing; Military; Militia

ARMY, STANDING: amendment needed to limit, 124; Antifederalists require two-thirds majority of both houses, 241; Constitution will not endanger with, 49–50, 230, 241; criticism of amendment limiting, 195; criticism of Congress' power to have during peacetime, 67, 133; defense of, 329–32; endangers liberty, 55, 349; Federalists said to favor, 389; limited in U.S. by

two-year appropriation maximum, 15, 475; Md. minority amendments limits, 475, 476; needs to be limited, 135–36; needs two-thirds vote of both houses of Congress, 180; no British provision against, 50; Parliamentary approval required in Bill of Rights, 51n; prohibited except by vote of two-thirds of both houses of Congress, 56; sometimes necessary, 125, 259; used as a foil by Antifederalists, 249; Va. Convention amendment limiting, 51n, 55; Va. Declaration of Rights allows when necessary, 49–50; Va. Declaration of Rights states danger from, 44. *See also* Army; Military; Militia
ARNOLD, PELEG (Smithfield, R.I.): id., 458
—letter from, 86
ARNOLD, WELCOME (Providence, R.I.)
—letter to, 86
ARSENALS. *See* Forts, magazines, and arsenals
ARTICLES OF CONFEDERATION: amendment process, 82n; called a compact, 27; defects of, 14, 41, 50, 62, 89, 202, 242, 333, 364, 365–66, 374, 420, 425; described as a rope of sand, 219, 392, 430; happiness not possible under, 10; needs changing, 335, 439; no coercive power over states other than warfare, 342; old Union under is dead after nine states ratify Constitution, 85–86; only gave Congress enumerated powers, 74; protects rights, 24–25; survival of Union under is questionable, 223; tottering, 225; requires nine state approval of treaties, 435; U.S. cannot flourish under, 364; Va. has abided by, 44; violated by Constitutional Convention, 77, 80, 122, 122n–23n; weakness was it couldn't act on people, 289; would forever need amendments, 274
—Article II, 27n, 103, 105n, 106, 107, 108n, 121n; is defective, 50; referred to as a bill of rights, 27; reserves powers to states, 95, 96n
ARTISANS: Constitution will benefit, 423
ASSEMBLY, RIGHT OF: protected in Va. Convention amendments, 55
ATHERTON, JOSHUA (Amherst, N.H.): id., 458
—speech in N.H. Convention, 67; quoted, 58
—letter from, 57–59; cited, 53n, 57n
—letter to, cited, 57, 57n
ATTAINDER, BILL OF: prohibition of refutes reserved powers theory, 74; used in Va. against Josiah Philips, 28, 30n
AUSTIN, BENJAMIN, JR. (Boston): id., 302n, 458; as author of "Honestus," 302n

BACKHOUSE, RICHARD (Durham, Bucks Co., Pa.): attends Bucks Co. meeting, 172; as delegate to Harrisburg Convention, 177; elected to Harrisburg Convention, 174
BAIL, EXCESSIVE: danger of under Constitution, 25; defense of Constitution's lack of protection from, 33; prohibited in Va. Convention amendments, 55
BAIRD, RICHARD (Pa.): as delegate to Harrisburg Convention, 177
BAKER, HILARY (Philadelphia): member of Philadelphia committee of correspondence, 186n
BALDWIN, ABRAHAM (Augusta, Wilkes Co., Ga.): id., 458
—letter from, 376–77
BALTIMORE, MD.: attempts in to eliminate party names, 124
BANCKER, ABRAHAM B. (Ulster Co., N.Y.): id., 459
—letter from, 135
—letter to, cited, 135
BANCKER, EVERT (New York City)
—letter from, cited, 135
—letter to, 135
BANKRUPTCY: defense of Congress' power to enact laws concerning, 370
BARBER, ROBERT (Albany Co., N.Y.): as printer of the *Albany Register*, 81n
BARLOW, JOEL (Hartford, Conn./France)
—letter to, 376–77
BARTLETT, JOSIAH (Kingston, N.H.): as candidate for U.S. Senate, 337–38
BECKLEY, JOHN (Henrico Co., Va.): estimates majority of Antifederalists in Va. House of Delegates, 284
BELL, JAMES (East Pennsborough, Cumberland Co., Pa.): Cumberland Co. meeting at house of, 166n
BENNET, GEORGE (Tinicum, Bucks Co., Pa.): attends Bucks Co. meeting, 173
BERKS COUNTY, PA.: incorrectly said not to have been represented in Harrisburg Convention, 188, 189
BIBLICAL REFERENCES: Absalom's attempt to dethrone his father David, 394, 395n; Adam, 281, 330; all the world will worship the beast (Revelations), 394, 395n; Apostles' Creed, 75, 82n; David said of Goliath's sword, 193, 193n; Ethiopian cannot change skin (Jeremiah), 242, 243n; fall of Adam, 390; giants the sons of Anak, 324; Goliath, 80, 82n, 193, 193n; he sweareth to his own hurt he changeth not, 391, 395n; hewers of wood and drawers of water, 390; Israelite spies in Canaan, 324; Jesus says the gates of hell shall not prevail

INDEX 483

against Peter, 116, 117n; laws of Moses, 393; lead us not into temptation, 93; Pharisees pay tithes but omit important matters, 75, 82n; Simon a tanner, 195; Ten Commandments, 66; thus far you have come and no further (Job), 16, 18n; wanting to be a slave, 393; we will have a King over us, 394, 395n; yoke of bondage, 391, 395n

BIENNIAL ELECTIONS: criticism of for U.S. House of Representatives, 119

BILL OF RIGHTS: Americans favor, 26; Antifederalists disagree over, 257; Antifederalists would be satisfied with, 361, 386, 438, 445, 447; Article I, section 9 is not equivalent of, 30; Article II of Articles of Confederation referred to as, 27; benefits from, 258–59; called parchment barriers, 257; can be adopted after Constitution is implemented, 29; Congress can protect in laws without altering the Constitution, 433; danger of in not listing every right, 64, 97, 101–2, 109–10, 218, 287; endangers liberty under a monarchy, 16; federal officers should take an oath not to violate states', 390–91; Federalists agree to but via Congress, 405; general provision needed to protect rights, 9; have been violated when most needed, 257; implications from are dangerous, 96, 97n; James Madison favors, 257; majority of states have, 27; may be dangerous in a republic, 12; Monroe supports principles of, 13; necessary in a monarchy, 97; necessary without a reservation of power clause, 107; needed, 9, 13, 14, 23–27n, 30, 44, 48, 65, 67, 94, 95, 97, 103–4, 110, 111, 124, 125, 134, 135, 140, 212, 334, 360, 437, 454; no objection to these kinds of amendments, 222; not endangered by Constitution, 231; not included in Harrisburg Convention's amendments, 194; not needed, 9–10, 12, 29, 63, 96, 101, 105, 109, 225, 389; not needed in republics, 12; N.Y. constitution does not include, 60; N.Y. constitution serves as, 61; N.Y. constitutional convention considers, 61n; N.Y. legislature enacts (1787), 61n; originated in England, 101; as part of N.Y.'s ratification, 394; people favor, 137; praise of, 13; proposed by Va. Convention, 8n, 456; protection of rights amendments will be obtained from first Congress, 262; questionable, 225; rejection of by Va. Convention previous to ratification of Constitution, 43; some states do not have, 12, 28, 95; some states have while others do not, 95;

as standard for trying public acts, 258; of states endangered by Constitution, 286, 473, 476; used as a foil by Antifederalists, 249; Va. charter was not a bill of rights, 32; Va. Declaration of Rights is no reason for, 27–28; will be adopted, 137, 400; William III and, 60

BINGHAM, WILLIAM (Philadelphia): nominated as candidate for U.S. House of Representatives, 368
—letter to, 174

BISHOP, JOHN (Pa.): as delegate to Harrisburg Convention, 177

BLACKSTONE, WILLIAM (Great Britain). See Political and legal writers and writings

BLAND, THEODORICK (Prince George Co., Va.; id., BoR, II, 490): asks for roll call in Va. Convention, 43n
—letters from, 291–92, 339–40n
—letter to, 255

BLITAZ, HENRY (Millford, Bucks Co., Pa.): attends Bucks Co. meeting, 172

BLOODWORTH, TIMOTHY (New Hanover Co., N.C.): id., 459
—speeches of in N.C. Convention, 97–98, 110–11n; responses to, 99, 111–12
—letter from, cited, 53n

BLYTH, BENJAMIN (Cumberland Co., Pa.): id., 459; chairs Cumberland Co. meeting, 164–65; on committee to draft Cumberland Co. circular letter, 166n; signs Cumberland Co. circular letter calling Harrisburg Convention, 166; as delegate to Harrisburg Convention, 177
—letter from, 164

"BON MOT—À PROPÔS": text of, 59

BOSTON: favors amendments when experience warrants, 429–30; newspapers in oppose amendments, 191; should elect Federalists to U.S. House of Representatives, 423; strongly Federalist, 219

"A BOSTONIAN": text of, 432–33

BOWDOIN, JAMES (Boston)
—letter to, 151

BRADLEY, DANIEL (Pa.): as delegate to Harrisburg Convention, 177

BRAND-HOLLIS, THOMAS (England): id., 459
—letter from, 315–17n

BREADING, NATHANIEL (Fayette Co., Pa.): signs election certificate for Harrisburg Convention, 170

BRISON, JAMES (Westmoreland Co., Pa.): Westmoreland Co., Pa., Antifederalist committee of correspondence, 132

BROADSIDES, PAMPHLETS, AND BOOKS: John Adams, Defence of the Constitutions, 127, 128n, 220, 221n, 315; Augustine Davis compilation of proposed amendments, 129, 208, 208n, 256–57, 260n, 473n; John Francis Mercer declares candidacy, 436–37, 437n; George Richards Minot's History of Shays's Rebellion, 151, 151n; N.Y. Convention Debates, 71n; William Paca's amendments in Md. Convention, 472n–76; Philadelphia procession of 4th of July 1788, 91n; "Truth," 230–31; Va. Convention Debates, 8n, 162, 244n; Va. Convention Journal, 162; James Wilson's oration on 4th of July 1788, 389, 389n. *See also* Political and legal writers and writings

BRYAN, GEORGE (Philadelphia): criticized as Antifederalist leader, 333; elected to Harrisburg Convention, 174, 174n, 175; as delegate to Harrisburg Convention, 177, 184, 194; fake letter from citing that Quakers opposed Constitution, 190, 191n

BUCHAN, EARL OF. *See* Erskine, David Steuart

BUCKS COUNTY, PA.: meeting and resolutions to elect delegates to Harrisburg Convention, 172–74; meeting of praised for moderation, 186, 187n, 203, 206n

BURKE, AEDANUS (Lower District, S.C.)
—letter from, cited, 53n

BURNLEY, HARDIN (Orange Co., Va.): id., 459
—letter from, 425–26

CABELL, WILLIAM, SR. (Amherst Co., Va.): id., 459; supports James Monroe's candidacy for U.S. representative, 421, 456–57, 457n
—letter to, cited, 255n

CADWALADER, LAMBERT (Hunterdon Co., N.J.)
—letter to, 182

CALDWELL, DAVID (Rowan Co., N.C./Iredell Co., N.C.): id., 459
—speech of in N.C. Convention, 117–18

"CAMILLUS," 244n; text of, 238–39; response to, 232–33

CAMPBELL, ARTHUR (Washington Co., Va.): id., 459; as author of "Many," 66n

CAMPBELL, CHARLES (Westmoreland Co., Pa.): Westmoreland Co., Pa., Antifederalist committee of correspondence, 132

CANADA: militia needed to protect U.S. from, 125

CANNON, DANIEL (Fayette Co., Pa.): signs election certificate for Harrisburg Convention, 170

CAPITAL, U.S.: Congress' jurisdiction should be limited to police and good order, 181; danger of, 67, 77; danger of Congress' jurisdiction over, 120; debate over location of in Confederation Congress, 160, 201,

224, 390; defense of Congress' jurisdiction over, 396–98; denial that juries in will be tools of political parties, 37; New York City wants to remain, 149–50; New York City will lose if N.Y. doesn't ratify, 87, 393; Philadelphia will become if N.Y. doesn't ratify soon, 87; population of will be diverse, 37

CAPTURES: no jury trials in cases of, 34. *See also* Admiralty law

CAREY, MATHEW (Philadelphia)
—letter to, 87

CARLISLE, PA.: Antifederalists celebrate 4th of July in, 82–83n. *See also* Cumberland Co., Pa.

CARMICHAEL, WILLIAM (Chestertown Co., Md./Spain)
—letters to, 137, 445; cited, 137

CARRINGTON, EDWARD (Powhatan Co., Va.; id., BoR, II, 491): opposes Va.'s resolution calling on Congress to call a second convention, 344; wants to publish Madison's letter supporting amendments, 356
—letters from, 123, 253–54n, 261–62, 272–73, 284–85, 352–54, 360, 378, 449; cited, 91n, 272, 273n, 284, 311, 312n, 352, 360, 378n
—letters to, cited, 253, 360

CARTER, CHARLES (Stafford Co., Va.)
—letter to, quoted, 84, 85n, 276n

CARTER, ROBERT (Westmoreland Co., Va.)
—letter to, cited, 439n

"CASSANDRA": text of, 64–66n

"CASSIUS": text of, 196–98

CATHOLICS: Antifederalists say that Roman Catholicism will be established church in America, 270

CELEBRATIONS: Antifederalists celebrate 4th of July in Carlisle, Pa., 82–83n; New York City procession is being planned, 91; Philadelphia procession account in newspaper, 91; throughout the U.S. for 4th of July and ratification, 90–91; Windham, Conn., celebrates N.H. ratification, 68–69

CENSUS: direct taxes apportioned based upon, 308

"CENTINEL" (Samuel Bryan), 324n; quoted, 367n; revival of cited, 364–65, 367n; text of, 250–52, 282–84, 348–49

CHASE, SAMUEL (Baltimore, Md.): 237n; id., 460; as candidate for Md. House of Delegates, 209, 210n, 211–13, 211n, 213n; continues opposition to Constitution after Md. ratification, 243; defended, 238, 297; favors a second convention, 243; favors acquiescence by Antifederalists, 212
—letter from, cited, 53n

INDEX 485

CHECKS AND BALANCES: insufficient in Constitution, 412
—needed, 382; but should not be excessive, 429; to protect property, 16
See also Impeachment; Separation of powers
"CHRISTIAN FARMER," 282n; text of, 280–82
CHRISTIANITY: best religion to make good members of society through morality, 117
"A CITIZEN OF NEW-HAVEN" (Roger Sherman), 436; text of, 433–36
CIVIL WAR: American Revolution was, 304; Antifederalist fears of are dismissed, 305; Antifederalists predict if amendments are not adopted, 190, 194n, 204, 234; danger from Antifederalists, 168, 176; danger if Constitution is defeated, 265; danger of under Constitution, 166, 432; delegates to Harrisburg Convention unable to kindle, 184; fear of in postwar America, 382; hated, 278; if N.Y. rejects Constitution, 393; opponents of amendments willing to provoke, 376; possible without federal control over militia, 209; second convention will lead to, 422
"CIVIS": text of, 192–93
CLARK, ABRAHAM (Essex Co., N.J.): id., 460; participates in Congress' transmittal of Constitution to the states, 91, 92n
—letter from, 91–92
CLASSICAL ANTIQUITY: Amphyctionic Council, 116; ancient republics rested liberty on general feeling and opinion, 407; Caligula, 256; Euclid, 365; Herculean task, 424; Horace, *Satires, Epistles and Ars Poetica*, 326, 327n; Livy, *History of Rome*, 316; Nero, 256; Philip of Macedon, 116, 117n
—Rome: compared unfavorably to future U.S. capital, 77; dictatorial powers in during crises, 74, 81n; had a medley of constitutions, 326–27
CLAY, JOSEPH (Chatham Co., Ga.): id., 460
—letter from, 145
—letter to, 437–38
CLERGY: prohibited from holding office in some state constitutions, 443, 445n
CLINTON, CHARLES, JR. (Ulster Co., N.Y.)
—letters to, 191–92n, 378n
CLINTON, DE WITT (New York City): id., 460
—letters from, 191–92n, 378n
CLINTON, GEORGE (New York City/Ulster Co., N.Y.; id., BoR, II, 492): criticized by Hamilton before publication of Constitution, 139n; sent letters from Va. Antifederalists, 52n; as a violent Antifederalist, 396
—speeches of to N.Y. legislature, 5–6, 448, 448n

—letters from, 413; quoted, 52n
—letters to, 136; cited, 413n
CLINTON, SAMUEL (Huntingdon, Pa.): rioter in Huntingdon, Pa., 171
COGSWELL, THOMAS (Gilmantown, N.H.; id., BoR, II, 492): as author of "The Farmer," 85n
COINAGE: Congress should have power to coin money, 132. *See also* Money; Paper money
COLLIN, NICHOLAS (Philadelphia): id., 460; as author of "Foreign Spectator," 264n
—letter from, cited, 264n
COMMERCE: Americans interested in, 332; conflict between navigating and non-navigating states, 72; Congress should have power to regulate, 65, 132, 432; Congress' power over needs further explanation, 181; Constitution will promote, 232, 245, 323, 422, 423; Constitution would benefit Philadelphia, 230; defense of Congress' power to enact laws for with simple majority, 371; importance of union with North and South, 89, 302, 328; is improving, 328; laws concerning should be approved by two-thirds vote of both houses of Congress, 476; merchants favor the Constitution, 388; N.Y. dominates commerce of N.J. and Conn., 73, 141, 142n; smuggling always a problem in America, 306; suffering under Confederation, 266; Union beneficial for, 89
COMMON DEFENSE: can only be secured by a confederacy of republican states, 179; Constitution will protect against foreign enemies, 288; danger of foreign conquest if Constitution is defeated, 265; endangers rights, 45–46; as the great object of government, 321. *See also* Army; Army, standing; Militia; Military; War
COMMON LAW: adopted in Va., 24, 34; Constitution will allow Congress to replace with civil law, 25; defense of omission of protection for in Constitution, 28, 34; different trials under, 100; fortified by English Bill of Rights, 36; frequently changed in England, 34; jury trials under in England, 25; not included in Constitution, 24; sometimes changes needed in, 34–35. *See also* Political and legal writers and writings, William Blackstone
COMPACT THEORY OF GOVERNMENT: Articles of Confederation referred to as, 27; should not give up natural rights, 53; Constitution is a defective compact, 46–47; Constitution is not a compact of states, 103; Constitution is with enumer-

ated powers, 32; Constitution will destroy compact between Va. and the people, 24; natural rights need to be reserved in, 140; nature of, 44, 104; Va. Declaration of Rights as, 23; violated if election not exercised worthily, 247
CONCORD, N.H.: as site of second session of the N.H. Convention, 59n
CONCURRENT POWERS: criticism of, 104; danger of, 97–98; defense of, 105
CONDORCET, MARQUIS DE (France): strictures on Constitution sent to Edmund Randolph, 138
CONFEDERATION CONGRESS: cannot enforce treaties, 106; died in June 1788, 292; inability to collect taxes, 296; needs power over commerce, 65, 132, 432; ordinance implementing Constitution, 150, 160, 182, 183, 222, 309, 364, 390; resolution of 21 February 1787 read in N.C. Convention, 94n; too weak, 14, 65, 94, 135, 333, 411; transmits Constitution to states, 91
CONGRESS, U.S.: alone allowed to propose amendments, 193; amendments via preferable, 455; amendments will be first order of business in, 139, 233, 359, 409; Antifederalists should be elected to, 318, 250–51; Antifederalists should not be elected to, 215, 276; Antifederalists striving to elect, 203; anxious to see actions on amendments, 151; can do anything that is not prohibited, 30; cannot adopt amendments, 7; Constitution requires sitting at least annually, 15; power to regulate elections is not dangerous, 194–95, 231; criticism of power to regulate, 67, 133, 180, 217, 475; criticism of requirement to publish journals, 15; danger from, 165; danger that it will be too cautious and timid, 226; denial it will have too much power, 365, 371; everything depends on its successful governing, 223; Federalists alone should be elected to, 245, 246–48; Federalists who oppose amendments should not be elected to, 161; future government of U.S. will take tone from, 251; Harrisburg Convention nominates candidates for, 163n, 183, 196, 206; importance of first appointments to, 229; importance of in gaining support of the people, 387; limitations in Article I, section 9 are insufficient, 30; members of ineligible for other offices, 434, 476; members of would be elected to a second convention, 457; must be given the chance to perform well, 408; needs more power than Confederation Congress, 132; no danger from as they are

representatives of the people, 109; opposition to two-thirds vote in each house for laws, 433–34; prohibitions on defended, 287; receives Va. and N.Y. resolutions requesting second convention, 6; should consider amendments recommended by state conventions, 42–43; should have all general powers, 179; should not be able to reduce its size, 133; should propose amendments, 255, 313; voters must not elect those who favor tyrannical government, 160; will be servants of the people, 10; will be virtuous, 409; will have too much power, 24, 26, 67, 119, 133, 334; will not propose amendments, 281; will propose some amendments, 285
CONNECTICUT: Convention of would have preferred amendments, 224–25; Convention Antifederalists acquiesce, 205, 206n; Federalists dominant in, 293; has ratified, 90; N.Y. dominates commerce of, 73, 141, 142n; N.Y. out of the Union would be threatened by, 73, 80
CONSCIENCE, LIBERTY OF: Constitution does not endanger, 42, 269, 365; Constitution endangers, 77, 120; endangered in Va., 257; public opinion in U.S. would restrict, 257; should be guaranteed to everyone, 362; will be protected by amendments, 444–45; will be protected if needed, 408
CONSCIENTIOUS OBJECTION: amendment needed to protect, 362; Constitution will not endanger, 363; protected in Md. minority amendments, 476; protected in Va. Convention amendments, 56
"CONSISTENCY": text of, 421–23
CONSTITUTION, U.S.: as an entire revolution without war or bloodshed, 123, 411; best plan offered to the world, 275; copy sent to Jefferson, 90; defective most capitally, 43; described as beautiful combination of strength and liberty, 197; excellence of consists in its brevity and perspicuity, 218; is imperfect, 41, 64–65, 164–65, 217, 250, 268, 276, 312, 334, 367, 389, 412; is imperfect but not as bad as Articles of Confederation, 420; not lacking fundamental principles, 5; transmitted to states by Confederation Congress, 91, 92n; unique in history, 40
—ambiguity of, 24, 26, 35, 40, 74, 111, 113, 119, 121, 140, 177, 243, 303, 304; will be explained by amendments, 35; will be explained by members of Congress, 35; none about Congress' power to emancipate slaves, 46

INDEX

—described as metaphor: this Bantling, 361; the building agreeably to the most modern taste, 274; a complex machine, 266; the fabric, 123, 313, 324, 401; the fair fabrick, 152; the federal edifice, 69n; a fiend come from the regions of darkness to enslave, 266; the glorious fabrick of American greatness, 233; glorious system of Federal Government, 425; a good canvas, 124; the grand system, 141; the guardian angel of America, sent from Heaven, 266; the harbinger of future peace and prosperity, 219; hitherto unequalled fabric, 247; the legitimate offspring of the people, 218; a machine, 199; the Magna Charta of America, 227–28; a messenger of good tidings, 219; the most magnificent edifice of government and liberty, 68; our fœderal barque, 187; our glorious fabric, 141; the sheet anchor of our hope as a people, 425; the Ship, 292; The Ship Constitution, 355; a stately edifice, 274; the whole fabric, 445; wisdom of ages reduced to practice, 315; a wolf in Sheep's clothing, 439
CONSTITUTIONAL CONVENTION: defense of delegates, 143, 205; denial of celestial influence over, 26; had to contend with jarring and discordant views, 275; needed, 333; R.I. refused to send delegation to, 149, 149n; resolution of implementing Constitution not adopted by states, 292; small group of selfish and artful men gained control of, 334; sought general welfare, 275; thanked, 108; Va. appoints delegates to, 88; was only a first step laying a foundation, 281–82
—criticism of for: management, 198; not having prayers at beginning of sessions, 282; violating Articles of Confederation and instructions, 77, 80, 122, 122n–23n; violating instructions and Congress' resolution, 118; exceeding its powers, 94, 120, 281–82; Pa. Antifederalists censure Pa. delegates to, 163n
—praise of, 112, 121, 142, 184, 227, 236, 268, 276; delegates for understanding their infallibility, 274; delegates as patriots, 268
CONSTITUTIONAL CONVENTION, SECOND: amendments should be submitted to, 135; Antifederalists will support in U.S. Congress, 123; can be called by Congress on request of two-thirds of states, 145; cannot be limited, 240, 244; could destroy Constitution, 146–47, 214, 377, 448; dangerous, 136, 145–46, 147, 175; delegates to

should not be given instructions, 138; favored, 137, 179; hard to get, 67; hopeful for success of, 198; influence of N.Y. circular letter in Va. in calling, 188; is premature, 153, 326; Madison opposes, 130; Mass. should not oppose, 225; might cause anarchy and confusion, 214; opponents of want discord and convulsion and are U.S. enemies, 374; opposition to, 62, 183, 290, 313, 361, 401, 454–56; Patrick Henry favors, 208; probably will not succeed, 435; resolution for in Va. House of Delegates, 339, 340n; should be delayed, 222; should be immediately called to meet in three years, 254; should meet as soon as possible, 178–79, 318, 373; should meet in three or four years, 221; should only be called on extraordinary occasions, 455; state legislatures can call, 7; sufficient number of state legislatures will not request, 253; support for N.Y.'s circular letter call for, 88n, 145, 146, 149, 158, 221–22, 262; uncertainty of, 147, 150; Va. resolution requesting Congress to call, 4; will be actuated by party spirit, 262; will be called by first federal Congress, 175; will be called immediately after ratification of Constitution, 92; will delay implementation of Constitution, 142, 216; will fail, 141; will not be called, 449; will not represent both the people and states, 454; will take too long to amend Constitution, 197, 244. See also Amendments to the Constitution; Antifederalists
"CONSTITUTIONALIST," 432, 433n
CONSTITUTIONS, STATE: based on best models and noblest principles of civil liberty, 333; cannot be abrogated by any federal power, 440; Congress should not pass laws that subvert, 134; defects of, 444; endangered by U.S. Constitution, 286, 473; federal officers ought to take oath not to violate, 390–91; guarantee jury trials in civil cases, 15, 279; guardians of liberty, 364, 407, 412; have all powers not expressly reserved, 32; inferior to U.S. Constitution's supremacy clause, 36–37; most excellent in the world will be destroyed by U.S. Constitution, 334; need bills of rights, 102; only grant enumerated powers, 75; protect rights, 23, 65, 76; protect freedom of the press, 122, 122n; provide equal representation for unequal counties, 443; reserved rights are specified in, 10; rights protected in remain under U.S. Constitution, 180; should stay in effect under U.S. Constitution, 180; some do not have bills

of rights, 12, 28, 95; some have bills of rights while some do not, 95; treaties should not violate, 476. *See also* Bill of rights
CONTEE, BENJAMIN (Charles Co., Md.)
—letter from, cited, 264n
CONTINENTAL CONGRESS, SECOND: resolution calls for drafting state constitutions, 60, 61n
CONTRACTS, OBLIGATION OF: Constitution's prohibition of impairment of, 397; federal judiciary can hear cases involving, 452–53; violated under Articles of Confederation, 257. *See also* Paper money; Tender acts
CONVENTIONS, STATE: most favor amendments, 281, 301; adopt Constitution by small majorities, 281, 318, 373, 386; amendments proposed by should be adopted, 179; Antifederalists in have acquiesced, 68, 203, 335; criticism of those that recommended amendments, 265; favor a bill of rights, 137; recommend amendments, 266; R.I. has not called, 3, 90, 217; six have adopted the Constitution without recommended amendments, 138–39; some instruct future members of Congress to seek amendments, 193; sovereignty resides in, 7. *See also* Antifederalists; Ratification, process of
"THE CONVERSION": text of, 406–7
CORBIN, FRANCIS (Middlesex Co., Va.): id., 461; opposes Va.'s resolution requesting Congress to call a second convention, 344, 347; in Va. House of Delegates, 297–98
—letter from, 263, 344
CORRUPTION: danger of monopolies from Congress because of, 280; guarded against in election of President, 403; likely under Constitution and Senate, 251, 419; unlikely in Senate, 419; likely under Constitution because of small House of Representatives, 133; unlikely in Congress unless the people are corrupt, 350; will probably not affect Senate in impeachment trials, 427–28
COULTER, JOHN (Baltimore, Md.): as candidate for Md. House of Delegates, 210n
COUNSEL, RIGHT TO: defense of Constitution's lack of protection for, 384; in Va. Convention amendments, 54
COXE AND FRAZIER (Philadelphia): id., 461
—letter from, 327
COXE, TENCH (Philadelphia; id., BoR, II, 492): as author of "An American Citizen," 8n, 445n, 456n; as a member of Philadelphia committee of correspondence, 183n, 186n
—letters from, 130–31, 203; quoted, 8n, 409n
—letters to, 150–51, 183, 293; cited, 51n, 186n
CRAWFORD, JOHN (Warwick, Bucks Co., Pa.): attends Bucks Co. meeting, 172; elected to Harrisburg Convention, 174
CREVECOEUR, ST. JOHN DE (France/New York City): id., 461
—letter from, 151, 395–96
CROOKS, JAMES (Pa.): as delegate to Harrisburg Convention, 177
CUMBERLAND COUNTY, PA.: circular letter calling Harrisburg Convention, 3, 165, 169, 170–71, 172, 176, 176n, 184, 186, 186n, 189, 190, 204; meeting calls for amendments, 164–65, 167. *See also* Carlisle, Pa.
CUTTING, JOHN BROWN (Boston/London): id., 461
—letter from, 215–16
—letters to, 86; cited, 215

DANA, FRANCIS (Cambridge, Mass.)
—speech of in Mass. Convention cited, 301
DAVIE, WILLIAM R. (Halifax Town, N.C.): id., 461
—speech of in N.C. Convention, 105–6; reference to, 113; response to, 94
DAVIS, AUGUSTINE (Richmond, Va.): id., 129; as compiler of pamphlet edition of amendments, 129, 208, 208n, 473n; as printer of *Virginia Independent Chronicle*, 66n
DAWES, THOMAS, JR. (Boston)
—speech of in Mass. Convention quoted, 279, 280n
DAWSON, JOHN (Spotsylvania Co., Va.): id., 461
—letter from, 290
—letter to, 413
DEBT, U.S.: Constitution will help payment of, 160; foreign creditors might resort to violence if Constitution is defeated, 266; holders of military certificates fear for payment under Constitution, 69; U.S. is loaded with, 217
DEBTORS: endangered by British creditors access to U.S. Supreme Court, 41; should pay their debts to British creditors, 11
DEBTS, PRIVATE: Americans loaded with, 217; Constitution will alleviate problems of, 423; hard for creditors to get payment of, 266; widespread in postwar America, 381

INDEX 489

DECLARATION OF INDEPENDENCE: lists violation of jury trials as a violated right, 100, 102n, 278, 280n; quoted, 61, 61n, 393. *See also* American Revolution
DELAWARE: has ratified, 90
DEMAGOGUES: Antifederalists are, 268, 270; danger of if Constitution is rejected, 35; gain election in postwar America, 381; Patrick Henry denies he is one, 47; trimmers not to be trusted, 447
DEMOCRACY: will disappear under Constitution, 128; democratic government best suited for dignity of human species, 357. *See also* Government, debate over nature of; Republican form of government
DESCENT: Congress can enact laws concerning, 452
"A DESPISER OF DEMAGOGUES, WOULD-BE-ATS, AND WHEELBARROW-MEN": text of, 193
DESPOTISM: Constitution will create, 70, 132, 283–84, 348, 406; God will protect America from, 127. *See also* Tyranny
DICKEY, JOHN (Pa.): as delegate to Harrisburg Convention, 177
DISCOURSE: candor and reason needed, 62, 88, 414, 455; civil debate in Va. Convention, 88; civility to be used in essays by "Republican," 89; important to keep on solid basis of truth, 280–81; necessary in a free society, 303–4; need temper and moderation in discussing amendments, 296; needed in debating Constitution, 205; needed in N.Y. Convention, 72; praise of debate over ratification, 90; praise of public debate on the Constitution, 265–66
DIVISION OF POWER: defense of Constitution's provision for, 286, 366; Mass. Convention amendments will provide correct balance, 309–10; necessary through transfer of power under Constitution, 444; proper division should be made, 334; sharp line cannot be drawn in infant America, 286, 288–89. *See also* Government, debate over nature of; Sovereignty
DOMESTIC INSURRECTION. *See* Civil war; Insurrection, domestic; Order; Violence
DOUBLE JEOPARDY: prohibited in Md. minority's amendments, 473
DRUSBACK, SIMON (Pa.): as candidate for Harrisburg Convention, 195
DU PONCEAU, PETER S. (Philadelphia): id., 461
—letter from, 357–58
DUER, WILLIAM (New York City): id., 461–62
—letter from, 377

"E": text of, 336n–37n
EASTERN STATES: Antifederalists in acquiesce, 126; New Englanders object to Constitution's prohibition of religious tests, 257. *See also* North versus South
EDUCATION: importance of, 363
ELECTIONS: beware of lies during, 226; free and frequent needed, 16, 63; free and frequent needed in Va. Convention amendments, 54; officeholders should regularly stand for re-election, 54
ELECTIONS, U.S.: amendment to limit Congress' power to regulate is unnecessary, 194–95; Congress' power to regulate will not perpetuate representatives for life, 231; criticism of Congress' power to regulate, 67, 133, 180, 217, 475
"AN ELECTOR," 430, 431n; text of, 424–25
ELLIOT, BENJAMIN (Huntingdon Co., Pa.): id., 462; as delegate to Harrisburg Convention, 177; as sheriff of Huntingdon, Pa., and potential violence, 171–72
—letter from, 171–72, 172n
EMOLUMENTS: only for public service in Va. Convention amendments, 54; defense of Constitution's provision concerning, 398–400
ENUMERATED POWERS: cannot list all that might be needed, 287; Congress has only, 42, 96, 97, 101, 109, 113; Congress should only have, 132, 473; Congress will have with only a few implied powers, 365; Constitution is a compact with, 32; Constitution only has, 10, 14, 28, 29; of Constitution will not violate rights, 32; denial that Congress is limited to, 30; Harrisburg Convention amendment limiting Congress to, 179; Harrisburg Convention amendment limiting President and judiciary to, 180; only given to government in state constitutions and Articles of Confederation, 74, 81n. *See also* Reserved powers
EQUITY JURISDICTION: different trials under, 100; no jury trials in, 111–12
ERSKINE, DAVID STEUART (Earl of Buchan) (Scotland)
—letter to, 216–17
ERWIN, NATHANIEL (Warrington, Bucks Co., Pa.): attends Bucks Co. meeting, 173; elected to Harrisburg Convention, 174
EUROPE: cases involving should come before federal courts, 450–51; countries in do not have reserved powers, 23; danger to U.S. from, 330; opposition in to re-eligibility of President, 136; pleased with Constitution, 313–14; relies heavily on excise taxes, 307; would view second convention

as a dark and threatening cloud, 313–14. See also Governments, ancient and modern; Great Britain
EVIDENCE: access to in Va. Convention amendments, 54
EX POST FACTO LAW: Constitution prohibits, 30–31, 323; criticism of use of to protect speculators in Continental currency, 30–31; danger from Constitution's prohibition of, 31, 40; defense of Constitution's prohibition of, 384
EXCISE TAX. See Taxation
EXETER, N.H.: as site of first session of the N.H. Convention, 59n
EXPENSES OF GOVERNMENT: privy council would be costly, 417; will be too high under Constitution, 91; will not be expensive to carry case to Supreme Court, 38–39
EXPORTS: Pa. minority amendment would allow taxes on, 294; tax on prohibited, 370
EXTRADITION: Constitution's provision concerning, 397

"THE FARMER" (Thomas Cogswell), 85n
FARMERS: U.S. House of Representatives will have fellow-feeling with, 35; most yeomen are Antifederalists, 47. See also Agriculture; Planters
FARRES, JAMES (Plumstead, Bucks Co., Pa.): attends Bucks Co. meeting, 173
FAYETTE COUNTY, PA.: election certificate for Harrisburg Convention delegate, 170
"A FEDERAL CENTINEL," 203, 203n, 249n; text of, 203–6
"FEDERAL COMMONWEALTH": text of, 237–38
"A FEDERAL REPUBLICAN": text of, 410–13; thought to be Melancton Smith, 413n
"FEDERALISM," 238, 239n, 297n; text of, 233–37
FEDERALISM: Constitution would create federal government dominant over states, 61. See also Division of power; Government, debate over nature of; Republican form of government
"A FEDERALIST" (multiple items), 155n, 161, 265n; texts of, 156–58, 239–42, 273–74, 364–67, 367–68
"The Federalist" (Publius) (Alexander Hamilton, James Madison, and John Jay), 158, 360
"A FEDERALIST WHO IS FOR AMENDMENTS": text of, 372–74
FEDERALISTS: accused of selfish motives, 80; agree that Constitution is imperfect, 64–65, 92, 334; agree that some amendments should be approved, 401; allegedly never supported amendments, 191, 349; criticized for opposing amendments, 153–54; deception of, 58, 144, 239, 251, 256, 280, 318, 349; disregard voice of the people, 153–54; divide over amendments, 340, 353, 360; have brought together union of sentiment throughout U.S., 327; in Mass. Convention praised for conciliation, 156; in Mass. support amendments, 314; and use of word "federal," 81n, 392; must be vigilant but mild against Antifederalists, 131; in N.C. Convention are hopeful, 92; in N.Y. Convention uncertain about ratification, 87; in N.Y. renege on their promise in Convention, 412–13; opponents of amendments called the real friends to our country, 236; oppose amendments, 231–32, 391; questionable support for amendments, 354; seek federal offices, 153, 333; should be elected to U.S. House of Representatives, 152–53, 159, 238, 245, 246–48, 260, 421; should be elected to Md. House of Delegates, 209, 210; should be elected to Pa. Assembly, 185; some want protecting individual rights, 257; still have differences with Antifederalists, 239–42; vilify Antifederalist leaders, 282; want amendments proposed by Congress, 3
—called: "Consolidarians," 58; arbitrary Aristocraticks, 161; Aristocratical tyrants, 160; blind persecuting zealots, 65; headstrong aristocrats, 153; men of abilities and established reputation, 338; a scheming junto, 162
—strength of, 449; strong in Boston, 219; dominant in Conn., 293; control newspapers in N.H., 58; gain ground in Va., 152; will have a majority in U.S. House and Senate, 415
—in Va.: divided in House of Delegates, 353, 360; fear Antifederalists in House of Delegates, 298; gain ground in, 152; have a majority in House of Delegates, 158; in Convention favor amendments, 69
FINDLEY, WILLIAM (Westmoreland Co., Pa.): did not attend Harrisburg Convention, 195; nominated for U.S. House of Representatives, 336, 344, 368, 376
FINES, EXCESSIVE: danger of under Constitution, 25; not endangered by Constitution, 384; prohibited in Va. Convention amendments, 55
FINLEY, JAMES (Fayette Co., Pa.): as delegate to Harrisburg Convention, 175; signs election certificate for Harrisburg Convention, 170

INDEX

FITCH, JOHN (N.J.)
—letter to, 87
FLACK, SAMUEL (Warwick, Bucks Co., Pa.): attends Bucks Co. meeting, 172
FLEMING, CHARLES (Springfield, Bucks Co., Pa.): attends Bucks Co. meeting, 172
FLEMING, GEORGE (Richmond, Va.): as safe Antifederalist conveyance for mail, 52n, 355
FLORIDA: militia needed to protect Americans from, 125
FOREIGN AFFAIRS: diplomatic immunity provided in law of nations, 37n; as a main point in Constitution, 209; sole area for federal government, 334; U.S. should stay aloof from Europe, 331. *See also* Europe; Treaties
FOREIGN OPINION OF THE U.S.: amendments will help raise, 309–10; Constitution will raise, 10, 123, 152, 154, 202, 305, 333, 374, 414, 422, 443; low under Confederation, 10, 266, 382; will fall if Constitution is rejected, 145; will suffer if Americans are oppressed, 334
"FOREIGN SPECTATOR" (Nicholas Collin), 264n; text of, 264n–67, 285–89, 293–96, 305–9, 321–23, 329–32, 341–44, 349–52, 361–63, 368–72n, 379–81, 383–86, 396–400, 402–5, 417–19, 426–29, 440–42, 449–53
FOREIGNERS: impediments imposed on by state constitutions, 443–44; American debtors endangered by British creditors access to U.S. Supreme Court, 41; American debtors should pay their debts to British creditors, 11
FORTS, MAGAZINES, AND ARSENALS: defense of Congress' jurisdiction over, 396, 397–98; militia needed to guard, 125
FRANCE: experiencing unrest, 304; Henry IV killed, 362; struggle in for liberty, 314; U.S. dangerously allied with, 155; uses civil law, 25
"FRANÇOIS DE LA E——.": text of, 388–89
FRANKLIN, BENJAMIN (Philadelphia; id., BoR, II, 494): defense of as delegate to Constitutional Convention, 205
—last speech in Constitutional Convention quoted, 84, 85n
—letter from, 285
—letters to, 171–72; cited, 171, 172n
"A FREEMAN" (multiple items), 190n, 288, 289n; text of, 184, 189–90, 246–48
"A FRIEND OF SOCIETY AND LIBERTY," 131; text of, 145
"A FRIEND TO AMENDMENTS," 311n; text of, 153–54, 337–39

491

"A FRIEND TO CONSISTENCY AND STABILITY IN GOVERNMENT": text of, 274–76
"A FRIEND TO GOOD GOVERNMENT": text of, 92
"A FRIEND TO LIBERTY AND UNION": text of, 332–37n; response to, 364–67, 367n
"A FRIEND TO THE PEOPLE," 339n; text of, 310–11
"A FRIEND TO TRUTH AND FREEDOM": text of, 332–33
FRUGALITY: Va. Declaration of Rights says it is needed to maintain liberty, 14. *See also* Virtue

GALBRAITH, ROBERT (Huntingdon Co., Pa.)
—letter from, 171–72, 172n
GALLATIN, ALBERT (Fayette Co., Pa.): id., 462; as delegate to Harrisburg Convention, 177; election certificate for as Harrisburg Convention delegate, 170
GALLAWAY, JAMES (Rockingham Co., N.C.): id., 462
—speech of in N.C. Convention, 94
GARDNER, JOSEPH (Pa.): as delegate to Harrisburg Convention, 177, 195
GARDOQUI, DON DIEGO DE (Spain): negotiates with John Jay, 110, 111n
GEDDIS, HENRY (Plumstead, Bucks Co., Pa.): attends Bucks Co. meeting, 173
"GEHENNAPOLIS": quoted, 264n–65n, 267n
GENERAL WARRANTS: Constitution will allow use of, 44; are dangerous and thus prohibited in Md. minority amendments, 474; defense of Constitution's lack of protection from, 26, 33, 49, 384–85; federal judiciary will not allow, 33; prohibited in Va. Convention amendments, 55; state judiciaries will not allow, 33
GENERAL WELFARE: amendments will not serve, 146; Americans support over local interests, 151–52; Antifederalists don't seek to benefit, 249; compromise necessary to support, 93; Congress needs power for, 287; Constitution would not benefit, 348; Constitutional Convention sought, 275; danger from broad interpretation of, 9; as end of government, 53, 73, 476; will empower Congress to emancipate slaves, 46
GENERAL WELFARE CLAUSE: danger from, 27
GEORGIA: has ratified, 90; prohibits clergy from holding public office, 445n
GERMANS: address to in Md., 211–13; none attend Harrisburg Convention, 190
GERMANTOWN, PA.: Blair M'Clanachan elected from to Harrisburg Convention, 174; meeting appointed delegates to Lan-

caster Convention, 254; meeting called to elect delegates to Harrisburg Convention, 167–69n
GERRY, ELBRIDGE (Cambridge, Mass.): as candidate for U.S. Senate, 153, 154n, 191
GIBSON, THOMAS (Plumstead, Bucks Co., Pa.): attends Bucks Co. meeting, 173
GOD: asked for help in defeating amendments, 219; asked to give N.Y. Convention wisdom, 87; a constitution from would be opposed by Antifederalists, 325; Constitution is not given by, 64–65, 282; did not order prevalence of tyranny in the world, 456; even a constitution created by would be inadequate without good administration, 248; gave man natural rights that are inalienable, 104; has protected Americans, 80, 127, 153, 154, 155, 157–58, 161, 302; hope for intervention to stop civil war in western Pa., 168; only knows how debate over amendments will end, 223; sent Constitution to save America from impending ruin, 266; some say Constitution came from Heaven, 397; will protect America from anarchy, 127; will protect America from despotism, 127
GORDON, JAMES, JR. (Orange Co., Va.): id., 462
—letter from, 158–59
—letter to, cited, 158
GOVERNMENT, DEBATE OVER NATURE OF: aim of is common benefit, protection, and security of people, 53; all power derived from the people, 9–10, 16–17, 42, 53, 61, 63–64, 74, 106–7, 247; Americans are learning process of governing, 205; Americans better acquainted with nature of government, 106–7; Americans know more about defining and delegating powers, 304; compromise must be sought, 329; Congress should only have minimum necessary powers, 133; Constitution creates a consolidated government, 78, 91, 95, 120, 132, 252; Constitution is a defective compact, 46–47; Constitution is based on people not on states, 106; Constitution is best form of government, 217; Constitution is not a compact of states, 103; a constitution is nothing without wise and honest administration, 424; Constitution will create an energetic government, 68, 364, 443, 447; Constitution will create government of men and not of laws, 39; Constitution will lead to unwieldy government, 334; Constitution will prove people can govern themselves, 221; Constitution would create a dominant federal government, 61; contracting parties are people of the states and state governments, 408–9; conventions are dangerous, 175; danger of constantly changing government, 275; danger of too little power in government, 259; danger of U.S. as national government instead of federal, 155; democratic government best suited for dignity of human species, 357; difficulty forming government to secure liberty and happiness, 73; efficiency of government to consist in giving power to great men, 357; end of government is impartial administration of justice, 277; end of government is safety, peace, and welfare of people, 73; energetic government needed, 35, 62, 185, 231, 255, 324; energetic government needed with amendments, 283; every society must estimate power of government and liberty, 281; in free governments majority rules but conciliatory, 192, 275; freest states have been ever the most powerful, 334; governments once established hard to regain liberty without violence, 173; government is strong when it protects rights of the people, 48; government like a mad horse, 80; governments are made up of three different branches, 277; governments with implied constitution need a bill of rights, 60; happiness as end of, 16, 106, 476; impossible to support free government opposed by many people, 373; improvement in came about through experience, 41; jealousy necessary to protect rights, 76, 116; liberty as end of, 16; liberty can only be secured by republican form of government, 132; liberty needs society to exist, 41; limited power can lead to relaxation of proper controls, 259; more efficient government needed, 178; national disputes not amicably settled via reason and equity, 265; natural rights cannot be given up in a compact, 53; nature of social compact, 44; need for a wise, energetic and free government, 231, 255; need to revisit fundamental principles, 14; new federal government will be somewhat national, 321, 323; no government can operate well without confidence of people, 6; origins of government, 73; party is the species of corruption in free states, 428; patriots will yield to torrent reserving strength for later, 358; perfection not to be expected, 62; powers delegated ought not to be indefinite or ambiguous, 304; powers once given are hard to recall, 85, 281, 455;

INDEX 493

rights and privileges of the people as end of government, 48; rights given up will be hard to regain, 79; rulers always try to abuse their power, 110; science of government still in infancy, 274; the simpler the government the easier to put it in motion, 357; social compact theory, 44, 104; some constructive power needed (implied), 286–87; stability and ease of government depends on custom and habit, 296; strong government needed to rule diversity in U.S., 151; those subverting government have advantage, 392; tyranny is a danger from wherever real power lies, 258; where power exists wrong will generally be done, 258. *See also* Despotism; Division of power; Separation of powers; Tyranny

GOVERNMENTS, ANCIENT AND MODERN
—France: experiencing unrest, 304; Henry IV killed, 362; struggle in for liberty, 314; U.S. dangerously allied with, 155; civil law used in, 25
—Germany: no reserved powers in, 23; civil law used in, 25
—The Netherlands: Antifederalists misquote as examples, 11; loan from obtainable because of expected new constitution, 314; tyranny of King Philip in, 73, 76, 81n
—Poland: election of king in, 136
—Prussia: treaty with U.S. prohibits letters of marque and reprisal, 316
—Rome: compared unfavorably to future U.S. capital, 77; dictatorial powers in during crises, 74, 81n; had a medley of constitutions, 326–27
—Russia: case of arrest of ambassador of, 36, 37n
—Spain: King Philip's oppression, 76; and negotiations over navigation of Mississippi River, 110, 111n; no reserved powers in, 23; tyranny of in The Netherlands, 73, 81n; uses civil law, 25
—Switzerland: Antifederalists misquotes as examples, 11; happiness thrives in, 155–56; no domestic insurrection in, 156; not involved in war, 156; U.S. government modeled on thirteen cantons of, 155
See also Europe; Foreign affairs; Great Britain

GRAND JURY INDICTMENT: danger of Constitution's lack of protection for, 279–80

GRAYDON, ALEXANDER (Dauphin Co., Pa.): id., 462
—letter from, 182

GRAYSON, WILLIAM (Prince William Co., Va.; id., BoR, II, 495): corresponds with N.Y. Antifederalists, 51n; elected U.S. senator from Va., 290, 339, 340, 361, 378, 405, 449; said to favor very strong government, 16; strongly opposes Edmund Randolph, 273; will probably be elected U.S. senator, 298
—speech in Va. Convention, 27; responses to, 16, 29
—letter from, cited, 52n

GREAT BRITAIN: bribery and corruption in, 63; dangerous use of general warrants to collect excise taxes in, 474; and U.S. debtors owe British creditors, 11, 41
—acts and charters: Declaratory Act (1766), 9, 84, 304, 305n; Intolerable Acts (1774), 105n; Stamp Act (1765), 98, 98n, 100; Sugar Act (1764), 98n
—and American Revolution: caused by oppression from, 24, 32, 41, 65, 72, 98, 100, 105, 230, 234, 250, 302, 333, 364, 374, 407; Gen. William Howe's incompetence during, 219, 220n; problem with smuggling in American colonies, 306
—Bill of Rights: defends only enumerated rights against king's prerogative, 14–15; fortifies common law, 36; settles disputes over king's powers, 9; originated because of king's oppression, 101; present some danger, 63; protects against king's prerogative, 12; protects right to jury trial, 41; restores primitive principles, 11
—constitution of: is changeable by Parliament, 37–38; future convention in would need representation from all branches of government, 456–57; has separated powers, 277; no reserved powers in, 23; oppose principle of reserved rights, 23; people share in government, 277; rights of in are enumerated, 14
—historical events: Civil War, 410–11
—House of Commons: size of, 435–36
—House of Lords: tries impeachment cases, 434
—legal and judicial system of: admiration in for jury trials, 100–101; common law frequently changed in, 34; common law jury trials in, 25; judiciary of does not protect right to challenge jurors, 38; judiciary praise of Jeffrey and Mansfield, 279; jury trial in the vicinage used under common law in, 26n–27n; jury trials in civil cases, 37–38, 277, 474; Star Chamber's oppression, 76, 82n; vice admiralty courts, 98n
—liberty in: burning of heretics abolished in, 35, 36n; liberty of the press not protected in, 15, 15n; protection for rights in, 28; religious tests in, 115; and suspension of habeas corpus, 44, 125

—Magna Carta, 475; admired by Americans, 63; defends only enumerated rights, 14–15; defends rights of the people, 11; originated because of king's oppression, 101; re-affirmed, 64n
—military of: standing army limited in, 15, 50, 51n
—monarchs: Cabal under Charles I, 394, 395n; Charles I as a tyrant, 60, 278, 410–11; Charles I executed, 278; dangerous powers of king, 63; king can do no wrong, 417, 419n; monarch at maximum strength, 63–64; prerogative powers of, 9, 12, 28, 95; William I, 63, 64n, 362; William III, 15, 209
—Parliament: constitution of is changeable by, 37–38; can suspend habeas corpus, 379; defends individual rights, 36; is supreme, 101, 102n; needs to approve a standing army, 50–51n; passes law punishing officers who arrest diplomats, 37n; restraints on in raising a standing army, 475; should meet frequently, 15
—Petition of Right, 60, 63
—political leaders of: Sir Edward Coke on Parliamentary supremacy, 102n; Cromwell, 410–11; John Wilkes case and general warrants, 385
—political, legal, philosophical, and literary writers and writings: John Hampden, 278; James Harrington, 316; John Milton, 73, 81n, 202, 202n, 316. *See also* Literary references
GREENSBURGH, WESTMORELAND CO., PA.: Antifederalist meeting supporting amendments, 131–34
GRIER, JOSEPH (Hilltown, Bucks Co., Pa.): attends Bucks Co. meeting, 173
GROUT, JONATHAN (Petersham, Mass.): as candidate for U.S. House of Representatives, 388
GURNEY, FRANCIS (Philadelphia): member of Philadelphia committee of correspondence, 186n

HABEAS CORPUS, WRIT OF: in cases of insurrection, 125; Constitution does not endanger, 230, 379–81; criticism of Constitution's provision concerning, 30, 31; importance of, 112; needs to be protected, 124, 135, 316; praise of, 27, 379; praise of Constitution's protection for, 15, 100; protected in England, 44, 125; protection for in Constitution disavows reserved power theory, 134; secured in N.Y. constitution, 74; sometimes necessary to suspend, 259

HAMILTON, ALEXANDER (New York City; id., BoR, II, 495): criticized George Clinton before publication of Constitution, 139n; plan of in Constitutional Convention, 121n
—letters from, 340, 377; cited, 378n
—letters to, 314–15n; cited, 51n, 314, 378n
HANCOCK, JOHN (Boston; id., BoR, II, 495): favors amendments, 5, 218, 314; opposes second convention, 5; proposed amendments in Mass. Convention, 220, 256, 299, 309–10
—speech of to Mass. General Court, quoted, 5, 84, 85n; draft of, 309–10
HAND, EDWARD (Lancaster, Pa.): nominated for U.S. House of Representatives, 368
HANNA, JAMES (Newtown, Bucks Co., Pa.): attends Bucks Co. meeting, 172; elected to Harrisburg Convention, 174; as delegate to Harrisburg Convention, 177; as leader of secret association of Antifederalists, 184; as secretary Bucks Co., Pa. meeting, 173, 174
—letters from, 169–70; cited, 176, 176n
HANNA, JOHN A. (Harrisburg, Pa.): id., 463; as delegate to Harrisburg Convention, 177; as secretary of Harrisburg Convention, 177, 181
HAPPINESS: absent under Articles of Confederation, 382; amendments needed for, 228, 302, 437, 456; Americans seek political happiness, 47; Americans will determine whether they have, 387; Antifederalists more concerned about themselves, 448; Antifederalists threaten, 205; bill of rights needed to preserve, 48; can only be secured by a confederacy of republican states, 179; colonies mostly experienced under British rule, 98; Constitution endangers, 41, 122, 472n; Constitution will promote, 10, 14, 16, 58, 121, 127, 152, 154, 217, 325, 327, 333, 374, 384, 389, 422; Constitution with amendments will promote, 309, 375; dependent on Constitution, 177, 233, 436; dependent on choice of government between a republic or aristocracy, 388; dependent on judiciary, 474; dependent on defeat of unamended Constitution, 348; dependent on people who are elected, 93; dependent on republican principles, 302; difficult to form government that would secure, 73; Edmund Pendleton attached to, 62; as end of government, 16, 106, 476; government suit genius of people to have, 26; hope for U.S., 144; as a natural right, 53; only a federal government could provide,

178; Pa. Antifederalists oppose for confederated America, 332–33; right of revolution should be used to obtain, 225; at stake in election of Congress, 247; thrives in Switzerland, 155–56; Union promotes, 41, 89; virtue needed for people to be, 152; Washington will promote as first President, 229; will occur in governments securing essential rights, 291
HARRIS, JOHN (Cumberland Co., Pa.): id., 463
—letter from, 293
HARRISBURG CONVENTION, 163–98; aim is not to amend but destroy Constitution, 197; amendments of are similar to Pa. Convention Antifederalists', 234; amendments of are unimportant, 196; amendments proposed by, 4, 180–82; amendments proposed by are unnecessary, 194; Antifederalists disappointed with, 188, 192; call of, 4, 130, 163n, 164, 165–66; called an unconstitutional and insignificant body, 196; called the Antifederal Conclave, 176; carried on with harmony and moderation, 186, 192; condemnation of, 197–98; danger from, 175; disparagement of delegates to, 193, 194; election of delegates to from Bucks Co., Pa., 172–74; no Germans or Quakers attend, 190; nominates candidates for U.S. House of Representatives and Pa. Assembly, 185, 187, 196; prefers amendments via a second convention, 244; proceedings of will be printed, 183, 188, 195, 222n; proceedings, resolutions, and petition, 4, 176–82; proposes that Pa. Assembly request Congress should call a convention, 243; purpose was to nominate candidates for U.S. House of Representatives, 188–89, 189–90; purpose was to nominate candidates for Pa. Assembly, 209; to recommend amendments, 175; secrecy in calling, 191, 254, 374; small and flawed representation to, 190–91; some delegates were hampered by instructions, 184; soon to meet, 149; Southern States prefer different amendments, 222; ticket of, 374–75
HARRISBURG, DAUPHIN COUNTY, PA.: originally called Louisburg, 182n
HARRISON, BENJAMIN (Charles City Co., Va.): strongly opposes Edmund Randolph, 273
HARTLEY, THOMAS (York Co., Pa.; id., BoR, II, 465)
—letters from, 183; cited, 186n
HAZARD, EBENEZER (New York City): id., 463
—letter from, 87
HEATH, WILLIAM (Roxbury, Mass.; id., BoR, II, 496): criticism of, 157–58, 158n; criticism of speech of in Mass. Convention, 157, 158n; as possible author of "Solon," 155n, 156, 201n, 232n; praise of, 161
—letter to, cited, 158n
HENDERSON, ANDREW
—letter from, 171–72, 172n; cited, 171, 172n
HENRY, PATRICK (Prince Edward Co., Va.): id., 463; asks for roll call in Va. Convention, 43n; continues opposition to Constitution after Va.'s ratification, 243; corresponds with N.Y. Antifederalists, 51n; favors second constitutional convention, 208, 222, 297–98; fear of his opposition to Constitution, 311; influence of in N.C., 146, 159; as leader of Va. House of Delegates keeps quiet, 273, 277; opposes James Madison, 356, 421; opposition of to Constitution grows, 208; as possible U.S. senator from Va., 261, 290, 378; power of in Va. House of Delegates, 158, 214, 299, 359, 401; proposed declaration of rights criticized, 50; proposes amendments in Va. Convention, 48, 49n; resolution of in Va. House of Delegates concerning second convention, 298, 347; says he is not a demagogue, 47
—speeches of in Va. Convention, 8–9, 23–27n, 30–32n, 36–37, 39–41, 43–49; quoted, 244, 244n; responses to, 10–11, 11–12, 14–15, 32, 34, 40, 49–51
—speeches of in Va. House of Delegates, quoted, 4; cited, 297
—letters from, 354–55; quoted, 52n; cited, 52n
HENRY, THOMAS (Plumstead, Bucks Co., Pa.): attends Bucks Co. meeting, 173
HERKIMER, NICHOLAS (Tryon Co., N.Y.): as deceased hero, 79, 82n
HESSIAN FLY: has caused agricultural damage, 287, 289n
HIESTER, DANIEL (Montgomery Co., Pa.): nominated for U.S. House of Representatives, 336, 344, 376
HIGGINBOTHAM, JAMES (Va.): sent letter supporting James Monroe's candidacy for U.S. representative, 457n
HOGE, JONATHAN (Cumberland Co., Pa.): as delegate to Harrisburg Convention, 177
"HONESTUS" (Benjamin Austin, Jr.): text of, 267–72, 299–303n, 327–29
HOOVER, HENRY (Millford, Bucks Co., Pa.): attends Bucks Co. meeting, 172
HOPKINSON, FRANCIS (Philadelphia; id., BoR, II, 496): account of Philadelphia procession, 91n
—letter from, 90–91
—letter to, 438–39

"HORTENSIUS": text of, 151–52
HOUSE OF REPRESENTATIVES, U.S.: amendment mongers should not be elected to, 226; checks Senate, 50; control of important for amendments and appointment of officers, 188; will not propose amendments endangering liberty, 455; election of in Pa., 415; Federalists must be vigilant in elections for, 187; Federalists should be elected to, 152, 159, 185; Federalists will have majority in, 415; Harrisburg Convention to nominate candidates for, 166; majority of representatives are from states that recommended amendments, 139–40; money bills must originate in, 50; no danger from, 35; nomination of candidates main purpose of Harrisburg Convention, 187, 189–90; praise of fellow-feeling with farmers and planters, 35; praise of role in electing President, 403; represents the people, 408, 444; should be compromise of Federalists and Antifederalists, 416; size of can be trusted to Congress, 435–36; size of precludes bad laws, cruel and unusual punishment & excessive bail, 33; too small, 75, 133, 180, 412; two-year term criticized, 119; two-year term praised, 316; will be aristocratic, 252; wisest and best men should be elected to, 187
HOWARD, JOHN EAGER (Baltimore, Md.)
—letter to, cited, 264n
HOWELL, DAVID (Providence, R.I.): id., 463; as author of "Solon, jun.," 86n, 149n
—letter from, quoted, 86n, 149n
HUGHES, ALEXANDER (Bedminster, Bucks Co., Pa.): attends Bucks Co. meeting, 172
HULTGREN, MATTHIAS (Sweden)
—letter to, cited, 264n
HUMAN NATURE: depravity of, 103, 419; desire for power, 119; dignity of prizes virtuous freedom, 154; fall victim to tyranny, 457; falsehood shrinks away from enquiry, 332; force of habit is great, 147; generally governed by passion and not reason, 414; guided more by conveniences than by principles, 221; human heart is wandering and mortals are whimsical, 363; imperfect, 92; jealousy between colleagues is more common than indulgence, 418; men will be honest if they dare not be villains, 93; not expected that few should be attentive to interest of the many, 278; no man infallible in politics, 227; passions run high in extraordinary assemblies, 455; popular favor should not be sought by those who prize honor, 312; truth and certainty are always grateful to the human mind, 215; well attached to one's own interest, 39; where power exists wrong will generally be done, 258; will abuse power, 119, 234
HUMPHREYS, DAVID (Derby, Conn.): id., 463–64
—letter from, 381–82
HUNTER AND PRENTIS (Petersburg, Va.): prints Va. Convention debates, 8n
HUNTINGDON, PA.: election of delegates to Harrisburg Convention, 171–72; violence in, 171
HUNTINGTON, SAMUEL (Norwich, Conn.): id., 464
—letter from, 224–25
—letter to, cited, 224–25n
HUTCHINSON, JAMES (Philadelphia): elected to Harrisburg Convention, 174, 174n
HUTCHINSON, THOMAS (Boston/England): Samuel Adams and Elbridge Gerry compared to, 153, 154n, 161

IMMIGRATION: Antifederalists say that people will be taxed if they attempt to leave a state, 271; Constitution will encourage, 244
IMMUNITIES AND PRIVILEGES: cases will fall under federal judiciary, 453
IMPEACHMENT: as check on President, 241, 417; defense of Senate's power to try cases of, 418–19, 434; criticism of Senate's power to try cases of, 278, 426–29; House of Lords tries cases of in Great Britain, 434
IMPLIED POWERS: Congress and President do not have, 42; Congress should not have, 132, 473; Constitution will not have, 15; danger from possessed by Congress, 45; could be used to emancipate slaves, 45–46; some constructive power needed, 286–87. *See also* Necessary and proper clause
IMPOST: benefits and detriments of, 306–7, 321; defense of accrual of revenue from to the federal government, 241–42; Md. amendment would retain revenue in state where collected, 294, 476; N.C. Convention amendment proposes state to match federal, 225n
IMPOST OF 1783: disliked and defeated, 242
INDIANS: an army needed to protect against, 330; Antifederalists compared to, 144; Constitution endangers rights and property of, 41; criticized as lawless and unable to frame government, 135; God saved Americans from, 80, 82n
INGENHOUSZ, JAN (England)
—letter to, quoted, 67n

INDEX   497

"AN INHABITANT": text of, 445–47
INSTALLMENT LAWS: defense of Constitution's prohibition of, 443
INSTRUCTIONS: Antifederalist delegates to N.C. Convention told to oppose ratification, 119; force some Va. Convention delegates to vote against ratification, 68; Mass. Convention gives to future members of Congress to seek amendments, 207, 208n, 225, 231; possibly from Williamsburg to Edmund Randolph to oppose second convention, 262; representatives should abide by, 226; right of guaranteed in Va. Convention amendments, 55; should not be given to delegates to second general convention, 138; some conventions give their future members of Congress to seek amendments, 193; some delegates to Harrisburg Convention were hampered with, 184; Va. Convention gives to future members of Congress to seek amendments, 454–55. See also Petition, right to
INSURRECTION, DOMESTIC: danger of, 266; and habeas corpus, 124–25; importance of pardons in quelling, 405; likely if previous amendments are not adopted, 48; N.C. amendment restricting Congress' power to declare state in rebellion, 341–42; non-existent in Switzerland, 156; previous amendments will prevent, 47–48; restraining as great object of government, 321. See also Civil war
INTERESTS: clash throughout U.S., 92. See also Debtors; Farmers; Lawyers; Merchants
IREDELL, JAMES (Edenton, N.C.; id., BoR, II, 496)
—speeches of in N.C. Convention, 99–102, 108–10, 111–13, 114–17; reference to, 113; responses to, 102–3, 104, 110, 111
IRVINE, WILLIAM (Carlisle, Pa.): nominated for U.S. House of Representatives, 336, 344, 368, 376
—letter to, 186
IRWIN, ALEXANDER (Huntingdon, Pa.): beaten in Huntingdon, Pa., 171

JACK, WILLIAM (Westmoreland Co., Pa.): as chair of Antifederalist meeting, 134; on Antifederalist committee of correspondence, 132
JARVIS, CHARLES (Boston)
—speech of in Mass. Convention quoted, 301, 303n
JAY, JOHN (New York City; id., BoR, II, 497): negotiates with Gardoqui over Mississippi River, 110, 111n

—letters from, 221, 254–55n
—letter to, quoted, 255n
JEFFERSON, THOMAS (Albemarle Co., Va./France; id., BoR, II, 497): tally sheet listing state approval of amendments, ii
—letters from, 66–67, 86, 124–25, 135–36, 137, 360–61, 386–87n, 400, 438–39, 445; quoted, 67n; cited, 137, 215
—letters to, 90–91, 146–47, 159–60, 215–16, 221–22, 256–60, 285, 381–82, 401–2, 415; quoted, 86n, 149n; cited, 66, 91n, 146, 150n
JOHNSON, THOMAS (Frederick Co., Md.): id., 464
—letter from, quoted, 253n
—letters to, quoted, 252n; cited, 253n
JOHNSON, WILLIAM SAMUEL (Stratford, Conn.; id., BoR, II, 497)
—letter from, 222–23
JOHNSTON, SAMUEL (Perquimans Co., N.C.): id., 464
—speech of in N.C. Convention, 97; response to, 97–98, 103
—letter from, cited, 224–25n
—letter to, 224–25
JOHNSTON, ZACHARIAH (Augusta Co., Va.): opposes second convention in Va. House of Delegates, 298
JONES, EDWARD (Wilmington, N.C.)
—letter to, 357–58
JONES, JOHN
—letter to, 255n
JONES, JOSEPH (King George Co., Va.): id., 464–65
—letters from, 262, 368; cited, 292n
JORDAN, JOHN (Cumberland Co., Pa.): on committee to draft Cumberland Co. circular letter, 166n; as delegate to Harrisburg Convention, 177
JUDICIAL REVIEW: could lead to anarchy, 429; people declare that laws are unconstitutional, 107
JUDICIARIES, STATE: endangered by U.S. judiciary, 104, 474; could be given jurisdiction in revenue cases, 473; need reforming in Va., 415; will not allow general warrants, 33; federal judiciary will be more impartial than, 452
JUDICIARY: danger of courts without juries, 84
JUDICIARY, U.S.: amendments proposed concerning, 450; Antifederalists want amendment prohibiting inferior courts, 240; criticism of amendment prohibiting inferior courts, 195; danger from, 75, 77, 91; danger from appellate jurisdiction in law and fact, 39, 120, 181, 473, 474; danger of concurrent powers of, 97–98; defense of,

105–6; ecclesiastical courts may be established, 120; ecclesiastical courts will not be established, 122; endangers state judiciaries, 104, 474; inferior courts should be limited to admiralty jurisdiction, 181; judges should be prohibited from holding other offices, 474; limits on inferior courts, 473, 474; necessity of inferior courts, 240; remedies should be available in Va. Convention amendments, 55; shall not be limited in criminal cases, 452; should alone deal with cases involving foreign countries, 450–51; should hear cases between a state and citizens of another state, 451–52; should hear cases between citizens of different states, 451; Supreme Court should not try impeachment cases, 428; will be more impartial than state judiciaries, 452; will be regulated by congressional laws, 435; will determine whether Constitution or bill of rights is supreme, 12; will not allow general warrants, 33; will not be expensive to carry case to Supreme Court, 38–39

JURY TRIAL IN CIVIL CASES: amendment needed to guarantee, 124; British threats to cause American Revolution, 98, 278, 280n; Constitution does not endanger, 99, 230; Constitution endangers, 8, 13, 24–25, 31, 39, 40, 41, 43, 67, 75, 98, 104, 110, 120, 134, 271, 278–80, 391, 474; defense of Constitution's lack of protection for, 11, 15, 33, 37, 99, 108, 111–12, 121; different practices in different states, 100; guaranteed in all state constitutions, 15, 279; importance of, 66, 97–98, 104; needs to be safeguarded, 63, 135, 144, 447, 473; not included in Harrisburg Convention's amendments, 194; not needed in admiralty law cases, 279; protected in Va. Declaration of Rights, 38, 39n; protection for in Va. Convention amendments, 55; right to challenge jurors is secure in U.S., 38; secure in England, 37–38; secure in U.S. Constitution, 38; secure in Va., 38; sometimes lacking in Va., 38; states have different provisions for, 99, 108

JURY TRIAL IN CRIMINAL CASES: Constitution endangers, 75; Constitution guarantees, 15, 32, 100; disavows reserved powers theory, 134; importance of, 112; mentioned as argument for jury trials in civil cases, 110, 383; protection for endangers in civil cases, 279; verdict not always unanimous, 83

JURY TRIAL IN THE VICINAGE: Constitution's provision for in state where crime committed, 397; criticism of lack of protection for in Constitution, 24, 25, 40, 75–76, 98, 103, 104–5; defense of Constitution's lack of protection for, 28, 39, 384; protected by common law in England, 26n–27n; protected in Va. Declaration of Rights, 40; in Va. Convention amendments, 54; will be secure in U.S., 38

JURY TRIALS: challenge of jurors in not endangered by Constitution, 38, 384

JUSTICE: Constitution will endanger, 75; Constitution will promote, 14, 202, 217, 324; end of government is impartial administration of, 277; importance of, 11; lack of under Articles of Confederation, 14, 217, 443; more obtainable from federal judiciary than from state judiciaries, 452; needed to preserve liberty, 14; uncertain under Constitution, 221; Va. espouses, 11

KAMMERER, HENRY (Philadelphia): member of Philadelphia committee of correspondence, 186n

KEAN, JOHN (Pa.): as delegate to Harrisburg Convention, 177

KELLER, JOHN (Haycock, Bucks Co., Pa.): attends Bucks Co. meeting, 172

KELLY, MOSES (Plumstead, Bucks Co., Pa.): attends Bucks Co. meeting, 173

KERR, WILLIAM (Huntingdon, Pa.): house of as site for election of Harrisburg Convention from Huntingdon, Pa., 172

KINGSLEY, MARTIN (Hardwick, Mass.): as candidate for U.S. House of Representatives, 388

KNOX, HENRY (Boston/New York City)
—letters to, 315, 449

LAFAYETTE, MARQUIS DE (France; id., BoR, II, 498)
—letter from, 123

LAMB, JOHN (New York City): as chair of New York Federal Republican Committee, 51n
—letters from, cited, 57, 57n, 69
—letters to, 51–57n, 57–59, 69–70; quoted, 52n; cited, 52n, 147n

LANCASTER, PA., 186n; incorrectly said not to have been represented in Harrisburg Convention, 188, 189
—Federalist convention held in: described, 284n; held in to nominate candidates for U.S. House of Representatives, 254; will be a deception, 283, 284n; will be one-sided, 293; ticket, 367n, 375

LANCASTER, WILLIAM (Franklin Co., N.C.): id., 465
—speech of in N.C. Convention, 122–23n

INDEX 499

LANGDON, JOHN (Portsmouth, N.H.): id., 465; defense of as candidate for U.S. Senate, 337
—letter from, 136
LANGDON, WOODBURY (Portsmouth, N.H.): as candidate for U.S. House of Representatives, 416
LANSING, ABRAHAM G. (Albany Co., N.Y.)
—letter from, quoted, 60n
—letter to, cited, 60n
LANSING, JOHN, JR. (Albany, N.Y.): id., 465; as possible author of undelivered speech in N.Y. Convention, 71n
—speech of in N.Y. Convention, cited, 71n
LARGE VERSUS SMALL STATES: no real conflict between, 72
LAW OF NATIONS: Congress can define, 29; diplomatic immunity provided in, 37n, 473; no jury trials in, 34
LAW OF THE LAND: protection under in Va. Convention amendments, 54–55. *See also* Supremacy clause
LAWS: are more effective than recommendations, 364; Congress can enact concerning descent and distribution of property of deceased, 452; Congress limited in defining crimes, 365; Congress should not pass laws that subvert state constitutions, 134; Congressmen would be subject to, 100; Constitution will create government of men and not of, 39; under Constitution will have good effect, 305; danger in providing for jury trial protection by, 279; easier to change than constitutions, 99–100, 108–9, 112–13; federal laws should act on people not states, 107, 365–66; no treaty shall violate federal law, 440; N.Y. legislature should pass prohibiting oath to support Constitution, 390; people declare unconstitutionality of, 107; remedies should be available for unlawful violations of liberty in Va. Convention amendments, 55; rights can be protected via, 433; treaties should not violate state or federal, 181; will be binding on people under Constitution thus need for bill of rights, 103–4; will be wise, mild, and equitable under Constitution, 384
LAWYERS: criticism of, 73, 381; favor the Constitution, 388; should not be elected to U.S. House of Representatives, 376
LEE, CHARLES (Fairfax Co., Va.): id., 465–66
—letter from, 4, 297–98
LEE, HENRY (Westmoreland Co., Va.; id., BoR, II, 498): and Eleazer Oswald's visit to Va., 51n
—speech of in Va. Convention, 9–11
—letters from, 213–14, 401; cited, 51n, 214
—letters to, 223–24, 382–83; quoted, 4
LEE, RICHARD BLAND (Loudon Co., Va.; id., BoR, II, 499): wants to publish Madison's letter supporting amendments, 356, 358, 359
—letters from, 298–99, 358–59, 413–15
—letters to, cited, 358, 413
LEE, RICHARD HENRY (Westmoreland Co., Va.; id., BoR, II, 499): as Antifederalist leader, 377; corresponds with N.Y. Antifederalists, 51n; decides not to stand for Va. Convention, 70; elected U.S. senator, 261, 290, 298, 339, 340, 354, 361, 378, 405, 449
—letters from, 69–70, 255; quoted, 96n; cited, 52n, 64n, 70, 70n, 96n, 255n, 361, 361n
—letters to, 61–64, 291–92, 339–40n, 354–55; cited, 69
LEGISLATURES, STATE: Antifederalist seek control of to elect U.S. senators, 209, 213; are guardians of liberty, 205, 392; cannot propose amendments to Constitution, 211; Constitution will weaken powers of, 24; danger from if controlled by Antifederalists, 235–36; elected delegates to Constitutional Convention, 281–82; have enacted bad laws concerning debts, 443; important to elect Federalist to who oppose amendments, 130; power to call constitutional conventions, 7, 205; praise of their election of U.S. senators, 419; protected by Article V's provision to call a convention, 243–44; should have power to recall U.S. senators, 180, 194; sovereignty resides in, 7; will consider amendments, 233; would retain supremacy if Congress didn't have direct tax power, 130. *See also* Constitutions, state; Sovereignty
LENOIR, WILLIAM (Wilkes Co., N.C.): id., 466
—speech of in N.C. Convention, 118–21; response, 121
LIBERTY: amendments needed to protect, 4, 164n, 173, 227, 296, 303, 309–10, 317, 335; amendments protecting will be proposed by Congress, 442; American Revolution fought for, 24, 32, 41, 65, 72, 98, 100, 230, 250, 302, 333, 364, 374, 407; Americans favor, 47; Antifederalists threaten, 205; based on state constitutions, 364, 412; bill of rights needed to preserve, 48; bill of rights not needed to protect, 12; can only be secured by a confederacy of republican states, 179; can only be se-

cured by a republican form of government, 132; Constitution does not endanger, 9–11, 34, 62, 93, 121, 143, 269–70, 305, 384, 407; Constitution endangers, 40–41, 58, 68, 72, 77, 79, 80, 85, 91, 94, 118, 164–65, 250, 251, 283, 334–37, 347, 348, 439, 472n; Constitution will promote, 9–11, 230, 408, 422; defeat of Constitution is last chance to save, 283; difficult to form government that would secure, 73; as end of government, 16; endangered under a national government, 155; general provision needed to protect, 9; is a trust for future generations, 79; justice needed to preserve, 14; Magna Carta protects, 11; as a natural right, 53; need society to exist, 41; no danger to in U.S. from ecclesiastical power, 407; only a federal government could protect, 178; at stake in election of Congress, 247, 325; state legislatures are guardians of, 205, 392; virtue needed to maintain, 154. *See also* Rights

LINCOLN, BENJAMIN (Hingham, Mass.): id., 466; as candidate for U.S. House of Representatives, 201
—letters from, 182–83, 228–30; cited, 289
—letters to, 152–53, 225–26, 289–90; quoted, 4

LITERARY REFERENCES: Colley Cibber, 420, 420n; William Congreve, *The Old Bachelor*, 228, 228n; James Harrington, 316; Lucretius, 156; John Milton, *Paradise Lost*, 73, 81n, 202, 202n, 316; Matthew Poole's *Synopsis of the Critics*, 74, 81n; Alexander Pope *The Sixth Epistle of the First Book of Horace*, 420, 420n; Alexander Pope, *An Essay on Man*, 389, 389n; Alexander Pope, *The Rape of Lock*, 406, 407n; Don Quixote, 385; Shakespeare, *Hamlet*, 87, 87n; Shakespeare, *Henry VI*, 291, 291n; Geard Van Sweeten, *Commentaries on Boerhaeven's Aphorisms*, 74, 81n; 'tis from experience that we reason best (poem from Boston oration 1777), 425. *See also* Political and legal writers and writings

LITTLE, JOHN (Huntingdon Co., Pa.): and violence in Huntingdon, Pa., 171–72

LIVERMORE, SAMUEL (Campton/Holderness/Thornton, N.H.): defense of as candidate for the U.S. Senate, 337; opposition to as candidate for the U.S. Senate, 310

LIVINGSTON, ROBERT R. (New York City)
—speech of in N.Y. Convention cited, 72, 79, 81n

LLOYD, THOMAS (Philadelphia): takes shorthand notes of Pa. Assembly, 176

LOCKE, MATTHEW (Rowan Co., N.C.): response to speech of in N.C. Convention, 111–12

LONG ISLAND, N.Y.: will secede from N.Y. if Constitution is rejected, 91

LOUIS XVI (France): hopes things get better for, 304. *See also* France

LOVINGUIRE, CHRISTOPHER (Westmoreland Co., Pa.): on Antifederalist committee of correspondence, 132

LOWNDES, RAWLINS (Charleston, S.C.)
—letter from, cited, 53n

"LUCULLUS": text of, 324; response to, 348–49

LUZERNE COUNTY, PA.: not represented in Harrisburg Convention, 182n, 184n

LYTLE, JOHN (Pa.): as delegate to Harrisburg Convention, 177

M'CLENACHAN, BLAIR (Philadelphia): id., 466; as chair of Harrisburg Convention, 174, 174n, 175, 177, 81, 183–84, 196; as delegate to Harrisburg Convention, 177, 195; and Germantown meeting, 167–68, 168n; nominated for U.S. House of Representatives, 336, 344, 376; praise of, 195

M'CUNE, WILLIAM (Huntingdon, Pa.): rioter in Huntingdon, Pa., 171

MCDOWALL, JOSEPH OF QUAKER MEADOWS (Burke Co., N.C.): id., 466–67
—speeches of in N.C. Convention, 98, 102–3; response to, 100

M'ELROY, WILLIAM (Huntingdon Co., Pa.): and violence in Huntingdon, Pa., 171–72

MCGREGOR, COLLIN (New York City): id., 467
—letter from, 323–24

MCHENRY, JAMES (Baltimore, Md.): id., 467; on appointment of presidential electors, 213; as candidate for Md. House of Delegates, 209, 210n, 211n, 213n
—letters from, 124; cited, 126
—letters to, 126–27; cited, 124n

MCKEAN, THOMAS (Philadelphia; id., BoR, II, 499)
—letter from, 175

M'KEE, ROBERT (Pa.): as delegate to Harrisburg Convention, 177

MACLAINE, ARCHIBALD (Wilmington, N.C.): id., 467
—speeches of in N.C. Convention, 96–97, 106–7; response to, 107–8n

MCLENE, JAMES (Franklin Co., Pa.): id., 467
—letter from, 186

MCMECHEN, DAVID (Baltimore, Md.): as candidate for Md. House of Delegates, 209, 210n, 211n, 213n

INDEX 501

MADISON, JAMES (Orange Co., Va.; id., BoR, II, 499); as candidate for U.S. House of Representatives, 353, 414, 415–16, 426, 431; as candidate for U.S. Senate, 261, 290, 298–99; defeated for U.S. Senate, 298, 312, 339, 340, 354, 356, 358, 414, 449; defense of on amendments, 414; effort to print his letter on amendments, 413–14, 415, 415n, 420; and Eleazer Oswald's visit to Va., 51n; election district for U.S. House of Representatives, 420, 425–26; not in Va. House of Delegates, 214, 223–24; opposes a second convention, 130; praise of speeches of, 10–11; prefers to be in U.S. House of Representatives instead of Senate, 311
—letters from, 136–37, 145–46, 146–47, 149–50, 188, 201, 221–22, 256–60, 262–63n, 311–12, 312–14, 382–83, 401–2, 405–6n, 415; quoted, 4; cited, 51n, 88n, 137n, 138n, 146, 150n, 158, 263n, 311, 353, 354n, 356, 357n, 358, 359n, 360, 377n, 387, 413, 415n, 436n
—letters to, 124–25, 137–38, 158–59, 198, 203, 208, 245–46, 261–62, 263, 272–73, 276–77, 284–85, 290–91, 298–99, 340–41, 344, 345–46, 352–54, 356–57, 358–59, 360–61, 368, 377, 378, 387, 401, 413–15, 415–16, 420–21, 425–26; quoted, 8n, 314n; cited, 88n, 145, 272, 273n, 284n, 292n, 298, 311, 312n, 341n, 352, 360, 377n, 420
MADISON, JAMES, SR. (Orange Co., Va.)
—letter to, 201
MADISON, REV. JAMES (Williamsburg, Va.): favors second convention, 198
MAGAW, ROBERT
—letter to, 175
MAGAZINES: Philadelphia *American Museum*, 288, 289, 289n. *See also* Broadsides, pamphlets, and books; Newspapers
MANUFACTURERS: address to in Baltimore, 226–28; Constitution will promote, 232, 422; increase in home manufactures will reduce revenue from excise taxes, 306; Union necessary to benefit, 302
"MANY" (Arthur Campbell): text of, 66
MARQUE AND REPRISAL, LETTERS OF: criticism of power to grant in Constitution, 316
MARSHALL, JAMES (Pa.): as delegate to Harrisburg Convention, 177
MARSHALL, JOHN (Richmond, Va.): id., 467
—speeches of in Va. Convention, 37–39, 40; response to, 39–40
MARTIAL LAW: danger of militia under during peacetime, 134

MARTIN, LUTHER (Baltimore/Harford Co., Md.): criticism of, 245; wants state legislatures to elect members of U.S. House of Representatives, 247
MARYLAND: difficulty of electing U.S. senators in, 150
—Convention: address of minority in favor of amendments, 272n; amendments merely a conciliatory measure, 267; fails to recommend amendments, 253; had a small minority, 285; minority's amendments, 472n–76; has ratified, 90; should not have taken so long in ratifying Constitution, 267–68
"A MARYLANDER" (Otho Holland Williams), 210n, 210n–11n; text of, 208–12n, 453–54
MASON, GEORGE (Fairfax Co./Stafford Co., Va.; id., BoR, II, 500); chairs Va. Antifederalists committee that sends amendments to N.Y., 501n; correspondence with N.Y. Antifederalists, 51n; criticism of, 245; signs Va. Convention amendments, 56n; wants amendments, 126, 127n
—speech of in Va. Convention, 29; praise of, 31; response to, 37–38
—letters from, 51–57n, 162–63, 431–32n; quoted, 52n; cited, 52n, 147n
—letter to, cited, 52n
MASON, JOHN (Fairfax Co., Va./France)
—letters to, 162–63, 431–32n
MASSACHUSETTS: declaration of rights is part of constitution, 12; legislature disagrees with Va.'s call for second convention, 5; has ratified, 90
—Convention recommended amendments, 57, 59n, 65, 67, 86, 92n, 161, 218, 285, 303, 445; were merely conciliatory, 220, 256, 273, 391–91; were not merely conciliatory, 299–300; reserving powers, 64, 64n; are not local, 301; not sufficient enough, 53; as part of form of ratification, 231, 300; instructed future representatives to Congress to seek adoption of, 280
MATHEWS, THOMAS (Norfolk Borough Co., Va.): chairs committee of the whole of Va. Convention, 42
MAZZEI, PHILIP (Italy)
—letter to, 405–6n
MECHANICS: address to in Baltimore, 226–28; Constitution will benefit, 245, 423; favor the Constitution, 388
MERCER, JAMES (Pa.): as delegate to Harrisburg Convention, 177
MERCER, JOHN FRANCIS (Anne Arundel Co., Md.; id., BoR, II, 500): opposition to as U.S. representative, 454

—declares candidacy for U.S. House of Representatives, 436–37
MERCHANTS: favor the Constitution, 388. *See also* Commerce
MIFFLIN, THOMAS (Philadelphia Co., Pa.; id., BoR, II, 500): and Pa. Supreme Executive Council, 168, 169n, 175–76
—letter from, 245
MILES, SAMUEL (Philadelphia): member of Philadelphia committee of correspondence, 186n
MILITARY: criticism of amendments concerning, 329–32; limit on appropriations for may be insufficient, 331; for military limited to two years in Va. Convention amendments, 56; praise of Constitution's two-year limit on appropriations for, 15, 50, 241, 343; should be subordinate to civil law, 55, 134
MILITIA: amendments concerning, 349–50; best defense of a country, 349; Constitution could endanger calling out, 391; criticism of amendment limiting federal service to two months, 195; defense of Constitution's provisions concerning, 350–52; federal service should be limited to two months, 181; Federalists said to favor federal control over, 389; importance of in U.S., 125; as a main point in Constitution, 209; states should provide for, 181; Va. Declaration of Rights states as best defense, 44; Va. law concerning, 49n
—dangers concerning: can be disarmed, 120; will be moved to federal capital, 120; will be given to foreign monarchy to pay U.S. debt, 271; should not be subject to martial law except when in federal service, 181, 271, 475; of federal control over, 78, 475
MISSISSIPPI RIVER: criticism of Congress changing Jay's instructions, 110, 111n
MONARCHY: abuses of power likely under, 258; Antifederalists say Constitution will lead to Prince William Henry becoming king, 271; Antifederalists had supported at beginning of Revolution, 248; bill of rights endangers liberty under, 16; bill of rights necessary in, 97; Constitutional features of, 119; danger President will become, 136; endangers liberty, 16; fear of in postwar America, 382; support for in U.S., 116, 381–82; William Grayson said to favor, 16. *See also* Great Britain, monarchs; President, U.S.
MONEY: defense of Congress' power to borrow, 371; scarcity of in postwar America, 266, 381

MONEY BILLS: must originate in U.S. House of Representatives, 50
MONOPOLIES: amendment needed to prohibit, 124; danger from grants of Congress through corruption, 280; encourages ingenuity, 125; justified in certain cases, 369–70; should be prohibited, 135–36; useful in literary works and inventions, 259–60
MONROE, JAMES (Spotsylvania Co., Va.): id., 468; address supporting candidacy for U.S. representative, 456–57; has supported amendments, 455; opposes Madison in election for U.S. House of Representatives, 378, 414, 416, 421, 426, 431
—speech of in Va. Convention, 13–14
—letter from, cited, 253
—letters to, 135–36, 253–54n
MONTGOMERY COUNTY, PA.: not represented in Harrisburg Convention, 182n, 184n, 191
MONTGOMERY, DANIEL (Pa.): as delegate to Harrisburg Convention, 177
MONTGOMERY, RICHARD (Dutchess Co., N.Y.): as deceased hero, 79, 82n
MONTGOMERY, WILLIAM (Northumberland Co., Pa.): nominated for U.S. House of Representatives, 336, 344, 368, 376
MONTMORIN, COMTE DE (France)
—letter to, 128–29n
MOORE, JOHN (Westmoreland Co., Pa.): chairs Antifederalist meeting in Greensburg, Pa., 131, 132
MORRIS, ROBERT (Philadelphia), 361
MORTON, THOMAS (Westmoreland Co., Pa.): Westmoreland Co., Pa., Antifederalist committee of correspondence, 132
MOUSTIER, COMTE DE (France): id., 468
—letter from, 128–29n
MUHLENBERG, PETER (Montgomery Co., Pa.): nominated for U.S. House of Representatives, 336, 344, 368, 376
MURRAY, THOMAS (Pa.): as delegate to Harrisburg Convention, 177

NATURAL RIGHTS: amendments needed to protect fundamental rights of people without damaging Constitution, 447; Americans enjoy, 315; Americans know more about than any other people, 140; are God given, 104; are not given up under Constitution, 109; cannot be given up in a compact, 53, 104; Constitution endangers, 94, 119
NATURE, STATE OF: people in before state constitution, 60. *See also* Compact theory of government; Natural rights

INDEX 503

NAVY: Congress should have power to raise and maintain, 132; Federalists said to favor, 389; small navy needed to guard against smuggling, 306; would not be a danger under Constitution, 230. *See also* Military

NECESSARY AND PROPER CLAUSE: danger of, 9, 13; defense of, 35, 96–97, 97n, 286–89; misquoted by Archibald Maclaine, 96, 97n. *See also* Implied powers; Reserved powers

NESBIT, CHARLES (Carlisle, Pa.): id., 468
—letter from, 216–17

NEW HAMPSHIRE: ratification of celebrated in Windham, Conn., 68–69; state constitution quoted on separation of powers, 418
—Convention of: Antifederalists have a majority in, 58; adjourns to later date, 59n; ratifies Constitution, 3, 57n, 90; recommends amendments, 67

NEW JERSEY: commerce of dominated by N.Y., 73, 141, 142n; has ratified, 90; as a threat to N.Y. out of the Union, 73, 80

NEW YORK: Antifederalists command, 130; commercial dominance over neighbors, 73, 141, 142n; discouraged by Va.'s ratification, 431; importance of, 141; influence of Va. on, 162; New York City, Staten Island, and Long Island will secede from if Constitution is rejected, 91, 393; resolution of requesting Congress to call a second convention, 6, 396n; would be endangered out of Union, 73
—prospects for ratification by: doubtful, 86; hesitating, 90; uncertain, 86, 87, 91; ratifies Constitution, 3, 128, 136, 140; will ratify, 86, 137; with Va. are least disposed to Constitution, 217; expected to reject by N.C. Antifederalists, 146

NEW YORK ANTIFEDERALIST SOCIETY: proceedings of meeting on calling second convention, 317–26

NEW YORK ASSEMBLY: resolution requesting Congress to call second convention, 6, 396n

NEW YORK BILL OF RIGHTS: N.Y. legislature enacts, 61n

NEW YORK CIRCULAR LETTER, 345; adoption of, 319–20, 431; calls for second convention, 153, 162, 163n; criticism of, 136, 138, 141, 149, 191, 325; criticism of it being called "Clinton's Letter," 372; danger of, 150–51, 158, 223; danger of coalition supporting from N.Y. and Va., 261; defense of, 155; encourages Antifederalists, 145, 146, 149, 158, 201, 214, 221–22, 262; impact of could delay implementation of Constitution, 216; influence of in Va., 145, 188, 253; N.C. rejection of Constitution will support, 182; Pa. Assembly does not recommend to next Assembly, 245, 245n; praise of, 88n, 135; read in Conn. legislature and tabled, 293, 315; received by N.H. president, 136; sent by R.I. to town meetings, 378, 378n; sent to Va. Gov. Edmund Randolph who will have it printed, 137; as standard for Antifederalists, 214; submitted to joint committee of Mass. General Court, 314; submitted to N.Y. legislature, 6; in Va. House of Delegates, 263, 290, 298, 378

NEW YORK CITY: Antifederalists in hope for N.Y. ratification, 87; procession in being planned, 91, 91n; will secede from N.Y. if Constitution is rejected, 91
—as federal capital: likelihood of, 149–50, 160, 201, 222; will lose if N.Y. does not ratify Constitution, 87

NEW YORK CONSTITUTION: all power derived from the people, 74, 81n; does not include a bill of rights, 60; prohibits clergy from holding public office, 445n; quoted by "Sydney," 60n; safeguards habeas corpus, 74; serves as a bill of rights, 61

NEW YORK CONSTITUTIONAL CONVENTION (1777): considers a bill of rights, 61n

NEW YORK CONVENTION: amendments from criticized, 138; amendments recommended by will destroy Constitution, 128, 135, 141; Antifederalists in change because of amendments, 87; Antifederalists in influenced by Va.'s recommended amendments, 86; Antifederalists win majority of delegates, 51n, 58–59, 59n; better to have defeated Constitution than approve circular letter, 136–37, 149–50; God asked to give it wisdom, 87; instructs future members of Congress to work to obtain N.Y. amendments, 391; opposes direct taxes for Congress, 158; praise of, 281; printed *Debates* allegedly biased against amendments, 71n; ratification by affects Pa. Antifederalists, 130; ratified Constitution to obtain amendments, 148–49; ratified Constitution despite two-thirds Antifederalist majority, 162; ratified Constitution with recommended amendments and circular letter, 6; recommends amendments, 123; undelivered speech in, 71n–82n; wants amendments through a second convention, 393; will recommend amendments, 87

NEW YORK FEDERAL REPUBLICAN COMMITTEE: correspondence with Va. Antifederalists, 51–57n
—letter from, cited, 147n; response to, 57

NEWSPAPERS: importance of, 66

—IN CONNECTICUT
—*Connecticut Courant*: cited, 374n
—*Connecticut Gazette*: printed, 68–69, 141–42; cited, 191n, 282n
—*New Haven Gazette*: printed, 433–36; cited, 436n
—*Norwich Packet*: printed, 280–82

—IN MARYLAND
—*Maryland Gazette* (Annapolis): cited, 272n, 346–47, 472n
—*Maryland Gazette* (Baltimore): printed, 208–12n, 211–13, 226–28, 232–33, 238–39, 239–42, 453–54; cited, 210n, 210n–11n, 239n, 472n
—*Maryland Journal*: printed, 175, 233–37, 243–44, 267–72, 447; quoted, 276n; cited, 29n, 128, 237n, 238, 239n, 297n, 472n

—IN MASSACHUSETTS AND MAINE: in Boston oppose amendments, 191
—*American Herald*: printed, 387–88; cited, 85n
—*Boston Gazette*: printed, 160–61, 161–62, 425; quoted, 336n–37n; 85n, 391, 430, 431n
—*Boston Globe*: cited, 154n
—*Herald of Freedom*: printed, 215, 219, 305, 388–89, 421–23, 423–24, 424–25, 432–33
—*Independent Chronicle*: printed, 154–55, 199–201n, 206–8n, 208, 218–19, 231–32, 299–303n, 303–5n, 327–29; cited, 85n, 153–54, 156, 161, 192n, 201, 218n, 219n, 232n, 302n, 395n
—*Massachusetts Centinel*, 237–38; printed, 59, 151–52, 156–58, 196, 198–99, 201–2, 219–21n, 242–43, 273–74, 324, 355–56, 400, 406–7, 420, 429–30, 438, 448; quoted, 69n; cited, 154n, 155n, 161, 201, 201n, 206, 207n, 208, 208n, 218–19, 218n, 219n, 221n, 256n, 424n, 432, 433n
—*Massachusetts Spy*: printed, 255–56, 277–80, 436; quoted, 272n; cited, 273, 274n, 280n, 395n
—*Salem Mercury*: printed, 386–87

—IN NEW HAMPSHIRE: controlled by Federalists, 58
—*Freeman's Oracle*: printed, 58, 83–85, 310–11, 337–39; cited, 59n, 83, 85n, 311n, 339n
—*New Hampshire Spy*: printed, 67, 416; cited, 59n, 416

—IN NEW YORK
—*Albany Gazette*: cited, 59n–60n
—*Albany Journal*: cited, 58–59, 59n
—*Albany Register*: founding of, 81n; printed, 71–82n; cited, 71n

—*Daily Advertiser*: printed, 167, 372–74; cited, 139n, 359n, 415n
—*Daily Gazette*: quoted, 267n; cited, 264n, 265n
—*New York Journal*: printed, 389–95, 410–13; quoted, 59–61, 59n, 96n; cited, 81n, 139n, 394, 413n
—*New York Packet*: printed, 186–87

—IN NORTH CAROLINA
—*Martin's North Carolina Gazette*: printed, 139–40

—IN PENNSYLVANIA: in Philadelphia oppose amendments, 191
—*Carlisle Gazette*: printed, 82–83n, 145, 364–67; cited, 163n
—*Federal Gazette*, 329–32; printed, 196–98, 245, 246–48, 248–49, 260–61, 264–67, 274–76, 305–9, 332–37n, 345, 349–52, 374–75, 379–81, 383–86, 407–8, 426–29, 442–45, 449–53, 454–56; quoted, 264–65n, 267n; cited, 348, 367n
—*Freeman's Journal*: quoted, 284n
—*Independent Gazetteer*: printed, 155–56, 176–82, 176–82n, 230–31, 250–52, 282–84, 348–49, 375–76; quoted, 376n; cited, 135n, 139n, 144, 163n, 164n, 191n, 264n, 324n
—*Pennsylvania Gazette*: printed, 7–8, 67–68, 135, 138–39, 169–70, 170–71, 174, 176, 184, 189–90, 190–91, 203–6, 325, 345n, 457n; cited, 91n, 131n, 144, 144n, 190n, 191n, 203n, 206n, 222n, 249n, 409n
—*Pennsylvania Mercury*: printed, 193, 254; cited, 87n, 187–88
—*Pennsylvania Packet*, 176–82; printed, 67–68, 69, 163, 172–74, 192–93, 367–68; quoted, 49n; cited, 91n, 164n
—*Pittsburgh Gazette*: printed, 131–34, 183–84, 194–96

—IN RHODE ISLAND
—*Providence Gazette*: printed, 147–49; cited, 149n; prints essays by "Solon, Jr.," 86n
—*United States Chronicle*: cited, 256n; prints essays by "Solon, Jr.," 86n

—IN VIRGINIA AND KENTUCKY
—*Kentucky Gazette*: printed, 448–49
—*Virginia Centinel*: printed, 345
—*Virginia Gazette* (Petersburg): printed, 92–93
—*Virginia Herald*: cited, 85n
—*Virginia Independent Chronicle*: printed, 66, 87–90, 325–27; cited, 87n, 96n, 138n, 191n–92n
—*Virginia Journal*: cited, 36n

NICHOLAS, GEORGE (Albemarle Co., Va.; id., BoR, II, 501)
—speeches of in Va. Convention, 14–15, 27–30n
NICHOLSON, JOHN (Cumberland Co., Pa.): id., 166n
—letter to, 164
NIXON, JOHN (Philadelphia): member of Philadelphia committee of correspondence, 186n
NOBILITY, TITLES OF: defense of Constitution's prohibition of, 398–400; prohibition of refutes reserved powers theory, 27, 74
"NOBODY": text of, 420
NON-RESISTANCE, DOCTRINE OF: opposition to in Md. minority amendments, 476; opposition to in Va. Convention amendments, 54
NORTH CAROLINA: Antifederalist U.S. Senate would induce ratification by, 209; needed to assist in obtaining amendments, 148; follows Va., 93; influence of Patrick Henry in, 146, 159, 354; in interest of to be in the Union, 159; must ratify because of Va. and S.C. as neighbors, 93; must ratify Constitution to have voice on amendments, 358; out of the Union, 148, 437; paper money policy of, 382; prohibits clergy from holding public office, 445n; rejection of encourages Antifederalists, 201; unknown action on Constitution, 129; Va. influences, 146; willing to accept Constitution only conditionally, 217; won't vote on implementing Constitution in Confederation Congress, 150
—prospects for ratification by: hopeful, 92–93, 216; expected to ratify but it rejects Constitution, 146; will ratify, 137, 169, 290, 382, 437; nothing heard from, 135, 137
NORTH CAROLINA CONSTITUTION: one-year terms for Commons and Senate, 121; prohibits clergy from holding public office, 445n
NORTH CAROLINA CONVENTION: amendments proposed by, 129, 215n, 225n; amendments from are similar to Va.'s, 445; refuses to ratify Constitution without amendments, 3; Antifederalists have majority in, 92, 281; rejection of Constitution by rejects republican principle of majority rule, 215; rejects Constitution, 138, 144, 145, 146, 147, 162–63, 182, 215n, 431, 437; declines to ratify or reject Constitution, 386, 445; does not ratify, 159, 159n, 382, 405; extract of journal transmitted to state governors, 224, 225n; Federalists in are hopeful, 92; is sitting, 90
—speeches in on amendments, 94–123n
NORTH CAROLINA HOUSE OF COMMONS: one-year term of office, 119, 121n
NORTH CAROLINA SENATE: one-year term of office, 119, 121n
"NORTH END": text of, 423–24
NORTH VERSUS SOUTH: importance of union with North and South, 89, 302, 327–28. *See also* Northern States
NORTHAMPTON COUNTY, PA.: not represented in Harrisburg Convention, 182n, 184n, 188, 188n, 189, 190n, 191
NORTHERN STATES: don't have common interest with Southern States, 45; Southerners fear under Constitution, 150; will have a majority in Congress, 46

OATHS: Constitution requires of all state and federal officers, 12–13; denial that they imply a religious test, 363; needed for warrants in Md. minority amendments, 474; necessary to obtain warrants in Va. Convention amendments, 55; N.Y. officeholders to delay until N.Y. amendments are confirmed, 224; required of all state and federal officeholders, 104, 113–14, 390
OFFICEHOLDERS: federal and state led during the war, 407–8; only friends to liberty ought to be elected, 93; should regularly stand for re-election, 54
OFFICEHOLDERS, STATE: Antifederalists are, 248; in N.Y. legislature have short terms, 61; oppose Constitution for selfish reasons, 138, 139n, 197, 325, 448; supporters of amendments said to be, 303
OFFICEHOLDERS, U.S.: Antifederalists desire positions, 188–89; Federalists seek positions, 153, 333; must vacate Va. state offices, 340; members of Congress prohibited from holding other offices, 476; opponents of amendments accused of being, 376; terms of are too long, 61; are trustees and servants of the people, 476; will multiply under Constitution, 251–52, 279, 284, 400; would not increase much under Constitution, 230
OFFICEHOLDING: not descendible in Va. Convention amendments, 54
"AN OLD GERMAN": text of, 226–28
OLIGARCHY: fear of in postwar America, 382
ORDER: Constitution will promote, 217; special conventions endanger, 175. *See also* Insurrection, domestic

ORTH, ADAM (Dauphin Co., Pa.): as delegate to Harrisburg Convention, 177
OSWALD, ELEAZER (Philadelphia): as Antifederalist courier, 51n, 52n, 70n

PACA, WILLIAM (Harford Co., Md.): opposition to as U.S. senator, 210; proposed amendments in Md. Convention, 210, 472–76; support for as U.S. representative, 453–54
—speech of in Md. Convention quoted, 472n
PAGE, JOHN (Gloucester Co., Va.): opposes Va.'s resolution requesting Congress to call a second convention, 344; wants to publish Madison's letter supporting amendments, 356
PAINE, TIMOTHY (Worcester, Mass.): as candidate for U.S. House of Representatives, 388
PAPER MONEY: abused under Articles of Confederation, 257; Constitution will stamp out fraud from, 324; defense of Constitution's prohibition of issued by states, 443; N.C. Convention amendment concerning, 225n; opposition to, 84; will be prohibited except for what is already circulating, 370
PARDONS: defense of President's power to grant, 404–5; defense of President's power to grant in treason cases, 434; limit put on President's power in cases of treason, 402
PARIS, ISAAC (Montgomery Co., N.Y.): as deceased hero, 79, 82n
PARTISAN POLITICS: causes opposition to amendments, 437; second convention will be actuated by, 262; should be avoided, 329; subsiding in Pa., 142. *See also* Discourse; Political parties
PATRIOTISM: Antifederalists called patriots, 162, 284, 303; Antifederalists lack, 188–89, 249; lack of in U.S., 150; needed, 223; needed in first federal elections, 229; praise of Nicholas Collin for "Foreign Spectator" series, 265n; and prudence needed in early federal government, 153; those with should be elected to Congress, 247
PEABODY, NATHANIEL (Atkinson, N.H.): as candidate for U.S. House of Representatives, 416
—letter from, cited, 57n
PEACE: amendments endanger, 202; amendments needed for, 47, 309–10, 456; Constitution will promote, 202, 219; depends on Federalist control of Congress, 421;

Edmund Pendleton attached to, 62; as end of government, 73; no danger to in U.S. from ecclesiastical power, 407
PENDLETON, EDMUND (Caroline Co., Va.): id., 468
—speech of in Va. Convention, 16–18
—letters from, 61–64, 245–46
—letters to, 262–63n; cited, 64n, 70, 70n
PENNSYLVANIA: Antifederalists in western part of combine with those in N.Y., 130; has ratified, 90
PENNSYLVANIA ASSEMBLY: resolution of rejecting call of second convention, 5; Federalists should be elected to because amendments will be considered, 185; Harrisburg Convention requests it to ask Congress for a convention, 243; Harrisburg Convention's main purpose was to nominate candidates for, 209; importance of election to, 206; Pa. constitution calls for men of wisdom and virtue to be elected to, 191, 193; receives petitions to de-certify Pa. ratification, 163n; rejects N.Y. circular letter, 376n; rejects Va. resolution for second convention, 5, 376n; seceding Assembly confused with Dissent of Minority of Pa. Convention, 234, 237n; seceding assemblymen criticized, 194, 196n; wisest and best men should be elected to, 187
PENNSYLVANIA CONSTITUTION (1776): calls for men of wisdom and virtue to be elected to Pa. Assembly, 191, 193
PENNSYLVANIA CONVENTION: does not allow amendments, 193; small number of voters elect delegates to, 49
—Dissent of the Minority of, 49n; criticism of, 194, 196n; lists amendments desired, 189; quoted, 237n; confused with Pa. seceding assemblymen, 234, 237n
THE PEOPLE: adhere to republican principles, 301–2; all power is in, 9–10, 16–17, 42, 53, 61, 63–64, 74, 106–7, 247; amendments are contrary to sentiments of, 220; are sovereign, 7, 8, 16, 258; common benefit, protection, and security of as end of government, 53; Congress will be servants of, 10; Constitution based upon, not on states, 106; endangered from majority violating bills of rights, 257–58; danger of licentiousness of, 9; elect delegates to ratifying conventions, 8; expect greatest political benefits from Constitution, 309; favor a bill of rights, 137; Federalist disregard voice of, 153–54; government is strong when it protects rights of, 48; have reserved powers under Constitution, 10; have sanctioned Constitution, 203; hearts

INDEX 507

and affection of do not support Constitution, 454; joyful with ratification of Constitution, 93, 151; laws operate on under Constitution, 107; laws should apply to, 366; like Constitution better unamended than with amendments, 275; want amendments, 200, 292; majority of Americans feel Constitution is dangerous, 65; most don't understand political disquisitions, 66; must have confidence in their government, 300; need to be virtuous to attain happiness, 152; no government can operate well without confidence of, 6; only few are qualified and able to serve in public office, 457; opinion of is important and must be considered, 328–29; not endangered by representatives of in Congress, 109; rights and privileges of as end of government, 48; Shays's Rebellion as example of danger from, 151; still attached to principles of Revolution with liberty, 65; tyranny emanates from majority of, 9, 257–58; when rightly informed will decide correctly, 143; will decide merits of Federalists and Antifederalists, 220; will elect friends of amendments to U.S. House of Representatives, 153; will no longer be deceived by Antifederalists, 365; will of should rule, 358; will see through Federalist lies and deception, 303; James Wilson has contempt for, 284

PERSON, THOMAS (Granville Co., N.C.)
—letter from, cited, 53n

PETERS, RICHARD (Philadelphia Co., Pa.): id., 468
—letter from, 188–89

PETERS, SAMUEL (England)
—letter to, 222–23

PETITION, RIGHT TO: protected in Md. minority amendments, 476; guaranteed in Va. Convention amendments, 55. *See also* Instructions

PETITIONS: Harrisburg Convention sends to Pa. Assembly, 4, 164n, 179–82, 196; Pa. Antifederalists to de-certify Pa. ratification, 163n; Pa. Assembly should send to first Congress requesting a second convention, 178–79

PETTIT, CHARLES (Philadelphia): elected to Harrisburg Convention, 174, 175; as delegate to Harrisburg Convention, 184, 194; nominated for U.S. House of Representatives, 336, 344, 368, 376
—letter to, 142–43

PHILADELPHIA: Constitution would commercially benefit, 230; newspapers in oppose amendments, 191; as possible federal capital, 87, 160; procession of, 91, 91n; proposed meeting in to elect delegates to Harrisburg Convention, 170

PHILADELPHIA COMMITTEE OF CORRESPONDENCE
—letter from, 185–86; cited, 183n

PHILADELPHIA COUNTY: meeting appoints delegates to Lancaster Convention, 254

PHILIPS, JOSIAH (Princess Anne Co., Va.): bill of attainder case of, 28, 30n

PICKERING, TIMOTHY (Salem, Mass.)
—letters to, 185–86; quoted, 409n; cited, 183n

PIPER, GEORGE (Bedminster, Bucks Co., Pa.): attends Bucks Co. meeting, 172

PIRACY: Congress can define and provide punishment for, 29

PLANTERS: U.S. House of Representatives will have fellow-feeling with, 35. *See also* Agriculture; Farmers

POETRY: Lucretius, 156; John Milton, *Paradise Lost*, 73, 81n, 202, 202n, 316; Alexander Pope, *The Sixth Epistle of the First Book of Horace*, 420, 420n; Alexander Pope, *An Essay on Man*, 389, 389n; Alexander Pope, *The Rape of Lock*, 406, 407n; Shakespeare, *Hamlet*, 87, 87n; Shakespeare, *Henry VI*, 291n, 292. *See also* Literary references

POLICE POWERS: belong to states, 334

POLITICAL PARTIES: attempt to eliminate names of in Baltimore, Md., 124; criticism of, 186–87, 367–68, 410–11; is species of corruption in free states, 428; often pursue same ends in different ways, 410; in Pa., 209, 210n; partisanship should be avoided, 329; partisanship subsiding in Pa., 142; should drop "anti" from name of Antifederalists, 186–87; will increase likelihood of impeachments, 428; will lead to charges of treason, 429. *See also* Partisan politics

POLITICAL AND LEGAL WRITERS AND WRITINGS: advanced American thinking on principles of freedom, 407; John Adams, *Defence of the Constitutions*, 127, 128n, 220, 221n, 315 not always complete title; Marchese di Becarria, *Crimes and Punishments*, 304, 305n; James Burgh, *Political Disquisitions*, 436, 436n; William Coxe, *Sketches of . . . Switzerland*, 156, 156n; David Hume, *History of England*, 394, 395n; Abbé de Mably, *Observations of Establishment of U.S.*, 138, 138n; Comte de Mirabeau, *Reflections on the Observations on the Importance of the American Revolution*, 81n; Montesquieu, *Spirit of Laws*, 304, 305n; Thomas Paine, "The American Crisis" V, 219,

220n; Jonathan Swift, *A Tale of a Tub*, 250, 252n; Adam Smith, *Wealth of Nations*, 309, 309n, 369, 371; Emmerich de Vattel, *The Law of Nations*, 392–93, 394, 395n
—William Blackstone: *Commentaries*, 36, 36n, 37n, 379, 381, 381n, 386, 386n; on king can do no wrong, 417, 419n; on Parliamentary supremacy, 102n; on residuum of human rights, 96n; on danger of courts without juries, 84; on importance of impartial administration of justice, 277, 280n; quoted by R. H. Lee, 96n
See also Literary references
POLL TAXES: Antifederalist amendments prohibit, 294; criticism of amendment to prohibit, 195; defended, 294; Federalists said to favor, 389; opposition to Congress' power to levy, 133, 476; Constitution will allow, 391. *See also* Taxation, direct taxes
POPULATION: majority of favors amendments to Constitution, 226–27; number of free blacks in Va., 49n
POST OFFICE: Congress should have power to operate, 132; limited franking privileges should be allowed members of Congress, 316; limited postage advocated, 316
POWERS, JAMES (Cumberland Co., Pa.): on committee to draft Cumberland Co. circular letter, 166n
PRESBYTERIANS: Antifederalist say it will be established church in America, 270
PRESIDENT, U.S.: criticism of connection with Senate, 119, 134, 251; defense of connection with Senate, 417–19; criticism of powers of, 48, 67, 248; danger of being elected by Antifederalist electors, 235; defense of powers of, 418; has only enumerated powers, 42; impeachment as check on, 241, 417; importance of first appointment to, 229; long term of is beneficial for treaty making, 440–41; praise of Constitution's provisions for, 315–16; procedure for election, 309, 310n, 402–3, 418; qualifications of defended, 117; Washington will be first, 81n, 127, 137, 214, 229, 285, 356, 396; will be virtuous, 409
—re-eligibility of, 125; objection to, 136, 137, 360, 438–39; objection to rotation in office requirement for, 434
—military powers of: defense of, 403–4; defense of lack of prohibition on field command of, 241; opposition to field command of, 56, 402, 476; should have knowledge of theory of war, 403
PRESS, FREEDOM OF THE: Constitution does not endanger, 11, 42, 122, 230, 365; Constitution does not protect, 26, 31; Constitution endangers, 8, 14, 43, 67, 75, 120; defense of Constitution's lack of protection for, 34, 385–86; federal government will never restrain, 125; importance of, 66, 249, 385; needs to be protected, 63, 124, 135–36, 144; not included in Harrisburg Convention's amendments, 194; not protected in Great Britain, 15, 15n; praised as bulwark of liberty, 316; praised, 26, 278; protected in U.S., 15; protected in Md. minority amendments, 475; protected in Va. Convention amendments, 55; secured in all state constitutions, 122; taxes on books and printing presses should not be allowed, 316; will be protected by amendments, 444–45; will be protected if needed, 408
PRICE, RICHARD (England): praise of, 220
—letter to, 364
PRIMOGENITURE: disallowed in Va., 34, 36n
PRIVY COUNCIL: opposition to, 417; should be created, 476
PROPERTY, PRIVATE: Constitution endangers, 31, 46, 58, 73, 77, 98, 251, 474; Constitution will protect and increase value of, 323; derived from William the Conqueror, 64n; as a natural right, 53; no danger to from ecclesiastical power in U.S., 407; protected by suffrage, 16; protected from arbitrary search and seizure in Va. Convention amendments, 55; protection of at stake in election of Congress, 247; should be protected, 96n; should be taxed to provide revenue for defense, 321–22; state constitutions violate rights of foreigners to, 444
PROSPERITY: Constitution will promote, 219, 443; Constitution with amendments will promote, 309; depends on Constitution, 436; depends on Federalist control of Congress, 421. *See also* Anarchy
PRUSSIA: treaty with U.S. prohibits letters of marque and reprisal, 316
PSEUDONYMS: "A.B.," 174, 211–13; Albert, 243–44; Alfred (Caleb Strong), 255–56, 273, 274n, 277–80, 280n, 395n; Alfredus (Samuel Tenney), 83–85, 85n; An American, 424n; An American Citizen (Tench Coxe), 7–8, 407–8, 409n, 442–45, 456–57; An Inhabitant, 445–47; Anti, 248–49; Antilocalis, 448; A Bostonian, 432–33; Brutus, 36n; Camillus, 232–33, 238–39, 244n; Cassandra, 64–66n; Cassius, 96n, 196–98; Centinel (Samuel Bryan), 250–52, 282–84, 324n, 348–49, 364–65, 367n; Christian Farmer, 280–82, 282n; A Citizen of New-Haven (Roger Sherman), 433–36;

INDEX 509

Civis, 192–93; Consistency, 421–23; Constitutionalist, 432, 433n; The Conversion, 406–7; A Countryman (De Witt Clinton), 81n; A Despiser of Demagogues, Would-be-ats, and Wheelbarrow-men, 193; "E.," 336n–37n; An Elector, 424–25, 430, 431n; The Farmer (Thomas Cogswell), 85n; A Federal Centinel, 203, 203n, 203–6, 249n; Federal Commonwealth, 237–38; A Federal Republican, 410–13, 413n; Federalism, 233–37, 238, 239n, 297n; A Federalist, 161; A Federalist (multiple items), 155n, 156–58, 161, 239–42, 265n, 273–74, 364–67, 367–68; A Federalist who is for Amendments, 372–74; The Federalist (Publius) (Alexander Hamilton, James Madison, and John Jay), 158, 360; Foreign Spectator (Nicholas Collin), 264n, 264n–67, 285–89, 293–96, 305–9, 321–23, 329–32, 341–44, 349–52, 361–63, 368–72n, 379–81, 383–86, 396–400, 402–5, 417–19, 426–29, 440–42, 449–53; François de la E——., 388–89; A Freeman, 184, 189–90, 190n, 246–48, 288, 289n; A Friend of Society and Liberty, 131, 145; A Friend to Amendments, 153–54, 311n, 337–39; A Friend to Consistency and Stability in Government, 274–76; A Friend to Good Government, 92; A Friend to Liberty and Union, 332–37n, 364–67, 367n; A Friend to Society and Liberty, 131, 131n; A Friend to the People, 310–11, 339n; A Friend to Truth and Freedom, 332–33; Gehennapolis, 264n–65n, 267n; Honestus (Benjamin Austin, Jr.), 267–72, 299–303n, 327–29; Hortensius, 151–52; An Inhabitant, 445–47; Laco, 153, 154n; Lucullus, 325, 348–49; Many (Arthur Campbell), 66; A Marylander (Otho Holland Williams), 453–54; Nobody, 420; North End, 423–24; An Old German, 226–28; One of the People, 29n; A Real Federalist, 71–72, 71n; A Real German, 128; A Real Patriot, 374–75; Republican (Edmund Randolph), 87–90, 137, 138n, 139n, 191n; Republican (defense of George Clinton), 139n; A Republican, 160–61; Senex, 219–21n; Sidney (Abraham Yates, Jr.), 389–95; Solon (William Heath), 154–55, 161, 192n, 199–201n, 201n, 231–32, 232n, 303–5n; Solon, jun. (David Howell), 85–86, 86n, 147–49, 149n; Steady, 198–99; Switch, 296–97; Sydney (Abraham Yates, Jr.), 59–61; Tarantula, 232–33, 239n, 244, 244n; A True Federalist, 359n, 387–88, 415n; Truth, 230–31; The Voice of the People, 218n, 218–19; A Word to the Wise, 187; "X," 141–42, 191n

PUNISHMENTS, CRUEL AND UNUSUAL: Constitution does not prohibit, 31; danger of under Constitution, 25, 36; no danger of under Constitution, 33, 384; prohibited in Va. Declaration of Rights, 29; prohibited in Va. Convention amendments, 55

QUAKERS: none attend Harrisburg Convention, 190; persecuted in Mass. by Presbyterians, 270
QUARTERING SOLDIERS, 343–44; prohibited in Md. minority amendments, 475; prohibited in Va. Convention amendments, 55

RAMSEY, HUGH (Warwick, Bucks Co., Pa.): attends Bucks Co. meeting, 172
RANDOLPH, BEVERLEY (Cumberland Co., Va.): meets with Patrick Henry, 208; sends Va. resolution requesting second convention to Congress, 6
—letter from, cited, 413n
RANDOLPH, EDMUND (Henrico Co., Va.; id., BoR, II, 503): called a young Benedict Arnold, 431, 432n; criticized, 263, 273; criticizes Patrick Henry's proposed declaration of rights, 50; favors second constitutional convention, 188, 188n, 222, 273; as possible author of "Republican," 88n; resigning as governor and entering House of Delegates, 138, 138n, 262n, 292, 292n, 346, 353; suggests a compilation of proposed amendments be printed, 129; transmits N.Y. circular letter to Va. legislature, 4; will introduce resolution for second convention in Va. House of Delegates, 262, 263
—speeches of in Va. Convention, 11–12, 12–13, 32–36, 49–51; praise of, 10–11
—letters from, 137–38, 198, 208, 276–77; cited, 88n, 145
—letters to, 145–46, 188, 311–12; quoted, 96; cited, 88n, 137n, 138n, 311, 436n
RATIFICATION, PROCESS OF: Constitution only half established with ratification, 234, 281; Constitution will be implemented with approval of nine states, 11; eight states have ratified, 62, 127; eight states ratify by time of Va. Convention, 88; nine states have ratified, 124, 135, 406; eleven states have ratified, 123, 127, 128, 147, 160, 169, 173, 215, 217, 222, 268, 364, 386, 405, 411, 445, 446; enough states have ratified to put Constitution in motion, 200; if known Mass. style would have been used by early state conventions, 207; N.C. rejected by a large majority, 138; N.H. Convention will

meet soon, 58; N.H. as ninth state to ratify, 3; N.Y. has ratified, 136, 140; praise of process provided in Article V, 200; S.C. has ratified, 51n, 86, 90; situation changed after nine states ratified, 85; six states ratified without recommending amendments, 433; state conventions follow Mass. example, 218; ten states have ratified, 90, 122, 131, 165; importance of Va. to, 63; Va. as tenth state to ratify, 3; Va. has ratified, 67–68; violates Articles of Confederation, 77, 80, 122, 122n–23n. *See also* Conventions, state

RATIFICATION, PROSPECTS FOR: too far along to be rejected by any one state, 144
— New York: hesitating, 90; uncertain, 86, 87, 91; ratifies Constitution, 3, 128, 136, 140; will ratify, 86, 137; with Va. are least disposed to Constitution, 217; expected to reject by N.C. Antifederalists, 146; nothing heard from, 135
— North Carolina: hopeful because of Va. ratification, 92–93; expected to ratify but it rejects Constitution, 146; hopeful, 216; will ratify, 137, 169, 290, 382, 437; nothing heard from, 135, 137
— Rhode Island: will not ratify, 135; will ratify, 169
— South Carolina: will ratify, 86
— Virginia: will ratify, 86; nothing heard from, 135

"A REAL FEDERALIST": text of, 71–72; quoted, 71n
"A REAL GERMAN": text of, 128
"A REAL PATRIOT": text of, 374–75
RECALL: senators should be subject to, 180, 194
REED, JACOB (New York City): as safe conveyance for Antifederalist mail, 52n
REED, JOSEPH (Philadelphia): criticized by Federalists, 282
RELIGION: general principles of should be taught in public schools, 363; Christianity is best religion to make good members of society through morality, 117; clergy prohibited from holding office in some state constitutions, 443, 445n; Presbyterism will be established church in America, 271; Roman Catholicism will be established church in America, 270
RELIGION, FREEDOM OF: Catholic countries extend toleration, 114; Constitution will endanger, 31, 43, 75, 94, 113, 120; Constitution will not endanger, 11, 34, 115, 116, 121, 231, 269, 305, 361–63; Constitution will protect, 114; criticism of established religions, 75; does not apply to criminal acts based on religious errors, 125; needs to be protected, 124, 135–36, 165; protected in Md. minority amendments, 476; protected in Va. Convention amendments, 56; Va. Act for Religious Freedom, 260n; variety of sects will prevent oppression, 13, 332, 362

RELIGIOUS TESTS: defense of Constitution's prohibition of, 113, 114, 118; don't elect advocates of in Pa., 206; opposition to Constitution's prohibition of, 117, 257; praise of Constitution's prohibition of, 12–13, 388–89; praise of prohibition of, 121–22; denial that oaths imply a religious test, 363; S.C. amendment to insert the word "other" as a clerical error, 435, 436n

REPRESENTATIVES: need to live among constituents, 63; not adequately provided for in Constitution, 119; should regularly stand for re-election, 54. *See also* House of Representatives, U.S.; Republican form of government

"REPUBLICAN" (Edmund Randolph), 191n; essays sent to Madison, 137, 138n; text of, 87–90
"REPUBLICAN": defense of George Clinton, 139n
"A REPUBLICAN": text of, 160–61
REPUBLICAN FORM OF GOVERNMENT: abuses of power likely under, 258; Americans must choose between aristocracy and, 387–88; bill of rights not needed in and maybe dangerous, 12; can only secure political liberty, 132; common law sometimes needs changes in, 34–35; confederacy of republican states needed for liberty and happiness, 179; criticism of Constitution's guarantee of, 78, 120; defense of Constitution's guarantee of, 116, 154; don't elect Federalists who oppose, 154; love of liberty is vital principle of, 266; majority rules in, 215; necessity for delegation of power to representatives, 41; representatives needed in large countries, 16; standing army inconsistent with principles of, 133–34. *See also* Representatives
REPUBLICAN PRINCIPLES: are adhered to by the people, 301–2; standing army inconsistent with, 133–34; need to revisit fundamental principles, 14
REQUISITIONS: amendments would require, 294; Antifederalists want before direct taxes are levied, 69, 159, 240–41; Conn. fails to pay, 381; opposition to, 435
RESERVED POWERS: Constitution has, 10; Constitution protects, 14–15; denial of

INDEX

theory of, 9, 13, 24, 27, 30, 45, 74, 95, 103, 110, 111, 121, 134; need to be specified in amendments, 56, 121, 207; not applicable to Va. constitution, 28; remain with the states, 365; remain with the people, 42; theory of endorsed, 63–64, 96, 101, 106–7, 113, 257, 260n
—Article II of Articles of Confederation, 27n, 103, 105n, 106, 107, 108n, 121n; is defective, 50; referred to as a bill of rights, 27; reserves powers, 74, 95, 96n
—in amendments proposed by: Harrisburg Convention, 179; seven conventions, 286; in Md., minority's, 473; Mass. Convention, 64, 64n; Va. Convention's concerning actually strengthens Congress, 286
See also Implied powers; Necessary and proper clause
RHODE ISLAND: Antifederalist U.S. Senate would induce ratification by, 209; assistance needed to obtain amendments, 148; called that little trollop, 183; criticism of radical economic system, 372, 382; has not called a state convention, 3, 90, 217; has not done anything, 431; has not ratified Constitution, 382, 405; hope it doesn't ratify soon because it will support amendments, 136; in interest of to be in the Union, 159; is out of the Union, 137, 148, 437; leaves Confederation Congress, 150; not an important state, 386; opposes the Constitution, 281; opposition to by is reason for favoring, 372–73; receives N.Y. circular letter and sends it to town meetings, 372, 378, 378n; reference to "wiseacres," 220, 221n; refused to send delegation to Constitutional Convention, 149, 149n; will be supported by N.C.'s rejection and N.Y.'s circular letter, 182–83; will not ratify, 135; will ratify, 169
RICH VERSUS POOR: Constitution would not benefit rich, 230; well born attack Antifederalist leaders, 282–83. *See also* Aristocracy
RICHMOND, VA.: R. H. Lee fears sickness in, 70
RIGGS, CALEB S. (N.J.): id., 468
—letter from, 87
RIGHT OF REVOLUTION: people have in Md. minority amendments, 476; people have included in Va. Convention amendments, 53–54; whenever happiness of the people requires, 225
RIGHTS: cannot list all, 287; Constitution endangers, 94, 98, 120, 177; Constitution will not endanger, 34; endangered by ambiguity and indefinite expressions, 24, 26,

511

35, 40, 74, 111, 113, 119, 121, 140, 177, 243, 303, 304; endangered by Constitution, 36–37; future ones will be discovered, 64; only guarded in Article I, section 9, 31. *See also* Bill of rights; Liberty; Reserved powers
ROBERTSON, DAVID (Dinwiddie Co., Va.): id., 8n
RODGERS, JOHN (Pa.): as delegate to Harrisburg Convention, 177
RODGERS, WILLIAM (Pa.): as delegate to Harrisburg Convention, 177
ROTATION IN OFFICE: importance of, 66; needed for Senate and President, 125, 136, 137, 360, 434, 438–39; requirement among Va. Convention amendments, 54; objection to rotation in office requirement for President, 434
RUCKMAN, JAMES (Plumstead, Bucks Co., Pa.): attends Bucks Co. meeting, 173
RUGGLES, TIMOTHY DWIGHT (Boston/Nova Scotia): Samuel Adams and Elbridge Gerry compared with, 153, 154n
RUSH, BENJAMIN (Philadelphia; id., BoR, II, 503): attacks Antifederalist leaders, 282; criticism of, 348; member of Philadelphia committee of correspondence, 186n
RUTLEDGE, EDWARD (St. Philip's and St. Michael's Parishes, Charleston, S.C.)
—letter from, quoted, 255n
—letter to, 254–55n

SATIRE: "The Conversion," 406–7; reference to Don Quixote chasing windmills, 385; "Truth," 230–31
SEABRING, HENRY (Solesbury, Bucks Co., Pa.): attends Bucks Co. meeting, 173
SEAGLE, BENJAMIN (Richland, Bucks Co., Pa.): attends Bucks Co. meeting, 173
SEARCH AND SEIZURE: danger of general warrants under Constitution, 26, 44, 271; defense of lack of protection from general warrants, 33; protection against in Md. minority amendments, 474; protection against in Va. Convention amendments, 55; in John Wilkes case, 385
SECRECY: necessary in treaty-making, 441; and Harrisburg Convention, 171, 175, 176, 189, 191, 193, 196, 197, 204–5, 206; Congress' journal will be kept secret, 31; criticism of Antifederalists for, 31, 184, 237, 332–33; in government condemned, 184; some Antifederalists attempt to destroy Constitution using, 153
SECTIONALISM: fear of under Constitution, 150. *See also* North versus South; Northern States

SEDGWICK, THEODORE (Stockbridge, Mass.; id., BoR, II, 503)
—letters from, 225–26, 314–15n; cited, 314
—letters to, 182–83, 340
SELF INCRIMINATION: defense of Constitution's lack of protection against, 384; prohibited in Va. Convention amendments, 54
SENATE, U.S.: appointments to have favored Federalists, 387; checked by House of Representatives, 50; controlled by Antifederalists would induce ratification by N.C. and R.I., 209; criticism of connection with President, 119, 134, 251; defense of connection with President, 417–19; criticism of power of to try impeachments, 278, 426–29; defense of power to try impeachments, 418–19, 434; criticism of six-year term of office, 119; danger if elected by Antifederalist-controlled state legislatures, 235–36; danger of corruption in, 251, 419; difficulty of electing in Md., 150; equality of states in, 444; Federalists will have a majority in, 415; lack of rotation in office requirement, 125, 136, 137, 360, 434, 438–39; from Mass. will oppose amendments, 201–2; no danger from, 35; praise of long term, 440–41; praise of staggered election of, 429; should be subject to recall, 180; Southern States want amendment allowing voting by proxy in, 163; Va. will probably elect two Antifederalists to, 327; will be aristocratic, 251; will represent interests of the states, 366, 408, 444, 455
—candidates for and elections to: Samuel Adams nominated for, 153, 154n, 191; Josiah Bartlett as candidate for, 337–38; Elbridge Gerry nominated for, 153, 154n, 191; William Grayson elected to, 290, 339, 340, 361, 377, 405, 449; John Langdon as candidate for, 337; Richard Henry Lee elected to, 261, 290, 298, 339, 340, 354, 361, 377, 405, 449; Samuel Livermore as candidate for, 310, 337; James Madison as candidate for, 261, 290, 298–99; James Madison defeated for, 298, 312, 339, 340, 354, 356, 358, 414, 449; John Sullivan as candidate for, 337–38
See also Privy council
"SENEX": text of, 219–21n
SEPARATE CONFEDERACIES: denounced, 90. *See also* Union
SEPARATION OF POWERS: alone will not secure liberty, 76; Constitution praised for, 221, 315–16; criticism of insufficiency of in Constitution, 24; criticism of connection of President and Senate, 119, 134,

251; defense of connection of President and Senate, 417–19, 418; espoused by John Adams in *Defence of the Constitutions*, 315; Great Britain has, 277; necessity of in Va. Convention amendments, 54; praise of, 418
SHAW, JOHN (Plumstead, Bucks Co., Pa.): attends Bucks Co. meeting, 173
SHAYS'S REBELLION: beneficial in showing government shortcomings, 382; as example of dangerous domestic insurrection, 168; honest men condemn, 84; serves as example of danger from the people, 151; transmittal of printed history of, 151, 151n
SHERMAN, ROGER (New Haven, Conn.): as author of "A Citizen of New-Haven," 436n
SHIELDS, JOHN (Westmoreland Co., Pa.): Westmoreland Co., Pa., Antifederalist committee of correspondence, 132
SHIPPEN, THOMAS LEE (Philadelphia/Europe)
—letters to, 66–67, 175–76, 361
SHIPPEN, WILLIAM, JR. (Philadelphia): id., 468–69
—letters from, 175–76, 361
SHORT, WILLIAM (Surry Co., Va./France)
—letters to, 123, 395–96, 400
"SIDNEY" (Abraham Yates, Jr.): text of, 389–95
SINGLETARY, AMOS (Sutton, Mass.)
—speech of in Mass. Convention cited, 257, 260n
SINNICKSON, THOMAS (Salem Co., N.J.)
—letter to, 91–92
SLAVE TRADE: Constitution condemned for not prohibiting, 80; criticism of Constitution's provision limiting Congress' prohibition of, 31, 77–78
SLAVERY: Congress will be able to emancipate during a war, 45; denounced but impractical to emancipate, 46; detested, 45; as a local matter which Congress should not interfere with, 46; Va. acts allowing emancipation of, 46, 49n
SMILIE, JOHN (Fayette Co., Pa.): as delegate to Harrisburg Convention, 170, 177, 186
SMITH, ABIGAIL ADAMS (Queens Co., N.Y.): id., 469
—letter from, 144
SMITH, ABRAHAM (Huntingdon Co., Pa.): and violence in Huntingdon, Pa., 171, 171–72
SMITH, JOHN (Huntingdon Co., Pa.): and violence in Huntingdon, Pa., 171–72
—letter to, cited, 413n

INDEX   513

SMITH, JOHN (Springfield, Bucks Co., Pa.):
    attends Bucks Co. meeting, 172
SMITH, MELANCTON (New York City/Dutchess Co., N.Y.): thought to be "A Federal Republican," 413n
—letter from, cited, 413n
SMITH, MERIWETHER (Essex Co., Va.): id., 469; copies Va. Convention amendments, 56n
—campaign address of, 439
—letter from, cited, 439n
SMITH, ROBERT (Pa.): as delegate to Harrisburg Convention, 177
—letter from, cited, 51n
—letter to, 130-31
SMITH, SAMUEL (Buckingham, Bucks Co., Pa.): attends Bucks Co. meeting, 173
SMITH, SAMUEL (Rockhill, Bucks Co., Pa.): attends Bucks Co. meeting, 172; chairs Bucks Co. meeting, 173, 174
SMITH, THOMAS DUNCAN (Huntingdon Co., Pa.): id., 469
—letters from, 171-72; cited, 171, 172n
SMITH, WILLIAM (Baltimore, Md.): support for as U.S. representative, 454
SMITH, WILLIAM (Suffolk Co., N.Y.)
—letter to, 224
SMUGGLING: always a problem in America, 306. See also Commerce; Impost
SNODGRASS, BENJAMIN (Warwick, Bucks Co., Pa.): attends Bucks Co. meeting, 172
SNODGRASS, JAMES (Newbritain, Bucks Co., Pa.): attends Bucks Co. meeting, 172
SOLIDAY, DANIEL (Bedminster, Bucks Co., Pa.): attends Bucks Co. meeting, 172
"SOLON" (William Heath), 161, 192n, 201n, 232n; text of, 154-55, 199-201n, 231-32, 303-5n; William Heath as possible author of, 155n, 156
"SOLON, JUN.": text of, 85-86, 147-49; David Howell as probable author of, 86n, 149n
SOUTH CAROLINA: Convention of recommends amendments, 65, 285; has ratified, 51n, 86, 90; will ratify, 86; constitution of prohibits clergy from holding public office, 445n
SOUTHERN STATES: favor different amendments than Harrisburg Convention, 222; want an amendment allowing senators to vote by proxy, 163. See also North versus South
SOVEREIGN IMMUNITY: amendment proposed guaranteeing, 450; Constitution allegedly does not allow individuals to sue states, 216, 216n
SOVEREIGNTY: definition of, 7; located in the people, 7, 8, 16, 258; resides in ratifying conventions, 7; resides in state legislatures, 7; resides in the people in electing all officers, 8; retained by states except where expressly vested in Congress, 180; states will lose under Constitution, 58, 61, 78, 128, 132; should retain sovereignty, freedom and independence in Va. Convention amendment, 56; and sovereign immunity, 216, 216n, 450
SPAIGHT, RICHARD DOBBS (Craven Co., N.C.): id., 469
—speeches of in N.C. Convention, 99, 121-22
SPAIN: King Philip's oppression, 76; and negotiations with U.S. over navigation of Mississippi River, 110, 111n; no reserved powers in, 23; tyranny of in The Netherlands, 73, 81n; uses civil law, 25
SPEECH, FREEDOM OF: protected in Va. Convention amendments, 55
SPEEDY TRIALS: defense of Constitution's lack of protection for, 33, 384; in Va. Convention amendments, 54
SPENCER, SAMUEL (Anson Co., N.C.): id., 469
—speeches of in N.C. Convention, 94-96n, 103-5, 107-8n, 111, 118; responses to, 96, 97, 105, 106-7, 108, 109
SPRAGUE, JOHN (Lancaster, Mass.): as Mass. candidate for U.S. House of Representatives, 388
SPRINGER, ZADOK (Fayette Co., Pa.): signs election certificate for Harrisburg Convention, 170
STANLY, JOHN WRIGHT (New Bern, N.C.): id., 469
—letter from, 437-38
—letter to, 145
STATEN ISLAND, N.Y.: will secede from state if N.Y. rejects Constitution, 91
STATES UNDER ARTICLES OF CONFEDERATION: defend rights, 78; are experiencing anarchy, 68, 135, 142, 197, 266, 333, 412. See also Constitutions, state
STATES UNDER THE CONSTITUTION: amendments needed to preserve, 65; endangered, 40; laws operate on people not on states, 107; non-ratifying states must shift for themselves, 85-86; should retain sovereignty, freedom and independence in Va. Convention, 56; and sovereign immunity, 216, 216n, 450; of Senate will represent interests of, 366, 408, 444, 456; weakened so as not to endanger justice, 324; will be abolished, 132, 249, 412; will lose sovereignty, 61, 78, 128; will not be abolished, 105, 288, 365

"STEADY": text of, 198–99
STERETT, SAMUEL (Baltimore, Md.): id., 447n, 470; praised, 454
—circular letter and address on his candidacy for representative, 447
STERRETT, WILLIAM (Cumberland Co., Pa.): on committee to draft Cumberland Co. circular letter, 166n; as delegate to Harrisburg Convention, 177
STEWART, THOMAS (Newbritain, Bucks Co., Pa.): attends Bucks Co. meeting, 172
STEWART, WALTER (Philadelphia): member of Philadelphia committee of correspondence, 186n
STILES, EZRA (New Haven, Conn.): id., 470
—letter from, 127–28n
STILLMAN, SAMUEL (Boston)
—speech of in Mass. Convention quoted, 273, 274n
STRONG, CALEB (Northampton, Mass.): id., 470; as author of "Alfred," 256n; as possible author of "Solon," 155n
STUART, DAVID (Fairfax Co., Va.): wants to publish Madison's letter supporting amendments, 356
—letter to, cited, 214
SULLIVAN, JOHN (Durham, N.H.): as candidate for U.S. Senate, 337–38
SUMNER, INCREASE (Roxbury, Mass.)
—speech of in Mass. Convention quoted, 301, 303n
SUPREMACY CLAUSE: criticism of, 36–37, 95; criticism of treaties as, 36, 113; defense of, 288; negates protections in state constitutions, 334
SUSPENDING LAWS: not allowed in Va. Convention amendments, 54
"SWITCH": text of, 296–97
SWITZERLAND: Antifederalists misquote as examples, 11; happiness thrives in, 155–56; no domestic insurrection in, 156; not involved in war, 156; U.S. government modeled on thirteen cantons of, 155
"SYDNEY" (Abraham Yates, Jr.): text of, 59–61

"TARANTULA," 239n, 244, 244n; text of, 232–33
TAXATION: Congress should be left free to exercise, 296; Congress should have impost power, 132; Congress will have too much power under Constitution, 26, 67, 78, 130, 217, 283; Constitution will alleviate problems of, 423; danger Antifederalists will weaken Congress' power over, 138; danger of combined power of purse and sword under Constitution, 24, 61, 67,

120; defense of Congress' power over, 294; defense of federal judiciary control over enforcement of cases of, 105; difficulty of creating equitable system of, 322–23; high in postwar America, 381; must be approved by the people or their representatives, 54; state judiciaries could be given jurisdiction in revenue cases, 473
—direct taxes: benefits of, 308, 321–23; Congress needs power over, 158–59; danger of under Constitution, 24, 120, 133, 400; needed for Constitution to succeed, 146–47, 209, 421; amendments require requisitions to precede, 69, 180, 240–41, 294, 295–96, 476; opposition to requisitions preceding, 159, 306, 435; Federalists said to favor, 389; Edmund Randolph defends, 222; N.Y. Convention opposes, 158–59; opposition to called very mischievous, 445
—excise taxes: benefits and detriments of, 307, 321; danger from Constitution, 391; defined, 307; Federalists said to favor, 389; would be laid on home manufactures, 271; as a main point in Constitution, 209; Congress' power to levy should be defined, 133; N.Y. amendment restrictions on American manufactures limited to ardent spirits, 295; Va., N.C., and Md. minority amendments provision for, 294, 308
—poll taxes: amendments prohibit, 294; criticism of amendment to prohibit, 195; defended, 294; Federalists said to favor, 389; opposition to Congress' power to levy, 133, 476; should be prohibited, 144, 180; Constitution will allow, 391
TENDER ACTS: Constitution prohibits, 323, 324, 370, 443; advocates of should not be elected, 206; opposition to, 84
TENNEY, SAMUEL (Exeter, N.H.): as author of "Alfredus," 85n
TERRITORIES: can be given up in treaties, 441–42; federal government needs to provide for education in, 363
THATCHER, GEORGE (Biddeford, Maine)
—letter from, cited, 214
—letters to, 140, 214–15
THOMAS, DAVID (Newbritain, Bucks Co., Pa.): attends Bucks Co. meeting, 172
THOMPSON, JOHN (Tinicum, Bucks Co., Pa.): attends Bucks Co. meeting, 173
TILGHMAN, JAMES (Philadelphia): id., 470
—letter from, 150–51
TILLINGHAST, CHARLES (New York City): as secretary of New York Federal Republican Committee, 59n

INDEX

515

TOASTS: supporting speedy and unanimous adoption of amendments, 82; in Windham, Conn., confusion to amendments, 68
TORRENCE, JOSEPH (Fayette Co., Pa.): signs election certificate for Harrisburg Convention, 170
TORTURE. *See* Punishments, cruel and unusual
TRANQUILITY: hope for U.S., 144. *See also* Insurrection, domestic; Order
TREASON: Antifederalists accused of against majesty of the people, 202; danger of excessive charges of under Constitution, 25; defense of Constitution's provision concerning, 28–29, 342–43, 365, 384; political parties will lead to charges of, 429; states cannot be guilty of, 342–43; and suspension of habeas corpus, 124–25
TREATIES: amendments proposed concerning, 440; to be enforced by federal government instead of state assemblies, 242; Confederation Congress unable to enforce, 106, 257; Congress should have power to approve, 132; criticism of as supreme law of the land, 36, 113; enforcement of is necessary, 106; nine states needed to ratify under Articles of Confederation, 111n, 435; objections to ceding territories needing three-fourths of both houses, 434–35; ratification of as a main point in Constitution, 209; secrecy needed in making, 441; should not violate state bills of rights or constitutions, 476; should not violate U.S. or state laws unless approved by U.S. House of Representatives, 181. *See also* Foreign affairs
TREATY OF PEACE (1783): U.S. citizens violate, 106
TREDWELL, THOMAS (Suffolk Co., N.Y.): id., 470; as possible author of undelivered speech in N.Y. Convention, 71n
TRUBY, CHRISTOPHER (Westmoreland Co., Pa.): Westmoreland Co., Pa., Antifederalist committee of correspondence, 132
"A TRUE FEDERALIST," 359n, 415n; text of, 387–88
TRUMBULL, JONATHAN, JR. (Lebanon, Conn.): id., 470
—letter from, 293
—letter to, 387
"TRUTH": text of, 230–31
TUCKER, ST. GEORGE (Chesterfield Co., Va.)
—letter to, 252
TUCKER, THOMAS TUDOR (Charleston, S.C.; id., BoR, II, 505–6)
—letter from, 252

TURBERVILLE, GEORGE LEE (Richmond Co., Va.; id., BoR, II, 506)
—letters from, 263, 290–91, 340–41, 345–46, 356–57, 415–16, 420–21; quoted, 314n; cited, 298, 341n, 420
—letters to, 312–14; cited, 263n, 353, 354n, 356, 357n, 358, 359n, 413, 414, 415n
TYRANNY: Constitution will lead to, 67, 73, 122, 169, 291, 334, 406, 456; danger of from wherever real power lies, 258; of King Philip in The Netherlands, 73, 81n; majority of people threatens, 258; ninety percent of globe lives under, 456; will not occur as long as people are armed with a noble spirit, 331; without jury trial can be opposed only by civil war, 278. *See also* Despotism

UNION: advantageous for commerce, 89; advantageous for N.C. and R.I., 159; advantageous to Va., 89; amendments endanger, 202, 209; amendments will promote, 47, 178, 200, 354–55, 447; Americans support, 151–52; Antifederalists endanger, 50, 237, 376, 402; under Articles of Confederation is dead after nine states ratify Constitution, 85; Constitution will promote, 142, 202, 203, 333; Constitution with amendments will help maintain, 309; danger of disunion, 35, 202; depends on Federalist control of Congress, 421; endangered by promise of subsequent amendments, 47; endangered if Constitution is not adopted, 42; endangered under Articles of Confederation, 178, 223; energetic government needed to preserve, 62; everything that tends to disunion should be avoided, 435; Federalists will preserve, 210; Harrisburg Convention opposes, 197; majority of Antifederalists in Va. firmly attached to, 68; must be firmly established with experience before amendments added, 266–67; N.C. and R.I. will be out of, 148; N.C. will be out of if it requires previous amendments, 122; necessity of, 62, 93, 109, 265, 327–28, 382; needed for freedom, happiness and independence, 41; non-ratifying states are out of, 85–86; not desirable under Constitution, 80; N.Y. amendments will keep N.Y. out of, 87; N.Y. would be endangered out of, 73; opponents of will attend a second convention, 262; and preservation of liberty will make Americans great and happy, 335; promotes happiness, 41, 89; R.I. is out of, 137; as reason for ratifica-

tion of Constitution, 389; as reason why N.Y. Antifederalists agreed to ratify Constitution, 317, 318, 319; second convention could destroy, 435; should not be dissolved because of lack of a bill of rights, 29; threatened by opposition to amendments, 301; Va. espouses, 11
UNITED STATES: Constitution will secure freedom and establish national importance of, 246; in a crisis, 348, 375, 387, 422, 424, 436; a critical era for, 144, 265; extensiveness of needs a federal government, 178; founded on republican principles, 301–2; made up of the people at large and thirteen local governments, 444; miraculous union of sentiment throughout on Constitution, 327; revolution in sentiment, 381; serves as important example to the world, 314; special era in world history, 304; strong government needed to rule over diversity of, 151. *See also* Americans
UTT, JACOB (Bedminster, Bucks Co., Pa.): attends Bucks Co. meeting, 172

VANDEGRIFT, JACOB
—letter to, 169–70
VANDEGRIFT, JOHN
—letter to, 169–70
VANSANT, NATHAN
—letter to, 169–70
VERMONT: would threaten N.Y. out of the Union, 73, 80
VICE PRESIDENT, U.S.: John Adams as possible first, 127, 314, 356, 356n, 377, 378; should not take field command in Va. Convention amendments, 56
VIOLENCE: Bucks Co., Pa., resolution opposing, 173; in Huntingdon, Pa., 171–72; possible in western Pa. from Antifederalist activities, 168; will occur if N.Y. rejects Constitution, 87. *See also* Civil war; Insurrection, domestic
VIRGINIA: Antifederalists in encouraged by N.C. rejection, 182; calls Annapolis Convention, 88; favors a second convention, 201, 214, 290, 422; importance of in federal measures, 223–24; importance of to ratification process, 63; influences N.Y., 162, 317, 431; influences N.C., 146; lays foundation for change in Confederation government, 88; and N.Y. are least disposed to Constitution, 217; other states will follow lead in calling a second convention, 214; will ratify, 86; ratifies Constitution, 3, 43, 52n, 67–68, 90; rejection of

Constitution by would be a disaster, 66–67; Virginians are too proud and vain, 263
VIRGINIA CHARTER: not a bill of rights, 32; protected rights of Englishmen, 32
VIRGINIA CONSTITUTION (1776): Declaration of Rights not part of, 12, 32, 38; does not have reserved powers, 28
VIRGINIA CONVENTION: Antifederalists in acquiesce, 68; civil debate in, 88; *Debates* to be published, 162; evenly divided, 52n, 53; George Wythe's resolution for ratification, 42–44; journal of transmitted, 162; long debate ends with ratification, 90; should discuss Constitution only by clauses, 11; some Antifederalists in remain staunchly opposed to Constitution, 68; some delegates instructed to vote against Constitution, 68; favors calling general convention for amendments, 456
—amendments in: should recommend, 42; influences N.Y. Antifederalists, 86; proposed by, 53–56, 69, 445, 456–57; recommended by are a concerted plan, 130; N.C.'s amendments are similar to, 162–63; N.Y.'s amendments are similar to, 162; Patrick Henry proposes, 48–49n; majority in favors, 70; instructs future representatives to Congress to seek adoption of, 456; rejects previous amendments, 68; speeches in on, 8–51; Va. Declaration of Rights as source of, 57n
VIRGINIA DECLARATION OF RIGHTS (1776): adoption of, 9; allows standing armies when necessary, 49–50; as a compact, 23; does not provide protection in all cases in Va., 28; is no reason for a federal bill of rights, 27–28; justifies adoption of Constitution, 14; not part of Va. constitution, 12, 32, 38; praise of, 30; praised as guardian angel, 32; prohibits cruel and unusual punishments, 29; prohibits general warrants, 26, 27n; protects against powers of sword and purse, 30; protects jury trial in the vicinage, 40; protects jury trials in civil cases, 39n, 40; protects rights, 23; says men are equally free and independent, 14; as source for Va. Convention amendments, 57n; states danger from standing armies, 44; states that militia is best means of defense, 44; violated, 29, 257; violations of will be nugatory under U.S. Constitution, 31
VIRGINIA HOUSE OF DELEGATES: Antifederalists control, 284, 312; divided between Federalists and Antifederalists on all issues, 426; Federalists divided in, 353; Fed-

INDEX   517

eralists have majority in, 158; letter from to George Clinton delayed, 413; resolution and letters to governors, 356–57, 359, 360, 378, 378n, 386, 401, 431, 455; resolution of requesting Congress to call second convention, 339, 340, 340n, 341n, 449; resolution of requesting second convention printed in Boston, 409, 410
VIRGINIA LEGISLATURE: to request Congress to call second convention, 297; will agree with N.Y. circular letter, 263
VIRTUE: cannot trust that representatives under Constitution will have, 25; cause of requires adoption and implementation of Constitution, 374; Constitutional Convention praised for, 236; most necessary for peace in U.S. because people are free, 363; needed for people to be happy, 152, 225; needed to maintain freedom, 154; needed to preserve liberty, 14; not used to get Pa.'s ratification, 169; Pa. constitution calls for in assemblymen, 191; those with should be elected, 206; those without are demagogues, 414
VOGLE, GEORGE (Nockamixon, Bucks Co., Pa.): attends Bucks Co. meeting, 173
"THE VOICE OF THE PEOPLE," 218n; text of, 218–19

WADSWORTH, JAMES (Durham, Conn.): as Antifederalist leader in Conn., 381; in Conn. legislature, 293, 293n; lost his influence in Conn. Assembly, 315
WADSWORTH, JEREMIAH (Hartford, Conn.; id., BoR, II, 506)
—letter from, 315
—letters to, 123, 245
WAIT, THOMAS B. (Portland, Maine; id., BoR, II, 506)
—letter from, 140
WALKER, WILLIAM (Warrington, Bucks Co., Pa.): attends Bucks Co. meeting, 173
WALKER, WILLIAM (Warwick, Bucks Co., Pa.): attends Bucks Co. meeting, 172
WAR: Americans are averse to, 331–32; defense of Congress' power to declare, 341; preparation for will help prevent, 331; Switzerland not involved in, 156. See also Civil war; Foreign affairs
WARD, ARTEMAS (Shrewsbury, Mass.): as candidate for U.S. House of Representatives, 388
WASHINGTON, GEORGE (Fairfax Co., Va.; id., BoR, II, 506): constrained to attend Constitutional Convention, 143; criticized by Antifederalists, 430; defense of as delegate to Constitutional Convention, 205; favors retirement, 143; as first President, 81n, 127, 137, 214, 229, 285, 356, 396; praise of, 220; praised by Mirabeau, 81n
—letters from, 126–27, 142–43, 152–53, 159–60, 223–24, 289–90, 359, 387; quoted, 4, 84, 85n, 252n, 276n; cited, 66, 124n, 158n, 253n
—letters to, 124, 136–37, 149–50, 188–89, 213–14, 221, 228–30, 293, 297–98, 383, 386–87n; quoted, 4; cited, 126, 289, 290n
WEAVER, JACOB (Tinicum, Bucks Co., Pa.): attends Bucks Co. meeting, 173
WEEDEN, GEORGE (Fredericksburg, Va.): wants to publish Madison's letter supporting amendments, 356
WEST, BENJAMIN (Charlestown, N.H.): as candidate for U.S. House of Representatives, 416
WESTERN PENNSYLVANIA: "A Friend of Society and Liberty" addresses inhabitants of, 145
WESTMORELAND COUNTY, PA.: Antifederalist meeting supporting amendments, 131–34; Antifederalists in profess federal sentiments, 132; not represented in Harrisburg Convention, 182n, 184n
WHITE, ALEXANDER (Winchester, Va.; id., BoR, II, 507)
—letter from, 387
—letter to, cited, 387
WHITEHILL, ROBERT (Cumberland Co., Pa.): and call of Harrisburg Convention, 195; on committee to draft Cumberland Co. circular letter, 166n; as delegate to Harrisburg Convention, 175, 177; nominated for U.S. House of Representatives, 336, 344, 376
WIDGERY, WILLIAM (New Gloucester, Maine; id., BoR, II, 507)
—letter from, 214–15
—letter to, cited, 214
WILLARD, JOSEPH (Cambridge, Mass.): id., 471
—letter from, 364
WILLIAMS, OTHO HOLLAND (Baltimore, Md.): id., 471; as probably author of "A Marylander," 210n
WILLIAMSBURG, VA.: might instruct Edmund Randolph to oppose second convention, 262
WILLIARD, SAMUEL (Mass.): as candidate for U.S. House of Representatives, 388
WILLING, THOMAS (Philadelphia)
—letter from, 174

WILSON AND BOYD
—letter to, 327
WILSON, JAMES (Philadelphia): alluded to as writer of an aristocratic Constitution, 283–84; and reserved powers theory, 94, 96n, 257, 260n
—speech of says bill of rights can be dangerous by not including some rights, 97
WILSON, SAMUEL (Nockamixon, Bucks Co., Pa.): attends Bucks Co. meeting, 173
WINDHAM, CONN.: celebrates N.H. ratification, 68–69
WITNESSES: must be brought before juries, 32
WITNESSES, RIGHT TO CONFRONT: confronting of in Va. Convention amendments, 54; defense of Constitution lack of protection for, 384
"A WORD TO THE WISE": text of, 187
WRIGHT, THOMAS (Plumstead, Bucks Co., Pa.): attends Bucks Co. meeting, 173

WYTHE, GEORGE (Williamsburg, Va.): id., 471; resolution of ratification by read in Va. Convention, 42, 44
—speech of in Va. Convention, 41–42; responses to, 43, 46
—text of resolution for ratification in Va. Convention, 42–43

"X," 191n; text of, 141–42

YATES, ABRAHAM, JR. (Albany, N.Y.; id., BoR, II, 508): as author of "Sydney," 59n–60n
—letters from, 224; cited, 60n
—letter to, quoted, 60n
YATES, ROBERT (Albany, N.Y.): as chair of N.Y. Convention Antifederalists corresponding with Va. Antifederalists, 52n
—letter from, cited, 52n
YORK COUNTY, PA.: not represented in Harrisburg Convention, 182n, 184n, 188, 188n, 189, 190n, 191
YOST, MANUS (Haycock, Bucks Co., Pa.): attends Bucks Co. meeting, 172

Article 1.

Congress shall make no law respecting an establishment of religion, or prohibiting the free exercise thereof; or abridging the freedom of speech, or of the press, or the right of the people peaceably to assemble, and to petition the Government for a redress of grievances.

Article 2.

A well regulated Militia, being necessary to the security of a free State, the right of the people to keep and bear Arms, shall not be infringed.

Article 3.

No Soldier shall, in time of peace be quartered in any house, without the consent of the Owner, nor in time of war, but in a manner to be prescribed by law.

Article 4.

The right of the people to be secure in their persons, houses, papers, and effects, against unreasonable searches and seizures, shall not be violated, and no Warrants shall issue, but upon probable cause, supported by Oath or affirmation, and particularly describing the place to be searched, and the persons or things to be seized.

Article 5.

No person shall be held to answer for a capital, or otherwise infamous crime, unless on a presentment or indictment of a Grand Jury, except in cases arising in the land or naval forces, or in the Militia, when in actual service in time of War or public danger; nor shall any person be subject for the same offence to be twice put in jeopardy of life or limb, nor shall be compelled in any Criminal case to be a witness against himself, nor be deprived of life, liberty, or property, without due process of law; nor shall private property be taken for public use, without just compensation.